OXFORD
TWENTY-FIRST CENTURY
APPROACHES TO LITERATURE

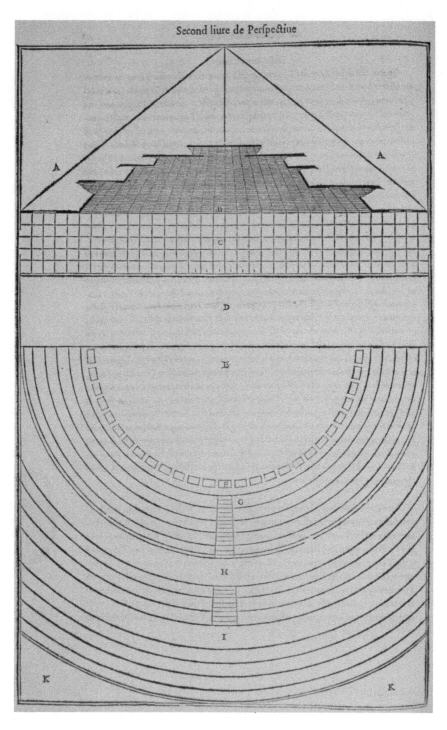

Diagram for a Theatre. *Le second Livre de perspective de Sebastian Serlio Bolognois, mis en langue franchoise par Iehan Martin* (Paris: Jehan Barbé, 1545), fol. 66 (photo: Library of Congress).

OXFORD

TWENTY-FIRST CENTURY

APPROACHES TO LITERATURE

Early Modern Theatricality

Edited by

HENRY S. TURNER

OXFORD
UNIVERSITY PRESS

OXFORD
UNIVERSITY PRESS

Great Clarendon Street, Oxford, OX2 6DP,
United Kingdom

Oxford University Press is a department of the University of Oxford.
It furthers the University's objective of excellence in research, scholarship,
and education by publishing worldwide. Oxford is a registered trade mark of
Oxford University Press in the UK and in certain other countries

© Oxford University Press 2013

The moral rights of the authors have been asserted

First Edition published in 2013

Impression: 3

Published in the United States of America by Oxford University Press
198 Madison Avenue, New York, NY 10016, United States of America

British Library Cataloguing in Publication Data
Data available

Library of Congress Control Number: 2013943771

ISBN 978-0-19-964135-2

Printed by
CPI Group (UK) Ltd, Croydon, CR0 4YY

CONTENTS

LIST OF ILLUSTRATIONS

LIST OF ABBREVIATIONS

EEBO	Early English Books Online
ELH	*English Literary History*
ELR	*English Literary Renaissance*
EMLS	*Early Modern Literary Studies*
JMRS	*Journal of Medieval and Renaissance Studies*
MLR	*Modern Language Review*
MRDE	*Medieval and Renaissance Drama in England*
OED	*Oxford English Dictionary*
PMLA	*Publications of the Modern Language Association*
REED	Records of Early English Drama
SEL	*Studies in English Literature, 1500–1900*
STC	A. W. Pollard and G. R. Redgrave, eds. *A short-title catalogue of books printed in England, Scotland and Ireland, and of English books printed abroad 1475–1640.* Second edition, revised and enlarged, begun by W. A. Jackson and F. S. Ferguson, completed by K. F. Pantzer. London: The Bibliographical Society, 1976–91, 3 vols.
TLN	through-line numbering [chapters 11 and 18]
TLS	*The Times Literary Supplement*

NOTES ON CONTRIBUTORS

Joel Altman is Professor Emeritus of English at the University of California, Berkeley. He is the author of *The Tudor Play of Mind: Rhetorical Inquiry and the Development of Elizabethan Drama* (California, 1978) and *The Improbability of Othello: Rhetorical Anthropology and Shakespearean Selfhood* (Chicago, 2010). jbaltman@berkeley.edu

Gina Bloom is Associate Professor of English at the University of California, Davis. She is the author of *Voice in Motion: Staging Gender, Shaping Sound in Early Modern England* (Penn, 2007) and has published essays in various journals, including *Renaissance Drama*, *Theatre Survey*, *English Literary Renaissance*, and *Shakespeare Studies*. gbloom@ucdavis.edu

Anston Bosman is Associate Professor of English at Amherst College. The author of 'Shakespeare and Globalization' in *The New Cambridge Companion to Shakespeare* (Cambridge, 2010), he is completing a book on transnational theatre in the early modern Germanic world and has just published a collaborative project on 'Intertheatricality' with Gina Bloom and William N. West. abosman@amherst.edu

Ann Baynes Coiro is Associate Professor of English at Rutgers University. Author of *Robert Herrick's Hesperides and the Epigram Book Tradition* (Johns Hopkins, 1988), co-editor of *Rethinking Historicism from Shakespeare to Milton* (Cambridge, 2012) and the forthcoming *Milton in the Long Restoration*, she has published widely on Milton's poetry, seventeenth-century court culture, and the interplay of early modern theatre and poetry. annbaynes.coiro@gmail.com

Mary Thomas Crane is the Thomas F. Rattigan Professor in the English Department at Boston College. She is the author of *Framing Authority: Sayings, Self, and Society in Sixteenth-Century England* (Princeton, 1993) and *Shakespeare's Brain: Reading with Cognitive Theory* (Princeton, 2000). mary.crane@bc.edu

Stephen Guy-Bray is Professor of English at the University of British Columbia. He is the author of three monographs, most recently *Against Reproduction: Where Renaissance Texts Come From* (Toronto, 2009). Forthcoming are a co-edited collection of essays on Thomas Nashe, a book chapter on Donne and Marvell, and an article on Milton. guybray@interchange.ubc.ca

Jonathan Gil Harris, Professor of English at George Washington University, is the author of five books on the drama and culture of Shakespeare and his contemporaries. His current book project, *The First Firangis: How to Become Authentically Indian*, will be published by Aleph Books in 2014.   jgharris@gwu.edu

Robert Henke is Professor of Drama and Comparative Literature at Washington University. He is the author of *Pastoral Transformations: Italian Tragicomedy and Shakespeare's Late Plays* (Delaware, 1997) and *Performance and Literature in the Commedia dell'Arte* (Cambridge, 2002). In St Louis, he is involved with the Catholic Worker movement and works as a resident scholar for Prison Performing Arts.   rhenke@artsci.wustl.edu

Blair Hoxby, Associate Professor of English, Stanford University, is the author of *Mammon's Music: Literature and Economics in the Age of Milton* (Yale, 2002). He is at work on two monographs, *What Is Tragedy?* and *Reading for the Passions*.   bhoxby@stanford.edu

Paul A. Kottman is Associate Professor of Comparative Literature at the New School for Social Research. He is the author of *A Politics of the Scene* (Stanford, 2008), *Tragic Conditions in Shakespeare* (Johns Hopkins, 2009), and the editor of *Philosophers on Shakespeare* (Stanford, 2009). He is also the editor of a forthcoming book series from Stanford University Press, entitled *Square One: First Order Questions in the Humanities*.   KottmanP@newschool.edu

Erika T. Lin is Associate Professor of English at George Mason University. She is the author of *Shakespeare and the Materiality of Performance* (Palgrave Macmillan, 2012), as well as of essays in *Theatre Journal, New Theatre Quarterly*, and various edited collections. She is currently writing a book on seasonal festivities and commercial theatre.   elin1@gmu.edu

Jeremy Lopez is Associate Professor of English at the University of Toronto. His work on the drama of Shakespeare and his contemporaries includes *Theatrical Convention and Audience Response in Early Modern Drama* (Cambridge, 2003) and a monograph, forthcoming from Cambridge, on the history of the 'non-Shakespearean' early modern dramatic canon.   jeremy.lopez@utoronto.ca

Julia Reinhard Lupton is Professor of English and Comparative Literature at the University of California, Irvine. Her most recent books are *Thinking with Shakespeare: Essays on Politics and Life* (Chicago, 2011) and *Citizen-Saints: Shakespeare and Political Theology* (Chicago, 2005). She is writing a book entitled *Shakespeare Dwelling: Habitation, Hospitality, and Design*. jrlupton@uci.edu

Ellen MacKay is Associate Professor of English at Indiana University. She is the author of *Persecution, Plague and Fire: Fugitive Histories of the Stage in Early Modern England* (Chicago, 2011). She is currently at work on two projects: one on sea spectacles and the epistemology of theatre illustration, and another on the early modern sub-rational.
                                                                                                                    emackay@indiana.edu

Scott Maisano is Associate Professor of English at the University of Massachusetts, Boston. His publications focus on Shakespearean Romance and the Scientific Revolution, Renaissance Humanism, and Posthumanist Theory. He is working on two books: *Shakespeare's Revolution: The Scientific Romances* and, with coauthor Holly Dugan, *The Famous Ape: Shakespeare and Primatology*.   Scott.Maisano@umb.edu

Madhavi Menon is Professor of Literature at American University. She is the author of *Wanton Words: Rhetoric and Sexuality in English Renaissance Drama* (Toronto, 2004),

Unhistorical Shakespeare: Queer Theory in Shakespearean Literature and Film (Palgrave Macmillan, 2008), and editor of *Shakesqueer: A Queer Companion to The Complete Works of Shakespeare* (Duke, 2011).   menon@american.edu

Paul Menzer is Associate Professor at Mary Baldwin College, where he is Director of the MLitt/MFA Shakespeare and Performance programme. His most recent book is *The Hamlets: Cues, Q's, and Remembered Texts* (Delaware, 2009). His most recent play is *Invisible, Inc.*, which premiered in Austin, Texas in 2013.   paulmenzer@gmail.com

Simon Palfrey is Professor of English Literature at Oxford University. He is a founding editor of the series *Shakespeare Now!* His books include *Late Shakespeare* (Oxford, 1997), *Doing Shakespeare* (Arden, 2005; revised edn. 2011), *Shakespeare in Parts* (Oxford, 2007, with Tiffany Stern), and *Connell Guide to Romeo and Juliet* (Connell, 2012). *Shakespeare's Possible Worlds* is forthcoming with Cambridge.   simon.palfrey@ell.ox.ac.uk

Richard Preiss is Associate Professor of English at the University of Utah, where he teaches Renaissance Drama and the history of theatre, especially traditions of comedy and clowning.   richard.preiss@utah.edu

Bruce R. Smith is Dean's Professor of English at the University of Southern California. A former president of the Shakespeare Association of America, he is the author of seven books on Shakespeare and early modern culture, including *Homosexual Desire in Shakespeare's England* (Chicago, 1991), *The Acoustic World of Early Modern England* (Chicago, 1999), *Shakespeare and Masculinity* (Oxford, 2000), *The Key of Green* (Chicago, 2009), and *Phenomenal Shakespeare* (Wiley-Blackwell, 2010).   brucesmi@college.usc.edu

Evelyn Tribble is Professor and Donald Collie Chair of English at the University of Otago, Dunedin, New Zealand. She is the author of *Margins and Marginality: The Printed Page in Early Modern England* (Virginia, 1993), *Writing Material: Readings from Plato to the Digital Age* (with Anne Trubek, Longman, 2003), *Cognitive Ecologies and the History of Remembering* (with Nicholas Keene, Palgrave Macmillan, 2011), and *Cognition in the Globe: Attention and Memory in Shakespeare's Theatre* (Palgrave Macmillan, 2011).   evelyn.tribble@otago.ac.nz

Scott A. Trudell is Assistant Professor of English at the University of Maryland, College Park. He has published articles in *Shakespeare Quarterly* and *Studies in Philology* and is currently working on a book about song culture, media theory, and literary form in early modern England.   trudell@umd.edu

Henry S. Turner is Associate Professor of English at Rutgers University, New Brunswick. He is the author of *The English Renaissance Stage: Geometry, Poetics, and the Practical Spatial Arts, 1580–1630* (Oxford, 2006), *Shakespeare's Double Helix* (Continuum, 2008), and editor of *The Culture of Capital: Property, Cities, and Knowledge in Early Modern England* (Routledge, 2002).   henry.turner@rutgers.edu

Laura Weigert is Associate Professor of Art History at Rutgers University, New Brunswick. She is the author of *Weaving Sacred Stories: Narratives of Saints and the Performance of Clerical Identity* (Cornell, 2004) and of *Images in Action: The Theatricality of Late Medieval French Art* (Cambridge, forthcoming). Her articles have appeared in *Art History, The Oxford Art Journal, Gesta, Studies in Iconography, The Art Bulletin, Art Journal, EMF: Studies in Early Modern France*, and in numerous collections of essays.   weigert@rci.rutgers.edu

William N. West is Associate Professor of English, Classics, and Comparative Literary Studies at Northwestern University and co-editor of *Renaissance Drama*. He is the author of *Theatres and Encyclopedias in Early Modern Europe* (Cambridge, 2002) and co-editor of Robert Weimann's *Author's Pen and Actor's Voice: Writing and Playing in Shakespeare's Theatre* (Cambridge, 2000) and his *Rematerializing Shakespeare: Authority and Representation on the Early Modern Stage* (Palgrave, 2005).   w-west@northwestern.edu

Phil Withington is Professor of Early Modern History at the University of Sheffield. His most recent book is *Society in Early Modern England: The Vernacular Origins of Some Powerful Ideas* (Polity, 2010). Current projects include a social history of the Renaissance and the history of early modern intoxicants.   p.withington@sheffield.ac.uk

Michael Witmore is Director of the Folger Shakespeare Library. He is the author of *Shakespearean Metaphysics* (Continuum, 2008), *Pretty Creatures: Children and Fiction in the English Renaissance* (Cornell, 2007), *Culture of Accidents: Unexpected Knowledges in Early Modern England* (Stanford 2001), and co-editor of *Childhood and Children's Books in Early Modern Europe, 1550–1800* (Routledge, 2006).   mwitmore@folger.edu

Susanne L. Wofford, Dean of the Gallatin School of Individualized Study at New York University and Professor of English, is author of *The Choice of Achilles* (Stanford, 1992) and editor of *Hamlet: Case Studies in Contemporary Criticism* (St. Martin's, 1994), among other works. Her essay 'Foreign Emotions' appeared in *Theatre Crossing Borders: Transnational and Transcultural Exchange in Early Modern Drama* (Ashgate, 2008).

susanne.wofford@nyu.edu

Peter Womack is Professor of Literature and Drama at the University of East Anglia. His books include *Ben Jonson* (Blackwell, 1986), *English Renaissance Drama* (Blackwell, 2006), and *Dialogue* (Routledge, 2011).   P.Womack@uea.ac.uk

CHAPTER 1

GENERALIZATION

HENRY S. TURNER

There are reasons to think that professional criticism of early modern drama is emerging from a period of consolidation, comforted by a sense of the canonical importance of its object but nagged by a certain intellectual restlessness. Few fields can claim to have undergone a more radical reinvention over the past forty years, and arguably no field has had a greater impact on the way that literary scholarship as a whole has come to be practised in the academy. In retrospect, the rise of 'historicism' as an international critical orthodoxy can be traced directly to the studies of Shakespeare, Jonson, Marlowe, and their contemporaries that were published during the 1980s and early 1990s by New Historicist and Cultural Materialist critics working in both the United States and the United Kingdom. When I entered graduate school, these methods were being reinvigorated by a turn to the history of the book, through which drama was coming to be regarded primarily as a printed form; today, the study of print culture and the history of reading still arguably forms the dominant mode of historicist inquiry in the field, although this may be changing as I write these words—the very existence of this volume implies a new direction. This shift towards the history of the book was possible partly because of the strong grip that sociological and materialist methods held on the critical imagination; it can also be understood as part of a more general drive towards an 'objective' criticism based on archive and fact, one that would allow literary studies to stand next to History as a royal discipline in the Humanities division of the university (and one that would make literary study newly amenable to research funding). But whatever the causes, there are good reasons for its currency: thanks to the path-breaking work of textual scholars and critics, the kinds of evidence that we might consider have been significantly expanded; plays we had come to know well suddenly look very different when their variant editions are examined for their interpretive value; we have a much more subtle grasp of the ways in which publishers shaped the dramatic market-place; and we realize how

unstable and non-unified a so-called 'play', as well as its many meaningful elements, really turns out to be.[1]

It seemed to me then, however, and it still seems to me now, that in a paradoxical
way the specifically *theatrical* history of drama has faded from view.[2] Shadowed by
the history of the book, critics writing on early modern theatre have faced several
unsatisfactory alternatives. Behind, an increasingly dated New Historicism, for
which the trope of 'theatricality' proved vital to the analysis of power and culture
but which left more to be said about how the theatrical fictions of the period actually came to life.[3] To one side, the excavations of theatre historians, rich in detail but
often cautious in argument; to the other, performance reviews that remain focused
on a singular event or studies of adaptation that assemble a pastiche of cultural
moments.[4] In the distance, the theoretical abundance of Performance Studies,
already beginning to cede its ground before the shimmer of New Media (which will
itself either fade into a quirk of humanities scholarship or grow to swallow us all).
In response, a growing number of critics have found renewal in omnivorous profusion: the recent turn to science and technology, phenomenology, philosophies

---

[1] Lesser and Stallybrass's arguments about the commonplacing of *Hamlet* and its implications for
early modern definitions of the 'literary' as a category of value stand out as an excellent recent example
of what new textual criticism can achieve; see Zachary Lesser and Peter Stallybrass, 'The First Literary
Hamlet and the Commonplacing of Professional Plays', *Shakespeare Quarterly* 59.4 (Winter, 2008),
371–420; also Lesser's *Renaissance Drama and the Politics of Publication* (Cambridge: Cambridge University Press, 2004) and Douglas Brooks, *From Playhouse to Printing House: Drama and Authorship in
Early Modern England* (Cambridge: Cambridge University Press, 2006). See also Lukas Erne, *Shakespeare as a Literary Dramatist* (Cambridge: Cambridge University Press, 2003), which did much to
reframe discussions of early modern drama as 'the intersection of theatricality and literariness' (220),
and Margreta De Grazia and Peter Stallybrass, 'The Materiality of the Shakespearean Text', *Shakespeare
Quarterly* 44.3 (1993), 255–83, an essay that still strikes me as paradigm-shattering and that provides
a kind of model for the approach adopted here vis-à-vis 'theatricality'.

[2] See Henry S. Turner, *The English Renaissance Stage: Geometry, Poetics, and the Practical Spatial
Arts, 1580–1630* (Oxford: Oxford University Press, 2006), esp. 1–3.

[3] Naturally there are exceptions, notably Stephen Greenblatt's analysis of Christopher Marlowe's
Tamburlaine in *Renaissance Self-Fashioning* (Chicago: University of Chicago Press, 1980); the work of
Stephen Orgel on the masque, *The Jonsonian Masque* (Cambridge, MA: Harvard University Press,
1965) and *The Illusion of Power* (Berkeley: University of California Press, 1975); the work of Louis
Montrose, especially ' "Shaping Fantasies": Figurations of Gender and Power in Elizabethan Culture',
Representations 2 (1983), 61–94 and *The Purpose of Playing: Shakespeare and the Cultural Politics of the
Elizabethan Theatre* (Chicago: University of Chicago Press, 1996); and Jean E. Howard, *The Stage and
Social Struggle in Early Modern England* (New York: Routledge, 1994), for whom a concept of
'theatricality' includes a pronounced formal and generic dimension as well as its commercial, institutional, and political realities. The notes that follow can only hope to touch on the enormous debt this
collection owes to earlier scholarship on early modern theatre and performance; the citations are not
meant to be comprehensive but represent the work that has been especially influential on my own
thinking while preparing the volume. I have deliberately refrained from citing the prior work of contributors to the collection, since their essays represent them better than a brief note could; the references and Further Reading that accompany their essays provide a wealth of additional bibliography.

[4] See, however, the exemplary work of Barbara Hodgdon, *The Shakespeare Trade: Performances and
Appropriations* (Philadelphia: University of Pennsylvania Press, 1998) and of M. J. Kidnie, *Shakespeare
and the Problem of Adaptation* (New York and London: Routledge, 2009).

of action, the spatiality of stage directions, actor's parts, globalization, political philosophy, religion and ethics, the history of the senses, props and prosthetics, environmental criticism, the life of animals, music and acoustic performance—to name
a few areas of active research—manifests how creative and eclectic current criticism
of early modern drama is becoming.

Some of this work has arisen as an attempt to recover areas that New Historicism
tended to marginalize: the history of rhetoric, classical philosophy and its diffusion,
the history of science. Some work sets out to advance theoretical problems that
New Historicism made central but determined in too narrow a way: the nature of
sovereignty and power, now resituated in relation to humanism and political theology; the history of gender, sexuality, and desire, especially in relation to queer subjectivity; the nature of 'race' and other forms of geographic difference, with an eye
to the East and not simply to the New World; the possibilities of drama as a mode
of ideological critique, now of the category of the 'human' rather than of the 'subject'. And good recent work has begun to dig more deeply into topics that have long
been of enduring interest to historicist literary criticism, in all its varieties: the relation between drama and religious thought, drama and civic identity, the economic
dimension to drama, drama in relation to ritual and performance.

Twenty-First Century Approaches to Early Modern Theatricality has been designed
to capture the energy that is emerging around the study of early modern theatre and
to sow the seeds for theoretical and methodological innovation of the type that has
characterized the study of printed drama and the history of the book more generally. We have seen how powerful a 'New Textualism' or a 'new New Bibliography'
can be as an engine for genuinely new and interesting arguments about major literary problems. So what would a 'New Theatricality' look like? The essays that follow
provide some answers. The goal has been to provide what engineers call an 'exploded
view' of early modern theatricality: a blueprint that isolates functional parts, mag-
nifies them for analysis, and then reintegrates them into the theatrical apparatus.
Taken collectively, the essays identify a cluster of mimetic and symbolic techniques:
the objects, bodies, conventions, signs, and collective habits of apprehending performance that 'theatricality' conveniently designates.[5] The abstraction of the term is

---

[5] The bibliography surrounding the notion of theatricality is obviously too long for a single note, but
useful points of departure, taken from a variety of disciplinary, methodological, and theoretical back-
grounds, include a special issue of the journal *SubStance* 31.2–3 (2002), ed. Josette Féral, including
Féral's own 'Forward' (3–13), her 'Theatricality: The Specificity of Theatrical Language', trans. Ronald
P. Bermingham (94–108), a helpful general bibliography on 'Theatricality and Performativity' (280–7),
and many highly relevant essays, including surveys of meanings and usage by Marvin Carlson, 'The
Resistance to Theatricality' (238–50) and Janelle Reinelt, 'The Politics of Discourse: Performativity
meets Theatricality' (201–15). See also Féral's earlier and influential 'Performance and Theatricality:
The Subject Demystified', trans. Terese Lyons, *Modern Drama* 25.1 (1982), 170–81; Erika Fischer-
Lichte, *The Semiotics of Theater*, trans. Jeremy Gaines and Doris L. Jones (Bloomington, IN: Indiana
University Press, 1992; first pub. 1983), esp. 139–41; Fischer-Lichte, 'Theatricality: A Key Concept in
Theatre and Cultural Studies', *Theatre Research International* 20.2 (1995), 85–9 and, in the same issue,

meant to mark a certain distance from the specificities of actual theatres and individual performances; it designates an open set of features—formal procedures, expectations, attitudes and perceptual experience, patterns of interaction, economic and social structures—that are shared across individual theatrical occasions and that even motivate performances that take place outside of a conventional theatre building. As a generalizing term, 'theatricality' opens up the terrain of possible examples while also holding those examples together. But for this reason it also circumscribes the field, limiting its extension. Like all acts of generalization, therefore, 'theatricality' should be understood as retaining a certain plasticity as it expands and contracts within certain limits. New examples, situations, and critical contexts will always refresh the term, which finds its definition only in this ongoing movement between particularity and abstraction.

In keeping with this approach, each essay in the collection has been designed as an exercise in what I have come to think of as 'the art of creative generalization': rather than attempting to capture the historical dimensions of the field in its entirety or to summarize existing scholarship, I have invited contributors to bundle together a set of historical, formal, and philosophical questions into a single topic, chosen by them, that could stand for the idea of theatricality as a whole. The collection might best be viewed, therefore, as a kind of handbook to the *Handbook* and as a companion to the *Companion*, since it shares with these projects an interest in compiling a large-scale picture of theatre but places its emphasis less on comprehensive synthesis than on a method of emblematic sampling.[6] Some topics that strike readers as being fundamental will inevitably have been left out, but the collection will have been successful only if it generates fresh possibilities for interpretation that other scholars subsequently take up, seeing the theatre in a new way through rubrics that they themselves discover and that do not appear here, but could have.

As is the convention in large collections of this type, the essays have been grouped into clusters so as to draw out shared ideas and problems, although I have eschewed part divisions and part headings, which often seem to me to be arbitrary and to raise more questions than they answer. Reading the essays in

---

Fischer-Lichte, 'From Theater to Theatricality—How to Construct Reality', 97–105; Elin Diamond, 'Introduction' to Diamond, ed., *Performance and Cultural Politics* (New York: Routledge, 1996), 1–12; Patrice Pavis, 'Theatricality', in Pavis, *Dictionary of the Theatre: Terms, Concepts, and Analysis*, trans. Christine Shantz (Toronto: University of Toronto Press, 1998), 39–97; Tracy C. Davis and Thomas Postlewait, eds., *Theatricality* (Cambridge: Cambridge University Press, 2003), 1–39; and Samuel Weber, *Theatricality as Medium* (New York: Fordham University Press, 2004).

[6] The recent *Oxford Handbook of Early Modern Theatre*, ed. Richard Dutton (Oxford: Oxford University Press, 2009) has done a superb job of gathering together the best recent scholarship on the state of the field and will undoubtedly become the measure of its type. Other notable collections include John D. Cox and David Scott Kastan, eds., *A New History of Early English Drama* (New York: Columbia University Press, 1997) and Peter Holland and Stephen Orgel, eds., *From Script to Stage in Early Modern England* (Basingstoke and New York: Palgrave Macmillan, 2004), animated throughout by the distinction between theatre and drama.

sequence will reveal many immediate continuities among them. But readers will also discover many resonances among essays that lie further apart: innumerable diagrams might be generated to map their overlaps, their departures, and their common concerns. Chronologically, the scale of inquiry for the collection has been expanded backward to the mimetic and spatial conventions of the late-medieval stage and forward across the chasm of the Interregnum, when theatricality putatively ceased to exist, into the new theatrical imagination of the Restoration. The *terminus a quo* for the volume has been set by Laura Weigert's essay on 'Stage', in which she speculates about transitions in theatrical representation from the multiple presentation areas of the medieval pageants to the fixed stage of the Renaissance period and tracks some of the performative conventions that persisted, among them the use of statues, paintings, and fabric to personify ideas, alongside the more conventional body of the actor. This is followed by Richard Preiss's essay on 'Interiority', on the way the enclosure of the theatres made possible not only a newly commercialized drama but also characterization and plot-structure that depended on an implied but unrevealed depth; and then by Peter Womack's essay on 'Off-stage', which examines how early modern performance replaces the absolute, sacred, and cosmic space of medieval performance with a newly secularized space of representation that could become fictional in a way that the medieval stage could not.

Phil Withington's essay on '*Honestas*', Ann Baynes Coiro's essay on 'Reading', and Blair Hoxby's study of 'Passions' together then mark a final perimeter for the volume. Withington traces the emergence of a specifically theatrical notion of personhood in the mid-seventeenth century, one that had its roots in earlier humanist notions of *honestas*, *decorum*, and civility but that had been modified by antitheatrical discourse and by new attempts to imagine a performative public sphere. During the Interregnum, Withington argues, theatricality really *did* become reality, as the antitheatricalists had feared, since it now informed new ideas about how to be a sociable person by playing the roles that were appropriate to the shop, the salon, or the street. Withington concludes with a close analysis of *Othello*, which captures in the figure of Iago the danger that a newly theatricalized notion of *honestas* presented to early modern contemporaries. Coiro, too, traces the fortunes of 'theatricality' after the closing of the public theatres and into the Restoration, showing how the plays of Shakespeare and Jonson, Beaumont and Fletcher were revived by the companies of Thomas Killigrew and William Davenant and gradually transformed into a more readerly form of literary drama by the publishing efforts of Humphrey Moseley and by the retrospective judgement of John Dryden's *An Essay of Dramatick Poesie*. During the Restoration, 'the London theater was crowded with old theatrical memories and new demands', Coiro argues, and it had been fundamentally altered by its passage into print. Hoxby, finally, follows the theory of the passions from the classical period through to the neoclassicism of the late seventeenth, eighteenth, and early nineteenth centuries to show how the later period developed a new understanding of character and of dramatic form that underwrites the criticism of our own moment. Pointing out that Dryden and Milton both regarded the passions, not 'character', as the most important objects of imitation, Hoxby reconstructs a critical and poetic world in which the 'personation' of passion was thought to be essential to the formal capacities of theatre and the source of the profound collective experiences it made possible.

Whatever its particular focus, however, each essay also engages with problems that recur across the collection as a whole, and since readers will inevitably move through the volume in different sequences, it will be helpful to survey these large issues briefly before turning the inquiry over to the contributors themselves—the account that follows reflects my own trajectories of reading and collaborating with them. The first concerns the interplay between the notion of 'theatricality' and that of 'performance'. Although it is often conventional within Performance Studies to regard 'theatre' as a subset or specialized mode of 'performance', for instance, readers of this collection should be alert to differences between the terms and even for an inversion of their topological relationship—for it is equally conventional, after all, to view 'performance' as a component of 'theatricality' rather than vice versa, and especially for theatre historians and theatre critics.[7] Some contributors will use the terms as rough synonyms for one another, but others will push them apart. There are many ways to draw distinctions between them, depending on the tradition one bears in mind. Where 'performance' might emphasize the immediacy, singularity, and evanescence of a present event—the 'Now', as Scott Maisano puts it in his essay, building on the work of Peggy Phelan—'theatricality' gathers that singularity into the reiterated, enduring conventions for representing actions, objects, and ideas on stage, conventions that are necessary to any individual performance but that exceed any particular occasion.[8] When 'performance' finds in ritual, in everyday behaviour, and in institutions of all kinds the enduring cultural codes that make action meaningful, 'theatricality' examines how the symbolic action of everyday life has been further concentrated by a translation into a specific mode of art. If a theoretical interest in performance once accompanied an attempt to deconstruct the subject and its attendant categories, 'theatricality' could be understood as performance beyond the subject—the subject distributed into the collective formations of groups, masses, audiences, and crowds—or with the subject subtracted, leaving in its place a variety of non-human elements, forces, affects, and things (and

---

[7] See for instance Richard Schechner, *Performance Theory*, rev. edn. (New York: Routledge, 1988; first pub. 1977), esp. 'Drama, Script, Theater, and Performance' (66–111), 'From Ritual to Theater and Back: The Efficacy–Entertainment Braid' (112–69), and 'Toward a Poetics of Performance' (170–210); helpful discussions of the problem with reference to early modern drama, specifically, may be found in Barbara Hodgdon and W. B. Worthen, eds., *A Companion to Shakespeare and Performance* (Oxford: Blackwell, 2005) and James C. Bulman, ed., *Shakespeare, Theory, and Performance* (New York: Routledge, 1996).

[8] Peggy Phelan, *Unmarked: The Politics of Performance* (New York: Routledge, 1993).

in this way also intersecting with some of the most challenging recent work in Performance Studies itself).[9]

At the same time, theatre always draws on performance, even as performance often manages to spill out of the theatrical enclosure. Gina Bloom's essay on 'Games' and Erika T. Lin's essay on 'Festivity' both drive a wedge between 'theatre' and 'performance' in order to see what each term—considered separately, and then refolded together—can bring to a new understanding of an art we feel we know well. Bloom shows how early modern card and board games would have trained theatre audiences in the performative conventions of a newly commercialized stage; under Bloom's eye, theatricality itself becomes a kind of game whose rules are explored, modified, and constantly reinvented through their performance by actors and the audiences who watched them. Lin argues that early modern playgoers would have responded powerfully to performative cues that they recognized from the holiday calendar, as playwrights reshaped traditional symbols and sounds into a commercial theatre system. The result, Lin maintains, is nothing less than a transformation in how time was experienced as a medium for communal identification: the cyclical calendar of the holiday year took a new shape as a homogeneous, bounded medium with beginning, middle, and end, which playwrights could fill with their theatrical fictions. Jonathan Gil Harris's essay on 'Becoming-Indian' meanwhile, focuses on how travellers to the New World and to India made sense of their encounters by framing them specifically in reference to the performance techniques and even the architecture of the theatre, in ways both positive and negative. In the case of Thomas Coryate, England's first travel writer, as Harris shows, theatrical performance became a means of self-transformation in both mind and body, an act of imaginative self-incorporation that blurred subject with object and dissolved the boundaries of cultural identities.

Harris's essay forms part of a larger cluster of essays that demonstrate how early modern theatricality was always an international, travelling phenomenon, taking shape out of shared performative techniques, overlapping legal regulations, networked patronage systems, and creative materials that circulated across the borders of Europe in the form of textual sources, recycled plot scenarios, marked styles of playing, and character-types. Robert Henke's essay on 'Poor' looks at how the

---

[9] See, for instance, Una Chaudhuri and Shonni Enelow, 'Animalizing Performance, Becoming-Theatre: Inside Zooesis with The Animal Project at NYU', *Theatre Topics* 16.1 (2006), 1–17; the essays collected in a special issue of *TDR: The Drama Review* 51.1 (2007) on 'Animals and Performance', ed. Chaudhuri; 'On Animals', a special issue of *Performance Research* 5.2 (2000), ed. Alan Read; and, in early modern studies specifically, the work of Bryan Reynolds, especially *Transversal Subjects: From Montaigne to Deleuze after Derrida* (New York: Palgrave Macmillan, 2009); Reynolds, *Transversal Enterprises in the Drama of Shakespeare and his Contemporaries: Fugitive Explorations* (New York: Palgrave Macmillan, 2006); Reynolds, *Performing Transversally: Reimagining Shakespeare and the Critical Future* (New York: Palgrave Macmillan, 2004); and Reynolds, *Becoming Criminal: Transversal Performance and Cultural Dissidence in Early Modern England* (Baltimore: Johns Hopkins University Press, 2002).

experience of poverty followed players wherever they travelled, furnishing the European theatre with some of its most popular tropes while at the same time persisting as a raw, brute reality throughout all of its formal translations and displacements. By setting the drama of England, France, Italy, and Spain against the backdrop of the new modes of capitalist accumulation that were beginning to transform European society, including the commercial theatre itself, Henke reveals the seams of impoverishment, hunger, and degradation that ran throughout the plays of the period as a source of amusement, humiliation, and restless improvisation.

Susanne L. Wofford's essay on 'Foreign' picks up where Henke leaves off, concentrating on the importation into English drama of elements that had their roots in European theatre as well as in classical sources and in English imaginations of the ancient past. Wofford shows how the plays of Marlowe, Shakespeare, Dekker, Middleton, and Marston absorbed this foreign material, becoming fully international even when they appeared to be most local; she offers several methodological categories for thinking in new ways about the problem of cultural translation that had come to define English theatre by 1600, including the need to recognize the 'formal agency', as she puts it, of the theatre's many different parts—the tropes, genres, emotions, characters, geographies, and ideas that imported a richly overdetermined set of foreign cultural meanings onto the English stage. Much like Wofford, Anston Bosman identifies three primary modes of theatrical 'Mobility' in the early modern period: geographical mobility from place to place, by both actors and scripts; a formal mobility among different modes of presentation and representation, including acting styles, characterization, and other embedded techniques of performance; and an ontological mobility that put into question the very notion of identity itself. Itinerancy was the norm for acting companies in the period, as Bosman shows, both within and outside England, and as the actors *moved*—over borders and among languages, across the boards and into the characters and plays of any given repertory—they carried with them a theatrical art that depended on many different modes of translation and cultural adaptation.

A second major problem running throughout the collection concerns the need to distinguish the notion of 'theatricality' from a notion of 'drama', although as in the case of 'performance' the terms will always remain closely related and will be marked in idiosyncratic ways by individual contributors.[10] The essays by Coiro and Hoxby, for instance, both demonstrate how 'drama' becomes an artefact of print culture as well as of critical or theoretical discourse: 'drama' is what theatre looks like from the perspective of the book, as it were, or from the vantage point of a critical tradition that was rooted in Greek and Roman categories but beginning to identify its own novel vocabulary, prescriptions, and judgements of value. Not all the contributors would agree with this characterization of drama or use the terms

---

[10] The distinction is central to the project of Hans-Thies Lehmann, *Postdramatic Theatre*, trans. Karen Jürs-Munby (New York: Routledge, 2006), esp. 29–45.

'theatre' and 'drama' in the same way. Some would emphasize the performative dimension to drama, for instance, and define it as the coincidence (if not synthesis) of scripted writing, live action, and audience presence in a single event.[11] For Aristotle, as we know, the term 'drama' derived from the Greek *drontas*, or 'men acting and doing', and Aristotle obviously had in mind a theatre that had everything to do with public performance and nothing to do with print. But as Paul A. Kottman's essay on 'Duel' argues, philosophy from Aristotle to Hobbes to Hegel has always separated a notion of drama from its conditions of performance in the theatre, and it has done so in order to idealize a notion of 'action' that has been denuded of its concrete and collective embeddedness. Kottman shows how Shakespeare presents us with a kind of infinite theatricality that is no less philosophical but that differs absolutely in its mode: in Shakespeare, theatre is not subordinated to philosophy but discloses the innumerable and unique circumstances—social, historical, and ethical—necessary to constituting humanity as such.

The relationship between theatre and drama, stage and page, has been the subject of some of the best criticism in recent years.[12] We know that early printed editions of plays provide our most important evidence for how theatrical performance unfolded on early modern stages, and we owe a significant debt to those modern editors who consider questions of staging sensitively as they reassemble the play and compose their apparatus.[13] And even as these theatrical conventions left their mark in print, ideas about drama that had been shaped by printed plays, both classical and contemporary, in turn contributed to how theatrical performance on stage was understood. Focusing squarely on this problem, Jeremy Lopez engages in a close analysis of the 'Dumb show' to examine how the theatre sought to legitimize itself in the shadow of the printed page's authority over what drama could and should look like. In the dumb show, Lopez finds an especially complex and self-conscious encounter between word and action, diegesis and mimesis,

---

[11] Along with the works cited in prior notes, see Kier Elam, *The Semiotics of Theatre and Drama*, 2nd edn. (London and New York: Routledge, 2002; first pub. 1980); W. B. Worthen, *Drama: Between Poetry and Performance* (Oxford: Wiley-Blackwell, 2010), esp. 1–34 and 35–93.

[12] See especially Julie Stone Peters, *Theatre of the Book, 1480–1880: Print, Text, and Performance in Europe* (Oxford: Oxford University Press, 2000); Charlotte Scott, *Shakespeare and the Idea of the Book* (Oxford: Oxford University Press, 2007); Robert Weimann and Douglas Bruster, *Shakespeare and the Power of Performance: Stage and Page in the Elizabethan Theatre* (Cambridge: Cambridge University Press, 2008); the essays collected in Peter Holland and Stephen Orgel, eds., *From Performance to Print in Shakespeare's England* (Basingstoke and New York: Palgrave Macmillan, 2006); Orgel, 'Acting Scripts, Performing Texts', in *The Authentic Shakespeare and Other Problems of the Early Modern Stage* (New York: Routledge, 2002), 21–47; Anthony B. Dawson, 'The Imaginary Text, or the Curse of the Folio', in Hodgdon and Worthen, eds., *Companion to Shakespeare and Performance*, 141–61; David Scott Kastan, *Shakespeare and the Book* (Cambridge: Cambridge University Press, 2001), esp. 7–9.

[13] On this problem see esp. M. J. Kidnie, 'Text, Performance, and the Editors: Staging Shakespeare's Drama', *Shakespeare Quarterly* 51.4 (2000), 456–73 and Kidnie, 'Where is *Hamlet*? Text, Performance, and Adaptation', in Hodgdon and Worthen, eds., *A Companion to Shakespeare and Performance*, 101–20.

presentational vehicles and represented fiction. As a moment of extraordinary semiotic density and redundancy, the dumb show was at once too readerly for the stage and too spectacular for the printed book, Lopez argues, and as such it marks 'a threshold between *drama* (a play as textual artefact) and *theatricality* (the quality of experience a play provides live and in real time)'.

As many essays in the collection aim to show, widening the analytic space between theatre and printed drama allows for a more precise focus on the cumulative cloud of codes, affective experiences, micro-forms, and large-scale combinations of elements that make the early modern theatre seem so distinctive as an artful practice. We see more clearly the different types of physical ability, for instance, that were integral to the period's notion of dramatic 'action' but that remain only in the interstices of printed plays, as Bosman shows in his essay on 'Mobility' and Evelyn Tribble describes in her essay on 'Skill'. For Tribble, theatre must be relocated onto a continuum with other occasional public games and entertainments, all of which required special combinations of physical, verbal, and cognitive abilities. Attending to the traces, gaps, and fissures in playtexts that open a space for these embodied performance practices, Tribble argues, allows us to discover ways of apprehending and evaluating the theatrical experience that are quite different from those of much twentieth-century criticism and that require a more complex cognitive and environmental approach to the theatrical event. Distancing theatricality from print also gives us a better grasp of the many different media and spectacular elements that might capture an audience's attention, as Scott A. Trudell recovers in 'Occasion'. Pointing out that poetic verse was a relatively insignificant element in the entertainments, pageants, and shows of the period, Trudell argues that print became a way to transform the contingencies of occasion into an enduring 'poesy': in print, the noise, rain, mud, crowds, bored monarchs, tired children, and sheer formal incoherence of the event all resolved into a grand and silent art. Distinguishing between theatre and drama, finally, also reveals surprising things about the nature of a 'play': in many respects, the play was *not* the thing for early modern audiences, or not the only thing, as William N. West argues in his essay on 'Intertheatricality'. These audiences would have apprehended a play not only, and perhaps not even primarily, as a scripted unity but rather as 'collections of enacted words, gestures, and interactions', in West's terms, that extended across many plays simultaneously and that were reiterated over years of performance. Playgoing implied the ability to pick out many different types of theatrical elements, at many different scales; what appears to us as a textual crux or lacuna, West suggests, may signify an especially dense point on a system of intertheatrical references that has been lost.

Trudell's and West's essays both also suggest how separating theatre from a notion of printed drama can help us clarify the difficult problem of how 'text' in general might relate to theatricality, a third recurring problem in many essays. For Roland Barthes, to take a classic formulation, 'theatricality' depends on the subtraction of 'text':

What is theatricality? It is theater-minus-text, it is a density of signs and sensations built up on stage starting from the written argument; it is that ecumenical perception of sensuous artifice—gesture, tone, distance, substance, light—which submerges the text beneath the profusion of its external language...There is no great theater without a devouring theatricality—in Aeschylus, in Shakespeare, in Brecht, the written text is from the first carried along by the externality of bodies, of objects, of situations; the utterance immediately explodes into substances.[14]

For Barthes, as for Artaud before him, dissociating 'theatricality' from a notion of 'text' opens a space to examine the play as an event integral to itself rather than as a mere realization of a prior script.[15] But as clarifying as Barthes's definition may be, recent work has shown his notion of 'text' to be too singular and hence also too sharply oppositional in its relation to theatricality, which is arguably best understood as a particular *interaction* between scripted writing and the 'embodied, kinesthetic means of nonverbal action', as W. B. Worthen has succinctly described it.[16] Tiffany Stern, meanwhile, has demonstrated how differentiated a notion of dramatic 'text' actually was in the early modern period, as well as how integral it was to the process of theatrical rehearsal and theatrical performance.[17] 'Text' might include the source material, whether classical or contemporary, printed or manuscript, that playwrights borrowed and transformed for the stage; the written scripts, roles, and parts that consisted primarily, but not exclusively, of words to be spoken by the actors; other technical documents, such as plotts, playbooks, and annotated promptbooks, that assisted in the production of the play; 'arguments', 'inventions', and other digest or sketch-forms of a play that might be used at many different stages of production; songs, musical parts, designs for choreography and larger processional movements.

Many of the essays attend to one or more aspect of this 'textual' dimension to early modern theatricality: Stephen Guy-Bray's essay on 'Source', for instance, takes up the crucial question of just what playwrights thought they were doing when they adapted the texts of classical poetry to a new theatrical medium, which even they

---

[14] Roland Barthes, 'Baudelaire's Theater', in *Critical Essays*, trans. Richard Howard (Evanston: Northwestern University Press, 1972), 25–31 (26).

[15] Antonin Artaud, *The Theater and Its Double*, trans. Mary Caroline Richards (New York: Grove Press, 1958).

[16] W. B. Worthen, 'Intoxicating Rhythms: Or, Shakespeare, Literary Drama, and Performance (Studies)', *Shakespeare Quarterly* 62.3 (2011), 309–39 (313). The relationships among text, drama, theatre, and performance have been central to Worthen's work; see in particular *Shakespeare and the Force of Modern Performance* (Cambridge: Cambridge University Press, 2003), esp. 1–27; Worthen, *Drama: Between Poetry and Performance*; Worthen, 'Drama, Performativity, and Performance', *PMLA* 113.5 (1998), 1093–1107. See also Kidnie, *Shakespeare and the Problem of Adaptation*, arguing that 'a play...is not an object at all, but rather a dynamic *process* that evolves over time' (2).

[17] Tiffany Stern, *Documents of Performance in Early Modern England* (Cambridge: Cambridge University Press, 2009); Stern, *Rehearsal from Shakespeare to Sheridan* (Oxford: Oxford University Press, 2000); and Simon Palfrey and Tiffany Stern, *Shakespeare in Parts* (Oxford: Oxford University Press, 2007).

understood to be a mode of representation with lower prestige. Bray identifies moments of what he calls 'meta-adaptation', i.e. those moments in plays when play-wrights seem to become especially self-conscious about the locus of literary author-ity, as they compare the formal capacities of theatre to that of poetry—in linguistic style, in characterization, in plot structure—and when they begin to explore ways in which theatre might become a self-sufficient 'literary' mode. Paul Menzer, in his essay on 'Lines', narrows in on the gradual emergence of one of the most obviously 'textual' units of early modern theatre: the poetic verse we recognize as character-istic of early modern drama and for which Marlowe and Shakespeare, in particular, became famous. Menzer shows that before the line became a formal verse element, it persisted as a graphic mark, a technology of performance shared by musicians and singers as well as by actors and playwrights. Only later, through the printing of plays and poems, did the line become the immaterial metaphysical unit we associ-ate with the period's finest 'literary' writing.

Below the scale of the line but still within the category of 'text' we find the word, perhaps the most elemental but also the most complex element of early modern theatricality. For as soon as a word has been spoken on stage, it serves as more than a unit of communication, becoming one of many instruments to be taken up in the course of performance, just as the gesture, the prop, the garment, the dance, the song, or the image might function as an ingredients in the scenic composition. All of these elements remain at some level both presentational and representational, to adapt the terms of Robert Weimann, since they are at once medium and message, or form and content, the furniture of a fictional world and the means by which the theatre goes about creating the worlds it needs to furnish.[18] But because words often bestow a second identity upon a staged thing, and because words can create things that do not appear on stage in a concrete way at all, language has an even more important role to play in early modern theatricality than it does in other kinds of theatre or in other media. As Joel Altman's essay on 'Ekphrasis' shows, the unusu-ally flexible capacity of the staged word meant that it could be used for a wide range of theatrical techniques, including the usual sense of 'word-painting' but going far beyond it. Ekphrastic passages might bundle together several classical and contem-porary allusions into a single speech, create lingering subjectivity effects, or activate the emotional and psychological processes without which theatricality would be impossible. For Altman, ekphrasis creates nothing less than what he calls 'the psy-che of the play', a mode of theatrical transference, as it were, that takes place among

---

[18] See Robert Weimann, *Author's Pen and Actor's Voice: Playing and Writing in Shakespeare's Theatre*, ed. Helen Higbee and William N. West (Cambridge: Cambridge University Press, 2000), esp. 98–108. Weimann's work provides a template for many of the essays in this volume; see his *Shakespeare and the Popular Tradition in the Theater: Studies in the Social Dimension of Dramatic Form and Function*, ed. Robert Schwartz (Baltimore: Johns Hopkins University Press, 1978); Weimann and Bruster, *Shake-speare and the Power of Performance*; Weimann and Bruster, *Prologues to Shakespeare's Theatre: Per-formance and Liminality in Early Modern Drama* (London and New York: Routledge, 2004).

the actors themselves—some of whom may be so overtaken by their ekphrasis that they cease to 'act' and begin to live the role—and that is necessary to the management of the audience, whose attention is gathered and absorbed, their reactions managed and coaxed (as a playwright such as Jonson perceived so keenly).

The essays by Guy-Bray, Menzer, Altman, and many others also remind us, in different ways, of the degree to which texts, especially printed drama but also manuscripts, are often understood to be repositories for literary value, a major question in recent scholarship on the publication of early modern plays. This work raises a large question for critics of early modern theatre: what precisely would we gain by describing theatricality as 'literary'? Are we ready to cede the definition of drama as a 'literary' object to the history of print? Or, to put the problem somewhat differently, if the category of the 'literary' at the turn of the seventeenth century depends in some fundamental way on print—a statement that seems broadly true to me, with some qualification (poetry begins not in writing, after all, but in song)—then what alternative category to the 'literary' might operate in the theatre? What term of value are we to use, and what evaluating categories did early moderns use? How are we to categorize those plays that seem especially self-conscious of their own theatricality (*Hamlet* has always been the paradigmatic case, but there are many others), plays that deliberately try to condense into themselves an entire repertory of techniques and sensibilities? Early modern plays, after all, present us with some of the best examples we could hope to find, in any era or medium, of art's capacity to discover singularity within convention, to assemble new patterns of experience, from enjoyment to terror and everything in between (or both at once, as Aristotle perceived), to find a source of gratification in frustrated expectations and to feed new forms to a cultivated taste. And all of this while turning on itself to reflect on how it does so, and all by means of the very theatrical resources it is deploying!

One of the aims of this volume has been to re-approach the problems I have just outlined by foregrounding the category of 'form', dissociating it from its usual stylistic, poetic, or narrative associations in order to explore how it might become a resource for analysing the unusual density and ontological complexity of early modern theatricality. The concept of form is such a complicated one, and the legacies of formalism in literary criticism so overdetermined, that the term must be used carefully.[19] Current scholarship employs it to describe everything from small-scale linguistic effects (rhetorical, stylistic, poetic) to large-scale structural principles of composition, to material, institutional, or social formations of all kinds—the

---

[19] I have broached the topic elsewhere in reference to the history of science and the work of Bruno Latour, and I will add simply that I think the early modern theatre offers one of the best examples—because one of the most *complicated* examples—of how form can function as a principle of 'translation' in the way that Latour understands it; see Henry S. Turner, 'Lessons from Literature for the Historian of Science (and Vice Versa): Reflections on Form', *Isis: Journal of the History of Science Society* 101.3 (September 2010), 578–89, with additional bibliography on the renewed interest in form in literary studies more generally.

difficulty is partly one of analytic differentiation (among different uses or categories of form) and partly one of application (a more subtle attention to *how* formal categories generate meaning or determine ontological problems). Here contributors approach the problem of form in ways that will often seem familiar to readers, since they focus on the significant elements that allowed the theatres to function as a specific mode of representation, one that was distinct from prose narrative, or poetry, or architecture, or painting, but that extended into the large domain of what we could call a 'non-theatrical theatricality', or what Lin calls 'para-theatricality': the holiday games and pageants, the aristocratic entertainments, royal progresses, and Lord Mayors shows that were all also often written by commercial playwrights. As Trudell shows, for instance, all of these events share formal features with the commercial theatre: they have actors with speaking parts, use rhetorical language and figurative imagery, employ props and costume, and rework generic source materials into large-scale scenic compositions. And yet occasional entertainments also employ formal effects that either did not appear in the public theatres or appear there in a limited way: machinery, pyrotechnics, elaborate musical ensembles, actual landscapes and buildings, lakes, waterworks, and more. One premise of this volume is that we can gain valuable insights by grouping all of these techniques together: not (or not only) with the goal of achieving a newly enhanced understanding of, say, the *Tempest*, or *Cymbeline*, or *Cynthia's Revels*, all of which employ several of these elements, but so that we have a better understanding of 'theatricality' across the landscape of the period as a whole. The collection is thus especially interested in identifying formal attributes that earlier criticism has tended to overlook, or discuss in a cursory way, or treat in a descriptive manner. Early modern theatricality often behaves in ways that we might not expect—so much so that today, even after several decades of state-of-the-art criticism, we are still learning how to understand it.

At the same time, many essays employ the notion of 'form' in ways that may strike some readers as unorthodox, since they do so to describe a continuous process of transformation rather an idealized, ontologically prior abstraction that remains distinct from particular substances or situations. Here, 'form' designates an invariant quality, of whatever type, in whatever medium, and at whatever scale. It is the sign of an always provisional coherence and minimal legibility, the result of an active, perpetual process of reconstitution. It is a 'performative' notion of form, indeed, in the strong philosophical sense, although with the emphasis placed less on difference or negation than on persistence and recurrence. Approaching the problem of form in this way allows for two kinds of insights, each occupying an opposite pole on our spectrum of intellectual attention. On the one hand, it is form that allows us to generalize creatively about phenomena, as I have described already: to group things together and to explain why we have done so; to capture, in way that is at once intuitive and informed, the subtle variations among a given collection of examples and hold their differences in suspension. Generalizing in this way not

only yields true understanding (as every teacher will recognize) but keeps thinking flexible, elastic, unpredictable, and thus pleasurable. 'Form' is thus always, in
my view, a mode of generalization, which has the integrity of the cloud or the
cluster and not that of the block or the sphere. On the other hand—and this follows from the act of thinking I have been describing—the power of form is that it
permits for specification, for precision; it allows us to mark differences and to
make discriminations. 'Art' is, at root, a 'formal' procedure because it engages in
acts of specific generalization: although we are most familiar with generalization
in language, it is probably better to consider acts of artistic expression such as
theatre as modes of generalization using substances that have very different properties and capacities than language does. Through form we glimpse, suddenly, the
appearance of a new thing for which we are unprepared but for which we have, at
the same time, somehow been made ready. Something is there, and once there it
has already become significant, even if we have yet to understand what this significance is; it is an apprehension over which meaning spreads, like fogged breath
on a cold window.

This approach to form as a guiding category of analysis leads to another emphasis
that appears in many of the essays, namely a turn to what Bert O. States has called
the phenomenology of theatre: its power to disclose persons, actions, ideas, and
things with an existential acuteness that we can never anticipate in advance.[20] For
States, the full event of theatre cannot be described exhaustively through the use of
semiotic approaches, modelled as they are on language:

> ...there is a sense in which signs, or certain kinds of signs, or signs in a certain stage
> of their life cycle, achieve their vitality—and in turn the vitality of theater—not simply
> by signifying the world but by being *of* it.[21]

For this reason, theatre can never simply be understood as 'literary', taking the literary, literally, as 'lettered', as worth reading and able to be read, as a special kind of
language that can be decoded with the right kind of intelligence and attention. Nor,
more radically, can theatre be adequately defined as a 'representation' of another
world, through whatever combination of modes we might identify (mimetic, diegetic,
'poetic'). Instead, theatre absorbs *our* world into itself, and as a consequence it alters
our sense of the very here and now that we occupy. Theatre is a mode of appearance
whose purpose, like all art, is to make present before us familiar things as we have
never apprehended them before; 'its object', States writes, 'is to strip signs, to empty
them of received content and to reconstitute them as a beginning':[22]

> The magic that Artaud and Grotowski talk about is that of transformation or alchemy;
> it is not only that the eye can be tricked into seeing almost any object as something

[20] Bert O. States, *Great Reckonings in Little Rooms: On the Phenomenology of Theater* (Berkeley:
University of California Press, 1985), 128.

[21] States, *Great Reckonings*, 20.   [22] States, *Great Reckonings*, 109.

else, but that an object that does not represent something *in advance* becomes a blank check, an open presence; it becomes the source of something *not yet here*, a thing without a history, or rather a thing whose history is about to be revised.[23]

The fact that everything is in view, lying in wait, gives the stage a great deal of its optical and temporal interest. This quality of still silent participation is one that not even the film, a medium exceptionally hospitable to realistic representation, can duplicate.[24]

Theatre never simply 'means': theatre pauses, and then, suddenly, it *does*; it acts and creates; it collects people together, and it does so in living time.

This collective force of theatre is central to Julia Reinhard Lupton's essay on 'Hospitality', which mediates on the longstanding associations between theatre, households, and what she terms 'acts of reception': the performed rituals of welcoming, accommodating, sharing, and dwelling, as well as their more inhospitable alternatives. Like the theatre, hospitality can be understood as the art of creating saturated symbolic occasions in which we disclose ourselves as members within a tissue of enduring ethical and political relations. Hospitality welcomes us across a threshold, inviting us to join in the collective practice of meaningful life that provides theatre with both its form and its content. But hospitality also exposes us to the forces that strain that life, if not negate it: to hypocrisy and betrayal, to thirst and hunger, to service and subordination to the absolute will of others. Michael Witmore's essay on 'Eventuality' similarly finds in Shakespeare's plays an activation of our capacity for sensation, and especially for shared, collective encounters. Building on a diverse philosophical tradition of inquiry into the nature of the event and sensation, Witmore turns to phenomenology to describe what happens when the event gets theatricalized: when it becomes embedded in a complex, multi-stranded texture of actions, at many different scales, any of which might exert a causal force; when it is exposed to the contingencies of performance that might emanate from actor, from architecture, or from audience; when it shakes free, momentarily, from our familiar categories of knowing the world and of experiencing one another.

In looking to phenomenology as a source for new approaches to early modern theatricality, Witmore's essay joins a number of others in the collection. Bruce R. Smith's essay, for instance, finds in the different usages of the term 'scene' an enduring continuity of meaning that illuminates the scene's conceptual and phenomenological importance for our own current criticism. Pointing out that much theatre does without scenic units, Smith shows how the notion entered haphazardly into English printed drama, even as other techniques for 're-marking the scene' during performance generated a spectrum of connotations around the term. Across these multiple meanings, Smith argues, early modern plays retained a tight connection between the physical structure of the stage and the mimetic or diegetic illusions the stage made possible. 'It is the inclusiveness of "scene"—from

---

[23] States, *Great Reckonings*, 109.   [24] States, *Great Reckonings*, 68.

stage structure on the one hand to a perceptual phenomenon on the other—that recommends the term at this particular juncture in performance criticism', Smith proposes, allowing us to combine the methods of textual scholarship, architectural history, phenomenology, performance theory, and social practice into a genuinely interdisciplinary amalgam.

Mary Thomas Crane's essay on 'Optics' could also be said to contribute to what Smith himself has called 'historical phenomenology' by taking as its point of departure theatricality's etymological origins in seeing and watching.[25] Crane examines how the conceptual and phenomenological relationships among sight, spectacle, and illusion that defined theatre were being reconfigured by contemporary developments in optics and the changing epistemological status of vision in the period immediately prior to the scientific revolution. By transforming optics into a deceptive, magical practice, early modern plays persistently delegitimize visual technologies in order to assert the theatre's distinctiveness and legitimacy as a mimetic medium, one whose predominantly verbal fictions are at once more wondrous, more powerful, and, paradoxically, more *real* than the images produced by mirrors and lenses. In this moment of transition, Crane argues, we encounter a theatre struggling to accommodate a new representational regime grounded in the mechanical image, a regime to which film and other new media technologies are the heirs and in which theatre threatens to become an anachronism.

Ellen MacKay's essay on 'Indecorum', too, takes inspiration from the phenomenological work of States but soon moves well beyond it. MacKay trains our attention on the ways in which the traffic between life and stage is always governed by a set of social, ethical, and interpretive norms, the violation of which threatens to humiliate (at best) or physically harm (at worst) the spectator. Playwrights faced the impossible task of placating an audience of many different sensibilities and status-positions while still defending their authority over their own plays—a dilemma that, if it could never be satisfactorily evaded (much less resolved), could at least be converted into the special metatheatrical pleasure of writing plays that pulled the audience *into* the world of drama, where the different possibilities for spectatorial interaction could be exaggerated or contained. MacKay finds in the figure of the female playgoer a model for indecorous participation, one that knowingly exploits the tensions between actuality and theatricality in order to sustain the play while also revealing its dependence upon the absorption and judgement of its audience.

As MacKay argues, the perceptual contract that makes theatrical fiction possible must be upheld by the spectator in so many different ways at once—imaginatively,

---

[25] In addition to the work of Smith, see Gail Kern Paster, *Humoring the Body: Emotions and the Shakespearean Stage* (Chicago: University of Chicago Press, 2004); Paster, Katherine Rowe, and Mary Floyd-Wilson, eds., *Reading the Early Modern Passions: Essays in the Cultural History of Emotion* (Philadelphia: University of Pennsylvania Press, 2004); Elizabeth D. Harvey, ed., *Sensible Flesh: On Touch in Early Modern Culture* (Philadelphia: University of Pennsylvania Press, 2003).

affectively, ethically—that it may dissolve at any moment; indeed, any act of theatre worth the same will always seek deliberately to push this contract to its limit. Scott Maisano's essay on 'Now' takes up this precise problem, singling out a fundamental formal and phenomenological dimension to theatrical experience—time—and showing us how Shakespeare's *The Winter's Tale* amounts to nothing less than a theatrical experiment in the nature of time itself as at once a perceived, represented, and actualized series of events. Building on the foundational work of Artaud, Maisano undertakes to rethink the problem of theatrical occasionality; he argues that the temporal unit favoured by Performance Studies—the presentness of the 'now'—must be abandoned in favour of an alternative idea of temporality that is at once as old as Parmenides and Zeno and as new as Einstein and string theory. The character of Time in *The Winter's Tale* is a singular and strange choric figure, granting us a metaphysical view of time and of life beyond what we know from our mundane, earthly, individual human existences, Maisano argues, and in the process the play upends the truisms of Aristotle (the *Poetics*, the *Physics*) as well as of much theatre criticism.

Maisano's essay takes inspiration from twentieth- and twenty-first-century philosophies of science, and especially of physics, which has produced its own deconstruction of linear time and its unit, the 'now'. And the analogy to physics was one that States, too, embraced at several moments. Theatre is simultaneously a space of metaphysics and of colliding substances, States argues, of force and language, of images so saturated with ontological presence that they shimmer with a kind of special fullness or surface tension. 'The stage becomes a kingdom held together by a physics of metaphorical attraction', he writes—I think it would be difficult to describe plays such as *King Lear* or *The Tempest* more concisely.[26] For Simon Palfrey, too, in his essay on 'Formation', 'theatricality' describes not a technology of *mimesis* nor even a kind of enacted philosophy but rather a kind of physics: a world in which bodies, ideas, affects, and figures combine and recombine to generate the plays we watch, read, react to, and think about today. Palfrey finds in Leibniz's philosophy of monads an inspiration for rethinking theatre as a living, changing, moving environment that is given shape by a series of actions-in-form, across many different scales. For this reason, Palfrey's essay shows us the value of the category of 'form' and uses it to address several of the major methodological problems that animate the entire collection's inquiry into early modern theatricality: the need to further specify its alphabet of significant properties (or its 'vocabulary', to use a term from Alan Dessen's path-breaking work);[27] the recurrent patterns and recombinations

---

[26] States, *Great Reckonings*, 57.

[27] Alan Dessen, *Recovering Shakespeare's Theatrical Vocabulary* (Cambridge: Cambridge University Press, 1995). Dessen's work shows how far textual evidence can take a critic into theatricality and provides a blueprint for the approach adopted throughout this collection; see especially Dessen, *Elizabethan Drama and the Viewer's Eye* (Chapel Hill: University of North Carolina Press, 1977) and Dessen, *Elizabethan Stage Conventions and Modern Interpreters* (Cambridge: Cambridge University Press, 1984).

of elements that circulate both inside and outside the theatres, at many different scales; and the varieties of perception and experience, affective response, and intellectual understanding that are activated in the theatrical encounter and that give it its peculiar life.

To these problems I would now like to add a fourth, which has already appeared briefly and which the category of form, too, helps bring into focus. At the risk of some pretension, it could be described as the problem of the ontology of theatre and its creations. This is not a problem of arriving at an essential definition for theatre (what theatre 'is') but a problem of specifying the multiple *ways* in which theatre 'is', or *how* it is, in its modes, functions, and effects. The problem implies, too, the pluralized notion that there might different *kinds* of being that theatre can bestow on its actors, audiences, characters, ideas, and things. In her essay on 'Skill', to take one example, Evelyn Tribble cites a passage from Thomas Heywood's 'Prologue' to Christopher Marlowe's *The Jew of Malta*, added upon the occasion of its revival at the Cockpit in 1633, to show how powerful the memory of the actor Edward Alleyn remained on the stage after his death. What precisely does Heywood mean when he declares that:

> ... by the best of Poets in that age
> The Malta-Jew *had being, and was made*;
> And He, then by the best of actors play'd (A4ᵛ; my emphasis)

For Heywood, Barabas the character in some sense precedes Alleyn the actor and is entirely distinct from him, a being all his own. But what kind of being is he? For States, the character is 'the actor's first person', an image of a person who 'passes through' the actor's voice and body;[28] he is a bundle of events, a combination of action, *ethos*, and thought[29] that comes to life upon the actor's frame. 'One might think of a play', States suggests (quoting Kant):

> ... as a closed society of 'substances' coexisting in 'dynamical communion.' These substances of course are characters represented by actors...[30]

> Thus plays, in their fashion, are efficient machines whose parts are characters who are made of actors. All characters in a play are nested together in 'dynamical communion,' or in what we might call a reciprocating balance of nature: every character 'contains in itself' the cause of actions, or determinations, in other characters and the effects of their causality... And, as in the physical world, if a character's properties are altered his place in the play's nature is altered as well.[31]

Each character exhibits a principle of 'directional lifelikeness'[32] that allows him or her to move in relation to the other characters; this 'lifelikeness' is not incomplete but is, to the contrary, entirely complete because *that is all there is*. However much we may infer additional details or 'real-ize' a theatrical character, who 'continues to

---

28 States, *Great Reckonings*, 124–5.   29 States, *Great Reckonings*, 131.
30 States, *Great Reckonings*, 144–5.   31 States, *Great Reckonings*, 146–7.
32 States, *Great Reckonings*, 150.

live in the dotted-line real of etcetera behavior' the minute he or she leaves the stage, as States puts it,[33] this imaginative realization is unnecessary to the illusion taking place on the stage before us, which supplies for us, whether through word or action, everything necessary to the play world. Reciprocally, States points out, we 'fictionalize'[34] the real-world people who surround us as the supporting actors in a play that unfolds continuously and seems to occupy 'a circumference with our consciousness at its center':[35]

> Each of us regards our own history from the perspective of a self that has survived it, and in this fact is lodged the whole mystery of time and memory. All of this is condensed, miraculously, into the two-hour traffic of a play. The thing we call our *self*—the 'I' that is always speaking, the eye that is always perceiving—has its analogue in the drama in the fact that Hamlet is always Hamlet. The deep creatural sympathy we feel for Hamlet arises from the fact that the man who says, 'The rest is silence', is the same man who a little earlier (three hours by the theater clock) said, 'A little more than kin and less than kind.' These are Hamlet's first and last words. In the interim we have essentially been through a whole life. We have, as we say, empathized with Hamlet—by which we mean that Hamlet's history has been the interim project in which the attention of our senses has been consumed. We have lived another life, peculiarly inserted into our own here and now, which has produced the effect of an entelechial completion, dimly like the effect of an out-of-body experience in which we are presumably able to see ourselves from an impossible perspective.

In their own ways, many of the essays in the collection take up the problem of the theatrical 'life' that States describes so evocatively, from Richard Preiss's discussion of how changes in early modern stage architecture, economics, and dramaturgy combined to produce the illusion of a fictional being endowed with secret depths, motives, and drives—a 'modern' sense of character that only becomes further reified by eighteenth- and nineteenth-century preferences for reading plays rather than attending theatre—to Madhavi Menon's essay on 'Desire'. Menon trains her attention on the absence of the Indian boy in Shakespeare's *A Midsummer Night's Dream*, an absence that indicates to us the disembodied, immaterial nature of *all* dramatic character, whether from the point of view of print (where all bodies are imaginary) but also, more unexpectedly, on the stage itself. For the theatrical character, too, never has a proper body; although we tend to think of the character as borrowing the actor's body and living with it, inside it, or upon it—although we always *desire* a body for the character and supply a body for it—strictly speaking, bodilessness turns out to be a condition for the character's mode of existence: the experience of fiction, we could say, turns out to be a state of perpetual desire for a body that always remains absent.

No doubt this 'bodiless body' and its persistent absence is possible on stage because theatricality in general was never exclusively a material phenomenon.

---

[33] States, *Great Reckonings*, 151.   [34] States, *Great Reckonings*, 151.
[35] States, *Great Reckonings*, 152.

Certainly theatre is 'material' in the sense that specific objects, bodies, and structural elements become integral aspects of a performance and make it possible. And we know that the theatres were embedded in complex networks of institutions, commodities, and work, as some of the best materialist work has shown us.[36] But theatre is also always intellectual, mental, fictional, abstract; it is driven by problems and ideas as much as by props, by concepts and figures, as much as by bodies. Theatre parades its ideas around on stage before us by embedding them in substances, scattering them like seeds in speech, 'personating' them in assembled characters; it opens a space in which the persistent linking of ideas to persons in a fictional mode can be staged, to be at once reflected upon and vividly experienced. And since theatre is always a *collective* art, it invites us to inquire into the source of its magnetic ideas—those ideas that are powerful enough to hold us together. And so perhaps the promise of 'theatricality' is nothing less than a new ontology of ideas (which was, after all, one of the exciting things about materialism in the first place): a new account of the specific and plural modes of being that ideas assume, of how we live with them and of how they often live parasitically through us.[37] As I have suggested, this new ontology of ideas would quickly become an ontology of fiction, and especially of 'fiction experienced collectively in a live form', which I would propose as another working definition for the notion of 'theatricality' that organizes the essays in this collection. To enter into an imaginative contract with a play, whether actively and disruptively or passively and silently, means acknowledging its ethical stakes and thus granting the play a power that extends beyond its fictional bounds. But it is also to recognize that this power originates *in* a fictional state: a strange condition that is at once real and imaginary, immaterial and embodied, present before us and yet somehow also always inaccessible.

[36] See, for instance, Steven Mullaney, *The Place of the Stage: License, Place, and Power in Renaissance England* (Chicago: University of Chicago Press, 1988); Mary Bly, *Queer Virgins and Virgin Queans on the Early Modern Stage* (Oxford: Oxford University Press, 2000); Marjorie Garber, 'Dress Codes, or the Theatricality of Difference', in *Vested Interests: Cross Dressing and Cultural Anxiety* (New York: Routledge, 2002), 21–40; Ann Rosalind Jones and Peter Stallybrass, *Renaissance Clothing and the Materials of Memory* (Cambridge: Cambridge University Press, 2001); the essays collected in Natasha Korda and Jonathan Gil Harris, eds., *Staged Properties in Early Modern English Drama* (Cambridge: Cambridge University Press, 2002); Andrew Sofer, *The Stage Life of Props* (Ann Arbor: University of Michigan Press, 2003); Ric Knowles, *Reading the Material Theatre* (Cambridge: Cambridge University Press, 2004); Will Fisher, *Materializing Gender in Early Modern Literature and Culture* (Cambridge: Cambridge University Press, 2006); Jean E. Howard, *Theater of a City: The Places of London Comedy, 1598-1642* (Philadelphia: University of Pennsylvania Press, 2007); Valerie Forman, *Tragicomic Redemptions: Global Economics and the Early Modern English Stage* (Philadelphia: University of Pennsylvania Press, 2008); Natasha Korda, *Labors Lost: Women's Work and the Early Modern English Stage* (Philadelphia: University of Pennsylvania Press, 2011); Mario DiGangi, *Sexual Types: Embodiment, Agency, and Dramatic Character from Shakespeare to Shirley* (Philadelphia: University of Pennsylvania Press, 2011).

[37] I am inspired by Gilles Deleuze, 'The Method of Dramatization', in *Desert Islands and Other Texts, 1953-1974*, ed. David Lapoujade, trans. Michael Taormina (New York: Semiotexte, 2004; first pub. 2002), 94–116, and by Martin Puchner, *The Drama of Ideas: Platonic Provocations in Theater and Philosophy* (Oxford and New York: Oxford University Press, 2010).

As I conclude, I would like to thank several people who were vital to assembling this collection: Sezen Unluonen, who brought her keen eye and meticulous attention to each of the essays as I was preparing them for publication; Sarah Hopkinson, who assisted in many of its final stages; the generous assistance of the Undergraduate Research Partnership Program at the Radcliffe Institute for Advanced Study, Harvard University; my research assistants at Rutgers, Lauren Devitt and Stephanie Hunt; James Swenson, Dean of Humanities at Rutgers, and Douglas Greenberg, Dean of the School of Arts and Sciences at Rutgers, for their support of the Program in Early Modern Studies and for the leave time during which I assembled the volume; Alastair Bellany, Director of the Rutgers British Studies Center, Meredith McGill, Director of the Center for Cultural Analysis, Curtis Dunn at the CCA, and Kathryn Fisher at the RBSC, all of whom made possible the conference at which contributors were able to present preliminary versions of their essays; Gina Bloom, Erika Lin, Scott Trudell, William West, Mary Ann Frese Witt, and the three readers at Oxford University Press, all of whose comments helped refine my approach to the volume in significant ways; Paul Strohm and Andrew McNeillie, who first suggested that I edit a volume in the Twenty-First Century Approaches series; Jacqueline Baker, who gave the project new life, and Rachel Platt, Jenny Townshend, Elizabeth Chadwick, and Gillian Northcott Liles, who expertly brought it through production. An earlier version of my introduction first appeared until the title 'Toward a New Theatricality?', written for the special 40th anniversary issue of *Renaissance Drama*, n.s. 40 (2012), 'What is Renaissance Drama?', ed. Jeffrey Masten and William N. West (29–35); I am grateful to Northwestern University Press for granting me permission to reproduce it here. A section of Gina Bloom's essay on 'Games' first appeared in Gina Bloom, '"My Feet See Better than My Eyes": Spatial Mastery and the Game of Masculinity in Arden of Faversham's Amphitheatre', *Theatre Survey* 53.1 (April 2012), 5–28, copyright © 2012 by the American Society for Theatre Research, and is reprinted here with the kind permission of Cambridge University Press. Permissions for all images may be found in their captions.

FURTHER READING

Davis, Tracy C. and Thomas Postlewait, eds. *Theatricality* (Cambridge: Cambridge University Press, 2003).

Deleuze, Gilles. 'The Method of Dramatization', in *Desert Islands and Other Texts, 1953–1974*, ed. David Lapoujade, trans. Michael Taormina (New York: Semiotexte, 2004; first pub. 2002), 94–116.

Doran, Madeleine. *Endeavors of Art: A Study of Form in Elizabethan Drama* (Madison: University of Wisconsin Press, 1954).

Dutton, Richard, ed. *The Oxford Handbook of Early Modern Theatre* (Oxford: Oxford University Press, 2009).

Féral, Josette, ed., special issue on 'Theatricality', *SubStance* 31.2–3 (2002).

Hodgdon, Barbara and W. B. Worthen, eds. *A Companion to Shakespeare and Performance* (Oxford: Blackwell, 2005).

States, Bert O. *Great Reckonings in Little Rooms: On the Phenomenology of Theater* (Berkeley: University of California Press, 1985).

CHAPTER 2

STAGE

LAURA WEIGERT

What can several foundational images pertaining to the history of the European stage tell us about the nature of early modern 'theatricality': the practices, representational strategies, and organizing principles that defined dramatic performance from the late fourteenth century through to the sixteenth? In what follows, I will be focusing on a period of change from the performance of mystery plays, ceremonial entries, and other occasional events, all of which often took place across multiple staging areas, to the fixed buildings designated for the performance of plays that we associate with the early modern stage. And the story of this transition begins with the following picture (Figure 1).[1] Serving as frontispiece to a written script of a Passion play performed in the northern French city of Valenciennes in 1547, the coloured ink drawing depicts a series of buildings in a frieze-like arrangement upon the length of a rectangular platform. Textual tags on these architectural structures identify them as the location of key events in the play, including heaven on the left, hell on the right, and Jerusalem and Herod's palace in between. The inscription along the top informs us that what we see is the 'stage or theatre'—'le hourdement ou théâtre'—just as it was when the play was performed. Theatre historians have taken this picture and the text that identifies its content at face value: in both scholarly and popular accounts, the picture illustrates what is referred to as 'the Medieval stage'.[2]

However important images such as the Valenciennes frontispiece may be to our history of medieval and early modern theatricality, they do not contribute to it in

---

[1] Paris, Bibliothèque Nationale de France, MS. fr. Rothschild I-7-3, fols. 1v–2 bis.

[2] A few examples of the use of the image in English-language publications include A. M. Nagler, *The Medieval Religious Stage: Shapes and Phantoms* (New Haven: Yale University Press, 1976), cover illustration; George Altman et al., *Theater Pictorial* (Berkeley: University of California Press, 1953), 56–7; John Wesley Harris, *Medieval Theatre in Context* (London: Routledge, 1992), figure 6. David Wiles has shown how other types of pictures contributed to the mischaracterization of the pre-modern English theatre; see his 'Seeing is Believing. The Historian's Use of Images', in Charlotte M. Canning and Thomas Postlewait, eds., *Representing the Past: Essays in Performance Historiography* (Iowa City: University of Iowa Press, 2010), 215–39.

the direct, evidentiary way that theatre historians have usually assumed. Indeed, I will argue that the image actually *obscures* our understanding of what was unique, strange, and exciting about the variety of performances that took place during the fifteenth and sixteenth centuries, not in 'theatres' but in churches, courts, and city streets and squares. Other images, less frequently associated with the history of theatre, preserve a vestige of the distinctiveness of such events; the vocabulary associated with these performances testifies to their multiplicity and in many ways unexpected components. Bridging the artificial historical division between late medieval and early modern, these pictorial and written artefacts expand and refine our understanding of the nature of 'theatricality' in the period.

From my study of these diverse pictures and contemporary written documents, two arguments will emerge. First, I will propose that what we understand in the singular as an epochal 'medieval stage' or 'early modern stage' must be understood rather as a plurality of stag*es* and staging practices, across spatial configurations of performance that could never be captured by a single image. Second, these forms of performance were not limited to, nor did they privilege, the human body as a primary conveyor of meaning: they were populated by many different kinds of entities—both animate and inanimate—all of which contributed to the living art of performance in the period. In many ways, the Valenciennes frontispiece is recognizable to us because it imagines a performance that took place in 1547 through the lens of another performance tradition, one that more closely resembles the modern playgoing experience. Implicit in the conception of the stage that guided the picture's making, a conception that the picture in turn supports, is the existence of a fixed site upon which events are performed, a site, moreover, that is separate from the one reserved for an audience. It is only a slight move from this particular 'stage' to considering 'the stage' in general as a distinct medium, and it is the history of these concepts of 'stage' that the Valenciennes illustration both captures and conceals.

The stage as performance site

To make the first point it is useful to re-evaluate the Valenciennes frontispiece. The 'stage or theatre' it depicts certainly looks different from those associated with the modern playgoing experience: the proximity and juxtaposition of geographically removed locations along the platform; the grandiose machinery that emitted smoke and flames; and the moralizing dichotomy between heaven on the left and hell on the right, let alone the presence of the characters who inhabit these realms. These features, all of which appear in vibrant and exuberant colours, have made the Valenciennes frontispiece particularly appealing both to scholars and the general public. Indeed, the multi-sensory impact of these performances was a crucial component of the experience they promoted. The complex machinery that produced these

Figure 1 Hubert Cailleau, 'Stage' or 'Theatre' for the 1547 Passion play in Valenciennes. *Le Mystère par personages de la vie, passion, mort, resurrection et ascension de Notre Seigneur Jésus-Christ en 25 journées.* Paris, Bibliothèque Nationale de France, MS. fr. Rothschild I-7-3, frontispiece (photo: BnF).

effects was expensive and became the object of specialized knowledge transmitted from one generation to the next. God and his terrestrial representatives and the devil and his legions were involved in much of the action.

Yet the picture distorts the fundamental spatial configuration of the performance tradition it commemorates. The event that took place in Valenciennes in 1547 is a good example of the explosion in scale of urban performances that began during the first third of the sixteenth century.[3] The standard length of these

---

[3] Raymond Lebègue, *Le Mystère des Actes des Apôtres, contribution à l'étude de l'humanisme et du protestantisme français au XVIe siècle* (Paris: H. Champion, 1929).

performances had commonly been three or four days.[4] In Valenciennes, the story unfolded over a period of twenty-five days, during which the action moved between geographically dispersed sites.[5] Here, however, the depiction of the platform as a single and self-sufficient unit already limits the space on which the events were actually performed. The two-dimensional surface of the picture plane and the thick black border around its edges reinforce this delimitation of the playing area.

[4] Jean-Pierre Bordier, *Le Jeu de la Passion. Le message Chrétien et le théâtre français (XIII–XVIe siècles)* (Paris: Champion, 1998); Véronique Dominguez, *La scène et la croix. Le jeu de l'acteur dans les Passions dramatiques françaises (XIVe–XVIe siècles)* (Turnhout: Brepols, 2007); Graham Runnalls, 'Time and the Mystères or: How Long Did French Mystery Plays Last?', in Barbara I. Gusick and Edelgard E. DuBruck, eds., *New Approaches to European Theatre of the Middle Ages: An Ontology* (New York: Peter Lang, 2004), 3–12.

[5] Paris, Bibliothèque Nationale de France, MS. fr. Rothschild I-7-3; Elie Konigson, *La Representation d'un Mystère de la Passion à Valenciennes en 1547* (Paris: Editions du Centre National de la Recherche Scientifique, 1972).

The drawing slices the 'stage or theatre' from its urban environment and places it against the white background of the pages of paper. In turn, it positions the viewer of the picture and by implication the spectator of the play at the centre and in front of this structure. That the picture appears before the written summary and dialogue of each day and the other twenty-five illuminations that accompany the text, however, establishes the 'stage or theatre' as an unchanging backdrop to the play in its entirety. Its placement at the beginning of the manuscript suggests that these sites remained stable components of the scenery and action throughout the duration of the performance.

Other textual additions in the manuscript assert the historical authenticity of the image in the frontispiece. The inscription claims that the 'stage or theatre' appears 'as it was when the Passion of our Lord was performed in Valenciennes'.[6] In a colophon on the final folio of the manuscript, the artist Hubert Cailleau is credited not just with the illuminations in the manuscript, including its frontispiece, but also with the design of the 'hourdement ou théâtre', constructed for the performance of the Passion play.[7] These textual additions strengthen the claim that this image corresponds to the one that a viewer of the 1547 performance would have seen. However, we need only note the absence of key locations in the Passion narrative, such as Golgotha or the Mount of Olives, to assume that our view of the sites at which the events transpired is partial. The sheer number of place marks mentioned in the text and included in the sequence of twenty-five illuminations corresponding with each day of performance belies the claim made in the inscription above the frontispiece that it depicts the 'stage' in its entirety.

The fact that the terms 'théâtre' and 'hourdement' are used in the inscription to refer to the same thing confirms that the former was not understood as an enclosed and permanent structure.[8] In her detailed analysis of twelfth- and thirteenth-century uses of the word 'theatrum', Mary Marshall differentiates between what she calls the learned antiquarian and the contemporary everyday usage: the latter describes not an enclosed structure but an open or public place, such as a city square or market-place (*locus communis*).[9] When used in this way, the Latin 'theatrum' and the French 'théâtre', which first appears in the late fourteenth century, emphasize an

---

[6] *Le theatre ou hourdement portraict comme il estoit quant fut joué le Mistere de la Passion notre seigneur Jesus Christ anno 1547* (Paris, Bibliothèque Nationale de France, MS. fr. Rothschild I-7-3, fol. 1v–2 bis).

[7] 'Il donna aussy le portraict du teatre ou hourdement avec Jacques de Moelles tel come il est painct au comenchement de ce present livre et come il estoit audit jeu' (Paris, Bibliothèque Nationale de France, MS. fr. Rothschild I-7-3, fol. 378v).

[8] The term 'theatre' has a long history and has been the object of nuanced studies, including, Mary H. Marshall, 'Theatre in the Middle Ages: Evidence from Dictionaries and Glosses', *Symposium* 4.1 (1950), 1–39 and *Symposium* 4.2 (1950), 366–89; Dino Bigongiari, 'Were There Theaters in the Twelfth and Thirteenth Centuries?', *Romanic Review* 37.3 (1946), 201–24; William N. West, *Theatres and Encyclopedias in Early Modern Europe* (Cambridge: Cambridge University Press, 2002), 43–56.

[9] Marshall, 'Theatre in the Middle Ages', 382.

audience and its primarily visual experience, underscoring the derivation of the words from the Greek *thea*, or a site from which to view. Yet in another colloquial use of the vernacular 'théâtre', the emphasis shifts from the audience to the perceived action or event of performance. In these cases the word refers to the site, location, or structure on which the objects or action to be viewed are placed, but not in the sense of a fixed building: it denotes the constructions made for the historical, mythological, and religious enactments that lined the route of festival or entry processions. The term is used in this sense, for instance, in the captions accompanying the illuminations depicting the temporary structures erected along the processional route during the entries of rulers into Valenciennes in the first illustrated history of the city.[10] These 'theatres' do not enclose a performance within walls; rather, they expand the geographic scope from which the different actions or events it contains were made visible. The number of such structures meant that a performance was not located in one site but took place at multiple sites that were distributed throughout the city.

Like this second use of the term 'théâtre', 'hourdement' referred to the structure in which different performances were seen: large-scale urban, processional, or banquet entertainments. The word seems to have been used interchangeably with 'eschafaudage' ('eschaufaudage', 'eschafaudaige').[11] Both refer initially to a basic wooden structure, the equivalent of the modern French use of 'éschafaudage', and of the English words, 'scaffold' or 'platform'. Carpenters commonly appear in records, and their contribution is often the focus of the descriptive accounts of a city's preparations.[12] The scale and format of these structures varied based on the occasion and the location at which the performance took place. According to the contemporary description of the entry of Philip the Good into Ghent, which displayed the same theme as that of the city's well-known altarpiece of the Holy Lamb, the scaffolding ('stellaghie') was three storeys high and measured fifty feet in length and twenty-eight feet across.[13] An anonymous burgher's account of a royal entry into Paris reports that the series of platforms on which the Passion was performed stretched

[10] Louis Wicart (de la Fontaine), *Les Antiquités de la Ville de Valenciennes*, 3 vols., 1553 (Douai, Bibliothèque Municipale, MS. 529). The painter, Hubert Cailleau, was responsible for the illuminations of both these processional 'theatres' and of the Passion play manuscript.

[11] The term is first used in conjunction with military fortification: the wooden platform constructed at the summit of a tower. At the end of the thirteenth century 'hourd' is the word used to describe the platforms constructed for the observers of tournaments. And in 1397 it is used as a synonym for scaffold (*Trésor de la Langue Français*, vol. 9, 954).

[12] See, for instance, the lengthy description of materials and labour involved in the making of the 'eschaffauts' for the entry of Charles VIII into Troyes in 1486 (Bernard Guenée and Françoise Lehoux, *Les Entrées Royales Françaises de 1328 à 1515* [Paris: Editions du Centre National de la Recherche Scientifique, 1968], 284–7).

[13] Elizabeth Dhanens, *Het Retabel van het Lam Gods in de Sint-Baafskathedraal te Gent. Inventaris van het kunstpatrimonium van Oostvlaanderen* VI (Ghent: Bestende Deputatie van de Provinciale Raad van Oostvlaanderen, 1965), 96.

to one hundred feet in length.[14] The account books for a mystery play performed in Mons also specify the dimensions of the scaffolding constructed to house the various locations in which the action of the play would take place, enabling Gustave Cohen to produce a diagram of these structural elements that spanned around the periphery of the market square in the city of Mons.[15]

What stands out in descriptions of the wooden constructions made for diverse performances is that the action took place on a series of structures—on *stages*, not on a stage.[16] The carpenter enlisted for the preparation of the 1547 Passion play in Valenciennes, for instance, was paid for the stages of the performance, the 'hourdements' or 'hourts'.[17] These payment records provide one explanation for the absence of important place marks along the length of the 'hourdement' depicted in the Valenciennes frontispiece. The picture could include just one of what were multiple platforms on which the action of the Passion play took place.

As Gordon Kipling has argued, attempts to produce strict classifications of medieval stages deny the interaction between these constructions and the site in which they were built.[18] Each wooden structure was built according to the requirements of the physical environment in which the event took place and signified in relation to its surroundings. The engagement of large-scale urban productions with the topography of urban communities was in many ways similar to that of dramatic events that accompanied processions into a city.[19] Both kinds of performances moved through and within the city and incorporated this immediate setting into the fictional setting of the stories they told. The location of a performance in a particular city or court contributed to the meaning of the event.

These temporary structures were erected to call attention to, elevate, and enclose the animate and inanimate carriers of meaning. They were not empty containers

[14] *Journal d'un bourgeois de Paris 1405–1449, publié d'après des manuscrits de Rome et de Paris*, ed. Alexandre Tuetey (Paris: Champion, 1881), 291.

[15] Gustave Cohen, *Le livre de conduite du Régisseur et le compte des dépenses pour le mystère de la Passion joué à Mons en 1501, publiés pour la première fois et précédés d'une introduction* (Strasbourg: Publications de la Faculté des Lettres de l'Université de Strasbourg, 1925).

[16] Graham Runnalls, 'The Staging of André de la Vignes's *Mystère de Saint Martin*', *Tréteaux* 3 (1981), 68–79 (71). For multiple scaffolds added to or removed in preparation for the different 'days' of a Passion performance in Montferrand, see: André Bossuat, 'Notes sur les Representations théâtrales en basse-Auverne au XVe siècle', in Georges Gougenheim, ed., *Mélanges d'histoire du théâtre au Moyen Age et de la Renaissance offerts à Gustave Cohen par ses collègues, ses élèves et ses amis* (Paris: Nizet, 1950), 177–83 (179); André Bossuet, 'Une Representation du Mystère de la Passion à Montferrand en 1477', *Bibliothèque d'Humanisme et Renaissance* 5 (1944), 327–45.

[17] G. A. J. Hécart, *Recherches Historiques, Bibliographiques, Critiques et Littéraires sur le Théâtre de Valenciennes* (Paris: Hecart, 1816), 31, 33, 34, 36.

[18] An example is Elie Konigson's division of medieval stages into five distinct types (Elie Konigson, *L'Espace Théâtral Médiéval* [Paris: Editions du Centre National de la Recherche Scientifique, 1975]); Gordon Kipling, 'Theatre as Subject and Object in Fouquet's "Martyrdom of St. Apollonia"', *Medieval English Theatre* 19 (1997), 26–80 (66).

[19] Alan Knight, *Aspects of Genre in Late Medieval French Drama* (Manchester: Manchester University Press, 1983), 117–40.

available to house the enactment of whatever theme is chosen, the common understanding of the 'platform stage', but are considered an integral part of the overall effect and message of a particular performance. They contributed a setting, background, or additional figures to the topic at hand. That such constructions made an impression on their contemporary audiences is suggested by their inclusion in the observers' accounts of these events. The court chronicler Remy de Puys calls attention to the complexity of the wooden constructions when he writes:

> We would do well to make known that all of the scaffoldings that were large and high, some in the form of castles others in the form of towers and many with doorways and loggias, were all from top to bottom of carpentry of beautiful craftsmanship and fabrication, from the doors to the windows to the towers and steeples.[20]

What is absent from descriptions of the 'stages' of these performances is their delimitation of an area distinct from and facing one reserved for the audience. The position from which the spectators perceived the action was not always differentiated from that in which the action took place. In numerous instances the audience and actors intermingled throughout the course of the performance, and the players moved into the site occupied by spectators. Moreover, the arrangement of these platforms was not limited to one side of the open area on which they were placed but most often stretched around at least three sides. The audience therefore was not positioned in front of the action but observed it from various and changing position points, none of which offered viewers the possibility to perceive the area in which the performance took place in its entirety. The action surrounded the audience, bringing it into the centre of the action and prompting an experience that was not just visual but also corporeal and participatory.

The potential participation of the audience in the performance and the site on which it took place is suggested in the semantic range of the words 'hourdement' and 'théâtre'. Each one can refer in contemporary documents to the site on which the action of a performance occurred, to that which housed its audience, or to the two sites simultaneously.[21] A similar structure could house those participating in the action of the play, those watching it, or both. In both words the semantic fluidity between the designation of sites for an audience and for the action points to the audience's shifting position as concurrently part of and as observer of a performance.

---

[20] 'On fait bien ascavoir que tous les eschaffaulx qui estoient haultz et larges aulcuns en forme de chasteaulx aultres de tours et plusieurs de portes et galleries furent de hault en bas toute charpenterie belle forte et artificielle tant portes que fenestres tours et tourelles' (Vienna, Oesterreichische Nationalbibliothek, MS. 2591 and printed as *La tryumphante Entrée de Charles Prince des Espagnes en Bruges 1515* [Paris: Gilles de Gourmont, 1515]). A facsimile of the printed version was published with an introduction by Sydney Anglo, *La tryumphante Entrée...* (Amsterdam: Theatrum Orbis Terrarum, 1973), Bii[v].

[21] Runnalls, 'The Staging of André de la Vigne's *Mystère de Saint Martin*', 74.

Figure 2 Terence, *Comedies* (Lyons: Jean Trechsel, 1493), frontispiece (photo: Washington, National Gallery of Art, Department of Prints and Drawings).

A pair of pictures offers a visual confirmation of the dual meaning that the word 'théâtre' took on within this performance tradition. Two different woodcuts preface the earliest printed editions of Terence's *Comedies* (Figures 2 and 3). The subject matter, authorship, textual transmission, and association with the 'theatre' of Antiquity differentiate Terence's plays from the types of performances contemporary with their printing in the late fifteenth century. As a pair, however, the two pictures that preface the *Comedies* illustrate the semantic flexibility of the word 'theatre' at the time. The print included in the Lyons edition by Jean Trechsel (1493) (Figure 2) provides an overview of the spatial organization of a structure in which a performance takes place. This 'theatre' is a building situated amongst the city's brothels; within it, an audience faces a proscenium arch and curtained stage. The 'theatre' of the second woodcut, used in J. Grüninger's Latin edition of the *Comedies* (Strasbourg, 1496) as well as in the French edition printed and illuminated in Paris (Anthoine Vérard, 1499) (Figure 3), also depicts an architectural structure. However, the occupants of this structure are situated around its exterior, rather than within it. The building thereby provides the seating for an audience, a large-scale pedestal from which to perceive the performance. Together these depictions of a 'theatre' incorporate the two functions of the structure referred to in contemporary texts: to house a performance and to offer a site from which to view it.

Two other images preserve a trace of the multiple stages of this performance tradition. The sketches that accompany a manuscript of a Passion play performed in Lucerne in 1583 depict the performance sites within the central city square as they were arranged over the course of the two days of the play (Figures 4 and 5).[22] Each one presents a detailed ground plan of the market square and surrounding buildings at a particular juncture in the performance. The diagrams do not present the spatial configuration of the play's setting from the perspective of a viewer but survey it from a bird's eye view. The copious inscriptions that span the surface of each plan identify the distinct components of the staging of the play. This concern to accurately preserve the staging relates to the function of the plans as both potential models for a future production of the Passion play and as commemorative accounts of an event in the city's history. We are not led to believe that we are seeing the staging in the way in which we would have seen the actual performance. Nevertheless, together the plans capture an essential feature of the experience of these performances. As we move from one drawing to the other, we become aware of the transformation of the setting from one day of performance to another. Rather than a fixed

---

[22] The two sketches attributed to Renward Cysat are preserved in Lucerne at the Blättersammlung. Cysat's detailed explanation of these sketches appears in the same library (MS. 172 V and MS. 172 III). A facsimile to scale of the sketches is reproduced in Carl Niessen, *Das Bühnenbild: ein Kulturgeschichtlicher Atlas* (Bonn: K. Schroeder, 1924–7, plates 8 and 9). M. Blakemore Evans devotes a chapter, called 'Stage', to the 'theatrum' on which the action took place, the actors' stations, and the spectators' stands in *The Passion Play of Lucerne: An Historical and Critical Introduction* (London: Oxford University Press, 1943), 138–75.

Figure 3 Terence, *Comedies* (*Thérence en françois*) (Paris: Anthoine Vérard, 1499), frontispiece (photo: BnF).

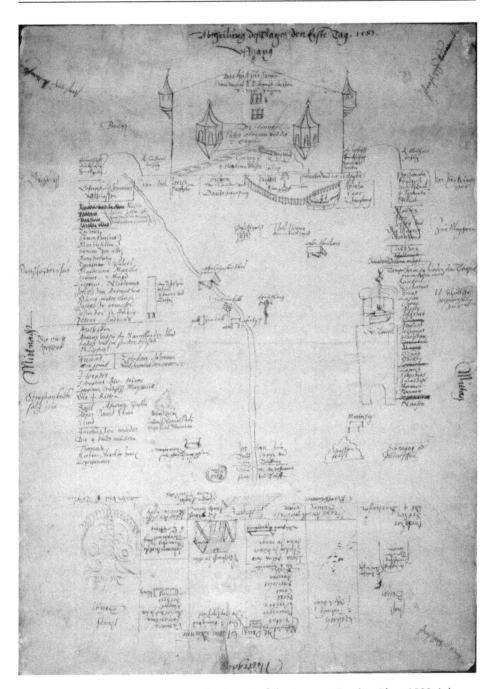

Figure 4 Renward Cysat, Diagram for Day 1 of the Lucerne Passion Play, 1583 (photo: ZHB Luzern Sondersammlung [Eigentum Korporation]).

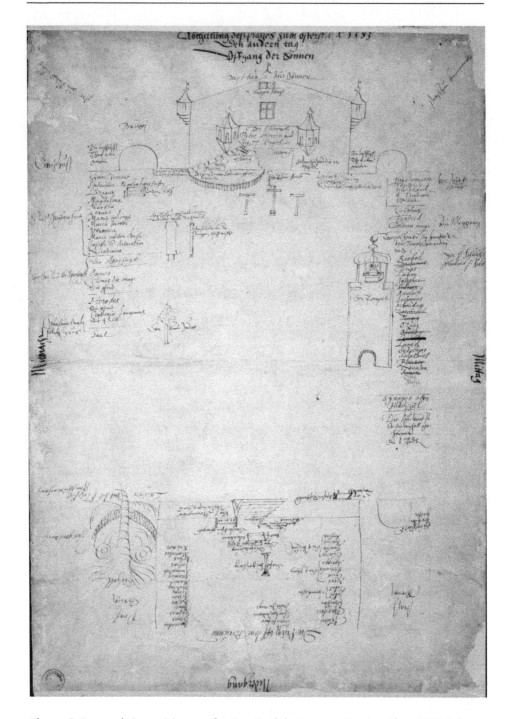

Figure 5 Renward Cysat, Diagram for Day 2 of the Lucerne Passion Play, 1583 (photo: ZHB Luzern Sondersammlung [Eigentum Korporation]).

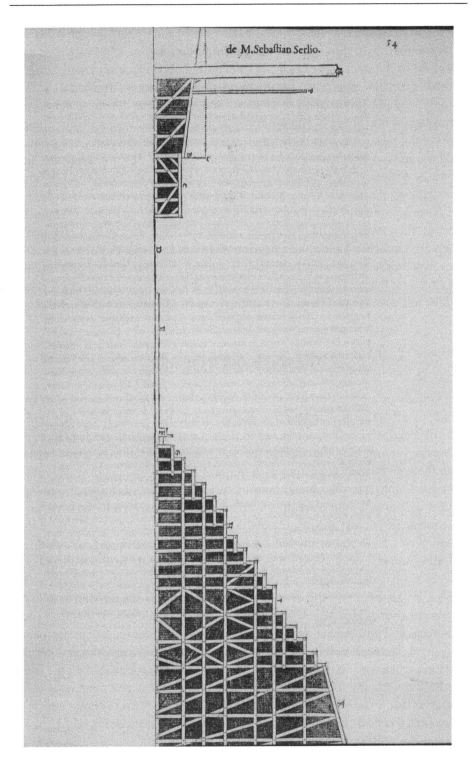

de M.Sebaftian Serlio.   54

Figure 6 Diagram for a Theatre. *Le second Livre de perspective de Sebastian Serlio Bolognois, mis en langue franchoise par Iehan Martin* (Paris: Jehan Barbé, 1545), fol. 64 (photo: Library of Congress).

and stable structure, the physical setting that housed and framed the action, as well as its relationship to those participating in and observing the play, varied on each day of the performance. The impact of this constant reconfiguration of the 'stage' is evoked as the viewer perceives the differences between the two drawings.

In the case of both the Terence woodcuts and the Lucerne drawings, the viewer's perception of one image in conjunction with the other recreates essential components of this past performance tradition. The use of similar structures to contain an audience and a performance event is visualized in the two Terence woodcuts. Yet it is only as viewers actively engage with the pair of pictures that they enact the audience's shifting perspective from spectator to participant in a performance. Each of the Lucerne drawings documents specific features of a day's performance, but together they evoke the multiplicity of stages and their distribution amongst or around the audience. Unlike the Valenciennes frontispiece that claims to represent a 'stage or a theatre', these two sets of pictures confirm that the scale and disposition of the structures that were typical of fifteenth- and sixteenth-century theatrical culture and the way a viewer perceived them could never be captured in a single image.

The stage and its media

The second assumption behind references to 'the stage' (whether 'medieval' or 'early modern') is that the term designates a distinct medium in which the human body is the privileged vehicle of meaning. But in the types of occasional performances that I have been considering, this was not the case; indeed, the signifying agents referred to in these performances encompass a range of representational forms that are by no means limited to the human body. Their descriptions suggest that inanimate figures and animate figures are subsumed together within a broader set of performance practices. For instance, the use of the word 'personnage' to describe the impersonation of a historical or mythical actor through a human being, a sculpture, a painting, or a tapestry indicates that animate and inanimate figures were not considered to be materials specific to two distinct and separate artistic practices. The French 'personnage' was the most common word used to identify the human figures representing characters within large-scale urban religious plays, banquet entertainments, and processional drama, as well as to refer to these types of performances in general. The word developed in a different direction from its Latin counterpart, 'persona', when used in relation to performances. In its association with the masks of classical antiquity, 'persona' focuses on one side of this operation, that is, the character that is conveyed through the body of the actor.[23] And although the word 'personnage' served as a way to differentiate performances involving human beings

---

[23] John Parker, 'Persona', in Brian Cummings and James Simpson, eds., *Cultural Reformations: Medieval and Renaissance in Literary History* (Oxford: Oxford University Press, 2010), 591–608.

engaged in role-playing from other kinds of performances, it was also used to refer to the inanimate figures of diverse pictorial media, which, like their human equivalents played the roles of fictional and historic characters.[24]

For these documents, neither 'actor' nor 'character' is an adequate translation: an 'actor' implies a human being, while 'character' refers exclusively to a fictional referent. 'Personnage', in contrast, does not refer either to the individual playing the role or to the role that this individual assumes but incorporates both sides of this signifying operation. It is better understood as an activity: the activity of assuming a role through different representational forms. So in the case of a statue, 'personnage' refers not to the material object but to the relationship that is established between this object and the human or divine being which it evokes. In reference to a performance involving human beings, the term refers both to those human beings and their everyday status and to the role they assume within the framework of the performance.[25]

Human, sculpted, woven, or painted figures were all seen within a similar set of circumstances. The same types of temporary structures, the 'hourdements' or 'théâtres', were erected to contain them. The arrangement of candles around these wooden platforms created a frame for the event transpiring on them, defining and heightening its visual impact. In many cases, textiles covered or revealed posed figures to view or created a space to enclose them. As processions passed by these temporary constructions, the curtains were parted, 'first concealing and then revealing to the gaze' what appeared within.[26] The variety of the colours of the textiles enclosing and spanning the top of such platforms, as well as the curtains hanging on either side, added colour to the sequence of orchestrated events along the route, linking individual ones together, or creating contrasts that would instil a rhythm in the broader viewing experience.

In addition to these practical and linguistic overlaps, a conceptual parallel between static and living materials also emerges in the descriptions. Animate and inanimate figures were considered to create the same constellations of meaning or to prompt homologous experiences on the part of their audiences. Bodies of human beings and those fabricated from other materials could potentially create the same scenario. Diverse representational forms could be arranged in similar ways, or alternatively could be incorporated together on a single platform or a sequence of them: automata and effigies, with sculpture and other two-dimensional images,

---

[24] 'Personage', *Trésor de la Langue Française*, vol. 13, p. 139, column a (Paris: Centre de la Recherche National, 1988).

[25] Dominguez, *La scène et la croix*, 292.

[26] '...qui pretereuntium cum oportunitate tum requesta cortinis ad hoc aptatis nunc velebantur nunc patebant obtutibus que nedum gestorum congrua fictione ac mirabilis pomposoque apparatus...' '[W]hen they are passed by, at the requested moment, the joined curtains first conceal and then reveal in order to gaze not only at the appropriate feigning of the gestures but also on the wonderful and opulent apparatus which conveyed most fittingly the tropology...' (Berlin, Kupferstichkabinett MS. 78 D 5, fol. 32).

with human beings. The ability to move and gesture, moreover, was not the exclusive domain of human beings, since sculpted figures could also be animated by mechanical means and the manipulation of textiles determined the duration of the viewing experience, essentially putting the stagings in motion. An address to the viewer could be achieved through the gestures of a human or sculpted figure or by an inanimate prop.

The individuals who designed these figures considered the human body as one potential raw material among others to be used in the orchestration of an event. For instance, following the recipes for edible dishes included in the compilation entitled 'Le Viandier' and attributed to Guillaume Tirel, known as Taillevent, are those that come under the heading, 'Interludes of Painting'.[27] Here the author refers alternately to a human body or to an image in two or three dimensions as supports for different 'personnages'. In the discussion of how to create a scenario for a tower, for instance, he describes first the components of the structure itself: it is made of painted cloths that contain four windows, within which are painted Sarrasins and Moors, 'pretending to shoot at the Wild Man'. To make the Wild Man, he continues, 'one needs a handsome man, tall and with good posture, dressed in a gown of cloth, socks and shoes, all of one piece—the gown entirely covered in painted hemp'.[28] The tall handsome man with good posture is one of several material elements required for this 'personnage', along with the one-piece costume with which he is clothed. In another example, the human body is interchangeable with one produced through paint. After a brief description of a staging of Saint Martha and the Dragon, the author concludes that these 'personnages' can be created either with human beings or with painted figures of the desired height and width.[29]

Both animate and inanimate figures were referred to as 'vif' ('alive' or 'enlivened') when their efficacy was appreciated. After describing the various 'personnages' made for the Labours of Hercules, the accounts for the banquet in honour of Charles the Bold's wedding (1468) commend the artists for making them 'as life-like as possible'.[30] The lamb in the staging at Philip the Good's entry into Ghent is described in the *Kronyk van Vlaenderen* as 'a figure of a lamb, made close to living'.[31] The staging

---

[27] Taillevant (Guillaume Tirel), 'Cy commence le viandier Taillevant, maistre queux du Roy de France, ouquel sont contenues les choses qui s'ensuivent', in *Le Viandier de Guillaume Tirel dit Taillevent*, ed. Jérôme Pichon, Georges Vicaire, and Paul Aebischer (Paris: Techener, 1892; reprint Lille: R. Lehoucq, 1991), 131–6.

[28] 'il faut un bel homme, haut et bien droit, vêtu d'une robe de toile, de chausses et de souliers d'une seule pièce—la robe étant entièrement recouverte de chanvre peint' (Pichon et al., eds., *Le Viandier*, 133–4).

[29] Pichon et al., eds., *Le Viandier*, 135–6.

[30] 'le plus près possible du vivant' ('Compte des ouvrages, entremets et peintures faits à Bruges, pour les noces de Monseigneur le duc Charles [1468]', in Léon de Laborde, ed., *Les Ducs de Bourgogne. Etudes sur les Lettres, les Arts et l'Industrie Pendant le XVe siècle et plus particulièrement dans les Pays-Bas et le duché de Bourgogne* [Paris: Plon, 1851], vol. 2, 324–5).

[31] 'eenen figuren van eenen lame, ghemaect near dlevende' (Dhanens, *Het Retabel*, 98).

of the four evangelists in Rouen for the entry of Charles VIII incorporates a mixture of animate and inanimate figures: the angel was a human being, while the eagle, the ox, and the lion were sculpted. According to the account of Pinel, a citizen of Rouen, 'the four evangelists were made so neatly that they all seemed to be alive,'[32] and the staging of the Agnus Dei was 'made artificially, very much close to living'.[33] All these cases suggest that the technical skill with which a figure was fabricated made it appear to be alive.

Such an interchangeability of painted and living figures is strikingly demonstrated in the documentation on the adornment of the Bruges procession of the Holy Blood. In 1395 and then again in 1397, civic accounts specify that the group designated as the 'ghesellen van den spele' (company of players) would provide 'tafele' (usually 'pictures') of the Apostles and Evangelists for the procession; in 1397 the accounts refer to this group's portrayal of the same figures in the procession as 'spele' (usually 'plays').[34] But there is no contextual evidence to allow us to determine whether these documents refer to pictures or plays: 'spele' and 'tafele' are both used to describe the same subject matter. It remains an open question whether the individuals who comprised the group made paintings that they carried or displayed in the procession or if they took on the role of apostles and evangelists themselves.

The ambiguity of these references to 'personnages' does not imply that contemporary authors were unconcerned about the medium for their performative message, only that they considered the boundaries between different representational forms to be more fluid than we might expect. Nor is this to claim that people couldn't see the difference between a human being pretending to be Saint George or a painting that pretended to be Saint George: the difference simply did not matter in the same way it does to us, with our assumption that the primary representational medium of the stage is the human body. In the fifteenth and sixteenth centuries, pictures and plays formed part of a theatrical culture in which overlap and interchangeability among forms of media were so common that the distinction between them is not a useful way of differentiating between types of theatrical performance. Nor was the spoken word inherent to the process of impersonation: staging involved non-speaking figures as often as it involved ones who spoke. When figures 'spoke', they often did so through textual inscriptions, or scrolls, or non-linguistic noises, or by words ventriloquized by human actors either concealed from or visible to the

[32] 'et aux quatre coingz dudit chercle les quatre Evangelistes hault troussés, et dont les trois estoient moullés, c'est assavoir ung aigle, ung beuf, ung lyon, et l'ange estoit vif; le tout des quatre evangelists fais si proprement qu'ils sembloient estre tous vifz' (Guenée and Lehoux, *Les Entrées Royales Françaises*, 248).

[33] 'Ledit Agnus Dei fait artificiellement auprès du vif treffort eslevé dedens ledit escu comme en armarie' (Guenée and Lehoux, *Les Entrées Royales Françaises*, 248).

[34] Léo van Puyvelde, 'Het Ontstaan van het Modern Tooneel in de Oude Nederlanden. De Ouste Vermeldingen in de Rekeningen', *Verslagen en Mededeelingen der Koninklijke Vlaamsche Academie voor Taal-en Letterkunde* (1922), 918, 928.

audience. Distinctions in media didn't matter in the same way to early moderns because they privileged the artifice through which the characters could be staged: the disjunction between a painting and a person was not one the producers of theatrical events attempted to disguise. In other words, a human being was considered as much like Saint George—or, in fact as *little* like him—as was a picture of Saint George.

Making the stage

Many factors came into play to make 'the stage' the presumed site of a performance and the human body the medium with which it was associated. In France, city streets remained the site of religious processions and ceremonial entries through-out the seventeenth century, but by the end of the sixteenth century the role of civic sponsors and citizens had become less significant in the organization, production, and actualization of these performances. Royal and municipal authorities exercised increasing control over these performances, which began to follow to a greater extent a predetermined script.[35] Municipal and clerical critiques of contemporary performances reveal their distrust of an event that exceeds the boundaries of a fixed and enclosed architectural structure. These accounts of performances and the legis-lation that accompanied them identified and delimited the site in which perform-ances could take place. A parliamentary decree of 1548 restricted the performance of large-scale urban drama in Paris.[36] The performance of mystery plays within public squares continued through to the end of the sixteenth century outside of Paris, coexisting with and, in some cases, conflicting with other forms of theatrical activity. The Parisian legislation makes it clear, however, that the civic authorities were concerned by instances in which plays were not confined by buildings. They argued that the spillage of religious drama into the city streets led to social disrup-tion.[37] From that point on, until the plays were prohibited altogether, they could only take place indoors, where the walls of the performance space limited the move-ment of both the actors and the spectators.

[35] Laurence Bryant, 'The Medieval Entry Ceremony at Paris', in Janos M. Bak, ed., *Coronations: Medieval and Early Modern Monarchic Ritual* (Berkeley: University of California Press, 1990), 88–118; Gordon Kipling, 'The King's Advent Transformed: The Consecration of the City in the Sixteenth-Century Civic Triumph', in Nicholas Howe, ed., *Ceremonial Culture in Pre-Modern Europe* (Notre Dame: University of Notre Dame Press, 2007), 89–128; Graham Runnalls, 'Mysteries' End in France: Perform-ances and Texts', in Sydney Higgins and Fiorella Paino, eds., *European Medieval Drama 1998: Papers from the Third International Conference on Aspects of European Medieval Drama, Camerino, July 3–5, 1998* (Camerino: Università degli studi di Camerino, Centro linguistico di ateneo, 1999), 175–86.

[36] Louis Petit de Julleville, *Histoire du Théâtre en France. Les Mystères*, 2 vols. (Paris: Hachette, 1880), vol. 1, 429.

[37] Graham A. Runnalls, 'La Confrérie de la Passion et les mystères: Recueil de documents relatifs à l'histoire de la Confrérie de la Passion depuis la fin du XIVe jusqu'au milieu du XVIe siècle', *Romania* 122 (2004), 135–201 (170, 171, 172, 176).

This regulation was accompanied by a narrowing of the representational forms associated with performance. In their critiques of certain contemporary performances, sixteenth-century religious and civic spokesmen increasingly assumed that the primary signifying agents of these events were human. Their most common argument was that the audience was prone to confuse an individual with the character he played in a performance, and since a player's social or moral standing was often inferior to that of his character, the confusion was particularly worrisome. One lawyer for the Parliament of Paris complained that lowly artisans assumed the roles of saints.[38] Preachers condemned a performance because the audience could recognize hypocrisy in the discrepancy between a character's spiritual commitment and an actor's conduct in everyday life. In a sermon delivered in 1506, Michel Menot denounced the audience's lack of concern over an actor's misconduct outside of performance: these spectators, he says condescendingly, praise the actor playing Saint Martin as holy but, following the performance, declare that 'the one who played Saint Martin is a nasty boy'.[39] This argument is an updated formulation of Tertullian's critique of the use of masks in Roman theatre, since 'the likeness of a god is put on the head of an ignominious and infamous wretch'.[40] Yet the assumptions implicit in Menot's remark, as in the larger antitheatrical discussion from which it emerges, overlook fundamental components of the theatricality they are characterizing. By assuming that the primary mode of signification of contemporary plays is the human body, antitheatricalists ignore the many kinds of materials with which a scenario might be orchestrated, whether human, woven, sculpted, or painted. Furthermore, they underestimate the audience's ability both to recognize and to appreciate the disjunction between theatrical figure and fictional referent. Audiences could delight in the correspondences or contrasts between actor and character, and they could accept a painting or sculpture as a legitimate and appealing representation of a 'personnage'.

At the same time that clerical and municipal groups formulated legislation to limit and control performance in cities, new texts and images appeared that provided more direct access to the 'theatre' of Antiquity and vividly captured the idea of a singular stage and the form of theatricality with which it was associated. This positive perception of the classical theatrical tradition resulted in part from the

---

[38] Runnalls, 'La Confrérie de la Passion et les mystères', 170.

[39] 'Ecce on ira querir unum juvenem et ludet sanctum Martinum...Cum sunt in ludo, habent magnum honorem: "O ille est sanctus, ille est domicella." Sed, ludo finito, dicetur: "O ille qui ludebat sanctum Martium, c'est ung mauvais garcon; et ille qui rex apparabat, c'estoit ung savetier"' (*Sermons choisis de Michel Menot [1508–18]*, ed. François Neve [Paris: Champion, 1924], 61).

[40] Tertullian, *Apologeticum* XV, 3 in *Latin Christianity: Its Founder, Tertullian. The Ante Nicene Fathers: Translations of the Writings of the Fathers down to A.D. 325.*, Vol. III, trans. Alexander Roberts and James Donaldson, revised by A. Cleveland Coxe (New York: Scribner, 1903), 30; *Corpus Christianorum Series Latina* I, *Tertulliani Opera Pars I* (Turnhout: Brepols, 1954), 114. Tertullian makes the same point in *Ad Nationes*: 'The mask of some deity, at your will, covers some infamous paltry head' (*Ad Nationes* I, 10, 45 [*ANF*, 120; *CCSL*, 29]).

printing of classical plays, as we have seen already, but also from the recovery of architectural drawings and textual descriptions of ancient Rome. The second book of Sebastiano Serlio's treatise on architecture was translated by Jean Martin into French and published in Paris in 1545.[41] The prints included at the end of the volume on perspective illustrated the spatial contours and distribution of a theatre, based on Serlio's design for one in Venice (Figure 6). Jean Gougon, the artist associated with a new classicizing trend in sculpture and the designer of triumphal entries of the French kings, illustrated the first French translation of Vitruvius's *De Architectura*, published in Paris in 1547.[42] His prints of the design of the Greek and Roman theatre adapted the designs included in the French edition of Serlio (Figure 7).

Through these prints and their descriptive texts, readers and viewers could imagine the sites in which diverse performances took place within Antiquity. This site consisted in a fixed stage, facing and elevated from the seats reserved for the spectators, and on which the scenery would change according to the play's content. The types of setting which this 'stage' could create were identified in terms of the types of classical drama: comic, tragic, and satyric; each one was adorned accordingly. In these images, the viewer of the picture is implicitly situated at a distance from the performance space; the images establish an ideal position from which to view the action, and the action is directed towards this point. As this position is fixed within the frame of the image, it offers the possibility that a position from which to perceive the stage in its entirety exists. The position the viewer of the image occupies is, in turn, one that replicates that of the viewer of the performance.

Serlio's and Goujon's illustrations make visible in a single image the spatial contours of the stage associated with one particular early modern playgoing experience. On the one hand, they represent a physical space that is strictly delimited and distinct from that reserved for the audience. On the other hand, they represent a symbolic space that creates the illusion of a world that is separate from the audience's lived environment. This fictional setting waits to be populated by living characters whose roles correspond with their function in plays designated as comic, tragic, or satiric. The stage these pictures represent fuses the theatre of Antiquity with that of the Renaissance and suggests the existence of an unbroken history that leads to what we call 'the stage' and the 'stage-based medium'. In its association with a theatre deemed medieval, the Valenciennes frontispiece fills what would be a lacuna in a history of the stage. What is relegated outside this history is a performance tradition with more permeable boundaries, one that could move into the streets of the city and that relied on an audience's ability to appreciate the range of media through which theatrical fictions could be represented.

---

[41] *Le second Livre de perspective de Sebastian Serlio Bolognois, mis en langue franchoise par Iehan Martin, secretaire de monseigneur reverendissime cardinal de Lenoncourt, avec privilege du Roy* (Paris: Jehan Barbé, 1545), fols. 63v–73.

[42] This volume was dedicated to Henry II (*Architecture, ou Art de bien bastir, de Marc Vitruve Pollion, auteur romain antique. Mis de Latin en Francoys, par Ian Martin... pour le Roy treschrestien Henry II* [Paris: Jacques Gazeau, 1547], fols. 70v–81v.

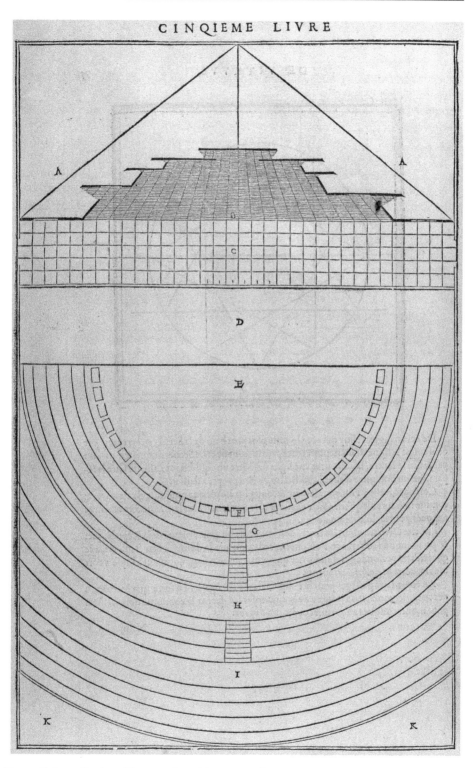

Figure 7 Jean Goujon, Diagram for a Theatre. *Architecture, ou Art de bien bastir, de Marc Vitruve Pollion, auteur romain antique. Mis de Latin en Francoys, par Ian Martin* (Paris: Jacques Gazeau, 1547), fol. 75 verso (photo: Marquand Library of Art and Archeology, Princeton University, Barr Ferree Collection).

FURTHER READING

Enders, Jody. *Death by Drama and Other Medieval Urban Legends* (Chicago: University of Chicago Press, 2002).

Kernodle, George. *From Art to Theatre: Form and Convention in the Renaissance* (Chicago: University of Chicago Press, 1944).

Kipling, Gordon. 'Theatre as Subject and Object in Fouquet's "Martyrdom of Saint Apollonia"', *Medieval English Theatre* 19 (1997), 26–80.

Symes, Carol. 'The Medieval Archive and the History of Theatre: Assessing the Written and Unwritten Evidence for Premodern Performance', *Theatre Survey* 52.1 (2011), 29–58.

Wiles, David. 'Seeing is Believing: The Historian's Use of Images', in Charlotte M. Canning and Thomas Postlewait, eds., *Representing the Past: Essays in Performance Historiography* (Iowa City: University of Iowa Press, 2010), 215–39.

Womack, Peter. 'The Comical Scene: Perspective and Civility on the Renaissance Stage', *Representations* 101 (2008), 32–56.

CHAPTER 3

INTERIORITY

RICHARD PREISS*

O pardon: since a crooked Figure may
Attest in little place a Million,
And let vs, Cyphers to this great Accompt,
On your imaginarie Forces worke.

— *Henry V*

For teachers of early modern drama, 'interiority' usually means class time lost to a reaction common among students: the sense that characters have lives, histories, and thoughts in excess of what is dramatized. Maybe she's not tamed, just faking; maybe pretending to be crazy has driven him crazy; maybe she had a child, and it died. Our own reactions are just as familiar: this is a play, we explain, not real events involving real people. Its ambiguities can't be decided by appeals to missing information; if the play wanted us to know other things about its characters, it would tell us. All the evidence we have are the words on the page. And yet student reactions point no less to the words on the page and are not altogether to be dismissed. They derive from an interiorized, predominantly verbal experience of the play, in which the burden of realizing character, setting, and action rests entirely on the imagination. They alert us, that is, to the historicity of dramatic interiority as a product of reading culture, and to early modern English drama's near-total absorption in that culture—indeed, to how reading culture grew up around it.

The fascination with 'interiority' has always had a whiff of antitheatricalism about it: a desire to escape space, to experience instantaneously and vividly all the mental transports of dramatic discourse, to inhabit others without the mediation and friction of bodies. Yet character infatuation is as old as early modern theatre itself:

* I am grateful to Tiffany Stern, David Kathman, and James Marino for research suggestions. My largest debt is to Henry Turner, who read an earlier draft meticulously and thoughtfully.

> Vpon a tyme when Burbage played Richard III. there was a citizen grone soe farre in liking with him, that before shee went from the play shee appointed him to come that night vnto hir by the name of Richard the Third.[1]

You know the rest: Shakespeare, overhearing her request, intercepts the rendez-vous, and sends Burbage a merry message about William the Conqueror. John Manningham's diary entry of 1601 is unverifiable, but the salient detail is its premise: it considers perfectly plausible the notion that a spectator might be so enamoured of a fictional character that she would want to import him into the real world, and to have sex with him—not the actor, but the *character*, for here anyone under that name will do. Plays were routinely titled for their most promi-nent person; subtitles of printed playbooks often advertise the more memorable characters; plays were packaged in cycles, stretching source material across mul-tiple instalments, or adding extra instalments if the first proved a success—Falstaff is not the only character to migrate across plays and across genres.[2] Seemingly made of denser stuff than the plays around them, detachable, mobile, and capable of acquiring new experiences, character exerted a 'reality effect' on early modern audiences as well: it was an expansion bracket, a growth market.

However much dramatic interiority flourished in the act of reading, in other words, it originated on the stage. The impulse to reify character is an artefact of the plays themselves, a response to something in their enactment no less than their textuality—perhaps, indeed, it is an impulse to conjoin the two domains, construct-ing character as a kind of inner space stretched across stage and page. But this 'interiority': whence did it spring? Why start doing it, if you haven't done it before? When and why did early modern theatre become invested in this delicate, tangen-tial business of psychological depth?[3] Early modern theatre, after all, was not just a metadiscourse, as New Historicism sometimes has it: it was—or at least was striving to be—an autonomous entertainment industry, with its own formal grammar, intel-lectual heritage, and economic imperatives. When we consider the world *inside* it, fittingly, rather than the world around it, we can better understand interiority as a site-specific technology, a practical invention not only consonant with the needs of plays but intimately connected to what Coleridge would later call their 'barbarous shapelessness'.[4]

---

[1] John Bruce, ed., *Diary of John Manningham, of the Middle Temple* (Westminster: J. B. Nichols, 1868), 39; from MS Harleian 5353, fol. 29b, 13 March 1601.

[2] Titles survive for over forty plays which seem to have contained more than one part. See Alfred Harbage and Samuel Schoenbaum, *Annals of English Drama, 975–1700*, 2nd edn. (London: Methuen, 1964), and Nicholas Grene, *Shakespeare's Serial History Plays* (Cambridge: Cambridge University Press, 2007).

[3] On early modern interiority see, among others, Katharine Eisaman Maus, *Inwardness and Theater in the English Renaissance* (Chicago: University of Chicago Press, 1995), 31.

[4] In approaching dramatic form as spatial practice, I am indebted to Henry S. Turner's *The English Renaissance Stage: Geometry, Poetics, and the Practical Spatial Arts 1580–1630* (Oxford: Oxford University Press, 2006).

Vicious circles

One can date the beginning of dramatic interiority surprisingly precisely: 1576, upon the opening of the Theatre in Shoreditch, the first permanent, dedicated play-house in England since Roman times. Although the Red Lion (1567) also had a durable stage and scaffolds, it lacked the one feature that made the Theatre unique: 360-degree outer walls. Like its London counterparts the Bull, the Bell, the Bel Savage, and the Cross Keys, the Red Lion was an inn, with a main yard accessible to coaches. And like every public gathering place in use by professional players in England since the Middle Ages—streets, market-places, town squares—it was thus a space to which ingress could not be controlled. This constraint had dictated the most basic fact about player finances: their method of payment. Fees were collected during or after the show, by 'passing the hat', and if a set amount were expected, it could not readily be compelled, because by then the play was either already underway or already finished. Though it often goes unremarked, the key innovation of the Theatre was not just a fixed venue, or the players' ownership therein, or their better protection from civic restraint thereby. It was the ability to charge admission, at standardized prices, ensuring a predictable revenue from each performance and irrevocably transforming the business model of the enterprise.[5]

Influenced in design by bull- and bear-baiting arenas, the first playhouses were circular, tiered structures, offering three viewing areas (yard, galleries, lord's rooms) priced according to luxury and visibility, and arrived at via separate entrances, where the corresponding fees were extracted. A circle both includes and excludes: in a very real sense, the opening of the Theatre meant the *closing* of theatre, its categorical restriction, for the first time, only to paying customers. 'Whoever cares to stand below only pays one English penny', observes the Swiss tourist Thomas Platter in 1599, 'but if he wishes to sit, he enters by another door, and pays another penny, while if he desires to sit in the most comfortable seats...where he not only sees everything well but can also be seen, then he pays yet another English penny at another door.'[6] Theatre still leaked out, of course, in the city-wide playbills advertising the day's performance, and in the parasitic forms of commerce that developed adjacent to it.[7] Yet its ritual modes of calling performance to

---

[5] David Kathman argues that this practice predated the Theatre, tracing it instead to the 1540s, when professional players began renting inns, taverns, and guildhalls for their own purposes. The fascinating documentation he compiles, however, confirms only his supposition that here players '*could* charge admission' (29), not that they did; such performance also appears to have remained relatively infrequent. His one piece of dispositive evidence for preposterous payment before 1576 I incorporate later in this essay. See 'The Rise of Commercial Playing in 1540s London', *Early Theatre* 12.1 (2009), 15–38.

[6] Clare Williams, ed. and trans., *Thomas Platter's Travels in England* (London: Jonathan Cape, 1937), 137.

[7] On playbills, see Tiffany Stern, *Documents of Performance in Early Modern England* (Cambridge: Cambridge University Press, 2009), 36–62; on bookstalls around the playhouse, see Stern, 'Watching

order—the hoisting of flags, the blast of a trumpet—were always initiated from within it, significations seemingly intended only for those already inside. No longer borrowed from existing social space by the cry of 'make room', theatre was now a room of its own, with barriers to segregate passers-by from patrons and to segment patrons from each other. Walled off from the outside world, all theatrical space suddenly became interior space.[8] However magnificent the scale and variety of the sights it held, 'theatre' now began by passing through the narrowest of apertures: a door.[9]

Such a threshold was without precedent in the history of early English playing, and just as the new architecture enabled a new economics, it also complicated them, determining the poetics that would emerge in response. From a playgoer's perspective, the disorientations of a closed playhouse must have been manifold. They are evident even in Platter's casual overview of playhouse pricing, which leaves unresolved what precisely those prices are *for*. Does one pay for one's seat, or—since seats were not reserved—for entry to the playhouse in general? And what about the play itself? The public theatre made playgoing at once a voyeuristic and an exhibitionist activity, so that even for a novitiate like Platter, 'see[ing] everything well' competes with 'be[ing] seen' as a primary interest. What one 'see[s]' is not just the stage but the rest of the audience, whose perspective always includes itself. Is the cost of playgoing the cost of the play, if the play is only a part of the theatrical experience? What, in absolute terms, does 'a play' cost, when that cost varies with one's vantage? If a play has no fixed price, does it have any inherent economic or aesthetic value?

Yet in another sense, that price had also become more fixed than ever. Whereas formerly playgoers were free to determine a play's value themselves by giving what they chose at the end of the performance, now every play cost the same, upfront. Excluding incidentals—food, beer, other divertissements available for purchase— the cost of one's seat suddenly became the *only* variable in the overall cost of playgoing. When one paid a penny to see a play, one did so irrespective of its genre, theme, author, relative novelty, venue, weather, audience, quantity of spectacle, quality of

as Reading: The Audience and Written Text in Shakespeare's Playhouse', in Laurie Maguire, ed., *How to Do Things With Shakespeare* (London: Blackwell, 2008), 136–59.

[8] See Steven Mullaney, *The Place of the Stage: License, Play and Power in Renaissance England* (Chicago and London: University of Chicago Press, 1988), esp. 1–59.

[9] This liminality—how one *entered* theatre as an integral component of its experience, producing not just expansion but contraction—has been neglected by previous studies of the influence of playhouse design on dramatic form. See Alvin B. Kernan, 'This Goodly Frame, the Stage: The Interior Theater of Imagination in English Renaissance Drama', *Shakespeare Quarterly* 25.1 (Winter 1974), 1–5, and Kent T. Van den Berg, *Playhouse as Cosmos: Shakespearean Theater as Metaphor* (Dover: University of Delaware Press, 1985), esp. 23–44, which stresses (via Karl Jaspers and Gaston Bachelard) the tendency of space, 'when it is experienced from the inside', to connote self-concentration and wholeness. But theatre was a journey *from* an outside to an inside, such that this wholeness may not necessarily pass to the occupants but reside purely in the structure itself.

execution, or the particular actors staging it.[10] Most importantly, one did so whether one liked the play or not. The opportunity to monetize judgement had been removed: payment preceded performance. Together with the playhouse architecture that facilitated it, this new custom of preposterous payment radically clouded the economic identity of theatre, rendering it something of a paradox. More than ever before, theatre was present, a visible, material, physical feature of the skyline and an institutional force to be reckoned with. More than ever before, theatre was also an absence, a void, an unknown, its principal commodities invisible at the instant one reckoned for them, sheltered from appraisal and ineligible for refund or return. For the first time, it became possible to see a play and not get one's money's worth.

Theatre now approximated those leisure industries that charged money not for tangible goods or services but for contingent, future experience—the very industries it geographically neighboured and whose buildings it copied.[11] The profits of suburban bear-gardens, bull-gardens, cockpits, bowling alleys, and dicing halls similarly rested on admission fees, hosting entertainments on whose outcome patrons could wager. Their 'product' was merely the invitation to gamble, to enjoy something not yet produced.[12] In 1596, William Lambarde describes playgoing procedure in terms reminiscent of Platter's, undifferentiated from those of gambling: 'such as goe to Parisgarden, the Bell Sauage, or Theatre, to beholde Beare baiting, Enterludes, or fence play', he writes, cannot enter 'unlesse they first pay one pennie at the gate, another at the entrie of the Scaffolde, and the third for a quiet standing'.[13] The playhouse offered the same uncertainty and risk, only without the chance to recoup one's admission; the gamble was the admission fee itself.

At the same time as interiority endowed theatre with an inside to which one gained privileged access, it intensified a pressure to clarify what that inside *produced*—whether it had any content, or whether this 'inside' was really just another outside. This ambiguity is the great theme of the early commercial theatre's most ardent theorists, its Puritan opponents, whose self-contradictory arguments bespeak the incoherence of their object. If the moralists were horrified by the

[10] This is necessarily to generalize in the service of a larger point. The advent of hall theatres in the 1580s and again in the 1600s introduced significant differences in both price as well as quality of experience, and amphitheatre prices gradually inflated during the early 1600s; as a rule, furthermore, prices doubled for a play's première. Nevertheless, none of these minor fluctuations much disturbs the constants: prices were standardized at *individual* playhouses and were almost never a function of the particular play itself—even repertory plays, whose value the market had already had time to assess.

[11] Intriguingly, Jason Scott-Warren suggests that 'the pleasure of animal-baiting...followed from the way that the bearpits and cockpits enabled animals to become objects of knowledge, exposing their inner natures to outward view' (74); see his 'When Theaters were Bear-Gardens; or, What's at Stake in the Comedy of Humors', *Shakespeare Quarterly* 54.1 (Spring 2003), 63–82.

[12] In the present volume (and elsewhere) Gina Bloom further explores the relationship between playgoing, gambling, and other early modern forms of ludic activity.

[13] William Lambarde, *Perambulations of Kent: Conteining the Description, Hystorie, and Customs of that Shyre* (London: Edm. Bollifant, 1596), 233.

proliferation of playhouses during the 1570s and 1580s, they were also awed by them. The phrase 'Theaters and Curtins' often appears in the antitheatrical litera- ture as a collective noun, as if both singular and plural at once; they are given demonic epithets such as 'Venus Pallace', 'Sathans Sinagogue', and 'the chapell *Adulterinum*'. William Rankins's allegorical *A Mirrour of Monsters* (1587) casts the theatre as its main character, making it the site of an infernal wedding masque whose lavish, shuddering description fills nearly the entire narrative.[14] In 1579, John Stockwood could not help but take note of how '*gorgeous*' is 'the Playing place erected in the fieldes'; preaching on the collapse of Paris Garden in 1583, John Field prophesied that 'by frequenting the *Theater*, the *Curtin* and such…one day those places will like wise be cast downe by God himselfe, & being drawen with them a huge heape of such contempners and prophane persons vtterly to be killed and spoyled in their bodyes'.[15] In the eyes of the antitheatricalists, the theatre's spa- tial and moral architectures reinforced one another: like its physical structure— built around a sunken yard—theatre is cavernous, concave, encircled, always a process of falling or being pulled inward. It is a 'puddle', a 'sincke', a 'pitte', a 'well', 'the gulfe, that the Diuell by playes hath digged to swallowe you', in the words of Anthony Munday, who warns that 'it behooueth you to be verie warie…how you thrust your selues into' them, for 'none can come within those snares that maie escape vntaken'.[16] For Stephen Gosson, it is simply 'Charybdis'—inwardness and involution epitomized, a place of total enclosure and darkness, its interior compa- rable to 'the Troyans hal[l]e in the horse'.[17]

From the nauseating *topos* of the playhouse, in turn, the Puritans drew *topoi* for the corporeality of playgoing itself, and for its insidious, nebulous pathways. 'You are no sooner entred' (7), Gosson advises, than theatre enters you through the 'pri- uie entries' (15) of the senses, therein to 'assault' you (43).[18] To come in contact with the playhouse is invariably to become it: fixated on its points of entry as figures for theatrical affect, as the point where self and other blend, the antitheatricalists can- not seem to decide if the playhouse is virus or host, the thing you are inside or the thing inside you. The city that tolerates playhouses in its suburbs is an infiltrated body that 'suffreth the enimie to enter the posterne', and so the private body that would resist theatre must take on its attributes: Gosson bids the pious to 'close vp your eyes, stoppe vp your eares', and Rankins counsels them to 'infence their

[14] William Rankins, *A Mirrour of Monsters* (London: T. H., 1587).

[15] John Stockwood, *A Sermon preached at Paules Crosse* (London: George Byshop, 1578), 134; John Field, *A godly exhortation, by occasion of the late iudgement of God, shewed at Parris-garden* (Robert Waldegrave and Henry Carre, 1583), C5v.

[16] Rankins, *Mirrour*, E1r, G4r; Stephen Gosson, *Playes Confuted in Fiue Actions* (London: Thomas Gosson, 1582), E2v; Anthony Munday, *A second and third blast of retrait from plaies and theaters* (London: Henrie Denham, 1580), 71, 97.

[17] Stephen Gosson, *The Schoole of Abuse* (London: Thomas Woodcocke, 1579), F4r; *Playes Con- futed*, B5r.

[18] Gosson, *Schoole*, A6v, B7r, F4r.

mindes…and bulwark theyr soules'.[19] Those whom the theatre infects inevitably assume its qualities. For the core trait of the playhouse libertine is an opacity and self-enclosure that conceals an essential unknowability. Despite the fact that 'comedyes make our delight exceede' itself, writes Gosson, opening the 'Pandoraes boxe' of carnal desire by which we are ever 'passing our boundes, going beyond our limits, neuer keeping ourselues within compasse', this eruption always remains bottled, bubbling beneath the surface and impossible to locate.[20] The playhouse is the site of contraction, never of symptomization, and Gosson can only wish that the lewdness it licenses 'were as well noted, as ill seene; or as openly punished, as secretly practised'.[21] An affair between two playgoers is conceived in, and concealed by, a furtive glance; the audience seethes with 'open corruption' and 'secret adulterie'; 'euery wanton and his paramour…euery John and his Joane, euery knaue and his queane, are there first acquainted', withdrawing to feed their lust behind closed doors. 'These goodly Pageantes beyng doen', cringes Philip Stubbes, 'euery mate sortes to his mate…and in their secret conclaues (couertly) they plaie the *Sodomits*, or worse'.[22] Theatricality: a parenthesis in daily life, concealing a not-so-secret transgression.

Perpetually passed over, of course, are the specific details of these 'Pageantes', in which their pornographic power would seem to inhere. This—the radioactive agent of all this silent tumescence, 'the poyson creeping on secretly'—is twice as invisible, and Gosson comes no closer than certain 'impressions of the mind…secretly conveyed ouer to ye gazers'.[23] But vagueness is the point: paranoiacally alive to a playhouse atmosphere redolent with conspiracy and resonant with menace, the moralists can only guess at the source of influences so pervasive they escape detection altogether. Theatre's mode of transmission, like its effects, is occult, such that its ultimate content becomes secrecy itself, the inwardness of its own architectural form. After numerous pages on the dangers of 'open theates', John Northbrooke admits that they are not 'open' at all, for 'I haue rather giuen but an ynkling hereof, than opened the particular secrets of the matter'.[24] For Gosson, likewise, 'there is more in them than we perceiue…the abuses of plaies cannot be showen, because they passe the degrees of the instrument, reach of the plummet, sight of the minde'.[25] Every indictment rests on the mere fact of occlusion, and perpetuates it: 'I intende not to shewe you al that I see', says Gosson, 'nor halfe that I heare of these abuses'.[26] Theatre, like the playhouse that framed and obscured it, fundamentally resists disclosure or comprehension—even by its own practitioners, for there is 'more filthines in [plays], then Players dreame of'.[27]

---

[19] Gosson, *Schoole*, F4v; Rankins, *Mirrour*, E1r.   [20] Gosson, *Schoole*, D3r, D1v–D2r.

[21] Gosson, *Schoole*, C1v.

[22] Gosson, *Playes Confuted*, G6r–v; *Schoole*, C2r; Phillip Stubbes, *The Anatomie of Abuses* (London: Richard Jones, 1583), N5r.

[23] Gosson, *Plays Confuted*, D8v, G4r.

[24] John Northbrooke, *A treatise wherein dicing, dauncing, vaine playes or enterluds with other idle pastimes…are reproued* (London: George Byshop, 1577), L1r.

[25] Gosson, *Schoole*, C4r–C5r.   [26] Gosson, *Schoole*, C3v.   [27] Gosson, *Plays Confuted*, C3v.

The box

And yet at the same time theatre perfectly discloses itself, revealing that there is nothing to reveal. Alongside the antitheatricalists' moral argument about the perils of playgoing runs an economic one that utterly contradicts it: in the same breath that they condemn playhouses as rank cesspools of hedonistic riot and semiotic overload, the antitheatricalists condemn plays as acutely *devoid* of content, as basically a rip-off. Here, the problem with theatre is not that it offers evil for one's money but that it offers *nothing* for one's money—hence its true, native criminality. 'Players', asserts Rankins, 'studie to *deceiue* the people with intising shewes'.[28] For Munday, 'the principal end of all…interludes' is 'to iuggle in good earnest the monie out of other mens purses'[29]; in his view, 'the people' are not just abused, but 'robbed'.[30] For Stubbes, plays are cheap tricks, elaborate sleights-of-hand; players are 'double dealyng ambodexters' whose fraudulence consists not just in their fictions but in their 'mak[ing] an occupation' of them.[31]

The claim that plays are insubstantial and counterfeit was not new to antitheatrical literature, and the Puritans rehearse it often. Neither was the claim that players are parasites, 'idle lubbers and buzzing dronets', 'their seruice…a kind of beggerie'.[32] What *is* new, however, is the claim that players have *forgotten* they are beggars: that they encourage the belief that plays are real, substantial goods, making their 'trade' not beggary but theft. William Prynne, synthesizing (and for long stretches largely reproducing) five decades of antitheatrical spleen, is most strident of all on the point that the playhouse itself is the ultimate swindle, allowing players to 'rather challenge as a due, then begge the almes of Play-haunters': 'all the coine they get by Playing, is stiled by themselves not Almes, but Wages: not Charity, but Desert…*and those who part with it, deeme it so*; who gratifie them onely for their Playing'.[33] Playgoers *think* they are paying for something, in other words, because 'they must pay deare, for their Admission, Seates and Boxes'. But in the final analysis, when the cost of the play is sifted from all the other 'vaine expences which Playes doe usually occasion', they are paying for nothing—donating only to 'Actors' rather then to poor mens' boxes, since 'whatsouever is given to Stage-players…is utterly lost'.[34]

Strangely, the image of the gathering box here starts to take on a dual reference, fusing both strains of antitheatrical anxiety into a single figure: the playhouse as a space of mystery into which one is swallowed, and the playhouse as a scene of gulling into which merely one's money is sucked—its contents otherwise bare, never

---

[28] Rankins, *Mirrour*, B2v.   [29] Munday, *Blast*, 116.
[30] Munday, *Blast*, 77.   [31] Stubbes, *Anatomie*, N2r, N6r.
[32] Gosson, *Playes Confuted*, E7v; *Schoole*, A3v; Stubbes, *Anatomie*, N5v; Munday, *Blast*, 76.
[33] William Prynne, *Histrio-mastix: The Players Scovrge, or Actors Tragedy* (London: Michael Sparke, 1633), 326 (my emphasis).
[34] Prynne, *Histrio-mastix*, 321–3.

fulfilling that illusory promise. Whereas for Gosson and Munday the playhouse is a black box, a trojan horse pulsing with incipient, explosive energy, for Prynne—and for all of them, simultaneously—it is an empty box, its final interior the player's purse. Here again, not just metonymically but metaphorically, theatre becomes synonymous with its system of payment, the blind drop of a coin into the abyss: 'never foster Playes or Players', Prynne obsessively concludes, 'by contributing to *their* boxes…the very contributing to *Players Boxes* (of which every common spectator must be culpable) is a Giant-like sinne'.[35]

At the root of the economic argument against playgoing, in other words, lies the same innovation responsible for the moral one: the enclosed shape of the playhouse, which, insofar as it imbues theatrical experience with a kind of extrasensory magic, also reduces it to a confidence scam. The patent contradictions of the antitheatricalists—their seasick vacillations between theatre's surface and depth, its sublimity and emptiness—are merely two unresolved topological interpretations of the theatre's new mode of commerce, which had polarized its outside and inside. Playhouses have interiors, but the plays within them do not; the body of theatre is three-dimensional, but the bodies it stages are never as real as it promises—never, indeed, as real as *it*. Locating theatre in its physical form of the playhouse, the antitheatricalists find its on-stage content emptier than ever, and oddly disappointing. There *must*, as Gosson put it, be 'more in [plays] then we perceiue', for otherwise there is nothing in plays that *cannot* be perceived, no secret, no mystery. Ultimately, the power of the playhouse is its mystification, convincing us that theatre actually contains something, or produces anything; it is literally 'gorgeous' in the dual senses of Stockwood's term, at once deep and vacuous, and thus Rankins dubs his archetypal theatre 'Hollow-well'. It is hollow, ironically, because the things inside it are *not*, *exactly* reducible to their surfaces—wearing their own insides, as it were, on the outside. 'Her guttes are turned outward', says Gosson of a character in a recent play, 'and all her secret conveighaunce, is blazed with colours to the peoples eye'.[36]

Antitheatricalists cannot entirely be trusted as drama critics, of course, but their appraisal of contemporary dramaturgy was essentially correct. Gosson is here not so much describing that character—'Love' in Robert Wilson's *The Three Ladies of London* (pr. 1584)—as paraphrasing her, which amounts to roughly the same thing.[37] Lady Love complains that this is what plays do to her (i.e. expose her secrets), and that that is why she hates them. Yet in saying so, of course, she is doing it to herself, still 'declar[ing] the nature of [her] disposition' and thereby turning her own 'guttes outward'. She is *called* 'Love', indeed, and her name both

---

[35] Prynne, *Histrio-mastix*, 327 (my emphases).   [36] Gosson, *Playes Confuted*, D2r.

[37] Conveniently, Gosson's passage corresponds to no scene in the unique 1584 quarto; this gave rise to the theory that the 1584 quarto was an abridged text, although better explanations can probably be offered. See Irene Mann, 'A Lost Version of *The Three Ladies of London*', *PMLA* 59.2 (June 1944), 586–9.

declares and delimits her nature: she is a personification, not a person, and personifications function only to voice the principles they nominate. Wilson's play is typical of the Puritans' exaggerations of theatre as a force for social corruption—it is a morality play, after all, and a quite innocuous one, hardly meriting the charge of scurrility—but it also bears out their aesthetic critique. As the prevailing genre of commercial drama in the 1570s and 1580s, the morality was a holdover from the mid-century repetories of itinerant companies, and it retained a strong didactic component reinforced by the use of allegorical characters, declamation, and pageant-like display. In so doing, as William N. West has argued, the morality plays descended from a humanist tradition that idealized 'theatre' as a space of encyclopedic, specular knowledge, where 'knowing [is] a species of seeing'.[38] Theatre, on this model, is an opening up, a space where all space is visible and nothing hidden; as an embodied medium, theatre *reveals*, and what cannot be revealed is not theatre.

'Character' does that revealing: literally a writing of and on the body, it is the abstract made manifest, a means of representation rather than its object. Morality protagonists are thus typically straw men, templates for identification designed precisely to let the viewer 'apply' them 'vnto themselves', as Munday put it. Similarly, we need never guess who the villains are, because they announce themselves; even when the Vice dons a disguise to fool the hero, he does not fool us, for he divulges his stratagems beforehand. Envy envies; Youth is young, and naïve; Dissimulation deceives, and says so; Justice is done, and what makes it just explained. Far from keeping secrets, morality seeks to dispel them, toiling in prologues, epilogues, and dumb shows to avoid misprision. It remains dedicated to a pedagogical vision of theatre where meaning is universal and immediate, in which 'what was seen was wholly contained and reproduced in what was said'[39] and 'all performed signs remain safely determinate'.[40]

The naming of the Shoreditch playhouse—'the Theatre'—acknowledged this tradition and in a sense brought it to fruition. Yet at the very instant that theatre achieved the status fantasized for it in humanist texts—the instant it became an allegory of itself—its moral dramaturgy suddenly became anachronistic, inadequate to the new theatrical structure and to the economic relations that it implied. Now performance unfolded across two different kinds of physical, symbolic, and moral space: playhouses are deep, but plays and players seem shallow; playhouses are closed, requiring acts of penetration and discovery, but plays seem open, transparently interpreting themselves. As the antitheatrialists watched drama in the 1570s and 1580s (or did not watch it, or pretended not to watch it), they were irked by the fact that it was qualitatively the same as the drama of the 1550s and 1560s, before

[38] William N. West, *Theatres and Encyclopedias in Early Modern Europe* (Cambridge: Cambridge University Press, 2002), 45.

[39] West, *Theatres and Encyclopedias*, 116.   [40] West, *Theatres and Encyclopedias*, 72.

there were playhouses to inflate our expectations of it. In their view, it is not that plays are confusing: they are too *obvious*, too flimsy, not sophisticated or challenging *enough*. A disjunction obtains between theatre's form and its content, and for the first time the entire institutional complex of theatre—not just its *mimeses*—can be analysed as a lie, a bait-and-switch, deceptive at the level of its very transaction.

Theatre professionals had reason to take this challenge seriously, because their customers sensed it as well. From the very advent of closed theatres to the closure of the theatres themselves, preposterous payment remained a source of endemic unease.[41] Prologues that introduced new plays to patrons newly alert to the possibility of failure and to the unavailability of redress faced the task of persuading the playgoer with fresh urgency, eagerly assuring playgoers that they *will be* pleased. Other prologues and epilogues of the period habitually equate patronage with censure, displacing guaranteed pleasure with the right to express displeasure. References to audiences' sitting in judgement on a play's life or death, or to their crying it down, are ubiquitous—and, as Tiffany Stern has shown, companies validated such suffrage not only by discontinuing plays after a bad première but by revising scenes according to audience reaction.[42] At the same time, companies insured themselves against failure by charging double for first performances, although if an audience paid twice as much to review a play, it could also feel twice as fleeced by it.[43] 'You shall haue Good Words for your Money', boasts the Prologue to *The Two Merry Milk-Maids* (1620), taking care also to inform them what they will *not* get—'no noyse of Guns, Trumpet, nor Drum'.[44] Similarly insecure notes are sounded by the Prologue to *No Wit, No Help Like A Woman's* (1613), which asks 'How is't possible to suffice / So many eares, so many eyes?', and by that of *The Roaring Girl* (1611), which fears that 'A play expected long makes the audience look / For Wonders', and many others.[45] *The Queen of Arragon* (1640), worried that 'no man may repent /

---

[41] The policy seems to have been rescinded after the Civil War. Collections then were taken only during the performance, which reputedly allowed gallants to deposit counterfeit money or to simply abscond after the first act. The Epilogue to Davenant's *The Man's the Master* (London: Henry Herringman, 1669) pillories those 'Town-Gallants' who 'visit our Plays, and merit the Stocks / For paying Half-Crowns of brass to our Box' after 'pass[ing] through our Scenes up to the Balcone'; others 'pretend / They come but to speak with a friend; / Then wickedly rob us of a whole Play / By stealing five times an Act in a day' (76).

[42] Stern, *Documents*, 82–93. See also Douglas Bruster and Robert Weimann, *Prologues to Shakespeare's Theatre: Performance and Liminality in Early Modern Drama* (Cambridge: Cambridge University Press, 2004); Brian W. Schneider, *The Framing Text in Early Modern English Drama: 'Whining' Prologues and 'Armed' Epilogues* (Farnham: Ashgate, 2011).

[43] For evidence of company business practices see Rosyln Lander Knutson, *The Repertory of Shakespeare's Company, 1594–1613* (Little Rock: University of Arkansas Press, 1991) and R. A. Foakes, ed., *Henslowe's Diary*, 2nd edn. (Cambridge: Cambridge University Press, 2002).

[44] J. C., *A Pleasant Comedie, Called The Two Merry Milke-Maids* (London: Lawrence Chapman, 1620), A2v.

[45] Thomas Middleton, *No Wit No Help Like a Womans* (London: Humphrey Moseley, 1657), A2; Thomas Middleton and Thomas Dekker, *The Roaring Girle* (London: Thomas Archer, 1611), A4r.

Two shillings and his time', goes so far as to list in advance 'the errors of [the] Play, / That who will, may take his money and away'.[46]

Some plays adopted an insouciant attitude to a newly explicit commercial transaction. In the Induction to *Bartholomew Fair*, Jonson's audience is reminded that they are already parties to his contract, having 'preposterously put to your Seales already (which is your money)'.[47] *The Careles Shepheardess* (c.1619) opens with a protracted 'Praeludium' in which a playgoer, Thrift, haggles with the gatherer— 'take this groat in earnest', he says, 'If I do like it you shall have the rest'—only to be told 'This is no market or exchange'. Sure enough, by the end of the Praeludium he has changed his mind, vowing to 'hasten to the money Box, / And take my shilling out again, for now / I have considered that it is too much'—long past the point when any real playgoer in attendance might do the same.[48] Joseph Hall's *Virgidemiarum* (1598) concludes its caustic tour of a day at the playhouse by watching it empty, and dwelling on a lone, dejected spectator:

> Now when they part and leaue the naked stage,
> Gins the bare hearer in a guiltie rage,
> To curse and ban, and blame his likerous eye,
> That thus hath lauisht his late halfe-penie.[49]

His anger is self-directed: he rues his waste of money on trifles. It is only at the end of the performance, however, when the stage shows itself 'naked', that his purse feels denuded, and he becomes a 'bare hearer'; he bought with a 'likerous' eye and is now repulsed by the unvarnished sight of what he paid for. Yet Hall has just described a packed programme, a mighty tragedy that 'rauishes the gazing Scaffolders' with 'thundring threate', then a jig that makes 'the Theatre Eccho all aloud / With gladsome noyse of that applauding croud'.[50] This is nearly all the playhouse can offer, but perhaps it is still not enough—perhaps the spectator is always left wanting something *more*.

The further back in time we move, the less settled the custom of pre-payment becomes and the graver its stakes, with the money box continuing to serve as the focal point for a new kind of theatrical melancholy. During a performance by the Queen's Men at Norwich in June 1583, a fight broke out between a gatherer and a disgruntled playgoer, who 'would have intred in at the gate, but wold not have payed untyll he had been within'.[51] By the 1630s, it was routine for cheapskates to sneak

---

[46] William Habington, *The Queene of Arragon* (London: William Cooke, 1640), A2v.

[47] Ben Jonson, *Bartholomew Fair* (London: Robert Allot, 1631), A6r.

[48] Thomas Goffe, *The Careles Shepheardesse* (London: Richard Rogers and William Ley, 1656), B1v, B4v.

[49] Joseph Hall, *Virgidemiarum* (London: Robert Dexter, 1598), Lib. I, Satire III, B6r.

[50] Hall, *Virgidemiarum*, B5r-v.

[51] Transcribed by J. O. Halliwell-Phillipps, *Illustrations of the Life of Shakespeare*, Part I (London: Longmans, Green & Co., 1874), 118–21.

into plays 'after the *second Act*, when the *Doore* is weakly guarded', and for their 'forcible Entrie' to get no worse than 'a knock with a Cudgell'.[52] Yet this case is different: like Thrift, here the playgoer intended (or so he claimed) to pay in full, but only once he believed the play was worth it. He ended up dying for that conviction. Rapiers drawn, three players charged off-stage and pursued him into the street, killing him—but not before, in his violent 'thrusting in' to the playhouse, he managed to 'spill the money out of the gate-keepers hand' and to the ground, setting off a public frenzy of 'gathering up'.[53]

Clearly, early playgoers were wary of being charged entrance and of the risks it entailed: once their money had disappeared irrevocably into a common box, they demanded something uncommon in return. Their suspicions were periodically confirmed, not only by plays that failed to please—as the Norwich playgoer evidently expected—but by plays that failed to materialize at all. In 1602, Richard Vennar advertised a sham at the Swan called *Englands Joy*, purporting to allegorize the life of Elizabeth in a series of stupendous pageants and to be performed by gentlemen and gentlewomen. 'The price at comming in', reports John Chamberlain, 'was two shillings or eighteen pence at least'. 'When he had gotten the most part of the money into his hands', however, Vennar fled, and 'in the meane time the common people when they saw themselues deluded, reuenged themselues' by tearing the playhouse to shreds.[54] If the anonymous *Mery Tales* (1567) is to be believed, Vennar's ingenuity was surpassed decades earlier by a grifter named 'Qualitees', who perpetrated a similar fraud at Northumberland House. The very first recorded instance of pre-payment is a story of cozenage: posting bills for 'an antycke plaie, that both for the matter and the handelyng, the like was neuer heard before', Qualitees filled the hall to capacity, hiring 'two men to stande at the gate with a boxe (as the facion is) who toke of euery persone that came in, a peny, or an halfe peny at the least'. He then 'came to the gate, and toke from the man the boxe with the money', saying he would now 'fetche in the plaiers'. Whereupon:

> They went in, and he went out, and lockt the gate faste, and toke the key with him...The people taryed from twoo a clocke tyll three, from three to foure, styll askyng and criyng: Whan shall the plaie begyn? How long shall we tarye?...Shall wee loose our money thus? Shall we bee thus beguiled sayeth this man? Shulde this be suffered saieth that man? And so muttrynge and chyding they came to the gate to goe oute: but they coulde not...Now begynne they a freshe to fret and fume: nowe they swere and stare:

[52] Richard Brathwait, *Whimzies: or, a nevv cast of characters* (London: F. K., 1631), 134–5.

[53] Halliwell-Phillipps, *Illustrations*, I.118–21.

[54] The National Archives, Kew, S.P. 12/285/fol. 149v.; quoted in Elizabeth Thomson, ed., *The Chamberlain Letters* (New York: Capricorn, 1966), 32, and Herbert Berry, 'Richard Vennar, England's Joy', *English Literary Renaissance* 31.2 (Spring 2001), 240–65. See also Vennar's (predictably different) account in his own *Apology: written by Richard Vennar of Lincolnes Inne, abusively called Englands Joy* (London: Nicholas Okes, 1614).

nowe they stamp and threaten. For the locking in greeved them more, then all the losse and mockery before.[55]

Something more than mere theft occurs here: under Qualitees' ruthless direction, theatre undergoes precisely the topological slippage that its new transaction predicted and that would so vex the antitheatricalists. Lured into a box by the promise of a genuinely new experience, the playgoers put their pennies into the box it contains, only to discover that inside and outside have flipped: the hall has become the money box, and the novelty they anticipated replaced by the experience of being trapped inside it. Uncannily, Qualitees manages to give them exactly what they paid for, a play 'neuer heard before'—a theatre so profound it refuses to speak, returning to their increasingly frantic questions only impassive silence.

Despite its cruelty (and illegality), in Qualitees' minimalist *coup-de-théâtre* lay a distant lesson for his more respectable successors. The problem of theatre after 1576 was how to ensure that people got, or at least *felt* like they got, their money's worth, when that equation was inherently imbalanced. Prepayment, built into the structure of the new playhouses, always conditioned disappointment, arousing baroque desires antithetical to the medieval paradigm of elucidation and fixity. In form, theatre connoted pregnancy and mystery; in content, its dramaturgy predicated on the visible, the only mystery became where that mystery had gone, as if the money box had swallowed the drama around it. Yet there, as we have seen, the sense of mystery persisted, tracing a progress of theatre from interior to ever-smaller interior. The shape of the playhouse and the experience of entering it fostered the illusion that it possessed an inner working, an inner life, something just beyond the range of perception. Sustaining that illusion once an audience was there required *not* giving them what they paid for but deliberately giving them *less*. If the money box epitomized the new anxiety of commercial theatre—its most watched object, the one container that always stayed shut—the solution was to construct a dramaturgy around the problem: to make the play, in short, like the box.

Contracting characters

If the analogy between round amphitheatres and 'round', complex characters is an intuitive one, the culture of the money box supplies a material and conceptual linchpin linking early modern theatrical economics with its aesthetics. Following the money from incoming patrons to gatherer, one can almost watch the aura of uncertainty intensify and the walls of the playhouse contract until they are small enough to fit inside a person. To construct a hypothetical person around that box, in turn, and to put that person on-stage was finally to harmonize dramatic content

---

[55] Anon., *Mery Tales, Wittie Questions, and Quick Answeres* (London: H. Wykes, 1567), I3r–v.

and theatrical form—to reconceive 'character' along architectural as well as semiotic lines, as someone who holds within him or herself not only a 'meaning' but also the space that could contain it.[56] Doing so also reconceived the very function of theatre by making the object of *mimesis* no longer the world but theatre itself, so that the world might in turn be refashioned in the theatre's image. For what makes those characters seem round, complex subjects often consists not in what they tell us about themselves but in what they *don't* tell us, not in what they divulge but in what they stubbornly withhold. Whereas an earlier allegorical drama had occupied the domain of the visible, the expressible, or the manifest, now theatricality required secrets, unfathomable motives and unrepresentable desires.

It is no accident that the appearance of this new theatricality coincided with the first commercial blockbuster of the early modern stage, Thomas Kyd's *The Spanish Tragedy* (c.1587). To be sure, *The Spanish Tragedy* marks several more frequently recognized firsts. Together with Marlowe's *Tamburlaine* (1587), it established blank verse as the default metrical arrangement of late Elizabethan drama; adapting Senecan models, it inaugurated the signature genre of the next decade, revenge tragedy; boasting a veritable orgy of murders, suicides, executions, and mutilations, it set a new standard for graphic stage violence. As a result, there is a tendency to call the play hypertheatrical—and it certainly is that, when 'theatre' is understood as a medium of the senses. Endlessly cited and imitated, such sensationalism was quickly surpassed, however, and cannot fully explain the play's endurance in the contemporary public imagination—why people kept going to see it, that is, long after its novelty should have worn off. Perhaps it is because they felt there was always something more to see, for *The Spanish Tragedy* gives us characters who keep secrets from us.

How to introduce 'interiority' to audiences unfamiliar with it and into creatures alien to it? Psychological interiority is by definition unrepresentable as such, and every attempt to represent it both misses and destroys it. And theatre is an embodied medium, limited at the level of character to externalized words and actions. Whenever a character does a thing—speak, think, move, exist—he or she must do so with the body in order for us to know about it; from the moment a character enters until the moment he or she exits, the character is always communicating, always revealing, always converting a state of being into empirical signs. *The Spanish Tragedy*'s solution to the theatrical problem of interiority is not to construct it on the level of the individual character but to do so distributively, in coordination

---

[56] Jacalyn Royce offers a competing version of this etiology, privileging not the external circularity of early modern playhouses but the *interior* circularity specific to the Theatre and Globe; the square stage and rectilinear internal angles of the Rose, by contrast, were less conducive to simulating ' "real" people in "real" places' (487). Yet this exaggerates the difference in acting styles between venues—the Rose was the home of Tamburlaine, Faustus, and Barabas—and forgets the mobility of plays across them. See 'Early Modern Naturalistic Acting: The Role of the Globe in the Development of Personation', in Richard Dutton, ed., *The Oxford Handbook of Early Modern Theatre* (Oxford and New York: Oxford University Press, 2009), 477–95.

with other characters, as well as props, costumes, scenery, performance areas, dissonant narratives, and events—the entire stage, in other words, is conceived as a system of externalities in whose collective density its members, and even its audience, partake. Warping our perception of theatrical space, expanding, contracting, and folding it, the play generates an 'interiority effect' that is gradually transferred to its characters; interiority begins not as a psychic property but as a spatial one, as a property of the playing space itself—as the literal sensation of feeling both inside and outside something at once. For the playhouse already was an 'inside'; indeed, delineating the 'inside' without at the same time disclosing it seems to have been the primary signification of the playhouse. This signification is everywhere in *The Spanish Tragedy*, compounded, scattered, and compressed; a decade after the fact, it is a play truly written for amphitheatre performance, grasping all the resources at its disposal—structural, optical, cognitive—and using them in concert. If the stage had not just a *frons scenae* but a back, an extra, hidden dimension off-stage it could silently incorporate, so, perhaps, it could incorporate the things on that stage. In *The Spanish Tragedy*, in other words, people come to operate like playhouses.

Take for example 3.11, in which two Portingales are inquiring after Lorenzo and chat briefly with Hieronimo.[57] It is a throwaway scene: they do not find him, and there is no reason for it other than to play off Hieronimo's madness against some unsuspecting, nameless passers-by. When the First Portingale is told that the house before them is Lorenzo's, however, something remarkable happens, in the blink of an eye. '*He goeth in at one door*', reads the stage direction, '*and comes out at another*' (3.11.9.5). The specificity of the direction is as bizarre as its superfluousness. The utility of having two doors on the Elizabethan stage was to create a locality opposition: each implies a separate direction, so that when a character passes through one, they are coming from or going to somewhere *different* than had they used the other. But a house is a single locale; the Portingale should return via the same door by which he left. Does the house have two front doors? Has he entered at the front, and emerged at the back, still facing his original interlocutors in the street? Where has he travelled in between? Has he wandered the rooms, calling in vain for Lorenzo, all in the span of one line? How long has he been gone? As Peter Womack elaborates in his essay for this volume, the effect is to suggest that 'off-stage' is a place, where bodies continue to exist and move in space and time, rather than just 'not on-stage'. Events—wordless, unreported events—*happen* there. A flurry of new questions arises: where do the characters go when they are off-stage? Do they *go* there at all, or *come from* there? Do they remain there when the play ends? Is performance but the extrusion of some deeper, persistent reality? Suddenly, the topology of the playhouse inverts: we thought we were inside it, but we are still outside, aware of

<hr />

[57] I use the text and scenography of David Bevington and Eric Rasmussen, in Bevington et al., eds., *Renaissance Drama: A Norton Anthology* (New York and London: W. W. Norton, 2002).

a further interior we cannot see. The stage at its centre, where the visible play transpires, is not really the centre; it is a membrane, a skin, merely the lid of a box.

This is hardly an isolated occurrence. Relentlessly, in fact, *The Spanish Tragedy* toys with its own depth of field, telescoping in and out, tantalizing us with the prospect of an underside that either cannot be represented or that disappears the moment it is shown. Lorenzo instructs Pedringano to kill Serberine 'at Saint Luigi's Park; / Thou knowest 'tis here hard by behind the house'; the ensuing scene, at Saint Luigi's Park, thus takes place 'behind' the setting of the previous one, yet looks in every way identical to it (3.2.83–4). At 4.3, by contrast, we seemingly find ourselves backstage, watching Hieronimo ready his play for court—conversing with Castile, hanging up the title, checking his actors' costumes. Yet again, this 'backstage' proves just another 'on-stage', visually undifferentiated from the performance scene that follows. Where 'backstage' becomes briefly visible, rather, is in the moments of logical confusion that accompany these spatial disorientations; it is as if the play were continuously changing its mind, precisely to register that it has a mind to change. When Lorenzo, Balthazar, et al. murder Horatio, they enter '*disguised*', yet Bel-Imperia instantly recognizes them—'save him, brother! save him, Balthazar!'—making the ruse pointless (2.4.57). When Hieronimo finds her letter identifying the killers, the direction stipulates only that '*A letter falleth*' from above—Bel-Imperia is nowhere to be seen, and from whom or where it falls we never learn (3.2.23.5 ff). Pedringano goes to the gallows believing his pardon is in a box, at which Lorenzo's page gestures teasingly throughout his trial; we know it is empty, yet Pedringano is executed before he can discover that fact—and for us the new, second-order 'box' becomes why, after such careful preparation, the joke omits its punchline. Conspicuously and almost wilfully, the play violates the grammars it sets up, at once foregrounding and enshrouding its internal mechanics. Immediately after his wife Isabella's suicide, Hieronimo '*knocks up the curtain*' for his play, veiling her body; yet he notes her death in the next scene, even though the preceding scene-change was his only occasion to learn of it.[58] Does Hieronimo occupy two fictional places at once—simultaneously at court and at home? Or, even more bafflingly, does information *travel* from the perfunctory business of scene-changes (which we are trained to ignore) into the scene itself? When he next reopens the curtain, Isabella's corpse has been replaced by Horatio's. We never see the switch get made: it happens, by an unseen hand, backstage.

Something similar occurs a few scenes earlier, when Hieronimo is being beset by petitioners and lends his 'handkercher' to Bazulto, an old man likewise grieving for a son. Realizing it is Horatio's bloody napkin, Hieronimo retracts it, and instead offers a manic profusion of nondescript items, seemingly pulled from his pockets: 'But heere, take this, and this—what, my purse?— / Ay, this and that, and all of them

---

[58] Bevington et al., eds., *Renaissance Drama*, 4.3.0. Editors usually solve the problem by supplying a stage direction for Isabella to 'exit' at the end of 4.2, but she has just killed herself. The point of the staging crux, I think, is to be a crux.

are thine' (3.13.90–1). Except for his purse, none of them is named, and but for his sword, he should have no other objects on him; after all, he is just a stage character, carrying only what his role requires. What are they, then? Bel-Imperia's letter? His copy of Seneca from the start of the scene? Or of *Suleiman and Perseda* from several scenes later? Or are they objects of a purely personal nature, with no dramatic utility—a ring, a watch, a notebook—never before mentioned and never glimpsed again? Which objects an individual production chooses is beside the point; the question of where they come from will remain. The scene seeks to express Hieronimo's internal state, and to do so it must forcibly create that internality, physically endowing him with an 'inside' to be emptied out—a subcutaneous lining that, even as it is secreted, produces another secret in the process, in its implication of some private life beyond the scope of the play. How many more things, we wonder, are in there? What else is on, or in, his person? Until now the body of the play as a whole has been illegible, but here that illegibility becomes a feature of its individual bodies; suddenly, the character appears a stage in miniature, not just a 'without' but a 'within' as well.

From the ruinous finale of *Suleiman and Perseda*—in which we are kept ignorant of Hieronimo's intentions until his revenge is complete, and, behind a veil of foreign languages, simulated violence turns real—recent critics have contended that *The Spanish Tragedy* represents a total rejection of the morality play's didactic procedures, advancing instead a dramaturgy of sheer, anarchic confusion.[59] Yet what the play seeks to generate is not just the unintelligible but something subtler: the invisible, a category that requires not the refusal to make sense but the *inability* to make sense, as if there were more to the play than it itself knows. In morality drama, this effect is impossible; there is no more to a play than meets the eye or than can be translated into speech. *The Spanish Tragedy* preserves the hermeneutic assumptions of morality drama precisely to subvert them, exposing the very rift between word and image, sign and meaning that theatre claimed to bridge. Not only is what we see sometimes never explained, but what is explained fails to correspond to what we saw. The play teems with explication: faithfully mimicking allegorical drama, every inset performance—Hieronimo's Iberian masque for the King, Revenge's dumb show for Don Andrea—elicits the perplexity of its on-stage audience ('I sound not well the mystery', the King admits; 'Revenge, reveal this mystery', bids Don Andrea), followed by copious exposition. *Suleiman and Perseda* is no different. Only here, such explication produces not a one-to-one correspondence between action and

---

[59] William N. West, '"But this will be a mere confusion": Real and Represented Confusions on the Elizabethan Stage', *Theatre Journal* 60 (2008), 217–33, esp. 228 ff. On languages in the playlet and the play in general, see Carla Mazzio, 'Staging the Vernacular: Language and Nation in Thomas Kyd's *The Spanish Tragedy*', *SEL* 38 (1998), 207–32; Janette Dillon, '*The Spanish Tragedy* and Staging Languages in Renaissance Drama', *Research Opportunities in Renaissance Drama* 34 (1995), 15–40; and Peter Sacks, 'Where Words Prevail Not: Grief, Revenge and Language in Kyd and Shakespeare', *ELH* 49 (1982), 576–601.

narration, as in an earlier allegorical drama, but rather remainders and theatrical leftovers, since the play as a whole now functions by introducing more than was shown on-stage. And the repository in which these remainders accumulate is the characters themselves.

The disclosure of Lorenzo and Balthazar's murder may be shocking, but it works in a relatively linear way. Introducing nothing we did not already see, it merely forces us to revise our interpretation of what we saw: Hieronimo and Bel-Imperia's intention had all along been to kill them, and their pretended dagger-thrusts were in fact real (or as real as dagger-thrusts on stage can ever be). Yet embedded in that revelation is the enigma of Bel-Imperia's subsequent suicide, news not just to us but even to Hieronimo. She 'missed her part in this', he sighs, 'For though the story saith she should have died, / Yet I of kindness and of care to her / Did otherwise determine of her end' (4.4.141–3). Now we are processing information that we *didn't* see, and that the play didn't either. On top of the catastrophe's two levels of reality, its gloss adds an entirely gratuitous third: Bel-Imperia's role called for her to die in the original script, to survive in Hieronimo's version, and to die in her own version, which she improvised. Not only was this final, self-directed dagger-thrust real as well, but the motive for it, unlike the others, remains opaque. Why did she decide to do this? And when? The masterstroke of *Suleiman and Perseda* turns out not to be its murders committed in plain sight but the self-slaughter conceived out of sight—off-stage, as it were—and hidden even from its architect: this is not, Hieronimo says, the resolution he planned. If 'off-stage' has hitherto localized the play's animating force, its ability to deviate from and author itself, with Bel-Imperia's suicide that agency enters visible space. For the first time, off-stage comes on-stage, projected into not just a body but a mind. In the history of English drama, she is the first character to keep a secret, and really *keep* it. And she does so, seemingly, for no other reason than to do so.

She is not the last. We never *see* Bel-Imperia's secrecy, of course: the moment it is born, she is dead, a mind only after the fact. It is one thing to be told retroactively that someone did not tell us something; it is quite another to hear them say so in the flesh—or, perhaps, not hear. *The Spanish Tragedy* has one more mystery up its sleeve, involving not so much an exposition that fails to explain as an exposition that fails even to register, that equates explanation with mystery itself. The strangest fact of Hieronimo's outpouring at the end of *Suleiman and Perseda* is the number of times he is made to confess, as if each time his efforts are inadequate.[60] 'See here my show! Look on this spectacle!' he cries, plunging into a sixty-three line recapitulation of the play: he accuses the princes; declares his madness feigned; brandishes

---

[60] Though Hieronimo's failed (and later retracted) confession has hardly escaped critical notice, it has been dismissed either as just another quirk, or as anticlimax; see e.g. Sheldon P. Zitner, 'The Spanish Tragedy and the Language of Performance', in A. L. Magnusson and C. E. McGee, eds., *The Elizabethan Theatre XI* (Port Credit: P. D. Meany, 1990), 75–93, esp. 91–2.

the bloody handkercher; extols the elegance of his plot; meticulously lists who killed whom; proclaims himself 'author and actor in this tragedy', which, now done, 'my heart is satisfied'; and finally, vowing to 'conclude my part' in suicide, urges 'no more words; I have no more to say' (4.4.89–152). Yet he is prevented from hanging himself: 'Save Hieronimo!' the Viceroy interjects. Save him for what? They know the princes are dead—'Brother', says the King, 'my nephew and thy son are slain'— but still, somehow, do not know why. 'Do but inform the King of these events', the Viceroy pleads. 'Speak, traitor!' barks the King, 'Damnèd bloody murderer, speak!' (4.4.154–63).

But what is Hieronimo to speak that has not been spoken? 'Why', asks the King, 'hast thou done this undeserving deed?' He has already told them, yet he begins again, now distilling his account into its most basic elements: 'My guiltless son was by Lorenzo slain, / And by Lorenzo and that Balthazar / Am I at last revengèd thoroughly' (4.4.171–3). Yet the King again repeats his demand, as if it has not been met in the slightest: 'Why speakest thou not?' What Hieronimo has been saying, seemingly, does not even count as speech to those around him; it is almost as if, to them, he has *not* been speaking but standing mute and motionless the entire time, staring wildly, his dagger dripping blood. Has he been? Have inside and outside switched places? Do the King, Castile, and the Viceroy, standing right beside Hieronimo, occupy a different reality? Has the rest of the stage, and the rest of the playhouse, somehow become the interior of Hieronimo's head, reverberating with words he never actually says aloud? When he began the play-within-the-play by having Castile 'throw me down the key' to the chamber doors, his intent was to lock the royals in: but it turns out we are the ones locked in, and the chamber is Hieronimo himself.[61]

And then, something extraordinary happens. Having twice said all, Hieronimo now proceeds to *confirm* the delusion that there is more to say—by refusing to say it. 'What lesser liberty can kings afford / Than harmless silence? . . . Sufficeth I may not, nor I will not, tell thee'. 'Fetch forth the tortures!' the King rages. It is immaterial whether he has heard this refusal, since hearing and not hearing are now the same. 'Thou mayst torment me', Hieronimo continues, 'as his wretched son / Hath done in murdering my Horatio'—yet another explanation—'But never shalt thou force me to reveal / The thing which I have vowed inviolate'. The third, even more atomic synopsis of the plot tucked into this defiance can be only for our benefit now, since clearly no one else apprehends it. And its sole purpose, seemingly, is to differentiate this 'thing', 'the thing which I have vowed inviolate', from virtually *everything* else in the play we have seen until this point. Did we miss something?

---

[61] Thus, when during their interrogations of Hieronimo the Viceroy cries 'break ope the doors!' (an order unfollowed by any direction for attendants to do so), they may not really be trying to get *out*—there are no further calls for escape—so much as *into* the place where Hieronimo, and we, already are.

A promise to Bel-Imperia? To Isabella? To Horatio? When? To keep *what* a secret? What 'vow'? What 'thing'? Hieronimo never says—and just to be certain, bites out his own tongue. Suddenly, in a movement gruesomely miniaturized by the disgorgement of that organ, inside becomes outside again. If a moment ago we were in Hieronimo's skull, given access to his private, unexpressed thoughts, now that inside discovers another inside, a further inner chamber sensible only on collision with its outer wall. No sooner has 'off-stage' engulfed the stage, and us with it, than it spits us out, shrinking and receding behind a door that inexplicably swings shut. Now the stage is just a lid again, and we are the King and the Viceroy, locked out of a play and a protagonist we cannot comprehend. Now we are Qualitees' audience, locked in a theatre that declines to speak, to show, to reveal. Now we are Pedringano, convinced that the box before us contains something, because it is a box.

The box, of course, is empty.[62] There is no 'thing which I have vowed inviolate'; Hieronimo is the first, and perhaps the only, dramatic character ever to keep a secret from himself, his being so tightly coiled around it that he could not impart it even if he wished. Its efficacy, though, lies not in any putative answer: the real secret is the secret itself, why Hieronimo *thinks* he has one. Unlike the visceral shock of *Suleiman and Perseda*, whose on-stage victims would still have done (despite Hieronimo's boasts) 'as tragedians do: die today…and in a minute, starting up again, / Revive to please tomorrow's audience', this secret does not exhaust itself upon repeat viewings (4.4.78–82). Rather, it is designed to *instigate* repeat viewings, to *make* tomorrow's audience, by frustrating the most basic conventions of theatrical experience. The revised quarto of 1602 truncates Hieronimo's interrogation, running his confession directly into his self-mutilation—signalled only by the line 'now to express the rupture of my part'.[63] Yet without his 'secret' or the reiterated commands to speak that generate it, the act is still continuous with his 'part' until now, an act of self-destruction. It is his baffling silence in 1592, by contrast, that constitutes both a new kind of 'part' and a 'rupture' of the old, by creating, at the very last second, a character who does *not* rupture, who does not disclose, who is no longer a 'character'—such that he is not, in any functional sense, on-stage at all.[64]

---

[62] Both Dillon and West view Hieronimo's self-mutilation as a refusal to 'help the spectators make sense' of the carnage they have witnessed ('Staging Languages', 35–6), 'implying the existence of a now-lost secret that might make sense of everything' ('Confusions', 232), but it is *the secret itself* that does not make sense—not what it purports to explain, which has already received sufficient explanation. What we cannot make sense of is the *need* to make sense of anything to begin with; the mystery is why the play pretends there is one. The Hitchcockian 'McGuffin' is a good cinematic approximation.

[63] Thomas Kyd, *The Spanish Tragedie* (London: Thomas Pavier, 1602), M1r. The revised text also directs attendants to '*breake in, and hold Hieronimo*' at the Viceroy's 'Break ope the doors!' (N4v), and even settles the question of the King's audition: 'Be deafe my sences, I can heare no more'.

[64] *The Spanish Tragedy*'s opening, in fact, foregrounds exactly this representational paradox. The ghost of Don Andrea must initially identify itself a ghost, not a living person—despite the contrary evidence of the actor playing him. To say 'When this eternal substance of my soul / Did live imprisoned in my wanton flesh' (1.1.1–2) is to say, ultimately, 'I have no body; though you may see me, I am not really here'.

Hieronimo has hitherto performed merely the character of 'madness'; this is the madness *of* a character, his withdrawal from the economy of dramatic representation, and it invents a new theatrical epistemology. By the end of *The Spanish Tragedy*, there can be no end to *The Spanish Tragedy*: the play's meaning has retreated into Hieronimo's mind, its immanence coterminous with the impossibility of its recovery.[65] Despite its printed title, for the next fifty years dramatists and spectators alike universally referred to *The Spanish Tragedy* simply as 'Ieronimo', as if the character really had swallowed the play and subsumed it.[66] When a sequel inevitably appeared, in 1605, it was titled *The First Part of Ieronimo*, and it was not a sequel but a prequel, covering 'the Warres of Portugall, and the life and death of Don Andræa', perhaps tempting playgoers with the prospect of some key buried in previous events that might unlock the later ones. We do not get it. *The First Part* fills in a backstory to *The Spanish Tragedy* that can be gleaned from the play itself; solving none of its riddles, it only deepens them.[67]

Fittingly, the play even spawned what might be called an 'inquel': a full-scale treatment of its play-within-the-play, *Soliman and Perseda* (1592). Doubtless indebted to *The Spanish Tragedy* yet shorn of any reference to it, *Soliman and Perseda* is literally the play's inside exploded, and made its own, freestanding dramatic world; indeed, since Hieronimo claims to have authored it, it is his inside as well. Each attempt to drill into *The Spanish Tragedy* either bounces off, or unspools new, fractal interiors. By its 1615 printing, the play had acquired its famous subtitle, 'Hieronimo is mad againe'. There is no such line in the play: instead, it conveys something like the play's reception, the entire public response to it reduced to a gnomic catchphrase. Hieronimo is already mad; Hieronimo is still going mad. In its weird, Janus-faced present tense, its mixture of familiarity and fascination, it struggles to capture the strangeness of a play and a protagonist that seem greater than the sum of their accumulated performances, that are somehow *still*

---

[65] Having assured Don Andrea that all his enemies have died and gone to Hell, Revenge concludes the play by vowing only 'there [to] begin their endless tragedy' (4.5.48).

[66] See Ben Jonson, *The fountaine of selfe-loue, Or Cynthias reuels* (London: Walter Burre, 1601), A4v, and *Bartholomew Fair* (London: Robert Allot, 1631), A5v; John Marston, *The Malcontent* (London: William Aspley, 1604), A4r; Francis Beaumont, *The Knight of the Burning Pestle* (London: Walter Burre, 1613), B2r; Thomas May, *The Heir* (London: Thomas Jones, 1622), B1r; John Gee, *New Shreds of the Old Snare* (London: Robert Mylbourne, 1624), 20; Thomas Rawlins, *The Rebellion* (London: Daniell Frere, 1640), I2r. Publishers' playlists always adopt the shorthand as well.

[67] Even if, as scholars have argued, *The First Part* is the lost play Henslowe calls 'Don Horatio' or 'Spanish Comedy', performed in 1592 alongside its counterpart and intended to precede it, priority of composition does not finally matter. By 1602, it has *become* a prequel: Hieronimo is here just a supporting role, but it is nevertheless 'his' *First Part*, eclipsed and devoured by the protagonist of the other play. Midway through 1592, indeed, Henslowe himself starts calling it 'comodey of Jeronymo' and never reverts to the former title. For the opposing view, see Lukas Erne, *Beyond the Spanish Tragedy: A Study of the Works of Thomas Kyd* (Manchester: Manchester University Press, 2001), 14–46.

happening—to express, in temporal terms, the atemporality of what we call the literary. No matter how often one sees the play, one cannot *see* it, because the full measure of its reality lies always just out of sight—behind the curtain or the stage door, or beneath the clothes and words of a speaker who is himself a curtain, and a door.

In these attributes we can recognize the distinctive qualities of the drama to come: the play's resistance to closure, its messiness and overcomplication, and the 'interiority' of its characters, which emerges in direct correlation with their malfunction as characters. We call these innovations 'early modern theatre', but they are theatrical only in a narrow, self-reflexive sense, by reference to the physical structure that conditioned them—a sense we have naturalized, indeed, in our very spatial calibration of meaning to 'closure' rather than 'openness'. In a closed playhouse, what a play like *The Spanish Tragedy* completes is not communication with its audience but simply with itself, orbicular and recursive; the play has its own interiority, of which its characters' develops only epiphenomenally. In later revenge plays, characters would likewise construct interiority as negative space—speaking the unspeakable only to unspeak it, exposing inner stages on which they refuse to perform, limning boxes whose content is their outline. At the end of *The Jew of Malta* (*c*.1592), Barabas hints that 'to what event my secret purpose drives, / I know', when his purpose (unless there is another?) is not a secret. Aaron ends *Titus Andronicus* (*c*.1594) by unpacking a life of hideous, motiveless crimes, grieving 'that I cannot do ten thousand more'. Alexander in *Alphonsus* (*c*.1594), taken in the act of murder, is asked 'what hast thou done?' only to reply 'When I haue leasure I will answer thee'. Eleazar in *Lust's Dominion* (*c*.1600) dies lamenting that 'had I but breath'd the space of one hour longer, I would haue fully acted my reuenge', when he has none left to pursue. Iago smirks 'what you know, you know, / From this time forth I never shall speak word'; Hamlet says he has 'that within which passes show', and our only proof is that he says so.[68] At these moments, characters are not people so much as playhouses, propagating the illusion of depth after depth has run out. Manufactured from the outside in, 'interiority' in the early modern theatre begins as merely its exterior reinscribed—the dwindling of its circle into the body of the actor until it became a point, elemental and 'inviolate'. To justify paying for what they could not see, playgoers had to believe that they could never see it: that 'theatre', organic and alive in every part, now inhered in the invisible.

---

[68] Christopher Marlo[we], *The Famous Tragedy of the Rich Ievv of Malta* (London: Nicholas Vavasour, 1633), I4r; [William Shakespeare], *The Most Lamentable Romaine Tragedy of Titus Andronicus* (London: John Danter, 1594), I2v; ?George Chapman, *The Tragedy of Alphonsus, Emperour of Germany* (London: Humphrey Moseley, 1654), K1v; Anon., *Lust's Dominion: Or, The Lascivious Queen* (London: F[rancis] K[irkman], 1657), 150; Shakespeare, *The Tragedy of Othello, The Moore of Venice* (London: Thomas Walkley, 1622), N1r; Shakespeare, *The Tragicall Historie of Hamlet, Prince of Denmark* (London: Nicholas Ling, 1604), B4v.

FURTHER READING

Kathman, David. 'The Rise of Commercial Playing in 1540s London', *Early Theatre* 12.1 (2009), 15–38.

Kernan, Alvin B. 'This Goodly Frame, the Stage: The Interior Theater of Imagination in English Renaissance Drama', *Shakespeare Quarterly* 25.1 (1974), 1–5.

Maus, Katharine Eisaman. *Inwardness and Theater in the English Renaissance* (Chicago: University of Chicago Press, 1995).

Royce, Jacalyn. 'Early Modern Naturalistic Acting: The Role of the Globe in the Development of Personation', in Richard Dutton, ed., *The Oxford Handbook of Early Modern Theatre* (Oxford and New York: Oxford University Press, 2009), 477–95.

Van den Berg, Kent T. *Playhouse as Cosmos: Shakespearean Theater as Metaphor* (Dover: University of Delaware Press, 1985).

CHAPTER 4

OFF-STAGE

PETER WOMACK

The Countess's horses

There is a striking moment in *The Insatiate Countess*, the tragedy left unfinished by John Marston on his enforced retirement from the stage in the summer of 1608, and completed by William Barksted and Lewis Machin for performance by a children's company at the Whitefriars some time between 1609 and 1613.[1] Isabella, Countess of Swevia, is a young widow who abruptly drops her mourning to marry a man named Roberto, but then immediately after the marriage feast elopes with a new lover, Rogero. There is a brief love scene between them, which, according to the 1613 quarto, ends:

> ROGERO.　　　To horse, to horse:...
> 　　　　　　　　　　　　lead by more powerfull charme;
> 　　　　　　Ide see the world winne thee from out mine arme.
> 　　　　　　　*Exeunt. Enter at severall doores, Claridiana and Guido.*
> GUIDO.　　　Zounds, is the Huritano comming? *Claridiana* what's the matter?
> CLARIDIANA.　The Countess of Swevia has new taken horse.[2]

In the margin, next to Guido and Claridiana's lines, is an additional stage direction: 'A trampling of Horses heard'. The layout is muddling, but the sequence of theatrical events is unambiguous. The 'trampling of horses' is understood to be the sound of Rogero and Isabella's departure, so it must follow their exit. And then Guido and Claridiana are understood to be reacting to the noise, so it must precede their

---

[1] The troubled genesis of the script we have is reconstructed by Giorgio Melchiori, the Revels editor (John Marston and others, *The Insatiate Countess* [Manchester: Manchester University Press, 1984], 1–17). He argues convincingly that the 1613 quarto, which is the only authoritative text, is not the acting version, but an incomplete draft opportunistically patched up for the press.

[2] John Marston, *The insatiate countesse A tragedie: acted at White-Fryers* (London, 1613), D3. The confusion in the text extends to the names of several characters, including the lover with whom Isabella elopes here. Modern editors regularize the speech-headings in various ways; I have simply quoted the episode as it was printed. Since the positioning of the unedited stage direction matters to my argument, this quotation is from the 1613 text. All subsequent quotations are from Melchiori's edition.

entrance. In short, there must be a moment when the stage is empty and the audience is listening to an off-stage sound effect.

Nothing in the plot compels the writers to do the Countess's flight in this way. Early modern dramatic characters often leave the stage in order to ride somewhere, and the audience understands what is happening without needing to hear the sound of the horse. *King Lear* offers a conclusive example: in 1.4–5, Lear twice calls for horses to be prepared for his departure from Goneril's house, attended by his hundred knights. While this large-scale exodus is being organized, Oswald and Kent both leave separately and hurriedly. The whole sequence is shaped by exits 'to horse', but there are no equestrian sound effects. The power of off-stage sound is being saved up for the thunder. In *The Insatiate Countess*, then, the 'trampling of horses' is not a narrative expedient but a deliberate theatre effect—a fairly noisy one, if 'Huritano' (hurricane) is an appropriate word. And what is startling about it, put straightforwardly if impressionistically, is that it is a *modern* effect. That emptied room, disturbed by noises off, is the native territory of classic realism: this is Nora shutting the door of the doll's house, the axes in the cherry orchard heard from the deserted interior, the revving of the engine as Willy Loman drives away. It provokes a distinctive *frisson*: staring at the silent furniture, we listen to the sound of decisive action elsewhere, unable to see what is happening, but knowing only too well. They've gone; they're not coming back.

One reason the effect feels modern is that it is illusionistic: the vivid intimation of a contiguous location enchants the set and makes us believe for a moment that we are in that drawing room, that back yard. But how does the effect work in an early Jacobean play, written for a cast of boys on a non-scenic stage, and adhering, as we understand it today, to theatrical conventions that are not naturalistic but rhetorical, or emblematic, or poetic? The authors seem to have smuggled in a device from the wrong dramaturgic repertoire. And this is not just a conceit of mine: as Melchiori suggests, this particular play, with its multiple authorship and its badly integrated double plot, owes its slightly chaotic air to experimental curiosity, not just to incompetence.[3] It is likely enough that somebody saw the possibility of a sensational effect, and threw it in regardless of its compatibility with the rest of the play. If so, the Countess's horses are an instance of what T. S. Eliot called, in a tone somewhere between modernist recognition and classical disapproval, the 'artistic greediness' of Elizabethan dramatists, 'their desire for every sort of effect together, their unwillingness to accept any limitation and abide by it'.[4]

This unprincipled inventiveness makes it impractical to define the conventions of 'Elizabethan drama' as if it were an organic artistic entity governed by immanent laws. We cannot be sure that we know what these playwrights were capable

---

[3] Melchiori, ed., *Insatiate Countess*, 35.

[4] T. S. Eliot, 'Four Elizabethan Dramatists', in *Selected Essays*, 3rd edn. (London: Faber and Faber, 1951), 116.

of. It seems more productive, and more in tune with the energies of early modern theatricality, to think of the surviving scripts as traces of a distinctive spatial practice.[5] The practice was disorderly but not formless: the business of playing gave rise to a socially and architecturally definite environment, and developed its powers within it and along with it. The playing was shaped by the space, which was shaped in its turn by what the players did in it. And among its fundamental coordinates is the one that confronts us in the form of the Countess's horses: the opposition between shown and hidden, stage and backstage, 'on' and 'off'. The empty stage and the hoofbeats give 'off-stage' a sudden prominence that is at once clumsy, portentous, comical, and uncanny. Exactly because their effect is so uncertain, they offer a way in to the history of this deeply questionable place.

On/off

To the extent that we are still the audiences of Ibsen and Chekhov, we read the duality of on-stage and off-stage metonymically. If the stage is a drawing-room, the characters are entering it from the dining-room; if it is a street, the upstage door leads into somebody's house; if it is a cliff edge, a character gazing out front is surveying the ocean. Hearing the Countess's horses, we infer that her exit led to a road down which she is now riding. The formula could be called *fictional adjacency*, and it is so familiar to us that it can look like a universal fact about the way theatre works. So it is worth reminding ourselves that it is not.

We may take for an example a theatrically sophisticated medieval script such as *Mankind*.[6] The show is introduced by the authoritative figure of Mercy, whose address to the audience is interrupted by the impertinent arrival of the Vices; he tells them they are not wanted and with some difficulty gets them to leave. Then Mankynde himself is introduced, and Mercy counsels him, making it clear that he himself is about to depart. The rowdy sounds of the Vices are heard from off-stage, and as soon as Mankynde is left alone they come on and try to distract him from his life of piety and labour. Like Mercy before him, Mankynde speaks to them angrily and eventually drives them off. This skeletal outline, covering nearly half the script, shows how much the action is shaped by entrances and exits. In allegorically transparent fashion, the Vices try to impose their presence while the virtuous characters try to get rid of them: the theatrical question is who is coming on, who is staying on, and who is going off. Off-stage space is therefore dramatically significant, but those who go off are not going *to* anywhere—they are merely ceasing to be present.

---

[5] The term is Lefebvre's, though I am not using it to import his entire conceptual structure. See Henri Lefebvre, *The Production of Space*, trans. Donald Nicholson-Smith (Oxford: Blackwell, 1991), 33, 38.

[6] Text in Greg Walker, ed., *Medieval Drama: An Anthology* (Oxford: Blackwell, 2000).

Mercy, for example, says 'Wythin a schorte space I must nedys hens' (260). 'Hence' means nothing but not-on-stage.

The next section of the play belongs to the Vices alone, so Mankynde has to vacate the stage. He explains that he is going to buy seed (one aspect of his representative humanity is that his work consists of digging in the earth). Here, for the first time, there is a faint suggestion of an off-stage 'world'—he goes somewhere, and later re-enters with a bag. The movement is interesting because it suggests that the authors of *Mankind* are not ignorant of fictional adjacency as a device: if it is little used in early English plays that is not because it is in some way unavailable to the medieval imagination. Rather it is that medieval theatre is actively doing something different.[7] This difference is underlined in the next scene. Beaten by Mankynde, the Vices resort to their master, the devil Titivillus. His voice is heard from off-stage, but the Vices tell the audience that if they want to see 'hys abhomynabull presens' (466), they must put money in a hat that is evidently going round. In other words, Titivillus is not coming from an imagined 'elsewhere'; he is explicitly hiding behind the scenes, promised, displayed, or withheld by the performers like a fairground prodigy. Again, the on–off relationship is being deployed with comic intensity, but its logic has nothing to do with location. Fictional adjacency is irrelevant to it.

I have made the point in negative terms, but there are two ways of expressing it positively. The first is to point to the show's *immediacy*. This stage, where the Vices warm the spectators up for the devil's arrival, is not primarily a means of representing a location in a story: it is a space where costumed entertainers interact with an audience. Insofar as that is so, off-stage no more operates as a narrative signifier than it does at, say, a concert or a wrestling match. The performers come on, do their performance and leave, and nobody pretends that they are going anywhere except to their dressing rooms. The performance may generate a 'character' (a singer adopts the voice of a lover, a wrestler cultivates an artificially aggressive stage personality); but if so, the character does not acquire enough imaginative solidity for us to attribute continuing life to it. Rather, it is a trope, or a colour, within the always dominant discourse of the performance itself. The entrances and exits of the performers can be highly significant (marked for example by applause or abuse from the audience), but their significance is not fictional.

Secondly, there is the universal scope of the play's allegory. If the title is to be taken literally, 'Mankynde' is all humanity, and the ground he tills is the world; the

---

[7] My impression is that it is indeed little used in early English plays—that *Mankind* is in that sense representative. A supporting instance of an extremely different kind is the famous *Second Shepherds' Play* in the Towneley cycle (also in Walker). Here there are three dramatically essential locations: the moor, the thief's house, and the biblical stable. On the moor there are (presumably unstaged) sheep; and the scenes at the thief's house often turn on exchanges between characters who are inside and those who are outside, knocking on the door. Fictional adjacency seems an almost inescapable resource for staging such a scenario, but the script always does something else.

stage does not stand for a *part* of something bigger but rather presents a totality. The force of this totality is felt at the very end, when Mercy draws the lessons of the play, and Mankynde prepares to leave:

> MANKYNDE. Syth, I schall departe, blyse me, fader, her then I go.
>   God send ws all plente of Hys gret mercy.
> MERCY.   *Dominus custodit te ab omni malo*
>   *In nomine Patris et Filii et Spiritus Sancti.* Amen.
>
> *Hic exit Mankynde.* (900–3)

The moment is ambiguous. Although the parting benediction suggests the hour of death, the character in the story is not dying; this is simply his exit at the end of the play. But since the stage is the earth in general, the end of the character's performance upon it cannot help signifying the end of his life. Whereas the principle of fictional adjacency is synecdoche (the audience imagine a whole on the basis of the part they are shown), here the theatrically effective figure is metaphor.

The off-stage dimension is lacking in imaginative solidity, then, because the on-stage space is *complete*. Whether one looks at it as a real-world encounter between the players and the audience or as an allegory of all humanity, the show has almost no investment in its connections with elsewhere, because everything that matters to it is present on the stage. This is drama in what Lefebvre calls 'absolute space', that paradoxical place that 'has no place because it embodies all places'.[8] In other words, this is *spatially*, as of course it is thematically, religious drama. Conversely, the intense apprehension of off-stage events, such as we see in the moment from *The Insatiate Countess*, is the trace of a general deconsecration of the theatre.

You that way; we this way

According to the performance bond governing its construction in 1567, the Red Lion, London's first purpose-built playhouse, was to have three separable components: 'galloryes' surrounding a courtyard, 'one Skaffolde or stage' within the enclosed space, and then, upon the scaffold, 'one convenyent turret of Tymber'.[9] The first two of these are self-explanatory: there needs to be a platform to act on and, around it, raised galleries so that paying customers can see the show. A good deal of the document, however, concerns the third and less obvious element, the turret. This was to be thirty feet high, with a floor seven feet from the top, and the whole structure secured with metal braces. This sizeable and solid building was apparently as important as the stage and the auditorium. Its importance could

---

[8] Lefebvre, *The Production of Space*, 236.
[9] Janet S. Loengard, 'An Elizabethan Lawsuit: John Brayne, his Carpenter, and the Building of the Red Lion Theatre', *Shakespeare Quarterly* 34.3 (Autumn, 1983), 298–310 (309).

be explained in two ways. One explanation is economic: if a company makes an open-air amphitheatre its base, even for a few weeks, it needs a lock-up where costumes, props and documents are safe from thieves and the weather. The Red Lion's imposing turret, then, can be seen as a sign of the actors' emerging autonomy. Whereas medieval actors had normally performed under the auspices of larger institutions—a church, a noble household, a guild—here the theatre is a piece of private property.

The other explanation is phenomenological: it is that the structure of a theatre is such that the open space where the actors appear entails, as its complement and condition, a closed space where they are concealed—a place, you could say, to appear *from*. This idea is vividly presented in an anecdote told by the twentieth-century designer and director André Barsacq.[10] It describes his company, the Thé-âtre des Quatre Saisons, preparing a performance of *Le médecin volant* on an open air stage in a forest. The run-through *in situ* is not working. The actors are unable to impose themselves upon the natural setting, and their gestures seem weak and arbitrary. Then, moved by some intuition, Barsacq hangs two sheets across the back of the stage on a rope. This elementary device transforms the situation. Now there is a palpable silence: the set-up is no longer pointless, it is waiting for something to happen. An actor slips on to the stage through the place where the two sheets meet, and his entrance is already significant: he has come 'to tell us what was passing in that hidden world whence he emerged, and which none but he had the right to penetrate'. The miracle of theatre, Barsacq declares, has occurred.

This apotheosis of off-stage space is not about fictional adjacency. Barsacq does not say whether the concealed space had a narrative specification or not; that is not the point. Rather, the story is about magic: the miraculous conjuring up of a 'hidden world', and the transformation of the actor into a priestly messenger. It speaks, then, to the uncanny effect of off-stage intimations, the sense that the hoofbeats do not merely inform us of the Countess's flight but momentarily enchant the empty stage. The establishment of a closed backstage area thus appears as a way of reclaiming, in the secularizing theatre, the metaphysical authority of sacred drama. The stage, like the church, is the portal of an unseen realm.

As the Red Lion's model was copied and streamlined over the following decades, the turret metamorphosed into the 'Attyring house', or into what de Witt reverberantly calls it: *mimorum aedes*, the actors' house.[11] If the actors have a house, the stage has the character of a forecourt: the open space in front of the house. As far as

---

[10] Quoted in Richard Southern, *The Seven Ages of the Theatre* (London: Faber and Faber, 1962), 156–7.

[11] 'Attyring house' is glossed as the 'place where the players make them readye' in a deposition in 1592, Charles Wallace, *The First London Theatre: Materials for a History* (repr. New York: Benjamin Blom, 1969), 127. 'Mimorum aedes' is written on Johannes de Witt's drawing of the Swan Theatre, *c.*1596, reproduced widely, and carefully read by John B. Gleason, 'The Dutch Humanist Origins of the De Witt Drawing of the Swan Theatre', *Shakespeare Quarterly* 32.3 (Autumn, 1981), 324–38.

we know, there were no entrances and exits on the Elizabethan stage other than the upstage doors. From a modern point of view this seems intolerably restrictive. Since the seventeenth century, the obvious way to make an entrance has been to walk on from the wings: our stages are completely if covertly open at the sides, allowing actors to come and go by a sort of elementary magic. The Shakespearean stage has no wings; except for the back wall, it is bounded by the audience. The actors enter through one of the tiring-house doors and exit by the same route. Modern reconstructors often rebel against this limitation, for example by placing steps against the front of the stage and entering through the audience. But there is surprisingly little evidence that early modern actors made use of that possibility.[12] Rather, it seems that we are looking at a different type of performance space, one whose boundaries were mostly closed. The performers emerged from their house to entertain the public, and when they were done, they went back indoors.

This spatial emphasis on the turret and its descendants is consistent in London theatres from 1567 through to 1642. In the de Witt drawing the *mimorum aedes* is the most prominent part of the building, marginalizing both stage and galleries. In the elevations for the two 'Cockpit' theatres, Inigo Jones's for the commercial one (1616) and John Webb's for the court (1629), the neo-Vitruvian *frons scenae* has an architectural grandeur that reduces the stage to an ancillary space in front of it.[13] In the replica Globe of the 1990s, the floridly painted façade of the tiring-house is so massive as to threaten to dwarf the action taking place at its foot, and designers often seek ways of breaking up its visual unity so as to restore the focus to the actors. These theatres vary in scale and in cultural pretension, but what they have in common is a flamboyant insistence on the wall that marks the back of the stage.

Structurally, this dominant presence overdetermines the stage itself. The galleries and the yard are inhabited by the public: they buy places there; the gradations of the auditorium respect their social differentiations; the enclosed polygon and the natural light make them aware of their own collective presence. The space is theirs. Correspondingly, the tiring-house belongs to the actors: it is their habitation, the conspicuous repository of their property and their secrets. In between the two, the stage belongs to both and neither. It is attached to the tiring-house, but, unlike a modern stage, it is not embedded in a backstage technology of wings and lighting grids: rather, it sticks out into the audience's space, three-quarters surrounded by it like a promontory in the sea. At the beginning and end of the play the stage is empty, and the audience and the actors are confined to their respective enclaves, but during the performance it is the ground where the two worlds meet, the space of an unstable cohabitation.

---

[12] J. W. Saunders, 'Vaulting the Rails', *Shakespeare Survey* 7 (1954), 69–81, makes energetic but speculative attempts to demonstrate that actors made use of the yard at the first Globe (1599–1613).

[13] See John Orrell, *The Human Stage: English Theatre Design, 1567–1640* (Cambridge: Cambridge University Press, 1988), plates 38 (175) and 36 (170), respectively.

The terms of this cohabitation are glimpsed in the traces of a dispute about on-stage spectators. At the opening of *The Malcontent*, a children's company play adapted for adult performance at the Globe, an actor pretending to be a member of the audience is told that he must not sit on the stage, and protests that it is permitted 'at the private house'.[14] It seems, then, that it was normal to have some seats on the stage at indoor playhouses, but that the practice was less automatically accepted at open-air amphitheatres. The difference may not have been an artistic one but rather a result of the fact that the private theatres were further up-market: the elite audience asserted its status by denying the actors a monopoly of the space. What interests me is the fact of the uncertainty: whether the stage belonged to the actors or the audience was a matter for *social* negotiation.

Henri Lefebvre's notion of 'monumentality' helps us with this social understanding of theatrical space. As Lefebvre conceives of them, monumental spaces such as cathedrals, mausoleums, and palaces are theatrical in two senses. First, they transcend the merely discursive: their architectural form is meaningful, but by virtue of being *acted in*, not by virtue of being *read*. Second, his list of monuments literally includes theatres: the amphitheatres of classical Greece, he argues, because of what people came together to do in them, could stage a wholeness, an 'all-embracing presence of the totality', that erased aggression, negativity, and partiality and had the (temporary) effect of 'a profound agreement':

> A Greek theatre presupposes tragedy and comedy, and by extension the presence of the city's people and their allegiance to their heroes and gods. In theatrical space, music, choruses, masks, tiering—all such elements converge with language and actors. A spatial action overcomes conflicts, at least momentarily, even though it does not resolve them; it opens a way from everyday concerns to collective joy.[15]

To be in theatrical space, thus imagined, is to be virtually, even somehow literally, in the presence of everybody. And of course it is central to the whole conception that Attic theatre was inseparable, as Lefebvre notes, from the collective worship of the gods. Here, as in the medieval English theatricality we looked at earlier, the total and unified character of the space is associated with the religious meaning of the performance. Monumental space accommodates sacred drama, and vice versa.

Certainly there is a sense in which the amphitheatres of early modern London were, or aspired to be, or promoted themselves as, 'monuments' of this kind. The scale, the grandiose names—Theatre, Rose, Globe—and the vaguely classicizing circular design all promise something like collective joy: shaped, as it were, by the amphitheatre in which they gather, the citizens engage in a 'spatial action' that 'overcomes conflicts' and creates a single collective body. But this monumentality is also

---

[14] John Marston, *The Malcontent*, ed. G. K. Hunter, Revels Plays (Manchester: Manchester University Press, 1975), Induction, 1–2.

[15] Lefebvre, *The Production of Space*, 222.

a kind of fake, like the pillars supporting the Heavens, which appear to be marble but really are painted wood. Set against this inclusivity, literally disrupting the open ring of galleries, are the closed-off walls of the tiring-house, the company's private property, a reminder that this is not a communal festival but a commercial entertainment.

Towards the end of *Love's Labour's Lost* (1595), Shakespeare nearly makes this division vanish, first drawing his cast together around a festive play within the play, and then ratifying that oneness by confronting them with a shared intimation of death. But at the very end, one of the departing characters remarks, lightly, 'You that way; we this way'.[16] The actors disappear into their house, and the spectators start to leave the galleries. With delicate self-awareness, the play lets go of its dream of an unbroken circle and acknowledges the dual orientation of its stage.

Threshold dramaturgy

The playhouse stage, then, is not an 'absolute space' after all. On the contrary, it is irreducibly relational: a space-between, a threshold. Showing how this threshold might work in theatrical practice entails some fairly detailed reading, and I shall start with *Richard III*: the play inherits some of the vocabulary of moral drama and so displays the different spatial grammar clearly. I shall trace the sequence that leads up to the murder of Hastings, printed as the first four scenes of Act 3. It begins with the young Prince Edward's arrival in London following his father's death. He enters with Gloucester, Buckingham, and the Archbishop of Canterbury; they are met by the Lord Mayor of London, then by Hastings, who brings word that the prince's brother York has taken sanctuary. The Archbishop is prevailed upon to extract the boy from his refuge, and, with Hastings, leaves the stage to fetch him. By the time the two men return with York, it has been determined that both princes will spend the night in the Tower (a prospect they dread). When they exit, it is to go there.

Where does all this action happen? In one sense, the answer is vague. Some remarks about meeting people by the way suggest that the party is literally travelling and that the scene is therefore set in the street. But when the Archbishop goes off, it is hard to imagine that the most powerful people in England simply wait at the roadside. Surely they would commandeer some accommodation? Their situation is unclear. In a different sense, however, the location is precise. The opening line of the

---

[16] *Love's Labour's Lost*, 5.2.931. All Shakespearean quotations from *The Riverside Shakespeare*, ed. G. Blakemore Evans, 2nd edn. (Boston: Houghton Mifflin, 1997). My understanding of the line is not universally shared: John Kerrigan, for example, supports, on balance, the idea that the characters of the play are separating into two groups and leaving through separate doors (*LLL*, New Penguin Shakespeare, [London, 1982]). But since Don Armado, whose line it is, is by this point speaking chorically for the performers within the play, the metatheatrical sense seems to me the most elegant.

scene is 'Welcome, sweet Prince, to London, to your chamber' (3.1.1). That is: the action is taking place at the very entrance to London, imagined as a room in the house of the realm. As the party pauses on the decisive boundary between the country and the city, two questions arise: whether York will emerge from sanctuary and meet them, and whether they will go to the Tower. The stage, then, is topographically meaningful not because it stands for a specified location—it doesn't—but because it is the meeting-point of the routes to three other places: the provincial retreat the rightful king has just left, the sanctuary where he would be safe, and the Tower where he will be murdered. The *intersection* is the essential matter of the scene: Richard and Buckingham are working to get the princes out of two of these places and into the third. In a multiple and darkly ironic sense, the stage is a threshold.

In the next scene, the threshold is a literal one: Lord Stanley's messenger is knocking at Hastings' door at four in the morning. Hastings sends the messenger back to get his master up and bring him; then Catesby turns up wanting to talk to Hastings and they discuss the political situation until Stanley arrives, and all three are to set out to a council meeting in the Tower. Hastings lingers a moment to talk to a Pursuivant, then to a priest, and then to Buckingham, whom, it seems, he bumps into on his way to the Tower. Again, the scene is strongly located in a relational sense (Hastings comes *from* his house and is going *to* the Tower), but it does not represent a single place. Hastings talks with six separate interlocutors in the course of 120 lines: to imagine them all turning up on his doorstep in neat succession would be to assume that, formally speaking, the scene is farce. It is more accurate to think of the scene as the story of Hastings' last morning, and of the various people who spoke with him after he got out of bed and before he arrived at the Tower. The stage is effectively the *space between* those two end-points.

The Hastings sequence is interrupted by a brief scene (3.3) showing the Queen's relatives being led to execution at Pomfret Castle. Even this interlude similarly uses the stage as a transitional space: its first line is 'Come, bring forth the prisoners', and it ends with their being led off to death. In other words, the stage is the space of their short journey from the off-stage cells to the off-stage block. The council scene itself (3.4) does in a way bring this tensed scenic mobility to a stop: '*Enter Buckingham, Derby, Hastings, Bishop of Ely, Norfolk, Ratcliffe, Lovel, with others, at a table*'.[17] We are at the meeting; people are sitting down; the stage represents, as nineteenth-century editors might say, 'A Room in the Tower'. In practice, though, the stability of the location is immediately undermined. Richard is late, and so the meeting starts, tentatively, without him. He arrives, sends the Bishop of Ely on an errand, and then leaves again with Buckingham, so that when the Bishop returns, it is to a meeting which is still incomplete, still not sure whether it is in session or not. Then Richard returns, denounces Hastings and storms out, calling on everyone else to

---

[17] 3.4.0. This stage direction is verbatim that of the Folio.

follow him. They do so, leaving Hastings alone at the table with his executioners. Thus Richard controls the scene by a violent and unpredictable alternation of presence and absence: Hastings, who is on stage throughout, is the helpless object of moves made elsewhere. No less than in the preceding scenes, though in a different sense, the visible stage is meaningful only by virtue of its relationship with an inner space which is not seen. Hastings imagined that he was *there*, at the place where decisions are made. He was not; he was in the ante-room.

Throughout the sequence, then, the platform stage is spatially meaningful, but never in itself, always in charged relation to off-stage space. The tiring-house façade has the effect of giving the actor on stage the uncertain poise of someone hesitating in a doorway. Shakespeare exploits this unresolved dynamism with great flexibility, applying the 'threshold' scenic structure to varying geographical contexts and orders of magnitude. But if we look back over the sequence of four scenes from Act 3, it appears that in pursuing their variety I have overlooked a striking uniformity: that for the Princes, for Rivers, Vaughan, and Grey, and for Hastings, the off-stage space is where they go to die. Proximately, the doorway leads to this or that room, or castle, or city; but ultimately, every threshold is that of the tomb. The underlying metaphor is that of Walter Ralegh's famous (and formulaic) comparison of life to a play:

> Heaven the Judicious sharpe spectator is,
> That sits and markes still who doth act amisse,
> Our graves that hide us from the searching Sun,
> Are like drawne curtaynes when the play is done,
> Thus march we playing to our latest rest,
> Onely we dye in earnest, that's no Jest.[18]

Here Barsacq's 'hidden world' is specified, in self-consciously tragic and homiletic fashion, as death, the unappearing reality that concludes the dubious appearances of life. The on–off duality that drives the stage action is not only metonymic but, in the same breath, emblematic.

Within

In an open-air amphitheatre the tiring-house is literally a house, and the stage is literally outside it, under the sky. Consequently the ordinary term for 'off-stage' is 'within', and this usage persists even in plays written for indoor performance. This opposition does not constrain the referential function of the space: there is no difficulty about having the stage represent an interior, and so making the inside of

---

[18] The lyric was popular and variously printed. This text is from Robert Nye, ed., *A Choice of Sir Walter Ralegh's Verse* (London: Faber and Faber, 1972), 65.

the tiring-house stand for the outside world, as it does in the moment from *The Insatiate Countess* with which I began. A stage direction from *A New Way to Pay Old Debts* (1625) reads 'Noise within as of a coach': the author of such a phrase takes it for granted that the spatial relationships of the playhouse are simply incommensurable with those of the fiction.[19] All the same, a play that does in fact line them up, so that the actor's 'within' is the story's 'within' too, is going along with the logic of the building.

I have noted elsewhere that some such consonance was normal in Italian comedy.[20] The default setting is a generic street, with doors leading off to the brothel, the father's house, the inn. The characters disappear into these interiors to lead their private lives, and emerge to conduct the negotiations that constitute the dramatic plot. This configuration is a humanist one, not only in the sense that it is copied from Terence and Plautus, but also in that it is rhetorical: what it stages is not the characters' spontaneous behaviour, but the public advocacy that their private interests generate. It could certainly be transplanted to the London stage: there is something like it, for example, in Lyly's *Mother Bombie*, and in Shakespeare's *The Comedy of Errors*, both around 1591–2. But there were other ways of using the 'insideness' of the tiring-house, ways more organically linked to the structure of English playhouses.

Take a pioneering domestic tragedy, also from the early 1590s: *Arden of Faversham*.[21] A long first scene sets out the dramatic situation, introducing Arden, his friend Franklin, his wife Alice, her lover Mosby, and various servants and neighbours. It does this almost entirely by means of arrivals and departures at Arden's house. This involves two off-stage orientations: exits can lead either away from the house or else to rooms within it. The stage is thus the interface between the two. Examples of the inward orientation include the following:

> ARDEN. How, Alice!
> *Here enters Alice.*
> ALICE.   Husband, what mean you to be up so early? (56–7)

> ARDEN. Alice, make ready my breakfast: I must hence.
> *Exit Alice.* (299)

These entrances and exits designate a 'within' that includes a bedroom and a kitchen. The location therefore works in the same way as the Italianate street: a screened off interior contains the material life of the household (sex and food), while the stage is the place of its social life (visits and conversation). This allocation of space becomes

---

[19] Philip Massinger, *A New Way to Pay Old Debts*, 3.2.241, in *The Plays and Poems of Philip Massinger*, ed. Philip Edwards and Colin Gibson (Oxford: Clarendon Press, 1976), vol. 2.

[20] Peter Womack, 'The Comical Scene: Perspective and Civility on the Renaissance Stage', *Representations* 101 (Winter 2008), 32–56.

[21] Text in Thomas Heywood et al., *A Woman Killed With Kindness and Other Domestic Plays*, ed. Martin Wiggins (Oxford: Oxford World's Classics, 2008.)

pointed at the end of the scene, when Arden leaves for London and Mosby says, 'Now, Alice, let's in and see what cheer you keep' (636). Command of the interior space is what the plot is all about.

Conversely, here are three entrances from the outward-facing direction:

> *Here enters Adam of the Flower-de-Luce*
> ALICE.   And here comes Adam of the Flower-de-Luce.
>   I hope he brings me tidings of my love.
>   How now, Adam, what is the news with you?
>   Be not afraid; my husband is now from home.   (105–8)
>
> *Here enters Mosby*
> ALICE.   Yonder comes Mosby. Michael, get thee gone,
>   And let not him nor any know thy drifts.
>   *Exit Michael*
>   Mosby, my love!
> MOSBY.   Away, I say, and talk not to me now.   (175–9)
>
> *Here enters Greene*
> MOSBY.   Alice, what's he that comes yonder? Knowest thou him?
> ALICE.   Mosby, begone; I hope 'tis one that comes
>   To put in practice our intended drifts.
>   *Exit Mosby*
> GREENE. Mistress Arden, you are well met.   (446–50)

These moments illustrate the identification of the stage as public space. Whereas entrants from within join the on-stage conversation immediately, these external arrivals can be seen coming a few lines before they speak. And the casual greetings— 'How now', 'Well met'—do not imply a visitor coming into a private house; they sound like people meeting in the street. Mosby's line, in particular —'Away, I say, and talk not to me now'—is puzzling unless the lovers are in public view. Their situation is the one outlined earlier by Alice, when she sent a message bidding him:

> To come this morning but along my door
> And as a stranger but salute me there....   (128–9)

The meeting is not quite either inside or outside Alice's house: it is 'but along her door'.

Thus the stage seems to be a place where the family can see and be seen by passers-by. Yet at one point Alice brings Arden his (incompetently poisoned) breakfast; he sits to eat it and invites Mosby to join him; there must be a table and chairs. The scene as a whole, then, is asking the audience to 'see' a place that is part of the interior of Arden's house but is also open to the rest of the town. Early modern spectators might have found this hybrid, threshold-like space easy to recognize. Laura Gowing writes evocatively about the doorstep—the boundary stone of the household; the place (especially in ill-lit houses) where women sewed or knitted or nursed babies; the scene, in numerous recorded disputes, of abusive words or accusations (137).[22] In the crowded courts of London, a woman on the doorstep was at home and connected to the neighbourhood at the same time. In wealthier households, a comparable function was served by the front room that was also a shop; and still further up the scale, in the house of a rising landowner such as Arden himself, the room immediately inside the front door was often a large, multi-purpose hall with doors leading off it to more specialized spaces such as the kitchen or the counting house.[23]

Doorstep, shop, hall: the stage in *Arden* is linked with these sites not by a fixed logic of denotation but by a functional analogy. As in *Richard III*, it is not that the action is 'meant' to be happening in a certain place: as far as that goes, the acting area counts as inside for some purposes and outside for others. Rather, it is that the stage works *like* a doorstep. Behind the tiring-house doors is the family's private space. Out here is the public space where its affairs are gazed at and talked about. In between them is the place where the play happens.[24]

Woman's place

It is obvious from *Arden* that the domestic version of 'within' has one spatial signification in particular: it is the woman's place. A repeated trope in conduct books and sermons aligns 'out' and 'in' with 'male' and 'female'. The opposition is presented as both right and natural: 'The cock flyeth abroad to bring in and the dam sitteth upon the nest to keep all at home'.[25] Women who fail to sit upon the nest are said to be 'gadding', with the implication that their movement is frivolous and irregular and, further, that geographical wandering is the image and cause of sexual wandering. Good women are coded as indoors: private, stationary, closed. Women who are on the contrary public, mobile, and open are whores.

[22] Laura Gowing, "'The freedom of the streets": Women and Social Space, 1560–1640', in Paul Griffiths and Mark S. R. Jenner, eds., *Londinopolis: Essays in the Cultural and Social History of Early Modern London* (Manchester: Manchester University Press, 2000), 130–51 (137). See also Lena Cowen Orlin, 'Women on the Threshold', *Shakespeare Studies* 25 (1997), 50–8.

[23] Dekker stages shops as just such intermediate spaces in several plays, including *The Shoemakers Holiday* and *The Roaring Girl*. For the place of the hall in gentry houses, Amanda Flather, *Gender and Space in Early Modern England* (Woodbridge: Boydell and Brewer, 2007), 43; Sarah Pearson, *The Medieval Houses of Kent: An Historical Analysis* (London: Her Majesty's Stationery Office, 1994), 136; Catherine Richardson, 'The Table in *A Woman Killed With Kindness*', in Jonathan Gil Harris and Natasha Korda, eds., *Staged Properties in Early Modern English Drama* (Cambridge: Cambridge University Press, 2002), 139–43.

[24] There is an illuminatingly similar argument about early modern 'threshold paintings' in John Loughman, 'Between Reality and Artful Fiction: The Representation of the Domestic Interior in Seventeenth-Century Dutch Art', in Jeremy Aynsley and Charlotte Grant, eds., *Imagined Interiors* (London: V&A Publications, 2006), 72–97.

[25] Quoted, among several other instances of the same trope, in Flather, *Gender and Space in Early Modern England*, 17.

The insatiate countess illustrates this principle. The play's first image freezes her in the attitude of a widow:

The Countess of Swevia discovered sitting at a table covered with black, on which stands two black tapers lighted, she in mourning.   (1.1.0)

The tableau is presumably set up in the central opening, so it holds the Countess, motionless and darkened, in a place that is hardly on the stage at all. By remarrying, the Duchess moves away from her home position and begins to go 'abroad' among the men; her flight from her new husband is a second such movement, more violent and depraved than the first. The galloping horses represent, you could say, extreme gadding.

Marston is exploiting the moralized opposition of home and abroad in characteristically lurid fashion, but the opposition itself is already there in the spatial language of the theatre. It underlies, for example, one of the best known stage configurations in Elizabethan drama: the balcony scene in *Romeo and Juliet*. The 'balcony' must in practice be the gallery above the upstage doors, so Juliet at her window, like the Countess in mourning, is attached to the house, while Romeo moves around the platform in front of it.[26] This is the structure of their performing relationship for much of the play, in fact. Although the Chorus promises two houses, like in rank and dignity, only one is dramatically present. The Capulets' house, and later their tomb, figure repeatedly in the action as places that people try to get into or out of, but the Montagues appear only in the street; we take it that they have a house, but it is not part of the play. The opposition that counts in the theatre, then, is not one house against another, but inside against outside, the tiring-house against the platform. This asymmetry does not mark any narrative distinction between the Capulets and the Montagues: on the contrary, it is the point of the story that there is nothing to choose between them. Rather, it is dictated by the relationship of Romeo and Juliet themselves: that she is within and he is without is the spatialization of their gender difference, their mutual attraction of contrary principles.

As for the gallery itself, it is a permanent part of the theatre building, so its fictional character is redefined each time it is used. Here its force is sexual. Juliet is out in the open air above the stage, in touch rhetorically with the darkness and danger of her forbidden love; but at the same time off-stage sounds, and rapid exits and re-entrances, connect her with the rooms of the house, where she is under the government of her parents and her nurse. With an eloquence that perhaps explains its fame, then, the 'balcony' enables Juliet, considered as an ideological image, to have it both ways. Her connection with the interior aligns her with the virtues of

---

[26] The word 'balcony' nowhere occurs in the text or stage directions of *Romeo and Juliet*; its universal use to refer to what the play calls Juliet's 'window' reflects the requirements of a later stage. The architectural and theatrical emergence of the balcony is related in Adam Zucker, *The Places of Wit in Early Modern English Comedy* (Cambridge: Cambridge University Press, 2011), 118–23. It seems to have occurred in the early 1630s and to have been, not surprisingly, a highly sexualized development.

domestic femininity—constancy, modesty, chastity—and so secures her position as the play's heroine. But her window, open to the night, leaves her incompletely separated from the exterior world of the stage and the streets, the mobility, fantastical desire, and physical display of the city's young men. To 'talk with a man out at a window' is a byword for female looseness.[27] Thus the paradox at the heart of the tragedy's mythic power—that Romeo and Juliet are husband and wife but also illicit lovers, exponents of reckless passion but at the same time innocent victims—is staged as a sort of spatial equivocation. They meet on the precarious ledge between the enclosed house and the open stage.

Thus Shakespeare's theatrical production of the official doctrine of gender is both expressive and ambivalent. The ambivalence is not surprising; after all, when moralists spoke of urban women gadding about, one of the deplorable destinations they had in mind was the theatre itself.[28] The shared assumption that man and woman had their respective spaces, the one without, the other within, certainly helped the theatre to make intelligible representations of space, but as a social space on its own account it was widely seen as violating exactly that principle. Going to a play means participating in a crowded public circle, gaudy and fashion-conscious, a place for looking and being looked at, an occasion for unsecured emotions and promiscuous encounters. It means, in several linked senses, going out rather than staying in. It would be surprising if this environment produced an unambiguous idealization of domestic femininity. Rather, its deployments of gendered interiority run to violation, travesty, and innuendo.

All three are on display, for instance, in the episode of *Volpone* (1606) that concerns Celia, the wife of the merchant Corvino. In pursuit of her heavily guarded charms, Volpone dresses up as a mountebank and does a show under her window, at the end of which he manages to persuade her to throw down her handkerchief. Again, the desirable woman is confined in the gallery of the tiring-house while the man moves around the open space in front of it. But the fact that Volpone is giving a performance makes the relationship more knowingly metatheatrical. And then Corvino's possessive fury turns the image of domestic enclosure into parody. He will have the window blocked up, he will draw a chalk line two yards back from it and tear her to pieces if she crosses it—

> And, now I think on't, I will keep thee backwards;
> Thy lodging shall be backwards; thy walks backwards;
> Thy prospect—all be backwards; and no pleasure,
> That thou shalt know, but backwards.[29]

---

[27] William Shakespeare, *Much Ado About Nothing*, 4.1.309.

[28] See for instance the address to the 'Gentlewomen Citizens of London' that ends Stephen Gosson's *The Schoole of Abuse* (London, 1579).

[29] Ben Jonson, *Volpone*, 2.5.58–61, in *Complete Plays*, ed. G. A. Wilkes, 4 vols. (Oxford: Clarendon Press), vol. 3.

The explicit reference of 'backwards' is to back *rooms*: Celia is to be denied any approach to the front windows, so that no glance or appearance compromises her enclosure by the house. But the feverish projection that motivates this prohibition infiltrates the word itself, so that without Corvino quite realizing it, his fortress of virtue gets mixed up with his sexual fantasies. The doctrine of the modest wife is tricked into exposing its bad side, which turns out to be sadism.

Jonson is a satirist, in judgemental control of the comic reversals with which Corvino struggles helplessly. But what produces the reversals themselves is a dangerous spatial ambiguity. The feminization of the backstage space may be a moral statement, but it also constructs it as an object of desire. The acting area is a male domain, so the tiring-house can readily appear as the enclosed place which the actor is trying to penetrate. That, at any rate, is where *The Insatiate Countess* begins. Once the candle-lit tableau of the widow in the central doorway has registered, the first line is 'What should we do in this Countess's dark hole?' And a few moments later, when the Countess herself breaks her silence, it is to say, 'Ha, Anna, what, are my doors unbarred?', to which the sardonic male response is, 'I'll assure you the way into your Ladyship is open' (1.1.19–20). Through the curtain, under the arch, along the half-seen passage, the interior is coded as female in a way that is not so much moralized as grossly embodied.[30]

In this context, then, the exit into the tiring-house is drastically overdetermined. It indicates the reserved interior where decent women keep the house. But it also implies the woman's penetrable body, the very centre of sexual transgression. The unseen-ness of the off-stage realm signifies both modesty and obscenity.[31] At this point, the reading of the tiring-house as domestic chamber crosses over with a quite different tradition of off-stage space: the doctrine that certain things are withdrawn from view because they are forbidden.

Intus digna geri

non tamen intus
digna geri promes in scaenam, multaque tolles
ex oculis, quae mox narret facundia praesens;
ne pueros coram populo Medea trucidet,

---

[30] The gendering of the spatial duality has a sociological counterpart. Natasha Korda notes that in 1607–8 the backstage staff of the Whitefriars included a 'tyrewoman', that is, a dresser of wigs and headgear. Thus the Countess is a boy, but he has been got up to look like a woman by a real woman who remains concealed behind the scenes. See Natasha Korda, *Labors Lost: Women's Work and the Early Modern Stage* (Philadelphia: University of Pennsylvania Press, 2011), 34–9.

[31] The verbal connection between 'scene' and 'obscene' is traced back as far as classical Latin by the *OED*, which adds, however, that it is a false etymology.

> *aut humana palam coquat exta nefarius Atreus,*
> *aut in avem Procne vertatur, Cadmus in anguem.*
> *quodcumque ostendis mihi sic, incredulus odi.*[32]

(Yet you will not display on the stage what ought to be performed within, and you will keep many things from our eyes, which an actor's ready tongue will in due course narrate in our presence; Medea is not to butcher her boys before the people, nor is impious Atreus to cook human entrails in public, or Procne to be turned into a bird, or Cadmus into a snake. Whatever you show me in this way, I disbelieve and detest.)

Which actions and objects ought to be kept 'within', behind the scenes? By no means all off-stage effects fall into this category. We saw in *Richard III* how the Tower of London is built up as a portentous off-stage destination, but then, when it comes to the point, there is no difficulty about setting the next scene inside the building. One scene's off-stage becomes the next scene's on-stage and vice versa; the relationship is significant, but it does not signify a prohibition. Some things, however, are withheld from sight not adventitiously but necessarily: we are more or less explicitly told that a particular object must not be shown. Horace's authoritative formulation of this ban is interestingly mixed. The famous tag—*incredulus odi*—concisely combines two distinct grounds for excluding something from the stage: that it cannot be represented credibly (for example because it is miraculous), and that it should not be represented at all (for example because it is shameful or atrocious). Practical and ethical considerations overlap.

The practical ones can appear explicitly on early modern stages. In the fourth act of Thomas Heywood's *The Fair Maid of the West*, for example, when the heroine sets off on her privateering voyage through the Mediterranean, a Chorus admits:

> Our stage so lamely can express a sea
> That we are forc'd by Chorus to discourse
> What should have been in action.[33]

The playwright sounds naïvely helpless; the sea seems to him inherently unstageable; he would like to present it but is reluctantly 'forced' to consign it to the off-stage world. A similar logic is implicit when the sea is evoked by what Alan Dessen calls 'as from' entrances, as when characters enter wet or ragged from an off-stage shipwreck.[34] We are nearly shown the exciting event itself—but no, it can't be done. And it is possible to think of the Countess's horses in the same way. Bringing a horse onto the stage is not out of the question, but for obvious reasons it is normally just

---

[32] Horace, *Ars Poetica*, 182–8, in *Satires, Epistles and Ars Poetica*, Loeb Classical Library (Cambridge, MA: Harvard University Press, rev. edn., 1929). I have rephrased the Loeb translation.

[33] Thomas Heywood, *The Fair Maid of the West*, ed. Robert K. Turner, Regents Renaissance Drama Series (London: Edward Arnold, 1968), Part I, 4.5.1–3.

[34] Alan C. Dessen, *Elizabethan Stage Conventions and Modern Interpreters* (Cambridge: Cambridge University Press, 1984), 31–2.

one horse, moving carefully.[35] A mounted party at full gallop is impossible, so it is handled in the same way as an ocean or a pitched battle.

But this type of exclusion is almost never as self-evident as it might seem. For one thing, the definition of what is 'practical' is never simply given but is produced by the artistic conventions of the theatre in question. As is well known, the Noah plays in the medieval urban cycles unhesitatingly stage the building of the Ark and the inundation of the world: this is not because they possess resources that Heywood lacks but because their representational practices are different from his, and so their criteria of practicality are different as well. And as we have seen, Elizabethan stage conventions are themselves unstable, so the boundary of the practical is never fixed. It is easy, for example, to contrast the comic literalness of the lion in 'Pyramus and Thisbe', which appears on stage, with the poetic suggestiveness of the lion in *As You Like It*, which is purely narrated. This, we say, is Shakespeare adapting, more skilfully than Heywood, to the limits of what his stage can express. But then a bear appears in *The Winter's Tale*, disturbing our confidence that we know where the limits are.

Besides, this way of framing the issues assumes that the material elements of the story are *just there*, arbitrary problems of representation that the play bumps into and has to try and solve. This is the assumption of the performers of 'Pyramus and Thisbe': for them, the lion must somehow be provided because it is mentioned in the play, whose authority they suppose to be absolute. But their relationship with the script is comic precisely because we can see, as they cannot, that Lion and Wall and Moonshine are not given contingencies but imaginative productions, dramatic signifiers of danger and confinement and transformation. It is not that Heywood has resorted to a Chorus because he was confronted with the sea; the sea and the Chorus are, both alike, elements of the theatre text.

In other words, there is not really a class of objects that exist somewhere and are refused admission to the stage. Rather, some of the theatre's objects are produced *as* off-stage; their concealment is not so much prohibitive as constitutive; not to be seen is, so to speak, the making of them. And if we consider the members of this class that we happen to have mentioned already—the sea, wild animals, galloping horses—we see that it overlaps with the class of things that are said to be hidden because they are shameful: sexual intercourse, bodily functions and diseases, mutilation and violent death. It is not only that most of the latter challenge canons of 'practicality' too (on-stage decapitation demands a conjuror's skills; any action involving the literal presence of a female body is out of the question). It is also that all these off-stage phenomena have an irreducible and as it were anti-discursive physicality. As the classical formulation from Horace makes explicit, their on-stage opposite is the actor's tongue, the propriety of narration: again we see how

---

[35] See the entry for 'horse' in Alan C. Dessen and Leslie Thomson, *A Dictionary of Stage Directions in English Drama 1580–1642* (Cambridge: Cambridge University Press, 1999).

fundamentally the humanist stage is a rhetorical space. Off-stage is its non-verbal other: the space of that which is *unspeakably* itself.

There is a complex example of this unspeakability, at once paradigmatic and bizarre, at the climax of Jonson's tragedy *Sejanus*. The hubristic imperial favourite Sejanus has fallen, and a messenger describes his death. Sejanus, we hear, has been torn to pieces by the enraged Roman mob and his body so utterly destroyed that no part of him can be found for burial. Not only that, but a second messenger comes on to add that the new power in Rome, Macro, ordered the execution of Sejanus' family too. Because there is a customary prohibition on the execution of virgins, it was arranged that his young daughter should be raped by the hangman before she was killed.[36] This effect seems schematically, wilfully obscene in all the various senses of the concept. It is technically unstageable: the chaotic, innumerable crowd, the physical details of both deaths, all seems designed to put enactment out of the question on practical grounds. And beyond this, the hyperbolical atrocity of the violence breaks with any conceivable canon of propriety. One shouldn't stage such things even if one could; and one couldn't stage them even if one should.

These different negations are connected ideologically. The controlling standpoint of the play is patrician (its heroes are aristocratic republicans, and both Sejanus and Macro are low-born imperial protégés), and the messenger's speech represents not only the fall of the protagonist but also the terror and monstrosity of the mob. It is formless, leaderless, mindless—it explodes in violence today with no memory of what it felt or did yesterday. It cannot be given articulate form because it is, so to speak, inarticulacy as such. Thus from the dramatist's point of view, the mob resists representation for the same reasons that make it morally abhorrent. It is like an enormous beast, or like the sea: it is aligned with all the things that cannot appear on the scene. This is a heavy dramaturgic investment in off-stage monstrosity, and it is hardly coincidental that it happens in such a self-consciously Roman context. The learned regulation of the spectacle in the name of probability and decorum generates a converse unseen space, fantastical and jarring. The opposition between on-stage as verbal and off-stage as corporeal is set out especially clearly in the tragedies of Seneca, with their frigidly rhetorical tirades and their onslaughts of evoked or narrated bloodletting. Structurally, *Sejanus* is not particularly Senecan, but Jonson is too much a humanist not to produce the same binary logic: you hear the classical purist, not only in the heroic length and Latinate diction of the *narratio*, but also in the deliberate excesses of the narrated events, conscientiously pushing the effect towards pity and terror.

The unstageable mixture of violence and formlessness that we encounter in *Sejanus* finds its paradigmatic source in the messenger's account of the death of Hippolytus in the *Phaedra*, the sequence where the sea-god rises up and drives the

---

[36] Ben Jonson, *Sejanus His Fall*, Act 5, 795–822 and 839–44, in *Complete Plays*, ed. G. A. Wilkes, 4 vols. (Oxford: Clarendon Press), vol 2.

boy's horses mad with fear so that they pull his chariot to pieces and he is torn apart.[37] And if this passage lies behind the dismemberment of Sejanus it also, I think, echoes in Isabella's whirlwind departure. Hippolytus, after all, is racing away from his stepmother's frightening desire for him: the violence that mixes up the images comes in part from the agitation generated by a woman's sexual voracity. The uncontrolled horse is a conventional emblem of lust, appearing as such, together with the sea, in Isabella's own soliloquy earlier in the scene (2.3.42–65). This imagery is further associated with off-stage effects in a later scene that shows Isabella's seduction of Rogero's friend Gniaca. At the end of their duologue she exits, promising, 'I'll lead the way to Venus' paradise' (3.4.77), and before Gniaca follows her, he tells his page to sing. When the song is over the lovers reappear, and Gniaca says:

> I have swum in seas of pleasure without ground,
> Vent'rous desire past depth itself hath drowned.   (3.4.85–6)

Once again, the stage action pauses in mid-scene in deference to what is happening elsewhere; and this time, with startling crudity, the suspension between exit and re-entrance means that the characters are having sex. The horses are of course not 'obscene' in that banal sense, but they connect with the same cluster of associations; they too intimate the bodily abandon which is opposed to the play's controlled speech. With a new and uneasy emphasis, the tiring-house façade appears as what stands between the theatre audience and the *real thing*.

There's more behind

Formally, then, the dynamic construction of the off-stage space has the effect of rendering the stage itself radically incomplete. John Orrell quotes a dictionary definition of 'theatre' from 1611: 'a publike Playhouse; an halfe-round house wherein people sit to behold publike Playes'.[38] This precisely evokes the shaping energies of early modern theatre. Whether we imagine a quasi-Palladian horseshoe shape or an open-air London amphitheatre, *half*-round is the decisive form, an inclusive 'public' circularity cut across by a lateral barrier. The space where the action is presented to the audience is half of something, the other half being out of sight: heard, inferred, reported upon. Watching the actors in front of their ornate screen, we understand that the show is not all present: there's more behind.[39]

---

[37] Seneca, *Phaedra*, 1000–1113, in *Tragedies* 1, ed. and trans. John G. Fitch (Cambridge, MA: Loeb Classical Library, 2002).

[38] Orrell, *The Human Stage*, 201.

[39] The expression is from the closing speech of *Measure for Measure* (5.1.529, 539), a play to which it is especially appropriate.

In specifying this lack metonymically, Marston is arguably looking towards the future. As in the realist theatre, what is behind is more of the *same* world, the highway or the boudoir. The immediately off-stage sex scene, at once brazen and coy, anticipates the disenchanted dramatic vocabulary of Wycherley and Behn. But if we look backwards, from the Countess's horses to the Senecan ones, we can see the most obvious unseen force of all: what really destroys Hippolytus, after all, is not his horses and not his stepmother, but the god. The thing we don't see continues to carry suggestions of the thing we *can't* see; however the tiring-house may become domesticated as another room, it still feels like another world. And that is why Marston's sound effect strikes a note of terror as well as innuendo. Everything about early modern theatre space is incomplete, even its deconsecration.

FURTHER READING

Hodges, C. Walter. *Enter the Whole Army: A Pictorial Study of Shakespearean Staging, 1576–1616* (Cambridge: Cambridge University Press, 1999).

Redmond, James, ed. *Themes in Drama: The Theatrical Space* (Cambridge: Cambridge University Press, 1987).

Turner, Henry S. *The English Renaissance Stage: Geometry, Poetics, and the Practical Spatial Arts 1580–1630* (Oxford: Oxford University Press, 2006).

Wiles, David. *A Short History of Western Performance Space* (Cambridge: Cambridge University Press, 2003).

Womack, Peter. 'Noises Off', *Textual Practice* 1 (1987), 309–28.

CHAPTER 5

SCENE

BRUCE R. SMITH

'In his owne conceit the onely Shake-scene in a countrey'[1]: just what did Robert
Greene in his famous put-down imagine Shakespeare to be shaking? The context
in *Greenes, groats-vvorth of witte* (1592) suggests several possibilities. The scene
that Shakespeare shakes might be just what speakers of twenty-first-century English would think of first: a segment of a play, in particular a segment demarcated at
beginning and end by an empty stage.[2] In that case the scene to which Greene
alludes would be the stretch of text in *Henry VI, Part Three* that modern editions
mark as act one, scene four. York's verbal assault on Queen Margaret in the midst
of 1.4 includes a line ('O tiger's heart wrapped in a woman's hide!'[3]) that Greene
seizes upon for ridicule: 'for there is an vpstart Crow, beautified with our feathers,
that with his *Tygers hart wrapt in a Players hyde*, supposes he is as well able to
bombast out a blanke verse as the best of you' (sig. F1v). (The 'our' here embraces
Christopher Marlowe, Thomas Nashe, and George Peele, all of whom, like Greene
but unlike Shakespeare, were university graduates.) There is a problem with reading 'scene' this way, however, since neither the 1623 folio printing of the play nor
the 1595 quarto recognizes an entity labelled act one, scene four. The folio starts
the text by announcing '*Actus Primus. Scaena Prima*' in large italic type, but that
is the last time any notice is given to acts and scenes. Instead the text of the play

---

[1] Robert Greene, *Greenes, groats-vvorth of witte, bought with a million of repentance. Describing the
follie of youth, the falshoode of makeshifte flatterers, the miserie of the negligent, and mischiefes of deceiu-
ing courtezans. Written before his death, and published at his dyeing request* (London: J. Wolfe and
J. Danter for William Wright, 1592), sig. F1v. Further quotations are taken from the 1592 printing and
are cited in the text.

[2] *Oxford English Dictionary Online*, 2nd edn. (Oxford: Oxford University Press, 1989), online version December 2011 (http://www.oed.com, accessed at various times March through September 2012
[subscription needed]), 'scene', *n.*, I.5.a. Further quotations from the *OED* are cited in the text.

[3] William Shakespeare, *The True Tragedy of Richard Duke of York and the Good King Henry the Sixth*
(*Henry VI*, Part 3), 1.4.138, in *The Complete Works*, ed. Stanley Wells and Gary Taylor, 2nd edn.
(Oxford: Clarendon Press, 2005), 99. Unless otherwise noted, quotations from Shakespeare's plays are
taken from this edition and are cited in the text by act, scene, and line numbers.

unfolds continuously, entrance by entrance, line by line, speech by speech, exit by exit, just as it does in the quarto. No breaks. No indication that an empty stage is significant.

A second possibility for Greene's 'scene' is the big effect of what is being represented at the moment.[4] In that case we confront in 1.4 a Scene of Rage played out between York and Queen Margaret. Taken captive by Margaret and her troops, planted on a molehill, mocked with a paper crown, forced to view the napkin that has been used to sop up his murdered son's blood, York finally blurts out, 'Bidds't thou me rage? Why, now thou hast thy wish. / Wouldst have me weep? Why, now thou hast thou will' (1.4.144–5). Greene himself uses 'scene' this way in *Greenes farewell to folly* (1591), when he has the soldier Bernardino chide the scholar Peratio for attacking pride among soldiers: 'you sir, induce a souldiour as prologue to your comedie of pride, where as you schollers ought to be for most in the scene'.[5] Bernardino goes on to instance an actual site for such a Scene of Pride, the University of Padua. A third sense of 'scene', as fictional location (*OED* I.4), figures at least tangentially here: in an updating of Cicero's *Tusculan Disputations* the supposed setting for *Greene's farewell to folly* is a villa outside Florence. It is worth noting that 'scene' in this sense does *not* figure prominently in 1.4 of *Henry VI, Part Three*. In 1.2 York tells his kinsmen, 'You are come to Sandal in a happy hour' (1.2.63), but the geographical location of the ensuing battle and York's death, in the parish of Sandal Magna near Wakefield, Yorkshire, is otherwise never mentioned, despite the specification in Holinshed's *Chronicles*, Shakespeare's source, that the battle and York's death took place 'betwene his castel and the town of Wakefield', a detail emphasized by the marginal tag 'The battaile of Wakfielde'.[6]

Scene as a segment of dramatic action marked at beginning and end by an empty stage, scene as big effect, and scene as fictional setting have their origins on the stage as a physical structure. Indeed, it is probably the stage specifically that Greene is thinking about when he mocks Shakespeare's ability 'to bombast out a blanke verse'.

---

[4] The *OED* does not recognize this as a distinct definition, despite, as we shall see, numerous references in Shakespeare's time to a 'scene' of this passion or that passion, this action or that action, this effect or that effect. The closest the *OED* comes are the metaphorical senses 'The place where an action is carried on and people play their parts as in a drama' (II.8, with citation of 'the Scene of Fame' from Henry Constable's sonnet sequence *Diana*, new edn., ?1594) and 'A view or picture presented to the eye (or to the mind) of a place, concourse, incident, series of actions or events, assemblage of objects' (II.9.a, with earliest citation as 'the greatest Scene of Majesty' from a sermon by Jeremy Taylor, 1653). I am advocating a conflation of these two definitions, and at an earlier date than is recognized by the *OED*.

[5] Robert Greene, *Greenes farewell to folly* (London: Thomas Scarlet for T. Gubbin and T. Newman, 1591), sig. C2. It is in the subtitle to this little book that Greene boasts himself to be '*vtriusque Academiæ in Artibus magister*', master of arts of both universities. Hence his snobbery about Shakesscene as a robber of other men's honours.

[6] Raphael Holinshed, *Chronicles of England, Scotland, and Ireland*, 1577 edition, The Holinshed Project (http://www.english.ox.ac.uk/holinshed/texts.php?text1=1577_5324#p14921, accessed 17 March 2012).

The big effect may be rage, but the scene of that Scene of Rage is a fourth sense of 'scene' as the act of acting, 'the action or representation of a piece upon the stage' (*OED* †I.3.a, obsolete since the early nineteenth century). 'Bombast' as a verb suggests a fifth, still more physical sense of what Shake-scene might have been shaking: the very boards of the platform and the tiring-house wall. Like *skene* in Greek and *scaena* in Latin, the English word *scene* originally designated the stage structure of ancient Greek and Roman theatres, not only the façade through which the actors made their entrances and exits but also the platform on which they stood as they spoke (*OED* I.1). Transferred across the centuries to London's public playhouses, scene in this sense seems to have referred primarily to the tiring-house wall.[7] Vibration and sound-dispersal were among the main functions of that timber structure.[8] Hence Greene's 'bombast'.

Beyond the physical theatre, a real-world place may lurk in Greene's phrase 'the only Shake-scene in a countrey'. Since *country* in early modern English usually referred to a region or district (*OED*, 'country, *n*', I.1.a and I.2.a) rather than a nation (I.3), Greene may be locating Shake-scene in the Warwickshire of his humble origins, as opposed to the London *urbs* already claimed by Greene and his ilk. If so, Shakespeare the upstart crow is not only the *writer* of the scene but the *actor* of the scene in his player's hide, and what he shakes are feathers. Aesop, Martial, and Macrobius all cast crows as mimics and tricksters, and Horace in epistle 1.3 compares a writer who steals other writers' lines to a bird who steals other birds' feathers, but Greene may also be invoking the crow's stolen feathers as a sign of social ostentation, part of Shake-scene's 'conceit'.[9] Not only for the Prince of Wales did feathers constitute a heraldic device. 'To shake the feather' was to show off one's honours (*OED*, 'shake, *v*', †8.b). In doing so, Shake-scene was, in Greene's view at least, writing himself into a social scene where he had no place being. A dress rehearsal for the upstart crow attack is to be found in the story Greene tells in *Francescos Fortunes: Or, The second part of Greenes neuer too late* (1591) about the time Cicero and the actor Roscius met at a dinner party. When Roscius presumed to compare himself to Cicero, the famous writer exclaimed, 'why *Roscius*, / art thou proud with *Esops* Crow being pranct with the glorie of others feathers? of thy selfe

[7] The *OED*'s 'scene, *n*', I.1, is labelled 'Antiq.', with citations from no earlier than c.1612, all of them in specifically antiquarian contexts. However, the entry for 'scene' in Alan C. Dessen and Leslie Thomson, *A Dictionary of Stage Directions in English Drama 1580–1642* (Cambridge: Cambridge University Press, 1999), 188, admits 'the tiring-house wall' as one of two definitions, with two relatively late citations, one from Brome's *A Jovial Crew* (1641) and one from Shirley's *The Gentleman of Venice* (1636). The other definition recognized by Dessen and Thomson is 'a segment of a play'.

[8] On the physical structure of theatres like the Globe as instruments for the projection and circulation of sound see my chapter on 'Within the Wooden O', in *The Acoustic World of Early Modern England* (Chicago: University of Chicago Press, 1999), 206–45.

[9] Peter Berek, 'The "Upstart Crow," Aesop's Crow, and Shakespeare as a Reviser', *Shakespeare Quarterly* 35.2 (1984), 205–7, parses the two possibilities in interpretations of the attack: Shakespeare as actor or Shakespeare as plagiarist.

thou canst say nothing'.[10] *Our* feathers, *our* lines, *our* social distinction: not *your* scene.

By relegating Shake-scene to the provincial place and the trading sort he came from, Greene anticipates modern biographers such as Katherine Duncan-Jones and Stephen Greenblatt, who argue that the social scene in which Shakespeare conceived his own part and played it out was not London but Stratford-upon-Avon. The subtitle to Duncan-Jones's biography is 'Scenes from his life', with 'scenes' understood as a matter of 'topics or issues associated with particular periods', a definition of *scene* that the *OED* (II.10.a) dates to the late seventeenth century but that surely is anticipated in *As You Like It* by Jaques' 'All the world's a stage' spiel.[11] It is, in fact, a multivalent use of the word *scene* that gives Jaques his cue: 'this wide and universal theatre /', Duke Senior observes, 'Presents more woeful pageants than the scene / Wherein we play in' (2.7.137–9). And off Jaques goes. The curiously redundant prepositions in Duke Senior's last line perhaps point up the multiple senses of scene as fictional locale and/or big effect ('the scene *wherein* we play') and as physical acting-space and/or the act of acting ('the scene ... we play *in*').

If I read Greene aright, Shake-scene could thus be imagined to be shaking one or more of six things: scene as subdivision of a script, as big effect, as the act of acting, as sounding-board, as fictional setting, as an episode in real life. Add to this list senses of *scene* that postdate the 1590s—scene as synecdoche for theatre itself (*OED* I.2), as stage scenery (I.6.a), as tableau (I.6.b), as the sphere of a particular activity or interest (II.8.d, e.g. 'the jazz scene'), as a place where a certain set of people meet and carry on common pursuits (II.8.e, e.g. 'the SoHo scene'), as a picture of a place or an incident or an assemblage of objects (II.9.a, e.g. the painted and engraved scenes in Boydell's Shakespeare Gallery), as a display of exaggerated feelings in real life (II.11, e.g. 'making a scene')—and the complexities of this monosyllabic word become dizzying. But not so dizzying as to make us collapse into an aporia. Rather, the multiple meanings of the word *scene* invite us to search out the continuities among the differences and to appreciate how these multiple meanings of *scene* bleed into each other. The result will be an enhanced understanding of 'scene' as a concept, on multiple fronts: (1) as a feature marked in scripts written for the English stage from 1590 to 1642, (2) as a feature remarked upon in prologues, choruses, and dialogue during the same period, (3) as a post-1642 cross-over term linking theatrical performance, other media, and the practice of everyday life, and (4) as a concept with unrealized potential in contemporary criticism.

---

[10]   Robert Greene, *Greenes neuer too late. Or, A powder of experience* (London: Thomas Orwin for Nicholas Ling and John Busby, 1590), sigs. B4v–B5.

[11]   Katherine Duncan-Jones, *Ungentle Shakespeare: Scenes from his life* (London: The Arden Shakespeare, 2001), x. Stephen Greenblatt pursues a similar argument vis-à-vis Shakespeare's social aspirations in Stratford-upon-Avon in *Will in the World: How Shakespeare became Shakespeare* (New York: Norton, 2004). The *OED*'s definition II.10.a reads, 'An action, episode, complication of events, or situation, in real life'.

Marking scenes

Despite the thirteen senses of the word *scene* that I have distinguished—six in use from 1590 to 1642 and seven dating from later times—we need to confront what an odd concept 'scene' actually is. Dramatic performance in most of the world's cultures gets along quite well without it. In medieval drama, as Helen Cooper points out, there are no scenes in the sense of breaks in the story being represented. In the biblical cycle plays each pageant (the creation of the world, the fall, the flood, the crucifixion, the last judgement) is presented within a single, continuous configuration of space and time, regardless of lapsed time and changes in location. Between pageants the over-arching story of sin and redemption provides an even larger continuity that makes gaps in the narrative seem inconsequential. Shakespeare's two history cycles, Cooper argues, are structured on similar principles: the life of an individual king gives each play its own coherence, while the overarching story of conflict and resolution in the Tudor dynasty bestows unity of space and time across the entire sequence of plays. In saints plays (*Mary Magdalene* for example) and morality plays (*Mundus et Infans*) the protagonist's story is likewise presented as a continuous entity, often with the protago-nist present on-stage throughout. *Doctor Faustus*, despite its many episodes and shifts in location, displays this mode of continuous representation of space and time.[12] In Middle English *scena* (noun) and *scenicalle* (adjective) are rare, specialist words, used only to refer to the physical structure of the playhouses of ancient Rome.[13]

Given this rarity, it should come as no surprise that Richard Pynson in his 1495–7 editions of Terence's comedies—the earliest printings of classical play scripts in England—should include an explanation of just what a *scena* is. Following the example of continental editions, Pynson reprints the introduction and running commentary on Terence's plays by the fourth-century grammarian Aelius Donatus. After a life of Terence and two treatises, one on story (*De Fabula*) and one on com-edy as a genre (*De Comoedia*), Donatus' commentary proceeds play by play, act by act, scene by scene, line by line.[14] A new scene is marked whenever a character

---

[12] Helen Cooper, *Shakespeare and the Medieval World* (London: Methuen, 2010), 97–102.

[13] Citations for both words in *The Middle English Dictionary* come from John Trevisa's translation (1387) of Ranulf Higden's *Polychronicon* (composed *c*.1300–64). The citation for *scena*—cast in past tense—is quite specific to the theatre buildings of ancient Rome: 'Theatrum was a place i-shape as half a cercle, and in þe myddel þerof was a litel hous þat was i-cleped scena [L *scena*]; In þat hous poetes and gestoures upon a pulpet rehersede poysees . . and withoute were mynstralles þat counterfeted þe . . dedes þat þey speke in her gestes and songes'. The definition of *scenicalle* as 'theatrical' derives from this architectural sense of *scena* and again is cast in past tense: 'This disporte and institucion off disportes scenicalle began þro þe . . suggestion of the deuelle . . a chorle . . dremede in his slepe that he scholde say to the senate þat thei scholde ordeyne pleyes seenicalle' (*Middle English Dictionary*, http://quod.lib.umich.edu/m/med/, accessed 14 August 2012).

[14] A modern edited text of Donatus' preliminary treatises and play-by-play commentary is available at http://hyperdonat.ens-lyon.fr. Donatus' influence in the sixteenth century is charted in Marvin T. Herrick, *Comic Theory in the Sixteenth Century* (Urbana: University of Illinois Press, 1964), 58–60.

already on-stage leaves or a new character enters, whether or not the stage happens to be cleared in that action. (In French practice, scenes in scripts continued to be marked this way into the twentieth century.) The names of the speakers are listed at the start of each scene. Donatus took for granted that fourth-century readers of his commentary would know what an act and a scene are; Pynson seems not to have been so sure about his late fifteenth-century readers, people whose first-hand experience of drama was, after all, not classical comedies and tragedies but biblical plays, saints plays, and morality plays. Pynson therefore provides definitions of *actus* and *scena* that are not, to the best of my knowledge, to be found in editions of Terence published on the Continent:

> This comedy Andria is divided into five distinct parts which are called acts. These acts we will note in the appropriate places. Now any act contains multiple scenes, where we will see the coming-and-going throughout the comedies. For *scena* is a place shaded by arches, from which personae come forward and into which they return out of view of the seeing and hearing audience. It's as if a given act is an action divided into multiple parts; and these parts are called scenes.[15]

A 'scene', then, is what is *seen* at a given moment. This definition shifts the focus from the platform to the spectators, but it remains firmly grounded in the Middle English *scena*, specifically the *scaenae frons*, 'the front of the scene', the architectural ensemble (often with arches) that spectators in ancient Rome saw behind the actors. If a character entered from an opening in the *scena* or made his exit into it, the 'scene'—what was being seen by the spectators—changed. Hence, in the script, a change in scene whenever a new character enters or exits.

Students in sixteenth-century grammar schools and universities in England were taught about acts and scenes in the Latin plays they read, but when it came to writing plays of their own in English, they seem not to have taken classical precedent very seriously.[16] Among the approximately 230 scripts printed before 1630 that I have examined on Early English Books Online-Text Creation

---

[15] Terentius Afer [*Comoediae*] (London: Richard Pynson, 1497), sig. A2v, trans. Thomas N. Habinek. The Latin text goes as follows: 'Hec comedia Andrie dividitur in quinque precipuas partes: que actus dicuntur. Eos actus in suis propriis locis annotabimus. Quilibet aute(m) actus plures scenas co(n)tinet, ut per comedie decursu(m) videbimus. Est enim scena locus cortinis obumbratus: unde p(er) sona egrediuntur; in quem pariter e populi spectantis / et audientis conspectus redeunt. Quasi ergo actus sit queda(m) res gesta in plures partis destributa; atque ipse partes scene nuncupantur'. I am grateful to Tom Habinek, my colleague in Classics at the University of Southern California, not only for the translation but for help with the transcription of Pynson's highly abbreviated text. Although printed at different times, there is evidence that Pynson intended the six separate plays to be bound together. *Hecyra* bears the date 20 January 1595; *Andria* (which in most editions of Terence's complete works is printed first), the date 1497. The other four plays are undated.

[16] T. W. Baldwin's argument that Shakespeare took a cue from his grammar-school education and laid out his plays in five acts (*Shakspere's Five-Act Structure* [Urbana: University of Illinois Press, 1947]) has by now been discounted by most Shakespeare scholars, but the concept of 'scene' as a unit of dramatic design remains unquestioned.

Partnership (EEBO-TCP), most include no markings of acts and scenes at all. Of those that do, the majority mark five acts but, within each act, only scene one.[17] Writers for academic audiences, unsurprisingly, are the most assiduous markers. In the first 'regular' English comedy, Nicholas Udall's *Ralph Roister Doister* (1552), acts and scenes are scrupulously marked, entrance and exit rules rigorously observed, and the speakers' names duly listed at the beginning of each scene. Not once, however, does a character within the fiction remark on 'scene' as an idea. The same hold true for Thomas Sackville and Thomas Norton's academic tragedy *Gorboduc* (1565): acts and scenes are dutifully marked, but characters within the fiction are no more likely to remark on 'scene' as a concept than on 'act' as a concept.

The folio text of *Henry VI, Part Three* turns out to be fairly typical of how acts and scenes were marked in plays printed between 1590 and 1630: haphazardly. 'Actus Primus. Scaena Prima' is grandly announced on the first page of *Henry VI, Part Three*, but thereafter acts and scenes are forgotten entirely. The same holds true for the folio printings of five other plays: *Henry VI, Part Two*, *Troilus and Cressida*, *Romeo and Juliet*, *Timon of Athens*, and *Antony and Cleopatra*. In eighteen of the thirty-six texts in the 1623 folio—exactly half—act and scene divisions are marked throughout (or in a few cases *almost* throughout), in three plays acts only are marked, in one play (*The Comedy of Errors*) acts and scene one only of each act are marked, in eight others acts but no scenes other than scene one of act one are marked. The imperative to mark scenes seems to have slackened in the course of printing individual plays. A different kind of petering out is represented in the folio text of *Hamlet*, which begins with the marking of act one and all scenes therein, then act two (but no indication of scene one), then scene two of act two, and then...no marks whatsoever.[18]

---

[17] The playwrights whose scripts I searched on Early English Books Online-Text Creation Partnership (http://www.textcreationpartnership.org, accessed at various times between March and September 2012) include Francis Beaumont and John Fletcher, Richard Broome, George Chapman, Thomas Dekker, Robert Greene, Thomas Heywood, Ben Jonson, Christopher Marlowe, John Marston, Thomas Middleton, George Peele, William Shakespeare, James Shirley, and John Webster. The total number of scripts searched—some across several printings—amounted to approximately 230. Aside from Jonson's quartos and 1616 collected works and Shakespeare's 1623 folio, I found only five scripts marked throughout in acts and scenes (three of the five being by Marston). Among the plays in which acts and scenes are marked, the majority (seventeen scripts) label each act but, within each act, only scene one.

[18] Act and scene divisions are marked in *The Tempest*, *Two Gentlemen of Verona*, *The Merry Wives of Windsor*, *Measure for Measure* (except acts three and five, where scene one only is indicated in each case), *As You Like It*, *Twelfth Night*, *Winter's Tale*, *King John*, *Richard II*, *Henry IV, Part One*, *Henry IV, Part Two*, *Henry VI, Part One* (except acts one and two, where scene one only is marked in each case and act five, where no scenes are marked), *Richard III*, *Henry VIII*, *Macbeth*, *King Lear*, *Othello*, and *Cymbeline*. Acts only are marked in *Love's Labour's Lost* (but no act five), *A Midsummer Night's Dream*, and *The Merchant of Venice*. Acts and scene one of act one only are marked in *Much Ado About Nothing*, *The Taming of the Shrew* (except act four, where scene one is also marked), *All's Well that Ends Well*, *Henry V*, *Coriolanus*, *Titus Andronicus*, and *Julius Caesar*.

What is invariably present in all thirty-six plays in the folio is some version of 'Actus Primus. Scaena Prima' set in italics between two horizontal rules. Charlton Hinman has identified six variations on this formula ('Actus primus, Scena prima', 'Actus primus. Scoena Prima', etc.) and has explained why each play begins the same way: once a standard first page consisting of title plus the heading 'act one/scene one' had been set in type, the template was kept in place for printing successive plays.[19] But that begs several fundamental questions. Why mark acts and scenes in the first place? And why in Latin? Why mark the beginning of each of Shakespeare's plays as if it were a text by Terence or Seneca? Who made the decision to do so? John Heminges and Henry Condell as compilers? William Jaggard as printer? Two reasons for the decision come to mind: (1) the folio presents Shakespeare's scripts—plays that according to Ben Jonson outdo 'Tart Aristophanes, / Neat Terence, witty Plautus'[20]—in just the form schoolmasters prescribed for Aristophanes, Terence, and Plautus and (2) that's how Jonson presented his own plays—albeit in plain English 'acts' and 'scenes' rather than in Latin *actūs* and *scaenae*—not only in the 1616 folio of his collected *Workes* but in the quartos that had been printed previously.[21]

If Heminges, Condell, and/or Jaggard aspired to Jonson's thoroughness, they failed conspicuously. Fully half the plays in the 1623 folio of Shakespeare's *Comedies, Histories, and Tragedies* are imperfectly marked—or in the case of six plays not marked at all after act one, scene one. Among the eighteen scripts of Shakespeare's plays that had been printed in quarto before 1623, not a single one is divided up into acts and scenes: a conspicuous contrast with Jonson's plays in quarto. The same holds true for Webster's scripts printed before 1630: none are divided into acts and scenes. Among plays by Middleton printed before 1630 only two include any markings of acts and scenes: *The Family of Love*, 1608 (acts and scenes throughout) and *A Game at Chess*, ?1625 (act one, scene one only). Even among the university-educated playwrights for the public stage whom Greene counts among his fine-feathered friends (Marlowe, Nashe, Peele), marked acts and scenes are surprisingly rare. Only in the two parts of *Tamburlaine* (printed 1590) are acts and scenes marked, in this case scrupulously, in Latin, from beginning to end. (And that may be an affectation of the publisher, Richard Jones, whose edition of George Whetstone's *Promos and Cassandra* in two parts (1578) is likewise divided throughout, in Latin, into acts and scenes, which commence sometimes with a stage direction ['Enter ...']

[19] Charlton Hinman, *The Printing and Proof-Reading of the First Folio of Shakespeare*, 2 vols. (Oxford: Clarendon Press, 1963), 1: 178–9.

[20] Ben Jonson, 'To the memory of my beloved, The AUTHOR MASTER WILLIAM SHAKE-SPEARE, AND what he hath left us', prefaced to the 1623 folio and reprinted in Shakespeare, *Complete Works* (2005), lxxii.

[21] The exception is *Catiline* (printed 1611), where only acts are explicitly indicated, although scene divisions are implied by periodic lists of speakers that turn the ensuing dialogue into a unit. That arrangement—acts marked but not scenes beyond lists of speakers—was carried over when *Catiline* was reprinted in the 1616 folio.

but more often with a list of the speakers in the scene, just as they do in Jones' printing of *Tamburlaine*.) The same is true for Peele: there is no marking of scenes aside
from *The Arraignment of Paris* (printed 1584), a play put on at court by the scholar-
choristers of the Chapel Royal.

As for Greene himself, despite his pretensions to classical learning, despite his
penchant for the word 'scene' in his prose writings, acts and scenes are marked in
none of Greene's printed play scripts, and in only one, *Orlando Furioso*, is 'scene' a
subject of comment in the play itself. Count Sacrepant contemplates his impending
death at the hands of Orlando as 'Ending the scene of all my tragedie'.[22] The printed
script of *Orlando Furioso* (1594) is presented as one continuous action in which
speeches, not scenes, constitute the marked unit. The impression of an unbroken
arc of action, segmented into speeches, is confirmed by the chance survival of a
manuscript containing only Orlando's lines (a 'side' is the modern term) that was
used by Edward Alleyn in working up the role.[23] Written out on strips of paper
measuring about 16¼ by 6 inches (originally pasted together into a roll), the manuscript contains brief cues before each speech—but no markings of acts or scenes.[24]
The implication is that scene divisions did not matter to Alleyn, at least while he
was learning his lines.

The implication of all this evidence is clear enough: the marking of acts and
scenes in plays printed before 1630 seems to have been a task that some playwrights,
or at least some printers, felt they *should* attend to, but the will to follow through
was lacking. Aside from Ben Jonson, the whole business of marking acts and scenes
seems not to have been truly assimilated to English printing practice before 1630.
Thomas Heywood, whose career spans the first four decades of the seventeenth
century, suggests why in his dedication 'To the READER' of the quarto printing of
The Fair Maid of the West in 1631: with respect to acts and scenes, playhouse practice and printing practice were two different things. 'My Plaies,' he tells his courte-
ous reader, 'have not beene exposed to the publike view of the world in numerous
sheets, and a large volume'—probably an allusion to the folios of Jonson and Shakespeare—'but singly (as thou seest) with great modesty, and small noise'. His plays in
print, Heywood trusts, 'will prove as gratious in thy private reading, as they were
plausible in the publick acting'. In reading, his plays will not require a prologue to
explain the argument, 'the matter it self lying so plainly before thee in Acts and

---

[22] Robert Greene, *The historie of Orlando Furioso, one of the twelue pieres of France. As it was plaid before the Queenes Maiestie* (London: John Danter for Cuthbert Burbie, 1594), sig. G4.

[23] On the history of 'sides' see Simon Palfrey and Tiffany Stern, *Shakespeare in Parts* (Oxford: Oxford University Press, 2011), 1–39.

[24] A specimen strip of Orlando's side (now Dulwich MSS 1, Article 138) is reproduced in Andrew Gurr, *The Shakespearean Stage 1574–1642*, 4th edn. (Cambridge: Cambridge University Press, 2009), 130. A full description of the surviving strips is offered by R. A. Foakes at the Henslowe-Alleyn Digiti-sation Project (http://www.henslowe-alleyn.org.uk/essays/orlando.html, accessed 15 August 2012), where a digital image will eventually be offered.

Scenes, without any deviations, or winding indents'.[25] Acts and scenes, Heywood implies, are features of print, a matter of clear distinctions, if not ruled lines; playhouse performance is something messier, a matter of deviations and winding indents. It was in the 1630s, in the years just after Heywood's preface to *The Fair Maid of the West*, that division into numbered acts and scenes finally took hold in English printing, as exemplified in the plays of Broome and Shirley.

Re-marking scenes

Explicit marking (act one/scene one, act one/scene two, etc.) is only one way that scenes can be registered verbally in scripts: they can also be remarked upon by the characters in the fiction ('How many ages hence /,' Cassius observes in *Julius Caesar* 3.1.112–14, 'Shall this our lofty scene be acted over, / In states unborn and accents yet unknown!'). The distinction here is not unlike the distinction made in narratology and film criticism between extradiegetic and diegetic elements. Scene divisions marked by the author or by a typesetter or by an editor are, physically and dramatically, outside (*extra*) the fiction; scenes remarked upon by the characters are inside the fiction. Somewhere in between, outside and inside at the same time, are scenes remarked upon by prologues and choruses.

So we have two sorts of evidence to consider: not only marks but *re*-marks. As Derrida argues in *Dissemination* and *The Truth in Painting*, we can appreciate the significance of a mark like 'scene one' only when that mark is *re*-marked as an object of attention. In 'The Double Session', a deconstructive reading of Mallarmé's prose-text 'Mimique', Derrida finds in theatre itself a metaphor for acts of marking and re-marking that ultimately signify nothing beyond their own operation within the closed system of theatre: 'The stage [*scène*] thus illustrates but the stage, the scene only the scene; there is only the equivalence between *theater* and *idea*, that is (as these two names indicate), the visibility (which remains outside) of the visible that is being effectuated.'[26] To extrapolate: Cassius' remark upon 'our lofty scene' in *Julius Caesar* 3.1 reifies 'scene' as an idea even if there is no guarantor outside the system of theatre for just what a scene *is*. As it happens, the folio text of *Julius Caesar* marks acts but not scenes. In terms of marks, then, there is no entity in the 1623 printing of *Julius Caesar* that can be pointed to as act three, scene one. What Cassius seems to be gesturing toward is, in any case, not a unit of text but the tiring-house and platform or else enactment of the assassination he is urging on his fellow conspirators. Or, most likely, both.

---

[25] Thomas Heywood, *The fair maid of the vvest. Or, A girle worth gold. The first part* (London: Miles Flesher for Richard Royston, 1631), sig. A4.

[26] Jacques Derrida, *Dissemination*, trans. Barbara Johnson (Chicago: University of Chicago Press, 1981), 209.

When we shift attention from marks to *re*-marks, the concept of 'scene' becomes more conspicuous, but still peripheral in comparison with remarks about the dramatic unit that is *always* marked in scripts: speech. Characters within a fiction are much more likely to call attention to the speech they are making than the scene in which they are performing.[27] There are exceptions, of course. Shame-faced Face at the end of *The Alchemist* confesses, 'My part a little fell in this last *Scene*, / Yet 'twas *decorum*'.[28] Cassius in *Julius Caesar* is more typical: he remarks upon 'our lofty scene' in act three, but more characteristic of his metatheatrical remarks is the moment in act four when Brutus accuses Cassius of having 'an itching palm' to buy and sell offices: 'I, an itching palm? / You know that you are Brutus that speaks this, / Or, by the gods, this speech were else your last' (4.1.62, 64–6). Despite the much greater attention given to speeches, all six senses of *scene* in Greene's attack on 'Shakes-scene' are invoked in the fictions created by Beaumont and Fletcher, Broome, Chapman, Dekker, Heywood, Jonson, Marston, Middleton, Shirley, and Shakespeare. These six senses of *scene* can be ranged horizontally on a continuum that stretches from the most concrete and objective on the left to the most metaphorical and subjective on the right:

stage structure	subdivision of a script	big effect	act of acting	fictional setting	episode in real life

Among these meanings of *scene* the dominant ones for us today are, probably in this order, (1) subdivision of a script, (2) fictional setting, (3) big effect ('the love scene', 'the trial scene', 'the death scene'), and (4) an episode in real life. *Scene* as the act of acting has been obsolete for two hundred years, and *scene* as stage structure, the English equivalent of the Greek *skene* or the Latin *scaena*, has been relegated to the specialist status of the term in Middle English. In scripts written by Shakespeare and his professional contemporaries, the most often remarked meanings of *scene* include the two that have since dropped out of use, and the frequency of the four remaining terms is different than it is with us. According to my search of scripts on EEBO-TCP, the word *scene*, when spoken within the fiction in late sixteenth- and early seventeenth-century scripts, refers, in descending order of frequency, to (1) big effect, (2) subdivision of a script, (3) stage structure, (4) fictional setting, (5) the act of acting, and (6) an episode in real life—or very often to a combination of two or more of these meanings. Let us consider the possibilities.

---

[27] A search for <speech*> in Jonson's 1616 *Works* and Shakespeare's 1623 *Comedies, Histories, and Tragedies* turns up 32 hits in Jonson's plays, masques, and entertainments and not fewer than 159 in Shakespeare's plays.

[28] Ben Jonson, *The Alchemist*, 5.5, in *Workes* (London: W. Stansby for Richard Meighen, 1616), sig. Kkk3.

Scene as big effect, the most frequent usage, figures among Heywood's defensive gambits in *An Apology for Actors* (1612):

> Art thou proud? our Scene presents thee with the fall of *Phaeton*, *Narcissus* pining in the loue of his shadow, ambitious *Hamon*, now calling himselfe a God, and by and by thrust headlong among the Diuels.... Art thou addicted to prodigallity? enuy? cruelty? periury? flattery? or rage? our Scenes affoord thee store of men to shape your liues by, who be frugall, louing, gentle, trusty, without soothing, and in all things temperate.[29]

Heywood catalogues here Scenes of Pride, Scenes of Prodigality, Scenes of Envy, etc. Heywood's perspective is extradiegetic, of course—he is looking at plays from the outside—but characters within early modern dramatic fictions often testify awareness of the big effect of the scene currently in progress or about to happen. Hence Shakespeare's Scene of Rage in *Henry VI, Part Three*, 'lofty scene' in *Julius Caesar*, 'scene of fool'ry' in *Love's Labour's Lost*, 'tedious brief scene of.../ very tragical mirth' in *A Midsummer Night's Dream*, 'little scene / To monarchize' in *Richard II*, 'scene of rude impatience' and 'woe's scene' in *Richard III*, 'dismal scene' in *Romeo and Juliet*, and 'scene of mirth' in *Troilus and Cressida*. Characters in plays by other writers are no less apt to remark scenes as big effects: Jonson's 'scene of courtship' in *Cynthia's Revels* and 'tragic scene' in *Catiline*, Chapman's 'scene of foppery' in *May Day* and 'strange scene of impiety' in *The Widow's Tears*, Marston's 'scene of folly' in *Antonio and Mellida*, Middleton's 'scene of lust' in *The Changeling*, Beaumont and Fletcher's 'scene of blood' in *The Woman Hater* and *Rollo Duke of Normandy*, and Shirley's 'scene of sorrow' in *Love in a Maze*, 'scene of mirth' in *The Example*, 'scene of wrath' in *The Politician*, and 'scene for death' in *The Court Secret* and 'great scene of death' in *The Traitor*.[30] When characters in Shirley's *Hyde*

---

[29] Thomas Heywood, *An apology for actors* (London: Nicholas Okes, 1612), sigs. G1–G1v. Further quotations are cited in the text.

[30] Shakespeare, *Henry VI, Part Three* 1.4.144, *Julius Caesar* 3.1.112, *Love's Labour's Lost* 4.3.161, *Midsummer Night's Dream* 5.1.56–7, *Richard II* 3.2.160–1, *Richard III* 2.2.38 and 4.4.27, *Romeo and Juliet* 4.3.19, *Troilus and Cressida* 1.3.173; Jonson, *The fountaine of selfe-loue. Or Cynthias reuels* (London: R. Read for Walter Burre, 1601), sig. F2v, and *Catiline his conspiracy* (London: W. Stansby? for Walter Burre, 1611), sig. F3; Chapman, *May-day* (London: William Stansby for Iohn Browne, 1611), sig. B1, and *The vviddovves teares a comedie* (London: William Stansby for Iohn Browne, 1612), sig. K2v; Marston, *The history of Antonio and Mellida* (London: R. Bradock for Mathewe Lownes and Thomas Fisher, 1602), sig. F1; Middleton, *The changeling* (London: Humphrey Moseley, 1653), sig. I1v; Beaumont and Fletcher, *The vvoman hater* (London: Robert Raworth for John Hodgets, 1607), sig. K2: Fletcher, *The tragœdy of Rollo Duke of Normandy* (Oxford: Leonard Lichfield, 1640), sig. B4; Shirley, *Changes: or, Love in a maze* (London: George Purslowe for William Cooke, 1632), sig. G2; Shirley, *The Example*, sig. H3v; Shirley, *The politician, a tragedy* (London: Humphrey Mosley, 1655), sig. F4v; Shirley, *The Court Secret*, in *Six new playes* (London: Humphrey Robinson and Humphrey Moseley, 1653), sig. A1; Shirley, *The traytor. A tragedie* (London: John Norton for William Cooke, 1635), sig. D1, spelling and capitalization modernized in all cases.

Park and *The Royal Master* quip, 'The scene is changed', they are referring to changes in the big effect, due to changes in power dynamics, not changes in fictional location.[31]

Within early modern dramatic fictions *scene* as big effect (the most frequent meaning) or *scene* as subdivision of a script (the second most frequent meaning) or *scene* as stage structure (the third) is seldom just that one thing. The insinuation of *scene* as stage structure is especially likely when a prologue speaks or a chorus or on-stage commentators of the sort Jonson loves to assemble. These figures are not quite outside the fiction nor yet within it. Perhaps we should call them '*inter-diegetic*'. The physical *scene* is present to them (and, through them, to us as spectators) in a way that is more at hand, shall we say, than to characters within the fiction. Prime among such inter-diegetic spokesmen is the Chorus in the folio version of Shakespeare's *Henry V*. When the Chorus, speaking as prologue, wishes for 'A kingdom for a stage, princes to act, / And monarchs to behold the swelling scene' (Pro. 3–4), he is invoking multiple meanings of *scene*: as big effect ('the brightest heaven of invention' [2]), as real-life event (the historical deeds of 'warlike Harry, like himself' [5]), as the act of acting (the effort of 'flat unraiséd spirits that hath dared / ... to bring forth / So great an object' [9–11]), and as stage structure ('on this unworthy scaffold' [10]). When the Chorus reappears at the beginning of act two, he adds to these four meanings of *scene* two more: a division in the script (the very fact of the Chorus's reappearance, not necessarily anticipated by the original audience, marks a break in the illusion) and fictional location ('Unto Southampton do we shift our scene' [2.0.42]). By now, 'our scene' in the last line has become not just fictional location but all the meanings of *scene* accumulated so far. Those telescoped meanings continue in the Chorus's later speeches ('our swift scene' [3.0.1], 'so our scene must to the battle fly' [4.0.48]). The Chorus's pointed attention to scene as fictional location is actually unusual among early modern play scripts. Printed texts of early modern plays may mark 'The Scene: LONDON' or some other place before the text begins, but it is comparatively rare for a prologue to announce, 'In fair Verona, where we lay our scene' (*Romeo and Juliet* Pro. 2) or 'In Troy there lies the scene' (*Troilus and Cressida* Pro. 1). And what does 'scene' mean in these cases? It certainly includes the act of acting and the physical structure of the playing place as well as fictional location. What is remarkable about all the remarks upon 'scene' that I have assembled here is their solid grounding in scene as stage structure. This firm connection between physical means and theatrical ends in early modern usage constitutes the most significant difference from our own understanding of *scene*.

---

[31] Shirley, *Hide Parke a comedie* (London: Thomas Cotes for Andrew Crooke and William Cooke, 1637), sig. B3v; Shirley, *The royall master* (London: Thomas Cotes for Andrew Crooke and Richard Serger, 1638), sig. I3, spelling and capitalization modernized.

Realizing scenes in other media

The difference comes down to vision, to what we tell ourselves we are seeing in the theatre. To judge from the Chorus to *Henry V*, what spectators saw first in 1599 was the bare structure of the stage, 'this unworthy scaffold'. With his speeches, the Chorus would persuade them to see instead, or to see as well, an illusion of epic proportions. For us, despite a half-century of productions in black boxes or against exposed brick walls, the word *scene* implies an artful visual design (*OED*, 'scene, *n.*', I.6.a), For that predisposition we can credit not only a century of films but the painted scenery that black boxes and brick walls were supposed to make us forget. As it happens, one of the earliest uses in English of *scene* as stage scenery also includes, in the same sentence, one of the earliest uses in English of the word *landscape* in the sense of natural scenery. It is in the printed account of Jonson's *The Masque of Blackness* (acted 1605, printed 1608) that the two words *scene* and *landscape* begin their long association in art history, garden design, cinema, and tourism: 'First, for the *Scene*, was drawne a Landtschap, consisting of small woods, and here and there a void place fill'd with huntings'.[32] Scene as scenery may have started out as a feature specifically of masques, but by the 1630s visual design was also being remarked in stage plays, at least at indoor theatres like the Salisbury Court. Richard Brome's Prologue to *The Antipodes*, acted in that venue in 1638, laments that opinion 'has, of late, / From the old way of Playes possest a Sort / Only to run to those, that carry state/ In Scene magnificent and language high'.[33] A posthumous anthology of Brome scripts published in 1659, seventeen years after Parliament banned public performances, thus dashing Brome's career, contains a preface 'TO THE READERS' that the editor, Alexander Brome, wishes could be a preface '*to the Spectators*, if the Fates so pleas'd, these *Comedies* exactly being dressed for the *Stage*; and the often-tried *Author* (better than many who can but scribble) understood the *Proportions* and *Beauties* of a *Scene*'.[34] Here 'scene' hovers between spectacle and verbal artefact, between something purchasers of the book must imagine (or perhaps remember) for themselves and something they can read. 'Proportions' and 'beauties' both seem to be visual phenomena. Just a year later the ban on plays would be repealed by the new royalist government, and stage productions would be re-established, this time with painted scenery as *de rigueur*.[35]

---

[32] Ben Jonson, *The Masque of Blackness*, in *Workes*, sig. Ffff3.

[33] Richard Broome, *The antipodes a comedie. Acted in the yeare 1638. by the Queenes Majesties Servants, at Salisbury Court in Fleet-street* (London: I. Oakes for Francis Constable, 1640), sig. A3v.

[34] Richard Brome, *Five nevv playes,: viz. The English moor, or the mock-marriage. The love-sick court, or the ambitious politique: Covent Garden weeded. The nevv academy, or the nevv exchange. The queen and concubine* (London: A. Crooke for H. Brome, 1659), sig. A3.

[35] The transition of scenic design from masques to private theatricals to Restoration public theatres is traced in Dawn Lewcock, *Sir William Davenant, the Court Masque, and the English Seven-*

Thanks to Inigo Jones's surviving drawings, we have a very good idea of what the scenes in *The Masque of Blackness* and other court masques looked like. What about the visual evidence of scenes in earlier decades, in less sumptuous venues? Drawings like the tableau of characters from the story of Titus Andronicus in a manuscript attributed to Henry Peacham (*c.*1595) and title-page woodcuts like those that accompany scripts of *The Roaring Girl* (1611), *The Spanish Tragedy* (1615), and *Dr Faustus* (1616) stand in a problematic relationship to early modern staging practices.[36] Just what are we looking at in these images? A single moment excerpted from a segment of text marked at beginning and end by an empty stage? The big effect of that excerpt? The fictional setting? What a spectator might experience by taking the Chorus's cue in *Henry V* and amplifying the words in his or her imagination? Moll Cutpurse on the title page to *The Roaring Girl* stands on planks that could represent a stage platform, but Faustus stands on a tile floor amid furnishings not called for in Marlowe's script, including a shelf and a window, while the murder of Horatio on the title page of *The Spanish Tragedy* takes place on turf, in the fictional setting of a garden with a trellised arbour—a mental space, not a stage space. What is more, the depiction of Hoartio's murder conflates three separate dramatic moments in what modern editions of *The Spanish Tragedy* mark as two separate scenes, 2.4 and 2.5.[37] In all three of these title-page visualizations the scene—if that is what the woodcuts show—proves to be an elusive affair.

Title-page woodcuts in scripts printed before 1642 are, in fact, of a piece with later visual evidence: the scenes included in Nicholas Rowe's *The Works of Mr. William Shakespear...Adorn'd with Cuts* (1709), in print collections like *The Picturesque Beauties of Shakespeare* (1783), and in the paintings and prints in John Boydell's Shakespeare Gallery (inaugurated 1786). What is depicted in many of these pictures of places, incidents, and objects (*OED*, 'scene, *n.*', II.9, earliest citation 1653) is not anything a spectator would have seen in a theatrical performance but a mental image touched off by events that in some cases are only narrated in the plays: the panoramic shipwreck in *The Tempest*, for example, in Rowe's edition or Desdemona's drowning in *The Picturesque Beauties of Shakespeare* or the murder of the young princes in *Richard III* in Boydell's Shakespeare Gallery. In all these cases, a particular scene in the sense of a division of the text is cited, but the location of the

teenth-century Scenic Stage, c.1605–c.1700 (Amherst, NY: Cambria Press, 2008). The classic account is Richard Southern, *Changeable Scenery: Its Origin and Development in the British Theatre* (London: Faber, 1952).

[36] In his comprehensive catalogue of *Illustrations of the English Stage 1580–1642* (Stanford, CA: Stanford University Press, 1985), R. A. Foakes tries his best to connect Peacham's sketch and the title-page illustrations with scenes identified by act and scene number from modern editions. More often than not, however, he is forced to acknowledge that the illustration 'relates to' such-and-such a scene rather than its depicting what spectators in the theatre actually saw. Thus, the famous woodcut of Dr Faustus printed in the quartos of 1616, 1619, 1620, 1624, 1628, and 1631 'very possibly relates to Scene III as it was staged, with Faustus conjuring in a circle' (109).

[37] Foakes, *Illustrations of the English Stage*, 104.

visual image is the viewer's imagination, not a stage. In these eighteenth-century depictions we move towards scene as a subjective experience with only loose connections to theatrical performance.

From scenes as pictures to scenes in novels is no leap at all. Thus the full title of the 1775 edition of Fielding's *Tom Jones* bills the novel as 'comprehending such entertaining Scenes, Both in HIGH and LOW LIFE, As are not be met with in any History of the Kind'.[38] We still use 'scene' this way in reference to novels. And in reference to our first-hand experience of the world. We participate in the local poetry scene, we need a change of scene, we return to the scene of our childhood, occasionally an encounter with another person turns into 'a real scene'. *Scene* in all these senses is a component of the practice of everyday life in precisely the terms suggested by de Certeau. 'Scene' is, in fact, a favourite term of de Certeau's for the space—geographical, technological, political, psychological—where the tactics of individuals come into conflict with the strategies of institutions. He imagines cyberspace in particular as 'the scene of the Brownian movements of invisible and innumerable tactics', albeit a space in which the free movement of individuals is illusory. 'The system in which they move about is too vast to be able to fix them in one place', de Certeau concedes, 'but too constraining for them ever to be able to escape from it and go into exile elsewhere. There is no longer an elsewhere.'[39]

Talking about scenes

With de Certeau's 'scene' we find ourselves at quite a distance from *scaena* as tiring-house façade and/or platform stage but in touch with the potential of 'scene' as a concept in performance criticism. Most existing scholarship on scenes—Shakespeare's scenes, at least—accept the term at face value. In Emrys Jones's *Scenic Form in Shakespeare* (1971) a 'scene' is a division of the verbal text, demarcated at beginning and end by an empty stage. Indeed, in Jones's view a play in performance is all about entrances and exits. Actors come and go. While they are present, they create an intensely present world that engages the audience's complicity through patterns of speech and patterns of action. Those patterns—Jones calls them 'forms'—recur across scenes as well as within scenes. Individual scenes, like individual speeches, have a syntax, and so do sequences of scenes: 'The patterns set going make for easy comprehension, like a well-constructed sentence.'[40] Jones's project, inspired by

---

[38] Henry Fielding, *The humorous and diverting history of Tom Jones, a foundling* (London: publisher not specified, ?1775), title page. The original edition was published in 1749.

[39] Michel de Certeau, *The Practice of Everyday Life*, trans. Steven F. Rendall (Berkeley: University of California Press, 1984), 40.

[40] Emrys Jones, *Scenic Form in Shakespeare* (Oxford: Clarendon Press, 1971), 17. Further quotations are cited in the text.

structuralist linguistics, seeks to uncover these underlying patterns. Across scenes Jones argues that Shakespeare typically organizes a play into two 'movements' with a break in between. Often the movement is defined by having a similar scene or action at the beginning and at the end. Typically, but not always, the first sequence comprises what modern editions mark as acts 1-2-3, the second as acts 4-5. An example would be *Hamlet* 1.1 to 4.4, before and after Hamlet's voyage to England, framed by mention of Fortinbras in 1.1 and Fortinbras' actual appearance in 4.4. Fortinbras' return at the end of the second sequence, in 5.2, exemplifies what Jones calls 'structural rhyming' (71). A narrower definition of *scene* as 'a section of the play bounded by complete changes of on-stage personnel' informs Robert F. Willson, Jr's *Shakespeare's Opening Scenes* (1977) and Walter C. Foreman, Jr's *The Music of the Close: The Final Scenes of Shakespeare's Tragedies* (1977), though Foreman does take into account *scene* as big effect, for example the moment in *The Winter's Tale* 5.3 when Hermione's statue comes to life.[41]

The more ample definition of *scene* in Paul Kottman's *A Politics of the Scene* (2007) shifts the focus from script and stage to the audience. As Kottman points out, 'scene' has not been taken over as critical term by philosophers in the way other theatre-related terms have—terms like 'action', 'representation', 'stage', 'persona', 'mask', and 'theatre' itself. For his part, Kottman approaches the word *scene* via Edmund Husserl's phenomenology, specifically Husserl's idea of 'horizon' as the limit or boundary that frames an act of perception. In a theatrical performance the horizon is physical (the walls of the theatre) and social (the particular group of people who are joint witnesses to the performance): 'dramatic performance presupposes a sheer gathering, a human plurality whose commonality lies, at base, in the time and space that they collectively inhabit, in their ontological exposure to one another within a given spatial and temporal horizon.'[42] The audience figures, in Kottman's view, as *the* essential component of 'scene'. The sense of community fostered by a theatrical performance becomes, in Kottman's argument, the grounds for political identity and political action by communities outside the theatre. Kottman does not cite it as an example, but King Harry's St Crispin speech in *Henry V* enacts just what he arguing. In this scene, marked 4.3 in modern editions, King Harry creates a sense of community among his soldiers as he inspires them to think about St Crispin's Day in the future, when the heroic deeds they are about to perform in battle will be remembered and their identities as participants in the event will be envied. In the process, the actor playing King Harry also creates a sense of community among the auditors and spectators in the theatre, turning them into English patriots. As Kottman insists,

---

[41] Robert F. Willson, Jr, *Shakespeare's Opening Scenes* (Salzburg, Austria: Universität Salzburg, Institut für Englische Sprache und Literatur, 1977) and Walter C. Foreman, Jr, *The Music of the Close: The Final Scenes of Shakespeare's Tragedies* (Lexington: University of Kentucky Press, 1977). The quoted definition of *scene* is Foreman's (ix).

[42] Paul Kottman, *A Politics of the Scene* (Palo Alto, CA: Stanford University Press, 2007), 165. Further quotations are cited in the text.

it is the futurity of the present dramatic moment that enables such acts of community-building: 'A scene emerges only insofar as it immediately leaves behind the potentiality for a future, testimonial address between those who were on the scene' (139).

Some readers may object that Kottman's leap from theatre to the world at large is only a metaphor—indeed, he confronts that objection in the book's epilogue—but he does return us to an audience-centred definition of *scene* that has been present from the word's first appearance in modern English. As the note in Pynson's edition of Terence's *Andria* reminds us, a *scaena* in Latin drama is determined by what the spectators see at a given moment. *Scaena* as stage structure presupposes spectators to do the seeing as well as actors to do the speaking and moving about on the stage. It is the inclusiveness of 'scene'—from stage structure on the one hand to a perceptual phenomenon on the other—that recommends the term at this particular juncture in performance criticism. In this moment of consolidation and critical eclecticism, we should welcome a concept that allows us to combine bibliography and post-structuralist linguistics, performance history and the phenomenology of perception, building history and the practice of everyday life. In 'scene' we have such a concept.

To appreciate these potentialities of 'scene' let us take all the meanings of the word surveyed in these pages and arrange them, not horizontally as we did with the pre-1642 meanings, but vertically so as to visualize the layering of meanings. At the most fundamental level—the ground of it all—is 'scene' as *scaena*, as a physical structure against which, on which, or within which a dramatic performance takes place. As we move up from there, we encounter senses of 'scene' that may be increasingly remote from theatres as physical structures but that nonetheless maintain a vital connection with theatrical performance as a way of framing and understanding human experience:

frame of perception

↑

arena of communal identity and political action

↑

sphere of a particular activity or interest

↑

place where a certain social set meets

↑

episode in real life

↑

topics or issues associated with particular periods

↑

picture of a place, an incident, or an assemblage of objects

↑

synecdoche for theatre as an enterprise

↑

fictional setting

↑

the act of acting

↑

big effect

↑

tableau

↑

subdivision of a script

↑

stage scenery

↑

stage structure

The position of *scaena* as the ground of this vertical continuum should be clear enough. The position at the top of 'scene' as a perceptual frame may need some explaining. In Derrida's terms, any bestowal of significance involves some kind of marking: this or that thing is marked off from other things, and its significance is remarked. In Husserl's terms, other possible objects of attention are 'bracketed' off, and a particular object is attended to in an act that connects the perceiving subject with the thing being perceived. In Kottman's terms, the connection is not only with the object but with other people who are present at the moment of perception. Physical circumstances inevitably figure in these transactions and persist in the knowledge that results. A phenomenology of 'scene' keeps in play all of these layered meanings, from bottom to top and top to bottom.

Contemporary redefinitions of 'scenography' as encompassing the entire environment of performance, not just the *mise-en-scène*, take us upward from stage structure at least as far as 'scene' as synecdoche for theatre itself.[43] I would extend 'writing the scene' (that is what *skeno-graphia* literally means[44]) still further upward, to include all the extrapolations of 'scene' to painting, life-writing, and social activity that have proliferated over the past 400 years, including, at the most comprehensive level, 'scene' as a way of framing experience outside the theatre as well as within.

---

[43] Pamela Howard in *What is Scenography?* (London: Routledge, 2002), provides this definition: 'Scenography is the seamless synthesis of space, text, research, art, actors, directors and spectators that contributes to an original creation' (130). She provides separate chapters on each of these seven aspects of scenography.

[44] If we limit the Greek *skene* to the building out of which and into which actors made their entrances and exits, *skeno-graphia* means 'the writing of the stage space', a meaning that Howard in *What is Scenography?*, 123, happily embraces. *Scenography* in its earliest usage in English, like the French *scénographie*, was limited to 'The representation of a building or other object in perspective; a perspective elevation' (*OED*, 'scenography, n.', †1., earliest citation 1645). The more recent meaning, 'The design of theatrical scenery; scenic design' (3) is dated by the *OED* only to the 1990s. The broader application deployed by Howard is more recent still.

The stage is implicated in all these 'higher' meanings, just as those accumulated meanings inescapably colour, for us, the physical facts of a theatrical performance. In this view, 'scene' functions at every level not as a metaphor for theatre but as synecdoche, as a tangible part of a complicated whole, sited as much in the mind as on the stage.

FURTHER READING

Howard, Pamela. *What is Scenography?* (London: Routledge, 2002).
Jones, Emrys. *Scenic Form in Shakespeare* (Oxford: Clarendon Press, 1971).
Kottman, Paul. *A Politics of the Scene* (Palo Alto, CA: Stanford University Press, 2007).
McKinney, Joslin and Philip Butterworth. *The Cambridge Introduction to Scenography* (Cambridge: Cambridge University Press, 2009).

CHAPTER 6

LINES

PAUL MENZER

The line is the next of the building blocks—the next given. Each line has its own journey and energy, whether it's a regular iambic pentameter, or a different syllabic length or an irregular rhythm; fast-paced or slow-moving; broken by a pause or shared between characters. It's a block of syllables riding on the iambic energy, and a specific stage in a precisely calibrated journey of thought and emotion.

Patsy Rodenburg, *Speaking Shakespeare*[1]

Drama takes place. Drama also takes time. 'Theatricality' is what it gives back. Arts that occupy time and place puzzle description, however, since our vocabulary is better tuned to location than duration. Henri Bergson addresses this oddity, where (or when) he notes 'we are compelled to borrow from space the images by which we describe what the reflective consciousness feels about time'.[2] 'I was there', we say of memorable events, not 'I was then'. I was there, at the Globe, the Lyceum, Altamont, the Old Vic. I was there, at the Mudd Club, CBGB's, The National, the Courtyard. (I was there too. It was closed.) Thus terms designed to define space are pressed into service to describe time.

'Lines' are pre-eminently liable in this respect, as Patsy Rodenburg's bewildered epigraph indicates. Indeed, Rodenburg exemplifies the lability of the 'line' in habits of thinking that conceive it as the *essential* unit in the composition, reading, editing, interpretation, and performance of early modern drama. The line's ubiquity as a formal interpretive unit for the study and performance of verse drama is all the odder, however, since the line in performance has no tangible form—we might even heretically suggest that 'verse' has no apparent presence in performance.[3] Indeed, the difficulty of distinguishing what a line *is* in performance seems inversely proportionate to—or the generative cause for—the amount of attention it attracts from

---

[1] Patsy Rodenburg, *Speaking Shakespeare* (New York: Palgrave Macmillan, 2002), 103.
[2] Henri Bergson, *Key Writings* (New York: Continuum, 2002), 56.
[3] I am enormously indebted to Jeremy Lopez for responding to this chapter and for sharing his essay 'From Bad to Verse: Poetry and Spectacle on the Modern Shakespearean Stage' before it went to press. It is forthcoming in *The Oxford Handbook to Shakespeare's Poetry*, ed. Jonathan Post.

both prosodists and performers, between whom there is a general consensus that early modern playwrights—Shakespeare in particular—made meaning on, around, and through the line, and it is therefore at that level that performers today should engage the work. But drama takes both time and place, and the 'line' has hatched an empire of interpretation founded upon the confusion of the one with the other. A unit that once marked space has emerged as an ontology unto itself unmoored from its spatial dimension.

It is probably no more than a benign metaphor to say that actors 'speak lines of dialogue', even though they do not (actors speak words and each one is a mono-logue).[4] Or to say that playwrights 'write' them or that we might 'scan' them.[5] How-ever benignant, metaphors perform conceptual and therefore ideological work, and the object of this essay is to palpate these metaphors to see what they obscure. The exploration is the more imperative for the metaphor's ubiquity. Indeed, for the dis-parate constituents of the loosely connected 'Shakespeare industry'—actors, edi-tors, scholars, teachers, students, directors, dramaturges, etc.—the 'line' serves as an 'industry standard'—something like an universal track-width in railroading or a common plug-size among electricians. It is the formal unit around which all inter-pretive energies organize. We are all, in sum, beholden to the line and therefore bound and determined to understand it, lest it bind and determine us.

As a unit that attracts and arranges critical attention, the 'line' has evolved from a physical to a metaphysical form via a long recension through metaphor. This chapter, therefore, explores the line in two sections broadly convened around the physical line and the metaphysical one. The first section argues that the graphic, not the poetic, line was a fundamental organizing unit in the arrangement of early modern theatrics, though such lines did not make it into print; the second section examines the metaphysics of the line and thinks through the ideological implications of the line's centrality to performance practices today. While the conclusion here may be no more than the anodyne observation that it is an ideology of textuality that metaphors

---

[4] A symptom of the phenomenon I'm describing is that scholars and actors consistently imagine the 'size' of Shakespearean parts in terms of 'lines', as though the only account of an actor's participation in a play is the number of lines he or she speaks. This is, as I argue, part of a larger dispensation wherein we imagine performance in terms of physical dimensions as opposed to temporal duration. For instance in T. J. King's *Casting Shakespeare's Plays: London Actors and Their Roles, 1590–1642* (Cambridge: Cambridge University Press, 1992) he understands 'principall comoedians' (from Jonson's *Workes*, 1616) and 'principall Tragoedians' (*Sejanus*, 1603) to be 'defined empirically as those who speak more than twenty-five lines' (1). I am not certain that this is what 'empirically' means.

[5] Early modern playwrights often speak of writing in 'sheets' not lines. See, for instance, Robert Daborne's correspondence with Philip Henslowe, where he refers to having '2 sheets more fayr written' or having stayed up 'till past 12 to write out this sheet' or the manuscript play *The Telltale*, which is marked in sheets in the upper left corner, e.g. '6th sheete' etc. (W. W. Greg, *Dramatic Documents from the Elizabethan Playhouses: Stage Plots, Actors' Parts, Prompt Books—Commentary* [Oxford: Clarendon Press, 1931], 197, 205). On, in particular, the Daborne–Henslowe correspondence, see also Grace Iop-polo, *Dramatists and Their Manuscripts in the Age of Shakespeare, Jonson, Middleton and Heywood: Authorship, Authority and the Playhouse* (New York: Routledge, 2008).

of the line advance, it is nonetheless worth challenging such ideologies, particularly when we speak of theatricality. This chapter argues that attention to the line promotes not just textual but *typographical* (and therefore typological) understandings of performance, and that attention to the line holds us hostage to protocols of type largely unrelated to embodied fictions. The line did play a vital role in coordinating the time and place of early modern theatricality, but it did not play the determining one, and a re-examination of theatricality must therefore begin with a line reading.

The physical line

'
_____
                                                                    '

(The part of Orlando, Dulwich MS. I, fol. 268)

In the beginning was the line, which ruled the page before the word. Strips of papyrus latticed themselves into being, limiting inscription to the horizontal plane. Vellum required lateral scoring before a hand could incise its flesh. Boiled rags clung to chain lines, rationalizing gridded paper out of formless pulp. Indeed etymologically as well as materially, the line precedes the word, for in the Old English, Frisian, or Saxon forms, to 'write' was to score, cut, tear, or draw. Writing therefore follows the line, which anticipates the word, and this principle of linearity binds most writing systems across the ages, whether those practices inscribe from left-to-right, right-to-left, or boustrophedonicly (zig-zag, in the vulgar).[6] The line is the horizon of the word, both its destiny and its limit. From papyrus to parchment, from the vellum of an uterine calf to the thin film transistors of liquid crystal displays, before it can be written, it has to be ruled.

Given the necessity of the line to the word, it is unsurprising that the 'line'—more often the plural 'lines'—made a metonymic leap from the *site* of writing to its *sense*, so that by the fourteenth century Piers Plowman complains that he 'can nou3te rede a lyne'.[7] A remarkably plastic term, 'lines' in the literary sense could apparently convey to the early moderns at least three related but discrete meanings: (1) an incised sequence of handwritten letters, so that Winchester can ask if Gloucester comes with 'deep premeditated lines? / With written pamphlets?' (*Henry VI, Part One* 3.1.1–2)[8]; (2) a coincidence of well-kerned glyphs, so that a typesetter 'composeth words in a composing-stick, till a Line be made'[9]; and (3) some early inklings of the

---

[6] Certain Asian scripts such as Japanese kana and Korean hangul can, of course, be written both horizontally and vertically.

[7] *Piers Plowman* B. v. 428

[8] All citations from Shakespeare refer to *William Shakespeare: The Complete Works*, ed. Stanley Wells and Gary Taylor (Oxford: Clarendon Press, 1988).

[9] J. A. Comenius, *Orbis sensualium pictus*, trans. Charles Hoole (London, 1672), 190–1.

primary formal sense in which we use 'lines' today as a synonym for 'verse'—when Jonson praises Marlowe's 'mighty line' we presume he means Tamburlaine's iambic cadence, not Ithamore's limber prose. 'Lines' for the early moderns therefore trace the trajectory from the material site of writing and reading to the formal arrangement of poetic verse.

It would be incorrect, then, to claim that the 'line' possessed only a physical, graphic sense in the early modern period—since its use clearly previews the modern conception of the line as *the* foundational poetic form that determined the composition and performance of the period's verse drama. At the same time the line in the early modern period had not yet achieved escape velocity, had not detached from its physical origins to attain the metaphysical status that performance accords it today. In what immediately follows I argue that the 'line' (and more particularly the absence that gives it presence, the 'line break') was originally designed to organize the performance of music and words. The setting of verse drama as lines in the period's playbooks is therefore partly skeuomorphic, an archaic residue of an exhausted technology—the end-stopped line is print's equivalent of a shutter on a digital camera.

The line may be designed to coordinate performers (and performances) but not, principally, performers of drama. The etymological derivation of 'prick song' hints at the origins of the end-stopped verse line as an apparatus designed to fit lyrics to music. Parchment was ruled by pricking the skin with an awl, a pricked wheel, or a dry-point stylus, before ultimately giving way to ruling with lead.[10] (Contemporary illustrations of book-making frequently depict the ruling of the sheet, which precedes acts of copying and illumination.) 'Prick song' is therefore music sung from notes written or 'pricked' as opposed to recalled from memory (the period presumably considered 'prick poetry' a redundancy). To 'prick' (like to 'write') is to score the surface, to write out music on the surface of the page by pen or by prick. This is what we mean when we speak of a musical 'score'. For the sake of synchronization among singers, musicians, and dancers, phonemes that intend to keep time with music and dance were set into lines, the breaks of which might graphically orient divergent performance materials and methods (voices/hands/instruments/feet/bodies). While all parchment and paper had lines, not all had line breaks, for it takes absence or negative space to enforce the silences around which collaborative performance organizes its constitutive activities. Line breaks are primarily a technology of collaboration, so their utility to the solo reader is largely mnemonic if they have any use at all.

In the absence of scoring, typography turns to the end-stopped line, absence enforcing the line's dictates. Songs that appear in printed playbooks partly exemplify this phenomenon, the more so when contemporary musical settings survive. For instance, Ariel's 'Full fathom five' and 'Where the bee sucks' both exist in

---

[10] D. C. Greetham, *Textual Scholarship: An Introduction* (New York: Garland, 1994), 62.

Robert Johnson's musical settings in *Cheerfull Ayres or Ballads* of 1660, where they are literally 'scored', i.e. they appear beneath lines or bars of musical notations. The divergent typographical treatment of songs in Johnson's *Cheerfull Ayres* and in Shakespeare's 1623 folio provides a spectacular instance of the way line breaks mimic a scoring system designed to determine vocal performance. In Johnson's setting, the words follow the line, not the rhyme, and therefore break where the line ends. The line can go no further—because there is no more paper to score— and so begins again at the left margin below. In the folio, the compositor (probably following manuscript copy) produces a spatial field that, first, differentiates the song from the pentameter that surrounds it and, second, breaks the line to empha- size the rhyme. While Johnson's setting seems plainly designed to enable perform- ance, the folio is caught between the desire to produce it and to reproduce it simultaneously (this is of course an ontological quandary of playbooks every- where, cf. stage directions). While the divergent settings here concern an actor's sung, not spoken, words, the starkly different settings reveal 'lines' and line endings to be—far from an inevitability or a fact of nature—an historically con- tingent result of the collision (not collusion) of distinct writing and performance cultures.

Why then do poets who write for private contemplation—not public performance—break a line of verse before, strictly speaking, they have to? It is a critical commonplace that the period's lyric poetry is indebted to a great tradition of medieval and Tudor song, though it is unclear what portion of Wyatt's, Surrey's, or Grimald's lyrics were chiefly composed for music. For Sidney, at least, the rela- tionship of poetry to music was axiomatic, since the poet comes 'with words set in delightful proportion, either accompanied with, or prepared for, the well enchant- ing skill of music'.[11] In any event, it is not difficult to trace the transition of a spatial decorum from lyric *qua* lyrics to private poetry. The typographical spatiality of end- stopped lines recalled Sidney's 'delightful proportion' whether the poetry was meant to be sounded or not. It seems reasonable to conclude that poetry written to be read (rather than or in addition to being sung) owes typographical allegiance to methods of inscription designed to enable group performance.

With this reductive history in mind, we might ask why Surrey broke his transla- tion of the *Aeneid* into unrhymed enjambed pentameters—an act widely credited with the origin of English blank verse, the default 'line' of the early English stage. I am not asking what prompted Surrey to 'write' blank verse, but what prompted Surrey to 'score' blank verse. Writing and scoring are cognate but not identical activities, after all. Surrey could have, as could anyone, 'write' blank verse without breaking the line after five stressed beats. To be more precise, why do writers of *enjambed* verse break off their line after ten syllables and begin again at the left

---

[11] 'The Defense of Poesy', in Katherine Duncan-Jones, ed., *Sir Philip Sidney: A Critical Edition of the Major Works* (Oxford: Oxford University Press, 1989), 227.

margin?[12] What work does a line break perform for enjambed blank verse, at which it seems demonstrably at odds (particularly, to recall and anticipate one of this chapter's arguments, if a line break is undetectable in its live rehearsal)? This is not—not yet at least—a question of form but a question of typography, though, of course, the anterior argument of this chapter is that the two are inextricable and often confused. So often when we think we are speaking of poetry we are actually speaking of type.

In sum, why is blank verse set differently than prose? The obvious answer (which isn't necessarily wrong) is simply that blank verse is set differently than prose out of the easy habit of convention—that even when poetry divorces itself from music (lyric from lyrics), becomes solitary rather than social, silent not sung, it preserves the residue of its origins. Line breaks are fossils of performance preserved in typographical amber. The music has stopped, but the words keep dancing. This reasoning, however, begins to shy into what I call here 'the metaphysical line', the modern idea that in form we find performance (or even *pre-formance*), that the dead hand of the poet directs the living voices of actors via a vital line from the grave. I'm suggesting, however, that the residue of performance that line breaks preserve recalls a performance tradition other than dramatic—the synchronization of multimedia performers and materials of music, not the ensemble of personnel, parts, and props that occupied the stage.

Early modern drama is, of course, full of lines—long lines, short lines, regular lines, rough lines, half lines, even some broken and shared lines—but you will not find them in print. It was apparently outside the ambit of Renaissance compositors to typeset the thousands of graphic lines that hash and score the period's dramatic manuscripts. In other words, the 'line' was certainly a performance technology for the period's players and playwrights just as surely as it was for the Renaissance singer and musician. It was, however, not the end-stopped line of poetry that synchronized theatrical performance but the lines of demarcation that scored playwrights' manuscripts, playhouse plots, and players' parts—like the silent line quoted at the outset of this section. Printed playbooks do not reproduce the lines that coordinated early modern theatrical work, however, since those 'lines' scored silence instead of, as for singers and instrumentalists, scoring sound. Lines were, then, an essential unit of early modern theatricality—just not the lines we usually have in mind.

At line 450 of Act 2, Scene 2 of *Hamlet*, the actor says, 'If it live in your memory, begin at this line' (2.2. 450–2). 'At', not 'with'. A simple enough distinction, but one that registers how, for the theatrical community, a 'line' had still primarily a

---

[12] Gilbert Sorrentino, in his legendary novel *The Imaginative Qualities of Actual Things* (New York: Pantheon Books, 1971), 31, offers a wry explanation for line breaks, in his description of a bad poet: '... a tendency that Lou was never to shake shows up in his short verse, that is, the tendency to think that a bad or trite line, if set by itself, space above and below it, somehow transcends its own weary language'.

physical, indexical function. A line marks a site, not a sound. (Here, in a familiar metaphor, Shakespeare conceptualizes memory as a volume, the memory as archive of theatrical material that Hamlet indexes with the search term 'The rugged Pyrrhus …') Hamlet, recall, has asked the First Player to speak 'a speech' that he 'heard spoken once'. He does not ask him to speak lines, nor, I would argue, does the meaning of 'line' function here in precisely the same sense that I meant when I wrote just now 'at line 450 … the actor says …'. With the help of Hamlet, and with reference to manuscriptal remnants from the early modern commercial stage, I want to review briefly the function of the line in the literary materials that helped enable performance.

First, early modern dramatic manuscripts require that you read between the lines, since that's where the words are. The plots, playbooks, and parts that somehow survive from late sixteenth- and early seventeenth-century England share a system of scoring that uses graphic rules of different dimensions to indicate a variety of divisions, between lines, between speakers, among scenes, and among acts. To generalize, lines indicate stasis—silence or the lack of phonic or physical activity that gives definition and shape to the voices and bodies that animate the stage and organize them into legibly discrete temporal units. Drama, in Bert O. States's terms, makes time 'shapely', and two of the primary units of dynamic differentiation that contour theatrical time are silence and absence.[13] The lines that appear in theatrical manuscripts function, above all, to keep time, to divide and coordinate presence and absence, silence and sound.

To begin with a part, Edward Alleyn's side of Orlando from Greene's *Orlando Furioso* features lines of four lengths and functions. In nearly every instance, the lines score silence. The shortest lines strike through words—lines baffling lines—where, for instance, some hand scores through '~~Italiano p dio~~' (Dulwich MS. I, fol. 261, l. 47). Such lines say nothing. At one point in the Orlando fragment, however, thin rules set off a section of Latin verse, which indicates at the least that the 'rules' had no rule, no single set function. Most often, these longer lines—or 'tails'—set off the 'right justified' cues that prompt Alleyn to speak. Here, the lines dummy words that are none of Alleyn's business, since each line 'gestures toward anything and everything that might be said by other actors in between one's own speeches'.[14] His concern is merely with the two or three words that say 'speak' to him (all cues, whatever their semantic content, perform 'speak' as their speech act). Alleyn's longest graphic lines would stretch from gutter to margin were his part a book not a scroll; instead, the lines span the scroll and *seem* to indicate some interval of indeterminate length. W. W. Greg, for one, states that the part does not signal scene breaks to its owner: 'There is no indication of scene division, and it would be difficult to determine the distribution of the speeches in the play without recourse to

---

[13] See Bert O. States, *The Pleasure of the Play* (Ithaca: Cornell University Press, 1994), *passim*.
[14] Simon Palfrey and Tiffany Stern, *Shakespeare in Parts* (Oxford: Oxford University Press, 2007), 83.

the Book. In one place…the word "Enter" marks the entrance of the speaker at the beginning of a new scene; at another…the heading "Orlando" together with the marginal direction "*solus*" probably has the same significance.'[15] Because Greg is focused on a different kind of lines (those of dialogue), he does not address the fact that the scribe sometimes employed a thin, scroll-wide rule to indicate, it seems, that something intervened between Alleyn's last words in one scene and first cue in another. We cannot then know whether parts routinely informed players of scene breaks through some instantly recognizable typographical formula. (The 1594 quarto of *Orlando Furioso* is not much help as a point of comparison with Orlando's part, since Orlando's lines in that quarto are so dissimilar to his lines in part. The two documents simply do not synchronize with a fidelity sufficient to illuminate the question.[16]) What seems likely at least is that the longest graphic lines in Alleyn's part signify silence *and* absence on his part whereas cue lines merely indicate silence. At one point, famously, some hand has interlineally scrawled 'fcurvy poetry a litell to long' (Dulwich MS. I, fol. 265, btwn. ll. 264–5), but then most of Alleyn's lines are dumb.

The period's surviving 'plots' are even more explicitly ruled by lines than are parts. In fact, plots are instantly recognizable as such due to their lineated appearance. Plots use both vertical and horizontal rules to box discursive scenic descriptions within a rationalized, double-columned grid of—usually—about twenty to twenty-five 'scenes'. In Greg's examination of the period's seven extant plots, he briefly surveys the use of rules—standard and discrepant—to organize the plots' material. Dispensing with 'the material and formal arrangement of the Plots' he turns to what we considers 'their more essential character', that is, the words.[17] Yet the standardization of the plots' 'formal arrangement' into a recognizable grid of lines signals that the lines as well as the words convey much of the material's 'essential character'. For instance, each plot contains two columns, bounded by vertical lines (except for that of *The Seven Deadly Sins* and, possibly, *Fortune's Tennis*). These margins provide space for words such as 'musique' or 'alarum' or '& tyre man' or '3 violls of blood & a sheeps gather'. The columns and notes suggest a graphic system that conceptualizes on-stage and off-stage space (and the activities and responsibilities that pertain to those spaces) as without/within the ruled box. In the box = on the stage. In the margin = in the tiring-house. In fact, as Tiffany Stern recently suggested, the neat fit of text to box suggests that the vertical columns were made first; then the scribe wrote in the text, 'sealing each box with a line as it was completed'.[18] The sizes of the various boxes then observe a standard width but a varying

[15] Greg, *Dramatic Documents*, 180.

[16] See W. W. Greg, *Two Elizabethan Stage Abridgments: The Battle of Alcazar and Orlando Furioso: An Essay in Critical Bibliography* (Oxford: Clarendon Press, 1923).

[17] Greg, *Dramatic Documents*, 72–3.

[18] Tiffany Stern, *Documents of Performance in Early Modern England* (Cambridge: Cambridge University Press, 2009), 208.

height—a graphic representation of the interplay between fixed space (the stage) but flexible time (the duration of a scene).[19] This is perhaps a rudimentary equation, but it suggests that the lines of the plot carry theatrically essential information that logocentric analyses often overlook.

Plots are public documents—large foolscap sheets pasted flat on thin pulp boards that hung backstage for corporate use. Parts are private property—scrolled scripts occulted in the hands of the player who possessed them. One primary function of the plot is, therefore, presumably to coordinate the collaborate efforts of players whose individual parts provide but scant information about the entire theatrical project.[20] And yet, parts and plots do not share lines, at least not in the terms that we conventionally imagine 'lines'. Within modern terms, plots contain none of the 'lines' spoken on the stage, whereas parts contain *only* lines spoken on the stage. This can baffle analysis that attempts to understand the synchronic relationship of plots to parts. But, of course, parts and plots *do* share lines, those graphic rules that indicate silence and stasis. The cryptic lines across the width of Alleyn's part likely indicate the cessation of that actor's on-stage activity as surely as the lines that divide each scene description on a plot indicate a cessation of on-stage activity altogether. Greg argues that the lines drawn across the columns of a plot indicate 'the close of a scene' and are therefore redundant, since each scene description closes with an 'exit' or 'exeunt'.[21] But an 'exit' and a terminal line are not redundant. An 'exit' implies the action of an actor who must move his body off the platform, while the line that follows indicates the momentary cessation of word and body, the momentary silence and stasis that gives significant form to the performance event.

It is manuscript playbooks, however, not parts or plots, that provided copy for printed playbooks, and it is immediately evident that the transition from manuscript to print magnified one kind of line at the expense of another. The graphic line was a victim of print while the iambic-pentameter 'line' emerges at its expense. The final batch of manuscripts that we might scour for scores are therefore those manuscript playbooks that fell into the hands of early modern compositors. What becomes immediately evident is that print privileges the poetic line while ignoring the graphic, utile one. Print un-scores the text while unwittingly emphasizing the importance of verse as a formal performative feature, advancing poetry over performance. This is understandable, since printed playbooks are for reading, not reciting.

Unlike printed playbooks, however, manuscript playbooks are *full* of scores, and it is all the more striking that these lines do not survive print, particularly since

---

[19] See Evelyn Tribble, 'Distributing Cognition in the Globe', *Shakespeare Quarterly* 56 (2005), 135–55 (144).

[20] See also David Bradley, *From Text to Performance in the Elizabethan Theatre: Preparing the Play for the Stage* (Cambridge: Cambridge University Press, 1992); Stern, *Documents of Performance*, 201–31.

[21] Greg, *Dramatic Documents*, 76.

many of the period's compositors seem quite literal in their treatment of dramatic copy text—setting a range of para-textual materials such as proper names, stage directions, music cues, etc. In other words, Renaissance compositors set *all sorts* of material other than the 'words of the play,' yet lines uniquely evade this literalistic protocol. This may be due to the fact that, to be precise, scores are not para-textual but para-performative apparatuses. For the most evident lines in manuscript play-books of the period perform the function of those long lines in parts and plots: they serve to delineate one unit from another, and so say silence. Act 1, Scene 3 of the *The Lady Mother* (British Museum, MS. Egerton 1994. fol. 191ª) ends with an '*Ex'*' hard upon another '*Ex'*' just two lines previous and leaves the stage free of person-nel. Recalling Greg, a line of demarcation here might seem redundant, since the writer has cleared the stage of bodies, yet the playwright saw fit to score his book across the width of the page because, to repeat, an 'exit' that clears the stage is not strictly the same thing as the silent line that divides one eventful unit from another. An '*exit*' line is concerned with place, moving actors from on stage to off; a graphic line with time, marking a moment of silence or stasis that gives to drama a discern-ible shape. (Another hand has added a marginal entrance cue to lead off the top of Act 2, Scene 1, and has scrupulously written the proper names of the actors *below* the line that closes 1.3.) These are, strictly speaking, end-stopped lines—though they denote the end or momentary stop in the eventful sequence of a play in per-formance, not the putative pause for breath that prosodists and performers impute to the end of a pentameter line. After all, early modern playmakers conceived of drama as the movement of bodies, materials, and sound across bounded time, not the stately march of serried characters across the printed page.

Other long lines bracket, box, and set-off stage directions and entrance cues (as in the manuscript playbook of *Richard II* [BM, MS. Egerton, 1994, fol. 178ᵇ] where—even in facsimile—horizontal chain lines are still apparent) or indicate the insertion of marginal revisions (as in *The Lady Mother* cited already). These lines, too, escape the printer's notice, though the words they surround or mark off do not. We can detect here the collision/collusion of two writing systems, those of the hand and those of type. A manuscript like that of *The Two Noble Ladies* (BM, MS. Egerton 1994, fol. 235ᵇ) uses lines to box and therefore differ-entiate a stage direction like '*Enter 2. Souldiers dragging Justina. bound*', since it occupies the same horizontal plane as a piece of Cyprian's dialogue, 'Let's ftay, and fee th'euent' (l. 18). The snatch of dialogue referring to 'th'euent' and the description of the event itself are so close as to appear to be part of the 'same line'. This is because the writer is not rigidly observing a marginal decorum that reserves the medium for dialogue and the shoulders for directions and speech prefixes. The box around the description mitigates potential confusion. Print deploys its own set of devices to segregate dialogue from directions, both type face (roman versus italic) and a rigid enforcement of margin and/or white space between lines of dialogue, where italicized directions might appear. Everywhere, print leaves the graphic line behind as part of a sweepstakes conversion of manu-scriptal mess into typographical tidiness. Though they may look messy to the type-trained eye, manuscript playbooks had their own graphic conventions that presumably enabled prompters and part-writers to differentiate dialogue from directions. Like the ephemerality of the performances they enabled, *those* lines evade textual reproduction.

The shortest but most ubiquitous lines in manuscript playbooks are those that administer the theatrical convention of 'one at a time', that is, the convention of dialogue speaking that requires one speaker to wait until the previous speaker has finished before he begins in turn. It is probably as laborious to read a description of this convention as it is to write it, but this convention is no less odd for being so obvious; 'one at a time' is a manner of speaking at once highly 'unrealistic' and yet so theatrically common that we do not let it prevent us from frequently describing such dialogue as 'naturalistic'. Based on available evidence, playwrights quite com-monly incised a short hash mark between the end of one character's dialogue and the outset of another's.[22] (Fancifully, perhaps *this* is what Hamlet means when he says 'begin at this line'.) Since these lines mark the transition from one speaker to another, they resemble those lines that anticipate the cues on players' parts, graphi-cally coordinating a verbal conjunction. Just possibly, these short hash marks made it fractionally easier for the person charged with part-production to scan a dramatic manuscript and fracture the playbook at those points.[23] Alternatively (or as well), these hash marks allowed the swift-composing playwright to return to his work and fill in speech prefixes *after* rather than before writing dialogue.[24] Perhaps the hash marks served the plot maker and or prompter to attend to those seams in ensemble performance where collaboration gathers. Conventional, habitual, or utile, manu-script lines enable, facilitate, and coordinate a performance event involving multi-ple men and boys (both on stage and off) across a duration of time. The famous fragment of *The Booke of Sir Thomas Moore* that possibly features Shakespeare's hand sports these hash marks as well. For all of this fragment's notoriety, however, these are not the 'famous lines' of Shakespeare that occasionally appear in the back of his works. These are the lines that scored performance, and these are the lines that evaporate in print.

---

[22] Greg argues that these 'speech rules', as he calls them, 'derived from the medieval habit of separat-ing speeches by lines drawn right across the page ...' (*Dramatic Documents*, 208). William B. Long argues persuasively that these speech rules directed playwrights and scribes in the placement of speech prefixes, which, whether they were copying or composing, writers filled in only after the entire playtext was complete ('"Precious Few": English Manuscript Playbooks', in David Scott Kastan, ed., *A Compan-ion to Shakespeare* [Oxford: Blackwell, 1999], 414–33, esp. 416).

[23] On scribal part production, see esp. Stern, *Documents of Performance*, 236–45.

[24] Long, '"Precious Few"', esp. 416; also William B. Long, '"A bed / for Woodstock": A Warning for the Unwary', *Medieval and Renaissance Drama in England* 2 (1985), 91–118 (96); John Jowett, *Shake-speare and Text* (Oxford: Oxford University Press, 2007), 33.

While my emphasis here has been on the graphic scores, marks, and hashes that lineate the period's theatrical ephemera, dramatic manuscripts also feature 'lines' of verse in the sense that most modern commentators and practitioners use the word. That is, manuscript playbooks also feature written characters horizontally arrayed in a sequence of ten syllables, as well as lines that reach the margin. It is striking, however, that print differentiates these distinctions by an order of magnitude. Early modern drama frequently toggles casually between prose and verse (or, to be more precise, between lines of ten syllables and longer ones), but play *manuscripts* rarely make this immediately evident. The section of *The Lady Mother* mentioned earlier provides an exemplary instance since 1.3 ends in pentameter lines while 2.1 opens with lines that extend to the margin. The difference is, at first glance, not immediately clear. Manuscript plays like *The Captives* and *The Two Noble Ladies* present similar effects. Nor, as is well known, do pentameter lines in manuscript inevitably capitalize initial letters, a typographic indication that, here, the reader is dealing with lines of verse.[25] A particular hermeneutics of close reading that attends to minute shifts in metre and syllable units—and that rationalizes such work, in part, by claiming that it accesses early modern performance practice—relies, tellingly, on the translation of manuscripts into printed playbooks, a translation that alters the 'lines' of early modern verse drama out of the material form that *we know* those first actors employed. It is tempting to present a section of a dramatic manuscript to a certain variety of iambic fundamentalist and say, simply, 'scan this: I dare you'.

Printed playbooks are not scores. In fact, they have been muted. This is why textbooks and manuals on prosody and on the acting of verse drama introduce diacritics to mark patterns of stress. The print form of the received text needs to be re-marked, pricked out for performance to make it typographically sound—the text needs to be converted from a 'memorandum to excite the reader's recall of a previous performance', to one that 'serves as a score for future vocal reproduction'.[26] So however 'natural' the iambic beat and pentameter length, the stress needs to be marked and the pentameter indicated by a line break. We rely, in short, on typography to alert us to what we are simultaneously told is an effect as natural as breath itself.

One way, then, to appreciate that printed copies of verse drama are not performance scores is that they are called 'playbooks' and not 'prick plays'. The other way to appreciate that printed playbooks are not scores is that they are not scored. To point out that we have replaced one kind of line with another may be merely a pedantic

---

[25] This phenomenon carries over to print as well. *The Fair Maid of Bristow* (1605), sometimes referred to as a 'Bad Quarto', prints most successive verse lines without capital letters. Although the compositor was probably simply following copy, within traditional bibliography this typographical 'irregularity' is one mark of its badness.

[26] Lorenzo Charles quoted in Meta Du Ewa Jones, 'Jazz Prosodies: Orality and Textuality', *Callaloo* 25.1 (Winter 2002), 66–91 (77–8).

quibble—or the kind of line we might spring on a student who wanders in front of our hobby horse. The following section attempts to outline, however, a more than merely pedantic effect of this line of reasoning, or the ideological impact of the line metaphysical.

The metaphysical line

Line structure…can be expressive and liberating.…The way the grace of the ballet depends on the base of rhythmic structure from which the balletic leaps…the way much improvisation in jazz arises not from nothing, not from noise, but from a melodic or rhythmic base. The iambic line is like a 'bounded water' whose boundedness—that pause—gives resonance and definition to its waves and tides, its riptides and undertows.… [L]ine structure is a kind of esthetic mask, a structure, a fundamental (in the musical sense) that heightens expressiveness by playing up the tension between form and feeling within each line, tensions that would slacken, lose their riptides and overtones if lines were run around willy-nilly without the defining pause, or moment of *poise*, at the end.

Ron Rosenbaum *The Shakespeare Wars*[27]

Got that? The physical becomes metaphysical via the metaphoric vector. At some point, tenor uncouples from vehicle and the whole thing goes off the rails ('riptides' *and* 'overtones'?) Ironically, this breathless prose celebrates the breath, the pause or 'poise' that marks the end. This is a common feature of what might be called the school, or clerisy, of the metaphysical line. The metaphysical line depends upon—demands—its being appreciable, 'registered' in performance, where its lack of apparent presence might seem to undermine its import. Within a metaphysic of the line, therefore, it is only absence—only silence—that can register presence—the pause that defines in Rosenbaum's terms. For a particular kind of priesthood, the line is available only when it is over—so that a line is always latterly registered, a reminder that the speaker has reached the end of the line. Whereas for the early moderns the graphic line anticipates the word, for us the line is always belated. For them, the line indicated silence; for us, silence indicates the line.

What the physical and metaphysical lines share, then, is that they both attempt to regulate silence, though in manners as different as presence and absence. The graphic lines of early modern theatrical-textual ephemera coordinated performances—especially but not only vocal performances—by scoring the silences that separated actor from actor, voice from voice, voice from action, and scenic unit from scenic unit. In these terms, silence is a technology of collaboration. Oddly,

---

[27] Ron Rosenbaum, *The Shakespeare Wars: Clashing Scholars, Public Fiascoes, Palace Coups* (New York: Random House, 2006), 234–5.

modern work on the Shakespearean line in performance banishes silence uniquely at the moments of transitions between one performer and another—the much discussed 'shared lines' that we know to be *exclusively* a phenomenon of type. That is, the transition in speaking from one performer to another—what we might call 'collaboration'—is the moment where pauses *may not* occur. The pauses, the breaths, the silences and poises that define the metaphysical line in performance are entirely solipsistic, a method by which a modern actor conveys discovery, intent, meaning, and purpose. Silence for us is a technology of self-consciousness, a technology of subjectivity.

The origin for the pause is not hard to locate. In *Shakespeare's Metrical Art*, George T. Wright offers a definition of poetry that frames the question even as it forecloses comment: 'Poetry is language composed in verse, that is, language of which an essential feature is its *appearance* in measured units, either as written text or in *oral performance*' (emphasis added).[28] This agreeably succinct formula raises a problem, however: how does an actor make poetic language *orally appear*? Wright provides no answer but does describe precisely how to know poetry on the page:

> in literate cultures the *line* is the indispensable unit of verse and the one by which we recognize its nature. Paragraphs of prose lack this essential feature: in different printed versions the separate lines may end at different words without injury to meaning or form; different printed versions of poems must retain the lines as they are. If a line is too long to print on a narrow page or column, the print must use some conventional means to show that the leftover words belong with the ones they follow. Even when the sense of one line runs over to the next, it is important to the form of a poem that the lines be preserved intact.[29]

Conventions of *print* make verse *apparent*. As Wright points out, print even invents ways to register verse when it cannot deploy line breaks. Consider our convention of employing a '/' when threading verse into our prose. It takes lines (/) to make lines. This definition of poetry by one of the industry's most comprehensive scholars of metrical arts ends up implying that poetry is not, in performance, a discernible type of phenomenon, since poetry is a phenomenon of type. Paradoxically, it takes silence in performance to remind us that playbooks are printed in lines, so that plays in performance are at their *most* textual and *most* typographical when most silent.

The great paradox, therefore, is that for all the attempts to emancipate Shakespeare from the page—to give voice to his *theatrical* purposes—the metaphysical line converts performance back into type. But a play in performance is not a sequence of words. It is an order of events. In performance, the 'line' has no substantial presence. By 'substantial presence' I mean it has no 'substance' in the philosophical sense of 'substance' as that which underlies phenomena, the 'permanent

---

[28] George T. Wright, *Shakespeare's Metrical Art* (Berkeley: University of California Press, 1988), ix.
[29] Wright, *Shakespeare's Metrical Art*, ix.

substratum of things' (*OED* 3.a). Language in performance is all phenomena, however, hence the relentless search for a permanent substratum of 'things'—in this
case text or type—to authorize performance. The emphasis on breath, on the pause,
on the phonic expansion of sounds or silence into audio-acoustic space ends up,
ironically, saying, 'remember the text, remember typography' because the line, in
performance, *doesn't exist*.[30]

In any other than a strictly graphic sense, therefore, the line can *only* be metaphorically explained, as the lush fluorescence of fanciful descriptions of the pentameter line
demonstrates. The metaphors of the metaphysic line divide, roughly, between prosodists and performers. The 'line' is most frequently troped as an inert but stable structure upon which meaning mounts *or* as a quickening pulse of meaning itself. The
architectural sense of the line implies, demands stasis—it is often the 'scaffold' or
'structure' of a poem—versus the 'pulsing' 'heartbeat' or 'energetic' conveyer of feeling
in performance. With some exceptions, prosody treats 'lines' as the former; performance as the latter ('Don't let's ask what it *is*,' writes John Barton of the line, 'for it's nothing static, but let's ask what goes on in it.')[31] Whatever their differences, these tropic
varietals struggle over the line's syntactical, and therefore ontological, status. Is the
line subject or object? Maker of meaning or meaning to be made? Determinant or
determined? Thus a prosody handbook can describe the line as, at once, a structural
unit but one that moves—'poetry...moves...in LINES' (caps in the original)[32]—and
Barton can deny the line ontological status/stasis but nevertheless trope it as a vessel
of meaning, a travelling trunk of poetry ready to be unpacked.

The two approaches—let us call them 'static' versus 'mobile'—nevertheless unite
around the line as the 'natural' form of English dramatic verse (as Wright notes, the
line is how we 'recognize its nature') and therefore deploy a common conceptual
system founded in the human body. Thus, poetic form becomes human form and
vice versa. For the metaphysical line is always, foremost, a vital line, as common as
a heartbeat, as easy as breath. Prosody handbooks and acting manuals are littered
with tropes that base themselves in the respiratory system or in the cardiovascular
pump. (More recently, presumably prompted by the genome project, genetic metaphors abound as well: 'A foot is a specific order of syllable types almost like a poem's
Deoxyribonucleic Acid (DNA).'[33]) The iambic beat is 'the first and last we hear—
that of our heart'.[34] I'm not that kind of doctor, but doesn't the trochaic beat more

[30] In this regard, Alistair Fowler's casual reference to an 'illiterate Rusian of our own time [who] is
said to have composed a poem of 40,000 lines' prompts a kind of zen koan: do illiterate poets compose
in lines? (Alastair Fowler, *A History of English Literature* [Cambridge, MA: Harvard University Press,
1989], 2).

[31] John Barton, *Playing Shakespeare* (New York: Anchor Books, 1984), 27.

[32] Barton, *Playing Shakespeare*, 45.

[33] *What is the Function of Meter in Poetry?* (http://www.wisegeek.com/what-is-the-function-of-
meter-in-poetry.htm, accessed 30 August 2011).

[34] Rodenburg, *Speaking Shakespeare*, 84.

closely resemble the human heartbeat than iambic? Is Chaucer therefore closer to our hearts than Shakespeare? But I digress. Or, '[s]ince about ten syllables form a convenient breath unit in English...it is no mystery that iambic pentameter should be our characteristic line',[35] since it is 'the most speechlike of English meters'.[36] This is a means of essentializing the line to rationalize it as the essential form—calling it either the heartbeat or the 'natural breath' unit—so that the pentameter line becomes the inevitable unit of poetic expression.[37] It's almost too easy to puncture the 'logic' of these claims: given the classical French alexandrine of twelve syllables, for instance, we would have to develop a poetics of respiration that has the French breathing less often than the English (a notion that might appeal to the English far more than it does to our common sense, but this is the familiar collapse of the naturalistic with the nationalistic). Above all, poetic lines are an inevitability:

> To sum up, the line is a nearly universal rhetorical feature of poetry. When expression becomes memorably compact, rich, and emphatic, and is highly organized in linguistic detail, lines all but certainly *come into being.* (italics added)[38]

The line is imagined as the essential form of poetic expression because it is a thing of nature, like a leaf. The line is pure Platonic poetry, awaiting only our breath to give it form.

It is characteristic of all metaphysics to mystify while they explain. Thus pentameter can be both as available as breath and as cryptic as an Axis cipher. After all, the problem with naturalizing the pentameter line is that it makes it apparent to anyone with a heart. Accessibility is therefore simultaneously the pentameter line's great virtue but also its most troubling asset—for the naturalizing tendency of such explanations threatens to convert the metaphysical line into a hyper-physical one. The verse line is therefore subject to yet another tropic programme, one that mystifies it as a vessel of encrypted information to which we have lost the codes. John Barton is being merely characteristic when he writes that, 'the Elizabethan theatre actors knew how to use and interpret the *hidden direction* Shakespeare himself provided in his verse and prose'.[39] As W. B. Worthen has argued, this idea of hidden

---

[35] Karl Shapiro and Robert Beum, *A Prosody Handbook* (New York: Harper & Row, 1965), 48.

[36] Wright, *Shakespeare's Metrical Art*, ix.

[37] An adjunct of this strain of critique is the minor industry committed to lampooning other verse forms such as 'fourteeners', which, unlike the graceful pentameter, can be derided as 'clumsy' or 'galumphing', though Chapman's *Iliad* is composed in iambic septameter (see Bruce Smith, *The Acoustic World of Early Modern England* [Chicago: University of Chicago Press, 1999], 187; Fowler, *A History of English Literature*, 43). C. S. Lewis's disdain for the 'Poulter's measure'—a couplet made out of an alexandrine and a fourteener—provides a hilarious running joke in his *English Literature in the Sixteenth Century, Excluding Drama*. He calls it the 'draff and scum of contemporary English poetry' and characterizes its effect thus: 'Hence in a couplet made of two such yoke-fellows we seem to be labouring up a hill in bottom gear for the first line, and then running down the other side of the hill, out of control, for the second' (Oxford: Clarendon Press, 1954), esp. 109 and 233.

[38] Shapiro and Beum, *A Prosody Handbook*, 51–2.   [39] Barton, *Playing Shakespeare*, 4.

meaning that must be discovered before it may be realized in performance partakes of an ' "information theory" understanding of text-and-performance. . . . in
this view, dramatic writing functions like encoded data, which can be properly
(and identically) downloaded with the proper theatrical software'.[40] Shakespeare,
who was famously quite good with words, is imagined to have encoded his line
with 'how to use' instructions—ciphers from the past that now require the Bletch-
ley Park treatment.

Decryption depends upon scansion, first of all, the translation of metrical patterns into a specialized system of diacritical marks. Thus the breathing, beating line
of poetry is doubly encrypted, alleged to contain coded information that requires
translation into an inscrutable language of diacritical marks that themselves require
deciphering. However ancient the origins of 'scansion' (from the Latin *scandere*,
which meant 'to climb,' hence the emphasis on determining the rhythm of feet),
scansion today is a technicalized practice. Systems of scansion greet the natural line
through, primarily, medical tropes. Thus the great scholar of nineteenth-century
literature Chip Tucker can describe scansion as a means to penetrate the body's
mysteries. Scansion is a method of,

> taking an X-ray of the architecture of verse. This inner structure arises from the inter-
> play of meter (the bones of a poem) with rhythm (its flesh); of abstracted, regular pat-
> tern with the pulse of felt, voiced meaning. . . . There is simply no better way for readers
> to get an inside line on what versecraft is about.[41]

The line is simultaneously naturalized to and alienated from our understanding.
Iambic pentameter is as natural as the beating of our heart, but it takes expertise to
read an ECG.

As Tucker's imagery implies, poetic language needs to be penetrated to be understood, a familiar enough metaphor, since surface/depth might be *the* master trope
through which the academy rationalizes and conceives of interpretation. But this
conversion of interpretation into technology—metrical scansion become medical
scanning—can be puzzled by the very forms it attempts to penetrate. For instance,
Optical Character Recognition (OCR), which facilitates database searching, requires
a standardization of characters and a straightness of lines that the hand-press period
could never achieve because printing materials (types, spaces, leads, etc.) were
handmade and not turned to tolerances sufficiently uniform.[42] Therefore, as William Proctor Williams puts it, 'attempts to turn text images (digital or the real thing)

---

[40] W. B. Worthen, 'Performing Shakespeare in Digital Culture', in Robert Shaughnessy, ed., *The Cambridge Companion to Shakespeare and Popular Culture* (Cambridge: Cambridge University Press, 2007), 227–47 (241).

[41] 'U.Va. Professor Helps Students Examine Poetry "For Better for Verse"', *UVA Today* (http://www.virginia.edu/uvatoday/newsRelease.php?id=10899, accessed 25 August 2011).

[42] The quartos of plays like *Hoffman* (1631) and *Knave in the Grain* (1640) offer instances of play-texts that might exhaust the most inexhaustible OCR.

into machine readable, and therefore searchable, files have a failure rate of about 90% for books printed before 1600'. Searchable databases such as EEBO-TCP, ECCO, and English Verse Drama have therefore been rendered, usually by human hand, into machine-readable forms.[43] Once again, early modern plays have to be translated out of their initial forms (in this case the print forms that themselves required translation from manuscript forms) to undergo yet another translation so that they can be scanned by eyes more accurate—because inexhaustible—than human. The sounds and secrets of the metaphysical line will yield, but only to a range of various excavatory and incantatory systems that have to rule the line before it can be read.

As Barton's quote suggests, that which is only technically available to us was freely available to our predecessors. As Jeremy Lopez has recently critiqued, '[s]cholars generally agree that a heightened perception of blank verse during live theatrical performance *was* possible for early modern audiences', and he cites as an exemplary instance Coburn Freer's sense that:

> At the heart of the interest in dramatic poetry is a concern for the line itself. Audiences could hear the blank verse line emerge and take shape, and their ability to do this gives the point to literally hundreds of speeches and scenes in English renaissance drama.[44]

Cicely Berry also believes that the 'Elizabethan audience must have been so attuned to this pulse that they would have picked up immediately on the dramatic nature of the writing by the way the beat was behaving'.[45] Recalling Wright's emphasis on an oxymoronic 'oral' 'appearance', the binding irony of prosodists and performers is that to recognize the line in performance is to recognize that it is no longer here, but was once there. This idea of a now-vanished perceptivity to the line in performance doubles down on the line's belated appeal and coalesces the conflicting tropic programmes that struggle to locate the line's metaphysical substance. However natural, however available, however strongly the line once pulsed in theatrical Eden, we live in a fallen world. The vanishing line of past performances inevitably gives way to a wistful nostalgia for a vanished line of perceptive performers (and audiences). We are always too late for the line, too late to perceive with perfect clarity what was once before apparent to all—but then, a wistfulness for a vanished world is also a quality of most metaphysics.

---

[43] Communicated in a private email from William Proctor Williams. I am indebted to him for walking me through this process.

[44] 'From Bad to Verse: Poetry and Spectacle on the Modern Shakespearean Stage', forthcoming in Post, ed., *The Oxford Handbook to Shakespeare's Poetry*. The extended quote is from Coburn Freer, *The Poetics of Jacobean Drama* (Baltimore: Johns Hopkins University Press, 1981), 33.

[45] Cicely Berry, *The Actor and the Text* (London: Applause Books, 1989), 53.

Coda: the royal line

Only about fifty actors are left in the theater who really understand them [the principles of verse speaking].

Peter Hall, qtd. in Ron Rosenbaum, *The Shakespeare Wars*[46]

Like all nostalgia, this is encomium disguised as lament, and Hall's elegy (sung to the tune of 'we happy few') mourns while it celebrates a different kind of line—a venerable tradition of verse speaking, the phonic version of Kean's sword, bequeathed across the ages, increasing in lustre the fewer who handle it. In the same book, Hall speaks of attending a conference on verse speaking at the Royal National Theatre in 1999 where 'it was generally agreed that we are perhaps the last generation for whom Shakespearean speech will be immediately intelligible at *all*'.[47] Late of the Royal Shakespeare Company, Sir Peter Hall's obsession with line endings is, in these terms, the more explicable.

This form of latent nostalgia extends the pentameter line genealogically to performers and performances past. In these terms, early modern theatrically forms a province in the academic imaginary where short but large-eared Elizabethans attended to exquisitely metrical performances by precision-tongued performers. (There is no place in this imaginary for a contrasting idea of a rabble of men and boys in tatty costumes flogging away at a piece of sub-Senecan tragedy for a couple of hours or three.) The combination of fantasy and desire that propels this idea ironizes its own operation by attempting to reach the living heat of early modern performance through the cold technology of the printed page.

As I noted at the outset, it is by no means novel these days to critique Shakespearean performance as always and everywhere an overly textualized phenomenon. Inescapably, print preconceives nearly everything we imagine about early modern theatricality. Since our access to the words, world, work of early modern drama is so dominated by print, we are left to ask how the printed arrangement of the words on the page enact or record the concerns of players and playwrights. If we could determine, however, through theoretical investigation or historical scholarship, that the ten syllable line was indeed the fundamental *compositional* unit in which playwrights embodied their poetic ideas and theatrical ideals—a determination that does not seem, it is fair to say, totally implausible—the question would still remain whether that 'fact' or phenomenon has any impact or impression whatsoever in the uptake of meaning or aesthetic appreciation during an event of embodied expression.

I have attempted to argue that attention at the level of the line pushes performance towards the typographic, even advancing a kind of 'typographical acting' alert

---

[46] Rosenbaum, *The Shakespeare Wars*, 222.   [47] Rosenbaum, *The Shakespeare Wars*, 233.

to every piece of punctuation, every line break, every diacritically pricked out metrical inflection. If we insist that actors 'speak lines', however, why do we insist that they memorize them? Surely it is perverse to conceive of performance simultaneously in such typographical terms and then to banish the page from the stage (to invert the familiar jingle). Of course, we have a name for textual, typographical performances. We call them 'staged readings' (though we do not call the performance of a play a 'staged remembering'). Most audiences would rebel at the sight of actors 'on book'. Part of what they've paid for is an 'off book' performance—theatre as a kind of memory circus. This is understandable, since performance disguises the writing systems that enable it, which perhaps explains much of our attempt to turn performance back into text, to make everywhere visible that which performance attempts to vanish—an attempt to remind us, above all, that some *thing*—the text—abides beneath the ephemeral phenomenon of performance.

It is, finally, at the level of the line that critical attention most often attempts to materialize the vanished intentions and origins of early modern theatricality. The most available critique of such attention would be to point out that it 'privileges' print over performance and violates the ontology of the object it examines. From there, we *could* argue that 'theatricality' constitutes an uneasy alliance or productive antagonism between print and performance (as in Robert Weimann's equilibrium model of 'author's pen' and 'actor's voice'). Yet such a reading of 'theatricality' leaves the line in place as, in Rodenburg's terms, 'the given', maintaining its position as determinate and determining force. Theatricality might be better understood not as a harmony of print and performance but a balance of spatial and durational phenomena, in which lines play a fundamental but not determining part, scoring time and space with sound and silence, giving to early modern theatricality the force and intensities we still, at a great remove, attempt to apprehend.

FURTHER READING

Barton, John. *Playing Shakespeare: An Actor's Guide* (New York: Anchor Books, 2001).

Edelstein, Barry. *Thinking Shakespeare: A How-to Guide for Student Actors, Directors, and Anyone Else Who Wants to Feel More Comfortable With the Bard* (New York: Spark Publishing Group, 2007).

Hall, Peter. *Shakespeare's Advice to the Players* (London: Oberon Books, 2003).

Kaiser, Scott. *Shakespeare's Wordcraft* (New York: Limelight Editions, 2007).

CHAPTER 7

SOURCE

STEPHEN GUY-BRAY

In order to meet the increasing demand for plays, English playwrights of the late sixteenth and early seventeenth centuries drew on a wide variety of sources: historical chronicles, English and classical poetry, Italian *novelle*, books and pamphlets about current events, among other kinds of material. The original texts were not completely effaced by their new theatrical form, however, and there was a strong, if usually implicit, tension between the earlier and newer versions. This tension was greater in the case of plays based on well-known texts or events, and greater still if playwrights chose to make this tension part of the subject of their plays—to confront, more or less explicitly, the question of the secondary status of their own texts and, by extension, the secondary status of theatre itself as a form that was new in an English context and of lower status than poetry. My examples are Christopher Marlowe's *Dido, Queen of Carthage*, Ben Jonson's *Poetaster*, and William Shakespeare and George Wilkins's *Pericles*. In these plays, the earlier text (or texts) is never merely something to be mined for plots. These authors make both the process of adaptation and the question of the relation between dramatic and non-dramatic literature an important part of their plays. Theatrical representation depends on the sense of sight to which a poem can only allude, for instance, and the visual often emerges in these plays (and especially, as I will argue, in *Pericles*) as an aspect of theatre that is not only added to the poem but even in competition with it.

As is well known, *Dido, Queen of Carthage* adapts a work central to both literary and political traditions. In contrast, *Poetaster* has no direct source, although Jonson does translate some of Horace's and Virgil's poetry more or less literally as well as using other classical incidents and situations. But in the play as a whole, his source is what is usually seen as the golden age of Roman literature (and thus of literature as whole): the time of Virgil, Horace, and Ovid, all of whom are characters in the play. Jonson's source is Latin poetry, rather than an individual Latin poem. Indeed, Latin poetry and the social context in which it was written emerge as the source not only for the incidents and situations of *Poetaster* but also for characters and the relations among them. Finally, although the basic plot of *Pericles* exists in a number of versions, both ancient and modern, Shakespeare and Wilkins chose to identify John Gower as the author of their source and to make him a character in the play. Different as these three plays are, however, they are similar in that their playwrights chose to make the question of source material and how it is adapted for a play into a major feature of their theatre.

Dido, Queen of Carthage

Marlowe's version of the story of Dido and Aeneas is an adaptation of one of the most famous narratives of the *Aeneid* and of the role it plays within Virgil's poem as a whole. The story of Dido is only a small part of the *Aeneid*: it takes up part of Book I and all of Book IV, while Books II and IV are concerned with how Aeneas and his men got from Troy to Carthage and the remaining books deal with Aeneas's adventures after leaving Carthage. In other words, although Dido may well be one of the most memorable or perhaps even *the* most memorable of the poem's characters, it is clear that Aeneas is the protagonist. In contrast, in Marlowe's play Dido is of equal stature with Aeneas.[1] One effect of this parallel is that the play has a chiasmic structure: at the beginning, Aeneas is shipwrecked and destitute while Dido is a rich and powerful monarch; by the end, Aeneas is able to sail to Italy with a new fleet while Dido has killed herself. Profiting from this inevitable consequence of dramatizing only part of the poem, Marlowe makes the question of who the protagonist of the story is into one of the central themes of the play.

I shall begin with the first scene, however, in which neither Dido nor Aeneas appears. This scene—which has become famous as the most explicitly homoerotic scene in English Renaissance drama—has no direct source in the *Aeneid*, although it is clearly based on Virgil's list of the reasons for Juno's enmity to the Trojans: '*iudicium Paridis spretaeque iniuria formae / et genus inuisum et rapti Ganymedis honores*' (the judgement of Paris and the affront to her slighted beauty and the hated race and the honours paid to kidnapped Ganymede; I.27–8).[2] But while Virgil's lines look back, in that they provide the motives for things happening in the poem's present, Marlowe's scene looks forward, in that it gives us important information about the world in which his play takes place and, in particular, about Aeneas. At the beginning of this first scene we see Jupiter attempting to seduce Ganymede and Ganymede keeping him at a distance in order to extort presents. This part of the scene culminates with Jupiter's offer of 'these linked gems, / My Juno ware upon her marriage day' (1.1.42–3). The conversation of Jupiter and Ganymede is played for

---

[1] Or perhaps not: in the first performances, all the roles were played by boy actors, and Jackson I. Cope has argued that the actor playing Dido would have been taller than the actor playing Aeneas; see Cope, 'Marlowe's *Dido* and the Titillating Children', *English Literary History* 4 (1974), 315–25.

[2] All translations are my own.

laughs and for titillation, I think, but it also serves to draw attention to the power of youthful male beauty and to the commercial aspects of sexuality.

These factors will be important to the story of Aeneas, who is, after all, Ganymede's cousin; like Ganymede, Aeneas will achieve his purposes by using his beauty. Marlowe stresses the parallel between the two Trojans by having Dido give Aeneas similar presents after hc has agreed to be her lover:

> take these jewels at thy Lovers hand,
> These golden bracelets, and this wedding ring,
> Wherewith my husband woo'd me yet a maide   (3.4.61–3)

What is important here is not merely that both men are promised jewels for having sex, but also that these are wedding jewels. The jewels that form part of the ceremony that unites two people either at the highest possible level on earth—the marriage of a king and queen—or at the highest possible level cosmically—the marriage of the king and queen of the gods—can be reused for entirely less exalted purposes. In adapting wedding jewels to the purposes of seduction, Jupiter and Dido parallel Marlowe's own adaptation of Virgil for different and less metaphysical ends. In the world of the play, things are important for what they can do rather than for what we might assume to be their inherent qualities.

As the play goes on to demonstrate, Aeneas follows the precedent of his cousin Ganymede, and his eventual journey to Italy—the journey that is fated to lead to the establishment of the Roman empire—is made possible by the generosity of Dido (and, ultimately, of Iarbas). Aeneas's passivity and his reliance on his looks and charm make him a curiously feminine character. As if in compensation, Dido is in some ways a more conventionally masculine character than is usually the case, especially in response to Aeneas's exaggerated humility. This aspect of the adaptation is emphasized by the staging, in which boys played all the parts, and could have been further emphasized if some of the parts were doubled: the actor playing Ganymede, for instance, could have appeared again as Aeneas. The experience of seeing the play with an all-male cast would have increased the sense in Marlowe's play in which the relation between physical gender and gender roles is fluid and unstable. As well, Marlowe has in mind here the strong—if implicit—parallel between Dido and Aeneas: both are Asian royalty who fled westward to establish kingdoms in the central Mediterranean. The difference in the play is that Dido is already a monarch while Aeneas is virtually powerless. In telling her son about the flight of the Phoenicians to what would become Carthage, Venus famously says 'dux femina facti' (the leader of the expedition was a woman; I.364); we could say that Dido, Queen of Carthage presents us with a woman as the leader of the Trojan expedition.

Like the change to the characterization of Aeneas, the change in the characterization of Dido also has a precedent in the first scene. After the first fifty lines, the celestial boyfriends are interrupted by Venus, who comments crabbily on Jupiter's neglect of his duty. Marlowe has drawn this from the first book of the *Aeneid*, but the difference in context is important. In Virgil's poem, Jupiter is already thinking about Aeneas when Venus approaches him:

> *Libyae defixit lumina regnis.*
> *atque illum talis iactantem pectore curas*
> *tristior et lacrimis oculos suffusa nitentis*
> *adloquitur Venus*

(He fixed his eyes on the kingdom of Libya, and while he turned over these cares in his breast, Venus—saddened and her eyes bright with tears—appealed to him; I.226–9.)

And as might be expected, in the *Aeneid* Venus and Jupiter speak to each other with courtesy, whereas in *Dido, Queen of Carthage* Jupiter's dignified response appears out of character. While Jupiter's calm and measured tone in this passage is consistent with his behaviour in the *Aeneid* as a whole, Marlowe's Jupiter appears to have switched to a different dramatic register altogether.

But however suitably Marlowe's Jupiter speaks when prompted, the fact remains that it took a woman to recall him to his duty. This state of affairs will turn out to be paradigmatic: throughout *Dido, Queen of Carthage* it is the female characters— both Venus and Juno, but also Dido—who have the most agency.[3] As Simon Shepherd remarks, 'the assumption that rationality is male and passion female is challenged, and male desire is foregrounded at the start of a play about a woman who classically exemplifies destructive desire'.[4] In Marlowe's version of the story, it is the male characters that are most associated with forms of desire that are inimical to the established order and that work against epic elevation. In this first scene, both Ganymede and Jupiter are precedents for Aeneas: the former because he uses his looks to gain material advantage; and the latter because he has to be recalled to his duty. Most of the play's second half is taken up with the attempts (ultimately successful) to get Aeneas to do what he is fated to do. At the end of the invocation to the *Aeneid*, Virgil comments on the work involved in fulfilling the dictates of destiny by saying '*tantae molis erat Romanam condere gentem*' (such a great task it was to establish the Roman race; I.33); in Marlowe's version, Aeneas adds substantially to this task. He does not have the natural leadership and nobility of Virgil's Aeneas; Marlowe's stress on the more or less constant manipulation by both humans and deities required to get Aeneas to Italy can be seen as an on-stage representation of the work of adaptation performed by Marlowe in his recension of Virgil.

---

[3] For an excellent discussion of the play with particular reference to agency, see Clare Kinney, 'Epic Transgression and the Framing of Agency in *Dido, Queen of Carthage*', *Studies in English Literature 1500–1900* 40.2 (Spring 2000), 261–76.

[4] Simon Shepherd, *Marlowe and the Politics of Elizabethan Theatre* (Brighton: Harvester, 1986), 200. For a more recent discussion of the play as an interrogation of ideas about masculinity, see Alan Shepard, *Marlowe's Soldiers: Rhetorics of Masculinity in the Age of the Armada* (Aldershot: Ashgate, 2002).

The play abounds with examples of Aeneas's unfitness to be a hero, many of them comic. Here, I shall only look at the beginning of the second act, in which Aeneas first reaches Carthage. In both the poem and the play, the first thing he sees is the city walls of Carthage, which are decorated with scenes from the fall of Troy. The passage in the *Aeneid* is one of the most famous and often quoted passages in the entire poem. Here is part of Aeneas's speech to his companion Achates:

> *sunt hic etiam sua praemia laudi,*
> *sunt lacrimae rerum et mentem mortalia tangunt.*
> *solue metus; feret haec aliquam tibi fama salutem*

(Here then are the rewards of glory, here are the tears for what has happened and mortal affairs touch the mind. Dispel your fear; this renown may bring you some comfort; I.461–3.)

The artwork vividly and movingly recalls its bloody and tragic source, but transforms it into something that will help to bring about happier days. In looking backwards, Aeneas can also look forwards, a point that is made at greater length in the second and third books in his own narration of the fall of Troy and his wanderings.

In Marlowe's play, however, no such comfort is possible or, at least, Aeneas is not susceptible to the transformative power of art. Instead, he is overwhelmed by the pictures, something that has the effect of emphasizing the importance and power of visual representation in a theatrical performance. Marlowe transforms Aeneas's dignified tears into uncontrollable sobbing, and both his own son and Achates have to tell him to pull himself together. While Ascanius says only 'Sweete father leave to weepe' (2.1.35), Achates says '*Aeneas* see, here come the Citizens, / Leave to lament lest they laugh at our feares' (2.1.37–8). Aeneas cuts a noticeably poor figure here—something that is emphasized by the rags he wears—and Marlowe underlines this in Dido's first line to him: 'What stranger art thou that doest eye me thus' (2.1.74). In the *Aeneid*, the first meeting of the two is very different. Venus has restored Aeneas to his former beauty: '*restitit Aeneas claraque in luce refulsit / os umerosque deo similis*' (Aeneas stood there and shone in the bright light, his face and shoulders like a god's; I.588–9). The reaction of Virgil's Dido is also different: '*Obstipuit primo aspectu Sidonia Dido*' (Sidonian Dido was stunned at the first sight; I.613). The love that will follow and that will eventually destroy her has begun at this first moment.

In the play, however, Dido does not fall in love with Aeneas until she is forced to by Cupid, acting on Venus's commands. Marlowe's cruelly farcical staging of Dido's falling in love may rob her of the tragic stature she attains in the *Aeneid* and presents her as a victim, without the nobility of character that redeems tragic heroes and grants them their stature. In contrast, in the *Aeneid* Dido admits her love to her sister and then reaffirms her chastity:

agnosco ueteris uestigia flammae.
sed mihi uel tellus optem prius ima dehiscat
uel pater omnipotens adigat me fulmine ad umbras,
pallentis umbras Erebo noctemque profundam,
ante, pudor, quam te uiolo aut tua iura resoluo

(I recognize the traces of the old fire, but I would rather wish that the depths of the earth would open for me or that the all-powerful father would drive me with his thunderbolt to the shades, the pale shades and profound night of Erebus, before, Shame, I injure you or break your laws; IV.23–7.)

From this point on, Virgil's Dido is still a sympathetic figure, but she can nevertheless be considered culpable.

Marlowe's Dido has no equivalent speech, and the omission has the crucial effect of making her blameless in what happens. But in a sense Marlowe does not omit the speech altogether; instead, he writes an equivalent speech for Aeneas:

> With this my hand I give to you my heart,
> And vow by all the Gods of Hospitalitie,
> By heaven and earth, and my faire brothers bowe,
> By *Paphos, Capys,* and the purple Sea,
> From whence my radiant mother did descend,
> And by this Sword that saved me from the Greekes,
> Never to leave these newe upreared walles,
> Whiles *Dido* lives and rules in *Junos* towne,
> Never to like or love any but her   (3.4.43–51)

I have quoted the vow at length partly because of its many dramatic ironies—the odd reference to the gods of hospitality reminds us of Aeneas's mercenary nature, the reference to Cupid's bow reminds us that it was this bow that forced Dido to love him, the play's version of Aeneas's great narrative has made it clear that his sword had very little to do with his escape from the Greeks—but mainly because this speech is Marlowe's way of fixing the blame for the tragedy firmly on Aeneas. I think that this is the most important change Marlowe makes to the *Aeneid*. For the purposes of theatrical representation Marlowe was obliged to shorten drastically Aeneas's narrative; this promise to Dido is Aeneas's big speech in the play and thus takes the place that the story of the fall of Troy had in the poem.

In my discussion so far I have looked at the various ways in which Marlowe adapted the *Aeneid* for the stage. I want to close my discussion by looking at a passage that is simultaneously an adaptation and not an adaptation. This passage consists of six lines in Latin that Dido and Aeneas speak to each other in their parting scene:

> *Dido. Si bene quid de te merui, fuit aut tibi quidquam*
> *Dulce meum, miserere domum labentis: et istam*

Oro, si quis adhuc precibus locus, exue mentem
Aeneas. Desine meque tuis incendere teque querelis,
Italiam non sponte sequor.

(*Dido*. If I deserved well of you, if anything about me was sweet to you, take pity on a falling house: and this I pray, if there is still a place for prayers, put it out of your mind.

Aeneas. Cease to inflame yourself and me with your complaints, I do not seek Italy of my own will; 5.1.36–40.)[5]

There has been an extensive critical debate about why Marlowe included Latin lines in his play. Earlier critics tended to argue that he was inattentive or just careless; in 1977, however, Roma Gill suggested that 'Marlowe, perhaps more modest than he is usually thought to be, knew where he could not hope to excel'.[6] More recently, Clare Harraway has argued that 'It is...possible that the play recites its origins as a direct challenge to them'.[7] I think Harraway's argument is convincing: in reproducing the Latin—in refusing to *adapt* Virgil or even simply to translate him—Marlowe forces us to consider the extent to which the theatrical context he has provided for these lines is already enough to affect our understanding of them.

Perhaps most obviously, Aeneas's famous statement that he is not going to Italy 'sponte' (of his own will) is comic in a play that has frequently demonstrated how little will of his own Aeneas has demonstrated. As well, since Dido is the first to speak Latin, in his own speech Aeneas merely follows her and thus confirms our sense of him as someone who has little initiative of his own. But of course this is still an adaptation: Dido's lines are 317–19 of Book IV while Aeneas's are lines 360–1. What is more, Aeneas's lines are part of a long and moving speech, while Marlowe confines Aeneas in this scene to short and inadequate responses: he sounds petulant rather than dignified. What is more, many members of the play's audience would simply not have understood the Latin. They would have recognized it as Latin but would have been unable to follow what Dido and Aeneas are saying. We could say that the audience would experience this passage as form rather than content; another way to make this point is to say that the audience would experience these lines merely as sound, that is, as another aspect of theatrical presentation (like the importance of the visual) that a poem cannot convey.

My discussion of *Dido, Queen of Carthage* has suggested that Marlowe has in many ways profoundly refashioned his source and called attention to factors that become important in a theatrical version: the physical presence of the actors, for

---

[5] Dido also speaks Latin just before she kills herself: in fact, three of her last four lines are in Latin (5.1.310–11 and 313). I shall not discuss these here.

[6] Roma Gill, 'Marlowe's Virgil', *Review of English Studies* 28 (1977), 141–55 (153). Gill also has a useful summary of critical judgements on this point.

[7] Clare Harraway, *Re-citing Marlowe: Approaches to the Drama* (Aldershot: Ashgate, 2000), 109. See 108–38 for a good discussion of the play as an adaptation.

instance, as well as the abbreviation and reordering of many of the poem's elements. It is important to remember, however, that he was not the first to rewrite the character of Aeneas. Just over fifty years ago, Ethel Seaton demonstrated that Marlowe was able to draw on a strong medieval tradition in which Aeneas is portrayed as less than heroic and even as villainous.[8] Furthermore, Marlowe probably knew two plays on the subject from slightly earlier in the sixteenth century: Lodovico Dolce's *Didone* and Étienne Jodelle's *Didon se sacrifiant*, both of which take a critical view towards Aeneas's treatment of Dido. And in a recent article on Marlowe's play, Lucy Potter has convincingly argued that the *Aeneid* is already ambiguous, and especially so in its treatment of Aeneas himself.[9] In other words, we could say that *Dido, Queen of Carthage* has several sources rather than one: Virgil's *Aeneid* is only the first of many sources. The play thus stands as a useful corrective to the belief that a work's relationship to its source is dyadic: instead, there are many sources and perhaps no real original.

Poetaster

Nevertheless, *Dido, Queen of Carthage* has typically been seen as a work that is focused on the *Aeneid*, and Marlowe's attitude towards Virgil has typically been characterized as Ovidian.[10] This view rests on the assumption that Ovid and Virgil should be seen not primarily as near contemporaries but rather as rivals who represented radically different versions of what poetry should be. Whatever the claims to plausibility of this assumption, it is clearly a factor in Ben Jonson's *Poetaster*. Indeed, Tom Cain, the editor of the Revels edition, argues that *Poetaster*, which was first performed in 1601, represents Jonson's renunciation of the Ovidian model of poetry that had been so dominant in the 1590s and that was most famously exemplified by Marlowe.[11] The key support for this theory is Jonson's presentation of Ovid's disgrace; the argument is that Jonson endorses Augustus's opposition to sexual licence, a licence that was seen as typical of the poetry of the decade or so

[8] See Ethel Seaton, 'Marlowe's Light Reading', in *Elizabethan and Jacobean Studies Presented to Frank Percy Wilson*, ed. Herbert Davis and Helen Gardner (Oxford: Clarendon Press, 1959), 17–35.

[9] See Cope, 'Marlowe's *Dido* and the Titillating Children'.

[10] Perhaps the best statement of this prevalent belief is Patrick Cheney's *Marlowe's Counterfeit Profession: Ovid, Spenser, Counter-Nationhood* (Toronto: University of Toronto Press, 1997), 99–114.

[11] See Ben Jonson, *Poetaster*, ed. Tom Cain (Manchester: Manchester University Press, 1995), 19–23. For a useful comparison of the Ovid of this play with the Ovid in Jonson's later play *Epicoene*, see Joseph A. Dane, 'The Ovids of Ben Jonson in *Poetaster* and in *Epicoene*', in *Drama in the Renaissance: Comparative and Critical Essays*, ed. Clifford Davidson, C. J. Gianakaris, and John H. Stroupe (New York: AMS Press, 1986), 103–15. For a discussion of Jonson's feelings about the proliferation of print and about his relation to Marlowe, see Joseph Loewenstein, 'Personal Material: Jonson and Bookburning', in M. H. Butler, ed., *Re-presenting Ben Jonson: Text, History, Performance* (New York: St Martin's Press, 1999), 93–113, esp. 105–11.

before *Poetaster*.[12] But although Jonson obviously intended himself to be seen as Horace, the character of Ovid is actually more important for much of the play's first half, and whatever plot the play could be said to have is centred on him. In my discussion here, I want to begin with Ovid, as Jonson did, before turning to Virgil and to *Poetaster*'s famously emetic conclusion.

In one sense, *Poetaster*, like *Dido, Queen of Carthage*, has a classical source: the play is set in ancient Rome and most of the characters are famous from history: the most famous poets from the most famous era of Latin poetry as well as the emperor Augustus himself. On the other hand, unlike *Dido, Queen of Carthage* the play has no direct source: although translations of Ovid, Horace, and Virgil appear in the play and although the vomiting of words is adapted from Lucian, the plot is largely original to Jonson.[13] The play may be said to have a further source in what is often called the poetomachia among Jonson, Marston, Dekker, and other writers in the years before and after the appearance of *Poetaster*, and this is in a sense its true source. The poetomachia is not of particular interest to me here, but it is important that Jonson begins the play by denying this interpretation: in the Induction, Envy reacts with disappointed fury to the poem's setting: 'How might I force this to the present state?' (Induction, 34). The fact that the elaborate denial in the Induction would not deceive a more than usually stupid child is not especially important: what matters here to me is both the stress on the play's classical setting and the stress on interpretation.[14]

While the classical setting and, in particular, the presentation of himself as Horace give him a great advantage in his fight with his contemporaries, Jonson is not simply endorsing the ancients against the moderns. Instead, he also wants to make the typically Jonsonian point that classical learning must be accompanied by good judgement. The good reader must know not only how to read Latin but also how to judge it and how to make use of it in the present day: Latin vocabulary and literature should inform and enrich English, but pedantry should be avoided at all costs. We could say that this is Jonson's main point in *Poetaster*; I think that the best single illustration of this point comes when Crispinus says 'I am enamoured of this street now, more than of half of the streets of Rome again; 'tis so polite and terse' (3.1.32–3). The adjectives 'polite' (from '*polio*', I make glossy or smooth) and 'terse' (from '*tergeo*', I wipe) are certainly applicable to a well-maintained street, but only in Latin,

---

[12] There is no consensus about exactly how we are to take Augustus's severity. Perhaps the most interesting discussion is Alan Sinfield, '*Poetaster*, the Author, and the Perils of Cultural Production', *Renaissance Drama* 27 (1996), 3–18. A thorough discussion of the importance of Ovid to the play is James D. Mulvihill, 'Jonson's *Poetaster* and the Ovidian Debate', *SEL* 22 (1982), 239–55.

[13] Victoria Moul has recently argued that we should see *Poetaster* 'as a work both composed of and, in some sense, *about* the act of translation' (135). For Moul's detailed and perceptive analysis of the play see *Jonson, Horace and the Classical Tradition* (Cambridge: Cambridge University Press, 2010), 135–72.

[14] Many critics have discussed Jonson's focus on interpretation in *Poetaster*. I think the best recent account is Lynn S. Meskill, *Ben Jonson and Envy* (Cambridge: Cambridge University Press, 2009), 97–109.

since English has taken only the metaphorical meanings of these words. Here, as in the rest of the play, it is not that Crispinus is ignorant but that he does not how to use his education—in contrast to Jonson, and especially so at this point in the play, since the scene in question is Jonson's translation and expansion of the ninth poem in Horace's first book of satires. The dramatic irony is underscored by the fact that in this scene Crispinus is conspicuously neither polite nor terse.

Crispinus's inability to make proper use of his Latin vocabulary is a major failing in Jonson's eyes. For him, the classical heritage is not something merely to be learnt but rather something that requires a contemporary actively to engage with his source in a theatrical way. It is for this reason, I think, that Jonson begins the play with a scene of composition. As Ovid enters he says:

> *Thus, when this body falls in funeral fire,*
> *My name shall live, and my best part aspire.*
> It shall go so [*Writes*]   (1.1.1–3)

He is immediately interrupted by a servant; once the servant goes Ovid reads aloud the poem as a whole, prefacing it by saying: 'thus alone our ear shall better judge / The hasty errors of our morning Muse' (1.1.41–2). The poem is number fifteen of Ovid's first book of elegies. Its assertion of the enduring power of poetry would obviously have been dear to Jonson's heart, and that it was still a famous poem in his time demonstrates that Ovid's assertions are not empty boasts. But the fact that the poem is read in manuscript with the ink just dry demonstrates that poetry is something that takes work. What is more, while Jonson presumably aspires to some of the cachet of Latin poetry, the fact that the poem forms part of a dramatic speech demonstrates the subordination of the classical literary mode to the contemporary theatrical presentation.

In other words, this poem is not presented as something to be studied at school or read in an anthology but rather as something that is the result of what I have referred to as an active engagement: both the engagement of Ovid the character with his own text and Jonson's engagement with Ovid, an engagement that takes the form of a turn from poetry to theatre. Our sense of all this is increased because the poem is not actually Jonson's translation of Ovid's poem but rather Marlowe's, which is to say that it is the kind of active engagement with a source that we now call plagiarism; Jonson did only the sort of minor tinkering with his source with which we are all familiar from the more unfortunate undergraduate papers. The educated members of the audience might well have had in mind simultaneously the Latin original, Marlowe's translation, and Jonson's revisions. And while the fact that this poem was reproduced as one of Ovid's elegies indicates that the judgement to which Ovid refers was favourable, we also know that the poem continued to be judged favourably, to be thought worthy of translation, and to be thought worthy to open Jonson's play. That is to say that just as the composition of a poem takes work—and this work is of course increased both if the poem is translated and if the poem becomes part of a play—so judgement also takes work and may be a process spanning many centuries.

Although Jonson dramatizes two poems by Horace in the third act (the first is the encounter between Horace and Crispinus in the first half of the act; the second is 3.5, although this scene does not appear until the folio and is not thought to have been part of the original performance),[15] the next translation to be presented as poetry is Virgil's reading of a passage from the *Aeneid* in the second scene of the fifth act. By Act 5 the plot of the play has more or less concluded, and it seems that this final act is intended to show what real poetry is. Unsurprisingly, Virgil is presented as the greatest of the Roman poets, inspiring the respect of the Emperor himself. In the first scene, Augustus, Tibullus, Gallus, and Horace gather to discuss Virgil. The scene, in which a group of characters exchange platitudes about morality, is not especially dramatic, but it is important to Jonson insofar as it models appropriate responses to poetry. Perhaps the most important comment is made by Horace, who begins by saying 'I judge him of a rectified spirit' (5.1.100). As Act 4 ended with Ovid's disgrace on the grounds of sexual immorality, it is important to Jonson to show that however excellent Ovid may have been as a poet, critical judgement should always include moral evaluation of writers as well as literary appreciation of their works.

Virgil is important to Jonson here not just because he was considered the greatest of the Latin poets, and perhaps the greatest poet of all time, but also because the *Aeneid* was an unfinished work; indeed, Virgil famously left instruction in his will that the manuscript should be destroyed. As was the case in the first scene, Jonson points to the labour involved in poetry. The passage Virgil reads is lines 160–88 of Book IV. This is the scene in which Dido and Aeneas have sex for the first time—an act that will ultimately bring disaster to Dido—although the stress in this passage is not so much on her eventual death but rather on the rapidity with which Fama spreads the news of this sexual act throughout Carthage and on the birth of Fama. Both aspects of this passage—the condemnation of the illicit sex of Dido and Aeneas and the speed with which all things become public—are of course crucial to *Poetaster*. The first acts as an implicit comment on what many people might be tempted to regard as the excusable behaviour of Ovid and Julia and their guests in the preceding act; the second reflects the atmosphere of Jonson's Rome, in which everyone seems to know everything, even things that are not true. The Rome of *Poetaster* is a city in which everyone sits in judgement on everyone, and part of Jonson's task is to demonstrate what rational judgement (like the conversation about Virgil before his reading) would look like.

The scene as a whole is not a success as drama—one could call it slightly creaky— although the image of Virgil enthroned above the other actors and declaiming verse is an impressive spectacle. The most serious problem with this part of the scene is

---

[15] See Jonson, *Poetaster*, 287.

the translation itself. While the translation of Ovid's poem is essentially Marlowe's, and thus is good, and while the attempts to dramatize Horace are quite clever (if not entirely successful as drama), the translation of Virgil is an unmitigated disaster.[16] Jonson makes Virgil sound as if he were no better a poet than, say, Silius Italicus. If Virgil's poetry were really at the level of Jonson's translation of it, he would never have been a famous poet. Jonson's failure here is curious. Since the first scene demonstrates that he was not above a kind of plagiarism, I cannot understand why he did not simply use someone else's translation. There were several available to him, all much better than his. And his failure to translate Virgil adequately is not only a poetic failure: it is also a failure of judgement—the very quality whose importance Jonson has stressed throughout the play. If Jonson thought that his translation of Virgil adequately supported his claim that Virgil represents the peak of poetic achievement, then his own judgement cannot be trusted.

And yet if we cannot trust Jonson's judgement on poetry, then the play's dénouement does not work. The final scene shows him, as Horace the true poet (Jonson was not handicapped by either modesty or subtlety), correcting the errors of the poetaster Crispinus by means of a pill that forces him to vomit up all the words to which Horace has taken exception. After this purgation, Virgil gives Crispinus advice about which authors he should use as models and which he should avoid. Suitably, the advice is couched in culinary terms: Cato and Terence are fit to be imbibed, for example, while Plautus and Ennius are 'meats / Too harsh for a weak stomach' (5.3.530–1). We could say that the governing metaphor here is of the literary source—and, by extension, of learning as a whole—as a food source, and this metaphor should not seem strange to us if we think of the literal meaning of 'alma mater'. What is ingenious here is Jonson's return to the etymology of education as 'leading out'. Here what is led out (violently) is not the inherent talent or understanding of the pupil but rather the vocabulary that testifies to Crispinus's having absorbed various literary sources without the accompanying judgement that would have allowed him to distinguish the good from the bad.

I have already suggested that Jonson's translation of Virgil should lead us to doubt his literary judgement, and of course literary judgement is one of the most important criteria in the world of the play. Another important criterion, although it is implicit, is the judgement of literary time. Here, Jonson stacks the deck by setting his play in what was then the most celebrated era of literary production in all of history and by assigning himself the role of one of the most highly regarded poets of this era. But the judgement of time does not work in his favour in this scene. Here are the words vomited by Crispinus: retrograde, reciprocal, incubus, glibbery, lubrical, defunct, magnificate, chilblained, clumsy, puffy, inflate, turgidous, ventositous,

---

[16] For a more sympathetic treatment of Virgil's reading, see Margaret Tudeau-Clayton, 'Scenes of Translation in Jonson and Shakespeare: *Poetaster*, *Hamlet*, and *A Midsummer Night's Dream*', *Translation and Literature* 11 (2002), 1–23.

Interestingly, Moul sees Jonson's translation of Virgil as containing numerous allusions to *Dido, Queen of Carthage*; see Moul, *Jonson, Horace and the Classical Tradition*, 160–5.

oblatrant, furibund, fatuate, strenuous, prorumpt, clutched, and obstupefact. There are also five pairs of words: spurious snotteries, barmy froth, conscious damp, snarling guts, and quaking custard. About half of these are still in use, and while some are either formal or colloquial, others are now common words. Many of the ones that did not succeed are to be missed: I especially regret glibbery and oblatrant. These are matters of taste; the survival of some words rather than others is the luck of the draw, and that is precisely my point. In returning to a classical source, Jonson sought the authority to pass an authoritative judgement on proper English style, but it turns out that for us Marston and Dekker are as good a source as he is.

Pericles

At first glance, *Pericles* might seem to pose few problems for a study of source material, since Shakespeare begins the play by having the author of his source appear on stage: 'To sing a song that old was sung / From ashes ancient Gower is come' (1.1–2). In fact, the situation is much more complicated than it appears, for Gower was *not* the first author but simply one of many people to tell the story. Roger Warren, the play's editor, points out that there are two important Latin sources from the middle ages: Godfrey of Viterbo's *Pantheon* and the *Gesta Romanorum*. The former is the source of Gower's version in his *Confessio Amantis*; the latter, of Laurence Twine's prose version in *The Pattern of Painful Adventures* from 1576.[17] The play follows the *Confessio Amantis* fairly closely, but the contemporary audience would have been aware of other versions; there is a sense in which the character of Gower could be described as merely the presenter of the story rather than its real author, in the sense that Virgil is the real author of the *Aeneid*.[18] That is, to name Gower as the author of the work may be somewhat arbitrary—we could say that rather than being the author he embodies the author function—and in identifying his play's source as a medieval English poem, Shakespeare may be seeking to give *Pericles* a higher status than it would have if the source were a folk tale or a relatively recent English prose work.[19]

[17] See William Shakespeare, *Pericles*, ed. Suzanne Gossett (London: Arden Shakespeare, 2004) and George Wilkins, *Pericles*, ed. Roger Warren (Oxford: Oxford University Press, 2003), 13.

[18] For a discussion of the difference between the poet Gower and the play's Gower, see Stephen Lynch, 'The Authority of Gower in Shakespeare's *Pericles*', *Mediaevalia* 16 (1993), 361–78. For a discussion of what Gower would have meant to the contemporary audience, see Christine Dymkowski, 'Ancient [and modern] Gower: Presenting Shakespeare's *Pericles*', in Philip Butterworth, ed., *The Narrator, the Expositor, and the Prompter in European Medieval Theatre* (Turnhout: Brepols, 2007), 235–64, and Helen Cooper, ' "This worthy olde writer": *Pericles* and other Gowers, 1592–1640', in Siân Echard, ed., *A Companion to Gower* (Cambridge: D. S. Brewer, 2004), 99–113.

[19] On the other hand, Warren suggests (in my opinion, persuasively) that the name Pericles may be intended to suggest Pyrocles, the hero of the *Arcadia*. Sidney's work was extremely popular at the time, so this would have been a shrewd move. Furthermore, the decision to change the protagonist's name from Apollonius to Pericles is certainly inexplicable otherwise. See *Pericles*, 16–20.

A further complication in the choice of *Pericles* for a discussion of theatrical sources is that the play does not have a stable form or even a stable author; this is in marked contrast with *Dido, Queen of Carthage* and *Poetaster*, both of which have relatively simple textual histories. The original source of the play we call *Pericles* is an unusually bad quarto edition, and the play was not even included in the First Folio. In order to produce a text that can be used for study or performance, editors have resorted to a number of stratagems. The edition I have chosen accepts the hypothesis that the play was co-written by Shakespeare and a minor writer named George Wilkins and has fleshed out the text with additions from Wilkins's prose work *The Painful Adventures of Pericles Prince of Tyre*, which appeared the year after the play and was what we would now call a novelization. Unsurprisingly, this particular strategy has not been universally accepted. To cite Shakespeare as the source of a play is in effect to say that the play is exceptionally good and should be frequently read and performed; to cite George Wilkins as its source is to declare that the play is at most of historical interest. Thus, even before we turn to the play itself —insofar as such a thing could be said to exist—we find the notion of source problematized in more than one way.[20]

The presentation of Gower in the play certainly positions him as the source: he uses a number of words that had become archaic by the early seventeenth century, and many of his lines are in the tetrameter couplets that would also have appeared rather old-fashioned. But he does not speak in Middle English: his dialect bears the same relationship to its source in fourteenth-century spoken English as the play does to its original sources. Shakespeare and Wilkins want their play to have a certain historical flavour but not at the cost of being unintelligible or of seeming like a real medieval play. In his speeches, Gower strikes a similar balance between the contemporary and the historical. His function is most obviously to give the spectators crucial information about the background of the story and the connections between one scene and the next—and he certainly does a great deal of this— but he also serves to point out the differences between a play and its source. From this point of view Gower's role could be said to be metatheatrical, but it might be more accurate to characterize the play as a whole as a meta-adaptation, as a text that is centrally concerned with the differences between a poem and a play. From this point of view, Gower can be seen as a referee (admittedly, a biased one), adjudicating the respective merits of poetical and theatrical presentation of a narrative.

As I have just pointed out, Gower gives a great deal of useful information: in the first speech he introduces himself and sets up the story; in the final speech he sums up the events of the play with the moralizing that one would expect from him. But

---

[20] For Warren's discussion of his own editorial stratagems and theories, see *Pericles*, 2–8. I chose Warren's edition more or less at random and without any real stake in the debate: any editor of the play would have to have come up with some way of making the text coherent. Warren's method has the merit of ingenuity and, in its pairing of Shakespeare and Wilkins, of troubling our sense of what it means to cite Shakespeare as the source of a play.

he often does more or less than give useful information, and sometimes the information he gives is not what one would have expected. Once he has introduced himself in the first speech, for instance, he does not mention either Pericles or Tyre; instead, the setting is Antioch and we are told of Antiochus and his incestuous affair with his beautiful daughter. It is Antiochus himself who introduces Pericles in his first line. I would argue that the fact that the duties of exposition are divided between Gower and Antiochus points to a certain insufficiency in Gower: the source is not enough to understand the play. A similar point is made by Gower himself when he tells us that many of the daughter's suitors died trying to win her and then says 'As yon grim looks do testify' (1.40), gesturing towards the decapitated heads adorning the stage. This line represents an important turn to the visual—that is, to an aspect of the story that the play can provide but that the poem cannot; Gower underlines this turn in the final couplet of his first speech: 'What now ensues, to the judgement of your eye / I leave my cause, who best can justify' (1.41–2).

The theme is continued in Gower's second speech. After summarizing the events of the previous scenes, Gower says that 'tidings.../ Are brought your eyes. What need speak I?' (5.15–16). But while his first speech is followed by dialogue, this speech is followed by a dumb show, and, as Christine Dymkowski points out, the dumb show 'would in fact be unintelligible without [Gower's] explanation'.[21] In this case, then, the source turns out to be necessary after all, and dramatic presentation (admittedly of a kind that may have appeared old-fashioned to an early seventeenth-century audience) is shown to be inadequate.[22] For instance, the dumb show shows Pericles talking to Cleon, receiving a letter, showing the letter to Cleon, rewarding the messenger, and leaving. Gower adds the important facts that the letter is from Helicanus, that Pericles has been followed to Tarsus by an envoy from Antiochus who intends to kill him, and that Pericles decides to leave by sea. So although the dumb show does not appear to contain anything remarkable, Gower is able to point out that the information in the letter is crucial to the plot and then to add the information that the ship is torn apart by storms, that Pericles is washed ashore, and that this shipwreck (like Aeneas's in Book I of the *Aeneid*) will actually turn out to be good news for him.

But what has perhaps appeared to represent the ascendancy of the written source over the visual enactment does not last long. On his first appearance, Gower ended his speech before the scene he had described began, in this way creating a fairly clear demarcation between his speech and the action of the play itself.[23] In this case, however, Gower is forced to cut his speech short:

---

[21] Dymkowski, 'Ancient [and modern] Gower', 245.

[22] On the convention of the dumb show see Jeremy Lopez's essay in this collection.

[23] Directors have sometimes chosen to keep Gower on stage throughout the performance, a choice that would reduce the contrast between his speeches and the rest of the play. For good performance histories, see Warren, ed., *Pericles*, 20–30 and Dymkowski, 'Ancient [and modern] Gower', 248–64.

> Till fortune, tired with doing bad,
> Threw him ashore to give him glad.
> [*Enter Pericles wet*]
> And here he comes. What shall be next
> Pardon old Gower; this 'longs the text   (5.37–40)

In this scene, then, Gower does not introduce the action of the play but is instead interrupted by it. The visual enactment—in this case, the appearance of the epony-mous character dripping wet and naked—trumps the rhyming summary. After the interruption Gower humbly asks for pardon and recedes into the background once again.

Our sense of Gower's apology here is admittedly complicated by the fact that it is not entirely clear what he means when he says 'this 'longs the text'. In her recent Arden Shakespeare edition of *Pericles*, Suzanne Gossett has a very helpful footnote at this point; she calls the line 'an example of aural ambiguity, not merely a reporting error. . . . If 'longs' = lengthens, *this* refers in a deprecating manner to the chorus. If, as is more likely, 'longs' = 'longs, i.e. belongs to, *this* refers to the subsequent action and the line parallels the conclusion of Gower's other cho-ruses (222, note to 2.0.40).[24] My personal feeling is that the word means both 'belongs to' and 'lengthens', but that the former meaning is primary. I think that the 'text' in this sense is not, as we might expect, the written playtext but rather a text in the sense of 'the original form and order, as distinguished from a com-mentary, marginal or other, or from annotations' (*OED* text *n*.1 2.b.). In this respect, the final couplet of this speech differs from the conclusion of Gower's other speeches in being an unambiguous concession of the primacy of the dra-matic version of the story: the source of the play is no longer the real text but now only a gloss on it.

As if to underline this point, most of the rest of Gower's speeches (there are eight in total) are chiefly confined to summary and moralization. To mark this transi-tion to a role closer to that of the Chorus in *Henry V*, for instance, in Gower's next speech there is a dumb show that gives valuable information that the audience can understand without his help. Thus, rather than being a mode of dramatic presenta-tion dependent on Gower, the visual enactment of the story becomes self-suffi-cient. Nevertheless, once again the dominance of the visual mode is not complete. In the fifth and sixth scenes, Gower points out the inadequacy of dramatic repre-sentation. In the sixth, for instance, he says to the audience 'In your supposing once more put your sight' (20.21) and thus, as Dymkowski points out, he 'prob-lematizes the nature of enactment'.[25] A similar problematization occurred in his previous speech, when he commented on the dumb show that depicted Dionyza and Cleon pretending to mourn for Marina by saying 'See how belief may suffer by

---

[24] Gossett, ed., *Pericles*, 222, n. to 2.0.40.
[25] Dymkowski, 'Ancient [and modern] Gower', 247.

foul show' (18.23). Gower reminds us that we still rely on him to tell the truth of the visual representation.

In his fifth speech Gower also comments more explicitly than at any other time in the play on his role in telling the story. He begins by saying 'Thus time we waste, and long leagues make we short' (18.1) and goes on to comment, rather oddly, on the fact that the play is in English: 'By you being pardoned, we commit no crime / To use one language in each several clime' (18.5–6). Although Gower shows deference to the audience—it is their imagination that can make the stage seem like Antioch or any of the play's other settings and it is their pardon that he requires—he nevertheless stresses that what they hear comes from him:

> I do beseech you
> To learn of me, who stand i'th'gaps to teach you
> The stages of our story   (18.7–9)

In a sense, the image of gaps returns to the idea of the play as the main text and Gower as someone writing in the margin or gaps of the manuscript. The reference to 'the stages of our story' draws attention to the fact that, as F. David Hoeniger points out, 'Shakespeare, or whoever designed the play, chose to follow the order of Gower's original narrative and his characters most of the time with singular subservience'—something that is at odds with Shakespeare's usual strategies of adaptation.[26]

Pericles suggests that however different a play may be from its source, the source is still necessary: we still need the writing in the gaps. Indeed, all three plays suggest this to one extent or another. The sources from which these playwrights adapted their plays are not replaced by the plays they inspired; instead, what results is a kind of dialogue between each play and its source, or sources. This dialogue may seem essentially confrontational, as in *Dido, Queen of Carthage*, or essentially respectful, as in *Poetaster*; the dialogue is also a dialogue between the writers and the times in which they write. *Poetaster* probably demonstrates this most clearly, but to some extent each of these plays foregrounds the differences between the relatively low status genre of drama and the higher status genre of poetry which provided so many of the plots of Renaissance drama: each of these plays sets up an implicit comparison between its source, as a text that has stood the test of time, and itself, as a text that might not pass this test. Furthermore, each of these plays engages the question of whether plays are to be merely adaptations or whether they are to be works of literature that can stand on their own. I ended with *Pericles* partly because it is the latest chronologically, but also because it most explicitly raises these questions and because it raises them without ultimately answering them.

---

[26] David F. Hoeniger, 'Gower and Shakespeare in *Pericles*', *Shakespeare Quarterly* 33 (1982), 461–79. Hoeniger also points out that the final act of the play is the most dependent on Gower's presence (466–7); we could interpret this as a further act of resistance on Gower's part.

FURTHER READING

Dillon, Sarah. *The Palimpsest: Literature, Criticism, Theory* (London: Continuum, 2007).

Greene, Thomas M. *Light in Troy: Imitation and Discovery in Renaissance Poetry* (New Haven: Yale University Press, 1982).

Quint, David. *Origin and Originality in Renaissance Literature: Versions of the Source* (New Haven: Yale University Press, 1983).

CHAPTER 8

INTERTHEATRICALITY

WILLIAM N. WEST

Just before the newly crowned Henry V comes on-stage for the first time, in the second of the three plays in which Shakespeare included him, his Chief Justice expresses anxiety about the new ruler. His companion agrees: 'Indeede I thinke the yong King loves you not' (1597; *Henry IV, Part Two*, 5.2, 2783).[1] And indeed, when he appears, the new King Henry expresses his anger at the Justice:

> ...how might a prince of my great hopes forget,
> So great indignities you laid upon me?
> What, rate, rebuke, and roughly send to prison
> Th'immediate heire of England? (5.2, 2841–4)

A few lines later the justice makes the history of their dislike explicit: 'Your Highnesse pleased to forget my place, / ... And strooke me in my very seat of judgement' (5.2, 2850, 2853).

How did we miss this? Easily, it turns out: the gesture the scene is built around is nowhere in the play. Its fullest explanation is thrown away in a line four acts earlier, when Falstaff's page introduces the Justice as 'the noble man that committed the prince for striking him about Bardolfe' (1.2, 308–9) and Falstaff mentions 'the boxe of th'yere that the Prince gave you' (1.2, 445–6). No more is said of it. Because these scenes occur in the second part of a two-part play, we might assume that the striking of the chief justice took place in the first part. But it is not in *Henry IV, Part One* (1597), either, although that play perhaps recalls another of its outcomes, when King Henry complains to his son that 'Thy place in counsell thou hast rudely lost' (3.2, 1773), without explaining why.

---

[1] Except as otherwise noted, references to Shakespeare's plays are to *The Complete Works, Original-Spelling Edition*, ed. Stanley Wells and Gary Taylor (Oxford: Clarendon Press, 1986), providing act and scene numbers with through-lineation by play. Dates of the first performance of plays are given parenthetically at their first mention.

Here is what seems to have happened, according to several written accounts that Shakespeare may have used in composing these plays. One of the Prince's men was remanded to the Chief Justice for theft. The Prince asked that the man be released to his control; the Justice refused; the Prince struck the Justice. For this offence, the Justice had the Prince arrested and the King suspended his son from his Council. Modern editions of the plays usually refer their readers to earlier written sources to explain the backstory, as I have just done.[2] This thoroughly textual approach makes the referent of these suggestive lines and lacunas a mystery to be explicated; one finds a crux that resists comprehension and then sifts backwards for something to explain it. But there is another vantage from which the striking of the judge could be recalled. We tend to forget that the early modern playhouse was not always mediated by texts, as it is for us.[3] Early audiences seem to have understood what they saw there as a reverberant constellation of speeches, gestures, and interactions rather than as neatly circumscribed plays: in the Induction to *The Taming of the Shrew* (1592), for instance, the drunken Christopher Sly recalls a line from *The Spanish Tragedy* (1587), 'go by S. Ieronimie' (Ind. 1, 7), but does not recognize the Latinate word 'comedy' (Ind. 2, 62), familiar from the printed titles of plays but not necessarily from their performances. A playgoer might well—might better, perhaps—have remembered seeing Prince Harry strike the chief justice on another stage.

One such moment occurs in an earlier play performed by the Queen's Men, the anonymous *Famous Victories of Henry V* (before 1588), in which the Prince intervenes in a trial to save one of his men from hanging for stealing. When the justice refuses to release the thief, the Prince *'gives him a box on the ear'* (4.sd85).[4] So resonant was this gesture that it seems to have been able to leap from performance to performance, without any need for textual transmission. *Tarltons Jests* remembers one particular enactment, where the blow itself is impossible to locate fully:

> At the Bull at Bishops-gate was a Play of *Henry* the fift, wherein the Judge was to take
> a boxe on the eare, and because he was absent that should take the blow, *Tarlton* him-
> selfe (euer forward to please) tooke upon him to play the same Judge, besides his owne

[2] William Shakespeare, *The First Part of King Henry IV*, ed. A. R. Humphreys, Arden, 2nd edn. (London: Methuen, 1960), xxix–xxxvi, and *The Second Part of King Henry IV*, ed. A. R. Humphreys, Arden, 2nd edn. (London: Methuen, 1966), xxxviii–xliii, cites Holinshed (1587), Stowe's *Annales* (1592), Elyot's *Governour* (1531), as well as *Famous Victories*, although tellingly wonders how Shakespeare could have *read* the last (*First Part*, xxiv).

[3] Erika Lin, *Shakespeare and the Materiality of Performance* (New York: Palgrave Macmillan, 2012), 13, compares the size of print runs for plays to calculations of playhouse attendance and suggests that upwards of 97 per cent of all encounters with plays would have been in performance.

[4] Seymour M. Pitcher, *The Case for Shakespeare's Authorship of 'The Famous Victorie'* (New York: State University of New York Press, 1961), sc. 4, ll.30–1. The play remained popular: Henslowe records performances of 'Harry the v' in 1595 and 1596 in *Henslowe's Diary*, ed. R. A. Foakes, 2nd edn. (Cambridge: Cambridge University Press, 2002), 33–4, 36–7, 47–8. The earliest extant edition is from 1598 (although the Stationers' Register lists one in 1594) and thus not available when *Henry IV, Part Two* was first played.

part of the Clowne: and *Knell* then playing *Henry* the fift, hit *Tarlton* a sound boxe indeed, which made the people laugh the more, because it was he: but anone the Judge goes in, and immediatly *Tarlton* (in his Clownes cloathes) comes out, and askes the Actors what newes? O saith one, hadst thou beene here, thou shouldst haue seene Prince *Henry* hit the Judge a terribly [sic] boxe on the eare. What man, said *Tarlton* strike a Judge? It is true yfaith, said the other: no other like, said *Tarlton*, and it could not be but terrible to the Judge, when the report so terrifies me, that me thinkes the blow remaines still on my cheeke, that it burnes againe...[5]

If players and playgoers had already seen the prince strike the justice elsewhere, there is no need to ferret out the meaning of the Justice's lines in *Henry IV, Part Two*, because it is available to those at the play as a remembered gesture. It is no longer a mystery to be solved, but a present memory of another theatrical moment. Such a memory is not wholly past. It informs the present scene, and points towards future recollections, repetitions, and re-actions.

Once we remember the theatrical context for the buffet, the unspoken, unseen incident of the Prince's striking of the Chief Justice starts to seem surprisingly pervasive in Shakespeare's plays about Henry. Although it is never directly performed or even described, it is referred to and discussed, it motivates certain actions and moods, and it is even re-enacted throughout *Henry IV, Part One* and *Part Two*, and *Henry V*. But the blow itself exercises its action at a distance and remains elusive as an event. The encounter of the Justice and the former Prince in *Henry IV, Part Two* is full of puns that, in the context of the memory, recall a box on the ear without actually naming it: the Justice will '*arme*' himself against 'the condition of the time' (5.2, 2784–5, my emphases throughout); Warwick worries that the new king will require the nobility to '*strike* sail to spirites of vile sort' (5.2, 2792). The new King reconciles with the judge by offering 'There is my *hand*', and promising him 'mine *eare*' (5.2, 2890, 2892). *Henry IV, Part One* seems almost pointedly to skip over the occasion of the blow, enacting the Gadshill robbery (2.2) and Falstaff's hyperbolic report of it (2.5, 1045–1155), but omitting the scene of Harry's violent encounter with the Justice. In its place, the play substitutes a short interview between the Prince and the Sheriff—an office with a very different jurisdiction—in which Harry promises to resolve everything according to his own sense of justice rather than being called to account on another's: 'if he have robd these men, / He shall be answerable, and so farewell' (2.5, 1453–4). If we remember the blow from somewhere else, this exchange seems almost to emphasize its absence.

The episode seems to be recalled again in *Henry V*, when the King arranges for Fluellen to 'purchase him[self] a box a' th' eare' (4.7, 2585) from Williams, whom Henry challenged while wandering in disguise among the troops. Not the blow itself, but a related recollection of action occurs in *Sir John Oldcastle* (1599), where

---

[5] *Tarltons Iests* (London: John Budge, 1613), C2v–C3r.

one character remarks several times that 'the King has beene a Theefe himselfe';
even the King describes himself as a 'perfect night-walker'.[6] *Oldcastle* is partly a
response to Shakespeare's characterization of Falstaff, that 'old lad of the castle'
(*Henry IV, Part One*, 1.2, 148), and it firmly links King Harry to Falstaff, Poins, and
Peto, 'all my old theeves' (*Oldcastle*, F2v) who share one of his early vocations. But
'night-walker' seems also to glance at the 'little touch of *Harry* in the Night' (4.0.47)
from Shakespeare's *Henry V*, which had yet not been published except in and as
performance.[7]

Such omissions and misdirections have the insistence of a Freudian slip, pointing
us towards something they do not express. They recall actions, but they also direct
new ones, either repetitions or reactions of different kinds. Within a single play,
such repetitions are contained; they can be viewed as markers of the play's thematic
coherence, foreshadowing, or patterns of imagery, which of course they may be. But
when they recur between plays, it is harder to know what to make of them. One
possible response is to posit that the play is not the basic unit of early modern theatricality, and not the most privileged one. Prince Harry's mobile misdeeds suggest
a different model for understanding plays: as networks of traceable elements of
action, the form and pressures of which have left their mark in more fixed media
like scripts and texts.

The actions that make playing are elusive, especially in media other than their
own. They are transmitted most readily, although always imprecisely, through performance itself. Their relations to one another are necessarily less direct and less
clearly focused than traditional, textually based study of sources or allusions have
imagined them to be. To follow them is to trace the unconscious of theatre, with its
unthought at work in what is repeated and varied from performance to performance without being logically articulated to the plot or the play. To approach the
theatre of Shakespeare's era in this way also offers new methods for describing how
the players, playwrights, and audiences collaborated in doing the work of the theatre and in reflecting upon it. Instead of reading the historical record of early modern theatricality as a collection of allusions and references, it opens the possibility
of understanding theatre as made out of other performances. Rather than seeing
different patterns and forms of performance as variations on a fixed type—the brag-
gart soldier, the clever page, the plain speaker—it understands them as belonging
to a horizontally organized repertoire, never completed and slowly changing, of
lines, gestures, characters, situations, genres, and other smaller elements that

[6] *Sir John Oldcastle* (London: T[homas] P[avier], 1600 [for 1619]), D1r, F2v.
[7] Both *Oldcastle* and the quarto *Henry V* were first printed in 1600 for Thomas Pavier, but by differ-
ent printers. On performance as *publishing*, e.g. the Letters Patent of 10 May, 1574, allowing Leicester's
Men 'to shew publish exercise and occupy to their best commodity' in the city of London, see M. C.
Bradbrook, *The Rise of the Common Player* (London: Chatto & Windus, 1964), 55, citing *Malone
Society Collections* I: 3, 262–3.

cumulatively allow for new performances and new concatenations of actions. Let us call this way of looking at playing its 'intertheatricality'.[8]

Intertheatricality is theatre from the bottom up. It is recognizing how performances are made up out of other performances, treating performance as its own archive. Intertheatricality describes how theatrical performance thinks about itself, within its own medium. Intertheatricality takes note of how performance refuses to accept a local habitation and a name, even in its most local habitations and names. It is recalling or re-enacting that is neither wholly allusive nor wholly citational, in the sense that it does not primarily point towards a *single* past performance, much less an original one. To look for intertheatricality—to look in an 'intertheatrical' way—is to seek shared memories of actions that can be called up to thicken present performances, like the box on the justice's ear. Looking at playing intertheatrically means attending to the replayings of elements of performance, like costumes, gestures, phrases, or situations, within, for us, the theatre of early modern England. Intertheatricality resists subordinating such instances to organizing structures external to them, but instead traces how they spread horizontally in the enaction of new performances. Intertheatricality requires noting how the elements organize the system. This casts plays, or plots, or genres, or histories, or ideologies, as mobile, open compositions of instances recovered and replayed variously from other performances. To approach plays in this way is to understand them as nodes in an active relay of gestures, characters, situations, genres, and other elements, of activity and as partakers in a much wider range of other performances.

The play, in other words, is *not* the thing, or not the only one; looked at intertheatrically, Elizabethan performance seizes not on a unified plot but on the discrete elements—the scenes, phrases, words, and gestures—that the play could either order into a narrative arc or deploy singly, as recognizable set pieces. However artfully combined, the play remained the parts of its sum. The plot the players had was not an Aristotelian *muthos* or a conceptual order that governs the play; it was a schema of entrances, exits, music cues, and props that let the play run from scene to scene—not an overview, in other words, but a breakdown.[9] Plays became whole

---

[8] The term *intertheatricality* has been used by Jacky Bratton, *New Readings in Theatre History* (Cambridge: Cambridge University Press, 2003), 37–8, and by Jonathan Gil Harris, *Untimely Matter in the Time of Shakespeare* (Philadelphia: University of Pennsylvania Press, 2009), both of whom emphasize how theatrical means are ways of reflecting on theatre history. Anston Bosman's intertheatre treats the mobility of plays across cultural differences ('Renaissance Intertheater and the Staging of Nobody', *ELH* 71 [2004], 559–85). Many other writers have looked at performance continuities under other terms; see Further Reading.

[9] David Bradley, *From Text to Performance in the Elizabethan Theatre: Preparing the Play for the Stage* (Cambridge: Cambridge University Press, 1992); Henry Turner, *The English Renaissance Stage: Geometry, Poetics, and the Practical Spatial Arts* (Oxford: Oxford University Press, 2006), 173–5. This is also true of other 'playhouse documents'; see Tiffany Stern, *Documents of Performance in Early Modern England* (Cambridge: Cambridge University Press, 2009).

only in playing. Ultimately, to look intertheatrically is to unfix *plays* from more linear and exact relations with their precursors and inheritors, to let them blur and expand into a weblike institution of *playing*, a system of nodes and concentrations rather than discrete pieces, so as to study more closely how theatre reflects on its histories, its current means and capacities, and its potentialities.

No theatrical gesture (and few non-theatrical ones) can claim real spontaneity. All are more or less stylized and codified; all come with pasts; as Marvin Carlson notes, the theatre is haunted.[10] But intertheatrical actions foreground their isolatability and iterability, their participation in the network of theatre. Their mimetic relation to what they replay means they cannot be paraphrased, nor can they be traced or restored to a determining point of origin. They strike the Wittgensteinian bedrock of 'this is what we do', not to insist coercively that what we do must be so, but to call it into question. Is this what we do? Why do we do that? How else might it be done? These actions can be compressed or reframed, transformed if not reduced; that is, their transformation recalls earlier transformations and deformations without simply repeating them. The intertheatrical is thus simultaneously familiar—we see in it *this is what we do*, or *this is what was done*—and estranging—by pointedly replaying the familiar it calls attention to its preterativity. By evoking another performance, intertheatrical moments in early modern plays call on their audiences to witness for them, making the audiences, as it were, responsible for elaborations or explanations that the plays omit.[11]

This evocation of memory outlines a shared, fuzzily defined, physically and temporally dislocated experience that it also defines as particularly theatrical. This experience extends beyond the instantiation of any single moment, not to become timeless but to define the sense of timeliness itself, the rhythms and interruptions that make sequencing possible. The question an intertheatrical approach raises is not 'what does it mean?' but, 'how is this system organized so as to be meaningful?' Meaning—thought, consciousness, cognition, understanding—is one ongoing product of the early modern system of playing. But so were plays themselves, understood as the commodity around which the economic and cultural institutions of playing developed. Plays organize themselves through iterations and interrelations of actions; intertheatricality is consequently theatre's own theatre history, not a representation or reflection of a history given elsewhere but a history *made* by plays distancing themselves from performances that they designate as past and superseded. Intertheatricality thus describes the 'play' itself as a self-fashioning, not merely as a medium within which other selves might fashion themselves. It is the

---

[10] Marvin Carlson, *The Haunted Stage: The Theatre as Memory Machine* (Ann Arbor: University of Michigan Press, 2001).

[11] This strategy of representation is most familiar from *Henry V*, but it was widespread. See Alan C. Dessen, 'Thomas Heywood and the Playgoer's Imagination', in *Acts of Criticism: Performance Matters in Shakespeare and his Contemporaries* (Cranbury: Associated University Presses, 2006), 46–57.

closest that plays come to showing themselves as both *a play* (a fiction) and as *playing* (activity).

Intertheatricality orients us towards performance as an autopoietic system directed as much towards a making-possible of future performances as towards a history of given ones. An examination of Elizabethan and Jacobean playtexts that looks forward and sideways, as I propose here, yields a different picture than one that looks back. It implies a shift from a notion of *allusion*—which produces complexity of meaning by juxtaposing two or more *texts*—to a notion of the *analogue* as a resource of theatrical possibility, familiarity, and difference. A complete examination of early modern intertheatricality would include, from smaller to larger, instances at the level of the sound or phoneme (for example, 'sa, sa, sa' or 'ho ho ho'); the word ('*pocas palabras*'—in *The Taming of the Shrew*, Sly manages to fit both into a single utterance: 'Therefore *Paucas pallabris*, let the world slide: Sessa', Ind.1, 8); the phrase ('Be ruled by me'); the gesture (stalking); genre (revenge play; prodigal son play; traditionally recognized genres like tragedy or history); the repertory of the company or professional body; and finally the system of several companies, venues, and seasons.[12] The formal integrity, however minimal and changing, of these iterated elements is confirmed first by the fact of their repetition, and second by their recognition by companies and publishers as identifiable, marketable units in their own right, although on a different axis than that of the printed plays in which they are most clearly recorded now. They are often presented on title pages in parallel, as it were, to the plot (Figure 8). On the title page of the 1602 quarto of *Merry Wives of Windsor*, for instance, what we know as the play comes (more or less) first. But scarcely less prominently featured, and standing almost independently of what we know as the play, are some kinds of playing that take place within it. These 'humors' and 'vaine'—the old spelling suggests galenic fluidity, vectors of movement, vacuities—are 'entermixed' with 'conceited' (that is, well-conceived or plotted), textually oriented 'comedy'. The comedy is 'of' its principal characters. The vein and the humours are 'of' actions they perform.

The *vein* was one of the most widely distributed, and complexly self-conscious, examples, as when Falstaff offers to dramatize the king 'in King Cambises vaine' (*Henry IV, Part One*, 2.5, 1317) or when Bottom declares to his fellow players, 'This was loftie…This is *Ercles* vaine, a tyrants vaine' (*Midsummer Night's Dream*, 1.2, 286–7). Similar patterns of action might also be called *humours, conceits, parts*, or

---

[12] 'Sa, sa, sa' or its variants appear in at least nineteen plays between 1580 and 1642, *pocas palabras* in at least eight. 'Ho ho ho' is ubiquitous. Lawrence Manley suggested 'Be ruled by me', and I was. On the styles and repertories of particular playhouses and companies, see Scott McMillin and Sally-Beth MacLean, *The Queen's Men and their Plays* (Cambridge: Cambridge University Press, 1998); Mary Bly, *Queer Virgins and Virgin Queans on the Early Modern Stage* (Oxford: Oxford University Press, 2000); Roslyn Knutson, *Playing Companies and Commerce in Shakespeare's Time* (Cambridge: Cambridge University Press, 2001); Lucy Munro, *Children of the Queen's Revels: A Jacobean Theatre Repertory* (Cambridge: Cambridge University Press, 2005); Andrew Gurr, *Shakespeare's Opposites: The Admiral's Company, 1594–1625* (Cambridge: Cambridge University Press, 2009).

A

Moſt pleaſaunt and

excellent conceited Co-
medie, of Syr *Iohn Falſtaffe*, and the
merrie Wiues of *Windſor*.

Entermixed with ſundrie

variable and pleaſing humors, of Syr *Hugh*
the Welch Knight, Iuſtice *Shallow* , and his
wife Couſin M. *Slender*.

With the ſwaggering vaine of Auncient
Piſtoll, and Corporall *Nym*.

By *William Shakeſpeare*.

As it hath bene diuers times Acted by the right Honorable
my Lord Chamberlaines ſeruants. Both before her
Maieſtie, and elſe-where.

LONDON
Printed by T. C. for Arthur Iohnſon, and are to be ſold at
his ſhop in Powles Church-yard, at the ſigne of the
Flower de Leuſe and the Crowne.
1 6 0 2.

Figure 8 Title page. William Shakespeare, *A Most pleasaunt and excellent conceited Comedie, of Syr John Falstaffe, and the merrie Wiues of Windsor* (London, 1602). This item is reproduced by permission of The Huntington Library, San Marino, California.

other terms. *The Blind Beggar of Alexandria* (London: William Jones, 1598) is described as 'discour*sing his variable humours* in disguised shapes full of *conceite and pleasure*'; *A Knack to Know a Knave* (London: Richard Jones, 1594) is offered '*With KEMPS applauded Merrimentes* of the men of Goteham'; and plays regularly observe figures taking a *child's, woman's, knave's, gentlemanly*, or *bestial* part, or direct them to *play the man, fool, tyrant*, or *whore*. Earlier references to 'vein' associate it with a written style, whether lofty like Virgil's (*Glass of Government*, 1575) or low like blind Davy the ballad singer's (*Pap with an Hatchet*, 1589), but for both Falstaff and Bottom, more than words is involved; Falstaff, for instance, needs a cup of sack to make his eyes red. *Vein* is something like the actor's style, without the link to writing that *style* (Latin *stylus*, pen) suggests. It allows an actor to replay a tyrant, for instance, without actually representing one. Its gestures do not refer to any determinate event but to a more generalized technique that subsumes many similar actions, just as today one might make a Chaplinesque gesture without replicating any specific gesture Chaplin ever made or even referring to a particular Chaplin film.

[T]*he swaggering vaine of Aunciente Pistoll* (*Merry Wives of Windsor*, t.pp., 1602, 1619, 1630), *swaggering Pistol* (*Henry IV, Part Two*, t.p., 1600), or just *Auntient Pistoll* (*Henry V*, t.pp., 1600 [1619]) is not primarily textual, although it is marked textually by strong rhythms, inkhorn vocabulary, alliteration, inversions of normal word order, and frequent recall of lines from other plays. The insistent repetition of the word *swagger* and its cognates—fourteen occurrences in *Henry IV, Part Two*—hints at the physical performance that accompanied it, perhaps to 'speak big words and stamp and stare', as another Captain threatens in *The Puritan* (1607), or to 'roar like Tamerlin at the Bull' (*The Guardian*, 1642).[13] In contrast, no forms of the word *swagger* appear in *Merry Wives*, except on the title page, perhaps suggesting that having been named in *Henry IV, Part Two*, Pistol's vein is given entirely over the action. In *Henry V*, Williams remembers the disguised King as 'a Rascall that swagger'd with me' (4.7, 2536–7). Is this a cue that Henry copies his vein as a common soldier from Pistol, whom he encounters just before meeting Williams, perhaps in a physical analogy to his boasted ability to mimic language?

The other figures that Pistol's vein invokes are not worldly examples but theatrical ones. Pistol recapitulates some of the most notoriously tearcat lines from Marlowe's *Tamburlaine* (1587):

> Shall packhorses,
> And hollow pamperd jades of Asia
> Which cannot goe but thirtie mile a day

---

[13] Thomas Middleton, *The Collected Works* (Oxford: Clarendon Press, 2007), 3.5.84; Abraham Cowley, *The Guardian* (London: John Holden, 1650), 3.6, C3v. Peter Womack considers swaggering in his *English Renaissance Drama* (Malden, MA: Wiley-Blackwell, 2006), 308–11.

> Compare with Caesars and with Canibals
> And troiant Greeks?   (*Henry IV, Part Two*, 2.4, 1194–8)

from Peele's *Battle of Alcazar* (1589):

> Then feed and be fat, my faire Calipolis.   (2.4, 1209)

and, in 'have we not Hiren here?' (2.4, 1190, 1205), probably from Peele's lost *The Turkish Mahamet and Hiren the Fair Greek* (before 1594). Intertheatricality is less directly referential to particular precursors than what we usually call allusion, more mediated by a variety of forms and presentations, more cluttered with indistinct or incommensurate senses from other instantiations.[14] Rather than appropriating existing discourses, intertheatrical recall dispropriates them, unfolding a net of possible connections and necessary spaces rather than a particular meaning that might be transmitted directly and unidirectionally. Its very imprecision makes it less visible to academic readers, much of whose cultural competence relies on precise memory. What is recalled intertheatrically is not, however, incoherent; replaying and recollecting of actions fuses them into a shared impression. This abstraction from a number of particular actions or speeches demands, and reproduces, a kind of formal integrity, even a performative prescriptiveness, akin to that of an Elvis impersonator.[15] The 'vein', then, as well as being a recognizable complex of associations, includes a degree of theatrical self-consciousness. Rather than just indicating a kind of person or a character type, it indicated itself as a kind of theatre. It was a collection of actions that a man might play, performed elements that could be put on or taken off again by anybody, like a prop or a costume. In James Shirley's *Changes, or Love in a Maze* (1632), when one character misquotes and enacts some of Hieronimo's lines from *The Spanish Tragedy*, he 'turns' Hieronimo:

> *Simple.*   Oh eyes no eies but Mountaines fraught with teares!
> *Chrysolina.* Hee's turnd *Ieronymo.*
> *Simple.*   Goe by, *Ieronymo*, goe by, goe by.
>   *He passeth by them with disdaine.*[16]

To turn Hieronimo is to utter certain things or to act in a particular way, not to have a particular set of thoughts or kind of constitution.

Because it calls attention to the formal means of performance—the categories of stage action that made theatre recognizably 'theatrical'—intertheatre also has a metatheatrical component. But it also differs from what is often called metatheatre, perhaps most prominently the device of the play within the play. Metatheatre, we

---

[14] On the challenge of following cross-referencing, and the partiality of surviving records, see Holger Schott Syme, 'The Meaning of Success: Stories of 1594 and Its Aftermath', *Shakespeare Quarterly* 61 (2010), 490–525 (508).

[15] Joseph Roach, *Cities of the Dead: Circum-Atlantic Performance* (New York: Columbia University Press, 1996), on effigy, 36–7, 69–71.

[16] James Shirley, *Changes, or Love in a Maze* (London: Thomas Cooke, 1632), 54, 4.1.

might say, presumes an *idea* of the play; intertheatre, in contrast, concerns the practical act of *playing*.[17] Metatheatre promises to present theatre from some place outside it; intertheatre—*intratheatre?*—offers to show off how theatre works from within it. Jaques's familiar metatheatrical observation that 'All the world's a stage, / And all the men and women meerely Players' (1599; *As You Like It*, 2.7, 1062–3), does not have much else to say about this playing other than to notice it. That, in fact, is its main point—that what the men and women actually do, between their entrances and their exits, is not especially important, whether we understand them to be vainly strutting and fretting their hour upon the stage or performing in the theatre of God's judgement.[18] The recurring image of guilty creatures at a play, struck to the soul by what they see, in some sense inverts the figure, but it, too, tends to erase the particularity of theatrical performance into an index to the world outside it. As its name implies, metatheatre suggests a hierarchical framing, so that the point from which we look from comes *after* theatre itself. What is viewed metatheatrically is treated as inset or embedded, like the neatly nested performances of Kyd's *Spanish Tragedy*, *Hamlet*'s Mousetrap (1600), or Ford's *Roman Actor* (1626). Intertheatre, instead, makes specific horizontal connections among performances without privileging one over another. If all the world's a stage, then there is no place to step off to get a clearer view; one can only move within it for differently partial views. An intertheatrical approach sketches not a hierarchy of levels but a decentred network of intersections among different scenes and different stages. It promises no neatly concentric levels of intelligibility, with each succeeding remove allowing a more complete grasp of the whole. Consciousness of the scene is nowhere total, even in any given, or imagined, audience. It can always be expanded.

Recreating these intertheatrical networks requires following performances step by step rather than mapping them from an abstracting distance, and thus something more like a physics of memory than a metaphysics—an attention to what gets passed on, how it is remembered, what work it does, and what work is done on it. What this kind of attention finds is not always the same as the stories that are told about the theatres, or even the stories that playing tells explicitly about itself. Richly intertheatrical moments are also not always the moments that seem most striking textually. One line that Pistol recalls, 'Have we not Hiren here?', seems fairly unremarkable taken by itself, certainly less so than the brio of the hollow pampered jades or fat Calipolis with which Pistol yokes it in *Henry IV, Part Two*.

---

[17] On the idea of the play as a reification, see Anne Righter, *Shakespeare and the Idea of the Play* (New York: Barnes and Noble, 1962); William N. West, 'The Idea of a Theater: Humanist Ideology and the Imaginary Stage in Early Modern Europe', *Renaissance Drama* n.s. 28 (1997), 245–87.

[18] Louis Montrose, 'The Purposes of Playing: Reflections on a Shakespearian Anthropology', *Helios* n.s. 7 (1979–80), 51–74; William N. West, 'Knowledge and Performance in the Early Modern *Theatrum Mundi*', in Flemming Schock, Oswald Bauer, and Ariane Koller, eds., *Dimensionen der Theatrum-Metapher in der Frühen Neuzeit: Ordnung und Repräsentation von Wissen* (Hannover: Wehrhahn, 2008), 1–20.

Both the latter lines also recall powerful gestures from the stage: the entrance of Tamburlaine's kings in harness or of Muly Malocco with lion's flesh on his sword. It is not clear what gesture might have accompanied 'have we not Hiren here?', yet the line had a lengthy afterlife in the theatre. Besides being part of Pistol's repertoire, it appears in Dekker's *Satiromastix* (1601), in the mouth of the Pistolish Captain Tucca, himself an intermedial figure who also appears in Guilpin's *Skialetheia* (1598) and Jonson's *Poetaster* (1601). In *Eastward Ho!* (1605), the apprentice Quicksilver demands 'lend me some money! Hast thou not Hiren here?' (2.1.100); in Middleton's *The Old Law* (c.1618) two characters quibble over whether it should be Hiren or Siren (4.1.52–7, 89).[19] So durable was the line that in 1658, another staging of the story still replayed it, much as a retelling of Hamlet might pay homage to Yorick or to 'To be or not to be': 'Shines not the fair Irene here'.[20] Hiren's staying power is exemplary for another, more cautionary reason, at least to critics accustomed to a textual history of drama, since the play it comes from is now lost. We have, as it were, no originary text to allude to, only reactions that allow us to triangulate the unexpected force of a theatrical element whose significance remains at least partly illegible to us.

How does an intertheatrical element project its own repetition? Thomas Kyd's *Spanish Tragedy* offers another example of how the recall of a line can reveal traces of performance and how its use serves as resource for the making of further performances. As an object conserved and transformed through acts of performative remembering, the play outpaces all rivals; diligent scholarship has counted about 120 clear verbal references to the play across nearly 70 different works.[21] It is impossible to calculate how many plays in the period were influenced by its larger features: its theme of revenge, its complaining ghost, and its carefully constructed frame tales, in all of which Kyd seems to have innovated—although this, too, is impossible to verify, and from an intertheatrical stance it is less important. Whatever Kyd's originality, his innovation was quickly absorbed into theatrical practice, so that by 1600 his play had become a tissue of outdated dramaturgy. In that year Ben Jonson sniped on-stage at audiences who judged '*the old Hieronimo,* [as it was first acted] ... *the onely best, and iudiciously pend play of Europe*'.[22] But the play continued to appear in further editions, gaining at least one set of additions, by Jonson and perhaps others (1601): it acquired a prequel, which may or may not have had

[19] Jonson, Chapman, and Marston, *Eastward Ho!*, ed. George Petter, New Mermaids (London: A & C Black, 1994); Middleton, *An/The Old Law*, in *Collected Works*.

[20] Gilbert Swinhoe, *The Tragedy of the Unhappy Fair Irene* (London: J. Place, 1658). A contemporary poem by actor and poet William Barksted, *Hiren: or the faire Greeke* (London: Roger Barnet, 1611) does not recall this line. Did it perhaps demand theatrical business for its effectiveness?

[21] Claude Dudrap, *Dramaturgie et Société, XVIe et XVIIe siècles*, ed. Jean Jacquot, 2 vols. (Paris: Centre National de la Recherche Scientifique, 1968), 2:607–31, 628–31; Emma Smith, 'Hieronimo's Afterlives', in *The Spanish Tragedie with the First Part of Jeronimo*, ed. Emma Smith (London: Penguin, 1998), 133–59.

[22] Ben Jonson, *Cynthia's Revels*, Induction, in *Workes* (London: W. Stansby, 1616), 185.

anything to do with Kyd, performed by the King's Men and parodied by the Children of the Chapel (*c*.1604); it was made into a ballad (1620–40); it even travelled to the Low Countries and to Germany with troupes of English comedians.[23] In fact, *The Spanish Tragedy* may have been the most widely circulated play of the era.[24]

Much from *The Spanish Tragedy* is replayed on later stages, from the ghost's monologue that initiates the action of the play (itself a Senecan device) to Hieronimo's entrance in his nightshirt to discover the body of his murdered son, 'What out-crie cals me from my naked bed…Who cals *Hieronimo*?' (2.5.1, 4). In *Return from Parnassus* (1603) this passage, together with the opening soliloquy of *Richard III* (1592), is used to audition aspiring players. Among other lines particularly prone to intertheatrical recollection were a vigorously euphuistic soliloquy by Hieronimo ('Oh eyes, no eyes, but fountaines fraught with teares' [3.2.1]), and a love poem from Thomas Watson's *Hekatompathia* (1582; 'In time the savage Bull sustaines the yoake' [2.1.3]), with which the villains Lorenzo and Balthasar demonstrate both their bad taste in verse and their Machiavellian attitude towards love. The appeal of such lines and scenes seems fairly straightforward: exceptional opportunities for vehement acting and roaring to match.

But the most frequently remembered element from the play, appearing in fifteen separate works between 1598 and 1638, was the much less impressive-sounding '*Hieronimo* be ware, goe by, goe by' (3.12.31). It seems a strangely flat line to merit this hypertheatrical attention, especially in a play full of elaborate rhetorical effects and startling actions. Hieronimo utters it to himself when he is trying to tell the king of his son's murder. At the beginning of the scene, he has appeared, one would think memorably, '*with a poynard in one hand, and a rope in the other*'—as an emblem, that is, of despair. Just in case we don't notice, he '*flings* [them] *away*' twenty lines later, and then '*takes them up againe*' (3.12.sd19–20). And yet this vivid allegorical image is not what gets replayed; instead what is remembered is (part of) the bland utterance that arrives some dozen lines later. The line doesn't seem to mark *any* important aspect of the play, thematically, aesthetically, metatheatrically, or by any other measure I can think of. But although it may not seem especially noteworthy to us, it was clearly well-noted by early modern playwrights, actors, and audiences.

What exactly was replayed in 'Hieronimo, go by'? 'Beware' was not important to it—none of the moments in later texts recall that particular word or even preserve

[23] On the additions and continental performances, see Lukas Erne, *Beyond the Spanish Tragedy* (Manchester: Manchester University Press, 2001), 119–30. On the first part, see Erne, *Beyond the Spanish Tragedy*, 14–23; for the ballad, Smith, 'Afterlives', 153–9.

[24] *Spanish Tragedy* was printed in nine editions by 1633 (the most was *Mucedorus*, with thirteen by 1642); according to Henslowe's diary, it was the third most frequently performed play at the Rose between 1592 and 1597. Uniquely, by 1604 it seems to have been played by four companies and in as many as six venues.

a space for it. Nor, in fact, is the name 'Hieronimo' absolutely necessary; most of the references include it (it is the easiest way to be sure they are, after all, references), but several don't, in contexts that nevertheless suggest that they are thinking of this particular line from this particular play. A would-be actor is told in Marston's *Antonio and Mellida* (1600):

> Not play two parts in one? away, away: tis common fashion. Nay if you cannot bear two subtle fronts vnder one hood, Ideot goe by, goe by.[25]

The maid of *Shoemaker's Holiday* (1600) once uses Hieronimo's name ('if I were as you, Ide cry, go by *Ieronimo*, go by', 1.2.41–2) but in a second iteration says 'forrester, go by' (2.2.2).[26] The minimal index of repetition is 'go by', ordinary enough Elizabethan English for 'move along; never mind' and the figure of apostrophe, or direct address. As with 'Hiren here', what this line remembers, in its compression, is an element that has been lost in the records of the play's performance: its action, or a gesture that accompanies it, or some other element capable of being 'remembered' not just linguistically or mentally but physically, in playing. It marks a place in the text where something happened on-stage—something recognizable, iterable, or imitable—but something that is not visible in the text by itself. How does one reconstruct a missing gesture? The answer is pretty straightforward: one doesn't. It isn't there. But something remains—clues of various kinds in the texts, accounts that recall some reference to it. It is possible, sometimes and not always, to retrace the absence left behind, like the burning of Tarlton's cheek.

So let us try. One repetition, in *Blurt Master-Constable* (1601), concludes with the speaker insisting, 'walke, walke, walke', and Shirley's use in *Changes* directs: '*He passeth by them with disdaine*'.[27] These references hint that the words 'go by!' were somehow linked to physical *going*. Six of the fifteen theatrical rememberings of the line are clustered in the period 1598–1602, which saw productions of Shakespeare's *Hamlet* and Marston's *Antonio and Mellida*, both of which owe large debts to *Spanish Tragedy*. The play had also been revived just before this period, most likely as a vehicle for the great originator of Tamburlaine, Edward Alleyn, who had recently come out of retirement to speed his new venture in the Fortune playhouse. Though only in his thirties, Alleyn had made his strongest impression a decade earlier and might well have seemed like a revenant to Jonson and others who remembered Hieronimo.[28] Was 'go by' thus reactivated in

[25] John Marston, *Antonio and Mellida*, ed. W. Reavley Gair (Manchester: Manchester University Press, 1991), Ind. 78–9.

[26] Thomas Dekker, *The Dramatic Works of Thomas Dekker*, ed. Fredson Bowers, vol. 1 (Cambridge: Cambridge University Press, 1962).

[27] *Blurt Master-Constable, or The Spaniards Night-walke* (London: Henry Rockytt, 1602), F2v.

[28] S. P. Cerasano, 'Edward Alleyn, the New Model Actor, and the Rise of Celebrity in the 1590s', *MRDE* 18 (2005), 47–58 (51–3). Cerasano notes that Alleyn's 'valedictory' performances (the quotation marks are hers) were in the roles of Faustus and Hieronimo (52).

part by the return of Alleyn to the stage in the seasons of 1597 or 1600? Was recalling Hieronimo's 'go by' an opportunity to 'stalk', as Alleyn's Tamburlaine was so often described as doing? 'Stalking' is a gesture associated with Tamburlaine specifically—'like stalking *Tamberlaine*', Dekker characterizes it in *The Wonderfull Yeare* (1603)—although it also accompanies other parts in the tyrant's vein, and some distinctively world-encompassing gait seems to have been characteristic of many of Alleyn's roles.[29] Could the missing gesture of 'Go by!' have been a distinctive way of walking across stage that in some way remembered or repeated Alleyn's already distinctive stalking in Tamburlaine's or Cutlack's vein, or even Hieronimo's own, a gesture that somehow answered it or self-consciously displayed not its walking but its walking *in a distinctive way*—in short, its theatricality?

Whatever it was that Hieronimo did as he went by, the movement signalled how both it and the play it came to stand for belonged to a system of theatre, one that devised a history of itself in moving forward and replaying its own past, which can be understood to inhere in a set of iterable formal units at many different scales. Early modern drama continuously established its novelty by recalling, and usually making fun of, earlier plays and the styles in which they were performed. The imprecision of their recall, coupled with their assignment to the past, provides the possibility of organizing a specifically theatrical history. The noise and inexplicable dumb shows of *Hamlet* and the desperate dramaturgy of the mechanicals in *A Midsummer Night's Dream* (1595) are two obvious examples, but even as early as in the late 1580s, when our history of early modern drama customarily begins, Christopher Marlowe's *Tamburlaine, Part One* (1587) famously rejected 'the jigging veins of rhyming mother-wits' (Prol. 1) and *The Spanish Tragedy* mocked the taste for didactic theatre.[30] By rehearsing its own earlier lines, words, gestures, and other elements, early modern playing sets distance between what they did then and what we do now, between what they liked and what we prefer. Replaying Hieronimo going by, then, like Jonson's more explicitly articulated verdict in *Bartholomew Fair* (1614) that 'He that will swear, *Ieronimo*, or *Andronicus* are the best playes' shows his 'Iudgment...hath stood still these five and twentie, or thirtie yeeres',[31] makes sense of a current performance by pronouncing judgement on an earlier one and rendering it old-fashioned, imitable, and therefore, in a negative sense, theatrical: peculiarly void. What is recalled is something that happened before, for a less knowing

[29] Thomas Dekker, *The Wonderfull Year* (London: Thomas Creede, 1603), D1. Cf. Everard Guilpin, *Skialetheia* (London: I. R. for Nicholas Ling, 1598), B2v: '*Allens Cutlacks gate: /...* His eyes are lightning, and his words are thunder:.../ Stalking and roaring like to *Iobs* great devill'.

[30] Christopher Marlowe, *Tamburlaine Parts One and* Two, ed. Anthony B. Dawson, New Mermaids (London: A & C Black, 1997). On Kyd's rejection of a didactic dramaturgy for one that is effective but incomprehensible, see William N. West, '"But This Will Be a Mere Confusion": Real and Represented Confusions on the Elizabethan Stage', *Theatre Journal* 60 (2008), 217–33.

[31] Ben Jonson, *Bartholmewe Fayre* (London: Robert Allot, 1631), Induction, A5v.

audience, on another stage. It recalls theatre as a history of playings—perhaps even as the habit of playgoing itself.

As I have emphasized, however, memories of a line or a behaviour need not refer back only; they bring forward the accumulated instances and contexts of all their prior iterations as well. In so doing, they explore what is possible on the present stage, and what its limits are. With its impressive but limited array of props, costumes, settings, and performers, the means of the early theatres must frequently have been manifest to regular playgoers, as when a player doubled a messenger's part to announce the death of his previous role, for instance, or when in one part he recalls another; when the bodies of boy actors were teasingly offered for, then withheld from, scrutiny; when 'HIERONYMO's old cloake, ruffe, and hat' was repurposed for Surly's disguise as the Spanish Don in *The Alchemist* (1610); or when a prop circulated among several plays and functions in them.[32] Almost any resource of staging could recall other instances of its use: ordinary props such as beds could serve as sites of either love or death; chairs used both as thrones of power and as supports for invalids. Taken in isolation, the informational content of such resources is minimal; they are both simple and repeated. But in their repetition—drawing a sword, wooing, praying, appearing above—simple resources produce a system of recollections and expectations, which can be exaggerated, played against, disappointed, and worked with in a variety of ways to develop the complexity of their signification. Let a boy, for instance, appear 'above'. Will he act something like Juliet, looking over her garden for Romeo? Is he a prophet like Oseas in *A Looking Glass for London and England* (1588), overseeing and commenting on the action? (And was *Spanish Tragedy*'s Andrea in a similar position?) Do we remember the scene from *King John* (1591), when the young prince Arthur climbs over a wall and falls to his death? Will he remind us of a siege, as when in *Tamburlaine, Part One* the virgins of Damascus come out to entreat Tamburlaine to spare their city, or later when their 'slaughtered carcasses' are 'hoisted up' again on the walls (5.2.68)? Or of *The Changeling* (1622), when Deflores kills Alonzo as he leans out a window and throws his body down, which seems to repeat and invert elements of each of the situations of the other plays? All possibilities are present at once, until the next actions relimit them, and in so doing introduce new possibilities.

Even a more determinate situation can gain force by the theatrical contexts it recalls. There seems, for instance, to be a clear consensus on what ghosts do in

---

[32] Ben Jonson, *Alchemist* 4.7, in *Workes*, 664. On doubling, see Bradley, *From Text to Performance*, 40–6, 88, and Simon Palfrey and Tiffany Stern, *Shakespeare in Parts* (Oxford: Oxford University Press, 2007), 50–4; on the boy's body, Ann Rosalind Jones and Peter Stallybrass, *Renaissance Clothing and the Materials of Memory* (Cambridge: Cambridge University Press, 2000), 212–19; on the handkerchief and the skull, Andrew Sofer, *The Stage Life of Props* (Ann Arbor: University of Michigan Press, 2003), 61–115.

plays. The Induction of *A Warning for Fair Women* (1590), laments the tedious predictability of these scenes:

> ...a filthie whining ghost,
> Lapt in some fowle sheet, or a leather pelch,
> Comes skreaming in like a pigge half stickt,
> And cries *Vindicta*, revenge, revenge:...[33]

It is true that early modern theatre includes quite a few scenes of ghosts crying for revenge. *The Battle of Alcazar* requires 'Three ghosts crying Vindicta' and its Presenter observes 'Revenge cries Abdilmelecs grieved ghost'; a ghost in *Locrine* cries 'Revenge, revenge for blood.... *Vindicta, vindicta*' (*c*.1594; 3.5); the Prologue to the *True Tragedy of Richard III* (1591) features a ghost who cries for revenge in garboiled Latin, ending with a recognizable *vendicta* (Prol. 2).[34] But while crying revenge is what ghosts are supposed to do, it is a custom more honoured in the breach than the observance. Many ghosts neglect to cry for revenge. Other plays recall such crying vengeful ghosts as contrasts to their own ghostly presentations of silent reproach, as in *Macbeth* (1606), or measured speech and temperate revenge, as in *Hamlet* or *Antonio's Revenge* (1600). The complexity of the ghost in *Hamlet*, and the interest it provokes both within the play and outside it—a complexity that is at once metaphysical, ethical, spiritual, and psychological—derives in no small part from its re-staging of the much simpler, less differentiated ghosts of *True Tragedy, Locrine*, or *Warning for Fair Women*. Those recollected ghosts establish what Old Hamlet's ghost *is not*; or, rather, Old Hamlet's ghost is their negation. This difference is not developmental (in the sense that the later ghost improves on the earlier) but responsive. What enables each ghost to be meaningful is the ongoing presence of its other ghosts and their gestures in the theatre's memory. Every time the ghost's appearance is replayed, it summons its negated alternatives, the other possibilities that it might have been. The full significance of such an action appears only between its repetitions.

Early modern theatre even made resources out of its deficiencies. The well-known chorus in *Henry V* asks the audience, 'Thinke when we talke of Horses, that you see them' (1. Prol. 26). This particular request is a pointed one, since horses were one thing that audiences could feel confident they would *not* see in the theatre, as Peter Womack observes in his essay 'Off-stage' in this collection. Only three plays call for horses on-stage, one fewer than call for bears.[35] Of these, only *Thomas of Woodstock* (1592) seems to require an actual horse, which must be ridden, walked, and talked

---

[33] *A Warning for Fair Women* (London: Valentine Sims, 1599), Ind. 58–61, A2v.

[34] *Alcazar* in *The Stukeley Plays*, ed. Charles Edelman (Manchester: Manchester University Press, 2005), 2.Prol.8.sd and 19; *Locrine* (London: Thomas Creede, 1595), G1r–v; *True Tragedie of Richard the third* (London: Thomas Creede, 1594).

[35] Alan C. Dessen and Leslie Thomson, *A Dictionary of Stage Directions in English Drama, 1580–1642* (Oxford: Oxford University Press, 2001), under 'bear' and 'horse'. *Tragi-comoedia* (John Rowe;

to; of the others, one calls for a funeral procession with the corpse 'carried upon a horse' and the other a skimmington, which hardly demand real horses.[36] Horses *had* been actual performers in playing inns, notably one Marocco, who is recalled in plays nearly as often as Tarlton, and with whom Tarlton briefly had a rivalry.[37] They also appear on-stage in Restoration dramas.[38] But for whatever reason—the weight of convention, or just plain weight—horses almost never show up on Tudor or Stuart public stages.

But rather than simply passing over their absence in silence, plays are strangely chatty about horses. Missing horses are painstakingly excused, as in *Macbeth*, where one murderer explains why Banquo and Fleance will enter on foot although they have been riding (3.3). Similar justifications of the off-stage whereabouts of present riders' absent horses occur among all companies and across the entire period, in, among others, *Arden of Feversham* (1591; sc. 9), *Northward Ho!* (1605; 5.1), *Your Five Gallants* (1606; 4.2.15–16), *Cymbeline* (1610; 4.1), *A New Way to Pay Old Debts* (1625; 3.1), and *Tottenham Court* (1634; 2.3).[39] Horses are missed equally in scenes of grim seriousness and open comedy. In *Titus Andronicus* (1594) Demetrius and Chiron chillingly but superfluously explain 'We hunt not we, with horse nor hound / But hope to plucke a dainty Doe to ground' (2.2, 652–3); in *The Parson's Wedding* (1641), when a servant asks some gentlemen what he should do with their off-stage horses now that they have returned to London, one answers, 'Mine? take him, hamstring him, kill him, any thing to make him away...'[40]

Oxford: Henry Cripps, 1653), sig. *2v, a treatise against playing, records that in 1653, in an amateur provincial production, *Mucedorus'* bear was played by a man in furs. But given the close physical, financial, and personnel relations between playing and bearbaiting, I suspect it might have been easier to see bears on-stage than horses.

[36] *A Larum for London* and *Late Lancashire Witches*, respectively. In *Ricardus Tertius* (1579), a university play, a stage direction specifies that Richard's body is brought in 'on a horse'. W. J. Lawrence, 'Characteristics of Platform Stage Spectacle', in *Pre-Restoration Stage Studies* (Cambridge, MA: Harvard University Press, 1927), 251–76, 274–5, convincingly argues that this and other *horses* may be *hearses*. Henslowe's 1598 inventory of props includes a 'great horse with his leages [legs]' (*Diary*, 320), although we have no way of knowing if this is a horse to ride or something else, for instance a Trojan or stalking or vaulting horse.

[37] See Jan Bondeson, *The Feejee Mermaid and other Essays in Natural and Unnatural History* (Ithaca: Cornell University Press, 1999). On the rivalry of Tarlton and Marocco, *Tarltons Jests*, C2r-v: 'Banks [the handler] perceiving (to make the people laugh) sayes; Signior (to his Horse) go fetch mee the veriest foole in the company, the Jade comes immediatly, and with his mouth drawes *Tarlton* forth: *Tarlton* with merry words, said nothing, but God a mercy Horse:...'

[38] Lawrence, 'Characteristics', discussing a 1668 revival of Shirley's *Hyde Park* (1632).

[39] *Arden of Feversham*, ed. Martin White (London: A & C Black, 1982); Dekker, *Northward Ho!* in *Dramatic Works*, vol. 2; Middleton, *Your Five Gallants*, in *Collected Works*; Philip Massinger, *New Way*, in *The Plays and Poems of Philip Massinger*, ed. Philip Edwards and Colin Gibson, vol. 2 (Oxford: Clarendon Press, 1976); Thomas Nabbes, *Tottenham Court*, in *Plays, Maskes, Epigrams, Elegies, and Epithalamiums* (London: I. Dawson, 1639).

[40] Thomas Killigrew, *The Parson's Wedding*, in *Comedies, and Tragedies* (London: Henry Herringman, 1664), 1.3, 80.

Even absent, horses draw attention with curious regularity. In *George a Greene* (1590), George arrests a group of lords for turning their horses loose in the town's fields, and then discovers that they are also traitors to the King; the scene requires constant reference to what the horses are invisibly doing in the field.[41] The horse-courser scene in *Doctor Faustus* (1592) focuses on a missing horse that turns out to be no horse at all. Richard III's well-known line is part of a rich intertheatrical relay that runs from *The Battle of Alcazar* ('A horse, a horse, villain, a horse!', 5.1.96) and *True Tragedy* ('A horse, a horse, a fresh horse', H3r) to *What You Will* (1601; 'A horse, a horse, my kingdom for a horse! Looke the[e] I speake play scrappes', 2.1) to *The Iron Age* (1612; in which Sinon proposes the stratagem of the Trojan horse with 'A horse, a horse!' and is answered 'Ten Kingdomes for a horse to enter *Troy*') to the Ministry of Silly Walks and the Royal Hospital for Overacting in *Monty Python's Flying Circus* (1970).[42] In the *Mayor of Quinborough* (1618), two Cheaters posing as players reveal their unfamiliarity with the business of playing by declaring, 'We have a play wherein we use a horse' (5.1.92).[43] Even the hobby horse, ostentatiously forgotten by Hamlet (3.2, 1857), Moth in *Love's Labour's Lost* (3.1, 762), Will Kemp in his tract *Nine Days' Wonder*—'For ô, for ô, the hobby-horse is forgot!'—and comically recalled by the Clown in *The Witch of Edmonton* (1621)—'The Hobby Horse shall be remembered!'—may be complicit.[44]

The finicky explanations for the absence of horses, the elaborate descriptions of horses that will never appear (like Petruchio's in *The Taming of the Shrew* or those of the French in *Henry V*), the cries for horses like Richard's that always go unfulfilled: all work together to suggest something like an elaborate shared theatrical joke. Almost every time horses are called for, talked about, or otherwise invoked among the imaginative furniture of the stage, they signal an undercurrent of self-awareness: a sidelong glance at the limits of a medium that can span continents or leap over intervening years but cannot accommodate the most ordinary means of transportation. *Woodstock*, the one play that seems to require a horse to mount the stage, is the exception that proves the rule; the appearance of the horse in the playhouse reflects the absurdity of a scene in which a nobleman tends the horse of a social inferior.[45]

The missing horses of the playhouse are the very creatures of intertheatricality, running through any number of plays but wholly present in none. It is hard to gauge

---

[41] *George a Greene* (London: Cuthbert Burby, 1599), C2–C3v.

[42] John Marston, *What You Will* (London: G. Eld, 1607), C1r–v; Thomas Heywood, *The Second Part of the Iron Age* (London: Nicholas Okes, 1632), C3v.

[43] Middleton, *Collected Works*.

[44] *Kemps nine daies wonder* (London: Nicholas Ling, 1600), B2v; William Rowley, Thomas Dekker, and John Ford, *Witch of Edmonton*, ed. Etta Soiref Onat (New York: Garland, 1980), 3.1.56.

[45] A 'spruce courtier' rides into Thomas of Woodstock's castle and mistakes Woodstock for a groom, promising Woodstock a tip if he will walk his horse, *The first part of the reign of King Richard the Second; or, Thomas of Woodstock*, ed. Wilhelmina P. Frijlinck (Oxford: Malone Society, 1929), f. 173a, ll. 1423–74.

when the missing horse begins to appear, as it were, but as early as the interlude *Disobedient Child* (*c*.1560), an unhappy husband asks to return home, 'If some man to me his Horse wyll lende'.[46] No single horse, present or absent, can demonstrate the theatre's general destitution of horses, which is only visible as a negative pattern of repeated and marked failures to appear. Such a network reads both backwards and forwards, backwards by picking up on prior works, forwards by dictating the terms within which later iterations of the system will work. Similar dispositions of form appear throughout the emergent system of early modern English theatre. *Hamlet* or *Antonio's Revenge* look back to scenes and characters, gests and veins, laid out in *The Spanish Tragedy* and (we guess) the ur-*Hamlet*; concurrently they look at and engage with each other transactionally; finally, they feed forward into later works like *The Revenger's Tragedy* or even to *The Courier's Tragedy*, that belated Jacobean drama that Thomas Pynchon scripts into *The Crying of Lot 49* (1966). These iterations give rise to what it means to be a revenge tragedy, to be 'tragic' in a particular way, even to be 'Elizabethan' and to be 'drama'.

This past fashioned from a limited stock of gestures replayed in theatrical practice anticipates a more unbounded future for itself. Elizabethan recall of earlier drama is far from total—much is not picked up for comment or reproduction, but only certain elements. Over time and through iteration, some actions acquire a force of attraction that draws further actions to them as if they were its emblems. Hieronimo's 'go by' is one example; Hamlet's ghost, and Richard's horse are others. But why do these particular actions—the latter two still canonical—show such a quality of accretiveness? It seems to be a contingent and compounding force of familiarity: as plays or characters become more familiar, they draw more gestures to themselves, and as they draw more references, they grow yet more familiar, and finally come to seem natural and germinal. By the second half of Shakespeare's career, ghostly cries of revenge are associated more often with old Hamlet's ghost than with Seneca's, Hieronimo's, or stage ghosts in general.

Like other kinds of capital, cultural capital earns interest. This organizing force of attraction is not something new to our times, although the particular organizations we make are specific to us; it begins within a few years of Shakespeare's plays. As early modern plays are revised, and their gestures replayed, they tend to become more fully themselves, whether as more homogeneous and thematically coherent, more focused on particular emblematic gests, or both.[47] Thus in the 1602 additions of *The Spanish Tragedy* Hieronimo's madness is brought out earlier and more forcefully; the 1619 title page of *Merry Wives* omits Sir Hugh, Justice Shallow, and Master Slender to highlight Falstaff, Pistol, the wives, and the plot; in our own

---

[46] Thomas Ingelond, *Disobedient Child* (London: n.p., 1570?), F2v.

[47] Katherine Rowe, 'Memory and Revision in Chapman's *Bussy* Plays', *Renaissance Drama* 31 (2002), 125–52.

time, Yorick's skull has increasingly become an emblem for *Hamlet*.[48] In the model I am proposing, elements or works that have received more attention—that have benefited from the most connections to other works—tend to receive still more attention, and thus continue to grow in their perceived richness and their aptness for further appropriation. Viewed intertheatrically, *Hamlet*, for instance, might well be the richest play of the period, but not because of its inherent qualities; rather, its richness derives from its history, both that of the theatrical networks it drew on and that of its current status interlaced with its history of re-actions— other plays, productions, criticism. Treating theatre as an intertheatrical system will handle the temporalities of production and reception differently than much historicist criticism currently does, acknowledging (among other things) that an attempt to read *Hamlet* by itself is an attempt to reframe the system at the level of a play, rather than considering other scales, of gesture or genre. Approached inter-theatrically, *Hamlet*'s richness will not be visible in *Hamlet* alone; indeed, one might legitimately ask whether it is possible to appreciate *Hamlet* fully in isola-tion, on its own.

Attention to the intertheatrical forms in which theatrical performance makes and remakes itself concerns more than an aesthetics—a change of styles or an evolution towards some other theatrical mode. As the formal elements in circula-tion that intertheatricality discerns come into focus, they reveal themselves not only as forms, but as themes of theatrical performance as well. Intertheatrical moments show how a present mode of playing distinguishes itself from modes that precede it, but which it also preserves as a resource. In this way, they also reveal *all* modes of representation to be modes, which do not simply reflect the world but produce it, which are themselves in states of change, and which may one day be recalled in another vein. Its intertheatrical moments show early mod-ern playing to be always in motion, never static; not teleologically evolutionary but at once *dislocated* and *emergent*—a series of forms changing into something else while still remaining recognizable. Its intertheatricality is a fully historicizing mode of thought, or doing: history is not just its object, but a formal motion that carries all of us along.

FURTHER READING

Bloom, Gina, Anston Bosman, and William N. West. 'Ophelia's Intertheatricality, or, How Performance is History', *Theatre Journal* 65 (2013), 165–82.
Bruster, Douglas. *Quoting Shakespeare: Form and Culture in Early Modern Drama* (Lincoln: University of Nebraska Press, 2000).

[48] West, 'Mere Confusion', 230–1; Pascale Aebischer, 'Yorick's Skull: *Hamlet*'s Improper Property', *EnterText* 1.2 (2001), 206–25.

Clubb, Louise George. *Italian Drama in Shakespeare's Time* (New Haven: Yale University Press, 1989).

Dessen, Alan C. *Recovering Shakespeare's Theatrical Vocabulary* (Cambridge: Cambridge University Press, 1995).

Kidnie, Margaret Jane. 'Surviving Performance: Shakespeare's Contested Works', in *Shakespeare and the Problem of Adaptation* (London: Routledge, 2009), 11–31.

Lopez, Jeremy. *Theatrical Convention and Audience Response in Early Modern Drama* (Cambridge: Cambridge University Press, 2003).

Womack, Peter. 'Actions That A Man Might Play', in *English Renaissance Drama* (Malden, MA: Wiley-Blackwell, 2006), 261–311.

CHAPTER 9

SKILL

EVELYN TRIBBLE

How might our conceptions of early modern theatricality be altered by viewing it through the lens of skill? Early modern players traded in skill, and skill is what people paid to see. In the highly competitive arena of the early modern theatre, companies played before demanding audiences that were themselves expert in watching and evaluating skilled performance. Despite these facts, the skill of early modern players is not always accorded due attention, and skill is an undervalued—and certainly under-conceptualized—category within studies of the early modern theatre. This chapter seeks to reclaim a positive account of the skill and expertise of early modern players, arguing that attention to skill has the potential to reorganize the categories through which we view the early modern theatre. Skill links mind, body, and affect in intelligent action.

For a variety of reasons, skill is often neglected in accounts of early modern drama. When the foundational theatre historian E. K. Chambers suggests that such extra-dramatic 'feats' were something of a last resort and that players of the 1580s and early 1590s were 'ready at need to eke out their plays by musical performances and even the "activities" of acrobats' (2:550), he voices an implicit hierarchy that is still common in history and criticism of drama, in which the playtext is viewed as the central artistic element and feats of the body are regarded as peripheral and subordinate. Chambers dismisses such displays as extraneous to the text, tossed in to appease the taste of the groundlings.[1] And in doing so, he is following the lead of the early modern playwrights, who commonly complain in their prefaces and inductions about the preferences of audiences for fights and clowns. Ben Jonson

---

[1] E. K. Chambers, *The Elizabethan Stage*, 2 vols. (Oxford: Oxford University Press, 1945), 2:550. W. W. Greg speculated that the large number of calls for fights and clowning in *Orlando Furioso* showed that the play was designed for touring, a point that L. B. Wright echoed in his description of inset skill displays as 'variety entertainments'; L. B. Wright, 'Variety Entertainment by Elizabethan Strolling Players', *The Journal of English and Germanic Philology* 26.3 (1927), 294–303. Such descriptions smack of disdain towards the provinces that the REED (Records of Early English Drama) project has done much to dispel.

and his contemporaries often encourage us to see the play's words as the 'matter', with stage fighting, music, dancing, dumb shows, and sounds relegated to ephemeral concessions to popular taste. Jonson famously has his Stage-Keeper in *Bartholomew Fair* complain about the tyranny of 'master poets' (Induction, 23), who eschew the 'sword-and-buckler man' (12) and even refuse to countenance 'a juggler with a well-educated ape' (15), thus satirizing the tastes of playgoers who prefer 'the concupiscence of jigs and dances' (118).[2] In fact, much of our knowledge of ephemeral skill displays is derived from satire within the drama and paratextual complaints in prologues and the like—displays of skill often come to our attention only as they are mocked.

Taking skill seriously as a significant element of early modern theatricality demands that we question distinctions between the proper ambit of drama and so-called extra-theatrical displays. Regarding theatre as a form of entertainment with as many affinities to sport as to literature helps us to capture a fuller picture of the early modern stage. We should be wary of following received narratives too closely, and especially narratives constructed out of satirical material peddled by playwrights themselves and then echoed by theatrical historians. Since almost all of what survives of early modern drama is in the form of playtexts, the physical skills that were necessary to performing those texts must dwell in their interstices, in stage directions and implied action. If we read these gaps and interstices correctly, we may become aware of elements of early modern theatricality that have been overlooked. Displays of skill were avidly consumed and often far overshadowed the elements of the drama that modern critics tend to value.

One reason for the neglect of skill is the general predominance of author-centred accounts of the drama, in which players tend to be reduced to more or less successful functionaries of playwrights (a view that Jonson was only too happy to promote). The art of gesture employed by the early modern player is often dismissed as a static and old-fashioned set of codes rigidly applied to the text, as in Gurr's speculation about 'stock poses' used to cope with the heavy demands of performance.[3] Yet players considered gesture to be the very foundation of the art of *actio*: the deft yoking of the voice and body to produce the passions embedded in the speech. For early modern writers, 'action', often closely coupled with 'grace', was the term of art in which the skill of players was described. Despite the examples of rivalry between playwrights and actors and complaints about authorial tyranny and player ineptitude, it was acknowledged that the best players 'graced' or 'enlivened' the language through their graceful melding of word and gesture in the art of action. As Joseph Roach has shown, the skill of the player literally knits audience and player together

---

[2] Ben Jonson, *Bartholomew Fair*, ed. George Richard Hibbard and A. Leggatt (London: Methuen Drama, 2007).

[3] Andrew Gurr, *The Shakespearean Stage*, 3rd edn. (Cambridge: Cambridge University Press, 1992), 103.

through lines of force generated by the ability of actors to embody and communicate passion in a 'lively' portrayal.[4] Before it is a translation of the classical '*mythos*', '*praxis*', or our 'plot', action is in essence embodiment, and its successful performance is a result of the skill of the actor in the twin arts of pronunciation and movement, especially gesture. While the skills of pronunciation and gesture that made up *actio* are probably the most familiar elements in the repertoire of abilities possessed by the early modern players, they trafficked in many others, as we shall see.

While we have an increasingly rich body of evidence about early modern players, full accounts of their craft continue to evolve.[5] The skills of boy actors, for instance, are often either overlooked or subsumed into discussions of the dynamics of gender performance.[6] But boys in the adult companies, especially younger ones, seem to have offered displays of tumbling, dancing, and athletic skill. Certainly there seem to have been many more boys within a company than are usually called for in the plays themselves. Alan Armstrong has drawn attention to the possible nimbleness and athletic skill of the boy playing Arthur in Shakespeare's *King John*, arguing that his disguise as a 'ship-boy' just before his fatal leap might indicate his skill in climbing (and falling from) ropes.[7] The boy players in Lyly's *Campaspe* dance, tumble, and sing in quick succession.[8] At indoor theatres, boys performed *entr'acte* entertainments, especially dancing and singing; the Citizen wife in *Knight of the Burning Pestle* asks the boy whether he can tumble and breathe fire in addition to dance (Act 3 Interlude 3, 12–15).[9] Adult players, too, were called upon to display a wide range of physical abilities, as is evident from the many stage directions that open a parenthesis in the discursive action of the play for fencing, dancing, singing, or, less commonly, vaulting or wrestling. The many varieties of such inset skill displays, and the regularity with which they appear, give us some indication of the players' versatility. Terse stage descriptions such as 'Enter Richard and Richmond. They fight. Richard is slain' (*Richard III*, 5.8) or more simply 'fight' indicate more or less elaborate choreographies of movement that were fairly routine. More specialized directions, such as *As You Like It*'s 'Wrestle' (1.2), assume an audience with a sporting eye for the

[4] Joseph R. Roach, *The Player's Passion: Studies in the Science of Acting* (Ann Arbor: University of Michigan Press, 1993).

[5] John Astington, *Actors and Acting in Shakespeare's Time: The Art of Stage Playing* (Cambridge: Cambridge University Press, 2010); David Kathman, 'Players, Livery Companies, and Apprentices', in Richard Dutton, ed., *The Oxford Handbook of Early Modern Theatre* (Oxford: Oxford University Press, 2009), 413–28; David Kathman, 'Grocers, Goldsmiths, and Drapers: Freemen and Apprentices in the Elizabethan Theater', *Shakespeare Quarterly* 55 (2004), 1–49.

[6] Peter Hyland, 'A Kind-of-Woman: The Elizabethan Boy-Actor and the Kabuki Onnagata', *Theatre Research International* 12.1 (1987), 1–8; Marvin Rosenberg, 'The Myth of Shakespeare's Squeaking Boy Actor—or Who Played Cleopatra?', *Shakespeare Bulletin* 19.2 (2001), 5–6.

[7] Alan Armstrong, 'Arthur's Fall', *Shakespeare Bulletin* 24.1 (22 March 2006), 1–10.

[8] John Lyly, *Campaspe* (London, 1584), STC (2nd edn.) 17048a.

[9] Francis Beaumont, *The Knight of the Burning Pestle*, ed. Michael Hattaway, 2nd edn. (New York: W. W. Norton, 2002).

practice. Heywood's *Four Prentices of London* calls for pike-throwing,[10] and one of the dumb shows in *The White Devil* calls for vaulting, or at least credible preparation for it: 'Flamineo and Camillo strip themselves into their shirts, as to vault' (2.2).[11]

Beyond the evidence provided by the plays themselves, we have numerous accounts of extra-fictional feats of skill performed by players attached to companies or travelling with them. In 1588, the Admiral's Men were paid by the court both for presenting plays and 'for two Enterludes or playes ... and for showing other feates of activity and tumbling'.[12] Henslowe's *Diary* records an entry from 1601 for 'a payer of hose for nycke to tumble in before the quen'.[13] As Anston Bosman describes in his essay for this volume, players visiting the Continent are reported to have been paid both for playing and for feats of activities, as in the payment of Robert Brown in 1592 for 'qualitiz en faict de music, agilitez et joeux de commedies, tragedies et histories'.[14] Such displays were expected elements of the theatrical experience provided by the major companies. In 1582, Stephen Gosson's condemnation of playing assumes that the experience comprises much more than simply viewing a play:

> For the eye beeside the beautie of the houses, and the Stages, hee [the Devil] sendeth in Gearish appareil maskes, vaulting, tumbling, daunsing of gigges, galiardes, morisces, hobbihorses; showing of iudgeling castes, nothing forgot, that might serue to set out the matter, with pompe, or rauish the beholders with varietie of pleasure.[15]

Gosson is hardly an objective witness of theatrical practice, of course, but account books detailing payouts to players at the court and in the provinces tend to be quite specific about precisely what types of skill performance were being paid for.[16] And Gosson may not have been as far off as we sometimes think, since feats of theatrical skill did become an occasion for gambling. There are a number of tantalizing references to set competitions between players, with the outcome subject to wagering.[17] The Henslowe–Alleyn archive at Dulwich College contains a letter to Edward Alleyn

---

[10] Thomas Heywood, *The Four Prentices of London*, 2nd edn. (London, 1615), STC, 13321.

[11] John Webster, *The White Devil*, ed. Christina Luckyj, 2nd edn. (New York: W. W. Norton, 1996).

[12] David Cook and Frank Percy Wilson, *Collections VI*, Dramatic Records in the Declared Accounts of the Treasurer of the Chamber, 1558–1642 (Oxford: Malone Society, 1961), 25.

[13] R. A. Foakes, *Henslowe's Diary*, 2nd edn. (Cambridge, Cambridge University Press, 2002), 186.

[14] Chambers, *Elizabethan Stage*, 2:224.

[15] Stephen Gosson, *Playes Confuted in Fiue Actions Prouing That They Are Not to Be Suffred in a Christian Common Weale, by the Waye Both the Cauils of Thomas Lodge, and the Play of Playes, Written in Their Defence, and Other Obiections of Players Frendes, Are Truely Set Downe and Directlye Aunsweared*, 2nd edn. (London, 1583).

[16] For example, in Bristol in the 1589–90 season, the Queen's Men were paid 32 shillings in the week of 2 August for 'tumbeling—and also shewen by a Turke upon a Rope, with running on the same'; the following week they were paid 30 shillings for a play. See Mark. C. Pilkington, ed., *Records of Early English Drama—Bristol* (Toronto: University of Toronto Press, 1997), 136–7.

[17] Murray Bromberg, 'Theatrical Wagers: A Sidelight on the Elizabethan Drama', *Notes & Queries* (December 1951), 533–5.

proposing that he pit himself against the actors Bentley and Knell in a test of acting skill: 'I see not, how you canne anie we [way] hurt yor credit by this action, for if you excel them, you will then be famous, if equall them, you winne both the wager and the credit, if short of them we must and will say Ned Allen still'. An accompanying poem reads:

> Deny me not sweete Nedd, the wagers down
> and twice as muche, commaunde of me or myne
> And if you wynne I sweare the half is thyne
> and for an ouerplus, an English Crowne
> Appoint the tyme and stint it as you pleas,
> Your labor's gain; and that will proue it ease.[18]

Similarly, Thomas Dekker refers to the practice of adjudicating skill by means of competition. Dekker describes 'a pair of players growing into an emulous contention of one another's worth' who decline to compete head to head: they 'refus[e]d to put themselves unto a day of hearing (as any players would have done) but stood only upon their good parts'.[19] Numerous references also exist to 'acting for a wager'; one of Dekker's mock-suggestions to the gallant in *The Gull's Hornbook* is to 'let any hook draw you to a fencer's supper or to players that act such a part for a wager'.[20] These references raise a number of questions, of course—what exactly did the actors *do* to compete? How were the wagers adjudicated? Who exactly was laying money on the venture?—but the passages indicate that skill generated considerable interest in the period, among actors and audiences alike, as an independent quality that could be contested, enacted, and evaluated.

Towards an ecological model of skill

Before turning to a close analysis of the way that feats of skill inform our understanding of specific plays, it is important to establish some of the theoretical and methodological presuppositions that inform the approach to skill that I am proposing, one that can make sense of the many different kinds of codes that were shared between players and their audiences and that I will call an 'ecological' model of theatrical skill. Skill is a property of biological, neurological, social, historical, and material forces and is best studied through a systems-level framework capable of

---

[18] 'MSS 1, Article 6, 01 Recto: Letter From W. P. to Edward Alleyn About a Theatrical Wager, with Six Lines of Verse Beginning "Deny Me Not, Sweete Nedd, the Wager's Downe"', c.1590, *Henslowe–Alleyn Digistisation Project*, http://www.henslowe-alleyn.org.uk/images/MSS-1/Article-006/01r.html, accessed Sept. 2012.

[19] Thomas Dekker and George Wilkins, *Jests to Make You Merrie... Unto Which Is Added the Miserie of a Prison and a Prisoner, and a Paradox in Praise of Saints...* (London, 1607), B4r.

[20] Thomas Dekker, *The Guls Horne-Booke* (London, 1609), F2v.

considering all of these areas simultaneously. Skill is embodied but also extended and embedded into its environment; it is profoundly social yet builds upon a neuro-biological foundation. An ecological model of skill takes account of complex interactions among internal cognitive processes, embodied skill building, technologies, and cultural situations to ask how skill is inculcated, appraised, transmitted, valued, and evaluated. As Emma Cohen suggests, 'cultural transmission—i.e. the emergence, acquisition, storage, and communication of ideas and practices—is powerfully influenced by the physical context in which it occurs...the bodily, cognitive, neural, and social mechanisms that permit and constrain knowledge transmission are conjointly operative and mutually contingent'.[21] Cohen's point recalls Marcel Mauss's highly influential account of skill and culture in 'Techniques of the Body', which he defines as the 'physio-psycho-sociological assemblages of series of actions' that are taken for granted within a culture but that are also widely variable across cultures and historical periods.[22] To take a contemporary example from a somewhat different disciplinary context—a paper on fieldwork on the Brazilian art of capoeira—the anthropologist Greg Downey writes of his gratification at discovering at least one lacuna in the otherwise extraordinary skills of the capoeira practitioners: their ineptness at catching small objects with their hands. Ballistic skills were a lacuna in the Brazilian physical repertory: 'Just as cultural regimes of training produced a distinctive set of skills, such as capoeira techniques, these same regimes also left gaps of incompetence around peaks of virtuoso ability'.[23]

As Downey's example demonstrates, accounts of skill demand a close examination of the means of entrainment and skill acquisition, as well as an understanding of the relationship between embodiment and culture. Studying skill requires a renewed look at the rich vein of work on habitus and the body, as exemplified by Norbert Elias and Pierre Bourdieu, for example, both of whom have demonstrated the myriad ways in which the body is shaped through implicit (and, more rarely, explicit) forces and cultural codes.[24] These are influential models, of course, and Bourdieu's account of the habitus, in particular, has justifiably enjoyed a wide currency. But as an account of skill, it misses quite a bit. Bourdieu argues

[21] E. Cohen, 'Anthropology of Knowledge', *Journal of the Royal Anthropological Institute* 16 (2010), S193–S202.

[22] Marcel Mauss, 'Techniques of the Body', *Economy and Society* 2.1 (February 1973), 70–88 (85).

[23] G. Downey, 'Throwing Like a Brazilian: On Ineptness and a Skill-Shaped Body', in Robert R. Sands and Linda R. Sands, eds., *The Anthropology of Sport and Human Movement: A Biocultural Perspective* (Lanham, MD: Lexington Books, 2010), 297; Iris Marion Young, 'Throwing Like a Girl: A Phenomenology of Feminine Body Comportment Motility and Spatiality', *Human Studies* 3.1 (December 1980), 137–56.

[24] In contrast to a social science literature that sees skill primarily as the property of the individual, Bourdieu attempts to account for embodied practices as produced by the larger cultural field, or 'habitus', which he defines as the 'systems of durable, transposable *dispositions*' operating largely out of anyone's conscious control. As Bourdieu puts it, 'it is because subjects do not, strictly speaking, know what they are doing that what they do has more meaning than they know'. See Pierre Bourdieu, *Outline of a Theory of Practice* (Cambridge: Cambridge University Press, 1977), 183.

that in 'treating the body as a memory, [societies] entrust to it...the fundamental principles of the arbitrary content of the culture. The principles em-bodied [sic] in this way are placed beyond the grasp of consciousness, and hence cannot be touched by voluntary, deliberate transformation' (94). But 'voluntary, deliberate transformation' must be a component of skill, and all the more so in a society that placed heavy emphasis upon an apprenticeship model of enskillment. Greg Noble and Megan Watkins's brilliantly titled paper, 'So, How did Bourdieu Learn to Play Tennis?', nicely pinpoints the neglect of what they term 'bodily attention' in his model.[25] That is, Bourdieu provides a compelling model of the social shaping and the tacit values placed upon particular skill modalities, but his theory does not include a full account of the means by which skill is mastered and inculcated.

Early modern theatre provides numerous opportunities to investigate the ecologies of skill within which the players worked and in this way to fill in some of the gaps in Bourdieu's model. But an ecological model of theatrical skill also demands that we consider the audience's expertise in these performances, as well as the broader cultural values placed upon certain modes of displaying physical abilities. Theirs was a culture that prized highly some forms of skill and ignored or denigrated others; swimming, for instance, was apparently viewed as a highly arcane art in early modern England, in part because it was feared that it would 'perish the sinues both with cold and moisture'.[26] Some skills were discussed and evaluated differentially across both class and gender lines: tumbling and other forms of gymnastic display were popular forms of entertainment, but when performed by a mixed-sex troupe of acrobats—thus attracting huge crowds—the practice was condemned by Thomas Norton as the 'unchaste, shamelesse, and unnaturall tomblinge of the Italian weomen'.[27] Class and status were also heavily implicated in the performance of skill. The display of aristocratic skill in public was something to be undertaken especially carefully, as is demonstrated by the debates in Thomas Hoby's translation of *The Courtier* about the proper modes of skill display among the upper classes; the courtier is enjoined to dance, but not too well, as overmuch 'swiftnesse of feete and doubled footinges' are 'unseemely for a Gentilman'.[28]

Castiglione's caution here suggests an emerging conception of decorum, or a relationship among expert performance, spectatorship, and the aesthetics of skill display. Roger Ascham's *Toxophilus* is one of the earliest articulations of such a relationship:

> For this I am sure, in learning all other matters, nothing is brought to the most profitable use, which is not handled after the most comely fashion. As masters of fence have no stroke fit either to hit another, or else to defend himself, which is not joined with a

[25] Greg Noble and Megan Watkins, 'So, How Did Bourdieu Learn to Play Tennis? Habitus, Consciousness and Habituation', *Cultural Studies* 17.3 (May 2003), 520–39.

[26] M. West, 'Spenser, Everard Digby, and the Renaissance Art of Swimming', *Renaissance Quarterly* 26.1 (1973), 11–22.

[27] Chambers, *The Elizabethan Stage*, 2:262.

[28] Count Baldessare Castiglione, *The Courtyer*, trans. Thomas Hoby (London, 1561), M3r.

wonderful comeliness. A cook cannot chop his herbs neither quickly nor handsomely, except he keep such a measure with his chopping-knives as would delight a man both to see him and hear him. Every handcraftman that works best for his own profit, works most seemly to other men's sight. Again, in building a house, in making a ship, every part, the more handsomely they be joined for profit and last, the more comely they be fashioned to every man's sight and eye.[29]

For Ascham, fencing in particular stands out as a form in which comeliness is wedded to skill, serving as a template for other, very different arts (cooking, handicraft) that we might not normally associate with an 'aestheticized' skilful performance. And fencing *is* an excellent example of a more general theatrical ecology of skill display and consumption, for fencing performances not only pervaded the drama of the period but were, at the same time, a fixture of London civic life. Throughout the latter decades of the sixteenth century, public fencing displays or 'prize fights' held by the 'Masters of the Noble Science of Defence', were 'a regular popular feature of the life of London and its environs'.[30] The manuscript archive of the Society of the Masters of Defence records over one hundred of such prizes, and the avidity with which these spectacles were consumed points to a high level of audience expertise in the various forms of intra- and extra-theatrical martial display.

Fencing is thus an important example of what Donald Hedrick has described as the 'sportification' of the early modern theatre.[31] Since watching a fencing combat involves the education of attention of the audience, especially given the speed with which a match unfolds, theatre-goers were likely to have a high degree of domain knowledge of the sport. Indeed, the civic fencing matches were in some sense already elaborate theatrical spectacles, often conducted in playhouses themselves, and preceded by elaborate processions through the city, which civic officials often opposed because of their capacity for disorder. Henslowe rented out his theatre for one such contest and took in 40 shillings, more than he took for almost any single dramatic performance.[32] These performances were fought with short swords and targets (bucklers), a mode of fighting that remained popular throughout the early modern period but that was considered to be the purview of the lower class and of the foot-soldier. John Florio referred to the short sword as 'a clownish dastardly weapon and not fit for a gentlemen'.[33]

[29] Roger Ascham, *Toxophilus*, ed. Peter Medine (Tempe: ACMRS, 2002), 125.

[30] M. McElroy and K. Cartwright, 'Public Fencing Contests on the Elizabethan Stage', *Journal of Sport History* 13.3 (1986), 193–211 (194).

[31] Donald Hedrick, 'Real Entertainment: Sportification, Coercion, and Carceral Theater', in Peter Kanelos and Matt Kozusko, eds., *Thunder at a Playhouse: Essaying Shakespeare and the Early Modern Stage* (Cranbury, NJ: Susquehanna University Press, 2010).

[32] Ian Borden, 'The Blackfriars Gladiators: Masters of Fence, Playing a Prize, and the Elizabethan and Stuart Theater', in Paul Menzer, ed., *Inside Shakespeare: Essays on the Blackfriars Stage* (Selinsgrove: Susquehanna University Press, 2006), 135.

[33] John Florio, *Florio His Firste Fruites* (London, 1578); quoted in A. L. Soens, 'Tybalt's Spanish Fencing in *Romeo and Juliet*', *Shakespeare Quarterly* 20.2 (1969), 121–7 (122).

Skill display on the early modern stage

Such spectacles remained common in the theatre, despite being denigrated by supposedly more sophisticated writers. Players could expect an audience avid for action and well versed in the nuances of fencing, and it seems fair to assume that the audience's knowledge and appreciation for the fights was an important reason for their ongoing life in a theatrical ecology of performance. Players were in a particularly complex position, because they had to negotiate a range of skills and styles of display, each of which might correspond to the different social hierarchies of their audiences. On the one hand, players needed to give a credible emulation of aristocratic skill before audiences drawn from the highest orders of society. As Lois Potter writes, 'Men and women who had spent years learning to fence and dance would be critical of inadequate performance from characters purporting to be royal or aristocratic.'[34] On the other hand, players also had to perform credible sword-and-buckler fights in the manner of the civic contests before audiences who were fluent in these very different styles.

In *Romeo and Juliet*, to take a famous example, at least four separate styles of fighting are mentioned or displayed.[35] Sampson and Gregory, as servants, seem to have 'clownish' swords and targets, since they are described using the 'washing [slashing] blow' (1.1.62) afforded by the short sword (as opposed to the thrust of the rapier).[36] Old Capulet calls for his longsword, an old-fashioned weapon that he is almost certainly too feeble to even hold upright, as his wife witheringly notes (1.1.76). And, crucially, the young noblemen fence with dagger and rapier, using European styles that had displaced the sword-and-buckler techniques still common among the lower orders. Mercutio fences Italian style, which at this point had been appropriated as a native English style, a thrusting and fluid style, in which the rapier moves between 'stoccato' (low) or 'imbroccatta' (high) position. In contrast, Tybalt fights by the 'book of arithmetic' as Romeo kisses by the book: 'he fights as you sing prick-song, keeps time, distance and proportion. He rests his minim rests, one, two, and the third in your bosom' (2.4.21–4). George Silver's *Paradoxes of Defence* notes that fencers using the Spanish style hold their bodies rigidly: 'They stand as braue as they can with their bodies straight upright, narrow spaced with their feet continually moving as if they were in a dance.'[37] Tybalt's stiff upper body works to his

---

[34] Lois Potter, *The Life of William Shakespeare: A Critical Biography* (Blackwell Critical Biographies), 2nd edn. (Malden, MA: Wiley-Blackwell, 2012), 66.

[35] Borden, 'The Blackfriars Gladiators', 132–46; Soens, 'Tybalt's Spanish Fencing in *Romeo and Juliet*'.

[36] Unless indicated otherwise, all quotations are taken from William Shakespeare, *The Arden Shakespeare Complete Works*, ed. Richard Proudfoot, Ann Thompson, and David Scott Kastan (London: Methuen Drama, 2011).

[37] George Silver, *Paradoxes of Defence Wherein Is Proued the True Grounds of Fight to Be in the Short Auncient Weapons, and That the Short Sword Hath Aduantage of the Long Sword or Long Rapier* (London: Edward Blount, 1599), C3v.

advantage when Romeo 'beats down' the weapons, allowing Tybalt to thrust only slightly to pierce Mercutio with his death-wound. The technical expertise with which the duels are presented and described is testimony not just to the actor's skill but to the sophistication of the spectators.

The drama is rife with inset skill displays of feats of arms and on-stage evaluation of them. Stage directions often indicate extended conflicts:

> *He fighteth first with one, and then with another, and overcomes them both*
>   (*Orlando Furioso*, 1526–7)
>
> *they fight a good while and then breathe*   (*Orlando Furioso*, 1536)
>
> *alarum, a fierce fight with sword and target, then after pause and breathe*
>   (*Rape of Lucrece*, 252)
>
> *Alarum, fight with single swords, and being deadly wounded and panting for breath, making a stroke at each other with their gauntlets they fall*   (*Rape of Lucrece*, 252)

Some stage directions call for very complex and technical displays, such as:

> *throws his cloak on the other's point; gets within him and takes away his sword*
>   (*Bride*, 36)

or, more famously:

> *In scuffling they change Rapiers*   (Folio *Hamlet*, 3777, 5.2.302)[38]

The commentaries within the plays show the level of skilled viewing expected, as in Middleton and Rowley's *A Fair Quarrel*, when the seconds debate whether the stroke was a punto or a passado.[39]

A similar level of virtuoso display was evident in the frequent calls for dancing. Early modern dance was often closer to gymnastic display than ballroom dancing, with male dancers in particular vying to display athletic leaps and capers, a practice Shakespeare mocks in *Twelfth Night* when Sir Toby Belch encourages Sir Andrew Aguecheek to 'Let me see thee caper' (1.3.136). As with the range of technical fencing skills expected by dramatists, the plays routinely call for high technical and varied dances:

> *dancing a Coranto*   (*Duke's Mistress*, F 41)
> *dances the Spanish pavin*   (*Blurt*, 1.1.158, 4.2.32)
> *place themselves in a figure for a dance*   (*Hannibal and Scipio*, 220, 256, also 221)
> *dance after the ancient Ethiopian manner*   (*Amorous War*, E2v)[40]

As with fencing, dance performance had wide cultural currency, with spectators often attending London's many dancing schools to witness feats of skill among the

---

[38] Cited from Alan C. Dessen and Leslie Thomson, *A Dictionary of Stage Directions in English Drama, 1580–1642* (Cambridge: Cambridge University Press, 1999), 92, 39, 92, 92, 50, 176.

[39] Thomas Middleton and William Rowland, *A Fair Quarrel*, ed. George R. Price (Lincoln: University of Nebraska Press, 1976), 3.1.153–4.

[40] Dessen and Thomson, *A Dictionary of Stage Directions in English Drama*, 65.

young men performing galliards, leaps, and tricks.[41] Marston satirizes the intricacies of newly fashionable courtly dances in *The Malcontent*, when a dancing master explains the 'easy' steps to the 'brawl': 'Why, 'tis *but* two on the left, two on the right, three doubles forward, a traverse of six round; do this twice, three singles side, galliard trick-of-twenty, coranto-pace; a figure of eight, three singles broken down, come up, meet two doubles, fall back, and then honor' (4.2.6–10).[42]

Analogous to dancing and fighting in its physical prowess and finesse was the well-established stage tradition of clowning, which consisted of highly skilled and virtuosic sets of performances by men trained in physical and verbal gymnastics. William Kemp's athleticism in leaping over a ditch earned him a reward from the Earl of Leicester; his marathon morris dancing from London to Norwich attracted huge attention and incited numerous amateurs to attempt to match his pace and skill of dance.[43] But theatre historians have continued to denigrate clowning just as they denigrate displays of other physical accomplishments. Hamlet's advice to the players is often seen as reflecting Shakespeare's own views, the aggrieved playwright's complaint about the clown interfering with the 'necessary questions' of the play. In this view, the comic energy of the clown is gradually contained by the writer, as exemplified by Hamlet's advice to the players to control the extemporizing of the fool: 'let those that play your clowns speak no more than is set down for them—for there be of them that will themselves laugh, to set on some quantity of barren spectators to laugh too' (3.2.39–42). In a teleological view of the theatre dear to many theatre historians and critics, the clown is gradually brought within the purview of the dramatic fiction, and audiences, except for those at citizen's theatres such as the Red Bull, gradually abandon broad clowning and begin to integrate the clown in the fiction.[44]

We have already seen how *Romeo and Juliet* draws elaborately on the many styles of stage fighting and its cultural associations. I would now like to consider some further examples of how ecologies of skill came to define early modern theatricality and suggest how approaching the plays as collections of skilled performances might yield new interpretive possibilities for criticism. A notable example is Thomas Middleton and William Rowley's *The Changeling*, which is, as Lois Potter puts it, one of 'perhaps ten non-Shakespearean plays that are frequently edited, have performance histories, and are thus beginning to acquire something of the aura (made up of multiple page and stage interpretations) that makes Shakespeare's plays seem so

---

[41] See Skiles Howard, *The Politics of Courtly Dancing in Early Modern England* (Amherst, MA: University of Massachusetts Press, 1998); Walter Sorrell, 'Shakespeare and the Dance', *Shakespeare Quarterly* 8.3 (Summer 1987), 367–84.

[42] John Marston, *The Malcontent* (Regents Renaissance Drama Series), ed. M. L. Wine, Cyrus Hoy, and G. E. Bentley (Lincoln: University of Nebraska Press, 1969), 4:2:6–10.

[43] Mark Eccles, 'Elizabethan Actors III: K-R', *Notes & Queries* 39.3 (1992), 293–303.

[44] See Andrew Gurr, *Playgoing in Shakespeare's London*, 3rd edn. (Cambridge: Cambridge University Press, 2004), 157.

complex.[45] After a long period of neglect, *The Changeling* was revived in 1961 by Tony Richardson, followed by two 1978 productions (Peter Gill's Riverside production and Terry Hands's Aldwych production). As Roberta Barker and David Nicol have noted, the critical reaction to this revival focused almost entirely upon the daring psychological portrait of the leading characters DeFlores and Beatrice-Joanna: 'what passes for a "straight" interpretation of a classic playtext is often the one that most closely reproduces a particular culture's established assumptions about it'.[46]

The focus in modern productions and criticism is almost entirely on the main plot, with Rowley's madhouse subplot cut, ignored, or relegated to a thematic echoing of the madness of the main plot. The situation was very different in the seventeenth century; here ample evidence reveals that contemporary audiences highly valued the antic subplot of fools and madmen. N. W. Bawcutt has compiled numerous examples of the great popularity of Antonio, or The Changeling, once again drawing on satirical prologues. The prologue (almost certainly written by Richard Brome) to Thomas Goffe's play *Careless Shepherdess* stages a pre-play conversation among a countryman (Landlord), a citizen (Thrift), an Inns of Court man (Spark), and a courtier (Spruce). Spruce challenges Landlord to answer the question 'What part you think essential to a play?'[47] The answer, of course, is 'The Fool':

> I would have the Fool in every Act ...
> I heard a fellow once on this stage cry Doodle, Doodle Dooe
> Beyond compare. I'de give the other shilling
> To see him act the Changeling once again.

The citizen enthusiastically agrees:

> And so would I, his part has all the wit
> For none speaks Craps and Quibbles besides him:
> I'd rather see him leap, laugh or cry,
> Then hear the gravest Speech in all the Play
> I never say Rheade peeping through the Curtain,
> But ravishing joy enter'd into my heart.[48]

This mocking prologue refers to Timothy Reade, who succeeded William Robbins as the clown for Queen Henrietta's Men. Thrift and Landlord recall with pleasure Read's performances; his physical leaps and capers and virtuosic verbal skills

---

[45] Lois Potter, 'The Director's Tragedy or, Approaches to the Really Obscure Play', *The Hare*, http://thehareonline.com/article/directors-tragedy-or-approaches-really-obscure-play, accessed Sept. 2012.

[46] Roberta Barker and David Nicol, 'Does Beatrice Joanna Have a Subtext: *The Changeling* on the London Stage', *EMLS*, May 2004, http://extra.shu.ac.uk/emls/10-1/barknico.htm, accessed Sept. 2012.

[47] Thomas Goffe, *The Careles Shepherdess* (London: Richard Rogers, 1656), B2v.

[48] Goffe, *The Careles Shepherdess*.

apparently commandeered most of the attention of the audience. These performances are even recalled across parts and between different plays, working 'intertheatrically', to use William N. West's term in his essay for this collection, since the
reference to his cries of 'Doodle, Doodle, Doo' alludes to his part of Buzzard in
Brome's *The English Moor*. While this prologue is parodic, it nevertheless attests to an
economy of spectatorship and skill that foregrounds the physical displays of particular charismatic players. The popularity of the part of Antonio through the seventeenth century is also attested to by the appearance of the figure of 'The Changeling'
on the title page of *The Wits, or Sport upon Sport* (1662); the dangling arms of this
figure seem to represent a favourite gestural bit described by Landlord: 'O it does me
good / To see him hold out's Chin hang down his hands'. As Steggle argues, 'The
changeling routines described by Landlord and Thrift are certainly not mere add-
ons to the play from which they come.'[49] Verbal wit, gestural comedy, both innovative and referencing past performances (as when Reade imitates Tarlton's signature
curtain bit) and the physical skill demanded to perform leaps and capers: these acts
of skill lived in the memory of playgoers.

These many contemporary accounts of skill suggest that audiences had as much
interest in the player as they did in his character (perhaps much like cinema audiences today). These references also show that it was not only the clown who stood
out in the emergent celebrity culture of the early modern theatre. As the reference
to 'Ned Alleyn still' in the Dulwhich archive establishes, it was this actor who
loomed above all others. Susan Cerasano argues that 'the career of Edward Alleyn
fashioned a new and powerful professional model, ushering in an era in which players began to perform not only for contemporary audiences but, in a sense, for posterity as well. Actors, in addition to plays, became commodities to be marketed and
capitalized on by playhouse owners and theatrical companies.'[50] Her position is a
welcome corrective to critics who cast doubt upon Alleyn's skill, arguing that his
style was outmoded and exaggerated, in contrast to the more subtle style of Richard
Burbage, the primary tragedian of Shakespeare's company.[51] This invidious distinction has become a critical commonplace; a recent critic suggests that Alleyn's 'sten-
torial acting style no longer appealed to the younger generation of players and the
public'.[52]

Yet the evidence for this assessment is thin; in fact, Alleyn's shade looms large
upon the early modern stage as late as 1633. When Christopher Marlowe's *The Jew*

---

[49] Matthew Steggle, *Laughing and Weeping in Early Modern Theatres* (Aldershot: Ashgate, 2007),
76–7.

[50] S. P. Cerasano, 'Edward Alleyn, the New Model Actor, and the Rise of the Celebrity in the 1590s',
Medieval and Renaissance Drama in England 18 (2006), 47–58 (48).

[51] See, for example, Andrew Gurr, *The Shakespearean Stage 1574–1642*, 4th edn. (Cambridge:
Cambridge University Press, 2009), 137–9.

[52] David Mateer, 'Edward Alleyn, Richard Perkins and the Rivalry Between the Swan and the Rose
Playhouses', *Review of English Studies* 60.243 (2009), 61–77 (70).

of Malta was revived for a performance at the Cockpit in 1633, the role of Barabas, indelibly linked with Edward Alleyn, was played by his former apprentice, Richard Perkins. Thomas Heywood's 'Prologue to the Stage' emphasizes Alleyn's ownership of the role:

> ... by the best of poets in that age
> The *Malta-Jew* had being, and was made;
> And he, then by the best of actors play'd,
> In *Hero and Leander*, one did gain
> A lasting memory; in *Tamburlaine*,
> This *Jew*, with others many, th' other wan
> The attribute of peerless, being a man
> Whom we may rank with (doing no one wrong)
> Proteus for shapes, and Roscius for a tongue,
> So could he speak, so vary ...
>
> (*The Prologue to the Stage, at the Cock-pit*: 1–11)[53]

Interestingly, Marlowe is memorialized through his non-dramatic verse (the wildly popular *Hero and Leander*), whilst Alleyn is remembered though his personation of the roles. So overpowering is the memory of Alleyn, long absent from the stage even before his death seven years earlier, that Perkins, in reinhabiting the role, is said to have no wish to prove himself against his powerful predecessor and former master:

> ... Nor is it his ambition
> To exceed, or equal, being of condition
> More modest; this is all that he intends
> (And that, too, at the urgence of some friends):
> To prove his best, and if none here gainsay it,
> The part he hath studied, and intends to play it.
>
> (*The Prologue to the Stage, at the Cock-pit*: 13–18)[54]

The epilogue likewise simultaneously invokes and disavows the language of rivalry:

> In graving with Pygmalion to contend,
> Or painting, with Appelles, doubtless the end
> Must be disgrace; our actor did not so:
> He only aim'd to go, but not outgo.
> Nor think that this day any prize was play'd;
> Here were no bets at all, no wagers laid;

---

[53] Christopher Marlowe, *The Jew of Malta*, ed. Richard Van Fossen (London: Edward Arnold, 1965).

[54] Marlowe, *The Jew of Malta*, 6.

All the ambition that his mind doth swell
Is but to hear from you (by me) 'twas well.   (*Epilogue to the Stage*: 1–8)[55]

Far from establishing that Alleyn's style looked dated and outmoded, these paratextual materials playfully reinforce the powerful hold he had over the drama decades after his heyday. This material also invites us to re-examine the nature of his performances to see what was valued in them; as in the example of *The Changeling*, contemporaries may have prized very different qualities than are privileged today.

The Jew of Malta has often puzzled its commentators, who complain that the play 'degenerates into farce' and that 'Barabas has at the beginning of the play a humanity and dignity he soon loses'.[56] Barabas's over-the-top evil, as expressed in such lines as 'How sweet the bells ring now the nuns are dead', can be ascribed to Marlowe's characteristic over-reaching, but many critics have been put off by the apparent low comedy of other scenes. His seemingly random appearance 'with a lute, disguised' as a French musician with a comic accent seems at odds with the efficient and intelligent Barabas of the first act: 'Must tuna my lute for sound, twang twang'. Shortly thereafter Barabas is carried in 'as dead', is thrown over the walls, and pops up alive immediately thereafter. And at the conclusion of the play he is said to '*Enter with a hammer above, very busy*', directing carpenters in a complex mechanical contraption of cords, cranes, and pulleys designed to rig a 'dainty gallery, the floor whereof, this cable being cut, / Doth fall asunder, so that it doth sink / Into a deep pit past recovery' (5: 5:33–6). Barabas's spectacular fall into this very pit to conclude the play may be a moral come-uppance, but it is also a *tour de force* of physical theatre, however it was originally played. It reminds us that Alleyn was praised above all for his Protean nature, his skill in *variety*. Audiences seemed to have prized the widest possible variety of the display of skill.

A final point about skill needs to be made: however talented and resourceful the players, these plays did not write themselves. The prologues such as those I have mentioned here tend to give the impression that the relationships of players and playwrights were marked primarily by rivalry. But Lois Potter's new biography of Shakespeare provides another way of looking at this evidence. The figure of Shakespeare that emerges from Potter's biography is above all that of a craftsman. Her Shakespeare is meticulous, hard-working, with a good ear, a capacious memory, and keen alertness to potential material, both through the books available to him and through the thriving theatrical scene in which he worked. Potter emphasizes his developing skill in poetic language, pacing, and plotting. But above all Potter emphasizes the skill of Shakespeare—and other playwrights—in writing good parts for their actors. At one point she makes the speculative but extremely intriguing suggestion that Shakespeare may have reworked an old version of *Hamlet*, probably

---

[55] Marlowe, *The Jew of Malta*, 114.   [56] Marlowe, *The Jew of Malta*, xxvvii.

by Thomas Kyd, to provide Richard Burbage with an acting vehicle that would stand up against the revival of *The Spanish Tragedy* performed by Alleyn upon his return to the stage in 1600. Potter writes: 'Above all, perhaps, Hamlet is a composite of everything that Burbage did best, which is why he is everything that an actor wants to play, and everything that an audience wants an actor to be.'[57] In this reading, the apparent inconsistencies of Hamlet's character are at least partly explained if we imagine the part as purposely written as a vehicle for actorly skill display, a *tour de force* of variety that could be set against Alleyn's Hieronomo and Barabas. Perhaps more such re-readings may be available if we foreground skill in our account of early modern theatricality.

FURTHER READING

Brissenden, Alan. *Shakespeare and the Dance* (Atlantics Highlands, NJ: Humanities Press, 1981).

Edelman, Charles. *Brawl Ridiculous: Sword Fighting in Shakespeare's Plays* (Manchester: Manchester University Press, 1992).

Hedrick, Donald. 'Real Entertainment: Sportification, Coercion, and Carceral Theater', in Peter Kanelos and Matt Kozusko, eds., *Thunder at a Playhouse: Essaying Shakespeare and the Early Modern Stage* (Cranbury, NJ: Susquehanna University Press, 2010).

Lindley, David. *Shakespeare and Music* (London: Arden, 2006).

Potter, Lois. *The Life of William Shakespeare: A Critical Biography* (London: Wiley-Blackwell, 2011).

---

[57] Potter, *The Life of William Shakespeare*, 281.

CHAPTER 10

GAMES

GINA BLOOM*

There has been little serious critical attention given to the fact that the climactic murder scene of the anonymous *Arden of Faversham* takes place during a game of backgammon and that a card game is the setting in which the betrayed husband of Thomas Heywood's *A Woman Killed with Kindness* tests his wife's infidelity.[1] This is surprising: given the challenges of staging these particular games, why would dramatists choose them as settings for scenes that are of foremost importance to the plot? Unlike drama, which can be performed in an array of venues, backgammon and card games are designed to be played in intimate spaces such as parlours or taverns, where spectators can closely encircle the playing space to follow the action. Sixteenth- and seventeenth-century paintings, such as those of the 'Merry Company' genre, show spectators clustered around card and backgammon matches (see Figures 9 and 10) in part because, as is sometimes true today, players and spectators of these games typically wagered on their outcome and thus had a stake in following the ludic action closely. Theatrical staging of such games presents several problems, then, among them the fact that theatre audiences were positioned far enough from the dramatized game that they could not follow it in the ways to which they were accustomed. So what is to be gained by including these games at all, let alone at such crucial junctures in plays? *A Woman Killed with Kindness* and *Arden of Faversham* are particularly rich examples to consider together because they are often seen as sharing a dramatic genre, the 'domestic tragedy'; in fact, critics have often

* For valuable responses to earlier versions of this essay, I am grateful to Seeta Chaganti, Frances Dolan, Noah Guynn, Henry Turner, and Valerie Traub. I presented sections of the essay at the Columbia Shakespeare seminar and at the conferences 'Phenomenal Performances: Getting a Feeling for Shakespeare's Theater' at Northwestern University and 'Theatricality' at Rutgers University. My thanks to audiences at these venues, especially to Jean Howard (my formal respondent at Columbia) for their feedback, and to Christopher Wallis for editorial assistance.

[1] For the sake of simplicity and clarity to modern readers, I refer to tables as *backgammon*, a variation of tables that came to England at the turn of the seventeenth century. See H. J. R. Murray, *A History of Board-Games Other Than Chess* (Oxford: Clarendon Press, 1951), esp. chapter 6.

Figure 9 *The Card Players* (oil on canvas) by Jan Havicksz Steen (1625/26–79). Private Collection. Reproduced by permission of The Bridgeman Art Library.

Figure 10 *The Game of Backgammon* (oil on panel) by Dirck Hals (1591–1656). Musée des Beaux-Arts, Lille, France. Giraudon. Reproduced by permission of The Bridgeman Art Library.

argued that the parlour game is an important technique for producing a sense of the domestic in these plays.[2] While the plays certainly share generic features, I want to suggest that the games they stage point well beyond problems of dramatic form. They also speak, and speak in markedly different ways, to early modern *theatrical* form: staged scenes of cards and backgammon invited audiences familiar with these games to repurpose their gaming competencies in order to become skilled theatre-goers. As they offered audience members the chance to play vicariously staged games, these scenes taught early audiences—as they teach modern critics—one key component of early modern theatricality: the participatory demands of spectatorship.

In using games to understand the formal dimensions of spectatorship within the specific institution of the early modern theatre and the dramas staged within it, my essay takes part in a long tradition of performance studies scholarship at the same time as it questions the trajectory of that scholarship, which has led away from tra-ditional theatre and drama and towards study of the theatricality of everyday life. Games have been fundamental to the self-definition of performance studies, and the relation of theatre to games was a central preoccupation of several of the field's most influential scholars. The sociologist Erving Goffman used theatre to under-stand everyday social interaction as a game, and anthropologist Victor Turner resists distinguishing between recreational games and theatre when he argues that cultural performances can be read as 'social dramas'.[3] Anthropologist Clifford Geertz, though he disagreed with Turner's reliance on the genre of drama to understand social life, turned, nevertheless, to the theatre, and specifically to the experience of watching *Macbeth*, to illustrate his argument about the 'sentimental education' the cock-fight delivers to its audiences.[4] The links between games and theatre have been explored perhaps most influentially by Richard Schechner, who has written that 'theater has more in common with games and sports than with play or ritual'.[5] Nevertheless, instead of using games to help us understand how the theatre works, most performance studies scholars follow Schechner in using games to expand the concept of performance *beyond* the institution of the theatre and

[2] Lena Cowen Orlin, *Private Matters and Public Culture in Post-Reformation England* (Ithaca: Cornell University Press, 1984); Ann Christensen, 'Business, Pleasure, and the Domestic Economy in Heywood's *A Woman Killed with Kindness*', *Exemplaria* 9.2 (1997), 315–40; Rick Bowers, '*A Woman Killed with Kindness*: Plausibility on a Smaller Scale', *Studies in English Literature, 1500–1900* 24.2 (1984), 293–306; and Theresia de Vroom, 'Female Heroism in Heywood's Tragic Farce of Adultery', in Naomi Conn Liebler, ed., *The Female Tragic Hero in English Renaissance Drama* (New York: Palgrave Macmillan, 2002), 119–40.

[3] Erving Goffman, *Interaction Ritual: Essays on Face-to-Face Behavior* (New York: Pantheon Books, 1967); Victor Turner, *From Ritual to Theater: The Human Seriousness of Play* (New York: PAJ Publica-tions, 1996).

[4] Clifford Geertz, 'Deep Play: Notes on the Balinese Cockfight', in *The Interpretation of Cultures* (New York: Basic Books, 1972), 11.

[5] Richard Schechner, *Performance Theory*, revised edn. (London: Routledge, 2003), 15.

dramas performed in early theatres in particular. This approach to games is symptomatic of wider trends in the field of performance studies, which has tended to ghettoize if not abandon entirely the study of traditional and especially pre-modern drama, leaving much of the work of investigating early modern theatrical conditions to theatre historians, who are on the whole uninterested in theorizing performance. The bias of performance studies scholarship towards modern and contemporary performance and the fission between theatre history and performance studies is replicated widely in the profession, from conferences to publications. But attention to the conditions of early modern theatres and to the plays that theorize and dramatize those conditions has much to teach those in the field of performance studies about the experience of spectatorship. And I argue that this project can begin where performance studies itself began: at the intersection of theatre and games.

Games and/in the theatre

To understand how game scenes in drama taught early modern spectators theatre-going competencies, we need to attend not simply to the broad resonance between games and theatre—the approach of a range of critics in the fields of literary analysis, theatre history, and performance studies—but to the formal elements of the particular games early modern dramatists integrated into the action of plays. It matters that *A Woman Killed with Kindness* stages cards instead of, for instance, backgammon or chess, for though these are all parlour games played on a table, their particular forms—their rules and the materials used in play—provoke very different kinds of engagement on the part of players and, consequently, theatre audiences who watch these players. For instance, cards are two-sided and thus require the strategic concealment and revelation of information in a way that is formally analogous, as we shall see, to most comic, revenge, or domestic tragedy plots, as well as to how those plots are staged. *A Woman Killed* is a good example of a play that uses a card game to instruct audiences in how to engage with theatre as a game of 'imperfect information'. Approaching theatre as a card game, audiences find themselves not as passive observers of plot developments but as players with an epistemological stake in the action. The game of backgammon differs from cards in that it is played on a confined game board and thus demands a specifically spatial skill of placement and positioning. When staged in *Arden*'s climactic murder scene, backgammon reflects on and queries the socio-spatial dynamics of the early modern amphitheatre in which it was first performed: theatre seats offering a bird's eye view of the stage signalled playgoers' higher socio-economic status but compromised their capacity to interact with and influence the action on the 'boards'. Though doing so in very different ways, both staged games invited playgoers to work by way of phenomenological analogy through their experience of spectatorship in the theatre, reminding them that the theatre, like a game, is an interactive medium that demands cognitive, emotional, and embodied engagement from its participants. Competencies developed through playing games like backgammon and cards inside and outside the theatre could thus help audiences develop skills in participatory spectatorship.

Such skills were necessary because the commercial theatre in which these plays were first staged was a newly emerging mode of entertainment in early modern England. To be sure, traditional entertainments with a theatrical dimension had flourished for centuries before—and continued to compete throughout the period with—the commercial plays staged in the first public amphitheatres. But there were important differences between the commercial stage and its predecessors/competitors. In the first place, commercial theatres demanded audiences pay money upfront before a performance, an innovation with a number of consequences for how those performances were understood, as Richard Preiss argues in his essay for this volume. And secondly, though theatre's defenders often presented the goal of plays to be moral instruction, in truth the commercial theatre's goal was predominantly and openly pure entertainment. Other kinds of theatre, including religious drama, educational plays, and court performances, had very different goals and involved different systems of economic exchange. Street entertainments perhaps came closest to the commercial theatre in their aims: a secular performance put on for the public purely for entertainment purposes. But these performances would have been more informal in nature, and audiences only paid if they enjoyed the performance and/ or felt that it deserved their support; as continues to be the case today, the performers would send a hat around to collect contributions at the conclusion of the show. In contrast, the professional theatres developing in London in the late sixteenth century were open to anyone who could afford to pay the admissions price—a mere penny for standing room in the outdoor amphitheatres. This payment was rendered at the door, which meant that audiences who entered the theatre committed financially to the play before seeing any part of it. It is as if audiences took a wager on the play; they rendered money in advance expecting that they would be entertained and get back at least their money's worth, hopefully more.[6]

From our perspective today, where commercial theatre of this kind is widely available and, at least in the Western world, the norm, it is easy to underestimate the effects and implications of this commodification of performance. Michael Bristol argues that early modern audiences were well prepared for this 'transformation

[6] Donald Hedrick, 'Real Entertainment: Sportification, Coercion, and Carceral Theater', in Peter Kanelos and Matt Kozusko, eds., *Thunder at a Playhouse: Essaying Shakespeare and the Early Modern Stage* (Selinsgrove: Susquehanna University Press, 2010), 50–66.

of familiar performance practices into merchandise' through their exposure to London's flourishing commodity culture, which, like the commercial theatre, enabled consumers to obtain 'desired goods or amenities outside the complex networks of reciprocal obligation that prevail in a traditional community'.[7] While I concur that the public theatre aimed towards this kind of commodity status, I doubt that the transition was as easy as Bristol suggests. Audiences in London may have been familiar with the workings of a commodity culture, but they were not as accustomed to viewing plays in this way. In particular, where theatre was concerned, they were not used to 'more passive habits of cultural consumption'.[8] Audiences needed to learn *how* to approach something like theatre as a commodity. It is no wonder, as Erika Lin points out in her essay for this volume, that the professional theatre drew on traditional forms of entertainment, such as festive performances, inviting audiences to take a more participatory role in plays. To be sure, when the commercial theatres appropriated these more familiar forms of entertainment, they offered audiences a way to invest emotionally and intellectually in an otherwise alienating commercial production. But I would maintain that the goal was not, as Lin argues, to produce in the theatre the kind of communal affiliation found elsewhere but rather to teach audience members their proper place as consumers.[9] The commercial theatre needed to *bridge* festive performance practices with this new ethos of theatre as commodity, and I submit that parlour games, perhaps even more so than festive entertainments, were the perfect medium for doing so. Backgammon and cards invited spectators to play vicariously and, like festive entertainments, could thus prompt audiences' deeper engagement in the experience of play. But as betting games, they also helped audiences retain some distance from the object of spectatorship and treat the performance, like a game, as a commodity. Through the staging of these games, the theatre could take advantage of its patrons' expertise with and interests in competing forms of recreation in order to build a theatrical form that was new but felt familiar.

What kind of history of theatricality emerges when we consider drama as part of a network of other ludic engagements? The question has been pursued by a range of scholars. Medievalists have debated the extent to which games and dramatic plays—both of which were described using the same term, *ludus* —could be clearly distinguished from one another before the sixteenth century.[10] Historians of early

---

[7] Michael D. Bristol, 'Theater and Popular Culture', in John D. Cox and David Scott Kastan, eds., *A New History of Early English Drama* (New York: Columbia University Press, 1997), 231–48 (247–8). The argument is further elucidated in Michael D. Bristol, *Big-Time Shakespeare* (London: Routledge, 1996), esp. 30–41.

[8] Bristol, 'Theater and Popular Culture', 248.

[9] Erika T. Lin, 'Popular Festivity and the Early Modern Stage: The Case of *George a Greene*', *Theatre Journal* 61 (2009), 271–97.

[10] See especially Glending Olson, 'Plays as Play: A Medieval Ethical Theory of Performance and the Intellectual Context of the *Tretise of Miraclis Pleyinge*', *Viator: Medieval and Renaissance Studies* 26

modern theatre have examined the ways other forms of recreation were implicated in theatrical production, with some, such as Glynn Wickham, even arguing that early modern plays were treated less as literature than as game.[11] For instance, there has been much discussion of the fact that amphitheatres developed out of and may even have doubled as bear-baiting arenas.[12] And a number of cultural historians and literary scholars have examined the intersections between theatre and games and between theatre and sports, with special attention to festive culture and, most recently, to gambling.[13] But studies of the intersections between games and theatre have tended to follow one of two tendencies. Many studies, overly reliant on theories of play developed by social scientists Johan Huizinga and Roger Caillois, approach games and play as broad categories that, in most cases, reflect on the nature of pretence in drama, instead of looking at specific kinds of games in relation to theatre. This approach risks not only flattening important differences between games but also overemphasizing pretence as the key competency exercised by participants in gameplay and theatre-going, when, in fact, both call for a broader range of skills.[14] Those scholars who do attend to particular games tend

---

(1995), 195–222; V. A. Kolve, *The Play Called Corpus Christi* (Stanford: Stanford University Press, 1966), esp. chapter 2; Lawrence M. Clopper, *Drama, Play, and Game: English Festive Culture in the Medieval and Early Modern Period* (Chicago: University of Chicago Press, 2001).

[11] Glynne Wickham, 'Actor and Play in Shakespeare's Theatre', *Maske und Kothurn* 15 (1969), 1–5. This argument is extended in Glynne Wickham, *Early English Stages 1300–1660*, 3 vols. (London: Routledge, 1972), vol. 2, esp. chapter 2.

[12] In addition to Wickham, see Andrew Gurr, 'Bears and Players: Philip Henslowe's Double Acts', *Shakespeare Bulletin* 22.4 (2004), 31–42; Jason Scott-Warren, 'When Theaters Were Bear-Gardens; or, What's at Stake in the Comedy of Humors', *Shakespeare Quarterly* 54.1 (2003), 63–82; John R. Ford, 'Changeable Taffeta: Re-dressing the Bears in *Twelfth Night*', in Paul Menzer, ed., *Inside Shakespeare: Essays on the Blackfriars Stage* (Selinsgrove: Susquehanna University Press: 2006), 174–91.

[13] On festive culture and drama, see, in addition to Lin, C. L. Barber, *Shakespeare's Festive Comedies* (Princeton: Princeton University Press, 1959); Robert Weimann, *Shakespeare and the Popular Tradition in the Theater: Studies in the Social Dimension of Dramatic Form and Function* (Baltimore: Johns Hopkins University Press, 1987); François Laroque, *Shakespeare's Festive World: Elizabethan Seasonal Entertainment and the Professional Stage*, trans. Janet Lloyd (Cambridge: Cambridge University Press, 1991); Naomi Conn Liebler, *Shakespeare's Festive Tragedy: The Ritual Foundations of Genre* (New York: Routledge, 1995); Michael D. Bristol, 'Shamelessness in Arden: Early Modern Theater and the Obsolescence of Popular Theatricality', in Arthur F. Marotti and Michael D. Bristol, eds., *Print, Manuscript, Performance: The Changing Relations of the Media in Early Modern England* (Columbus, OH: Ohio State University Press, 2000), 279–306. Further references follow. On gambling and drama, see Linda Woodbridge, '"He Beats Thee 'gainst the Odds": Gambling, Risk Management, and *Antony and Cleopatra*', in Sara Munson Deats, ed., *Antony and Cleopatra: New Critical Essays* (New York: Routledge, 2004), 193–211; and Hedrick, 'Real Entertainment'.

[14] Johan Huizinga, *Homo Ludens: A Study of the Play Element in Culture* (Boston: Beacon Press, 1950). Roger Caillois, *Man, Play and Games*, trans. Meyer Barash (Urbana: University of Illinois Press, 2001). Examples of studies that approach play broadly include Louis A. Montrose, '"Sport by Sport O'erthrown": *Love's Labour's Lost* and the Politics of Play', *Texas Studies in Literature and Language* 18.4 (1977), 528–52; Marianne L. Novy, 'Patriarchy and Play in *The Taming of the Shrew*', *English Literary Renaissance* 9.2 (1979), 264–80; Anna K. Nardo, *The Ludic Self in Seventeenth-century*

to focus on spectacle-driven kinds of games or sports, such as bear-baiting, wrestling, traditional festive performance, and fencing, all of which were either performed in venues not unlike theatres or at least shared theatre's fundamental modalities: one or more 'performers' (human or animal actors) engage in some spectacular actions for the benefit of spectators.[15]

The games I examine here, with attention to their specific forms, are far less obviously suited to dramatization on the stage. And I would suggest that the tensions between theatres and the venues (such as taverns and parlours) where games like backgammon and cards were played were crucial to the project of bridging everyday leisure activities with commercial theatre. For although the theatre benefited by establishing links to games, it had economic and ideological reasons for distinguishing itself from competing ludic forms. Consumers had only so much time and money to spend on leisure, so the theatre needed to demonstrate, as Donald Hedrick argues, the 'relative entertainment value' of their product.[16] Another factor was the need to combat the rhetoric of antitheatricalists, who strategically collapsed theatre and games to argue that all pleasures were the same, no matter their form. The staging of parlour games precisely helped to underscore the formal *differences* among games and between games and theatre. Rather than simply exploit the game–theatre overlap, then, such scenes defamiliarized and put pressure on analogies built upon it. For unlike wrestling, fencing, or other more spectacle-driven entertainments, backgammon and cards drew attention to themselves as the kind of games that could not be played in a public theatrical space. As such, they called upon audiences not only to exercise their gaming competencies but to repurpose

English Literature (Albany: SUNY Press, 1991), esp. chapter 2; Alessandro Arcangeli, *Recreation in the Renaissance: Attitudes Toward Leisure and Pastimes in European Culture, c. 1425–1675* (New York: Palgrave Macmillan, 2003); Alba Floreale, *Game and Gaming Metaphor: Proteus and the Gamester Masks in Seventeenth-century Conduct Books and the Comedy of Manners* (Rome: Bulzoni Editore, 2004). A more nuanced version of this broad approach can be found in Tom Bishop, 'Shakespeare's Theater Games', *Journal of Medieval and Early Modern Studies* 40.1 (2010), 65–88. Bishop includes a range of games under the broad rubric of 'play' but provides a complex definition of game-playing competencies to include, in addition to pretence, 'competitive cooperation' (73) and 'improvisational interplay' (74).

[15] In addition to work on festive performance by Lin, Bristol, Weimann, and others, see Cynthia Marshall, 'Wrestling as Play and Game in *As You Like It*', *Studies in English Literature, 1500–1900* 33.2 (1993), 265–87; Jennifer A. Low, *Manhood and the Duel: Masculinity in Early Modern Drama and Culture* (New York: Palgrave Macmillan, 2003); Edward Berry, *Shakespeare and the Hunt: A Cultural and Social Study* (Cambridge: Cambridge University Press, 2001); Gregory M. Colón Semenza, *Sport, Politics, and Literature in the English Renaissance* (Newark: University of Delaware Press, 2003). Among the exceptions are essays on chess and its uses in Shakespeare's *The Tempest* and Middleton's *Women Beware Women* and *A Game at Chess*. Additionally, two short essays from the 1950s survey the appearance of parlour games in early modern drama but do not provide much in the way of analysis. See Joseph T. McCullen Jr, 'The Use of Parlor and Tavern Games in Elizabethan and Early Stuart Drama', *Modern Language Quarterly* 14.1 (1953), 1–7; Delmar E. Solem, 'Some Elizabethan Game Scenes', *Educational Theatre Journal* 6.1 (1954), 15–21.

[16] Hedrick, 'Real Entertainment', 56.

and adapt them. They pushed audiences to approach the play as a different *kind* of game, one that audiences would, nevertheless, be equipped to play.

Thus far, I have focused on the historical intersections between theatre and games, but it is worth noting that when it comes to games, conventional historical approaches are of limited use. To be sure, we can imagine reasons why parlour games would have become more popular during the rise of the commercial theatre. Given the spread of printing technologies, for instance, which made it cheaper to produce playing cards and gameboards and to publish instruction manuals for gameplay, games ostensibly would have been available to more people than ever before. But game rules, though they can be transmitted in writing, were (and continue today) to be transmitted orally; in fact oral transmission is arguably more suited to game rules, since these rules change almost as quickly as they are codified. Changes may be reflected in, but are not determined by, texts of gaming, such as boards, printed cards, and rule-books. For example, the game of 'tables', which we commonly call backgammon (one of its several versions) shows variations during the period in its number of players, the significance of capturing men, and the amount of interaction between men on the board—a board whose spaces historically have taken the shape of circles, spirals, and crosses. When exactly such variations in the game developed and how they did so are impossible to ascertain. Changes are even more difficult to track with cards, where an even greater number of games can be played using the same materials, the basic 52-card deck; the card game played in *A Woman Killed with Kindness*, Vide Ruff, was a precursor to Whist, which eventually became Bridge.

The prevailing theory about how games change over time is that players adapt game rules to create more pleasurable playing experiences, and variations of a game are reiterated over and over until they become institutionalized as the new rules of the game. Game rules, we could say, materialize through repeated performance. To be sure, somewhere along the line someone may publish the rules of Whist, whose main difference from Vide Ruff is that the former is played in silence. But the rule of playing in silence was, we might imagine, generated by players of Vide Ruff, perhaps because they realized that all the talking during the game was enabling players to cheat by communicating in code with their partners. In sum, the historicist's foundational question—*when did this occur?*—cannot be answered simply in relation to games. We cannot determine when changes to a game occur, and even if we could, the payoffs for doing so are insignificant.

Consequently, although my readings of games in *Arden* and *A Woman Killed* draw on available records for how the games were played in the early modern period, my goal is less to historicize the games themselves than to provide some specificity for what I would describe rather as a phenomenological approach. My method is akin to Bruce R. Smith's 'historical phenomenology' insofar as I suggest that in order to understand how games work in the theatre, we must not only historically contextualize but also '*inhabit* the evidence'.[17] Although I treat early modern game rules and objects as evidence, I also accept the invitation of historical phenomenology to view the present and the early modern past 'not as separate compartments but as relative points along a continuum', maintaining that we must supplement study of early modern materials of gaming with the modern critic's own experiences of game-play.[18] Historical phenomenology urges us to approach games not as something we simply read about, but something we and early moderns alike *do* with and through our bodies and our embodied minds. Scholars willing to engage in this more participatory form of criticism are better able to discover the participatory forms of spectatorship early modern audiences learned through the game scenes in plays. What is more, emphasis on how the body and mind *do* games reveals overlaps between games and theatre that are not only symbolic but experiential: games and theatre often look quite different, but to their participants they can feel somewhat similar. 'Included in the situatedness of the observer...are the *feelings* of the observer in the face of what he or she sees', Smith reminds us.[19] An historical phenomenological approach to games enables us to grasp not only the overlaps between games and theatre, but also the formal and phenomenological differences among various games. As my readings of cards and backgammon will suggest, there is much at stake for our understanding of early modern theatricality in attending to how playing backgammon *feels* different than playing cards.

Cards, imperfect information, and
A Woman Killed with Kindness

The card game staged in Heywood's *A Woman Killed* happens at a key moment in the play's primary plotline. The gentleman Frankford has just been told by a faithful servant that his wife Anne is having an affair with his best friend, Wendoll, something the audience knows to be true. Frankford seeks and finds corroboration through a card game with the suspected adulterers. Although critics of the play often mention the card game as among Heywood's most theatrically interesting scenes, few say much about it, and those who do are interested in its emphasis on domestic detail or in its intriguing use of double entendres.[20] For instance, critics observe that the name of the game played, Vide Ruff, puns on Anne's

---

[17] Bruce R. Smith, *Phenomenal Shakespeare* (Chichester: Wiley-Blackwell, 2010), 37.

[18] Smith, *Phenomenal Shakespeare*, 36.

[19] Smith, *Phenomenal Shakespeare*, 13.

[20] Keith Sturgess, ed., *Three Elizabethan Domestic Tragedies* (Harmondsworth: Penguin, 1985) calls this scene 'a masterpiece of sustained metaphor' (45). The most extensive commentary on the scene's use of double entendres is Thomas Moisan, 'Framing with Kindness: The Transgressive Theatre of *A Woman Killed with Kindness*', in Georgia Johnston, ed., *Essays on Transgressive Readings: Reading over the Lines* (Lewiston: Edwin Mellen Press, 1997), 171–84.

clothing, a symbol of her body and sexuality, and that Wendoll's knave card puns on his deceitfulness. By reading past the game's terminology to arrive more quickly at its symbolic function, critics miss a great deal: what actually *happens* in this card game? Why does it matter *to the game* that Wendoll draws a knave from the deck? What are the implications of Frankford learning about the sexual liaison through a card game rather than, say, a game of chess or, for that matter, through spying or intercepting a letter? To answer these questions, we need to attend to the formal aspects of card play, Vide Ruff especially, and to examine how the conventions of play invite audiences—like game players—to manage information in particular ways.

Arguing that all games are systems of information, modern game designer Celia Pearce theorizes four kinds of information that players have or pursue. There is information known by all the players (e.g. cards laid face-up on the table); information known to only one player (e.g. cards in a player's hand); information known to the game only (e.g. when there is a stack of cards lying face down, for players to draw); and randomly generated information (e.g. from the shuffling of the deck).[21] In all games information crosses between these categories as the private becomes public and sometimes vice versa. Indeed, the *drama* of many games comes from this movement between the known and the unknown. Additionally, variability in information—who knows what and how much is known—distinguishes one game from another. Thus, chess has been categorized as a game of 'perfect information' because both players can see the board and its pieces at all times. Cards, by contrast, are used in games of 'imperfect information', since they are designed to conceal what players know.[22]

As games of imperfect information, cards call for and teach a particular set of competencies. On the one hand, as card-players feel a rush of emotion in the moment before information is revealed, a card game encourages participants to take pleasure in their state of uncertainty. At the same time, the process of the game—which at every turn involves the revelation of previously unknown information—provokes participants to develop their interpretive skills so that they can figure out hidden information and use it effectively before other participants do. The better participants' interpretive skills and the more vigorously invested they are in applying interpretations, the more successful they will be in decoding the ludic action and figuring out what information to divulge and when to divulge it. While there are certain cognitive skills that can help a game participant excel in interpretation—for instance, a good memory helps a participant recall which cards have been played already—what distinguishes mediocre from expert players is both their

---

[21] Celia Pearce, *The Interactive Book: A Guide to the Interactive Revolution* (Indianapolis: Macmillan Technical Publishing, 1997), esp. 422–3.

[22] Katie Salen and Eric Zimmerman, *Rules of Play: Game Design Fundamentals* (Cambridge, MA: MIT Press, 2003). On cards see David Partlett, *A Dictionary of Card Games* (Oxford: Oxford University Press, 1992).

level of investment in deciphering the game's secrets and their familiarity with the conventions of the game, conventions which enable participants to reveal and conceal information through particular codes of play. The more one is familiar with the conventions of the game and intent on applying them, the richer one's interpretive skills and the more hidden information one can ascertain before others. In fact, the most skilled players—having rehearsed thoroughly and internalized the conventions of a particular game—may decipher an opponent's secrets almost intuitively, with little or any deliberative cogitation.

The complex epistemology of card play and its significance for the theatre is well-illustrated in the painting *Four Gentlemen of High Rank Playing Primero* by Master of the Countess of Warwick (*c.*1567–9) (Figure 11), which depicts four of Elizabeth I's most important advisers and friends—Sir Francis Walsingham, William Cecil, Henry Carey, and Walter Raleigh—in the heat of a game of Primero. Each figure is poised to execute his strategy, his fingers fixed on the card he aims to play. The epistemological drama of the moment is heightened for the viewer of the painting by its flirtatious revelations and coy occlusions of the status of the game: the left-most figure shows the viewer the card he will play, while the right-most figure openly reveals some of his cards and protectively obscures others, and the two central figures hide their hands entirely. The effect is to draw the viewer vicariously into the drama of the game, offering a glimpse, but only a glimpse, into the ludic experiences of its powerful players. Like each of the figures in the painting, the viewer is invited to decipher who will win this hand.

Figure 11 *Four Gentlemen of High Rank Playing Primero* (oil on panel), by Master of the Countess of Warwick (*fl.*1567–9). The Right Hon. Earl of Derby. Reproduced by permission of The Bridgeman Art Library.

Not surprisingly, the drama of card play is well-suited to the theatre stage. For like the Primero painting, staged card games extend to the spectator the epistemological experience of their represented card players. A comparison between chess and cards helps demonstrate this point. Consider the experience of watching a chess match in its more common venue in the early modern period, an intimate interior like a parlour or tavern. Having all of the same basic information as the game's players, spectators in these venues are invited to play along, projecting themselves into gamers' decision-making processes: if I were in that seat, what move would I make, and what would its repercussions be? This sort of future-oriented decision-making might be said to constitute a fundamental form of engagement in chess, for players and spectators alike. When a chess game is staged in a theatre, as it is in *The Tempest*, however, the audience has a far different phenomenological engagement with the game than the players: for while the latter experience a game of perfect information, the audience, unable to see the board, experiences one of imperfect information.[23]

Card games work differently, for even when played in an intimate space where audiences can see the card table, the game *always* remains one of imperfect information, inviting not a future-oriented mode of projection, as in chess, but a past-oriented mode of reconstruction. As new information becomes available (e.g. a player throws out a certain card), gamers and their spectators think back to the cards that have already been played (what's known as 'counting cards') in an effort to try to ascertain the content of cards still concealed. This experience of negotiating imperfect information extends to theatrical performances of card games, where both characters and audience grapple with partial knowledge, albeit of different degrees and kinds. Just as players cannot easily know what information their opponents hide, so audiences, positioned at a distance from the staged game, cannot easily know what cards are being played. Yet through characters' dialogue and gestures, a staged card game gives off partial information. As private information becomes public, audiences, like on-stage gamers, are invited to reconstruct what is known.

The drama of imperfect information takes a distinctive form in theatrical performance, in comparison with other kinds of fiction (i.e. novels and films), because theatre audiences cannot manipulate their medium to find out information sooner than it is revealed. Like a game, theatre is live and unfolds at its own pace. To be sure, an audience member who has seen or read the play before the performance will know more than someone who has not. But productions of a play differ widely; even the same drama put on by the same actors with the same props can play out differently from one day to the next. Whatever their prior experience with a particular play, audiences bring to the theatre a gamer's mindset: they cannot know

---

[23] I explore *The Tempest*'s use of chess to teach theatre-going competencies in an essay in Valerie Traub, ed., *The Oxford Handbook of Shakespeare and Embodiment: Gender, Sexuality, and Race* (Oxford University Press, forthcoming).

how this production will play out on every level (plot, actors' gestures/delivery, stage properties, costume, etc.), but if the play is at all successful, it will encourage audiences both to relish and to seek to overcome their lack of knowledge, whether through interpretive effort or through less deliberate forms of recollection.[24] Heywood's *A Woman Killed* demonstrates to audiences the benefits they reap if they learn or at least attempt to learn this skill of participatory spectatorship. For, as I shall demonstrate, only by playing vicariously the card game staged before them does the audience discover, along with Frankford, that Wendoll cheats at cards, manipulating the disparities in knowledge that are part of routine card play.

When Frankford first alludes to Wendoll's cheating during the card game, the accusations are subtle and the cause specious enough that Frankford seems to refer only to Wendoll's adulterous affair. Before the game begins, each character draws from the deck to determine the dealer. Although the audience does not know what card Frankford draws, the fact that he wins the right to deal after Wendoll and Anne draw a Knave and Queen respectively, indicates that Frankford draws something of higher value. As he takes the card deck, Frankford observes, 'They are the grossest pair that e'er I felt' (8.173).[25] Beyond its double entendre reference to the adulterous couple, Frankford's comment suggests that the card deck or the 'pair' (as it was known in the period) feels 'gross', or rough, a possible allusion to marked cards.[26] That Wendoll and Anne should both draw honour cards, and ones so befitting of their adulterous states (knave and queen, a pun on 'quean'—slang for prostitute), is somewhat suspicious but by no means confirms dishonest play, especially since it is usually the dealer who benefits from using marked cards. At the same time, however, Frankford's designation as dealer leaves Wendoll and Anne in charge of shuffling and cutting the deck, respectively: 'Shuffle, I'll cut' (8.174), says Anne. Again, there is nothing immediately suspicious about these actions, but they do, as Charles Cotton's exposition on card sharks explains, put Anne and Wendoll in the position to place high honour cards strategically in the deck, a point to which I'll return.

Once the cards are shuffled, cut, and dealt, the game begins and Frankford reports having 'lost my dealing' (8.175), to which Wendoll responds, 'Sir, the fault's in me. /.../ Give me the stock' (8.176–8), indicating that he has the ace of trumps (the

---

[24] On Tudor plays as structured by and productive of such epistemological crises, see Joel B. Altman, *The Tudor Play of Mind: Rhetorical Inquiry and the Development of Elizabethan Drama* (Berkeley: University of California Press, 1978). I explore a similar theatrical spirit of inquiry not in terms of the rhetorical arts, but in relation to the practice of gaming. For a discussion of how less deliberate forms of recollection shape playgoing (and play-making) competency, see Gina Bloom, Anston Bosman, and William N. West, 'Ophelia's Intertheatricality, or, How Performance is History', *Theatre Journal* 65 (2013), 165–82.

[25] Thomas Heywood, *A Woman Killed with Kindness*, ed. Brian Scobie (New York: Norton, 1991).

[26] Charles Cotton, *The Compleat Gamester: or, Instructions How to Play at Billiards, Trucks, Bowls, and Chess. Together With All Manner of Usual and Most Gentile Games Either on Cards or Dice* (London, 1674), esp. 118–19, explains how cards may be marked by nicking their edges.

most valued suit in the game) in his hand and wins the right to 'ruff the stock'—or exchange any of the cards in his hand for those in the pile of four left on the table after all the other cards have been dealt. As the game proceeds and Wendoll's good luck builds, the audience comes to read double entendres and asides concerning cheating as pertaining to his performance in the card game. The next game action the audience can ascertain comes from Frankford's declaration, 'My mind's not on my game /.../ You have served me a bad trick, Master Wendoll' (8.178–80). Someone familiar with Vide Ruff will know that Frankford appears to have lost the trick he led to Wendoll, who has now led with or 'served' a card that Frankford cannot beat, 'a bad trick'. After Wendoll responds, 'Sir, you must take your lot. To end this strife, / I know I have dealt better with your wife' (8.181–2), Frankford offers the audience the first clear indication that he suspects Wendoll is cheating at cards: 'Thou has dealt falsely then' (8.183). For Wendoll to be sure his card will win the trick, he must have some knowledge of Anne's hand, impossible unless they have illicitly shared information.

As the trick concludes, Frankford communicates to the audience absolute certainty about Wendoll's cheating. Anne, who is to put down her card after Frankford, asks, 'What's Trumps?' (8.184); Wendoll answers 'Hearts' and, presumably after Anne and Cranwell (Frankford's partner) play their cards, Wendoll takes the trick, 'I rub' (8.185). Engaging a homonymic pun on 'rub', Frankford responds in an aside,

> Thou robb'st me of my soul, of her chaste love;
> In thy false dealing, thou hast robbed my heart.
> Booty you play; I like a loser stand,
> Having no heart, or here, or in my hand   (8.186–90)

and then he abruptly ends the game, claiming illness. While the lines obviously work metaphorically in a cuckoldry plot—Wendoll has stolen Frankford's one true love, his 'heart'—to any audience following the dramatic arc of the game and counting cards, they also tell us that when Wendoll wins the trick, he takes Frankford's sole trumps card. This tells us that Wendoll has all of the highest trumps in the pack and, thus, should take every or almost every remaining trick. Frankford's subsequent outburst and sudden decision to end the game has been read by critics as evidence of his uncharacteristic loss of control,[27] but from the perspective of the card game, Frankford has simply realized not only that he and Cranwell have no chance of winning because Wendoll's cards are too good, but also that Wendoll has almost certainly cheated in order to achieve such a hand. For someone familiar with Vide Ruff, the cheating scheme would be fairly self-evident in retrospect: through marked cards and some sleight of hand techniques, Wendoll, with Anne as his accomplice, has managed to stack the deck so that he holds the top five trumps.

---

[27] For example, David Cook, 'A Woman Killed with Kindness: An Unshakespearian Tragedy', *English Studies* 45 (1964), 353–73 (359).

Critics who analyse this scene of the play have never noticed that Wendoll is cheating at cards. To be sure, this is partly because modern readers are unfamiliar with the rules of early modern card games. But the staged game would have been challenging to follow even for Heywood's original audiences (most of whom knew how to play Vide Ruff[28]), for, positioned at some distance from the scene's card table, audiences would have been unable to see the cards characters play. Wendoll's cheating at cards, then, is more than an allegory for or extension of cuckoldry; it is a metacommentary on the epistemologies of gameplay and theatrical spectatorship. More specifically, the revelation of Wendoll's character through the card game invites audiences to participate viscerally in Frankford's own dramatic journey of discovery.

In thinking about the way the play aligns its theatre audience with Frankford, I am to some extent following Katherine Eisaman Maus, who argues that in cuckoldry plays the audience's identification with the jealous husband foregrounds epistemological uncertainties for both audience and male protagonist, drawing a complex analogy between theatrical spectatorship and the emotional drama represented on the stage.[29] Moreover, Maus convincingly demonstrates that this identification, based on shared doubt, is accomplished, paradoxically, through disparities in knowledge between audience and characters: the audience knows about the cuckoldry before the husband does. Heywood's card game complicates her thesis, however, since the card game produces a disparity between audience and characters that is the inverse of the 'dramatic irony' in the play's larger plotline. Whereas the audience knows about the affair before Frankford and other characters do, in the case of the card game, the audience—who cannot see any of the cards on the staged game table—sees and thus knows less than Frankford does. If, as Maus maintains, the gap in knowledge between protagonist and audience prompts interpretive work on the part of the protagonist—the play's plot concerns his efforts to uncover the adultery—then, I would suggest, the card game shifts this interpretive work away from Frankford's character and towards the audience. Spectators of a game they cannot see completely and whose moves are available to them only through snippets of dialogue, the audience is called upon to reconstruct the moves of the card game, negotiating imperfect information in much the way the characters on-stage do. As a consequence, the audience's theatrical experience of the play doesn't map neatly onto the movement of its plot: while the plot builds towards the climax of the bedroom discovery scene, which comes later and is the focus of Maus's and most critical readings of the play—the climax of theatrical engagement and participation is, in fact, the card game scene.

---

[28] According to Cotton, Ruff and games like Whist are 'so commonly known in England in all parts thereof, that every Child almost of Eight years old hath a competent knowledg' of them (*The Compleat Gamester*, 114).

[29] Katherine Eisaman Maus, 'Horns of Dilemma: Jealousy, Gender and Spectatorship in English Renaissance Drama', *ELH* 54.3 (1987), 561–83.

Backgammon, spatial mastery, and *Arden of Faversham*

Just as critics have underappreciated the ludic action of the card game in *A Woman Killed*, so have they overlooked the significance of the choice of backgammon to the climactic murder scene in *Arden of Faversham* (*c*.1592). Indeed, some have even mistakenly presumed that the murder happens during a game of dice or cards.[30] These games do share some common features—backgammon, for instance, involves the use of dice—but the formal distinctions between them are significant and, as a consequence, the games call for and teach very different skills. *Arden of Faversham* stages and enacts the ludic competencies peculiar to backgammon in order to reflect on and help audiences to navigate socio-spatial relations in the early modern theatre. As is the case in cards, it is easier to appreciate the particular formal attributes of backgammon by comparing it with other similar games. Like chess, backgammon requires its players (usually two) to move 'men' strategically across a board and encourages aggressive interaction, as opponents attempt to capture each other's men.[31] Because the men are equally visible to players and spectators, backgammon resembles a game of perfect information, yet insofar as movement in backgammon is determined by the roll of dice, backgammon is also a game of imperfect information. Conjoining competencies involved in chess and cards, backgammon teaches the skill of mastering space in the face of aggressive opponents as well as unpredictable chance.

This was also a competency of theatre-going in the principal venue where the play was first staged, an outdoor amphitheatre. Amphitheatre patrons interacted physically with each other far more than is the custom in most theatres today: the pit was standing room only, there were no assigned seats anywhere, and without scheduled intervals between acts, theatre-goers would have needed to move around in order to buy refreshments and relieve their bladders, among other things. Aggressive interaction with other playgoers was enough of an expectation in amphitheatres that these first commercial playhouses instituted tiered seating, offering patrons of means a space apart, seats in the 'two-penny galleries'. Notably, and contrary to the pricing structure of theatres before (and since) this time, the space apart was also a space *above*. I would suggest that part of the allure of

---

[30] Viviana Comensoli, *'Household Business': Domestic Plays of Early Modern England* (Toronto: University of Toronto Press, 1996) mistakes this as a game of cards. Critics who refer to this as a dice-game include Frank Whigham, *Seizures of the Will in Early Modern English Drama* (Cambridge: Cambridge University Press, 1996), 116; and Tom Lockwood, 'Introduction', in *Arden of Faversham*, ed. Martin White (London: A & C Black, 2007), ix. My citations of the play follow White's edition.

[31] A useful primary source for the early modern rules of backgammon and other tables games is *Francis Willughby's Book of Games: A Seventeenth-Century Treatise on Sports, Games, and Pastimes*, ed. David Cram, Jeffrey L. Forgeng, and Dorothy Johnston (Burlington, VT: Ashgate, 2003). See also Murray, *A History of Board-Games*.

the two-penny galleries was that they offered patrons a bird's eye view and, thus, the fantasy of what Michael Dobson calls 'scopic control' of the theatre space.[32] They purported to offer playgoers a way to transform the chaos and unpredictability of the theatre into what Michel de Certeau has called a 'system of defined places'.[33] But when *Arden of Faversham* stages backgammon, it challenges the amphitheatre's appraisement of space, encouraging audiences to question the fantasy of complete knowledge and control promised by the bird's eye view and instead to accept and locate pleasure in the interactive and unpredictable features of theatre-going.

Arden's use of backgammon to invite critique of the amphitheatre's valuation of the bird's eye view may be usefully unpacked vis-à-vis de Certeau's treatment of the bird's eye view in cartography. De Certeau turns briefly to an analogy with board games to underscore his distinction between *place* and *space*. He compares the chequerboard to a 'system of defined places' because of the way it 'analyzes and classifies identities':[34] the act of gameplay in chequers, according to de Certeau, exemplifies the sort of transgressive spatial practices that disrupt any single viewer's fantasy of scopic and gnostic power. The *practice* of space 'opens up clearings; it "allows" a certain play within a system of defined places. It "authorizes" the production of an area of free play (*Spielraum*)' on the chequerboard.[35] We might say, then, that the game-board is to *place* what gameplay is to *space*. That is, the game as form—with its grid lines, specified positions, and conspicuous rules—is meant to discipline movement and furnish players with an intelligible plan for managing space. But the practicalities and pleasures of play necessitate less static, controlled, and abstract approaches to the board, instead requiring players to engage in dynamic, risky, and physically interactive navigations of space.

I have argued elsewhere that one of the ways *Arden* encourage audiences to critique fantasies of total spatial management is through its mockery of Arden's murderers, who insist on carefully locating each murder attempt but find that their strategy of emplacement fails repeatedly.[36] The play reserves its most trenchant critique of the murderers' 'scopic and gnostic' drive for the climactic murder scene itself, where Arden is killed while playing backgammon with Mosby. The tension of the scene stems from the way it materially links Arden's life to his

[32] Michael Dawson, 'The Distracted Globe', in Anthony B. Dawson and Paul Yachnin, *The Culture of Playgoing in Shakespeare's England: A Collaborative Debate* (Cambridge: Cambridge University Press, 2005).

[33] Michel de Certeau, *The Practice of Everyday Life*, trans. Steven Rendall (Berkeley: University of California Press, 1988), 106.

[34] De Certeau, *The Practice of Everyday Life*, 106.

[35] De Certeau, *The Practice of Everyday Life*, 106.

[36] Gina Bloom, '"My Feet See Better Than My Eyes": Spatial Mastery and the Game of Masculinity in *Arden of Faversham*'s Amphitheatre', *Theatre Survey* 53.1 (2012), 5–28.

competency at backgammon. Mosby has instructed the murderers to wait for him to utter the code phrase, 'Now I can take you' before rushing out. Thus theoretically, Arden may preserve his life if he manages to keep his men from being captured by Mosby. As the murderers wait on the sidelines while the game is played, they anxiously wonder if Mosby will ever manage to take one of Arden's men and speak the code phrase. As the game proceeds, Black Will complains, 'Can he not take him yet? What a spite is that!' (14.223). Finally, Mosby, in a climactic moment, declares that he is about lose his final opportunity to capture one of Arden's men if he cannot cast a one on his next roll of the dice: 'One ace, or else I lose the game' (14.227). The audience, like the murderers, wait with baited breath as Mosby throws the dice, turning up, Arden informs us, double aces (a one on both dice).

For playgoers familiar with the popular game of backgammon, Mosby's comment immediately conjures up a game puzzle: how might the board be set up so as to bring the match to this exciting crux? That the state of gameplay fascinated early playgoers is evinced by the famous frontispiece to *Arden*'s 1633 quarto, which not only represents this scene from the play, but highlights the game-board, dramatically tilting it so as to give readers a bird's eye view of the gamic action (Figure 12). The illustration helps demonstrate the oddly ambivalent effects of this staged game scene. On the one hand the illustration reveals this to be the climactic moment of the play, demonstrating how Mosby's report on the status of the game produces much needed dramatic tension. Such tension kept playgoers engaged in what easily could have become, but for theatrical success could *not* become, an anti-climactic murder scene: just about anyone in

Figure 12 Frontispiece of *The Lamentable and True Tragedy of Master Arden of Feversham in Kent* (London: Printed by Eliz. Allde dwelling neere Christ Church, 1633). Reproduced by permission of the Huntington Library, San Marino, CA.

the theatre could know from prior accounts that the historical Arden's murder happened during a tables match. On the other hand, however, and this is the point I would underscore, the illustration shows readers something that playgoers would never have seen. Like the murderers on the outskirts of Arden's parlour, playgoers do not have visual access to the game-board, whose details cannot be seen from afar. The spatial configuration of the scene thus belies a mythos of total spatial management, insisting that theatrical pleasure—the sense of climax experienced with Mosby's gesture of casting the dice—is possible only when spectators play along with the game, becoming involved (cognitively and emotionally, if not physically) with its unpredictable risks and aggressive interactions.[37]

There was more at stake in the denial of spatial management for early modern theatre-goers who had chosen and paid significantly more for seats with a bird's eye view of *Arden*'s stage. If the design of amphitheatres enabled these patrons to avoid some spatial frustrations of interactive theatre-going (the smells, sounds, and touch of groundlings, for instance), they did so at an aesthetic cost, for the gains in elevation that enabled a bird's eye view were accompanied by increased distance from the stage and diminished capacity to interact fully with the action on the 'boards'. Even if Elizabethan actors adapted their performance style to reach patrons further from the stage, communication with these patrons could not be as intimate as it was with groundlings, whose reactions to the play—laughter, inattention, commentary, sleepiness, and so forth—could be conveyed easily to actors through what Gay McAuley calls 'feedback loops'.[38] Significantly, patrons in the two-penny galleries, although put in the position of board-game players, could not directly manipulate any pieces on the boards. This paradox would have been all the more acute when actual board games were played on stage, for whereas groundlings, positioned below the stage, could not expect to follow such games visually, those in the high galleries were presented with an uncomfortable irony: they were the only patrons who shared the actors'/characters' bird's eye view of the staged gamic action, but because they were so far away, they could not, in fact, see any more than groundlings could. The staged backgammon game in *Arden* at once

---

[37] In theatre, as in board games, interaction could be intense even if it were not obviously physical. Cognitive science research on board games has found that players produce mental maps of a game-board, imagining different playing scenarios even when they are not physically manipulating pieces. See Pertti Saariluoma, *Chess Players' Thinking: A Cognitive Psychological Approach* (London: Routledge, 1995). In fact, this dynamic helps explain why board games can be engaging spectator sports, as they were in the early modern period and remain in some cultural contexts today. Such research on board games supports findings by scholars of embodied cognition and performance who argue for spectatorship as an active, indeed physically interactive, engagement, even when spectators do not make explicit physical contact with actors or the stage. See, for example, Susan Leigh Foster, 'Movement's Contagion: The Kinesthetic Impact of Performance', in Tracy C. Davis, ed., *The Cambridge Companion to Performance Studies* (Cambridge: Cambridge University Press, 2008).

[38] Gay McAuley, *Space in Performance: Making Meaning in the Theatre* (Ann Arbor, MI: University of Michigan Press, 2000), 246.

invites 'privileged' theatre-goers to identify through shared vision with the actors on stage at the same time as it encourages these audience members to become aware of the implicit limits of their socio-scopic power, suggesting that theatrical pleasure can better be found in the disorienting experience of becoming lost in and part of (the) play.

Games and early modern theatricality

As we have seen, staged parlour games in *Arden* and *A Woman Killed* call upon audiences to participate in theatre in ways that are reminiscent of traditional and rival entertainment forms. Audiences who expect 'alienation from direct par-ticipation in the creative process', treating plays simply as commodities that require no 'time-consuming burdens of skilled engagement',[39] miss a great deal of what the plays have to offer. The problem of imperfect information dramatized in the cuck-oldry plot of *A Woman Killed* may well be available to unskilled playgoers, but the playgoer who has even the slightest familiarity with card playing and who makes the effort to follow the game of Vide Ruff staged in the drama does not just observe, but *participates* viscerally in the experience of negotiating imperfect information. Yet, like the games staged in them, plays do not simply replicate the dynamics of traditional entertainments, where there was much more at stake in audience's will-ingness to invest time, money, and emotional energy. Audiences in the commercial theatre had little to lose if they chose not to become part of (the) play, unlike, for example, traditional parish entertainments: here, as Lin notes, there was 'significant peer pressure—financial, social, and moral' (283) on audiences to take a participa-tory role, whereas in the commercial theatre there were no serious ramifications if audiences ignored the play entirely, as some seemed to do. But the game scenes in plays underscore that closer involvement with the play (the action on-stage as well as the action within the broader theatrical environment of the playhouse) held out an added value to the audience. In effect, the commercial theatres did not simply appropriate traditional forms of theatrical interactivity for their own sake: they commodified them. And those who chose not to participate fully in (the) play ostensibly got less for their money.

I have suggested that games, especially when examined phenomenologically, are particularly useful for theorizing and historicizing these forms of spectator participation. Phenomenology takes as axiomatic the imbrication of subject and object, and thus of gamer and game; the game is defined largely by who plays it. By approaching the games staged in early modern theatres phenomenologically—attending to how early modern gamers as well as modern critics participate in games, wherever they are staged—we are led to put the experience of spectatorship

---

[39] Bristol, 'Theater and Popular Culture', 247.

at the centre of our definition of theatricality and to look much more closely at its modalities. Early modern theatricality was defined by an especially interactive form of spectatorship, which involved a range of cognitive, emotional, social, and embodied entanglements with actors/characters, dramatic plots, objects on the stage, theatre space, and other spectators. Like spectators of games, spectators of theatre were always already players, actively involved in producing the phenomena before them.

Although this essay has explored overlaps between games and theatre, my aim has not been to collapse these forms but to use games to reveal what is distinctive about theatre as a form of performance. In this way, the essay has also resisted the impulse of much scholarship on games and theatre to read theatricality as a subset of performativity. As Thomas Postlewait and Tracy Davis point out, with the emergence of performativity as a concept and its spread to explain everything, a polarity has emerged between 'theatricality (taken in its essentialist strain as the defining trait of dramatic and performance texts) and performativity (in its imperialist strain as the unifying idea for cultural and social behavior)'.[40] One unfortunate result is that theatricality is often subsumed by performativity, which tends to empty out the formal and historical specificity of the theatre as a space/institution for spectatorship: an audience is an audience no matter whether it engages in a performance on a street corner, in an office building, at the breakfast table, or in a traditional theatre space. If performance studies has helpfully opened up our sense of what constitutes theatre—leading to a broader canon of early modern performance that includes pageants, festivities, and royal entertainments as well everything from dinner parties to executions—its methodologies have not been sufficiently used to explore the experience of spectatorship in traditional theatre spaces, and particularly the spaces that housed early modern dramas. Studying these theatres need not lead to 'imperial applications for the idea of theatricality', against which Postlewait and Davis warn. Nor does it mean cutting the theatre off from everyday performance and treating it as a separate institution with its own exclusive, internal codes and semiotics. As I have suggested, the experience of gameplay in a tavern or parlour had direct relevance to the experience of spectatorship in a theatre. But game scenes in drama do not simply theatricalize the everyday activity of playing games in a tavern or parlour. Rather, they take advantage of the fact that the experiences of gameplay and of theatre-going were commensurate on a number of levels. This commensurability was vital to the success of the emerging commercial theatres, which had a stake in encouraging audiences to repurpose their gaming skills in order to develop competencies of participation that were necessary for skilled spectatorship in commercial theatres.

---

[40] Tracy C. Davis and Thomas Postlewait, 'Theatricality: An Introduction', in Davis and Postlewait, eds., *Theatricality* (Cambridge: Cambridge University Press, 2003), 31.

FURTHER READING

Adams, Jenny. *Power Play: The Literature and Politics of Chess in the Late Middle Ages* (Philadelphia: University of Pennsylvania Press, 2006).

Bateson, Gregory. 'A Theory of Play and Fantasy', in *Steps to an Ecology of the Mind* (New York: Ballantine, 1972), 177–93.

Bloom, Gina. 'Manly Drunkenness: Binge Drinking as Disciplined Play', in Amanda Bailey and Roze Hentschell, eds., *Masculinity and the Metropolis of Vice, 1550–1650* (New York: Palgrave Macmillan, 2010), 21–44.

Kavanagh, Thomas M. *Dice, Cards, Wheels: A Different History of French Culture* (Philadelphia: University of Pennsylvania Press, 2005).

CHAPTER 11

FESTIVITY

ERIKA T. LIN

Early modern holidays were often celebrated with dancing, music, athletic combat, informal role-playing, and scripted drama. In the professional theatres, however, these same activities functioned not as communal rituals but as commodified entertainments. How did one-off experiences tied to the cyclical rhythms of the seasons come to be understood as performances that could be enacted year-round—that is, rendered intelligible *as theatre* within linear models of historical time? And how did playing come to be imagined not only as a mode of sociality but also as a vendible commodity? In this essay, I take Thomas Dekker's *The Shoemaker's Holiday* as an exemplary instance for dealing with these broader theoretical questions.

Because seasonal rituals were primarily non-verbal traditions transmitted orally and kinesthetically, they have received far less attention than the canonical drama of Shakespeare and his contemporaries. Yet primary documents transcribed by the Records of Early English Drama (REED) project suggest the ubiquity of popular spectacles and games, such as Robin Hood gatherings, morris dances featuring stock characters such as the hobby-horse, and the election of May Lords and Ladies. These activities might be understood as both 'theatrical' and 'paratheatrical': they involved mimetic role-playing but often without scripted dialogue, and they included some characters and rudimentary plots but without a well-defined aesthetic frame. Text and narrative are two concepts to which our understandings of early modern theatricality are often (mistakenly) yoked. This essay pushes against these assumptions by arguing that early modern professional drama was fully imbricated in the representationally porous and generically hybrid forms of entertainment that characterized seasonal events.[1] The professional stage, I contend, was engaged in a complex project to situate its own performances in relation to existing festive practices, a process of negotiation required for theatre to be understood as a fully distinct cultural form.

---

[1] On cross-fertilization of performance practices, see William N. West, 'Intertheatricality', in this volume.

What was early modern festivity, then, and how do we locate it in the theatre? Although the central character in *The Shoemaker's Holiday*, Simon Eyre, has often been described as embodying 'festive spirit', this amorphous designation conflates several different understandings of the term. As the *Oxford English Dictionary* notes, the word *festive* can mean 'Mirthful, joyous, glad, cheerful' as well as 'Of or pertaining to a feast'.[2] Critical studies have often emphasized the former definition in examining figures such as Eyre or the more famous Falstaff, whose affinity for cakes and ale invokes holiday excess, and approaching festivity in this way has produced some fascinating accounts of plays by Shakespeare and his contemporaries. Yet it has also tended to privilege the thematic and ideological implications of characters, episodes, and allusions *within* the fictional action, with little attention paid to the ways in which seasonal practices were integrated into the medium of performance.[3] Rather than treating festivity as a personal characteristic, value, or mood, this essay focuses on its other sense of 'pertaining to a feast': I examine festivity as feast day by analysing the real-life holidays that took place around the time Dekker's comedy was originally performed, and I treat it as literal feast in considering the cultural resonances those temporal coordinates produced for the banquet at the play's end.

In *The Shoemaker's Holiday*, festivity functions on two levels at once. Within the world of the play we find morris dances, Shrove Tuesday celebrations, and frequent invocations of Saint Hugh, whose annual feast took place on 17 November, the day later appropriated for Queen Elizabeth's Accession Day. However, if we move beyond references to holidays described in the dialogue or depicted as occurring within the dramatic fiction, we can see that festivity was also central to the *presentational* medium through which that fiction was produced and communicated. That is, it permeated the generic conventions and semiotic practices of theatrical performance and profoundly shaped the affective experiences and interpretive modes of early modern audience members. Attending to these performance dynamics and playgoer responses is in some sense a phenomenological project, in that it considers the formal and structural dimensions of theatrical experience as crucial to how on-stage actions are perceived and interpreted. Where I depart from traditional phenomenological approaches, however, is in my view that performance functions as a culturally contingent experience, whose impact on spectators is conditioned by a vast network of

---

[2] *OED Online*, 2nd edn. (1989), under 'festive, *adj.*' (defs. 1a, 1b), published online September 2011, http://www.oed.com/ [subscription required].

[3] Important studies include, among others, C. L. Barber, *Shakespeare's Festive Comedy: A Study of Dramatic Form and Its Relation to Social Custom* (Princeton, NJ: Princeton University Press, 1959); François Laroque, *Shakespeare's Festive World: Elizabethan Seasonal Entertainment and the Professional Stage*, trans. Janet Lloyd (Cambridge: Cambridge University Press, 1988); and Leah S. Marcus, *The Politics of Mirth: Jonson, Herrick, Milton, Marvell, and the Defense of Old Holiday Pastimes* (Chicago: University of Chicago Press, 1986).

historically specific, habitual modes of thinking and feeling.[4] Moreover, I view theatrical performance as culturally productive: the very act of on-stage presentation itself—aside from and in addition to its function as representation—constructs social meanings and norms and produces material effects. The phenomenological impact of performance, then, must be carefully historicized *and* treated as itself an epistemology. In early modern England, festivity constituted a mode of embodied popular knowledge, and commercial theatre registered these beliefs on the level of theatrical form. Plays did not simply offer *depictions* of seasonal traditions but functioned as socially efficacious *enactments* of them, (re)producing cultural attitudes and beliefs not only through discourses and events within the dramatic fiction but also through on-stage physical actions and playgoer experiences. This material—and materializing—mode of cultural production had significant consequences. And one of its most important effects was to reshape what counted as theatricality, so as to render theatre a culturally legible and *fungible* category.

To explore this process of generic definition and commodification, this essay will focus on two key issues: first, on constructions of time, or how the ritual calendar was replicated through theatrical form; and second, on playing as commercial exchange, or how seasonal customs were commodified via the semiotics of performance itself. Dekker's comedy has often been read as a bourgeois fantasy of English civic identity and prosperity in an increasingly capitalist economy where actual social realities were much more grim.[5] When considered in relation to the presentational dynamics of festivity, however, the play's overt concern with issues of labour, work, and trade can be understood as both cause and effect of the reconfiguration of theatricality via the act of performance. My discussion will centre around

---

[4] In this, my essay connects up with accounts of affect in early modern studies and beyond. On the passions and theories of drama, see Blair Hoxby, 'Passion', in this volume. On affect studies and 'historical phenomenology', see Gail Kern Paster, Katherine Rowe, and Mary Floyd-Wilson, eds., *Reading the Early Modern Passions: Essays in the Cultural History of Emotion* (Philadelphia: University of Pennsylvania Press, 2004); Bruce R. Smith, *The Acoustic World of Early Modern England: Attending to the O-Factor* (Chicago: University of Chicago Press, 1999); and Smith, *Phenomenal Shakespeare* (Chichester: Wiley-Blackwell, 2010). In theatre and performance studies, see Susan Bennett, *Theatre Audiences: A Theory of Production and Reception*, 2nd edn. (London: Routledge, 1997); Nicholas Ridout, *Stage Fright, Animals, and Other Theatrical Problems* (Cambridge: Cambridge University Press, 2006); and Bert O. States, *Great Reckonings in Little Rooms: On the Phenomenology of Theater* (Berkeley: University of California Press, 1985).

[5] See, for example, Jonathan Gil Harris, 'Ludgate Time: Simon Eyre's Oath and the Temporal Economies of *The Shoemaker's Holiday*', *Huntington Library Quarterly* 71 (2008), 11–32; Jonathan Gil Harris, 'Properties of Skill: Product Placement in Early English Artisanal Drama', in Jonathan Gil Harris and Natasha Korda, eds., *Staged Properties in Early Modern English Drama* (Cambridge: Cambridge University Press, 2002), 35–66; David Scott Kastan, 'Workshop and/as Playhouse: Comedy and Commerce in *The Shoemaker's Holiday*', *Studies in Philology* 84 (1987), 324–37, repr. in David Scott Kastan and Peter Stallybrass, eds., *Staging the Renaissance: Reinterpretations of Elizabethan and Jacobean Drama* (New York: Routledge, 1991), 151–63; and Wendy Wall, *Staging Domesticity: Household Work and English Identity in Early Modern Drama* (Cambridge: Cambridge University Press, 2002), 146–57.

the ringing of the pancake bell, which symbolically opens the final banquet hosted by Simon Eyre. After showing how the temporal coordinates of the play's original staging at the Rose Theatre crucially shaped audience experiences of that sound in performance, I extend my analysis by tracing the bell's integration into the transnational financial exchanges that take place within the dramatic fiction. I then turn to the play's performance at court before Queen Elizabeth to explore the bifurcation of the traditional role of the mock king before concluding with some remarks on the centrality of festivity for the criticism and historiography of drama. What scholarly consensus deems the major 'themes' of Dekker's comedy, I contend, have relevance far beyond this play, since they constituted the underlying structure and implicit performance dynamics shaping the early modern dramatic canon as a whole. Professional theatre was in a curious position as it began to commodify the act of playing, which was traditionally offered up at holiday events as amateur entertainments. Negotiating between seasonal pastime and commercial enterprise, acting companies ended up integrating festivity into professional theatre not only by selecting and fictionalizing popular holiday traditions but also by integrating them into the formal and semiotic dimensions of playhouse performance. It was through this process—through the repeated act of on-stage presentation itself— that theatre was slowly prised apart from the unique occasions of its enactment. Only then could theatre eventually become intelligible as a distinct kind of reproducible entertainment commodity, whose function as representation came to be viewed as primary to the genre that today we call *drama*.

Holiday time

The final scene of *The Shoemaker's Holiday* consists of several short episodes culminating in the King's presence at a banquet hosted by Simon Eyre. The action of this part of the play begins immediately after the marriage plots are resolved: that is, Jane's wedding to Hammon is interrupted, and she is reunited with Ralph, while Lacy and Rose successfully elude their guardians and elope. It is at this point in the narrative that the pancake bell is rung, marking a transition from the confusions and tensions produced by the romantic separations in the earlier parts of the narrative to the feasting and celebrations attendant on Eyre's seemingly effortless rise to the office of Lord Mayor. In early modern England, the pancake bell was rung yearly on Shrove Tuesday morning to signal the start of the holiday also known as Pancake Day.[6] Despite the holiday's famous associations with disorderly apprentices sacking the theatres and brothels, misbehaviour was more typical of James's reign than Elizabeth's, and no actual violence is recorded before 1598. In practice, Shrove

---

[6] Ronald Hutton, *The Stations of the Sun: A History of the Ritual Year in Britain* (Oxford: Oxford University Press, 1996), 157.

Tuesday was usually observed through civic-, parish-, and household-sponsored events.[7]

The ritual eating of pancakes likewise functioned less as Carnivalesque gluttony than as reinforcement of the status quo. Indeed, the dish was often used as a metaphor for socially appropriate behaviour. In *Roome for a Gentleman*, for instance, Barnabe Rich condemns upwardly mobile citizens who demand coaches for their wives because they believe that 'to see a Lady to walke the streetes without a Coatch, is like my Lord Maior, when he comes from Westminster without a Pageant, or like a Shroue Tuesday without a pancake'.[8] Rich's comment seems particularly apt in the context of Dekker's play, which makes fun of Margery Eyre's *nouveau riche* airs. The pancake bell's associations with class pretensions can also be seen in John Phillips's *Sportive Wit*. Satirizing citizen wives and working class men touring Westminster at Easter, Phillips describes them as waiting at the gates and 'gaping for the Master of the Shew; presently they hear the keyes ring, which rejoyces them more than the sound of the Pancake-bell; and he peeping over the spikes, and beholding such a learned Auditory, opens the gates of Paradise'.[9] In both Rich and Phillips, social mobility is cleverly critiqued by contrasting the improprieties of class crossing with the appropriateness of pancakes on Shrove Tuesday. Shakespeare, too, draws on the pancake bell's associations with issues of social class to parody the verbal affectations of courtiers. In *As You Like It*, Touchstone jokes that he learnt the oath 'by mine honor' (TLN 228; 1.2.60) from 'a certain Knight, that swore by his Honour they were good Pan-cakes, and swore by his Honor the Mustard was naught' (TLN 230–2; 1.2.63–5).[10] In *All's Well That Ends Well*, when Lavatch wittily asserts that 'O Lord sir' (TLN 865; 2.2.41) is an 'answere that fits all questions' (TLN 838–9; 2.2.15–16), he insists that the phrase is as 'fit' as 'a pancake for Shroue-tuesday' (TLN 846–7; 2.2.23–4). In both plays, Shrove Tuesday pancakes are mentioned by clowns offering jabs at those who act above their proper station by mimicking aristocratic

---

[7] Hutton, *Stations of the Sun*, 152–5. Influential Bakhtinian readings of festive subversion have tended to obscure the holiday's conservative dimensions. See Michael D. Bristol, *Carnival and Theater: Plebeian Culture and the Structure of Authority in Renaissance England* (New York: Methuen, 1985); and Peter Stallybrass and Allon White, *The Politics and Poetics of Transgression* (Ithaca: Cornell University Press, 1986).

[8] Barnabe Rich, *Roome for a gentleman, or The second part of faultes collected and gathered for the true meridian of Dublin in Ireland, and may serue fitly else where about London, and in many other partes of England* (London, 1609), sigs. I1v–I2r.

[9] John Phillips, *Sportive vvit the muses merriment, a new spring of lusty drollery, joviall fancies, and a la mode lamponnes, on some heroic persons of these late times, never before exposed to the publick view* (London, 1656), 90 [sig. Ff5v].

[10] Quotations from Shakespeare's plays are taken from *The First Folio of Shakespeare*, ed. Charlton Hinman (New York: Norton, 1968) with through line numbers (TLN) followed by act, scene, and line numbers from *The Riverside Shakespeare*, ed. G. Blakemore Evans et al., 2nd edn. (Boston: Houghton Mifflin, 1997). On these lines as specifically reflecting the play's performance at court on Shrove Tuesday 1598/9, see Juliet Dusinberre, 'Pancakes and a Date for *As You Like It*', *Shakespeare Quarterly* 54 (2003), 371–405.

behaviour.[11] When the pancake bell rings in *The Shoemaker's Holiday*, then, it might seem at first glance that the holiday dish is invoked specifically to critique the class crossings in Eyre's rise to Lord Mayor and in the marriage of Lacy and Rose. Yet just as ringing the pancake bell was warranted only on Shrove Tuesday, social mobility was an acceptable practice only on holidays. Recast as festive inversion, class pretensions critiqued earlier in the play here function as ritual observance. Dekker's comedy honours this notion of festive time as set apart from the everyday by deploying the pancake bell as a sincere mode of celebration that reinforces the narrative resolution in the shift from romantic confusion to holiday feast.

Regarding such details from the perspective of the play's performance rather than from that of its dramatic fiction, however, complicates the play's festive meanings. The pancake bell situates the closing banquet in the early part of the ritual year, yet Dekker's comedy likely débuted at the Rose Theatre much later in the calendar cycle, in the autumn of 1599. The title page and opening epistle to *The Shoemaker's Holiday* state that it was performed before the Queen during the Christmas season of 1599/1600, specifically on 'New-yeares day at night'.[12] On 15 July 1599, Henslowe records lending £3 to Samuel Rowley and Thomas Downton to 'bye A Boocke of thomas dickers Called the gentle Craft'.[13] Given that plays were usually presented at court only during or after a successful run on the public stage, and given that public theatres tended to offer a particular play no more often than once or twice a fortnight initially and once every month or two thereafter, it is likely that performances took place at the Rose Theatre primarily in the autumn of 1599.[14] Tiffany Stern follows Roslyn Knutson in estimating that the typical amount of time required for preparing a new play was three weeks, though in practice the number of days varied a great deal from as few as three to as many as fifty-one.[15] Assuming

---

[11] For a similar, non-Shakespearean example, see James Shirley, *A contention for honour and riches* (London, 1633), sig. C1v.

[12] Quotations from the play are drawn from Thomas Dekker, *The shomakers holiday. Or The gentle craft VVith the humorous life of Simon Eyre, shoomaker, and Lord Maior of London* (London, 1600), with signature numbers from the original quarto followed by scene and line numbers from *The Shoemaker's Holiday*, ed. R. L. Smallwood and Stanley Wells, The Revels Plays (Manchester: Manchester University Press, 1979). All quotations have been cross-checked with *The Shoemaker's Holiday*, ed. Jonathan Gil Harris, New Mermaids, 3rd edn. (London: Methuen Drama, 2008).

[13] R. A. Foakes, *Henslowe's Diary*, 2nd edn. (Cambridge: Cambridge University Press, 2002), 122.

[14] Regarding the legal fiction that public performances were merely rehearsals in preparation for performance at court, see Tiffany Stern, *Rehearsal from Shakespeare to Sheridan* (Oxford: Clarendon Press, 2000), 92–3. On repertory schedules and frequency of performances, see Roslyn Lander Knutson, *The Repertory of Shakespeare's Company, 1594–1613* (Fayetteville: University of Arkansas Press, 1991), 32–4. A successful performance at court might also have spurred audiences to see the play at the Rose in the early months of 1600. However, as Knutson notes, playing companies sometimes stopped doing business during at least part of Lent (*Repertory*, 28–9).

[15] Regarding these numbers, the time of year also mattered. Since new plays were introduced constantly into the existing repertory, less time was available for learning new parts during those seasons when the professional companies were in residence and actively playing in London. Stern, *Rehearsal*, 54–5, 121; and Knutson, *Repertory*, 35.

that *The Shoemaker's Holiday* was not unusual in its production schedule, its initial début would not have taken place before August 1599 at the earliest, and Henslowe's gallery receipts suggest that an October opening is perhaps more likely, a possibility that concurs with Stern's and Knutson's descriptions of the typical annual cycle of play productions as tied in part to the academic calendar.[16]

For Dekker's original spectators, the Shrove Tuesday celebration depicted within the theatrical fiction would have resonated in curious ways with the autumn holidays when the play was first performed. One is particularly worthy of note: Queen Elizabeth's Accession Day on 17 November, which was famous for the ringing of bells.[17] Although plays were rarely performed on Accession Day itself,[18] the holiday's temporal proximity may have influenced how audiences perceived the sound of the pancake bell in Dekker's comedy. This conflation of the Queen's celebration with Pancake Day is reinforced by references within the fictional narrative to Shrove Tuesday as 'Saint Hughes Holiday' (sig. I4r; 18.224–5).[19] This patron saint of shoemakers traditionally had his feast day not in February but on 17 November, and he continued to be honoured throughout Elizabeth's reign in several different geographically distinct regions of the country.[20] The saint is also explicitly juxtaposed with the fictional monarch in the play when Eyre declares that, in thanks for the King's pardon to Hans/Lacy, Eyre and his fellow shoemakers 'shal set your sweete maiesties image, cheeke by iowle by Saint Hugh' (sig. K1v; 21.7–8).

The appropriation of Saint Hugh's Day for the Queen's celebration is often read as an effect of the Reformation, which transformed many Catholic holidays into Protestant state-sponsored events. Competition for control over holidays thus had a decidedly

---

[16] Foakes, *Henslowe's Diary*, 95, 120 (and compare 60); Stern, *Rehearsal*, 48–9; and Knutson, *Repertory*, 27–30.

[17] David Cressy, *Bonfires and Bells: National Memory and the Protestant Calendar in Elizabethan and Stuart England* (London: Weidenfeld & Nicolson, 1989), 50–7; and Hutton, *Stations of the Sun*, 387–91. Although bells were rung on various special occasions, Cressy argues that they were associated especially with royalty, particularly Queen Elizabeth (*Bonfires and Bells*, 70–6)—an interesting observation given the mock king traditions I discuss later. On royal pageantry's relation to festivity, see Scott A. Trudell, 'Occasion', in this volume.

[18] Knutson, *Repertory*, 28.

[19] On allusions to Saint Hugh in Dekker's play, see L. D. Timms, 'Dekker's *The Shoemaker's Holiday* and Elizabeth's Accession Day', *Notes & Queries* 32 (1985), 58; and Marta Straznicky, 'The End(s) of Discord in *The Shoemaker's Holiday*', *SEL* 36 (1996), 357–72. On the play's treatment of Saint Hugh's bones, see Phebe Jensen, *Religion and Revelry in Shakespeare's Festive World* (Cambridge: Cambridge University Press, 2008), 98–103.

[20] Cressy, *Bonfires and Bells*, 30; Hutton, *Stations of the Sun*, 389. Saint Hugh's ongoing popularity can also be seen in his feast day's being 'returned' to him after the Queen's death, with the new Stuart reign commemorated on 24 March instead. See Cressy, *Bonfires and Bells*, 57; and Alison A. Chapman, 'Whose Saint Crispin's Day Is It? Shoemaking, Holiday Making, and the Politics of Memory in Early Modern England', *Renaissance Quarterly* 54 (2001), 1467–94 (1491). Chapman also discusses the feast of Saints Crispin and Crispianus (25 October), also sometimes viewed as patron saints of shoemakers. However, the holiday was not widely celebrated in early modern England, so I have omitted discussion of it here.

political character.[21] Debates over the ritual calendar were also economic, bound up as they were with disagreements over the number of working days in a year. Dekker's comedy alludes to such difficulties when it stages the shoemakers' ancient prerogative to work on the Sabbath and rest on Mondays instead.[22] Such social struggles were embodied not only in the literary representation of shoemakers but also in the temporalities of on-stage presentation. Given the play's emphasis on Shrovetide, its many allusions to Monday may well have called to mind Shrove Monday, also known as Collop Monday, so named for the collops (slices) of meat that were eaten on that day along with pancakes.[23] If the play invokes shoemakers' ancient prerogative to refrain from work on Mondays, it equally calls to mind the consumption of food typical of the day immediately prior to the central holiday depicted in the play's final episode. Such Shrovetide feasting takes on added significance when considered in light of banquets held as part of Elizabeth's Accession Day celebrations.[24]

Moreover, Accession Day was never a holiday that officially sanctioned time off from work; Shrove Tuesday, by contrast, *was*.[25] The establishment of this custom is explicitly depicted in Dekker's comedy. Firk declares that once 'the pancake bel rings, we are as free as my lord Maior, we may shut vp our shops, and make holiday: Ile haue it calld, Saint Hughes Holiday' (sig. I4r; 18.222–5); and a general acclamation immediately follows as all cry, 'Agreed, agreed, *Saint Hughes Holiday*' (sig. I4r; 18.226). The play here collapses the distance between Accession Day and Shrove Tuesday, their similar forms of ritual commensality and aural modes of celebration, even as it highlights their differing relationships to release from work. Questions of labour that are central to the dramatic fiction are thus made materially at stake in the seasonality of its performance. Indeed, the play's thematic content here echoes its presentational dynamics: just as holiday feasting trumps labouring in the shop, so, too, does theatrical performance trump actual calendar divisions. In the ringing of the pancake bell, theatrical presentation pulls apart and reconfigures the temporal matrix—as if to imply that theatre is precisely that which enables reorganizing the calendar to privilege play over work. The multiple, overlapping meanings of 'play'—as rest from labour, as participation in games, as festive observance, as mimetic acting—are here

---

[21] See Chapman, 'Shoemaking'; and Straznicky, 'Discord'. I agree with Cressy that the ringing of bells 'could simultaneously satisfy conservative religious instincts and honour the Protestant queen' (*Bonfires and Bells*, 51). In my view, the feast's putative object was less important than the enactment of the ritual practices themselves.

[22] Chapman, 'Shoemaking', 1471, 1476.

[23] Ronald Hutton, *The Rise and Fall of Merry England: The Ritual Year, 1400–1700* (Oxford: Oxford University Press, 1994), 19; and Hutton, *Stations of the Sun*, 151. On Shrove Monday pancakes, see also John Taylor, *Divers crabtree lectures Expressing the severall languages that shrews read to their husbands, either at morning, noone, or night. With a pleasant relation of a shrewes Munday, and shrewes Tuesday, and why they were so called*...(London, 1639), sigs. B1r–B4v. Combining pancakes with meat is also implied in Touchstone's comment from *As You Like It*, noted previously, which mentions the holiday dish in relation to mustard.

[24] Cressy, *Bonfires and Bells*, 53–4; Hutton, *Stations of the Sun*, 387–91.

[25] Cressy, *Bonfires and Bells*, 53.

condensed and refigured by theatrical performance as no longer confined to tradi-tional holidays but associated specifically with the commercial theatre. Though Ref-ormation authorities abrogated numerous saints' feast days, in the theatres playgoers could 'shut vp our shops, and make holiday' *every* day. When Firk states that 'euery Shrouetuesday is our yeere of Jubile' (sig. I4r; 18.221–2), then, the word 'yeere' not only means 'annual', as editors have usually suggested,[26] but also reflects the disloca-tion of time asserted by the scene's performance dynamics: in the playhouse, if every day is Shrove Tuesday, it is like having a year full of holidays. Theatre, that is, alleviates the drudgery of the everyday by offering every day that which is festive play.

Commerce and community

Such interest in labour was perhaps inevitable. Audiences had to be trained, after all, into thinking of playgoing as an activity to be enjoyed on working days as well as on holidays.[27] Moreover, as professional theatre commodified the act of playing, it found itself in the awkward position of charging admission for mimetic activity normally understood to be the collective property of all. Informal role-playing games, such as the election of Summer Lords and Robin Hoods, continued to serve as parish fundraisers well into the seventeenth century.[28] Money collected during such events was folded back into the community and helped pay for repairs to church buildings and for other local needs. When spectators participated in such festive performance traditions, they not only received pleasurable entertainment but also reinforced important social bonds. Commercial theatre complicated these existing economic structures. Money offered to professional actors implicitly situated playing within a broader commercial nexus, one in which the social efficacy of the financial transac-tion at stake was less immediately obvious.[29] *The Shoemaker's Holiday* has often been read in terms of this larger capitalist network. However, thinking about the presen-tational dynamics of performance reveals how labour, work, and holiday in Dekker's comedy index a process of theatrical transformation: professional actors mobilized

[26] Smallwood and Wells, eds., *Shoemaker's Holiday*, 18.222n; Harris, ed., *Shoemaker's Holiday*, 18.202–3n.

[27] On representations of audience behaviour and implicit contracts in theatrical performance, see Ellen MacKay, 'Indecorum', in this volume. On habituating spectators to playgoing as a routine, see Paul Menzer, 'Crowd Control', in Jennifer A. Low and Nova Myhill, eds., *Imagining the Audience in Early Modern Drama, 1558–1642* (New York: Palgrave Macmillan, 2011), 19–36.

[28] Alexandra F. Johnston and Wim N. M. Hüsken, eds., *English Parish Drama* (Amsterdam: Rodopi, 1996); Alexandra F. Johnston and Sally-Beth MacLean, 'Reformation and Resistance in Thames/Sev-ern Parishes: The Dramatic Witness', in Katherine L. French, Gary G. Gibbs, and Beat A. Kümin, eds., *The Parish in English Life, 1400–1600* (Manchester: Manchester University Press, 1997), 178–200; and Sally-Beth MacLean, 'King Games and Robin Hood: Play and Profit at Kingston upon Thames', *Research Opportunities in Renaissance Drama* 29 (1986–7), 85–93.

[29] I discuss these issues in greater detail in Erika T. Lin, 'Popular Festivity and the Early Modern Stage: The Case of *George a Greene*', *Theatre Journal* 61 (2009), 271–97 (291–7).

cultural associations with festivity to negotiate the changing economic, and thus social, implications of their own commercial practices.

The tension between playing as parish pastime and as specialized skill can be seen in an earlier episode in *The Shoemaker's Holiday* that echoes—both figuratively and literally—the ringing of the pancake bell at the play's conclusion. According to Henslowe's *Diary*, when the play was originally staged by the Lord Admiral's Men, the acting company owned two 'stepells', or parish clock bells.[30] One of these was likely used for the pancake bell in Dekker's play.[31] In the scene when the Dutch merchant ship lands, the down payment on the cargo is described specifically in terms of church bells. The episode is crucial, since it is this investment that results in Eyre's eventual success, celebrated by the banquet at the play's end. When Hans sends his fellow shoemakers to fetch their master, Simon Eyre, so that he may invest in the merchant's cargo, Firk and Hodge describe what Eyre must do in order to secure the goods:

> *Firk.* Yea, but can my fellow Hans lend my master twentie porpentines as an earnest pennie.
>
> *Hodge.* Portegues thou wouldst say, here they be Firke, heark, they gingle in my pocket like S. Mary Overies bels.   (sig. D2r; 7.23–7)

In comparing the earnest money to the sound of bells, Hodge's figure of speech draws attention to the location of the play's performance: the Rose Theatre, a scant five-minute walk from Saint Mary Overy (now known as Southwark Cathedral) and well within that Bankside church's acoustic radius. Any actual church bells that audience members may have heard are here incorporated *into* the fictional world of the play.[32]

---

[30] Foakes, *Henslowe's Diary*, 319. The property list is dated 10 March 1598, just a year and a half prior to what was likely the first public performance of *The Shoemaker's Holiday*. Foakes argues that the date is in new-style format; if in old-style format with 25 March marking the start of the year, the inventory would be from earlier the same calendar year as Dekker's play.

[31] According to John Taylor, eleven o'clock on Shrove Tuesday was the usual time for the pancake bell, but 'the helpe of a knauish Sexton' might assure that it rang 'commonly before nine'. His comment implies that the same church bells regularly used to keep time were also used for the pancake bell— evidence that concurs with the conventional theatrical vocabulary of the stage direction itself, '*Bell ringes*' (sig. I3v; 18.192), which was used in other plays to signal the time. John Taylor, 'Iacke a Lent, His Beginning and Entertainment: with the mad prankes of his Gentleman-Vsher *Shroue-Tuesday* that goes before him, and his Foot-man *Hunger* attending', in *All the vvorkes of Iohn Taylor the water-poet Beeing sixty and three in number. Collected into one volume…* (London, 1630), sig. L4r; and Alan C. Dessen and Leslie Thomson, *A Dictionary of Stage Directions in English Drama, 1580–1642* (Cambridge: Cambridge University Press, 1999), 28.

[32] A similar thing happens in Shakespeare's *Twelfth Night*, when Feste compares Duke Orsino's money to the bells of Saint Bennet Paul's Wharf, a church located directly across the river from the Globe. After successfully extracting two gold coins from the Duke, the Clown attempts to get a third: '*Primo, secundo, tertio*, is a good play, and the olde saying is, the third payes for all: the triplex sir, is a good tripping measure, or the belles of S. *Bennet* sir, may put you in minde, one, two, three' (TLN 2187–90; 5.1.36–40). See *Twelfth Night, or, What You Will*, ed. Keir Elam, The Arden Shakespeare, 3rd series (London: Arden Shakespeare, 2008), 5.1.35n.

Moreover, the semiotics of hearing in the theatre are specifically imagined in relation to monetary exchange. This connection is foregrounded when Firk bungles the name of the Portuguese currency, which he calls 'porpentines' (that is, porcupines). After correcting his malapropism—'Portegues thou wouldst say'—Hodge immediately draws attention to the sound of the coins—'heark, they gingle in my pocket like S. Mary Overies bels'. But when Hodge shakes his purse and tells Firk to listen, his actions highlight the fact that, in the playhouse, the coin he refers to does not actually exist. Hodge cannot take one out to show his fellow shoemaker—or real-life spectators—because his purse contained not valuable Portuguese coins but rather small English ones functioning as theatrical props. The presentational dynamics of performance create an imaginative equation between the two currencies *through* embodied experience: the sound of gold is apparently not so different from that of copper. Just as Hans's fake Dutch covers over his true English identity, domestic coin is here disguised as foreign through sound. Like Firk, audience members must listen carefully to correctly decode the meaning of aural signifiers: actual church bells are to be understood as the jingle of coins; only the Admiral's Men's 'stepells' are to count as bells within the fictional representation. The episode repositions the social and financial exchanges that implicitly structured theatricality by integrating non-representational sounds that were part of the playhouse experience, but not part of the play world per se, into the very signifying systems through which on-stage action became fictional representation. Just as the tension between holidays within Dekker's comedy and the season of its performance reshaped theatricality's relationship to labour, the scene with the merchant ship mobilized the dynamic interplay between dramatic narrative and performance context in ways that reconfigured theatricality's relationship to economic exchange.

When the pancake bell rings later in the play, the audience's ability to interpret sound in performance is again foregrounded. Firk cries, 'O braue, hearke, hearke' (sig. I3v; 18.192), and all respond, 'The Pancake bell rings, the pancake bel, tri-lill my hearts' (sig. I3v; 18.193–4). The 'musical bel' (sig. I3v; 18.207) here functions not only as an aural experience akin to songs and instrumental music but also as a theatrical signifier with a specific phenomenological impact, a signifier whose purpose within the fictional world of the play only becomes clear through dialogue: verbal meaning is here imposed across aural sensation. The significance of an actual pancake bell rung during Shrove Tuesday would have been obvious from its temporal position within the festive calendar. In the playhouse, however, the bell's context is not self-evident but must be explicitly glossed for the audience. Through the device of bell ringing, the performance dynamics of the play link the two episodes together and register, on the level of embodied experience, the narrative relation between the earlier scene (which marks the beginning of Simon Eyre's economic good fortune) and the final one (which celebrates the happy fruits of his investment). Moreover, in foregrounding the semiotic process through which on-stage action comes to signify within the dramatic fiction, the two scenes highlight the very act of playing itself. That act is imagined as embedded in a commercial nexus—transnational trade and currency exchange—even as it recalls parish life in the sound of church bells on a holiday.

Festive monarchs

I have been arguing that the commercialization of theatre altered the economic exchanges at the heart of traditional festivity. For theatre-goers, playing was recreation; for actors, playing was work—spectators essentially purchased the labour of performers. This transaction gets obfuscated in a particularly clever way when, as in *The Shoemaker's Holiday*, audience members are positioned as festive participants who must be schooled in the rules of this new game. In this way, the performance medium effaced the social and economic consequences of commercial theatre by constructing itself as a kind of stand-in for festive observance. Moreover, theatre positioned itself as phenomenologically similar to the experience of actual holidays. When the pancake bell rings in Dekker's play, its aural presence—and present*ness*—bring together fictional story with real-life theatrical event, echoing audience members' sensory memories and re-embodying their lived experiences.

When *The Shoemaker's Holiday* was acted at court on New Year's Day, 1600, that audience included Elizabeth herself—and the aural experience of the bell thus activated further social meanings that tied together the temporal with the political. Whereas the banquets and bells of Accession Day in parishes throughout England celebrated the monarch in absentia, those same bells and banquets, when performed at the royal New Year's feast, specifically called attention to the presence of the Queen. In this context, Gloriana becomes a harmonious spirit presiding over the play's narrative shift from the discord of parted lovers to the concord of their union. When the fictional King sanctions Lacy and Rose's marriage, he brings together Lincoln and Oatley, gentleman and citizen, and declares, 'Ile haue you frends, / Where there is much loue, all discord ends' (sig. K3v; 21.120–1). The love to which the King refers is both the romance between the children and the civil harmony between their guardians. In this, the play taps into poetic metaphors circulating around Queen Elizabeth herself, metaphors in which political power is imaginatively interpolated into a discourse of erotic communion in which the mutual love between Elizabeth and her subjects legitimates her right to rule. It is, moreover, noteworthy that immediately after the King in Dekker's play finalizes the marriage between Lacy and Rose, he turns to Simon Eyre and asks for his opinion: 'What sayes my mad Lord Maior to all this loue?' (sig. K3v; 21.122). When the erstwhile-shoemaker-turned-civic-leader expresses his approval of the match, the King rewards him with 'One honour more' (sig. K3v; 21.130) and officially names Leadenhall. Although the play describes the building as having been put up at Simon Eyre's own expense—Firk calls it 'the great new hall in Gratious streete corner, which our Maister the newe lord Maior hath built' (sig. I3v; 18.198–9)—its naming is imagined as a royal gift, with Eyre and his wife humbly offering their thanks. Royal and civic authority are here depicted in happy harmony.[33]

The amity between the gentry and the citizenry, as epitomized by the marriage plot's resolution as well as by the congeniality between royal and civic authority, folds together the two feasts that represent the transformation of discord into concord: the one the Queen's winter feast, the other the Shrove Tuesday banquet taking place within the dramatic fiction; the one a royal revel, the other a Lord Mayor's feast. Moreover, as a symbol of Shrove Tuesday, the pancake bell marks the *end* of the cycle of seasonal celebration that begins with Christmas.[34] In the fictional world of the play, the next day will be Ash Wednesday, a time of repentance and preparation for the renewal of Easter; in the real world of performance, the next day will still be part of the twelve days of Christmas. Court and city are in this sense imagined as temporally analogous yet distinct. War will follow in the play—as the King in *The Shoemaker's Holiday* declares at its conclusion, 'Come Lordes, a while lets reuel it at home, / When all our sports, and banquetings are done, / Warres must right wrongs which Frenchmen haue begun' (sig. K4v; 21.194–6)—yet peace and harmony will reign in real life, a sentiment appropriately complimentary to the monarch and congruous with the setting of her New Year's feast.

Scholars have often read *The Shoemaker's Holiday* in terms of its relationship to history and have thus speculated extensively about which real-life monarch served as the basis for the character of the King.[35] Looking at this figure in terms of theatrical festivity, however, raises different questions: rather than focusing on linear time in which a historical past brushes up against the early modern present, the temporal model becomes cyclical. The actual historical personage represented by the fictional King becomes less important than the ritual embodiment of a festive monarch. These

---

[33] The play may also have enacted this harmony quite literally: the uniquely English form of bell ringing, known as change ringing, produced mathematically precise sequences that literally transformed disorderly noise into harmonious music. On change ringing during holidays, see Cressy, *Bonfires and Bells*, 70. For a fuller description of the system, see Ron Johnston, *Bell-Ringing: The English Art of Change-Ringing* (Harmondsworth: Viking, 1986).

[34] On early modern understandings of the two holidays as bookending the winter festive season, see Thomas Nabbes's masque in which personified figures representing Christmas and Shrovetide debate with one another before Lent and springtime appear. Thomas Nabbes, *The springs glorie Vindicating love by temperance against the tenent, sine cerere & Baccho friget Venus. Moralized in a maske. With other poems, epigrams, elegies, and epithalamiums of the authors Thomas Nabbes* (London, 1638). It is noteworthy that the Christmas holidays (including New Year) and Shrovetide were precisely the two seasons when professional players were most often brought to court. R. Chris Hassel, Jr, *Renaissance Drama and the English Church Year* (Lincoln: University of Nebraska Press, 1979), 3, 6.

[35] On conceptions of historicity in the play, see especially Harris, 'Ludgate Time'; and Brian Walsh, 'Performing Historicity in Dekker's *The Shoemaker's Holiday*', SEL 46 (2006), 323–48. On historical rulers, particularly Henry V and VI, as sources for the King, see Bethany Blankenship, 'Tennis Balls in Dekker's *Shoemaker's Holiday*', *Notes & Queries* 47 (2000), 467–8; W. K. Chandler, 'The Sources of the Characters in *The Shoemaker's Holiday*', *Modern Philology* 27 (1929), 175–82; and Michael Manheim, 'The King in Dekker's *The Shoemakers' Holiday*', *Notes & Queries* 4 (1957), 432–3.

mock king traditions are invoked in Dekker's play in ways that not only reinforce parallels between theatricality and holiday role-playing but also diffuse potential concern about the economic imperatives underlying commercial acting.

Just as associations with particular seasonal observances celebrated royal and civic cooperation, the play's deployment of the early modern custom of electing a holiday 'lord' positions different administrative authorities as working together in harmony. Dekker's comedy imagines the function of the festive ruler as split between two leaders: Simon Eyre and the King. The inclusion of two 'monarchs' echoes Eyre's favourite saying, 'Prince am I none, yet am I princely borne' (sigs. K1v–K2r; 21.35–6), which he reiterates throughout the play. The festive signifi-cance of this statement is underscored in the final scene when Eyre tells the King, 'My sweete Maiestie, let care vanish, cast it vppon thy Nobles' (sig. K1v; 21.33–5) and then repeats his famous tag line. The King turns to Cornwall for his opinion, then is interrupted by the entry of Lincoln, who says, 'My gracious Lord, haue care vnto your selfe, / For there are traytors here' (sig. K2r; 21.39). Actual nobles are here juxtaposed with festive ones—and the latter come out on top. The 'care' of actual treason 'vanish[es]' when events reveal that Lacy is the only traitor present. Preceding Lincoln's arrival, Simon Eyre's festive rule has already obtained royal pardon for his former shoemaker, Hans/Lacy. The division of the function of festive lord between two persons, which could poten-tially be interpreted as reflecting real-life tensions between the city of London and the Crown, is here imaginatively transformed into harmony between civic and royal authorities.

In the play's on-stage presentation, the inclusion of two festive leaders also serves as a proliferation of the trope of festive plenty. Within the imaginary world of the play, the King acts as a festive lord by enabling the class transgression implicit in the marriage of unequals. Pretending initially to 'diuide' (sig. K3r; 21.87, 21.89) Rose and Lacy, he makes sure they are then 'ioynd againe' (sig. K3r; 21.94), trans-forming the 'difference of birth, or state' (sig. K3r; 21.106) into mutual 'harmony' (sig. K3r; 21.98). Echoing the parish practice in which festive rulers presided over a mock court, the monarch in *The Shoemaker's Holiday* transforms Lacy into a knight and Rose into a lady—a performative production of class elevation by means of a festive lord. Moreover, at parish events, it was usually a churchwarden or other respected member of the community who played the part of the holiday king.[36] Dekker's play pushes the logic of festive role-playing to the next level when the fictional monarch takes on the role of God. In first joining, then divorcing, then re-marrying Lacy and Rose, the King is imagined as having the authority he ini-tially disclaims: to 'vntie, / The sacred knot knit by Gods maiestie' (sig. K2v;

[36] John Marshall, 'Gathering in the Name of the Outlaw: REED and Robin Hood', in Audrey Doug-las and Sally-Beth MacLean, eds., *REED in Review: Essays in Celebration of the First Twenty-Five Years* (Toronto: University of Toronto Press, 2006), 72–94; and James D. Stokes, 'Robin Hood and the Churchwardens in Yeovil', *Medieval and Renaissance Drama in England* 3 (1986), 1–25.

21.64–5). When the King reunites the lovers so that his 'heart be easde, / For credit me, my conscience liues in paine, / Til these whom I deuorcde be ioynd againe' (sig K3r; 21.92–4), he invokes early modern discourses about monarchs as divine agents, sanctioned by God to act on the basis of conscience in a way that their subjects were not.[37] The moment echoes the logic implicit in festive king games, which enabled the hierarchically low to play at being high. Role-playing as part of parish life, with all its attendant religious connotations, is here mapped onto role-playing in the theatre, embedded within a system of economic exchange. The question with which Dekker's play appears to be wrestling is how festivity fits into such worldly concerns. In holiday celebrations, inversion of earthly distinctions in degree ultimately enables heavenly harmony; in professional playhouses, the moral and social accord implicit in role-playing traditions could potentially be troubled by drama's commercial status. In setting up multiple analogies—between festive rulers and fictional characters, between parish customs and playhouse representations, between the religious and the secular—the performance dynamics of this episode smooth over such difficulties by replicating in its formal structure the logic of festive plenty.

The holiday excess of the theatrical form is further reinforced through the doubling of the mock king in the figure of Simon Eyre. In amateur seasonal games, both administrative duties for organizing revels and mimetic role-playing fell to festive leaders, known variously as Lords of Misrule, Robin Hoods, Christmas Princes, and Summer Lords.[38] In *The Shoemaker's Holiday*, Simon Eyre's role as host marks him as just this kind of figure. Although he is 'One of the merriest madcaps' (sig. I4r; 19.2), the new Lord Mayor is also 'serious, prouident, and wise' (sig, I4r; 19.7) in his actions. This duality is crucial since it enables both entertainment and charity, two pillars of traditional holiday feasting.[39] When Eyre declares, 'let wine be plentiful as beere, and beer as water' (sig. I4v; 20.9–10) and 'let sheepe whine vpon the tables like pigges for want of good felowes to eate them' (sig. I4v; 20.27–8), he not only deploys the hyperbolic discourse of festive plenty but also demonstrates that he is the one responsible for making sure the boards are not empty. In providing for a 'hundred tables againe, and againe' (sig. I4v; 20.15) till all have eaten their fill, the host takes on the role of mock king by displaying a kind of noble largesse.[40] As chief guest, the King in Dekker's play participates in the

---

[37] At court, the play's performance dynamics draw an implicit comparison between the fictional ruler's theatrical authority and the Queen's actual authority—and thus position Elizabeth as not only actual but also festive leader, honouring her authority as host of the New Year's feast. On conscience, see Marissa Greenberg, 'The Tyranny of Tragedy: Catharsis in England and *The Roman Actor*', *Renaissance Drama* 39 (2010), 163–96.

[38] I discuss the function of festive leaders in more detail in Lin, 'Popular Festivity', 285.

[39] On charity's relationship to entertainment, see Judith M. Bennett, 'Conviviality and Charity in Medieval and Early Modern England', *Past and Present* 134 (1992), 19–41.

[40] On feasting as a display of aristocratic generosity that enhanced the host's social status, see Felicity Heal, *Hospitality in Early Modern England* (Oxford: Clarendon Press, 1990), 12–14, 24–5, 389–93.

game by demanding that the new Lord Mayor 'put on his woonted merriment' (sig. I4r; 19.15). This request allows Eyre to entertain both fictional monarch and actual playgoers: immediately after these lines, Eyre and his shoemakers enter *'with napkins on their shoulders'* (sig. I4r; 20.0.s.d.), a visual reference to the morris they danced earlier (sig. F2v; 11.51–5). At the end of the scene, the enactment of an actual song and dance routine is implied in Eyre's request to 'friske about, and about, and about, for the honour of mad Simon Eyre Lord Maior of London' (sig. K1r; 20.63–5) and in Firk's lively response, 'Hey for the honour of the shoomakers!' (sig. K1r; 20.66). As both host and festive leader, then, Eyre enables the 'merriment' of playgoers, who are cast in the role of guests. Whereas the fictional King's actions reflect on the festive leader's role in creating heavenly harmony and on commercial theatre's imbrication in that practice, Eyre's instigation of music and dancing constructs the audience as festive participants. Moreover, with both Eyre and the fictional King taking on the role of festive leaders, the class crossings within the play—the marriage plot, the shoemaker's rise to civic office, the titles granted to Lacy and Rose—echo those literally enacted on the stage with professional actors embodying characters who are above their station. Actors are here likened to Eyre and the King, imagined as festive leaders; playgoers are positioned as guests and participants; and *The Shoemaker's Holiday* itself functions as the ritual observance of seasonal performance traditions.

Towards theatricality

In Dekker's play the structural shift from the marriage plot to the Lord Mayor's celebration is thus integrated into the presentational enactment of a transition in seasonal time that collapses different holidays and their customs into one. Festive time, the play suggests, is the eternal 'now'—and it is precisely this notion of 'present-ness' that theatrical performance also invokes.[41] Drawing on religious notions of holidays as holy and festivity as saintly feast, theatre appropriates universal Christian time for the secular playhouse. It imagines the phenomenological experience of the moment of performance as coextensive with the convergence of different temporalities at traditional seasonal nodes. Such moments in time were both cyclical and linear, each iteration of a feast day connecting a communal custom to the historical past while also reenacting it in the present. Professional theatre, Dekker's play implies, enables playgoers both to participate in festivity and to transcend the social institutions and temporal strictures that traditionally circumscribed those customs. Decoupled from the ritual calendar, theatre could conjure up the experiential dimension of holidays all year round.

---

[41] On temporality and the theatrical present, see Scott Maisano, 'Now', in this volume.

These shifting and overlapping discourses about time in early modern England have important implications for theatre historiography.[42] Before theatre can be thought of as a distinct aesthetic practice about which histories may be written, it must first be cordoned off from communal festivity. This notion of drama as separate from the season of its presentation may be dominant in much criticism today, but it has not always been so. Writing a proper history of early modern theatricality demands that we rethink our assumptions about the generic categories defining what we call 'theatre'. Moreover, examining festivity and theatre as interlocking pieces forces us to revise our ideas about theatrical form. The centrality of performance *qua* performance to both these practices points up certain structural similarities. The presentational dynamics of the late sixteenth-century professional stage repeatedly drew on, even as they exceeded, the calendar of seasonal observances. In doing so, early modern theatre echoed in its temporal structure the trope of festive plenty, not only by depicting but also by enacting holiday practices outside of the ritual confines usually ascribed to them.

Only by attending to the ways in which festive performance traditions were invoked and remade into commercial theatre, moreover, will we be able to reconstruct the unique temporal matrix of any given play or performance event and, in doing so, to grasp its significance even more precisely. More than simply a reflection of tensions between transnational exchange and traditional notions of guild practice and labour, *The Shoemaker's Holiday* is itself an enactment of early modern theatre's own complicated position in a culture for which performance was both festive and commercial. Playgoers could experience theatre as rest from labour only by transferring the money they earned as compensation for that labour to actors for whom playing *was* work. That commercial exchange is strategically effaced through the construction of Dekker's play as itself a kind of festive observance. Rather than simply holding a mirror up to nature, theatre was nature in another form: it was constituted by the very performance traditions that were essential to holiday rituals, and the cultural assumptions that undergirded those popular customs were integrated into professional drama's own presentational modes. It was the interplay between the structural and semiotic dynamics of the early modern stage, on the one hand, and the material conditions of its commercial operation, on the other, that ultimately produced critical changes in the social functions of theatricality. Performance slowly reshaped what counted *as* performance. And it was only with this shift that 'playing' could be reimagined as a commodity and as work.

Looking at early modern theatricality, then, allows us to see something about theatricality that is not otherwise visible in studies of subsequent periods, when theatre became a more defined and bounded aesthetic practice, one that was clearly linked

---

[42] On theatre historiography and temporality, see also Tracy C. Davis, 'Performative Time', in Charlotte Canning and Thomas Postlewait, eds., *Representing the Past: Essays in Performance Historiography* (Iowa City: University of Iowa Press, 2010), 142–67; and Jonathan Gil Harris, *Untimely Matter in the Time of Shakespeare* (Philadelphia: University of Pennsylvania Press, 2009). Foundational work on festive time includes, of course, Joseph Roach, *Cities of the Dead: Circum-Atlantic Performance* (New York: Columbia University Press, 1996).

to an established cultural institution and profession. Early modern theatricality was significantly more porous than the playhouse practices of later eras, and it served a distinctly different social function—one less about art and representation and more about full integration into social and communal life. The historic rift (now somewhat mended) between Theatre History and Performance Studies as disciplines is in part a function of the way theatre and performance have come to be defined. This conceptual divide would not have been possible in early modern England. For Dekker's original actors and audience members, the theatricality of scripted plays and the theatricality of everyday life were much more closely intertwined. Indeed, rather than collapsing the issue of theatricality into the familiar debate over when (and whether) theatre came to be tied to dramatic text, it is worth remembering that stage–page distinctions are themselves a function of later values. Focusing on early modern contexts, then, enables us to better see other social implications of theatre and performance. It highlights the ways in which theatricality serves and produces multiple—and, from a modern perspective, often unexpected—cultural functions and effects. Most importantly, studying *early modern* theatricality enables us to better understand the numerous and conflicting forces that produced the ontologically distinct aesthetic category that we know of today as *theatre*.

FURTHER READING

Chapman, Alison A. 'Marking Time: Astrology, Almanacs, and English Protestantism', *Renaissance Quarterly* 60 (2007), 1257–90.

French, Katherine L. *The People of the Parish: Community Life in a Late Medieval English Diocese* (Philadelphia: University of Pennsylvania Press, 2001).

Hutton, Ronald. *The Stations of the Sun: A History of the Ritual Year in Britain* (Oxford: Oxford University Press, 1996).

Jensen, Phebe. *Religion and Revelry in Shakespeare's Festive World* (Cambridge: Cambridge University Press, 2008).

Roach, Joseph. *Cities of the Dead: Circum-Atlantic Performance* (New York: Columbia University Press, 1996).

Weimann, Robert. *Shakespeare and the Popular Tradition in the Theater: Studies in the Social Dimension of Dramatic Form and Function*, ed. Robert Schwartz (Baltimore: Johns Hopkins University Press, 1978).

White, Paul Whitfield. *Drama and Religion in English Provincial Society, 1485–1660* (Cambridge: Cambridge University Press, 2008).

CHAPTER 12

OCCASION

SCOTT A. TRUDELL

Where is the early modern theatre? Productions inside buildings with consistent sets and performance environments were the exception, not the rule. Itinerant companies toured the same plays through open-air amphitheatres, indoor play-houses, royal chambers, and Inns of the Court. They travelled through the country, transforming inns, barnyards, and university halls into theatres; they adapted plays with unique prologues, revised scenes, cut sections, and added new songs. Plays involved a rich diversity of activity—including music, jigs, jests, dancing, and fighting—which was neither designed by a playwright nor proprietary to a play-house. There was not even a clear line between theatre and eating house: the 1988–91 excavation of the Rose Theatre found evidence that theatre-goers consumed beer, peaches, plums, figs, apples, hazelnuts, and oysters.[1] The period saw a constant migration of theatrical activity to diverse locales—most markedly of all in the occasional entertainment tradition, with its diversity of performative activity that processed through country estates and city streets.

When is the early modern theatre? The custom-built playhouses of the period were built out of cock-fighting pits, cathedral walls, and other evocative surround-ings, with lingering sounds, sights, and (as in the case of the Hope Theatre, which doubled as a bear-baiting pit) smells. Experiencing a play within a disused monastic refectory or surrounded by the timber from the Theatre in Shoreditch, which the Lord Chamberlain's Men surreptitiously ferried across the Thames to erect the Globe, would have summoned up a host of prior associations.[2] Plays ranging from

---

[1] Julian Bowsher and Pat Miller, *The Rose and the Globe, Playhouses of Shakespeare's Bankside, Southwark: Excavations 1988–91* (London: Museum of London Archaeology, 2009), 148–58. On play-house design and itinerant playing, see Glynne Wickham, *Early English Stages, 1300–1600*, vol. 2: *1576 to 1660*, Part II (London: Routledge, 1972); and Andrew Gurr, *The Shakespearean Stage, 1574–1642*, 4th edn. (Cambridge: Cambridge University Press, 2009).

[2] When Richard Farrant moved the Chapel Children into the former Blackfriars monastery in 1576, for example, he adopted the 'frater' or refectory as a playing space; and when James Burbage took con-trol of the space in 1596, he converted the 'upper frater', or great chamber above the old Priory, into a theatre. See Gurr, *The Shakespearean Stage*, 191–2, 200.

Twelfth Night, which débuted in the hall of the Middle Temple on 2 February 1602, on Candlemas, to *Bartholomew Fair*, whose plot is thoroughly lodged in the London fairground of 24 August, were shaped in diverse ways by the festival calendar.[3] Never, however, were performances so enmeshed in the immediate present as during the royal processionals, aristocratic entertainments, popular festivals, civic pageants, and other entertainments that could never be repeated and belied attempts to be recorded and preserved.

The volatility of occasional entertainments in space and time helps to show how adaptable the conventions of early modern playing could be. In the pageants, processionals, masques, and other entertainments composed and produced by Ben Jonson, Thomas Middleton, Thomas Dekker, and others, playing was not confined to a theatre building. Theatricality occurred at the private, aristocratic wedding of the son and daughter of Lord Anthony Montague, which included dancing in Venetian costume and verse lauding the family's connections to the Montagues of Venice.[4] It arose in the crowded, noisy streets of London, when a mythical 'King of Moors' upon a pageant float promised bounty and devotion to the 'Genius' of the City and its mercantile grandees.[5] It emerged on a man-made lake at the Earl of Leicester's country estate, in the form of a 'delectabl[e] ditty' sung by a child representing the Dionysiac poet Arion, atop a twenty-four-foot dolphin that floated toward the Queen while carrying a musical consort inside its belly.[6] Fully interactive with the richly physical and symbolic ecologies around them, occasional entertainments reveal especially clearly how a fixed stage was only one of many means by which early moderns designed and procured theatricality.

Several key semiotic tendencies make entertainments distinct (though, as we shall see, not wholly separable) from other types of early modern theatricality. Entertainments do not include the framing devices and technologies that set apart fictional representation in the theatre, such as the raised stage of the outdoor amphitheatre or the proscenium window of the indoor playhouse. They tend not to have stable viewing and hearing positions, and they generally employ allegorical 'personages' rather than dramatic characters. They do not make clear distinctions between their presentational and ambient components, and the narratives they produce are integrated with the lives of their participants. Above all, they are thoroughly embedded in and defined by the festive atmosphere that is their *raison d'être*: an entertainment cannot be divorced from its historical, performed

---

[3] Though its subject matter is shaped by the fairground atmosphere of 24 August, *Bartholomew Fair* was first performed at the Hope Theatre on 31 October 1614 and débuted at court the following day. On the influence of the festival calendar upon early modern drama, see Erika T. Lin's essay 'Festivity', in this volume.

[4] See E. K. Chambers, *The Elizabethan Stage*, vol. 1 (Oxford: Clarendon Press, 1923), 163.

[5] Thomas Middleton, *The Triumphs of Truth* (London, 1613).

[6] Robert Langham, *A Letter: whearin, part of the entertainment untoo the Queenz Maiesty, at Killingwoorth Castl, in Warwik Sheer, in this Soomerz Progress 1575. iz signified* (London, c.1576), C7r.

environment. Because of these special properties, scholars have often sidelined entertainments from the dramatic canon. The only type of early modern entertainment that has received ample scrutiny is the Stuart masque, and it is no coincidence that this is the only type of entertainment designed for a proto-modern, indoor stage.[7] Entertainments that took place in an outdoor environment—and that, therefore, disrupt our expectation of a consistent and clearly delimited playing space— have been under-studied. Those scholars who have turned their attention to pageants and processionals have tended to focus on political content and the performance of institutional power without dwelling on the unique challenges that outdoor entertainments pose to our assumptions about the dramaturgical, structural, and symbolic norms of the period.[8]

Yet these prominent art forms, upon which monarchs, nobles, and trade guilds routinely spent thousands of pounds, transforming whole cities into spectacular arenas of performance and artifice, are at the heart of the early modern theatrical imagination. Pageants for monarchs and mayors were ubiquitous, unavoidable events: guild members (including Ben Jonson, the bricklayer) were *required* to attend London's Lord Mayor's Show each year. Although entertainments require a critical vocabulary attentive to their unique semiotic tendencies, they share a host of similarities with the plays of professional companies, and they were designed by many of the most accomplished playwrights of the period. Shakespeare was one of the few major early modern playwrights *not* known to have had a hand in entertainments, and the misleading exemplarity that Shakespeare continues to enjoy in early modern drama studies has no doubt contributed to the relative neglect of pageantry. There is little question that Shakespeare himself was deeply influenced by entertainments, however: his plays are full of meta-entertainments, ranging from the rude mechanicals' extemporaneous performance in *A Midsummer Night's Dream*, to the spectacle of Muscovites in *Love's Labour's Lost*, to the outdoor

---

[7] David Bergeron's *English Civic Pageantry 1558–1642* (1971; revised edn., Tempe: Arizona State University Press, 2003) is the only comprehensive treatment of the outdoor entertainment tradition to date.

[8] Exceptions include Michael Witmore's discussion of the automated and miniaturized 'synchronization of song and action' that characterizes Tudor civic pageantry, in *Pretty Creatures: Children and Fiction in the English Renaissance* (Ithaca: Cornell University Press, 2007), 58–94, esp. 86. On city pageantry, see Wickham, 'The Emblematic Tradition', in *Early English Stages*, 206–44; and Lawrence Manley, 'Scripts for the Pageant: The Ceremonies of London', in *Literature and Culture in Early Modern London* (Cambridge: Cambridge University Press, 1995), 212–93. On Elizabethan progresses, see William Leahy, *Elizabethan Triumphal Processions* (Aldershot: Ashgate, 2005); and Jayne Elisabeth Archer, Elizabeth Golding, and Sarah Knight, eds., *The Progresses, Pageants, and Entertainments of Queen Elizabeth I* (Oxford: Oxford University Press, 2007). On the relationship between civic pageantry and the professional theatre, see Tracey Hill, *Anthony Munday and Civic Culture: Theatre, History and Power in Early Modern London 1580–1633* (Manchester: Manchester University Press, 2004). On the manuscript and printed cultures in which entertainment records were circulated, see Gabriel Heaton, *Writing and Reading Royal Entertainments: From George Gascoigne to Ben Jonson* (Oxford: Oxford University Press, 2010).

betrothal ceremony of *The Tempest*. More generally, entertainments took over whole scenes and even acts in the professional theatre, from the royal panegyric of Jonson's *Cynthia's Revels* to the procession of madmen in Webster's *The Duchess of Malfi*. As consumers and impresarios of the entertainment tradition, Shakespeare and his contemporaries were well aware of how closely performance could be tied to occasion. What, then, can occasion tell *us* about early modern theatricality?

Media dispersal

In the first place, entertainments bring out the upheaval and reinvention that characterized early modern theatricality—reminding us that playing flourished during this period not simply because it was supported by paying audiences and institutionalized within stable edifices. Poets, companies, patrons, and other entrepreneurs 'devise' entertainments, remaking them in response to shifting circumstances.[9] The process begins with elaborate planning: as a clerk for the guild of Skinners puts it in the record of preparations for the 1619 Lord Mayor's Show, 'Anthonie Mondaie, Thomas Middleton and Richard Grimston poettes, all shewed to the table their seuerall plottes for devices for the shewes and pagente against Symon and Iudes tide and each desired to searue the Companie'.[10] The poets' 'plottes' (structural and symbolic agendas) for their 'devices' (artificial and fanciful contrivances) are thus set in competition in order to determine which ones win the support of their patrons. Afterwards, rehearsal and construction—what Jonson calls the 'mechanic part' of the spectacle—introduce challenges of concrete physicality and embodiment.[11] And when the devices finally emerge into the occasions for which they have been designed, they encounter new levels of complexity and competition, including the noisy crowds that are at once fundamental to the pageant's symbolism and threatening to its formal coherence.

We can see the tension between background and foreground that is characteristic of the entertainment tradition in Orazio Busino's panoramic description of the 1617 Lord Mayor's Show:

---

[9] On the terminology for poetic 'devices', 'plots', and 'inventions' during the period, see D. J. Gordon, 'The Poet as Architect: The Intellectual Setting of the Quarrel between Ben Jonson and Inigo Jones', in *The Renaissance Imagination: Essays and Lectures by D. J. Gordon*, ed. Stephen Orgel (Berkeley: University of California Press, 1975), 77–101.

[10] 'Skinners' Court Books of 1619', in Jean Robertson and D. J. Gordon, eds., *Collections, Vol. III: A Calendar of Dramatic Records in the Books of the Livery Companies of London 1485–1640* (Oxford: Malone Society, 1954), 99. All quotations from livery company records are taken from the Malone Society *Collections*, Vol. III (henceforth *MSC* III), with the exception of records from the Merchant Taylors' Company. Note that the original records housed in Guildhall Library, London provide a wealth of context and detail not available in modern transcriptions.

[11] Ben Jonson, *Ben Jonson his Part of King James his Royal and Magnificent Entertainment* (London, 1604) in *Thomas Middleton: The Collected Works*, ed. Gary Taylor and John Lavagnino (Oxford: Clarendon Press, 2007), 273, l. 2549.

The [Lord Mayor] made his progress with the greatest possible pomp he could devise, always alluding to his line of trade with huge expenditure...We watched as a large flotilla, including the big vessels already mentioned, made an appearance accompanied by innumerable small boats of sightseers...The ships were very beautifully decorated, their balustrades festooned with various paintings, huge banners and an infinite number of pennants. Accompanied by thundering canon and fireworks, a very numerous and well-appointed group of musicians sang and played on fifes, drums, and other instruments. They were rowed swiftly upriver with the swelling tide, to the constant peal of firing ordnance. We saw the aforementioned barges carrying stages highly decorated with various devices, which later served as triumphal cars on the city's main thoroughfare.[12]

As it travels up the Thames from Westminster and into the City of London, the pageant attracts 'innumerable small boats of sightseers', accumulating components and performers as it migrates through its occasion. Eventually the procession will include the mayor, his aldermen, musicians, fireworks, pageant floats, acrobats, actors, singers, orders of guildmen, and enormous crowds lining the streets. All are collective contributors to the entertainment: since their very presence is part of the public display of celebration at the core of the pageant's design, they signify *within* the spectacle. Audiences in a theatre do something related when they laugh or shout at a play, but they nevertheless retain a position of witnessing and interpretation that implies a difference from the space of representation. In pageantry, by contrast, almost nothing is 'off-stage': theatrical space and time extends far beyond a platform at a designated interval, so that spectators and even ambient environments *participate* in the performance.

The open-endedness of this representational process leaves entertainments in need of vigilant and continuous assertions of limits, of all different kinds—ideological authority, political will, artisanal skill, and crowd management—in order to consolidate themselves and display their dominant characteristics and purpose. Given that everything from pickpockets working the crowds to the feasting and carousing of the mayoral procession is potentially included in an entertainment event, the critic who seeks to separate out what is 'part of' the pageant faces a daunting task. For those involved in producing the event, certain media (for example, the sound of a child's voice amidst the din of the crowd), surroundings (the parade route along Fleet Street, but not the everyday business that continued all around it), and artefacts (the emblematic artisanship on a pageant float, as opposed to the triumphal arches left over from a monarchal procession) must be painstakingly articulated over and against a great profusion of competition. Poets, princes, architects, 'whifflers' (stewards charged with maintaining order), and others constantly work to assemble an entertainment into a coherent system or form—a cultural consensus about the essential structure of the endeavour.

---

[12] Orazio Busino, 'Orazio Busino's Eyewitness Account of *The Triumphs of Honour and Industry*', trans. Kate D. Levin, in *Thomas Middleton: The Collected Works*, 1265–6. As chaplain to the Venetian ambassador, Busino observed the pageant from a privileged viewpoint.

This articulation of what we might call the representational outline of perform-ance—the process by which viewing positions, codes of interpretation, physical playing spaces, and boundaries of fictional signification are institutionalized—is common to all theatricality. At stake is not only what a particular performance 'means', but what entities and interests are understood to be intrinsic to it. There is no final resolution to this question: on the contrary, entertainments exemplify the impossibility of defining theatrical form in a permanent or universal way. Attend-ees of King James's coronation pageant of 1604, for example, would have approached the spectacle from radically diverse standpoints: for many, the essential content of the event would not have been royal panegyric but wine flowing from the city's water conduits. In his printed account of the entertainment, Jonson goes so far as to suggest that there is no point in explicating his allegorical inventions to the 'multi-tude', since 'no doubt but their grounded judgements gazed, said it was fine and were satisfied'.[13] Even King James and the poets commissioned to honour him had different outlooks on the fundamental components of the coronation, with James apparently uninterested in hearing some of the verse. As Dekker notes in his ver-sion of the events: 'Reader, you must understand that a regard being had that his Majesty should not be wearied with tedious speeches, a great part of those which are in this book set down were left unspoken'.[14]

How an entertainment comes to be 'set down', and what is included within or excluded from its cultural identity, are shaped by its *media*: the scripts, voices, bodily enactments, and artisanal machinery that bring it to life, as well as the mem-orabilia, spoken recollections, and printed books that preserve and transmit it. All of these count, in my parlance, as media: I deliberately use the term broadly to include not just written inscriptions but artistic crafts and embodied acts, since all of these are vehicles for the circulation of meaning.[15] The printed accounts that Dekker and Jonson provided for James I's coronation pageant allowed them to prof-fer influential viewpoints upon the array of activity that is included within or excluded from the pageant. Yet these written records are only a fraction of the story: banners, costumes, choirs, fireworks, musical instruments, and Stephen Harrison's magnificent architecture (including an enormous model of London atop the arch at Fenchurch Street) also transmit the experience of the coronation. Some media are more enduring than others: Harrison's arches, for example, remained in the streets of London for years to come, reminding passersby of the event and reinforcing its

---

[13] Jonson, *Ben Jonson his Part of King James his Royal and Magnificent Entertainment*, 241, ll. 762–4.

[14] Thomas Dekker, *The Magnificent Entertainment given to King James* (London, 1604), in *Thomas Middleton: The Collected Works*, 276, ll. 2720–3. Also see Gilbert Dugdale's discussion of 'his Highnes pleasure to be private', in his narrative account of the coronation, *The Time Triumphant* (London, 1604), in John Nichols, *The Progresses, Processions, and Magnificent Festivities, of King James the First*, vol. 1 (London: J. B. Nichols, 1828), 414.

[15] For more on media theory and its bearing on the early modern theatre, see my essay 'The Media-tion of Poesie: Ophelia's Orphic Song', *Shakespeare Quarterly* 63.1 (Spring 2012), 46–76.

importance. Mediation—the means by which communication is transmitted through technological structures and cultural protocols—is an ongoing, dynamic process, which is why there can be no final consensus on theatrical form. What we understand to be *The Whole Royal and Magnificent Entertainment of King James through the City of London* continues to change even to this day—for example, in R. Malcolm Smuts's 'ideal reconstruction, rather than an account of what anyone saw or heard on 15 March 1604', for the 2007 Oxford edition of Middleton.[16] Because theatricality can be delimited only tenuously and temporarily, it must be *remediated* again and again in order to be culturally recognizable and coherent.[17]

A stage within a fixed edifice, itself a 'medium' for the production and distribution of performance, has proven to be a robust means of defining theatricality. The stage effectively marks off the distinction between the occasional elements of a performance and its fiction, since the audience is drawn in and trained upon a presentational space that is raised and apart from them. Yet the codes of playing cannot be determined by architecture alone: music signals the beginning of the play, a jig in the outdoor amphitheatre marks its end, boys in the indoor playhouse sing between acts, and accumulated conventions and habits determine when to clap, jeer, or pay attention. Nor is the fine line between occasion and representation always clear: in the outdoor amphitheatre, the downstage *platea* space lay between external context and fictive *locus*, while wealthier patrons who perched in the terrace above the tiring-house were often presenting themselves to public view as much as they were spectating. Theatricality inevitably involves a negotiation between a dramatic representation and the elements that attend or surround that representation. What distinguishes entertainments is the degree of volatility that they introduce into this process: outdoor sites with unpredictable weather, crowds, and innumerable distractions make it especially tricky to impose symbolic design into a singular event. Immanently distributed through their environment, entertainments manifest the labour involved in carving theatricality out of occasion.

Noise, crowds, and weather

The struggle to fashion the boundaries of theatrical significance emerges particularly vividly in the Lord Mayor's Show. By the late sixteenth century, the procession honouring the annual accession of the new mayor had developed into London's largest and most elaborate spectacle of the festival year. Livery companies spent

---

[16] R. Malcolm Smuts, ed., *The Whole Royal and Magnificent Entertainment*, in *Thomas Middleton: The Collected Works*, 219.

[17] On reproducing and remaking mediation, see Jay David Bolter and Richard Grusin, *Remediation: Understanding New Media* (Cambridge, MA: MIT Press, 2000), 21–50.

lavishly on the manifold components of pageantry, including poets who composed allegorical verses, child actors dressed as mythological personae, and mobile floats finely wrought with painting and gilding. During pageants, the entire metropolis became a theatrical site in which guilds could assert their influence and consolidate their ranks. By conspicuously displaying the City's mercantile riches and alluding to royal and Ancient Roman processional traditions, Lord Mayor's Shows announced London as an increasingly powerful economic hub and signalled its legitimacy in relation to the Crown.[18] The shows also provided a means of celebrating the locations and people that held London together: the established parade route imbued with special significance the conduits, streets, and gathering places through which it passed, and the organization of participants and spectators into an elaborate order provided a means of reinforcing the City's hierarchy of officials and stakeholders.[19]

London had long been shaped by the competitive influences of Westminster and Guildhall, and pageantry was one means of working through that relationship.[20] The basic structure of the Lord Mayor's Show reflected a very old Crown–City dynamic by proceeding from the City of London towards the court, where the new mayor offered fealty to the monarch and then returned through London in celebration. What changed during the early seventeenth century were the increasingly elaborate allegorical tableaux and parade floats that greeted the Lord Mayor upon his return to the City—a development that coincided with London's growing commercial and political influence. City funds were an important source of revenue for the Stuarts, and, in turn, City merchants depended upon the Crown's military and tariff protection in order to trade. The Lord Mayor's Show provided a forum for the negotiation of these and other concerns. It allowed guildmen who could afford company livery to assert themselves over less wealthy citizens; it provided a means of courting and cultivating relationships with trading partners and ambassadors from Holland to India, who were often in attendance; and it advertised the City's special ability to communicate with, and manage, the lowest strata of the social ladder, the noisy crowd that populated and animated the spectacle.

In the course of the seventeenth century, James I and Charles I presided over an increasingly insular entertainment culture, confined largely to the indoor masque and unavailable to larger spectrums of the population. Royal entertainments no

---

[18] On the ways in which Lord Mayor's Shows advanced the interests of London's merchant elite, see Theodore B. Leinwand, 'London Triumphing: The Jacobean Lord Mayor's Show', *CLIO: A Journal of Literature, History, and the Philosophy of History* 11.2 (Winter 1982), 137–53.

[19] While key City officials including the aldermen and the mayor proceeded together with the pageant floats, citizens and guildmen stood alongside the parade route; see Busino's description of the guildmen in gowns who 'line the sides of the streets…accompanied by footmen and other officers to protect them from the press of the crowd', in 'Orazio Busino's Eyewitness Account', 1267.

[20] On the relationship between London and Westminster in the years preceding the Civil Wars, see Robert Ashton, *The City and the Court 1603–1643* (Cambridge: Cambridge University Press, 1979). On the ways in which this relationship was worked out through civic pageantry, see Manley, 'Scripts for the Pageant'.

longer served to advance courtly interests among wider publics ranging from boisterous popular crowds to the propertied classes (merchants, country gentry, and Puritans) that ultimately prosecuted the Civil Wars.[21] Meanwhile, the Lord Mayor's Show grew in size and scope, making plain the City fathers' ability to assemble London's crowds, which were central to the festive idiom of the Lord Mayor's Show. Although the crowds could neither have heard nor understood most of the speeches, the fact that movable floats proceeded sequentially through the streets allowed everyone in attendance the opportunity to gather some sense of the overall symbolic programme. This makes a stark contrast with the masque, which was designed around the viewing position of the monarch and which Inigo Jones developed into an intricate proscenium stage with illusions of perspective that only those seated at the centre of the hall could fully appreciate. Even Stuart royal entries and receptions in London, which (unlike the masque) came into contact with the threatening energy of public crowds, were designed and organized around the sovereign in a manner that was distinct from the Lord Mayor's Show. Divided into presentations at various stations or arches, the narrative of monarchal entries unfolded in such a way that only the royal procession experienced the entire display. Although Lord Mayor's Shows imitate the conventions of royal pageantry at many levels, that is, their narrative structure is more openly accessible—bearing out, to some extent, their rhetorical commonplace that a pageant is the gift to the City as a whole.

Because livery companies kept meticulous records of their expenditures for Lord Mayor's Shows, it is possible to piece together their shape and structure in some detail. For example, we learn from guild records that in order to put on the 1605 pageant *The Triumphs of Re-United Britania*, whose principal poet was Anthony Munday, the Merchant Taylors paid for an extraordinary variety of materials and services, ranging from brightly coloured costumes to stilts for a procession of giants.[22] The soundscape of this pageant was set to include twenty-four trumpeters, six drums, three fifes, the city waits (a traditional ensemble of street musicians), and several 'Greenemen', or adolescents dressed as savages who were in charge of setting off fireworks and explosions including '[the] doble discharging of 120 brasse chambers'.[23] The noise that resulted from such provisions is well documented; Orazio Busino notes in 1617 that the 'booming' and 'constant peal of firing ordnance' and 'perpetual shower of firecrackers' in that year's Lord Mayor's Show were matched only by the 'huge mass of people, surging like the sea', a 'chaotic mixture' of disorder and noise.[24] In his printed description of the 1633 Lord Mayor's Show, Thomas Heywood is

---

[21] On the decline of monarchal progresses during the Stuart era, see Bergeron, *English Civic Pageantry*, 67–76 and 110–12.

[22] Merchant Taylors' Accounts of 1605–6, transcribed in R. T. D. Sayle, ed., *Lord Mayors' Pageants of the Merchant Taylors' Company in the 15th, 16th & 17th Centuries* (London: The Eastern Press, 1931), 75–84.

[23] Sayle, ed., Merchant Taylors' Accounts of 1605–6, 78–9.

[24] Busino, 'Orazio Busino's Eyewitness Account', 1266.

inclined to agree with Busino, noting that it would be pointless to supply verses for a show designed for 'the throng, who come rather to see then to heare', since the 'words would be drown'd in noyse and laughter'.[25] Without careful preparation, as Munday points out in his account of the 1609 Lord Mayor's Show, 'the weake voyces of so many Children, which such shewes as this doe urgently require, for personating each devise, in a crowde of such noyse and uncivill turmoyle, are not any way able to be understood, neither their capacities to reach the full height of instruction'.[26]

The 'turmoyle' that Munday describes was particularly acute in 1605, when the guild's lavish preparations went disastrously to waste:

> this yere by reason of the greate rayne and fowle weather hapnyng, and falling upon the morrowe after Symon and Judes Day being the day my Lord Maior went to Westm[inster] the greate coste the Company bestowed upon their Pageant and other shewes were in mann[er] cast away and defaced.[27]

With their pageant destroyed before it could even begin, the Merchant Taylors sought to erect a smaller-scale production slightly later, at a fraction of the cost, but there was no pageant on Lord Mayor's Day that year. *The Triumphs of Re-United Britania* is thus an extreme but by no means isolated example of how pageant poetry could be drowned out by its occasional environment. Even when the skies were clear and the streets relatively free of mud (a rare enough occurrence in early modern London), diaries and other extant descriptions of Lord Mayor's Shows leave the impression of an unruly, even cacophonous atmosphere. The sixteenth-century diarist Henry Machyn reproduces the acoustic experience of the Lord Mayor's Shows of 1554 and 1555 with staccato repetition:

> guns and drums and trumpets, rowing to Westminster up and down…squibs [small fireworks] burning, and trumpets blowing, and drums and flutes, and then the bachelors with crimson damask heads, and then trumpeters, and the waits of city…with trumpets and drums, and all the crafts in barges and streamers; and at the 9 of the clock my new lord mayor and the sheriffs and the aldermen took barge at the 3 Cranes with trumpets and shawms [reed instruments], and the waits playing; and so rode to Westminster, and took his oath in the checker, and all the way the pinnace shooting of guns and playing up and down; and so after came back to Paul's wharf, and landed with great shooting of guns and playing; and so in Paul's church-yard there met the bachelors and a goody pageant, and a 66 men in blue gowns, and with goodly targets and javelins and a devil, and 4 tall men like wodys [madmen] all in green, and trumpets playing.[28]

[25] Thomas Heywood, *Londini Emporia* (London, 1633), B3v–B4r.

[26] Anthony Munday, *Camp-bell, or The Ironmongers Faire Field* (London, 1609), in *Pageants and Entertainments of Anthony Munday: A Critical Edition*, ed. David Bergeron (New York: Garland Publishing, 1985), 29.

[27] Sayle, ed., Merchant Taylors' Accounts of 1605–6, 83.

[28] *The Diary of Henry Machyn*, ed. John Gough Nichols (London: Camden Society, 1848), 73, 96. Because Machyn uses a difficult and idiosyncratic sixteenth-century spelling, I have modernized these passages.

Trumpets, drums, and gunfire recur as soundmarks throughout Machyn's and other diarists' accounts of the pageants, along with descriptions of iconographic detail and splendour.[29] Travellers to London are also taken aback by the size and rowdiness of the crowd. As Busino writes:

> the insolence of the crowd is extreme. They swing up onto the back of carriages, and if one of the drivers turns on them with his whip, they jump to the ground and hurl stinking mud at him...everything resolves itself with kicks and punches and muddy faces...Some men masked as wild giants strode through the crowd with wheels and fireballs, hurling sparks here and there at the bodies and faces of the multitude, but to no avail at making a wide and clear route for the procession.[30]

The Pomeranian traveller Lupold von Wedel confirms that policing this crowd had long been a problem, noting in his diary that the 1584 pageant was preceded by 'fire-engines ornamented with garlands, out of which they throw water on the crowd, forcing it to give way, for the streets are quite filled with people'.[31] These allusions to flames and even an early modern water cannon trained on spectators adopt a playful tone, but they may hint that organized violence could run alongside livery company propaganda.

Speech, print, and supplement

Throughout these descriptions, diarists rarely mention drama or verse, let alone record any; aside from a single reference to 'goodly speeches' in one of Machyn's six entries on Lord Mayor's Shows, for example, we would not know from his diaries that verse had a place in the festivities at all.[32] This could not be more different from the accounts of entertainments provided in printed pamphlets commissioned by guilds and produced by poets. In these accounts, poetry effectively eclipses everything else—downplaying or ignoring the overwhelming noise that may have made verse inaudible even to the child actors who recited it. What is more, poets boast their ability to represent the entire scene that took place on Lord Mayor's Day in a comprehensive, verisimilar manner. Claims on title pages such as that of John

---

[29] Note also the Russian ambassador Aleksei Ziuzin's emphasis on sound in his account of the 1613 *The Triumphs of Truth*: 'And the King's trumpeters trumpeted, and they beat the drums and they played on litavra [kettle drums] and there were all sorts of various instruments. And they fired a great salute from the ship in which the Lord Mayor sailed and from other ships which were there and from big boats and from the City wall. And from all the small boats there was a great shooting of muskets', 'An Account by Aleksei Ziuzin', ed. Maija Jansson and Nikolai Rogozhin, trans. Paul Bushkovitch, in *Thomas Middleton: The Collected Works*, 978.

[30] Busino, 'Orazio Busino's Eyewitness Account', 1266, 1268.

[31] Lupold von Wedel, 'Journey Through England and Scotland Made by Lupold von Wedel in the Years 1584 and 1585', trans. Gottfried von Bülow, in *Transactions of the Royal Historical Society*, New Series, Vol. IX (London: Longmans, Green, and Co., 1895), 255.

[32] Machyn, *The Diary of Henry Machyn*, 48.

Taylor's 1634 *The Triumphs of Fame and Honour*—'The particularities of every Invention in all the Pageants, Shewes and Triumphs both by Water and Land, are here following fully set downe'—are a staple of the genre, and poets including Munday emphasize their ability to capture the entire field of spectacle and sound.[33] In the printed pamphlet of *The Triumphs of Re-United Britania*, for example, Munday announces his intention 'to discourse the whole frame and body of our deuise, in this solemne triumph of re-vnited *Brytannia*', and provides (as was typical) descriptions of the pageant floats and other elements of the procession.[34] Yet Munday's record gives no indication that the procession was rained out and its floats destroyed; the title page goes so far as to claim that what we are about to read was 'Performed at the cost and charges of the Right Worship[ful] Company of the Merchant-Taylors, in honor of Sir *Leonard* Holliday kni[ght] to solemnize his entrance as Lorde Mayor of the Citty of *London*, on Tuesday the 29. of October. 1605'.[35] Munday's pamphlet departs from its performative occasion so entirely, that is, as to raise the question of whether such printed accounts served to record what happened on Lord Mayor's Day at all. It is unlikely that a printed record would knowingly ignore the fact that a pageant was cancelled, so pamphlets including this one were probably typeset in advance.[36] But this only heightens the sense that what actually occurred on 29 October was, in a way, beside the point.

Records of Lord Mayor's Shows differ so radically from their performative occasions largely because their goal is to elucidate the pageant's symbolic programme or 'invention'. Those unable to attend the pageant, and those who had witnessed the performance but were unable to apprehend its significance or hear its verse, could read the record and appreciate the allegorical design of the event. Borrowing from a discursive tradition dating back to Roman triumphs and medieval monarchal processions, poets produced records that (despite their rhetoric of faithful representation) functioned primarily as vehicles of edification. Pamphlets afforded authors the opportunity to redefine the meaning of the pageant invention on their own terms and assert their poet's control over the entire intermedia endeavour. This is true not only of the Lord Mayor's Show but of other types of entertainment as well: in the preface to George Gascoigne's account of the 1575 Kenilworth Entertainment for Queen Elizabeth, for example, the printer notes that many 'Pleasant and Poetical Inventions were there expressed, as well in verse as in prose' and claims that this publication 'plainly doth set down every thing as it was indeed presented, at large: And further doth declare, who was Author and Deviser of every Poem and Invention'.[37] As another

---

[33] John Taylor, *The Trivmphs of Fame and Honovr* (London, 1634), t.p.

[34] Munday, *The Trivmphes of Re-vnited Britania* (London, 1605), A4r.

[35] Munday, *The Trivmphes of Re-vnited Britania*, t.p.

[36] We cannot know exactly when the printings took place, though it is worth noting that payments to the printer by livery companies are sometimes recorded in entries dated before 29 October.

[37] George Gascoigne, *Gascoigne's Princely Pleasures, with the Masque, Intended to Have Been Presented Before Queen Elizabeth, at Kenilworth Castle, in 1575* (London: J. H. Burn, 1821), 2.

account of the festivities makes clear, however, Gascoigne's pamphlet excludes a wide array of events that occurred during Elizabeth's visit, including Coventry plays, morris dances, tavern stories, and a country marriage—all of which might have distracted from the official symbolism of the entertainment, not to mention the precedence of Gascoigne's poetry.[38]

Likewise, Munday's 1605 pamphlet responds to the threat of being 'drown'd in noyse and laughter' by downplaying the competition. Munday's priority is not to describe the pageant in neutral terms, but to communicate its symbolic content to learned readers in the style of a humanist instructor. Accordingly, Munday begins his account by outlining the mythological history of the names England and Britain, and he describes the floats not by reference to their procession through the muddy streets but by explicating their iconographical significance. He elaborates a symbolic apparatus that renders the circumstances of the occasion itself irrelevant (even if, as in the present case, they actually wiped out the performance). And he does so above all by underscoring the importance of his own verse, thereby asserting his authority and relevance. Take the following stanza from *The Triumphs of Re-United Britania*, in which the supposed founder of British civilization, Brute, justifies his temporal leap from the doldrums of British history to the new reign of King James:

> See, after so long slumbring in our toombes
> Such multitudes of yeares, rich poesie
> That does reuiue vs to fill vp these roomes
> And tell our former ages Historie,
> (The better to record Brutes memorie,)
> Turnes now our accents to another key,
> To tell olde *Britaines* new borne happy day.[39]

Here, 'rich poesie', a medium well-suited for recording and memory, enables the transition to James's reign and the commerce that prospers in it. Munday comes back to this theme repeatedly, emphasizing the 'powerfull vertue of Poesie (after such length of time) to behold *Britaniaes* former Felicity againe' and announcing that the 'lawes of Poesie grants such allowance and libertye' that pagan gods are able to reflect on present circumstances.[40] By Munday's account, poesie provides an optimal view of history as well as a sense of authorial control over the narration and significance of a pageant that would otherwise fail to cohere into a symbolic programme.

Munday and other poets who sought to outline the determining power of their inventions and verses were not, however, entirely successful. The medium of print may have insulated poets to some extent from the contingencies of performance, and Munday takes advantage of this in order to assert his own version of *The*

---

[38] See Langham, *A Letter*.
[39] Munday, *The Trivmphes of Re-vnited Britania*, B3r–B4v.
[40] Munday, *The Trivmphes of Re-vnited Britania*, B1v, B1r.

Triumphs of Re-United Britania as a unified and humanistic art form. But it does not follow that pageants were understood to operate separately from their occasions. It would be more accurate to describe Munday's comments about poesie as a *supplement* to a larger historical process, in which actors' speeches, architectural marvels, gilded pageant floats, and other media vie for influence. The events of 29 October would have been much more central to this process of mediation than Munday admits: recall that diarists and even poets themselves consistently define pageantry in relation to its exact occasion. To take another example, the title page of Middleton's *The Triumphs of Love and Antiquity* advertises what follows as 'Taking beginning in the morning at his lordship's going, and perfecting itself after his return from receiving the oath of mayoralty at Westminster, on the morrow after Simon and Jude's Day, October 29, 1619'.[41] The sheer scale of a Lord Mayor's Show, furthermore, suggests that it would have occupied a prominent place in the memory of thousands of Londoners, making the mere 500 copies of the poet's record that were typically printed a relatively small window into the larger experience and significance of the pageant. Indeed, Munday's wishful thinking about the transformative power of poesie is probably best understood as a type of compensation for an art form that was embedded in its occasion and mediated in countless ways that he could not control.

In fact, printed accounts of Lord Mayor's Shows were not even independent from the patronage system that governed the rest of the pageant, since they did not participate in the book *trade*. The records are generally not entered in the Stationers' Register, their title pages do not indicate that they will be sold, and livery company records suggest that poets would have expected to have profited directly from the guild (and presumably not from the printer):[42]

'It[e]m, to Mr. Munday for prynting the bookes of speeches in the pageant. } xxx [shillings]'

'It[e]m, more paid to [Mr. Munday] for printing the bookes of the speeches in the Pageant and the other shewes } vjli [shillings]'

'besides [Mr. Munday] is to furnish the Children with apparell and give into the Companie 500 bookes printed of the speeches'

'Mr Tho[mas] Decker the Poett and Mr Crismas...[agreed] to give the company 500 bookes of the declarac[i]on of the said Shewe'[43]

---

[41] Middleton, *The Triumphs of Love and Antiquity* (London, 1619), in *Thomas Middleton: The Collected Works*, 1399.

[42] Dekker's 1612 *Troia-Nova Triumphans* is a notable exception: it was entered in the Stationers' Register, and its title page indicates that it is 'to be sold by John Wright dwelling at Christ Church-gate'. Yet the Merchant Taylors made a payment to Dekker and his collaborator 'for the printing of the bookes of the Speeches' (Sayle, ed., Merchant Taylors' Accounts of 1612–13, 103), which suggests that the pamphlet is involved in the book trade *as well as* the livery company patronage system.

[43] Sayle, ed., Merchant Taylors' Court Books of 1602, 65; Sayle, ed., Merchant Taylors' Accounts of 1605–6, 78; Ironmongers' Rough Book, 17 October, 1609, *MSC* III, 73; Ironmongers' Court Books of 1629, *MSC* III, 114–15.

Records were consistently commissioned by guilds in this way, suggesting that they were designed not as commodities for a bibliographic market-place so much as memorabilia for the wider ceremony in which they were embedded. An entry in the Goldsmiths' Court Books of 1611 assigning Munday the responsibility 'to cause 500 bookes thereof to be made and printed to be deliuered to Mr Wardeins by them to be *disposed*' (my emphasis), supports the idea that the pamphlets were intended less for the bookseller than as tokens of remembrance that were distributed to guild members.[44] The printed record was thus an appendage of pageantry—one of many media that participated in its cultural definition. The history of pageants as books folds together with the history of pageants as performances in what I have called mediation: the ongoing process by which theatricality (and other arts) accrue meaning as they circulate through their environment.

Poets, impresarios, and 'The Whole Devyce'

That mediation is never finalized—that media always *go between* without an absolute end or final inscription—comes into focus in livery company records of payments to poets. Even as scholars of the early modern theatre have come to acknowledge the determining influence of performance practices upon drama, they continue to take for granted that playwriting is just that: writing. Yet closer inspection of guild records reveals that poets including Munday, Heywood, and Middleton were paid for a great variety of tasks, and that writing itself often appears to have played a surprisingly minimal role in their responsibilities. Take, for example, the following entry in the Grocers' Records of 1617 concerning Middleton's remuneration for his role in *The Triumphs of Honour and Industry*:

> Payde to Thomas Middleton gent for the ordering overseeing and writyng of the whole devyse for the making of the Pageant of Nations The Iland The Indian chariott The Castle of fame, trym[m]ing the shipp, with all the severall beastes which drewe them and for all the Carpenters worke paynting guylding and garnyshing of them with all other things necessary for the apparelling and fynding of all the p[er]sonages in the sayd shewes and for all the portage and carryage both by lande and by water for the lighters for the shew by water for paynting of a banner of the Lord Maiors armes and alsoe in full for the greenemen Dyvells and fyer workes with all thinges therevnto belonging according to his agreem[en]t the some of 282 [pounds].[45]

Charged with 'the ordering overseeing and writyng of the whole devyse', Middleton is entrusted with the massive sum of £282 in order to supervise a host of collaborators ranging from carpenters to fireworks specialists: his role is to commission and

---

[44] According to the *Oxford English Dictionary*, 'disposed' did not denote a monetary transaction during the period, http://www.oed.com (accessed August 2012) [subscription required].
[45] Grocers' Charges of Triumphs, 5 May 1618, *MSC* III, 92.

coordinate the work of painters, shipbuilders, architects, and other artisans. Other records suggest that Middleton was likely not just to have selected and costumed the child actors but to have chaperoned and even fed them: in the Drapers' Accounts of 1623, for example, we find a record of three pounds 'paide to Mr Middleton for the making of a Breakefast and fyer for the Children of the Pageants'.[46]

Guilds did not rely exclusively on poet-managers; they normally commissioned a committee of 'devisors' and 'surveyors' to organize a pageant, and they often jointly requisitioned a poet and a 'carver' (a kind of artisan–engineer) to oversee a subset of activities.[47] But poets were particularly prominent among a pageant's managerial figures, and they were rarely paid for writing alone. Munday was a particularly seasoned manager and contriver who was given broad latitude in his responsibilities: in 1611 the Goldsmiths note that 'Mr Mundye is to beare the charge of the tyreing and trymming of the children and whatsoeuer els is requisite to be done by him for the managing of the whole busyness', and he was sometimes compensated for his 'paines' even in pageants for which he did not write any verse.[48] The role of a poet was thus not unlike a modern-day contractor or film producer: overseeing the musical performance, gesture, oratory, feasting, fireworks, costumes, iconographical design, and other elements that collectively constituted a pageant. As we discover from expenditures (typical in Lord Mayor's Shows put on by the Grocers) 'for Nutmegges, Gynger, almondes in the shell, and sugar loves, w[hi]ch weare throwen abowt the streetes by those w[hi]ch sate on the Gryffyns and Camells', these efforts were not even limited to vision and sound.[49] Poets and others attempted to mould all of these components into a recognizable form, coordinating a multifarious series of moving parts.

Some poets, notably Thomas Dekker, are less interested in hewing to livery company propaganda than in embracing an occasion's eruption of activity and noise. In Dekker's 1612 *Troia-Nova Triumphans*, for example, Neptune draws our attention to the powerful influx of cheering and uproar from the crowd in a manner that betrays not anxiety about a lack of poetic control, but excitement and anticipation:

[46] Drapers' Wardens of the Bachelors' Accounts, 1623–4, *MSC* III, 106.

[47] In 1622, for example, we see a wide range of responsibilities assigned jointly to Middleton and Garret Christmas (who, together with his son John, was the principal 'carver' of early seventeenth-century Lord Mayor's Shows): 'Payde to Thomas Middleton gent and Garrett Christmas Carver for orderinge overseeing and wrytinge of the whole devise' (Grocers' Charges of Triumphs, 24 April 1623, *MSC* III, 104).

[48] Goldsmiths' Court Books, 7 September 1611, *MSC* III, 82. For example, Munday is paid fifty-five shillings 'for the hyer of a barne in Whitecrossestreete' to be used in the 1623 pageant for which Middleton was the chief poet (Drapers' Wardens of the Bachelors' Accounts, 1623–4, *MSC* III, 106); and he is paid two pounds for 'paines' not specified in a Lord Mayor's Show which is not extant but for which Ben Jonson apparently composed the verse (Haberdashers' Yeomanry Account for the Lord Mayor's Triumph, 1604, *MSC* III, 63).

[49] Grocers' Charges of Triumphs, 14 April 1614, *MSC* III, 88.

> Whence breaks this warlike thunder of lowd drummes,
> (*Clarions* and *Trumpets*) whose shrill eccho comes
> Vp to our *Watery Court*, and calles from thence
> Vs, and our *Trytons*?...what does beget
> These *Thronges*? this *Confluence*? why do voyces beate
> The *Ayre* with acclamations of applause,
> *Good wishes, Loue,* and *Praises*? what is't drawes
> All *Faces* this way? This way *Rumor* flyes,
> Clapping her infinite wings, whose noyse the Skyes
> From earth receiue, with *Musicall* rebounding,
> And strike the *Seas* with repercussive sounding.   (ll. 108–11, 116–23)[50]

Neptune not only allows us to revel in the dangerous 'thunder' of the crowd; he also makes plain how close its 'shrill eccho' is to the 'acclamations', 'Good wishes, Loue, and Praises' that are essential to the success and purpose of the pageant. Even Rumour, an element of misrule that threatens to erupt into disorder, has a 'repercussive' and 'Musicall' rhythm, connecting by way of counterpoint to the acoustic celebration of the Lord Mayor. This device comes to a climax with the agitations of Riot and Calumny, the deputies of the villainous Envy and (together with Rumour) allegorical figures associated with noisy disorder. Seeking to halt the mayoral procession, Envy invokes an infernal eruption of sound—'*Adders* shoote, hysse speckled Snakes...Vomit sulphure to confound her, / Fiendes and Furies (that dwell vnder) / Lift hell gates from their hindges'—after which 'Omnes' or 'All that are with Envy' proclaim, chant, or sing 'Shoote, shoote, &c' (ll. 297, 315–17, 323). Dekker is careful to note that these raucous lines, accentuated by strong alliteration, coincide with literal explosions—'Either during this speech, or else when it is done, certaine Rockets flye vp into the aire' (ll. 324–5)—and when Envy's minions 'discharge their blacke Artillery' at the Chariot of Virtue, 'their arrowes, which they shoote vp into the aire, breake there out in fire-workes' (ll. 288–9, 292–3).

Dekker is uniquely skilful at celebrating the radical openness of the Lord Mayor's Show to its occasion, channelling ambient surroundings into the core of a poetic invention. More often, as we have seen with Munday, poets work to disentangle an entertainment from its noisy and unstable environment. In Middleton's 1616 pageant for the investiture of Prince Charles, *Civitatis Amor*, the allegorical personage 'London' commands its subjects, 'Let not your loving, over-greedy noise / Beguile you of the sweetness of your joys. / My wish has took effect, for ne'er was known / A greater joy and a more silent one'.[51] Similarly, Orpheus in Middleton's *The Triumphs of Love*

---

[50] Dekker, *Troia-Nova Triumphans* (London, 1612), in *The Dramatic Works of Thomas Dekker*, ed. Fredson Bowers, vol. 3 (Cambridge: Cambridge University Press, 1958), 225–49, quoted by line number.

[51] Middleton, *Civitatis Amor* (London, 1616), in *Thomas Middleton: The Collected Works*, 1205, ll. 69–72.

and Antiquity (1619) explores how a public, occasional atmosphere might be ordered or coerced to silence:

> Just such a wilderness is a commonwealth
> That is undressed, unpruned, wild in her health;
> And the rude multitude the beasts o'th' wood,
> That know no laws, but only will and blood;
> And yet, by fair example, musical grace,
> Harmonious government of the man in place,
> Of fair integrity and wisdom framed,
> They stand as mine do, ravished, charmed, and tamed:
> Every wise magistrate that governs thus,
> May well be called a powerful Orpheus.[52]

Here, Middleton is not interested in idealizing the 'rude multitude' but in acknowledging its power in 'will and blood'—and perhaps those educated and privileged enough to read his pamphlet sympathized with the desire to charm, tame, and 'ravish' this crowd. Notice, however, that Middleton's language by no means dismisses the threatening force of the crowd and its noise. On the contrary, Orphic music is employed as a means of re-appropriating the crowd's uncouth sounds, subsuming the surroundings of pageantry into its assertion of power. The same is true of *Civitatis Amor*: the 'over-greedy noise' that Middleton's 'London' hopes to silence remains a potent source of expression.

Despite their diverse responses to crowds and noise, that is, Munday, Dekker, and Middleton all acknowledge the unsettling force that outdoor occasions introduce into the fabric of a poetic invention. Few early modern art forms compare to the Lord Mayor's Show in the sheer complexity of its representational process: highly mobile; extremely decorative; deafeningly loud; brimming with dignitaries, crowds, machines, horses, and architectural implements; so multi-sensory as to include not only sights and sounds but confections and sweetmeats thrown to the crowds. Instead of actors, pageants present a procession of honourees and patrons together with musicians, gymnasts, child actors, and other performers. Instead of paying audiences, they line the streets with the entire social spectrum, marking status distinctions by specifying the locations that City officials, liverymen, craftsmen, and subaltern labourers stand or walk. And instead of a definitive stage upon which a fictional world is located, the Lord Mayor's Show is characterized by a profusion of mimetic moments and spaces that are impossible to distinguish clearly from the sea of activity around them.

Nevertheless, 29 October was not the only time that an early modern Londoner could witness noisy, embodied activity in an unpredictable environment. The professional theatre was full of dancing, dumb shows, acrobatics, and much more,

---

[52] Middleton, *The Triumphs of Love and Antiquity*, ll. 155–64.

and playing remained a notoriously unwieldy and absorbing endeavour—this was part of its unsavory reputation, and part of its allure. Open-air amphitheatres such as the Globe, banished outside the city walls, were like circulatory organs that drew in audiences and exposed them to London's sights and sounds: collecting noise, amplifying it, and then projecting it into the air.[53] For Phillip Stubbes, the playhouse was a space of shocking oversaturation in spectacle and a magnet for the most disreputable and lascivious activity that London had to offer:

> marke the flockyng and runnyng to Theaters and Curtens, daylie and hourelie, night and daie, tyme and tide, to see Playes and Enterludes, where such wanton gestures, such bawdie speeches: suche laughyng and flearyng: suche kissyng and bussyng: suche clippyng and culling: suche winckinge and glancinge of wanton eyes, and the like is vsed, as is wonderfull to behold. Then these goodly Pageantes being doen, euery mate sortes to his mate, euery one bryngeds an other homewarde of their waie very friendly, and in their secrete conclaues (couertly) thei plaie the *Sodomits*, or worse.[54]

In spite of himself, Stubbes admits a sense of *wonder* at the continual, improvisational activity of the playhouse: daily and hourly, night and day, time and tide. This is a space of ongoing adaptation and renewal—an atmosphere not so far removed from the mobility and immediacy of the Lord Mayor's Show. Like pageantry on the street, 'Pageantes' on the stage migrated tantalizingly and dangerously into new and diverse locales, working their way into any 'conclaue' where their conventions and structures could take hold.

To put this another way, entertainments are an extreme case of the occasional dimension of *all* theatricality. Any dramatic fiction, no matter how carefully designed and produced, is open to the environment in which it is embedded. If it is impossible to disconnect an entertainment from its performative moment—the way in which it is literally constituted by the streets, crowds, mud, and weather of a particular festival day—it is also impossible to disconnect a professional play from foggy weather obscuring the players' gestures, a hungry and impatient audience, a drunken crowd on a festival day, and innumerable other occasional influences and distractions. The history of theatricality is, in this sense, like the history of the book. Just as every print shop, paper mill, bookseller, and binder contributes to the production of a material text, each country manor house, banqueting hall, Fleet Street arch, reconfigured monastery, professional company, trade guild, and public holiday shapes and defines the endeavour of playing. Theatricality is made possible, or impossible, by the outdoor amphitheatres constructed by Henslowe and Burbage, the cannons of *Henry VIII* which burned down the Globe, the rainstorm that destroyed *The Triumphs of Re-United Britania*, and the innumerable seasons, times

---

[53] On the outdoor amphitheatre as a sounding chamber, see Bruce Smith, *The Acoustic World of Early Modern England* (Chicago: University of Chicago Press, 1999), 206–45.

[54] Philip Stubbes, *The Anatomie of Abuses* (London, 1583), L4v–L5r.

of day, structures, viewing positions, celebrations, and other occasions that assemble its audiences and structure its meaning.

FURTHER READING

Hill, Tracey. *Pageantry and Power: A Cultural History of the Early Modern Lord Mayor's Show, 1585–1639* (Manchester: Manchester University Press, 2011).

Northway, Kara. '"To Kindle an Industrious Desire": The Poetry of Work in Lord Mayors' Shows', *Comparative Drama* 41.2 (Summer 2007), 167–92.

Palmer, Daryl W. 'Metropolitan Resurrection in Anthony Munday's Lord Mayor's Shows', *SEL* 46.2 (Spring 2006), 371–87.

Stock, Angela. '"Something Done in Honour of the City": Ritual, Theatre and Satire in Jacobean City Pageantry', in Dieter Mehl, Angela Stock, and Anne-Julia Zwierlein, eds., *Plotting Early Modern London: New Essays on Jacobean City Comedy* (Aldershot: Ashgate, 2004), 125–44.

Weber, Samuel. *Theatricality as Medium* (New York: Fordham University Press, 2004).

CHAPTER 13

OPTICS

MARY THOMAS CRANE

By virtue of its etymological derivation from the Greek verb θεάομαι, 'to see or behold,' the term 'theatricality' points to one of the most problematic aspects of early modern theatre: its vexed relation to sight, seeing, spectacle, and illusion.[1] Bert States has argued that 'a certain tension between seeing and hearing is a distinguishing feature of Shakespeare's theater' where 'naming—eloquently naming—anything constitutes the chief form of proof'.[2] This is not surprising given the 'particularly unsettled' status of vision in sixteenth-century Europe described by Stuart Clark, when for many reasons 'vision came to be characterized by uncertainty and unreliability'.[3] Huston Diehl attributes the ambivalence of early modern drama towards the visual to Protestant iconoclasm, but, as Clark reveals, a number of factors contributed to early modern interest in and distrust of, the properties of sight: the Reformation, to be sure, but also the development of perspectival and anamorphic techniques in art and the rediscovery of ancient scepticism.[4]

In this essay, I will argue that early modern optics impinged powerfully on the theatre and that it did so in surprising and contradictory ways. Like many fields of knowledge in the unsettled period just before the scientific revolution, optics bridged what we would call 'science' and 'magic' and, as Stuart Clark has argued, illuminates the ways in which the two domains were configured in relation to one another.[5] We have to reconstruct this history in an oblique relation to the theatre,

---

[1] I want to thank my research assistant, Deanna Malvesti, for her help with this essay.

[2] Bert O. States, *Great Reckonings in Little Rooms: On the Phenomenology of Theater* (Berkeley: University of California Press, 1987), 56, 55.

[3] Stuart Clark, *Vanities of the Eye: Vision in Early Modern Culture* (Oxford: Oxford University Press, 2007), 2.

[4] Huston Diehl, *Staging Reform, Reforming the Stage: Protestantism and Popular Theater in Early Modern England* (Ithaca: Cornell University Press, 1997), especially 64–73. Clark, *Vanities*, 3–4.

[5] Clark, *Vanities, passim*. 'Science' is an anachronistic term, of course; as Carla Mazzio notes, in the sixteenth century, 'science' referred to all knowledge, while what we would call 'science' today was called 'natural philosophy'. See Carla Mazzio, 'Introduction' to *Shakespeare and Science, c. 1600*, a special issue of the *South Central Review* 26.1–2 (2009), 1–23 (1–2). However, I am using 'science' to refer

however, because early modern plays resolutely refuse to stage optics as science. Optical devices and other phenomena that were widely known in the period as legitimate natural practices are reconfigured on the stage as products of demonic magic or as a fraudulent trick. Early modern theatre evidently preferred to align itself with the conjuring of demons or with fraud rather than with experiments in optics. We can only speculate about the reasons for this, but I will argue that while early modern plays were obsessed with probing the conditions and limits of visual illusion, they did so using a theatrical technology that was deeply ambivalent about its own implication in visual deception and that tended to create illusions verbally rather than visually. The Jacobean and Caroline court masque, to be sure, developed a very different theatrical style emphasizing visual illusions based on perspectival and other optical technologies. Plays written for the public and private theatres denigrate new optical technologies in order to define and defend their own verbal and visual medium. Several contradictory possibilities thus run throughout early modern theatricality: did theatre offer the audience a version of the truth or a deceptive illusion? Did it offer an illusion that had no effect on reality or one that could influence and transform it in some way? In what follows I will be looking at how these questions play out in four plays that work through the relationship between theatre and visual illusion in revealing ways: Robert Greene's *Friar Bacon and Friar Bungay* (c.1589), Ben Jonson's *The Alchemist* (1610), William Shakespeare's *The Tempest* (1611), and Thomas Tomkis's *Albumazar* (1615).

Setting the stage

Sixteenth-century England inherited optical theories from classical antiquity and from medieval scholasticism that were complex and that may seem to us to be paradoxical. Medieval optics was to some extent more forward-looking than other contemporary fields of natural philosophy because it was based on observation and on the mathematical analysis of natural phenomena. But medieval optics also provided the basis for influential theories of astrology and natural magic, areas that we tend not to regard as 'scientific'. Medieval optics emphasized the adequacy of human vision to provide reliable information about the world, but it also studied the ways vision could be distorted, and it extended its scope from visible phenomena to an interest in the invisible or 'occult'.

As Peter Dear and others have argued, Aristotelian natural philosophy was based on an epistemology that privileged ordinary experience of the world: the routine

---

to late sixteenth-century naturalistic understanding of nature and technology. In some cases this 'science' involves ideas (Copernican astronomy, a particulate theory of matter, the beginnings of a mathematical approach to nature) that we would associate with the scientific revolution, and in some cases with Aristotelian naturalism.

sensory observations of people over a long period of time.[6] Aristotelian optics held that vision was accurate under the right circumstances; as Clark notes, 'the object had to be suitably present and located, the medium adequately clear and accessible, the eye whole and healthy'.[7] Exactly how an image was transmitted into the eye could be explained by theories based on both extromission (the eye sent out a force that captured the image) and intromission (the object gave off some force that entered the eye). Scholastic philosophers in Paris and Oxford—including Roger Bacon, who influenced sixteenth-century English thinkers such as Kepler, Harriot, and Dee—as well as Islamic philosophers such as al-Kindi and Alhazen significantly refined and elaborated this basic Aristotelian optics. They rejected extromission theory and developed an intromission theory of vision which held that all objects produced what they called *species*, which radiated out, transmitting (or 'propagating') images through the medium of air into the eye. *Species* were captured by the eye and then transmitted to the brain, where they physically produced an image like an impression stamped by a seal in wax, or like a painting, or like a reflection in a mirror.[8] When Hamlet suggests that the function of a play is to 'hold as' twere a mirror up to nature' and 'to show the very age and body of the time his form and pressure', he applies the language of veridical optical transmission to the stage.[9]

Clark points out that to scholastic philosophers, 'under normal conditions the world was what it appeared to be and contained real qualities that matched those which were perceived'.[10] This neo-Aristotelian assumption involved bracketing off any phenomena that were not detectable by human senses as 'occult' or hidden and therefore considered to be by nature inexplicable. As William Newman and Clark have both emphasized, many contemporary scholars cling to an anachronistic definition of 'occult' as meaning supernatural or preternatural.[11] In fact, in the Aristotelian system, occult phenomena such as magnetism were assumed to have natural

---

[6] Peter Dear, *Discipline and Experience: The Mathematical Way in the Scientific Revolution* (Chicago: University of Chicago Press, 1995), 22. As Dear explains, 'experiments' were not able to reveal the truth about nature because they involved a single event. 'Experience' was based on the ordinary observations of a number of people over time.

[7] Clark, *Vanities*, 14.

[8] Clark, *Vanities*, 15. The Islamic philosopher Alhazen developed a way to use Euclidean geometry to study optics; since *species* could be seen to radiate from the object to the eye in the form of rays which travelled in straight lines, so lines and angles of vision could be understood geometrically, a practice that influenced the beginnings of modern optics in the work of Kepler and Harriot. See David Lindberg, *Theories of Vision from Al-Kindi to Kepler* (Chicago: University of Chicago Press, 1996).

[9] G. B. Evans, ed., *The Riverside Shakespeare* (Boston: Houghton Mifflin, 1974). 3.2.22–4. All citations to plays by Shakespeare are to this edition.

[10] Clark, *Vanities*, 17.

[11] See William Newman, 'Brian Vickers on Alchemy and the Occult: A Response', *Perspectives on Science* 17.4 (2009), 482–506 (485–8); see also Stuart Clark, *Thinking with Demons: The Idea of Witchcraft in Early Modern Europe* (Oxford: Oxford University Press, 1997), 215, who notes that ' "Magic," even more than "occult," is a word that is indispensable to the study of early modern natural philosophy and, yet, rendered almost unusable by its connotations.'

explanations—human beings were just unable to access them. Optics provided an influential basis for understanding occult phenomena with reference to what was already visible, while also providing possibilities for gaining control over them. Robert Grosseteste and Roger Bacon understood optical phenomena as, in Nicholas Clulee's words, 'the model or prototype of physical causality', such that occult phenomena could be explained by the radiation of invisible *species*.[12] They argued that invisible (or 'occult') species operated according to the same mathematical principles as visible light and therefore developed 'a mathematical interpretation of nature according to geometric optics based upon the behaviour of light as a model for all natural operations'.[13] For Bacon, natural magic was based on human manipulation of the invisible ('occult') forces given off by objects in the world. As lenses and mirrors could reflect and refract light, so too might they, and other technologies, be able to focus and control invisible forces.[14]

In sixteenth-century England, a number of circumstances conspired to intensify the paradoxes underlying optical theory, threatening the Aristotelian assumption that vision provided accurate information about the world but at the same time holding out the possibility that optics could provide new insights into occult phenomena. Copernican astronomy posed a particular challenge to veridical optics, since it offered a theory of the universe that was at odds with its appearance from the perspective of human vision on earth.[15] In this context, several natural philosophers in sixteenth-century England pursued a range of optical projects. William Fulke argued in his *Goodly Gallerye* (1563) that the atmosphere could reflect and refract light in ways that caused optical illusions, explaining away what others had interpreted as supernatural omens. He observes that 'oftentimes, men have seen, as they thought in the firmament, not only two sonnes, but oftener thre sunnes, and many more in number'; this phenomenon, though 'wonderful', occurs when clouds act like a mirror:

> they are nothing els but Idols, or Images of the sunne, represented in an equal smooth and watry cloude, placed on the side of the sunne, and sometime on both sydes, into which the sunn beames being received as in a glasse, expresse ye likeness of fashion and light, that is in the sunne, appearing as though there were many sunnes, where as in dede there is but one, and all the rest are images.[16]

---

[12] Nicholas Clulee, 'Astrology, Magic, and Optics: Facets of John Dee's Early Natural Philosophy', *Renaissance Quarterly* 30.4 (1977), 632–80 (665). Clulee argues that Dee's works (at least before 1558) were influenced most powerfully by al-Kindi, Grosseteste, and Bacon rather than the Neoplatonic or hermetic sources sometimes alleged to have influenced him.

[13] Clulee, 'Astrology, Magic, and Optics', 668.

[14] Clulee, 'Astrology, Magic, and Optics', 672.

[15] In Kepler's words: 'as regards Copernicus, however, this whole illusion (*phantasia*) of standing still and retracing of steps is demonstrated most beautifully from optics'. Johannes Kepler, *Optics: Paralipomena to Witelo and Optical Part of Astronomy*, trans. William H. Donahue (Santa Fe: Green Lion Press, 2000).

[16] William Fulke, *A Goodly Gallerye with a most Pleasant Prospect, into the garden of natural contemplation, to behold the natural causes of all kynde of Meteors* (London, 1563), 41r–41v.

Like John Dee, his associates Leonard Digges and Thomas Digges, and William Bourne, Fulke was interested in man-made as well as naturally occurring optical illusions. Optics thus provided ways to understand, naturalize, and potentially to control occult forces. Fulke offers a more elaborate explanation for the appearance of crosses, circles, armies, beasts, and other images in the sky: these apparitions 'perteyne to the knowledge of Optice and Catroptice, that teache howe by diverse refractions and reflections of beames, such visions are caused' (45r). Such images can be caused by reflections, 'the one artificially, the other naturally' (45v). Artificial apparitions are caused by 'certein glasses and instruments made according to a secret part of that knowledge whiche is called catoptrice' (45v–46r)—Fulke is evidently imagining something like a giant, aerial slide projector. Most such visions have natural causes, however, 'when the disposition of the ayre, hath been suche, that it hath received the image of manye thinges placed and done on the earth' (46r).

John Dee expanded on the work of Roger Bacon and attempted to develop a methodology for measuring and quantifying the powers of the heavenly bodies, using optics to provide a quantified natural basis for astrology.[17] He shared Fulke's interest in 'Catoptrics', arguing in his *Propaedeumata Aphoristica* (1558) that through 'Catoptrics' you could 'cause any one of the five planets to stand off very far from the earth…and finally in the winking of an eye, you may be able to draw it, as it were, to a new perigee',[18] referring probably to the effects of lenses and mirrors that made things appear both farther and closer. Like Bacon, he believed that lenses and mirrors could focus and amplify invisible heavenly rays just as a burning glass could concentrate the rays of the sun. In his *Mathematical Preface* to the first English translation of Euclid's *Elements* (1570), Dee gives optics a large role in astronomy and in natural magic, arguing that 'Perspective', or optics, is necessary so that 'of Astronomicall Apparances, perfect knowledge can be atteyned', providing insight into the ways 'our eye is deceived and abused' by various visible phenomena in the sky.[19] The eyes can be deceived by natural phenomena and also by human contrivance. Dee here gives an example of a 'glasse' that if you lunge towards it with a sword or dagger in hand,

> you shall suddenly be moved to give back (in maner) by reason of an Image, appearing in the ayre, between you & the glasse, with like hand, sword or dagger, & with like quicknes, foyning at your very eye, likewise as you do at the Glasse. (b1v)

---

[17] See Robert Dunn, 'John Dee and Astrology', in Stephen Clucas, ed., *John Dee: Interdisciplinary Studies in English Renaissance Thought* (Dordrecht: Springer, 2006), 85–94, who argues that in the *Propaedeumata Aphoristica* Dee provides 'a natural philosophically based mechanism for [the stars'] operation in the terrestrial realm and a mathematical method for their analysis' (87). Dee seems not to have believed in the predictive powers of traditional judiciary astrology but nevertheless practised it to meet 'market requirements' (93).

[18] John Dee, *Propaedeumata Aphoristica*, ed. and trans. Wayne Shumaker as *John Dee on Astronomy: Propaaedeumata Aphoristica (1558 & 1568)* (Berkeley and Los Angeles: University of California Press, 1978), 175.

[19] John Dee, 'Mathematicall Praeface' to *The Elements of Geometrie of Euclid of Megara* (London, 1570), b1r–b2r.

Dee insists that this glass really exists, 'in London', owned by 'a Gentleman' who will 'very willingly, let the Glasse, and profe be sene'.[20] Dee's interest in illusions also extends beyond lenses and mirrors to trace a range of technologies through which wonders are carried out 'by sundry meanes', including pneumatics, weights, and 'stringes strayned, or Springs, therwith imitating lively Motions' (Preface, A1v), including 'the brazen hed, made by Albertus Magnus, which dyd seme to speake', (Preface, A1v). Optics also plays a role here, since 'by Perspective also straunge thinges, are done...as, to see in the Ayre, a loft, the lyvly Image of an other man, either walking to and fro: or standyng still' (A1v).

In the 'Preface', Dee's discussion of these illusions is framed by a trope that is repeated in other contemporary treatises: the idea that educated people understand that such illusions are natural, explicable, and potentially controllable while the ignorant attribute such effects to magic. Dee insists that these 'marveilous Actes and Feates' are 'Naturally, Mathematically, and Mechanically, wrought and contrived' and complains that 'the folly of Idiotes, and the Mallice of the Scornfull' causes those who fabricate such wonders to be considered conjurors (A1v). Similarly, Dee's student Thomas Digges claims in his *Pantometria* (1571) that his father Leonard had constructed a telescope-like device:

> Sundrie times [he] hath by proportionall Glasses duly situate in convenient angles, not only discovered things farre off, read letters, numbered pieces of money with the very coyn and superscription thereof, cast by some of his friends of purpose uppon downes in open fields, but also seven myles off declared what hath been done at that instante in private places.[21]

In 1580 William Bourne, an expert in navigation, reported to Lord Burghley that 'Mr. Dee, and also Mr. Thomas Digges' had knowledge of technology for seeing at a distance and that a proper combination of plane and concave mirrors aimed at some distant thing 'will shewe the thinge of marvellous largeness, in a manner uncredable to bee believed of the common people'.[22] In his own book of *Inventions or Devises* (1578), Bourne similarly describes a telescope-like device similar to that constructed by Digges: 'to see any small thing a great distance of from you it requireth the ayd of two glasses'.[23] A final section, Device number 113, describes a number of 'Strange works that the world hath marvayled at, as the brazen head that did seeme for to speke'.[24] Bourne explains that 'while some thought it hath bene done by inchantment, which is no such thing, but it hath bene done by wheeles, as

[20] Dee, 'Mathematicall Praeface', b1v.

[21] Thomas Digges, *A Geometrical Practise, named Pantometria* (London, 1571), A3v.

[22] The passage from Bourne's report is cited by C. A. Ronan in 'The Origins of the Reflecting Telescope', *Journal of the British Astronomical Association* 101.6 (1991), 335–42 (339).

[23] William Bourne, *Inventions or Devises Very necessary for all Generalles and Captaines, or Leaders of men* (London, 1578), 96.

[24] Bourne, *Inventions or Devises*, 98.

you may see by Clockes, that doo keepe tyme, some going with plummets, and some with springs'.[25] Bourne concludes with the usual warning that 'the common people' assume that such things are 'done by Inchantment', whereas they are done 'by no other meanes, but by good Artes and lawfull'.[26]

On the stage

Huston Diehl has argued that Shakespeare responded to Reformation iconoclasm and to antitheatrical critique of a theatre that 'bleareth mens eyes', and can 'lead people with intising shewes to the divell', as William Rankins put it in his *Mirrour of Monsters*, by insisting on a theatrical aesthetic that avoided tricks of illusion and instead offered accurate reflection of nature.[27] As evidence, Diehl cites Hamlet's instructions to the players that they employ an acting style that faithfully mirrors human behaviour. When Hamlet attributes to the stage the same ability to faithfully transmit a mirror image or impression of the world that optics associated with *species* and the eye, however, he aligns the stage with the paradoxical and contradictory body of optical theory that I have been tracing thus far, since he aligns the illusory world of the stage (the actors are not really in Denmark) with claims about the capacity of vision to perceive the world as it really is. Hamlet's insistence upon accurate visual mirroring on the stage represents just one of many staged responses to the relationship between theatricality and illusion in the period, a response which, as Diehl has argued, counters accusations that the theatre deceives its audience with a claim that it accurately mirrors the world.[28] Like States, Andrew Sofer and Bruce Smith have, in different ways, emphasized the predominance of acoustic illusion-making on the early modern stage, and many early modern plays self-consciously take up the problem.[29] *A Midsummer Night's Dream* meditates on the relationships among imagination, dream, and theatre by using language to create the illusion that human actors are tiny fairies. *Macbeth*, as Stuart Clark has argued, echoes early modern preoccupations with atmospheric illusions when it blurs the boundaries between demonic magic and the power of thickened light, bubbles in the air, and mirrors to create illusory effects.[30]

But four plays in particular signal their ambivalent engagement with optics by representing the kinds of devices and practices identified in the treatises as natural

---

[25] Bourne, *Inventions or Devises*, 98.   [26] Bourne, *Inventions or Devises*, 99.

[27] Rankins, *A Mirrour of Monsters* (London, 1571), 85–6, as cited by Diehl, *Staging Reform, Reforming the Stage*, 71.

[28] Diehl, *Staging Reform, Reforming the Stage*, 85.

[29] See Andrew Sofer, 'How to Do Things with Demons: Conjuring Performatives in *Doctor Faustus*', *Theatre Journal* 61 (2009), 1–21. See also Bruce R. Smith, *The Acoustic World of Early Modern England: Attending to the O Factor* (Chicago: University of Chicago Press, 1999), especially chapter 8.

[30] Clark, *Vanities*, 236–65. Clark notes that air was 'an element of sleights and tricks', and that *Macbeth* features 'the thick air of illusion' (248–9).

and mathematical—as proto 'science'—but showing them instead as products of demonic magic, or as fraudulent tricks. Robert Greene's *Friar Bacon and Friar Bungay* stages the perspective glass and talking head that Dee and Bourne discuss but seems to align itself with the 'ignorant' by insisting that they were produced by necromantic spells. Three later plays, Ben Jonson's *Alchemist*, Shakespeare's *The Tempest*, and Thomas Tomkis's *Albumazar*, all first produced between 1610 and 1614, echo one another and experiment with different ways of delineating the relationship among theatrical illusion, new technologies for controlling nature, magical power, and fraudulent deceit. These plays use optical devices and other illusionistic techniques to work through questions about the nature of theatre: its relation to reality, its relation to illusion, its efficacy in the world.

Robert Greene, author of *Friar Bacon and Friar Bungay* (1589), was a Cambridge graduate, and there is evidence that he had reasonable knowledge about early modern optics and astronomy. Greene was the author of the *Planetomachia* (1585), a dialogue on astrology that reveals his knowledge of the kind of naturalistic rationale for it espoused by Dee.[31] As Henry S.Turner and Bryan Reynolds have argued, Greene was involved in a feud with Gabriel Harvey that involved criticism of his brother Richard Harvey's astrological predictions.[32] Gabriel Harvey was familiar with the writings of William Bourne, referring to several of his books in his marginalia, where he also mentions Dee and Digges.[33] Although we cannot prove that Greene had read Bourne's book, it is highly likely that he had come across at least one of the several published scientific accounts of the glass prospective and brazen head. And yet his play presents both the perspective glass and the talking head as produced by necromancy and conjuring.

Greene's play was probably written around 1589–90, possibly capitalizing on the popularity of Marlowe's *Doctor Faustus*. This double plot comedy pairs a cross-class romance between Margaret, the fair maid of Fressingfield, and the Earl of Lincoln with a plot centred on the magical exploits of Friars Bacon and Bungay at Oxford. Greene's depiction of Friar Bacon is based on legendary accounts of the same Roger Bacon whose exploration of optics inspired John Dee and whose interests in optics, astrology, alchemy, and Neoplatonism led to a popular reputation as a magician or conjuror, which coexisted with his reputation as a serious scholastic philosopher.

[31] Nandini Das, ed., Robert Greene's *Planetomachia* (Aldershot: Ashgate, 2007), 140–1. All citations to *Friar Bacon and Friar Bungay* are to Russell A. Fraser and Norman Rabkin, eds., *Drama of the English Renaissance I: The Tudor Period* (Upper Saddle River, NJ: Prentice Hall, 1976).

[32] Henry S. Turner and Bryan Reynolds, 'From *Homo Academicus* to *Poeta Publicus*: Celebrity and Transversal Knowledge in Robert Greene's *Friar Bacon and Friar Bungay*', in Kirk Meinikoff and Edward Gieskes, eds., *Writing Robert Greene* (Aldershot: Ashgate, 2008), 86.

[33] Harvey mentions Bourne's 'The Treasure for Travelers' (1578) in his marginal notes in Jerome Turler's *The Traveiler* (1575), and he owned, and made notes in Bourne's *A Regiment for the Sea* (1574). Harvey also noted in the margins of John Blagrave's *The Mathematical Jewel* (1585) that 'after the principles of geometry, and astronomy are canonically and empirically learned, there is nothing difficult in mathematics or in mechanical instruments or experiments'. See *Gabriel Harvey's Marginalia*, ed. G. C. Moore Smith (Stratford-Upon-Avon: Shakespeare Head Press, 1913), 212.

Popular stories about Bacon's magical exploits were collected in a tract called 'The Famous History of Friar Bacon', which Greene seems to have used as a source for the play: the failure of the talking bronze head, the perspective glass, the conjuring contest with Vandermast are all there.[34]

In his play, Greene insists that Bacon creates both the head and the glass through 'nigromancy' (illicitly conjured spirits of the dead) and through the agency of conjured demons. The distinction, underscored in contemporary treatises, between control of nature based on mathematical technologies and on the conjuring of demons is erased. Older criticism of the play tended to argue about whether Bacon's magic was benign 'white' magic or illicit 'black' magic.[35] These critics clearly pick up on the mixed signals offered by the play: what Bacon actually performs was described in the period as within the reach of natural magic (in the sense of a technology that could manipulate invisible natural forces), albeit easily mistaken by the ignorant for black magic. But Bacon himself repeatedly associates these feats with conjuration and necromancy. Bacon is introduced in a scene where a Master Burden doubts that Bacon can create a talking brass head. A colleague named Mason espouses the position of writers like Dee and Bourne when he explains that 'magic may do much in this', and 'he that reads but mathematic rules / Shall find conclusions that avail to work / Wonders that pass the common sense of men' (2.72–5). Burden insists that the talking head is 'more than magic can perform' (2.77) and Bacon answers him by conjuring a demon to bring Burden's illicit mistress from Henley to embarrass him. Bacon further admits that he will create the talking head through 'nigromantic skill' (2.146).

Although we do not see the magical construction of the 'glass prospective' that allows people in Oxford to see the happenings in Fressingfield (166 miles away), we are told that it presents 'shows / That nigromancy did infuse the crystal with' (13.82–3). When the glass leads to the deaths of two sons (who have seen their fathers back in Fressingfield kill each other and follow suit), Bacon breaks the glass and renounces his sinful use of black magic:

> It repents me sore
> That ever Bacon meddled in this art.
> The hours I have spent in pyromantic spells,

---

[34] Alongside these legends about Bacon as a magician was an account of his life that emphasized his standing as a scholastic philosopher with a serious interest in experimentation, especially in areas related to optics; see A. G. Molland, 'Roger Bacon as Magician', *Traditio* 30 (1974), 445–60, which traces Bacon's reputation as both respected philosopher and demonic magician. John Bale described Bacon in 1548 as a 'Juggler and necromantic mage' but later changed his mind and wrote that 'he was possessed of incredible skill in mathematics, but devoid of necromancy, although many have slandered him with it' (cited by Molland, 447); Dee also wrote a defence of Bacon, which has not survived.

[35] See Mark Dahlquist, 'Love and Technological Iconoclasm in Robert Greene's *Friar Bacon and Friar Bungay*', *ELH* 78.1 (Spring 2011), 51–77, who points to Barbara Traister, *Heavenly Necromancers* (Columbia: University of Missouri Press, 1984), 67, for the argument that Bacon's magic is benign (53–4), and Albert Wertheim, 'The Presentation of Sin in *Friar Bacon and Friar Bungay*', *Criticism* 16 (1974), 273–86, for the view that his magic is dangerous (54).

> The fearful tossing in the latest night
> Of papers full of nigromatic charms,
> Conjuring and adjuring devils and fiends,
> With stole and albe and strange pentagonon,
> The wresting of the holy name of God...   (13.85–92)

Bacon promises to spend the rest of his life 'In pure devotion, praying to my God / That he would save what Bacon vainly lost' (14.107–8). His talking head and prospective glass are acceptable as long as they have no discernible efficacy. If they have the power to affect the world they must be renounced.

Critics have recently begun to connect Bacon's endeavours to the new science but with only occasional attention to the deliberate theatricality of his inventions.[36] In fact, both mirror and brazen head are literally stage effects, although they work in different ways, with different relations to optics and to the epistemology of the stage. The mirror, is, of course, unnecessary on the stage, since different parts of the stage can easily represent different locations through the illusionistic verbal technology identified by States as 'eloquent naming': one end of the stage is Oxford, the other is Fressingfield, if characters in the play say that this is so. The stage directions in the 1594 edition of the play reflect this fact. When Edward looks into the glass to spy on Lacy and Margaret in Fressingfield, the stage direction reads '*Enter Margret and Friar Bungay*' (4.11) and some lines later '*Enter Lacy*' (4.46).[37] Their entrances represent the mirror's power to make events in Fressingfield visible because Friar Bacon names that power: 'Within this glass prospective thou shalt see / This day what's done in merry Fressingfield' (6.5–6). A telescopic device is unnecessary on stage because distance is understood to be completely subject to the fictional world of the play, which is established verbally.

A later play, *The Travels of the Three English Brothers* (1607) by John Day, William Rowley, and George Wilkins, makes the relationship between a perspective glass and the power of stage illusion even clearer. Here the glass is not explicitly attributed to magic, although it is wielded by Fame, a chorus figure who is associated

---

[36] Dahlquist has also linked the glass prospective to the glasses described by Digges and Bourne and argues that Greene sees the 'mirrors and optics of sorcerers such as Leonard Digges and John Dee' as offering 'the atheistic dream of an objective inner self'. The failure of the mirror and head are thus Greene's rejection of the idea that 'the wonders of the new science are similar to the miracles of God' (76). Henry Turner and Brian Reynolds argue that Greene has 'retrojected contemporary developments in mathematics into a romanticized medieval past'; see Brian Reynolds and Henry Turner, 'Performative Transversations: Collaborations Through and Beyond Greene's *Friar Bacon and Friar Bungay*', in Brian Reynolds, ed., *Transversal Enterprises in the Drama of Shakespeare and his Contemporaries: Fugitive Explorations* (Basingstoke: Palgrave Macmillan, 2006), 248. For Turner and Reynolds, the failure of the head, rendered on-stage as 'a useless, a ridiculous stage effect' shows Greene 'asserting the superiority of his own specialized language—poetics and dramatic representation—over the spurious incantations of B's device' (248); see also Reynolds and Turner, 'Homo Academicus', 79–81.

[37] Cited from *The honorable historie of frier Bacon, and frier Bongay* (London, 1594), C4r–v.

with the power of the play to 'charm your attentions in a gentle spell' (prologue, line 2).[38] Fame introduces the glass at the very end of the play to allow the brothers, who have not seen each other for many years, to experience a virtual family reunion. The power of the glass is dependent upon the chorus's power to name distant locations into being on the stage:

> But would your [the audience's] apprehensions help poor art,
> Into three parts dividing this our stage,
> They all at once shall take their leaves of you.
> Think this England, this Spain, this Persia.   (epilogue, 8–11)

A long stage direction follows, in which 'Fame gives to each a prospective glass: they seem to see one another and to offer to embrace, at which Fame parts them and so exeunt all except Fame' (Epilogue). Fame has served throughout the play as a figure who can conjure up locations or the passage of time. The prospective glass here becomes a technology of theatrical illusion tied only distantly to magical 'charms'.

The talking head in *Friar Bacon and Friar Bungay* is another matter, and ironically it may have relied on some of the technology described by Dee and Bourne. In *Magic on the Early English Stage*, Philip Butterworth discusses how talking heads in Greene's play and several others might have been staged, and he considers whether the mechanical devices described by Bourne might have been used.[39] He concludes that 'the mechanical devices suggested in Bourne's account may appear too complex or inflexible for the kind of theatrical use' found in Greene's play. However, he does argue that the head may have been made to speak by pipes or other devices as Bourne suggests.[40] Butterworth also points out that 'the conscious working of the reality-illusion relationship is not only central to the conventions by which theatre exists, but also to the creation of magic through conjuring, legerdemain or sleight of hand, ventriloquy and other forms of overt deception or pretence'.[41] In other words, an audience watching a play expects there to be a gap between what appears to be true and what is actually true. And the audience expects that gap to produce wonder, at least some of the time. Andrew Sofer, writing about the conjuration scene in Marlowe's *Doctor Faustus*, has argued that 'a thoroughly skeptical audience would have little use for the Elizabethan theatre',[42] since the success of that play

---

[38] *The Travels of the Three English Brothers*, in Anthony Parr, ed., *Three Renaissance Travel Plays* (Manchester: Manchester University Press, 1995).

[39] For a discussion of the relationship between the head and mechanical clocks in the period, see Todd Andrew Borlik, '"More than Art": Clockwork Automata, The Extemporizing Actor, and the Brazen Head in *Friar Bacon and Friar Bungay*', in Wendy Beth Hyman, ed., *The Automaton in English Renaissance Literature* (Aldershot: Ashgate, 2011), 135–42. Borlik speculates about the reasons for Greene's decision to 'mystify innovations in early modern automata' (134).

[40] Philip Butterworth, *Magic on the Early English Stage* (Cambridge: Cambridge University Press, 2005), 103–5.

[41] Butterworth, *Magic on the Early English Stage*, 98.

[42] Sofer, 'How to Do Things with Demons', 21.

depends on 'an unresolved tension in the Elizabethan imagination between conjuring as an act of deception (or "jugglery") and conjuring as a particular speech act—one with potentially magical effects'.[43] *Friar Bacon and Friar Bungay* plays on a slightly different tension, between the audience's awareness that it understands how the mirror and the glass work as theatrical illusions and their wonder at the magical illusion that is achieved within the fiction.

The epistemology of the theatre is thus quite different from that of writers like Digges, Dee, and Bourne. Their task is to explain the gap between the manifest and the occult, between surface appearances and their underlying causal reality. The task of the theatre is to exploit that gap. It would be pointless for the play to show Friar Bacon constructing a telescopic mirroring device according to Bourne's instructions, because the stage doesn't need it. It would be dangerous (and boring) to show him fashioning a brazen head that operates through springs and plummets, because the play depends in part on the wonderment of an audience that doesn't scrutinize what lies behind its marvellous effects. The comic failure of the brazen head is funny only if it is presented as having supernatural agency—a broken clockwork mechanism on-stage would be a technical difficulty, not a joke. Instead, the play effaces the optical and technological effects by translating them into demonic magic, in this way presenting theatre itself as a source of wonder that is safer and more orthodox. But the play does so, I would argue, by disavowing its own efficacy. Bacon's magic is praised and rewarded as long as it produces harmless shows like the ineffectual talking head, the prospective glass that lets people spy on their friends, the power to control Vandermast's Hercules figure and to transport other characters on and off the stage. When the mirror is shown to have power over what happens in the world by inspiring the deaths of the two sons, it must be renounced. Critics have long noticed that the play draws a parallel between Margaret and Bacon as characters whose gifts (beauty and magic) give them powers at odds with their social position that must be limited and circumscribed under the power of the king.[44] Something similar could be said about the play's view of theatricality itself.

In contrast, three plays clustered around 1610—the date of publication of Galileo's *Starry Messenger* and a traditional turning point in the development of 'the new science' in England—go beyond *Friar Bacon and Friar Bungay* in interrogating the status of theatrical illusion in relation to optical technologies for the control of nature and for the creation of perspectival illusions in the court masque. The plays are explicitly in dialogue with one another and represent the nature of optical, and

---

[43] Sofer, 'How to Do Things with Demons', 21.

[44] This argument goes as far back as William Empson in *Some Versions of Pastoral* (London: Chatto & Windus, 1935), 33, who saw beauty and magic as 'individualist, dangerous, and outside the social order'. Charles Hieatt, 'Multiple Plotting in *Friar Bacon and Friar Bungay*', *Renaissance Drama* n.s. 16 (1985), 17–34, argues that Margaret and Bacon test the limits of their powers and are brought back within an accepted social order by the king (23). Turner and Reynolds are also concerned with Bacon's social position as *homo academicus* in need of patronage.

theatrical, illusion in very different ways.[45] Unlike the other plays that I am discussing here, Ben Jonson's *The Alchemist* does not directly allude to optical devices or illusions, presenting alchemy (and astrology and magic) as the deceitful practices of con artists. *The Alchemist* goes even further than Greene's play in questioning the efficacy of theatrical illusion. Shakespeare's *The Tempest* does the opposite, representing Prospero's control over nature as real and magical (rather than illusory, fraudulent, or natural) and, like Greene, linking the power of his magic with the power of the theatre, although with a less circumscribing attitude. Finally, Thomas Tomkis's *Albumazar*, which echoes both the *Alchemist* and *The Tempest*, represents a fraudulent astrologer who claims to have invented various wondrous devices, one of which is based on Galileo's account of the telescope, which the play reveals to be a fraud. In a scene that returns us to Hamlet's 'mirror up to nature', Albumazar's devices reveal only the material world of the theatre, reflecting the audience present at the performance rather than far-off locations within the world of the play.

Ben Jonson probably knew more about the technologies of illusion than any other playwright of the period through his more than twenty years of collaboration with Inigo Jones in the creation of court masques. Jones relied on a range of illusionistic devices, including machines that rotated scenes, devices that allowed painted sets to be changed quickly, and elaborate optical effects such as 'mirrors, and magnifiers, colored lamps, and metallic or sequined costumes'.[46] As is well known, Jonson felt that the poetic text ought to be more important than elaborate scenery, and this feeling was exacerbated over time by the fact that, as Orgel argues, Jones's 'control of realistic visual illusions' threatened to make the poet's role 'superfluous'.[47] Jonson, of course, eventually quarrelled with Jones over the increasing primacy of the visual over the verbal in masque. His 'Expostulation with Inigo Jones' complains about Jones's view that 'painting and carpentry are the soul of mask'.[48] He criticizes Jones's pretensions as an architect in ways that link architecture with optics and other related mathematical technologies: Jones claims exaggerated knowledge of mathematicians like Euclid, Archimedes, Archytas, and Ctesibus; he panders to

---

[45] A number of critics have pointed out evidence linking Jonson's *Alchemist* with Shakespeare's *Tempest*; for a summary of arguments, see David Lucking, 'Carrying Tempest in his Hand and Voice: The Figure of the Magician in Jonson and Shakespeare', *English Studies* 85 (2004), 297–310. *Albumazar*, in turn, has a character named 'Truincalo', probably based on Shakespeare's Trinculo. There is some equivocal evidence that Tomkis's play was actually written in 1610–11, several years before its first recorded performance. Dryden claimed that Jonson based *The Alchemist* on *Albumazar* but this seems unlikely; see Hugh G. Dick, ed., 'Introduction' to Thomas Tomkis, *Albumazar: A Comedy* (Berkeley: University of California Press, 1944), 48–52.

[46] Stephen Orgel, 'Introduction', to *Ben Jonson: The Complete Masques* (New Haven: Yale University Press, 1969), 15.

[47] Orgel, 'Introduction', 23–5. Orgel also notes that English audiences in the period didn't quite know what to make of the scenic effects used in masques because they were so different from the verbal scene-painting in the theatre.

[48] Ben Jonson, *Poems*, ed. Ian Donaldson (Oxford: Oxford University Press, 1975), line 50.

public taste for 'the machine, and the shows' (l. 32) and 'the mere perspective of an inch-board' (l. 44); he appeals to 'the money-get, mechanic age' (l. 52) and uses optical technologies like the 'lantern-lurry: with fulginous heat / whirling his whim-sie' (ll. 72–3).

We should not be surprised, then, that Jonson does not share Greene's interest in staging optical devices. Jones provided elaborate scenery depicting an alchemist's laboratory in the masque *Mercury Vindicated from the Alchemists at Court* (1616), but Jonson, in *The Alchemist*, pointedly refuses to show Subtle's apparatus on-stage. His alchemical work is depicted entirely through his own lengthy and jargon-filled descriptions of it—it exists entirely in language and sound effect. Alvin Kernan has commented on the 'incredible density of *things* in this play', but he means 'things' that are conjured up only in words, in Subtle's lists of alchemical ingredients and Mammon's catalogues of decadence. Jonson seems to take delight in demonstrating the power of verbal illusion. However, as a number of critics have noted, Subtle and Face employ verbal illusion in the service of fraud. The alchemical apparatus that Subtle so powerfully calls into being by naming does not, in fact, exist: his long bravura descriptions are the means through which he draws in and fools his dupes. And critics have also understood that theatre is implicated in Jonson's exposure of alchemical deception. David Riggs has suggested that '*The Alchemist* is largely concerned with the institution of the theater and its place in the fantasy life of the popular audience'.[49] Although Jonson's prologue to the play promises that it will offer 'wholesome remedies' and 'fair correctives' to improve the audience, many critics have had a difficult time squaring this claim with its comic conclusion where Face's lies and deceptions seem to be forgiven, if not rewarded.[50] The play ridicules the idea that alchemy, and by extension theatre, can be an agent of transformation or 'perfection', to use Subtle's term. The dupes' aspirations to self-improvement are shown to be deluded.[51] Jonson, like Greene, may have intended to differentiate theatrical illusion from more dangerous contemporary optical and scenic practices, but *The Alchemist* reveals that the distinction is impossible to maintain.[52]

As for Shakespeare, Harry Levin was right, I think, to argue that *The Alchemist* and *The Tempest* treat 'clearly related themes' but nevertheless 'stand in polar opposition' to one another.[53] Several critics have argued that the plays respond to one another in some way, but it is impossible to be certain about the chronology and

---

[49] David Riggs, *Ben Jonson: A Life* (Cambridge, MA: Harvard University Press, 1989), 171.

[50] See Mary Thomas Crane, 'What Was Performance', *Criticism* 43.2 (Spring 2001), 169–87 (180). See also Riggs, *A Life*, 171–2.

[51] Crane, 'Performance', 180–1.

[52] For a very different take on the relationship among alchemy, science, and theatre, see Katherine Eggert, 'The Alchemist and Science', in Garrett Sullivan, Patrick Cheney, and Andrew Hadfield, eds., *Early Modern English Drama: A Critical Companion* (Oxford: Oxford University Press, 2006).

[53] Harry Levin, 'Two Magian Comedies: "The Tempest" and "The Alchemist"', *Shakespeare Survey* 22 (1969), 47–58 (57).

therefore about which is responding to which.[54] Where Jonson exposes alchemy as a fraud, Shakespeare presents a world where natural magic is powerfully efficacious; where Jonson shows that alchemy and theatre leave people 'basically unchanged', Shakespeare seems to remain hopeful that illusion fosters 'change and growth and diversification'.[55] Shakespeare's play is also pointedly unlike *The Alchemist* in that it makes use of an unusually large number of special effects: an illusory storm, a vanishing feast, flying spirits, a vanishing masque. Keith Sturgess argues that these 'quaint devices' are a function of its history of private performance and performance at Blackfriars, although Jonson's play was staged there as well.[56] Sturgess describes *The Tempest* as 'an experiment in metatheatre' which 'explores the baffling territory marked out by "magic," "illusion," and trick"', and suggests that 'the staging of the play is both design and meaning', a position that Jonson adamantly opposed.[57] Shakespeare, in other words, exploits the acoustic and optical properties of the private theatre stage in order to test the possibilities and limits of the greater control over audience perspective afforded by newly popular forms (like the masque) and venues (like Blackfriars).

But although he affirms the power of theatrical illusion on one level, Shakespeare also raises a set of related questions about the sources and nature of the magic that stands in for it in the world of the play. Perhaps because the play insists so strongly that Prospero's magic is derived from books and does not involve demonic agency, it stages something closer to the writings of sixteenth-century natural philosophers than the other plays discussed here. Its careful discrimination of Prospero's magic from the unseen and unstaged powers of his predecessor, Sycorax, for instance, might be seen to replicate the treatises' attempts to draw similar boundaries between natural and supernatural, lawful and unlawful practices. And this in turn may explain why *The Tempest* has been associated with the scientific revolution more frequently than other plays.[58] As in *Friar Bacon and Friar Bungay*, however, the play identifies as 'magic' phenomena that might have been explained by Dee and company as involving mechanical effects or optical illusions. Keith Sturgess has argued that Prospero may be linked to Dee by virtue of the fact that Richard Burbage probably would have played both Prospero and Subtle, who John Aubrey claimed was

---

[54] The induction to *Bartholomew Fair* takes a couple of jabs at *The Tempest*: 'If there be never a servant-monster I' the fair, who can help it? he says; nor a nest of antics? He is loath to make Nature afraid in his plays, like those that beget Tales, Tempests, and suchlike drolleries' (ll. 125–9). Fraser and Rabkin, eds., *Drama of the English Renaissance II: The Stuart Period*, 'Induction' to *Bartholomew Fair*, ll. 137–9.

[55] Levin, 'Two Magian Comedies', 57.

[56] Keith Sturgess, *Jacobean Private Theatre* (London: Routledge & Kegan Paul, 1987), 73–5. For the play as a commentary on the conditions of performance at Blackfriars, see Douglas Bruster, 'Quoting the Playhouse in *The Tempest*', in *Quoting Shakespeare: Form and Culture in Early Modern Drama* (Lincoln: University of Nebraska Press, 2000), 117–42.

[57] Sturgess, *Jacobean Private Theatre*, 73.

[58] See, for example, Elizabeth Spiller, 'Shakespeare and the Making of Early Modern Science: Resituating Prospero's Art', *South Central Review* 26.1–2 (Winter 2009), 24–41, as well as Denise Albanese, 'Admiring Miranda', in *New Science, New World* (Durham: Duke University Press, 1996), 59–91.

based partly on Dee.[59] Prospero's claim that he has 'bedimmed the noontide sun' and 'given fire' to 'the dread rattling thunder' (5.1.40–1, 45, 44), even Sycorax's alleged ability to 'Control the moon' (5.1.270)—all might have been plausibly explained as optical illusions or effects created by mirrors and lenses along the lines suggested by Dee in his *Propaedeumata*, where catoptrics is said to be able to move the heavenly bodies. His 'insubstantial pageant' that dissolves without a trace might have been catoptrically projected like the visions explained by Dee and Fulke, rather than enacted by spirits.[60]

The Tempest also queries the nature and sources of knowledge about the world and causes the audience to hesitate over whether it can trust what it sees or believe what it hears. Prospero's control over the world of the play and his command of illusion is shown to be problematic in several ways. The first two scenes of the play put the audience in a radically disorienting situation. From their perspective, they see an opening scene that creates a stage storm using the expected effects: squibs to produce the effect of lightning, drums and rolling cannonballs to produce thunder, pebbles revolved in a drum to produce the sound of the sea, strips of canvas turned on a wheel to produce the wind.[61] The audience suspends disbelief and accepts this storm as 'real' within the fictional world of the play. 1.2 then flirts with theatrical disaster by revealing that the storm was an illusion. The audience's suppressed knowledge that the storm was not real or natural is confirmed, but they are then told that it was created by magic. Prospero's magic is thus identified from the beginning of the play as an illusion created by special effects. The audience has been put through an exercise in the drawing of distinctions between art and nature, reality and illusion, but the play only continues to confound these distinctions. Prospero repeatedly insists that his magic is artificial, 'it was mine art, / when I arriv'd and heard thee, that made gape / The pine, and let thee out' (1.2.291–3). Prospero and Caliban both claim that Prospero has learned his magic from books: 'Remember / First to possess his books; for without them / He's but a sot as I am' (3.2.91–3). However, this is not what the play shows us: strikingly, there is no indication that we see any of his books on-stage.[62] The magic that we see him perform is mostly carried out by Ariel, who appears to be some kind of nature spirit; by Prospero's own

---

[59] Sturgess, *Jacobean Private Theatre*, 74–5.

[60] Spiller, 'Shakespeare and the Making of Early Modern Science', has convincingly argued that the play also reveals the role of art in mediating the shift from Aristotelian *scientia* to modern science: Prospero's artificial interventions in nature educate Ferdinand and Miranda from 'a kind of Aquinian wonder to Baconian science' (32). She acknowledges, however, that Prospero's knowledge comes not from the evidence provided by the senses but from deceiving them: for Spiller, the play is finally 'not an experiment' (36).

[61] Sturgess, *Jacobean Theatre*, 81, describes these effects. Bruce Smith, *The Acoustic World*, 233, argues that *The Tempest* 'exploits the acoustic potentialities of the new space to the full'.

[62] Andrew Sofer, 'Properties', in Richard Dutton, ed., *The Oxford Handbook of Early Modern Theatre* (Oxford: Oxford University Press, 2009), 569, argues that 'Prospero's magic books are never explicitly conjured by stage directions'.

admission, he didn't conjure Ariel up using directions found in a book but instead gained control over him when he managed to free him from the tree. He uses threats, not magic, to control Ariel, and for the most part controls Caliban with threats as well. As I have argued elsewhere, the long distance 'pinches' that he seems able to inflict are persistently described in natural terms: Prospero likens them to the pain caused by bees or hedgehogs ('urchins'), but Caliban describes an actual hedgehog attack: hedgehogs 'lie tumbling in my barefoot way, and mount / Their pricks at my footfall' (2.2.10–12). Caliban and Ferdinand are made to carry logs, Ariel is repeatedly threatened with confinement in another tree, and his enemies are chased through 'tooth'd briers, sharp furzes, pricking goss, and thorns' (4.1.180), a punishment that blends together with the pricking pinches supposedly inflicted by supernatural means. They are finally confined to a 'filthy mantled pool' and it isn't fully clear whether they are held there by magic or by mud.

It is not fully evident, then, that Prospero brought magic to the island with his books as he claims. Magic was already there, and as many critics have noticed, the demonic magic of Sycorax the witch as described by Prospero seems virtually indistinguishable from his own magic (as he describes it); both are said to control heavenly bodies and are able to wreak havoc with trees. Prospero claims that he and Miranda brought what they needed to survive on the island with them, but Caliban claims they owe their survival to his direct knowledge of its nature. As Denise Albanese has argued, the play shows the artful magic derived from Prospero's books to be limited and contingent. His books did not enable him to retain power in Milan, and 'it is Caliban who must show Prospero and Miranda the sources of fresh water and edible fruit'.[63] As opposed to Prospero, Caliban possesses empirical knowledge of the features of the island: 'fresh springs, brine pits, barren place and fertile'. Elizabeth Spiller has argued that Caliban's knowledge is that of an Aristotelian natural historian who describes rather than controls nature, and whose knowledge gives him no access to power.[64] But if Caliban did provide Prospero with initial knowledge necessary for survival, his loss of power may have more to do with Prospero's psychological manipulation of him and less to do with his relation to nature. The play suggests that Prospero's claims—that his power comes from a book, that his art conquers nature, that he brought with him sufficient means for survival on the island—are not necessarily true, or are not the only truth. The play thus questions Prospero's fantasy of the powerful book.

Ultimately, Prospero's 'magic' on the island is used not to gain power over nature but for the psychological manipulation of other people. And this is also what finally aligns his magic with theatre, since he commands Ariel to put on one show after another. The play self-consciously stages a contemporary shift towards a theatre of directed gaze, psychological manipulation, and optical effects, but it has deep

---

[63] Albanese, 'Admiring Miranda', 68.
[64] Spiller, 'Shakespeare and the Making of Early Modern Science', 34.

misgivings about these technologies. Of all the plays discussed here that take up the problematic relation between magic and science, *The Tempest* most fully stages the distinction-making struggles of the optical treatises. In the end, *The Tempest* is as ambivalent about art as it is about science, questioning both the ethical implications of his manipulative technology and also his claims that human learning, derived from books, can control nature.

Thomas Tomkis's *Albumazar*, performed during a visit of King James and his court to Trinity College, Cambridge, in 1615, marks a logical endpoint for my discussion, because it echoes both *The Alchemist* and *The Tempest* and puts the first optical device unambiguously associated with modern science—Galileo's telescope—explicitly on the stage.[65] Tomkis follows in the footsteps of Greene, Jonson, and even Shakespeare by refusing to acknowledge the telescope as a natural and legitimate technology for extending human vision, representing it, like alchemy in Jonson's play, as a fraudulent device used to deceive a gull whom the sham astrologer intends to cheat. In doing so, Tomkis goes farther than any of his predecessors in debunking both the power of optical technology and the power of theatrical illusion, as the 'perspicill' literally holds a mirror up to nature, allowing the gull to see only the theatre audience in front of him.

Tomkis based his play on Giambattista Della Porta's *Lo Astrologo*, but the staging of Galileo's telescope was Tomkis's addition. Della Porta was also the author of *Magiae Naturalis* (1589), a book of secrets somewhat similar to William Bourne's *Inventions or Devises* that offered instructions on distilling, cooking, grafting, and alchemy, and it included a chapter on burning glasses and other mirrors and lenses that could create optical effects. Della Porta described a telescopic device similar to those mentioned by Digges and Bourne, and was eventually put out that Galileo did not credit him with invention of the device (even though he never actually built one).[66] Della Porta's play satirizes what was called 'judicial' astrology, the making of specific predictions about human events based on the location of the heavenly bodies. But his treatise on natural magic reveals that he accepted 'natural astrology', the basic idea that heavenly bodies had power over nature.

Near the beginning of Tomkis's play, one of Albumazar's henchmen Ronca dazzles the gull Pandolfo with a 'Perspicill', which he calls 'an engine to catch starres' (l. 236). In language that resembles Prospero's claim that Sycorax could 'control the moon', Ronca claims that the device will 'draw the Moone so neere that you would sweare / The bush of thornes in't prick your eyes' (ll. 245–6). When Pandolfo looks

---

[65] The play alludes to Galileo's *Siderius Nuncius* when it echoes his name for the telescope, 'perspicillium', but calling it a 'perspicill' (1.3.279) and it mentions Galileo by name at 1.5.367. On these references see Hugh G. Dick, 'The Telescope and the Comic Imagination', *Modern Language Notes* 58 (1943), 544–8. All citations are to the edition of Dick (in note 45).

[66] See Stephen Jay Gould, 'The Sharp-eyed Lynx, Outfoxed by Nature: Galileo and friends taught us that there is more to observing than meets the eye', *Natural History* 107.4 (May 1998), pt I: 82–90, 116–21.

through the glass, however, he sees 'a Hall thrust full of bare-heads, some bald, some busht, / Some bravely branch't' (ll. 269–70). The play is set in London and Ronca tells Pandolfo that he is seeing a theatre audience made up of members of the university and the court in Cambridge 'forty miles hence' (l. 268). The actors playing Ronca and Pandolfo are, of course, standing on a stage in Cambridge pointing the telescope at that very audience. While *Friar Bacon and Friar Bungay* preserved the power of the stage to make Fressingfield visible in Oxford by naming it, *Albumazar* collapses that power into a joke. The perspicill can only show what is literally right in front of it. The play then extends this flattening of the theatre's powers into an acoustic realm when it introduces the auditory equivalent of the telescope, an 'otacousticon', shaped like a pair of asses ears, which can extend the power of hearing. Pandolfo puts on the device and says he is able to hear 'a humming noyse of laughter' (l. 290), which Ronca identifies as 'the Court / And Universitie, that now are merry / With an old gentleman in a comedy' (ll. 290–2). He then hears what he thinks is 'celestiall musick' and a song follows, which Ronca identifies as 'musick twixt the Acts' (l. 294) of the play in Cambridge. These devices have no power to extend the reach of human senses beyond what is actually present, and the theatre seemingly has no power to create the illusion of that extension or to show anything except what is literally there in the performance hall.

Albumazar goes farther than either *The Alchemist* or *The Tempest* in dampening the illusionistic power of the stage. Unlike *The Tempest*, it refuses to align the stage with magic. The 'celestial music' that Pandolfo thinks he hears in *Albumazar* is not like the mysterious music that Caliban is able to hear on the island, but it is instead identified as the music between the acts of the play. Unlike *The Alchemist*, it does not offer up a verbal display that can conjure up an alchemical laboratory out of nothing. As a university play, *Albumazar* may be more resistant to the kinds of optical experiments being carried out in London outside the sphere of the university, and as an academic drama it may be less interested in the complex nature of theatrical illusion. The play may also reflect emerging changes in theatrical taste. Stephen Orgel has argued that the 'perspective stages' constructed by Jones 'establish their particular kinds of reality by depending on a set of assumptions that the English spectator was not on the whole used to exercising in the theater' in the early years of the seventeenth century. He traces a gradual change, influenced by the aesthetics of the masque, towards theatrical productions dependent more upon elaborate scenery rather than verbal descriptions.[67] *Albumazar* may reflect a further point in this evolution, although it does not itself make much use of scenic effects.

Early modern playwrights seem to have been fascinated by contemporary developments in optics but wary of the theatrical potential of optical effects. Perhaps these writers intuited that the ability to project lifelike images in the air or at a

---

[67] Orgel, 'Introduction', 25, 39.

distance would one day pose a serious threat to the complex illusionistic practices developed for the stage, and to live theatre itself. States has argued that while Shakespeare and film are not 'incompatible', there is still 'a subtle competition between the two modes of scene painting and it becomes most apparent when the camera tries to duplicate imagery that is itself serving a cinematic function'.[68] Uncertain about its own relation to veridical visual perception, the early modern theatre could not afford to let audiences see new optical technologies represented directly, and instead depicts them as refracted through demonic magic or fraudulent tricks. And yet, the theatre remained drawn to new optical theories and technologies because they provided such rich possibilities for reflecting on the nature of theatrical illusion itself.

FURTHER READING

Clulee, Nicholas H. 'At the Crossroads of Magic and Science: John Dee's Archemastrie', in Brian Vickers, ed., *Occult and Scientific Mentalities in the Renaissance* (Cambridge: Cambridge University Press, 1984), 57–72.

Harkness, Deborah E. *John Dee's Conversations with Angels: Cabala, Alchemy, and the End of Nature* (Cambridge: Cambridge University Press, 1999).

Ronan, C. A. 'The Origins of the Reflecting Telescope', *Journal of the British Astronomical Association* 101 (1991), 335–42.

[68] States, *Great Reckonings*, 57.

CHAPTER 14

EKPHRASIS

JOEL ALTMAN

'We shall enrich speech by description of a thing when we do not relate what is done, or has been done, summarily or sketchily, but *place it before the eyes painted with all the colors of rhetoric,* so that at length it draws the hearer or reader outside himself *as in the theatre.*'[1] Thus Erasmus advises students of composition to embellish their themes, letters, and declamations by infusing their language with what the Greeks call *enargeia*, the Latins *evidentia*—thereby to fashion signifiers whose signifieds shine forth, whether read or heard, to form pictures in the imagination that rival the experience of actually seeing what is only told.

The passage appears in Erasmus's popular school text *De duplici copia verborum ac rerum*—first issued in 1512 and running through some 150 editions in the sixteenth century[2]—as part of his discussion of amplifying one's subject matter. This method, he writes, 'consists chiefly of the description of things, times, places, and persons.'[3] By 'things' (*res*) he means not only objects, but human actions and events, strange peoples, different ways of life, and political conditions such as democracy and tyranny; natural phenomena like storms, famine, living animals, and plants; and works of art, such as paintings and statues. In his usage, description (*descriptio* in Latin, *ekphrasis* or *hypotyposis* in Greek) is a statement filled with the *circumstances* surrounding the matter, expressed in vivid, concrete diction, ornamented with metaphors, similes, and other rhetorical figures chosen to pass through the eyes and ears into the imagination, where, shaped by fantasy, reason, and memory, it will secure emotional adherence and intellectual conviction.

By way of illustration, Erasmus quotes Quintilian, the revered first-century Latin rhetorician:

---

[1] 'Rei descriptione locupletabimus orationem, quum id quod fit aut factum est non summatim aut tenuiter exponemus, sed omnibus fucatum coloribus ob oculos ponemus, ut auditorem sive lectorem, iam extra se positum, velut in theatrum avocet.' *Desiderii Erasmi Roterdami Opera Omnia* (Amsterdam, 1988), vol. I-6, 202. English translation by Donald B. King and H. David Rix, *On Copia of Words and Ideas* (Milwaukee: Marquette University Press, 1963), 47, with minor emendation. Italics mine.

[2] Erasmus, *On Copia*, 2.   [3] *Opera Omnia*, 202; *On Copia*, 47.

If someone should say that a city was captured, he doubtless comprehends in that general statement everything that attends such fortune, but if you develop what is implicit in the one word, flames will appear pouring through homes and temples; the crash of falling buildings will be heard, and one indefinable sound of diverse outcries; some will be seen in bewildered flight, others clinging in the last embrace of their relatives; there will be the wailing of infants and women, old people cruelly preserved by fate till that day, the pillaging of profane and sacred objects, the running about of those carrying off booty and those seeking it, prisoners in chains before their captors, and the mother struggling to keep her infant, and fighting among the victors wherever there is greater plunder. For although the overthrow of a city involves all these things, it is nevertheless less effective to tell the whole at once than it is to relate all the particulars.[4]

Erasmus's advice is echoed in the sixteenth century by such vernacular writers as Thomas Wilson, Henry Peacham, and George Puttenham, heirs to Cicero, Quintilian, the author of the *Rhetorica ad Herennium*, and the late classical rhetorician Aphthonius (fourth century AD), whose Latinized *Progymnasmata* was an important English grammar school text in the period.

But the phrase 'as in the theatre' must give us pause.[5] Clearly, Erasmus and his fellow rhetoricians are not, in the first instance, giving advice to playwrights. Therefore, when they claim that writers or speakers who compose vivid *descriptiones* can transform mere readers or listeners into theatrical spectators, the question arises: what happens when the listeners are already spectators? For playwrights, too, employ ekphrases, especially in the Elizabethan and Jacobean theatres.[6] How might we describe their effect on the stage, and what is the relationship of ekphrastic speech and the ongoing action in which it is enunciated? These questions involve the role of the speaker and his or her verbal style, vocal pitch, and delivery, all of

[4] *On Copia*, 47–8; cf. Quintilian, *Institutio oratoria*, trans. H. E Butler, Loeb Classical Library, 4 vols. (Cambridge, MA: Harvard University Press, 1966), viii.3.67–70.

[5] The words are not exclusively Erasmus's. Some of the oldest texts suggest that the speaker who fashions vivid *descriptiones* has the power to turn his listeners into a theatrical audience, mere hearers into spectators. Notes Ruth Webb: 'The words *hup'opsin agōn* ("leading before the eyes") suggest the dramatist who literally produces characters and actions on stage, placing them before the eyes of the audience. And the term used by Nikolaos [fifth century AD] to express the transformed role of the audience of ekphrasis, *theatai*, more obviously refers to the *spectators* in a theatre than to viewers of a work of art. Theatrical imagery is frequently used elsewhere of vivid language, as in the scholia to the Shield episode in *Iliad*, 18 where Homer is said to "roll out (*ekkukleō*) the maker [Haiphaistos] as if on a stage and show us his workshop in the open"' (*Ekphrasis, Imagination and Persuasion in Ancient Rhetorical Theory and Practice* (Burlington, VT: Ashgate, 2009), 54. See also Bernard F. Scholz, '"Sub Oculos Subiectio": Quintilian on Ekphrasis and Enargeia', in Valerie Robillard and Els Jongeneel, eds., *Pictures into Words: Theoretical and Descriptive Approaches to Ekphrasis* (Amsterdam: VU University Press, 1998), 72–99 (80).

[6] Erasmus acknowledges this when he cites messenger speeches from Euripides, Seneca, and Sophocles, which 'are presented instead of the spectacle' and 'report the things which it is either impossible or inappropriate to present on the stage' (*Opera Omnia*, 204; *On Copia*, 48), but aside from reinforcing the idea that hearing a *descriptio* is as good as seeing an action performed, he offers no clue as to how the aural experience might enhance the visual.

which constitute a *punctum* in the flow of the plot and introduce a competing temporality to that of the action. They also involve the degree to which an extra-mental reality resides in the ekphrastic signified—be it natural object, emblem, statue, someone else's speech—and the synaesthetic and therefore psychological impact of the combinate form. Such matters have particular significance in a non-illusionistic theatre, one that by the early 1600s had begun to coexist with the stage adaptation of continental achievements in the visual arts; in the Jonson–Jones masque, for instance, the ancient paragone between the verbal and the visual, already implied in the rhetoricians' advice to use language as paint, would grow especially fierce.[7]

More practically, what *uses* are made of ekphrasis in a medium that is as visual as it is verbal, and what functions does it perform? Clearly it injects a certain elasticity into the action, allowing more to 'take place' than is shown, as Francis Berry demonstrated many years ago, distinguishing between the 'foreground' and 'hinterland' of a play on the analogy of religious paintings of the Italian and Northern Renaissance.[8] In doing so, however, it also expands what we might call the psyche of the play—what the play is mindful of—which necessarily includes the minds of both speaker and listeners. Of what sorts of things are they compelled to take note? For example, our mentor Erasmus observes that when ekphrasis aims largely at producing pleasure, it is related to epideictic rhetoric, the kind of speechifying that calls attention to the ingenuity of the speaker and often shifts the focus from content to rhetorical skill.[9] How might a shift in tone, syntax, and reference bring about a corresponding cognitive and emotional shift in the listener? And this raises an even more fundamental question: how was *any* ekphrasis thought to do its work—in the speaker and his or her audience? What went on inside their heads? Here we are concerned with psychic process, and especially the *expressive* potential of ekphrastic speech and its transmission to the listener: is the speaker merely a bringer of news? emotionally invested in his or her description? possessed by it? Are there instances in which what is being described is also viewed by auditors, who can judge the condition of the speaker's psyche? This opens ekphrasis to characterological and subjective analysis and to ironic uses as a mode of persuasion, whether directed to oneself, an on-stage auditor, off-stage auditors, or all three.

Finally, there is the matter of the *objects* of ekphrasis. By 'objects' I don't just mean that which is described but also that for the sake of which the description occurs. This involves consideration of the professional, social, and political functions that

---

[7] See Gary Schmidgall, *Shakespeare and the Courtly Aesthetic* (Berkeley: University of California Press, 1981); Roy Strong, *Henry Prince of Wales and England's Lost Renaissance* (London: Thames and Hudson, 1986).

[8] Francis Berry, *The Shakespearean Inset* (New York: Theatre Arts Books, 1965). This remains a valuable study, linking as it does a variety of 'insets' to stage position, vocal delivery, and grammatical tense. Berry is not explicitly concerned with ekphrasis and its extra-diegetical effects, but his analyses are nuanced and illuminating, and his concerns often overlap those considered here.

[9] *Opera Omnia*, 204; *On Copia*, 48.

ekphrasis may have performed on the early modern stage. For example, it has long been speculated that Oberon's description of a 'fair vestal, throned by the west' in Shakespeare's A Midsummer Night's Dream (2.1.158)[10] alludes to a royal entertainment, at Kenilworth or Elvetham, and extended an extra-diegetical compliment to Queen Elizabeth. But the line also must have functioned in a public theatre as a stimulus to commoner imagination, eager to participate vicariously in a royal event to which ordinary subjects would otherwise have no access. For both these purposes, that flesh-and-blood political entertainment is 'translated' (to use a favourite Dream term) into language that honours the Queen, gratifies the gentry, flatters the groundlings, and supplies new energy to the action. Similarly, the Chorus's vivid exhortations in Henry the Fifth to 'Piece out our imperfections with your thoughts /... And make imaginary puissance' (Prol. 23, 25) before an audience that was even then being conscripted for the Queen's Irish wars serve a political purpose, which is to displace anxiety and stir blood lust among those whose lives were being disrupted by Essex's mission and enable them to participate vicariously, as a foretaste of what they may expect to relish in combat, in Henry's already-realized victories in France.[11] In quite another register, Sir Epicure Mammon's voluptuary fantasies in The Alchemist, with its allusions to 'Elephantis, and dull Aretine' (2.2.44)[12]—the latter a clear reference to Giulio Romano's athletic drawings for 'I modi', published with Aretino's obscene dialogues in the early sixteenth century—invite inquiry into Jonson's bid for parity among the arts cognoscenti of early Jacobean London. In a more homely vein, we might think of the often-vexed relationship of the suburban theatres and the Common Council of the City of London, and consider the ways in which one stage playwright, Thomas Middleton, who worked in both venues, might have used ekphrasis to mediate the recurrent conflict by re-presenting in Middlesex, Surrey, or Blackfriars liberty the civic events that his audiences attended within the city's jurisdiction.

In the present essay it will not be possible to pursue all these paths, but I shall attempt to plot out the parameters of ekphrasis on the early modern English stage by offering a few salient examples of the ways in which ekphrasis instantiates early modern theatricality. I do so with the following considerations in mind:

(1) If we think of theatricality as a quality attending any performance—whether in a theatre, court, innyard, street, or river barge—that solicits the kind of attention not usually accorded the ordinary behaviour encountered in daily life, then ekphrasis is a distinctively verbal form of theatricality. In its very nature as a stop-action device—and in its relation to epideictic rhetoric—it calls attention to itself.

(2) If, on the other hand, we think of theatricality as a term that emphasizes the mimetic activity that occurs in any 'framed' setting—theatre, court, innyard,

---

[10] All Shakespeare quotations are from The Norton Shakespeare, ed. Stephen Greenblatt et al. (New York: Norton, 1997).
[11] See Joel Altman, '"Vile Participation": The Amplification of Violence in the Theater of Henry V', Shakespeare Quarterly 42 (1991), 1–32.
[12] All Jonson quotations are from Ben Jonson, ed. Ian Donaldson (Oxford: Oxford University Press, 1985).

street, barge, etc.—with whatever degree of verisimilitude, soliciting a commensurate suspension of disbelief in accordance with current convention, performance style, mode of representation, audience disposition and experience,
then ekphrasis augments mimesis through its own unique power to inform the
imagination.

(3) Ekphrasis, then, might be said to be quintessentially theatrical, since it can
invite critical attention to itself as performance yet also bracket that performance to infiltrate, captivate, and illustrate with images the mind of the listener,
effecting through the skilful mimetic expression of its content both intellectual
and emotional conviction—'as in the theatre'.

Before proceeding, it is only proper to explain why I am using the term *ekphrasis*
rather than 'description' or *descriptio*. First, the rhetoricians with whom early modern
playwrights were familiar distinguished between simple description or narration and
the kind infused with both *enargeia*—which makes words glowing and lifelike—and
energeia—a quality of description that seems to give it movement. To avoid ambiguity, I have chosen *ekphrasis*, even though these same rhetoricians more often used
descriptio and sometimes conflated the word with *enargeia, hypotyposis*, and even
energeia.[13] But there is a professional reason as well. During the second half of the
twentieth century, *ekphrasis* became an important critical term.[14] Its meaning, however, narrowed from its ancient and early modern usage to designate, in James
Heffernan's words, 'the verbal representation of a visual representation'; that is, *ekphrasis* is now commonly regarded as a vivid description of a work of art, in the manner
of Keats's 'Ode on a Grecian Urn' or of its ancient forebear, Homer's description of
Achilles' shield in *The Iliad*. Thus criticism has focused on intermedial exchange
between poetry and objects of plastic art. This has led to a comparative neglect of the
study of ekphrasis in early modern English drama, except in the case of Shakespeare.[15]

[13] See Webb, *Imagination and Persuasion, passim*, and Lucia Calboli Montefusco, '*Enargeia et Energeia: l'évidence d'une demonstration qui signifie les choses en acte*', in Mireille Armisen Marchetti, ed.,
Demonstare: voir et fair voir: forme de la demonstration a Rome (Toulouse, 2005), 43–58.

[14] See Jean H. Hagstrum, *The Sister Arts: The Tradition of Literary Pictorialism and English Poetry
from Dryden to Gray* (Chicago: University of Chicago Press, 1958); Leo Spitzer, 'The "Ode on a Grecian
Urn," or Content vs. Metagrammar', in Ann Hatcher, ed., *Essays on English and American Literature*
(Princeton: Princeton University Press, 1962), 67–97; Murray Krieger, *Ekphrasis: The Illusion of the
Natural Sign* (Baltimore: Johns Hopkins University Press, 1992); James A. W. Heffernan, *Museum of
Words: The Poetics of Ekphrasis from Homer to Ashbery* (Chicago: University of Chicago Press, 1993);
the essays by Tamar Yacobi, Claus Clüver, and Valerie Robillard in Robillard and Jongeneel, eds., *Pic-
tures into Words*; Heinrich F. Plett, 'Intertextualities', in *Intertextuality* (Berlin: Walter de Gruyter,
1991), 1–29, and 'Pictura Rhetorica: The Rhetorical Conceptualization of the Visual Arts and Pictorial
Poetry', in *Rhetoric and Renaissance Culture* (Berlin: Walter de Gruyter, 2004), 85–110.

[15] See Leonard Barkan, 'Making Pictures Speak: Renaissance Art, Elizabeth Literature, Modern
Scholarship', *Renaissance Quarterly* 48 (1995), 326–51; Rawdon Wilson, *Shakespearean Narrative*
(Newark: University of Delaware Press, 1995); Barbara Hardy, *Shakespeare's Storytellers: Dramatic Narration* (London: Peter Owen, 1997); Alison Thorne, *Vision and Rhetoric in Shakespeare: Looking
through Language* (New York: St Martin's Press, 2000); Richard Meek, *Narrating the Visual in Shakespeare* (Burlington, VT: Ashgate, 2009).

The dual aim of this essay, therefore, is to restore the term ekphrasis to its wider pur-view and draw attention to its use in early modern drama as a way to evoke a play's cultural surround.

Being there: performances past, present, and never

The first item of business is to recall the psychology motivating the use of ekphrasis. It rests upon an essentially Aristotelian tradition—fortified by Stoic epistemology and transmitted to Christian culture by Saint Thomas Aquinas—that was very much alive in the early modern period. This tradition distinguished between the perception of external stimuli by the bodily senses and the 'images' that were formed when these literally material influences arrived in the fantasy or imagination, and actual-ized it from its state of potentiality. There, these stimuli were reconstituted as immaterial *phantasmata* (Greek) or *visiones* (Latin) and transmitted to the mem-ory, where they mingled with prior *visiones*.[16] A *visio* can be re-activated when the fantasy is stimulated by a new perception or a thought. Therefore when ekphrases, using words of vivid particularity, pass through the ears of the listener into the fantasy and supply *visiones* no less persuasive than perceptions that pass through the eyes of the beholder, these *visiones* mingle with earlier *visiones* released by the memory. With the aid of reason the newly actualized fantasy shapes them into cognitions that tell the subject 'this is such and such', arousing passions appropriate to the cognitions. Which is why theorists and practitioners believed ekphrasis to be so powerful a stimulant to emotional response and action. It also suggests why ekphrasis was such a useful instrument to the playwright working in a largely non-illusionistic theatre. It could expand the visual resources of that theatre as far as his imagination could stretch and find expression in words.

To what ends, then, did the dramatist stretch his imagination and, through ekph-rasis, that of his auditors? We might first examine a Jonsonian fantasy, transmitted by Volpone as he woos Celia, who has been lured to the bedside of the supposed invalid by her avaricious husband:

> Nay, fly me not.
> Nor let thy false imagination
> That I was bed-rid, make thee think I am so:
> Thou shalt not find it. I am, now, as fresh,
> As hot, as high, and in as jovial plight
> As when in that so celebrated scene

---

[16] See Aristotle, *De Anima*, 427b27–8, 431b2; Malcolm Schofield, 'Aristotle on the Imagination', in Martha C. Nussbaum and Amélie Oksenberg Rorty, eds., *Essays on Aristotle's De Anima* (Oxford: Clarendon Press, 1992), 249–77 (273); and Dorothea Frede, 'The Cognitive Role of *Phantasia*', in Nussbaum and Rorty, 279–95 (290).

> At recitation of our comedy,
> For entertainment of the great Valois,
> I acted young Antinous, and attracted
> The eyes and ears of all the ladies present,
> T'admire each graceful gesture, note, and footing.   (3.7.154–64)

The place, let us recall, is Venice, and Volpone is claiming to have participated in one of the most lavish political events of the later sixteenth century, the visit to Venice of the French heir apparent, Henri Valois, in 1574.[17] The visit was widely celebrated, and it is possible that its splendours cast an after-glow even thirty years later, when *Volpone* was first performed by the King's Men at the Globe. But it is not the extravagance of the event that is evoked by Volpone; he refers to the occasion with the casual, if calculated, familiarity of an insider. Rather, he focuses on himself as he *once* was to persuade Celia of his virility *now*. It is a strange turn. He has leapt from his sickbed, insisting that she has a 'false imagination' of him—that is, she is carrying about an inaccurate *phantasma*—and to prove that he is in fact 'hot, high, and...jovial', he asks her to imagine him at the time he was performing in the Gelosi comedy for Henry III. Her false imagination is to be replaced by a true imagination, but that true imagination is a memory—his, perhaps hers (we can't tell, since he is his own press agent). Moreover, he is asking her to imagine not Volpone but Antinous, the role he played in that 'so celebrated scene'. It was as Antinous that he attracted the eyes and ears of all the ladies who followed gesture, voice, and step. Thus he is asking Celia—and the theatre audience—to undergo a double imaginative displacement—from now to then, from himself to the figure he personated. You get at a present truth, he implies, by imagining a past fiction.

That fiction itself is a bait for the cognoscenti. Young Antinous may have had visual and auditory appeal to all the ladies present, but as the Emperor Hadrian's lover, he may also have attracted the eyes and ears of the royal French guest. And that would have been another point of audience recognition. Henry III's sexuality was notoriously ambivalent—if not in 1574, then certainly by the date of *Volpone*. In 1589, the year he was assassinated by a scandalized monk, he was branded 'a buggerer, son of a whore, tyrant' by an outraged subject, near the end of a reign marked by fruitless attempts to father an heir, the culling of male favourites known as 'les mignons', reported episodes of cross-dressing, and futile attempts, encouraged by

---

[17] In 1574, Henry III, heir to the French throne and recently elected King of Poland, was returning to Paris from Warsaw via Venice, following the death of his brother Charles IX. He remained there for eleven days. A triumphal arch designed by Palladio greeted him on his arrival at the Lido, and he was entertained by regattas, jousts, banquets, concerts, sight-seeing trips, and performances by the famous theatrical troupe I Gelosi, who twice staged a comedy *all'improviso* and once a tragedy of Cornelio Frangipane in his honour. See Armand Baschet, *Les comédiens italiens à la cour de France sous Charles IX, Henry III, Henry IV et Louis XIII* (Paris: Plon, 1882), 59–61; Pier de Nolhac and Angelo Solerti, *Il Viaggio in Italia di Enrico III: Re di Francia e le Feste a Venezia, Ferrara, Mantova e Torino* (Torino: L. Roux e C., 1890), 94–154.

his mother Catherine de Medici, to placate his ambitious younger brother, François Valois, the 'Monsieur' of Chapman's tragedy *Bussy D'Ambois* (about which more follows)—which created for him the public image of an effeminate, ineffectual ruler.[18] Volpone's buoyant heterosexual seduction of Celia thus effloresces through his ekphrastic 'proof' of virility into intimations of polyvalent sexuality in the receptive imaginations of his audience. No matter that there is no such living creature as Volpone, and that he could not therefore have acted in Henry III's entertainment, or that, given the foregoing, the role of Antinous in that comedy may have been as much Jonson's invention as was Volpone himself.[19] Venetian Celia believes him, and English auditors, charmed to envision 'each graceful gesture, note, and footing' in this famous foreign extravaganza, are likely to have believed with her.

The moment opens a dizzying window on theatrical ekphrasis. At centre is the dramatis persona Volpone himself, whose *modus vivendi*, the audience knows, is acting. He envisions himself as an invalid and projects this *visio* into the imaginations of others. Now, defying logic if not lust, he reveals himself to dramatis persona Celia *as* an actor—moreover, one with a past—and his description of that past draws her and the hitherto sceptical audience into the same orbit of politics, performance, and memory in which he dwells! Acting, it would seem, is a particularly acute mode in which the psychology of ekphrasis is concentrated.

Ekphrasis could be used not only to waft an audience out of its own theatre to one in a distant land but could also function as a mirror in which the audience was invited to observe itself looking and listening; in this way, ekphrasis became a vehicle for concentrating an audience's theatrical self-awareness. In the second scene of Middleton and Dekker's *The Roaring Girl* (*c*.1610), presented at the Fortune Theatre, Sir Alexander Wengrave is entertaining friends in his parlour as they thank him for his hospitality and admire his furnishings. When Sir Davy Dapper calls it 'A very fair sweet room', the host replies in a manner that becomes increasingly ambiguous:

> Nay, when you look into my galleries—
> How bravely they're trimmed up—you all shall swear
> You're highly pleased to see what's set down there:
> Stories of men and women, mixed together
> Fair ones with foul, like sunshine in wet weather.
> Within one square a thousand heads are laid
> So close that all of heads the room seems made;
> As many faces there, filled with blithe looks,
> Show like the promising titles of new books
> Writ merrily, the readers being their own eyes,
> Which seem to move and to give plaudities.

---

[18] See Katherine B. Crawford, 'Love, Sodomy, and Scandal: Controlling the Sexual Reputation of Henry III', *Journal of the History of Sexuality* 12.4 (October 2003), 513–42.

[19] Antinous is a very unlikely character in a comedy *all'improviso*.

> And here and there, whilst with obsequious ears
> Thronged heaps do listen, a cutpurse thrusts and leers
> With hawk's eyes for his prey—I need not show him:
> By a hanging villainous look yourselves may know him,
> The face is drawn so rarely. Then, sir, below,
> The very floor, as 'twere, waves to and fro,
> And like a floating island, seems to move
> Upon a sea bound in with shore above.   (1.2.14–32)[20]

This fanciful ekphrasis of place, which begins as a cue to imagine a room where elegant pictures hang ('How bravely they're all trimmed up') quickly shifts to suggest a library ('see what's set down there.... Stories of men and women'), then redirects the listener to envision a square room of shelves laden with heads whose faces reveal pleasurable anticipation, much as book titles are indices to merry tales. But, 'the readers being their own eyes', the focus now moves from the putative books to the eyes themselves, 'Which seem to move and to give plaudities'. They are the eyes of theatre-goers.

So thickly metaphorical is Sir Alexander's ekphrasis that only now does it become fully evident that the walls he is describing are the square galleries of the Fortune Theatre, where 'obsequious ears' hang on his every word and pickpockets ply their craft among the 'thronged heaps'. Yet the picture conceit persists as Sir Alexander refuses to finger the cutpurse, so easily recognized because 'The face is drawn so rarely', and then shifts his attention to the floor of the room, the habitation of the groundlings, which, 'as 'twere, waves to and fro' like a floating island 'Upon a sea bound in with shore above'. This cunning bit of writing must have given deep pleasure as the audience became aware that Sir Alexander was talking about them and their 'obsequious ears' shook free of enchantment to admire the rhetorical wit that had seduced them. Still, the imaginative and cognitive processing demanded by this audio-visual journey could not have been easy. While the sensual eye was trained on Sir Alexander and followed his gestures toward the theatre galleries, the mind's eye, guided by the ear, was conducted on a tour of a London town house that rapidly underwent metamorphosis into the theatre that the sensual eye beheld—a theatre filled with guests of a different sort—paying guests, as it were—among whom the 'men and women' listening numbered themselves. They were all now part of the scene—groundlings included.

If in this instance audiences recognize themselves becoming absorbed into the *mise-en-scène* of the theatrical performance—which, from the playwright's point of view, also served to co-opt a potentially unfavourable reception—ekphrasis also worked to lift the audience, as it were, above the walls (and roof) of the theatre so as to provide a bird's eye view of the city in which the action is occurring. The effect is to extend the theatrical fiction into an actual social landscape. As the fourth act

---

[20] Thomas Middleton, *The Collected Works*, ed. Gary Taylor, John Lavagnino, et al. (Oxford: Clarendon Press, 2007).

opens at the Blackfriars production of *Eastward Ho!* (*c*.1605) by Jonson, Marston, and Chapman, a butcher's apprentice named Slitgut appears 'above', identifies the location as Cuckold's Haven, east of London Bridge, then shimmies up a pole to the third stage level and places a pair of ox-horns at the top of a tree 'to advance this crest of my master's occupation' (4.1.10–11) for St Luke's Day.[21] Once up there, he feels a tempest blowing and gazes out at the turbulent river:

Lord, what a coil the Thames keeps! She bears some unjust burthen, I believe, that she kicks and curvets thus to cast it. Heaven bless all honest passengers that are upon her back now; for the bit is out of her mouth, I see, and she will run away with 'em. So, so, I think I have made it look the right way;[22] it runs against London Bridge, as it were, even full butt. And now let me discover from this lofty prospect, what pranks the rude Thames plays in her desperate lunacy. O me, here's a boat has been cast away hard by! Alas, alas, see one of her passengers laboring for his life to land at this haven here! Pray heaven he may recover it! His next land is even just under me; hold out yet a little, whatsoever thou art; pray, and take a good heart to thee. 'T is a man; take a man's heart to thee: yet a little further, get up o' thy legs, man; now 't is shallow enough. So, so, so! Alas, he's down again! Hold thy wind, father! 't is a man in a night-cap. So! Now he's got up again; now he's past the worst; yet, thanks be to heaven, he comes toward me pretty and strongly. (4.1.16–40)

A moment later old Security the usurer appears on the platform stage sopping wet, in pursuit of his young wife, who has run off with Sir Petronel Flash. From his perch Slitgut tries to comfort him, but learning where he has landed, Security crawls away in shame. Whereupon Slitgut spies another drowning figure farther downstream: 'A woman, i' faith, a woman! Though it be almost at St. Katherine's, I discern it to be a woman, for all her body is above the water, and her clothes swim about her most handsomely' (73–7). She turns out to be Security's wife Winifred, entering below at St Katherine's with the man who has rescued her and now offers to save her reputation. On their exit, the scene returns to Cuckold's Haven, where Slitgut, still above, spies yet another shipwrecked party downstream being rescued at Wapping gallows: 'See, see! I hold my life, there's some other a-taking up at Wapping now!' (4.1.139–40). This introduces a longer sequence below, first at Wapping, then on the Isle of Dogs, then back at the Blue Anchor tavern at Billingsgate, whence they all took shipping. At this point the lines return to Slitgut: 'Now will I descend my honourable prospect, the farthest seeing sea-mark of the world; no marvel, then, if I could see two miles about me' (4.1.355–8).

These ekphrastic passages are remarkable first, for the way they invite the Blackfriars audience to view a two-mile stretch of the Thames through the excited Slitgut's eyes—'See, see!' is his frequent refrain—and thus to join him in a

---

[21] Quotations are from C. F. Tucker Brooke and Nathaniel Burton Paradise, eds., *English Drama 1580–1642* (Lexington, MA: D. C. Heath, 1933).

[22] Is this Slitgut the self-conscious ekphrastic artist speaking, savouring his equine metaphor?

carnivalesque celebration of their common London environment.[23] Second, Slitgut addresses not only the audience and himself, but the figures he descries struggling in the river—'take a man's heart to thee....Hold thy wind, father!'—thereby intensifying the audience's sense that they are witnesses. Third, the locations Slitgut specifies enlist familiar place-names as instruments of dramatic exposition, for they are apt landings for the people involved.[24] Thus this extended ekphrasis unites actions that are topographically and temporally separated in a vivid, meaning-laden continuum. Unlike the passage in *The Roaring Girl*, this one, beginning as a solo performance above an empty platform, serially combines narrative and dramatized action to move the plot forward. What Slitgut describes from his perch atop the tree materializes visually and aurally below as the predominantly verbal gives way to the balance of verbal and visual, which in turn relinquishes its power to the verbal again. The combined effect presents the audience with a detailed panorama of London on the north bank of the Thames through speech, supplemented by 'close-up' insets as the characters appear on the platform stage.[25]

Becoming mindful: cross-genre transfusions through word-painting

Erasmus remarks that classical dramatists used *descriptiones* to report events that they could not conveniently bring on-stage, and offers as examples the reported deaths of Polyxena, Iphigenia, Astyanax, and Orestes. Such 'messenger speeches' are frequently heard in the early modern theatre, intruding upon the ongoing action with varying dramatic effects. Gertrude's account of Ophelia's death, for instance, interrupts the increasingly vicious one-upmanship of Claudius and Laertes as they devise a fail-safe plot to kill Hamlet, providing a lyrical pause that looks outward onto a pastoral scene alien to the play at the same time that it seems to express the inwardness of Gertrude's growing despair:

[23] John Stow's Survey of London was published in 1598 and reissued only two years before our playwrights adapted its methods to the theatre.

[24] Cuckold's Haven is the ironically termed landing spot for Security, who has eagerly participated in what he believes to be the cuckolding of his lawyer Bramble by Sir Petronel; Winifred, whose willingness to run off with Sir Petronel remains ambiguous, finds herself saved from drowning, but in a home for dishonest women; Quicksilver, the conniving young gentleman who engineers her abduction, finds himself on shore by gallows where pirates are hanged; and Sir Petronel himself, along with Captain Seagull, comes ashore on the disreputable Isle of Dogs.

[25] Further integration occurs at the end of the play when the repentant Quicksilver, released from debtors' prison, says: 'Stay, sir, I perceive the multitude are gathered together to view our coming out at the Counter. See, if the streets and the fronts of the houses be not stuck with people, and the windows filled with ladies, as on the solemn day of the Pageant' (Ep., 1–6). The Pageant referred to is the annual Lord Mayor's show, which the play, as Henry Turner suggests, now assimilates to its citizen comedy. See Turner, *The English Renaissance Stage* (Oxford: Oxford University Press, 2006), 214. In doing so, its brief description performs that politic crossover between theatre and city suggested earlier and also anticipates in small the absorption of audience into scene that we observed in *The Roaring Girl*.

> There is a willow grows aslant a brook
> That shows his hoar leaves in the glassy stream.
> Therewith fantastic garlands did she make
> Of crow-flowers, nettles, daisies, and long purples,
> That liberal shepherds give a grosser name,
> But our cold maids do dead men's fingers call them.
> There on the pendent boughs her crownet weeds
> Clamb'ring to hang, an envious sliver broke,
> When down the weedy trophies and herself
> Fell in the weeping brook....   (4.7.137–46)

All forward action stops at Gertrude's entrance. Whatever the actors of Claudius and Laertes may do by way of gesture, their attention and the audience's is riveted on the speaker, who sets the scene retrospectively in meticulously observed detail— the reflection, for example, of the grey bottoms of green willow leaves in 'the glassy stream'. Mixing narrative, spatial and floral description, and natural lore—she cannot resist moralizing the names given to 'long purples'—Gertrude adapts the animating convention of pastoral elegy ('envious sliver', 'weeping brook') as though she were reflecting her own feelings about Ophelia. The speech is epideictic in the fullest sense—pointing to itself, its speaker, and its connection to a classical genre with roots in a world far from the political machinations of Elsinore.[26] Like the pirate tale in Hamlet's letter to Horatio (4.6), which draws romance material into tragedy, Gertrude's elegy reveals how a theatrical ekphrasis can serve as a strong cultural magnet, attracting other literary genres and conventions into the field of its own modality, thus expanding what I have referred to earlier as the psyche of the play.

But unlike the ekphrases we have examined, this one raises an epistemological question from within the diegetical core of the action. How does Gertrude *know* the details of Ophelia's death? Has she helplessly witnessed it? Has she heard it from someone who recounted it to her minutely? Did she hear it briefly told and with this seed generate an ekphrasis from her imagination? Perhaps this is to consider too curiously, yet it opens an important theatrical issue: the relationship of ekphrasis and the representation of subjectivity. In this case, there is insufficient textual evidence to assert that the ekphrasis arises from Gertrude's visual or aural experience. It is enough to note that the pastoral mode aestheticizes and naturalizes Ophelia, telling us that even in madness she fashions beauty, weaving garlands of wild flowers and singing old hymns, borne up by the stream 'like a creature native and indued / Unto that element' (4.7.178–9). Its tonality further suggests that Gertrude has changed profoundly from the opaque, evasive queen and mother of 1.2; the angry, frightened, and astonished mother, wife, and widow of 3.4; and the defensive queen and wife of 4.5. Yet this subjectivity effect is the result of word-painting delivered

---

[26] This may be why the speech has seemed so artificial to many critics. See the comments in the *New Variorum Edition of Shakespeare*, ed. H. H. Furness, 2 vols. (Philadelphia: Lippincott, 1877; reprint Dover, 1963), 1.370–3; and *Hamlet*, ed. Harold Jenkins (London: Methuen, 1982), 544–6.

sympathetically; we cannot trace its origin to Gertrude's own experience. It is 'characterological' rather than 'subject-revealing'.[27]

Before we proceed, a word about word-painting. This was a trope even more common than 'as in a theatre' when explaining ekphrasis. Introducing the concept of *enargeia* in *De Copia*, Erasmus writes, 'We use this whenever for the sake of amplifying, adorning, or pleasing, we do not state a thing simply, but set it forth to be viewed as though portrayed in color on a tablet, so that it may seem that we have painted, not narrated, and that the reader has seen, not read'.[28] In Aphthonius's widely read *Progymnasmata*, we find that '*Descriptio* is speech in which the whole matter that concerns us is, in a manner, an image painted by words'.[29] We must bear this in mind as we examine our next example of ekphrasis.

In a quite different mode, George Chapman adapts the messenger speech to report a death brought about by his problematic hero in *Bussy D'Ambois* (1607). His *descriptio* works formally, aesthetically, and psychologically to establish the pivotal question of the tragedy: can 'man in his native noblesse' (3.2.91) exist in contemporary society and defy its legal and moral conventions without corruption?[30] In formal terms, the Nuntius' speech follows two diverse species of dramatic dialogue with contrasting rhetorical effects: at the end of Act I, three of Henry III's supercilious 'mignons' trade lines mocking Bussy as an upstart wearing the cast-off clothes of Monsieur, who has entered him at court; overhearing them, Bussy issues a challenge, which they take up with careless bravado: 'Come, sir, we'll lead you a dance'. As Act II opens, Henry III is lecturing the Duke of Guise on envy, which he treats ekphrastically—indeed, emblematically—by personifying it as a kite feeding on entrails, when suddenly the Nuntius enters and declares: 'What Atlas or Olympus lifts his head / So far past covert, that with air enough / My words may be informed, and from his height / I may be seen and heard through all the world?' (2.1.25–8). He is poised to describe the sword fight between Bussy, his two friends, and Henry's three courtiers, and the level of style has suddenly risen to the *genus grande*.

Why this is so becomes clear once we realize that Chapman has chosen to pose the question of the naturally noble man in civil society as a palimpsest: he has taken the historical figure Louis de Clermont, Seigneur de Bussy (1549–79)—military hero, erotic adventurer, quarrelsome duelist, and brutal participant in the St Bartholomew's Day massacre—and overwritten historical memory in the language of epic. The result is an ekphrasis calculated to evoke wonder:

[27] Here I make a distinction between 'character'—the kind of self one appears to be, to oneself and others (including audiences)—and 'subject', the interior, fluid self, often unknown to oneself and others, but sometimes revealed in soliloquy and ekphrasis. See Joel B. Altman, *The Improbability of Othello* (Chicago: University of Chicago Press, 2012), esp. 235–83.

[28] *Opera Omnia*, 202; *On Copia*, 47. Cf. Thomas Wilson, *The Art of Rhetoric* (1560), ed. Peter E. Medine (University Park: University of Pennsylvania Press, 1994), 204, 219–20; Henry Peacham, *The Garden of Eloquence* (London, 1593), fol. Tiiiv; George Puttenham, *The Art of English Poesy*, ed. Frank Whigham and Wayne Rebhorn (Ithaca: Cornell University Press, 2007), 329.

[29] *Apththonii Progymnasmata* (London, 1650), 281–2, my translation.

[30] George Chapman, *Bussy D'Ambois*, ed. Nicholas Brooke (London: Methuen, 1964).

> But D'Ambois' sword, that lightened as it flew,
> Shot like a pointed comet at the face
> Of manly Barrisor, and there it stuck.
> Thrice plucked he at it, and thrice drew on thrusts
> From him that of himself was free as fire;
> Who thrust still as he plucked, yet (past belief!)
> He with his subtle eye, hand, body, scaped;
> At last, the deadly-bitten point tugged off,
> On fell his yet undaunted foe so fiercely
> That, only made more horrid with his wound,
> Great D'Ambois shrunk, and gave a little ground;
> But soon returned, redoubled in his danger,
> And at the heart of Barrisor sealed his anger.   (2.1.81–92)

The scene described is indeed 'past belief': Bussy's sword, flying towards, then sticking in Barrisor's face; his attempt to extract it three times as Barrisor, still pierced, thrusts at him with each attempt—the action boggles the mind but remains visualizable. Which is precisely what Chapman's poetics aims to accomplish. 'That *Enargia*, or cleerenes of representation', he writes, 'requird in absolute Poems is not the perspicuous delivery of a lowe invention; but high, and harty invention exprest in most significant, and unaffected phrase; it serves not a skilfull Painters turne, to draw the figure of a face only to make knowne who it represents; but hee must lymn, give luster, shadow, and heightening; which though ignorants will esteeme spic'd, and too curious, yet such as have the judiciall perspective, will see it hath motion, spirit, and life'.[31]

The governing terms here are 'significant' and 'judiciall'. Echoing the distinction Quintilian makes between the *perspicuitas* normally required in oratory and 'that ἐνάργια [*enargeia*] which Cicero calls *illumination* and *actuality* [*illuminatio et evidentia*], which makes us seem not so much to narrate as to exhibit the actual scene',[32] Chapman's hyperbolical ekphrasis, so far beyond common experience, is intended to arouse admiration in 'such as have the judicial perspective' and can recognize that his words signify an epic confrontation. It is an ambitious strategy, to add 'luster, shadow, and heightening' to a figure who often seems to be a wilful, irascible roughneck, and tests the limits of ekphrastic claims for the efficaciousness of word-painting. It does not convince the Duke of Guise, who cries, 'Oh, piteous and horrid murder!' (2.1.105), but this may show his ignorance. Henry himself is doubtful, and it takes Monsieur's additional argumentation to adjust his focus. Henry and Guise are not alone. Chapman's method, which involves not only epic but also mythic palimpsest, tugs the imagination and judgement, informed by what is seen

[31] 'To the Trulie Lerned, and my worthy Friende, Ma. Mathew Roydon', *Ovids Banquet of Sense*, in Phyllis Bartlett, ed., *The Poems of George Chapman* (New York: Russell and Russell, 1962; first edn. 1941), 49.

[32] Quintilian, *Institutio oratoria*, trans. H. E Butler, Loeb Classical Library, 4 vols. (New York: G. Putnam's Son and London: Heinemann, 1921–2), vi.2.32.

and heard, in opposing ways as the action proceeds to its powerful, ambiguous close.[33] Monsieur and Guise provide a choric introduction to Bussy's fall by debating whether Nature fashions great men 'to have rewards proportioned to their labours' or 'works at random', heedless of their ends (5.3.9, 29) as Bussy prepares to meet Montsurry, whose chaste wife he has seduced. Challenging the outraged husband to a heroic sword fight, he is shot ignominiously by Montsurry's hired guns, and dies in despair at having missed his promised greatness, while the Ghost of the Friar celebrates his apotheosis among the stars beside Hercules. In this play, word-painting becomes a complex expository device that tests its own premise by juxtaposing epic and mythic language to what often appears to be tawdry court intrigue. Ekphrasis itself thus becomes a tragic enterprise.

As my reference to Henry III's emblematic discourse on envy suggests, theatrical ekphrasis can be intermedial as well as intertextual. That is to say, it is sometimes used to render aurally forms of verbal art usually encountered in distinctive printed formats possessing a visual dimension, just as it describes more common forms such as painting and sculpture. At the trial of Vittoria Corombona in Webster's *The White Devil* (1610), for example, Cardinal Monticelso, believing he has sufficient evidence to convict the protagonist of whoredom, addresses her in familiar language:

> I will be plainer with you, and paint out
> Your follies in more natural red and white
> Than that upon your cheek.   (3.2.51–3)[34]

Adducing a wide range of circumstantial evidence to prove his charge, he replies to Vittoria's challenge—'Ha? Whore—what's that?'—by defining his term:

> Shall I expound whore to you? Sure I shall;
> I'll give their perfect character. They are first,
> Sweet-meats that rot the eater: in man's nostril
> Poison'd perfumes. They are coz'ning alchemy,
> Shipwrecks in calmest weather. What are whores?
> Cold Russian winters, that appear so barren,
> As if that nature had forgot the spring....   (3.2.77–84)

And so on for more than twenty lines. This is not your usual method of definition. It is the vivid, cumulative method of analogy, known rhetorically as *icon*, used in Sir Thomas Overbury's *Characters* (1614) to which Webster probably contributed. On the page the Character is unmistakably ekphrastic, as this sampling from 'A Whoore' will indicate:

[33] See Raymond B. Waddington, *The Mind's Empire* (Baltimore: Johns Hopkins University Press, 1974), 19–44.
[34] John Webster, *The White Devil*, ed. John Russell Brown (London: Methuen, 1965).

A Whoore

Is a hie way to the Divell, hee that lookes upon her with desire, begins his voyage: he that staies to talke with her, mends his pace, and who enioyes her is at his iourneys end: Her body is the tilted Lees of pleasure, dasht over with a little decking to hold colour: tast her she's dead, and fals upon the pallate; the sins of other women shew in Landscip, far off and full of shadow, hers in Statue, neere hand, and bigger in the life: she prickes betimes, for her stocke is a white thorne, which cut and grafted on, she growes a Medler...[35]

A whore, in other words, is anything but a whore. She is a cluster of metaphors—journey, drink, artwork, fruit—as the writer approaches (but never reaches) her supposed essence via a series of comparisons that prove morally or sensually bathetic. Webster's proleptic appropriation of 'their perfect character' in *The White Devil* not only reflects the growing popularity of the genre but uses similar formal means: title set apart from body of text, piled-up imagery, antithetical yet elusive structure.[36] But in his theatricalization of the Character at Vittoria's trial he goes further—suggesting how specious is its claim to represent anyone. 'This character scapes me', replies Vittoria as the Cardinal ends his speech, and the theatre audience must surely agree. Once again, cross-genre ekphrasis complicates tragic understanding.

Seeing within: Shakespeare and ekphrastic subjectivity

Shakespeare's work is especially rich and bold in the deployment of ekphrasis. I have briefly noted his open invitation to the audience at *A Midsummer Night's Dream* to participate vicariously in a famous royal entertainment and his strategy in *Henry V* to use the French wars to fashion support for the Queen's cause in Ireland. He also makes extensive use of ekphrasis as a psychological index, and signals this in a variety of ways—often with cues embedded in the text. I have argued that Gertrude's description of Ophelia's drowning in *Hamlet* gives off a 'subjectivity effect' without actually expressing subjectivity, since there are no cues that she has either seen the event or heard it recounted. In so doing, I distinguished between an ekphrasis that literally word-paints to convey information and exploit genre modality—suggesting character, as it were, from the outside—from one that reveals the interior workings of the speaker's mind.[37] The latter is

---

[35] *The 'Conceited Newes' of Sir Thomas Overbury and His Friends, a Facsimile Reproduction of the Ninth Impression of 1616 of 'Sir Thomas Overbury His Wife'*, commentary and notes by James E. Savage (Gainsesville: Scholars' Facsimiles & Reprints, 1969), 112–13.

[36] Joseph Hall's *Characters of Vertues and Vices* had been published in 1608.

[37] The former is also found in the Nuntio of Bussy, whose 'character', such as it is, is a function of his speech, which places an epic overlay on the protagonist.

heard when Ophelia reports that 'Lord Hamlet, with his doublet all unbraced, / No hat upon his head, his stockings fouled / Ungartered and down-gyved to his ankle', had entered her chamber, grabbed her wrist, searched her face 'As a would draw it' (2.1.78–80, 91), then sighed and departed, looking over his shoulder as he went. She not only recalls the event; she re-enacts it—'And thrice his head thus waving up and down' (94)—confirming our impression that she has directly experienced Hamlet's distraction. Certain moments linger so vividly that they are expressed in the present tense: 'he comes before me', 'goes he to the length of all his arm', and 'falls to perusal of my face' (85, 89, 91). The total effect of the speech is to suggest that Hamlet has taken up her entire field of vision; only the framing phrases, 'as I was sewing in my closet' and 'out o'doors he went', remind us that she was in her own private space when he intruded and so powerfully appropriated her imagination.[38]

Did Edgar ever stand on Dover cliff? It is hard to say. Yet his compelling description of doing so is a *tour de force* of Shakespearean theatricality. Its epideictic nature—calling attention to itself as a linguistic feat while at the same time seducing the listener from admirer to rapt believer—is underwritten by audibly calling attention to the flatness of the stage. 'Methinks the ground is even', says the blinded Gloucester; 'Horrible steep', Edgar replies; 'Hark, do you hear the sea?' 'No, truly', the old man responds (*King Lear*, 4.5.3–4). He speaks for the audience here, who plainly see the ground is even, and hear no murmuring surge. Yet when Edgar finds his stand ('here's the place: stand still') and begins to describe what he says he sees, the case is altered:

> How fearful
> And dizzy 'tis to cast one's eyes so low!
> The crows and choughs that wing the midway air
> Show scarce so gross as beetles. Half way down
> Hangs one that gathers samphire, dreadful trade!
> ....
>   I'll look no more,
> Lest my brain turn and the deficient sight
> Topple down headlong.   (4.5.11–15, 22–4)

Enchanted by his words, we may not realize that our initial question is beside the point: he didn't need to stand on Dover Cliff. Gloucester has planted the seed-image in his fantasy:

---

[38] Ophelia's ekphrasis also gives off what we might call an 'interiority effect' for Hamlet. Through her detailed description of his appearance and behaviour—and her truly frightened response—she enables the audience to 'see' what has happened to him since he declared his intention to put an antic disposition on. What had begun as a strategy for psychic and physical survival may have seeped into Hamlet's being. We don't know—which is why Ophelia's description produces only an 'interiority *effect*'. I owe this idea to Henry Turner.

> There is a cliff whose high and bending head
> Looks fearfully in the confined deep.
> Bring me but to the very brim of it.... (4.1.73–5)

Thus seeded, the image enters the memory, where it mingles with other mnemic traces until it is called forth by Gloucester's question: 'When shall I come to th' top of that same hill?' (4.5.1). Edgar's amplification of Gloucester's earlier speech recapitulates Quintilian's example of the captured city quoted here. It differs, however, not only in the immediacy of its sharply perceived verse, but in its etiology from the image planted five scenes before. It is Quintilian, we might say, biologized and theatricalized.

But is it believable? Richard Meek, among others, questions its representational integrity: are we to envision crows and choughs, or beetles? fishermen or mice? bark, cock, or buoy? These successive diminutions, he suggests, exceed the imagination's grasp. Moreover, *would* a man with increasing vertigo be able to take hold of so many details? Dr Johnson found the passage poor for that very reason: 'He that looks from a precipice finds himself assailed by one great and dreadful image of irresistible destruction. But this overwhelming idea is dissipated and enfeebled from the instant that the mind can restore itself to the observation of particulars and diffuse its attention to distinct objects.'[39] These are shrewd arguments, yet they underscore the fact that Edgar is *not* looking from a precipice but only trying to *sound* as though he is for Gloucester's benefit—to which end his imaginary vision moves vertically from the 'midway air' to 'half way down' to the 'fishermen that walk upon the beach', then laterally out to sea and 'yon tall anchoring bark', at once naming the objects one would see *and* shrinking them to the size they would appear to be from the top of the cliff.[40]

It would be more productive to consider that Edgar's speech, an intentional ekphrasis, follows the rhetorical principle that the greater the circumstantial detail, the greater the emotional response in the audience, for there is more to react *to*. The rhetoricians also emphasized that to achieve that response the speaker must himself produce internal *visiones* to which *he* responds. Having absorbed Gloucester's brief description of the cliff at Dover and elaborated it in memory and fantasy, Edgar persuades Gloucester and (presumably) many in the theatre audience that they stand at 'the very brim of it'. Caught up in his own feigning, might he even begin to *feel* what he describes, as many Renaissance critics believed actors did?[41] In which case, 'I'll look no more' may be more than mere play-acting—and ekphrasis an actor's tool with unexpected consequences.

---

[39] Meek, *Narrating the Visual*, 125–6.

[40] Jan Kott once compared the precision and clarity of Edgar's scene to a Breughel painting; indeed it sounds much like a word-painting of such a panoramic canvas as *The Fall of Icarus*. See Kott, *Shakespeare our Contemporary* (New York: Anchor Books, 1966), 143.

[41] See Altman, *Improbability*, 258–60, 290–2.

Shakespeare exploits the *intermedial* power of ekphrasis to express interiority when Hamlet confronts Gertrude with the 'counterfeit presentment of two brothers'—one with 'Hyperion's curls, the front of Jove himself, / An eye like Mars to threaten and command'—the other 'like a mildewed ear / Blasting his wholesome brother' (3.4.55–6, 63–4). Elizabethan audiences, unable to compare the two portraits themselves, may have taken Hamlet at his word or remained troubled by the same polarization they had had heard earlier in the play: 'So excellent a king, that was to this / Hyperion to a satyr'—when he had included himself in the equation: 'My father's brother—but no more like my father / Than I to Hercules' (1.2.139–40, 152–3). The referent is probably a pair of miniature pendants, but the signified is the distorted phantasma Hamlet sees with his mind's eye, an amalgam of the love, jealousy, hatred, guilt, and self-loathing that the text invites us to read in his behaviour. Thus 'a verbal representation of a visual representation'—in this case, two of them— as Heffernan describes ekphrasis, becomes a means of psychological exposition.[42]

Shakespeare had explored the gap between external referent and imagined signified even more explicitly some five years earlier, when Romeo views Juliet asleep in the 'borrowed likeness of shrunk death' (Rom. 4.1.104) upon her bier in the Capulets' vault. The audience knows that she is still in the deep slumber induced by Friar Laurence's potion, but as Romeo speaks they learn that signs of life are returning to her face as the drug wears off. The sight of Juliet's lips and cheeks beginning to glow with colour releases in him the fantasy of a post-mortem martial triumph: 'O my love, my wife! / Death, that hath sucked the honey of thy breath, / Hath had no power yet upon thy beauty.... Beauty's ensign yet / Is crimson in thy lips and in thy cheeks, / And Death's pale flag is not advanced there' (5.3.92–6). Here Shakespeare reveals a subject whose immersion in Petrarchan erotics leads him to fatally *misdescribe* the *living* Juliet he perceives before him, and the audience knows it.[43]

Witnessing transformation:
the liminal female body and ekphrastic actualization

The liminal state in which a female dwells—alive, but as if dead—seems increasingly to have become a subject of Shakespearean ekphrasis. We find her again in the swooning Hero of *Much Ado*, whose denunciation by Claudio at their marriage ceremony causes 'A thousand blushing apparitions / To start into her face, a thousand innocent shames / In angel whiteness beat away those blushes' (4.1.158–60) before her spirits are 'smothered up', as Don John so nicely puts it; in the sleeping Desdemona, whose 'whiter skin...than snow, / And smooth as monumental

---

[42] The size of the portraits and their provenance on-stage have been much debated. For useful commentary, see Jenkins, *Hamlet*, 516–19, and Thorne, *Vision and Rhetoric*, 129–30.

[43] Though Romeo describes what the audience cannot see, they will recognize what is happening by recalling Friar Laurence's words only a few scenes back (4.1.91–106).

alabaster' proclaims her innocence and intimates her present death (5.2.4–5); in the disguised Imogen, who unwittingly reprises Juliet's sleeping draught and is thus eulogized by Arviragus: 'Thou shalt not lack / The flower that's like thy face, pale primrose; nor / The azured harebell, like thy veins; no, nor / The leaf of eglantine, whom not to slander / Outsweetened not thy breath' (*Cymbeline*, 4.2.221–5). That the apparent death of a spirited female should call forth a lyrical ekphrasis that buries her in the masculine language of poetic art ought not be surprising in Shakespeare. When the language of art becomes a means of returning the female to life, that is notable, and this is precisely what happens when the most startling liminal female of all—Hermione's statue in *The Winter's Tale*—ostentatiously reverses the process.

In itself, the revival of the lady is not new. We see Juliet come back to life—as we do Hero and Imogen—though she then kills herself. Desdemona awakens, to be smothered in our presence into saintly silence. In Hermione alone, Shakespeare first denies the audience the opportunity to witness the process of mortification— our only cue is Paulina's 'Look down / And see what death is doing' (*The Winter's Tale*, 3.2.146–7)—and then recovery from sleep or swoon. The idea that Hermione has actually died is reinforced by Antigonus' ekphrasis of his vision: 'In pure white robes / Like very sanctity she did approach' (3.3.21–2). Obscuring its diegetic origins, Shakespeare focuses instead on the presentation of the statue and the responses of the on-stage audience, who perform a collective ekphrasis like a critical group of courtly connoisseurs: 'Her natural posture...But yet, Paulina, / Hermione was not so much wrinkled...So much the more our carver's excellence / Which lets go by some sixteen years, and makes her / As she looked now...Would you not deem it breathed...?...The very life seems warm upon her lip...The fixture of her eye has motion in it ...' (5.3.23–67).

The cumulative appreciations of 'life so lively mocked' are, in retrospect, preparation for Hermione's descent from the pedestal, her embrace of Leontes, her address to Perdita, and her resumption of life after great loss. But before these things happen, they are praises of a work of art. Why should Shakespeare's last liminal female be a living statue? Thematically, she makes explicit the process of reification that many of Shakespeare's women experience under the subjective gaze of their male lovers.[44] True, too, the play is much concerned with the entwined relations of nature, art, and sexual love, and that it draws upon literary precedent, in Ovid's Pygmalion, of an artist whose longing to vivify surpassed even that of Giulio Romano, alleged sculptor of the statue.[45] But it is must also be remembered that at this point in his development as a dramatist Shakespeare was influenced by the vogue of the court masque—witness the descent of Jupiter in *Cymbeline* and the masque of Ceres in

---

[44] To those above we might add Cressida and Cleopatra, fixed in their lability by the hero's compelling desire to comprehend their multiplicity. For further discussion, see Altman, *Improbability*, 241–2, 280–3.

[45] Cf. *The Winter's Tale*, 5.2.85–90.

The Tempest—which delighted to offer tableaux of royal and aristocratic participants striking statuesque poses, then miraculously easing their arms, legs, and
torsos into liquid movements exhibiting the grace of every gesture, note, and footing, as did Volpone as Antinous.[46] The final ekphrasis of *The Winter's Tale*, I suggest,
ushers psychological release from solipsism and physical release from mortification
into its own *mise-en-scène* even as, more largely, it honours the new theatrical form
fashioned for the royal Stuarts. 'The dignity of this act was worth the audience of
kings and princes, for by such it was enacted', says the First Gentleman, describing
the earlier reunion of Sicilia and Bohemia as though it were a masque performed
in the English court (5.2.72–3). His ekphrasis is actualized now. But that is part of
a longer tale.[47]

FURTHER READING

Baldwin, T. W. *William Shakspere's Small Latine & Less Greeke*, 2 vols. (Urbana, IL: University
of Illinois Press, 1944).

Gent, Lucy. *Picture and Poetry 1560–1620: Relations between Literature and the Visual Arts
in the English Renaissance* (Leamington Spa: James Hall, 1981).

Lear, Jonathan. *Aristotle: The Desire to Understand* (Cambridge: Cambridge University Press,
1988).

Mack, Peter. *Elizabethan Rhetoric: Theory and Practice* (Cambridge: Cambridge University
Press, 2002).

Schofield, Malcolm. 'Aristotle on the Imagination', in Martha C. Nussbaum and Amélie
Oksenberg Rorty, eds., *Essays on Aristotle's De Anima* (Oxford: Clarendon Press, 1992).

Scholz, Bernard F. '*Ekphrasis* and *Enargeia* in Quintilian's *Institutionis Oratoriae Libri XII*', in
Peter L. Oesterreich and Thomas O. Sloane, eds., *Rhetorica Movet: Studies in Historical
and Modern Rhetoric in Honour of Heinrich F. Plett* (Leiden: Brill, 1999).

[46] See, for example, Jonson's description of the masquers in *The Masque of Blackness* in *Ben Jonson:
The Complete Masques*, ed. Stephen Orgel (New Haven: Yale University Press, 1969), 49, 56–7.

[47] The play was, of course, performed at court on 5 November 1611, and again in 1612–13, though
not by royal actors. My last sentence refers to a project on *The Winter's Tale* in which I am currently
engaged.

CHAPTER 15

DUMB SHOW

JEREMY LOPEZ

Prologue: Hamlet's advice

As is the case with so many aspects of early modern theatricality—including verse-speaking and physical gesture—'Hamlet's advice to the players' (3.2.1–14) has done much to over-determine approaches and responses to the dumb show.[1]

> O, it offends me to the soul to hear a robustious periwig-pated fellow tear a passion to tatters, to very rags, to split the ears of the groundlings, who for the most part are capable of nothing but inexplicable dumbshows and noise. (8–12)

Hamlet bequeathed to modern critics a vocabulary for theatrical evaluation based upon oppositions between character and action, language and spectacle, and elite and popular plays or audiences. As B. R. Pearn said in his exhaustive survey of the different types of dumb show, this pervasive theatrical convention was 'of little assistance in a play whose object was primarily to portray the development of character'; rather, they were 'especially favoured by the mass of the audience, the "groundlings" of *Hamlet*, who no doubt enjoyed… as much incident and spectacle as possible.'[2] Of course, Hamlet may not be the most reliable judge of theatrical experience. At the very least he is proved to have a rather idealistic view of the transparent nature of audience response, and in any case the oppositions that structure his critique quickly break down under scrutiny. Hamlet's initial complaint is not about spectacle, but speech (*it offends me… to hear*); he then wavers between speech conceived as gesture (*tear a passion to tatters*) and speech conceived as violent noise (*split the ear*) before shifting the focus of his critique from the actor to the audience. What frustrates Hamlet is not merely a certain kind of acting, but a

---

[1] Unless otherwise noted, all citations are from the Arden *Hamlet*, ed. Harold Jenkins (London: Methuen, 1982).

[2] B. R. Pearn, 'Dumbshow in Elizabethan Drama', *Review of English Studies* 9 (1935), 385–405 (402).

kind of acting that implies a certain kind of audience. As these two terms, actor and audience, come to inscribe one another, Hamlet imagines the theatrical phenomenon connecting them alternately (or simultaneously) as one of silence and of sound: *dumb shows* and *noise*, opposites presented as appositives.

The paradoxes and oscillations of Hamlet's advice are endemic both to the theatrical experience provided by early modern dumb shows and to the critical tradition that has risen up around them. Dumb shows are, as I shall argue, a threshold between *drama* (a play as textual artefact) and *theatricality* (the quality of experience a play provides live and in real time), and they vividly represent not only the contest between text and performance for authority over theatrical meaning, but also the tendency of each to displace this authority onto the other. Moreover, in the canon of early modern drama and in the modern critical tradition, dumb shows are most frequently a sign of a derivative theatricality directed at a merely popular audience. With the exception of *Hamlet* and a few others—Kyd's *The Spanish Tragedy*, Webster's *The Duchess of Malfi* and *The White Devil*, Middleton and Rowley's *The Changeling*—most of the fifty or so extant early modern plays containing dumb shows are not likely to be considered great plays, plays (in Pearn's terms) for which the representation of character is paramount. Rather they are the early plays which toil in a too-rigid Senecan model—e.g. *Gorboduc*, *Jocasta*, and *Tancred and Gismunda*; or the episodic classical or folk histories of Munday, Heywood, and any number of anonymous playwrights; or the topical, quasi-didactic plays such as Barnes's *The Devil's Charter* or Dekker's *The Whore of Babylon*; or the later plays, such as *Four Plays in One* or *The Queen and Concubine*, which respond to the fashion for masques in the Jacobean and Caroline courts. From the perspective of a modern criticism that has internalized Hamlet's injunction to suit the action to the word, these are plays that seem, like the dumb shows they contain, to struggle mightily to express something that is either beyond or all too obviously within their reach.

In what follows I attempt to revalue the dumb show not simply by arguing that it is the source of complex theatrical effects, but also by arguing that the complex effects it achieves are closely related to the problems the convention presents for a criticism (or spectatorship) that privileges efficiency. Like the plays in which they most commonly occur, dumb shows seem to give us both more and less than we want. They cheapen spectacle by providing an excess of it, and cheapen language by rendering it merely or ambiguously supplementary to action. On the page, they suggest that the realization of text in performance might be more trouble than it's worth. On the stage, they have the potential to make it all too clear what theatrical experience actually is: laborious, solipsistic, imaginary activity that is always *this close* to lapsing into incomprehensible or meaningless self-referentiality. Dumb shows are a response to the problem of establishing a referent for theatrical activity, and in responding to this problem they exacerbate it. They occur most frequently in plays based upon essentially documentary material of one kind or another—*A Warning for Fair Women, Captain Thomas Stukeley*, Heywood's *Age* plays, Shakespeare's *Henry VIII*, etc.—where the playwright's and the spectator's awareness of an underlying textual tradition acts as an anchor for theatrical excess, even as that theatrical excess is meant to enlarge upon the text, or make it irrelevant.

Reduplication

(*Loud Musick*)
Enter four Lords, two Bishops, King, Prince: they sit; Eulalia in black, Crowned; a golden Wand in her hand, led between two Friers; she kneels to the King, he rejects her with his hand. Enter at the other door, a Doctor of Physick, a Midwife, two Souldiers; the King points them to the Bishops, they each deliver Papers, Kiss the Bishops Books and are dismissed. The Papers given to the King, He with his Finger menaces Eulalia, and sends her the Papers: she looks meekly. The Bishops take her Crown and Wand, give her a Wreath of Cypress, and a white Wand. All the Lords peruse the Papers. They shew various countenances: some seem to applaud the King, some pity Eulalia. Musick ceases. King speaks.

The foregoing passage is a stage-direction from Richard Brome's 1635 *The Queen and Concubine* (sig. C3v), which was printed in 1659 in a volume of Brome's plays called *Five New Playes*.[3] I have a hunch that you did not read all of this stage-direction. Why would you? One hundred and twenty-seven words, in italic font, describing a series of minutely choreographed actions in a play you have probably not read—or at least not read recently: eminently skippable. You probably assumed that this essay would direct your attention to those parts of the stage-direction that are most important and eventually give you enough context that you could return to it and read it in its entirety without your eyes glazing over. That is to say, you need to know something about the play in which it occurs before you can actually read the directions for a dumb show in any meaningful way. The quotation, then, is meant to dramatize two distinguishing characteristics of the dumb show. First, this most theatrical, or most embodied, of early modern theatrical conventions is necessarily transmitted to us in densely textual form. And second, what is recorded in this densely textual form often seems to some extent redundant in, or at least supplementary to, the words and action of the play 'itself'.

A third distinguishing characteristic of dumb shows is their opacity. Their stage-directions are, even under the best of circumstances, difficult to read: much like a detailed plot summary, even a summary of a play you already know quite well, the stage-directions for dumb shows move alternately too quickly and too

---

[3] This was the volume printed by Andrew Crooke, not to be confused with the 1653 *Five New Playes* printed by Thomas Roycroft.

slowly for the reading mind that is remembering or attempting to supply something beyond a mere record of actions and gestures. Dumb shows are also opaque in performance: they require a different form of attention. 'What means this, my lord?', Ophelia asks of the dumb show. Hamlet provides no help, and so Ophelia looks ahead to the play itself—'Belike this show imports the argument of the play'—or to the Prologue—'Will a tell us what this show meant?' (3.2.134–8). Watching a dumb show, you must not only work vigorously to interpret gestures that are almost necessarily of a different size and style from gestures elsewhere in the play; you must also put the act of interpretation into a kind of suspense, waiting for later action, accompanied by words, to help you sort out meanings: does this dumb show represent something that has happened, is happening, or is going to happen? Is its action expository, imaginary, or allegorical? On the page, dumb shows seem to demonstrate the primacy of embodiment in the creation of theatrical meaning; on stage, dumb shows seem to demand a form of 'reading' that is nearly textual in its intensity and its simultaneously forward and backward movement.

Playwrights were obviously aware of the difficulty involved in understanding dumb shows during a performance: when dumb shows are not accompanied by a Chorus or 'presenter' explaining the meaning of the pantomimed action, they are generally preceded or followed by detailed in-scene exposition that clarifies it. But the lengths to which playwrights will go in order to alleviate the problems of comprehension created by dumb shows only exacerbate another problem, namely their redundancy. Anthony Munday's *The Downfall of Robert, Earl of Huntingdon* (*c*.1598) begins with an elaborate dumb show that establishes in pantomime the antagonistic relationship between King Richard I, his mother, and his brother John; the love of Robin Hood and Marian; and the competition for Marian between Prince John and Robin Hood. This dumb show is called forth by the character of John Skelton, who is presented as the play's author, and says that he will act 'as Prologue, purpose to expresse / The ground whereon our historie is laied' (A2v). Skelton, however, says nothing during the dumb show's initial run, which is described in sixteen lines of text. Rather, at the end of it, he calls out: 'once more, bid your dumbe shewes come in; / That as they passe I may explaine them all' (A2v–A3r). The entire sequence of action is then re-run, only now in smaller segments, which are interspersed with Skelton's explications. On the page, the theatrical repetition is represented by textual repetition: the stage-directions for the actions accompanied by Skelton's narration repeat almost word-for-word the corresponding sections of the initial dumb show. Munday is widely considered to be a hack playwright, but even the dumb shows of acknowledged masters carry the burden of reduplication. *The Mousetrap* in *Hamlet* is introduced by a dumb show and then repeats exactly the dumb show's actions; and the dumb show direction, '*pours poison in the sleeper's ears*', is nearly exactly replicated by a stage-direction some 130 lines later: '*Pours the poison in the sleeper's ears.*'

How are we to understand this reduplication? Why does Munday choose to keep Skelton quiet the first time around rather than eliminate the first dumb show and accompany all pantomimed actions with Skelton's narration—similar to what, for example, Thomas Heywood did with his lengthy dumb shows in the contemporaneous *Four Prentices of London* (c.1594)? One conventional, and plausible, answer to this question would be that when Munday was writing, in the 1590s, dramatists were still learning how best to use the tool of the dumb show to achieve effects in a modern, commercial, quasi-realistic (as opposed to classical, academic, quasi-allegorical) theatre. Another answer might be that Munday worried that the link between Skelton's narration and the segments of pantomimed action would not be easily perceived in real time; therefore, he gave the audience a preview of what it was *going* to see, and then showed it to them again, in smaller pieces, where they would be under less pressure to assimilate visual meaning and could focus instead on the verbal explication. A similar argument has been made about the reduplicated action in *Hamlet*: having seen how the action of *The Mousetrap* will end, spectators need not worry too much about what the Player King and Player Queen are actually saying when the play is performed, but rather can focus their attention on the way Gertrude, Claudius, and Hamlet are *reacting* to the words and actions of the play.[4]

In his comprehensive study of the dumb show in the sixteenth- and seventeenth-century drama, Dieter Mehl gives both kinds of answer about the function of the redundancy in Munday's play.[5] In the broadest terms, Mehl traces an evolution of the dumb show from an external to an internal function: in its earliest forms it is wholly supplementary to the action—as in *Gorboduc* (1561), where the characters in the allegorical, between-act pantomimes are all different from the characters in the actual play—and in its later forms it is so fully integrated that it essentially disappears as such—as in Fletcher's *The Prophetess* (1622), where pantomimed action is used to stage a crucial plot-point, and moreover to 'make it dramatically effective by forceful gestures...rather than by dialogue'.[6] Plays like Munday's, still somewhat uncertain about whether the dumb show can function most effectively as an internal or an external development of the actions and perspectives of their characters, are at the approximate mid-point of this evolutionary scheme. In more local terms, Mehl finds Munday to be positively solicitous of his audience as he leads them into a dramatization of one of English folk-history's most famous episodes: 'The form of the scene shows that the desire to make it easy for the audience to understand the play was the main consideration'.[7] In this argument, Munday's redundancy is not understood as such—indeed, it seems to be construed, in advance, as an almost inevitable part of a scene. And it is consistent with what Mehl finds to be the

---

[4] See John Emery, 'The Dumbshow in *Hamlet*', *Notes & Queries* 7 (1960), 77–8.
[5] Dieter Mehl, *The Elizabethan Dumb Show* (London: Methuen, 1965).
[6] Mehl, *The Elizabethan Dumb Show*, 165.
[7] Mehl, *The Elizabethan Dumb Show*, 97.

primary function of the dumb show throughout the book: intensification. Dumb shows are the most vivid example of early modern dramatists' desire to

> make everything as clear and impressive as possible. Everything had to be said more than once, using different artistic means, in order to impress it on every single member of the audience.[8]

The idea of the super-communicative early modern theatre solves the problem of redundancy by distributing it across a fragmented audience wherein different sections will understand only what is directed at them: 'every single member' suggests a sweep from the nobility to the groundlings, each getting the same meaning in succession and by 'different artistic means'.

For Mehl, as for Pearn, dumb shows seem to involve an opposition between action and word. Both critics argue that playwrights take advantage of the temporal compression enabled by an absence of speech in order to (in Pearn's words) 'cram more incident into [a] play than was possible by normal methods'.[9] Coloured as it is, however, by Hamlet's prejudice against dumb shows as a popular form—Mehl says that they provided an 'easy way out' for dramatists seeking to transcend the temporal and geographical constraints of scene-writing[10]—the opposition between action and word gives way to an equivalence: dumb shows represent action as words might, or when words do not. They would not be necessary if everyone in the audience were equally appreciative of dramatic poetry. What is not accommodated by this essentially mimetic idea of the dumb show, where action is suited to word, is the convention's sheer excess and inefficiency. Big blocks of text erupting up into the space between the dialogue and action, simultaneously clamouring for and sapping our attention and our interpretive energy, dumb shows are almost always inefficient, on the page and on the stage, even when they explicitly announce that their purpose is efficiency.[11] As we can see from turning to the play with which this section began, the peculiar inefficiency of dumb shows—a redundancy that cannot be explained solely by the play's expository demands—is fully constitutive of their form and function. It is an inefficiency born of early modern dramatists' desire to go beyond mimesis, not only sundering the link between action and word, but attempting to put them back together in the form of the theatre's shadow: the text.

In *The Queen and Concubine*, the King of Sicily unjustly forsakes the love of his loyal, virtuous wife Queen Eulalia in order to take up with the ambitious, lascivious concubine Alinda. The King makes the switch official by putting Eulalia on trial for adultery, convicting her on false evidence given by suborned witnesses (hired by Alinda's courtier friend Flavello), banishing her, and then immediately and publicly

---

[8] Mehl, *The Elizabethan Dumb Show*, 12.   [9] Pearn, 'Dumbshow in Elizabethan Drama', 402.
[10] Mehl, *The Elizabethan Dumb Show*, 24.
[11] See, for example, Heywood's *The Brazen Age* (1611), where Homer introduces a dumb show at the beginning of act five by saying: 'Our last Act comes, which lest it tedious grow, / What is too long in word, accept in show'.

announcing that he will take Alinda as his wife. The dumb show represents the trial, including Eulalia's supplication (*she kneels to the King, he rejects her with his hand*); the giving of false evidence (*a Doctor of Physick, a Midwife, two Souldiers…each deliver Papers, Kiss the Bishops Books and are dismissed*); the King's judgement (*He with his Finger menaces Eulalia*); Eulalia's ritual deposition (*The Bishops take her Crown and Wand, give her a Wreath of Cyprus, and a white Wand*); and the court's reaction (*They shew various countenances*). Much of what we see in this pantomime has already been narrated in some detail by Flavello to Alinda in the immediately preceding scene, in which he has he told her how he has suborned the witnesses, why they were willing to do it, how much he paid them, what they said, and how the Queen not only patiently denied the charges laid by these witnesses but also 'wept / For their iniquity, and gave them a *God forgive ye*' (C3r). All that remains, Flavello says, is for the certain judgement to be passed against her.

As we know from plays such as *The Winter's Tale*, whose entire climactic reunion scene is given in narrated form, the exchange between Flavello and Alinda is more than enough exposition to establish both the trial's unjust form and Eulalia's patient bearing during it. Indeed, the subsequent dumb show, which backs up in time to show us what Flavello has just described, might very well diminish the power of Eulalia's sufferance, replacing her forgiveness of her accusers with a single, impressionistic gesture: *she looks meekly*. What the trial gains from the dumb show which it did *not* have in Flavello's narration, and which it might have lacked even if it had been staged with dialogue, is a theatrical sense of the solemnity of the ritual that the suborned witnesses are travestying with their false evidence. That solemnity is conveyed not only by the silent movements of the characters, set against the pomp of *Loud Musick*, but also by the quite specifically textual gestures they perform: delivering papers, transferring those papers to different characters around the stage for perusal, and kissing books. These documents are literally mute signs of the possibility of truth. Kept separate from the expedient, cynical, satirical language of the suborned witnesses and the sham trial, the documents gather up the power of Eulalia's meek looks. Then, in the next scene, we are given a dramatization of both the destructive power and the inefficacy of words: here the King speaks in self-consciously dilatory fashion about his reluctance to pass sentence; here the King pretends to be unable even to speak the word *Adultery*; and here Eulalia's loyal courtier Lodovico repeatedly but ineffectually interrupts, contradicts, or comments aside upon the King's judgement and sentence.

We might think of this sequence, from dialogue to dumb show and back again, as a triptych, where Brome is trying to achieve in three separate panels what he perhaps does not imagine he can achieve, or what cannot be achieved quite so well, in one.[12]

[12] I borrow the image of the triptych from Leonard Barkan's discussion of the 'non-syntactic' quality of dumb shows in 'Making Pictures Speak: Renaissance Art, Elizabethan Literature, Modern Scholarship', *Renaissance Quarterly* 48.2 (1995), 326–51. See especially 346–7.

Flavello's conversation with Alinda exposes the sham of the trial before it happens; the dumb show form of the trial gives us the sense of its impact and seriousness from Eulalia's point of view which Flavello's expedient cynicism could not; and the action of the trial which is *not* staged in dumb show dramatizes the close link between the King's manipulation of language and his manipulation of spectacle. To achieve this effect the play violates the theatre's nearly inviolable formal principle, forward temporal movement, with the potential result that a spectator will find language and action to be redundant, or that a spectator will initially perceive what turns out to be the transformation of language into action as the presentation of a new action, separate from the one already described. While this triptych-like effect might be seen in retrospect to have an obvious theatrical value—achieving a near simultaneity of affect and mode—it is nevertheless true that if you were to remove the dumb show from *The Queen and Concubine*, the play would be just fine without it. Brome's scene is inefficient because it places upon the audience the burden of separating, and also of reconjoining, language and spectacle. In this way it might be said to render mimetically the experience of the truth-finding ritual that is the trial. At the same time, its preoccupation with texts and the act of reading gestures beyond itself to the reconciliation of the King and Eulalia, effected in part by a letter written by Lodovico, which we see delivered to and read by the King, though we never hear what it contains (see H5v–H6r). This letter is itself somewhat superfluous: we can easily guess what it contains but it requires some generic good will to accept that the King is now receptive to the truth he's so wilfully ignored throughout the play. Even if it is only a sign of play-writing's necessary expediencies, Lodovico's letter, like the dumb show, reminds us that the fates of the characters, who seem to inhabit the most urgent present moment as they appear for our pleasure, are always bound within a text.

Like the dumb show in *Queen and Concubine*, the dumb show at the beginning of Munday's *Huntingdon* both makes explicit and occludes the textual basis of theatrical effects. 'Howe, maister Skelton: what, at studie hard?': the play opens with Sir John Eltam, cast as Little John in the forthcoming play, arriving at last after a delay at court. Skelton is, presumably, reading or writing something—reviewing the script, perhaps, or still labouring at the play's conclusion (at the end of the performance he will come on again to promise a yet-to-be-completed second part, L2v). The playwright calls out that the last actor has arrived, and suddenly

> At euery doore all the Players runne out, some crying where? where? others welcome
> sir *Iohn*, among other the boyes and Clowne.   (A2v)

The noise of the theatre erupts out of the scene of writing: the arrival of the actor achieves what the playwright alone in his 'studie' could not. The subsequent dumb show, once the actors have taken their places, puts the playwright in a subordinate relation to spectacle. When Skelton announces a prologue and the figures of King Richard, Prince John, Marian, and Robin Hood mutely pass over the stage, it seems that the actions of these storied figures can speak for themselves. But this turns out to be only half true: when Skelton calls for the dumb show to be repeated, he insists upon the very scriptedness of the action. And, after labouring to 'explaine them all', he asserts the authority of the poet: 'many talk of *Robin Hood* y[t] neuer shot in his bowe, / But *Skelton* writes of *Robin Hood* what he doth truly knowe' (A3v). He rounds out the induction with twenty-four lines of Skeltonic verse, verbally citing the poet's textual identity as the source of the performance's authority. Dumb shows, in short, occur at a moment where the theatre tries to do more than the theatre can—not by becoming more theatrical, but rather by acting more like a text.

Missing dumb shows

The expository superfluity of the dumb shows, and the prolific signs and analogues for meaning which they generate, seems to be an index of the theatre's power to provide multiple, disparate yet synchronous perspectives on a single event. But that theatrical power is made evident only through a form of writing which might actu-ally serve to neutralize it, for the textual rhetoric of the early modern dumb show has, since the beginning, been one of cipher and symbol. Here is an excerpt from the first dumb show in English drama, in Sackville and Norton's *Gorboduc*.

> Firste the Musicke of Violenze began to playe, durying whiche came in vppon the Stage sixe wilde men clothed in leaues. Of whom the first bare in his necke a fagot of smal stickes, which thei all both seuerallie and togither assaied with all their strengthes to breake, but it could not be broken by them.... Wereby was signified, that a state knit in unytie doth continue stronge against all force. But beynge deuyded, is easely destroied. As befell vpon Duke *Gorboduc* deuidinge his Lande to his two sonnes....　　　　　　　　　　　　　　　　　　　　　　　　　　(Q 1565, A2v)

The idiom, especially in phrases like 'Wereby was signified...' is decidedly non-theatrical. For Mehl, this non-theatricality seems to be deliberate: the scene 'could easily degenerate into a riot although of course no comedy of any kind was intended', and the playwrights present a counterweight to potential actorly improvisation by imagining 'a complete, rounded-off scene...its allegorical significance for the play...explicitly stated and commented on'.[13] Eric Rasmussen has a different view of the scene: its non-theatrical idiom, in particular the fact that it is written in the past tense, 'implies a report of a performance rather than an instruction for perform-ance'.[14] He argues that the 'yong man' who, lacking 'a litle money and much discretion', sold the play illegally to William Griffith in 1565, was probably one of the actors in

---

[13] Mehl, *The Elizabethan Dumb Show*, 30–1.
[14] Eric Rasmussen, 'The Implications of Past Tense Verbs in Early Elizabethan Dumb Shows', *English Studies* 67.5 (October 1986), 417–19.

the Inner Temple performance of 1561 and that he had to 'reconstruct the dumb shows from memory and insert them in their proper positions'.[15] Sackville and Norton, as in-house producers of their own play, would not have had to write out what they wanted to happen in the dumb shows, for they would have been able to explain it to the actors during rehearsal; we can infer that there is no authorial manuscript behind the dumb show directions because (for example) the direction quoted here calls Gorboduc *Duke* (rather than *King*) and that the error was preserved in the corrected quarto of 1570. In both Mehl's and Rasmussen's view of *Gorboduc*, the point at which the convention of the dumb show enters English theatre history is a point at which text seems to strive with performance, author with actor, for control of the play's meaning.

Rasmussen's and Mehl's arguments are partially conjectural, of course, but their conjectures illuminate both the odd formal relation between the dumb shows and the main play, and the contest between text and performance in establishing, or negating, the play's identity as a 'popular' form. For the first, to imagine that the existence of *Gorboduc*'s dumb shows was recorded for posterity only by means of an opportunistic actor's belated memorial reconstruction, or to think of them as opportunities for inexperienced actors to travesty the solemnity of the play's allegory, is to see immediately how contingent and tenuous is their relation to the play itself. If the text had come down to us with no dumb show directions, it would be perfectly legible; indeed, it might be considerably *more* legible, for we would not have to explain if and how particular dumb show actions (such as the attempt to break the bundle of sticks, for example) are re-presented in the main action. And we would not have to account for the disparate visual vocabularies used by the play's pantomimes—the 'wilde men clothed in leaues' in the first, the fable of a poisoned cup in the second, the rather straightforward iconography of mourning in the third, and the parade of furies and other classical figures in the fourth. For the second, John Day's address to the reader in the second quarto develops an elaborate metaphor in which the illegally printed text is conceived as a wronged maiden, taken from her friends by a young and irresponsible gallant and compelled to prostitute herself. It is in the bookstalls that the play will be clapper-clawed with the palms of the vulgar, and the elaborate, second-hand dumb shows might be seen as the gaudy attire that will attract them. Performance becomes text and text then shades back towards performance as the actor simultaneously cheapens and elevates, through augmentation, the authorial text. Rasmussen's narrative of dissemination recapitulates Mehl's narrative of chastened embodiment, where, even as the highly textualized dumb show seems to assert the primacy of literary interpretation over the potentially anarchic free-play of actors' bodies, the very explicitness of the textualized meaning makes it hard for the future reader to separate the text out from what must be imagined as a crude and

---

[15] Rasmussen, 'The Implications of Past Tense Verbs in Early Elizabethan Dumb Shows', 418. The story of the text's illegal sale comes from John Day's address to the reader in the 1570 edition, A2r.

didactic performance. As the play makes its way out of the Inner Temple and into the bookstalls, its spectacular dumb shows and all their noisy meaningfulness perhaps come to seem more like theatrical excrescences from the text than the solemn, symbolic pageants the playwrights might have intended them to be.

Rasmussen suggests that the actorly additions to the 1565 quarto of *Gorboduc* established the convention for subsequent texts: the past tense was used to record dumb shows in all those plays that were printed after *Gorboduc* but preceded the advent of commercial playing. Whether or not this is the case, it is clear and significant that with the rise of the commercial theatre came increased formal experimentation wherein the action of dumb shows was made simultaneous with the action of the main play. Thus in *The Spanish Tragedy* (c.1587) Revenge calls forth and interprets an allegorical pantomime to signal the direction of the play's dénouement; in *The Four Prentices of London* dumb shows are used to fill in large swaths of action quickly; a dumb show provides *most* of the action in the second play of *Four Plays in One* (c.1615); and in *The Queen and Concubine* a dumb show to some degree subsumes the play's temporal movement. It is also clear and significant that as the sale of dramatic texts became attached to the sale of public performances, the directions with which they were recorded came to be written in the present tense. This change in grammatical convention may take its origins from changes in theatrical practice: in the busy world of commercial repertory theatre, playwrights might not have had the leisure to work as closely with playing companies as Sackville and Norton could with their fellows at the Inner Temple. It was, perhaps, now a practical necessity for the playwright to write out detailed instructions for dumb shows which would then be presented to the actors. The reproduction of this new grammatical convention in printed texts, whatever its origin, had the effect of putting the reader in the position of the character or the actor. Present-tense dumb show text is one powerful means by which the reading experience is represented as coextensive with theatrical experience.

The present-tense experience that dumb show directions provide is always a past-tense experience as well. For readers in a future unthought of by early modern playwrights, these detailed instructions provide a vivid outline of early modern theatrical practice, and in particular its iconographic and symbolic conventions: the visual associations and habits of mind which might have structured an audience's experience even of plays without elaborate silent pageants. The dumb show provides a means to confront the alterity of the past. We might, indeed, see the critical tradition wherein the dumb show is found to be an essentially popular form as a manifestation of the desire to *honour* the alterity of the past—to imagine that, once, the largest possible audience was able to decipher a series of actions whose meanings are now significant only to the initiated specialist. Textual shadows cast by ephemeral performances whose character must have depended at least as much upon visual effects as verbal, dumb shows might disclose, if we could view them rightly, the essential component parts of theatricality itself. Certainly this would be the case for future historians of our own theatre reading accounts of the dumb show in the Royal Shakespeare Company's 2008 production of *Hamlet*—where the deployment of stage technology (a wire on which the poisoner was able to descend from the flies, head down, perpendicular to the stage), casting innovations (the poisoner was a comically sexualized black actor, the Player Queen was a hideous man in drag), and a pastiche of theatrical idioms (pantomime, sit-com, drag-show) lay open for analysis the modern classical theatre's dreams and nightmares about the secrets of the Shakespearean text.[16]

An epitome of this view of the dumb show—as a dream-like mediation of past and present in both its ephemeral present moment in the theatre as well as its permanent present tense in texts—might be provided by one of the more puzzling dumb shows of the early modern period which has its own strange textual history: the dumb show dramatizing Endymion's dream in 2.3 of Lyly's *Endymion*.

Musique sounds.

Three Ladies enter; one with a Knife and a looking glasse, who, by the procurement of one of the other two, offers to stab *Endimion* as hee sleepes, but the third wrings her hands, lamenteth, offering still to preuent it, but dares not.

At last, the first Lady, looking in the glasse, casts downe the Knife. *Exeunt.*

Enters an ancient man with bookes with three leaues, offers the same twice.

Endimion refuseth, hee readeth two, and offers the third, where hee stands awhile, and then Endimion offers to take it.

This dumb show did not appear in the 1591 quarto of Lyly's play but was first printed in Edward Blount's 1632 Lyly edition, *Six Court Comedies*. R. W. Bond speculated that it was not in the quarto because Lyly would have been able to tell his boy actors what to do. Bond's argument is cited both by Rasmussen in support of his own argument about *Gorboduc* and by David Bevington in his Revels edition of *Endymion*, but no one has addressed the question of the dumb show text's origin. If Lyly didn't need to write it out, why was it written out at all, and by whom?

It's hard to see why the dumb show is in the play: there is no dumb show in any other Lyly play; the exposition in *Endymion* does not require it, and in fact is not affected by it; and Endymion narrates the content of his dream in considerably more detail in 5.1, interpreting much of it as he does so. There are some small but perhaps significant differences between this narration and the dumb show direction. The direction calls for the lamenting lady to *wring her hands* and for the ancient man to enter with *books with three leaues*, but in Endymion's narration, the lamenting lady has *her armes crossed* and the ancient man (actually an *aged man*) carries *a booke with three leaues*. In Endymion's narration the aged man *rent* and *tore* the first and second leaves while in the dumb show direction he *readeth* them. There is no way to verify it, of course, but the dumb

---

[16] I have discussed this dumb show in detail elsewhere: see Jeremy Lopez, 'Shakespeare and Middleton at the RSC and in London, 2008', *Shakespeare Quarterly* 60.3 (2009), 348–65.

show direction almost seems as though it was written out after a not-very-careful reading of Endymion's speech in 5.1, as though it were added in specifically for the 1632 text. Perhaps someone (an actor? Blount himself?) recalled that there had been a dumb show when it was performed before the Queen's majesty at Greenwich on Candlemas.[17] Perhaps it is an interpolation, intended to give, in an idiom approximating that of Elizabethan dumb shows, a local habitation to Endymion's inscrutable yet crucial dream.[18] These are merely speculations, but they might provide an explanation for other graphical oddities of the dumb show in Blount's edition: the widely spaced way in which it is laid out on the page in an otherwise fairly close-ruled volume, the fact that most of it is printed in Roman rather than italic type, and the rather tortured, quite un-Lylean phrase *by the procurement of one of the other two.*[19] Whether the dumb show as it appears in the Blount edition is a version of what Lyly actually wrote or an idea about what he should have written, it is a strange textual eruption, perhaps the textualization of memory itself, which takes shape around a ritual of texts. In Endymion's narration of his dream in 5.1, he explains that the leaf he was left holding contained an allegory of Cynthia's triumph over treacherous, envious, and flattering courtiers. Staging the book in the dumb show, where rending has become reading, allows the audience to witness and experience the process of interpretation, to watch performance resolve itself into text, and to discover, with Endymion, that the truth is written down.

The King speaks

In a typically Shakespearean irony, Hamlet (and *Hamlet*) looks for truth—not only about the murder of old Hamlet, but about the theatre's capacity to represent and call forth from its audience something real—in the very medium he (and it) has just disavowed.

> *The Trumpet sounds. Dumbe show followes.*
> *Enter a King and a Queene, the Queene embracing him, and he her, he takes her vp, and declines his head vpon her necke, he lyes him downe vppon a bancke of flowers, she seeing him asleepe, leaues him: anon come in an other man, takes off his crowne, kisses it, pours poyson in the sleepers eares, and leaues him: the Queene returnes, finds the King dead, makes passionate action, the poysner with some three or foure come in againe, seem to condole with her, the dead body is carried way, the poysner wooes the Queene with gifts, shee seemes harsh awhile, but in the end accepts loue.*[20]

---

[17] I allude here to the title page of the 1591 quarto.

[18] In his edition of *Endymion*, Bevington notes that the dumb show is stylistically similar to those in *Gorboduc* and *The Misfortunes of Arthur* (1588). See John Lyly, *Endymion*, ed. David Bevington (Manchester: Manchester University Press, 1996), footnote at 2.3. 67.2.

[19] A Literature Online search turns up nine uses of the word *procurement* in dramatic texts printed between 1570 and 1642; with the single exception of *Endymion*, all are from texts composed after 1609.

[20] This is quoted from the 1604 quarto.

Imagine it in an outdoor theatre at the turn of the seventeenth century: there is no talking, but the dumb show is full of noises. The trumpet sounds; we hear the footsteps and the rustling of the long gowns of the King and Queen; when the Queen, finding the King dead, *makes passionate action*, we lean forward as though to hear the noise beneath her silence—perhaps in a particularly rapt theatre we hear the opening and closing of her mouth, her sighs of non-verbal exertion; then there is the sound of *some three or four* hoisting the dead King's body and bearing it off-stage—the sound of a curtain being pulled back and then dropped, or of a door opening and closing, as they disappear from view. And all around us there are the sounds of the audience, and of the world outside the theatre. If the experience is intense it is so in large part because of how much we have to block out in order to extract meaning from gesture alone, for there is nothing surprising about the dumb show's content. It is a reduplication of what we have heard the Ghost describe and what Hamlet has been saying about his father's murder. The meaning of its gestures are entirely clear, linked to Hamlet's point of view almost as though he were their author, and indeed we might even imagine that this dumb show is the dozen or sixteen lines he asked the players to add to their performance; the spectre of a text is always near at hand when actors are silent. Where everything starts to get unclear is in the second reduplication, when Gonzago speaks. His repetitive, archaic poetry calls attention to itself *as* text: someone is speaking lines that were written a long time ago. The characters, as immediate to us as to Hamlet in their muteness, suddenly come to seem distant and unreal. Then Hamlet announces the arrival of one Lucianus, nephew to the King, and what had seemed like a verbalized repetition of the dumb show's unequivocal meaning becomes an unexpected revision. The dumb show has become inexplicable, but only through the noise of the play.

In another typically Shakespearean irony—or an irony typical of scholarly attempts to come to terms with Shakespeare's plays—there is no known source for *The Murder of Gonzago*. That is, the play that follows the dumb show has no antecedent text except the text of *Hamlet*, unless it is the text of memory itself: Hamlet's recollection of the plot of *The Murder of Gonzago*, his attempt to follow his father's injunction to remember, his still-living memory of a speech (one that was never acted—or perhaps it was) that mourns the dead. Into the space between the text of memory and the text of the antiquated play, somehow incorporating or incorporated within the text of the lines Hamlet promises to give to the players, erupts the dumb show: a dream of revenge. When, after the show is over, Hamlet's hand is stilled by the King's mute, unknowably insincere performance of piety, the archaic conventions of staged performance (staged performance always teeters on the edge of archaism once it has been written down) stands accused for all its inert excess. 'I have heard / That guilty creatures sitting at a play...', Hamlet said earlier, unaccountably imagining the King to be the kind of rube who could be manipulated by spectacle and noise, the kind of person who is transported by a dumb show. It is a nostalgic idea, like a dumb show itself. To modify Mehl's evolutionary history of the form slightly, we might say that over the course of the early modern period the nostalgia of the dumb show becomes constitutive of theatricality in general. Belated playwrights, dreaming of an already fading golden age, deploy a dazzling range of formal vocabularies in an effort to evoke and supersede texts they did not write. No surprise then that the King indicted by the dumb shows of Brome's *Queen and Concubine* is named Gonzago.

The dumb show as such is no longer a meaningful theatrical convention. In a modern production of an early modern play a dumb show always feels old-fashioned, unless it is made quite deliberately to feel modern. The poisoner in the 2008 RSC *Hamlet* opened a heart-shaped box strapped to his crotch, and out popped a Slinky: such a provocation only acknowledges that the stage direction *anon come in an other man* conceals within itself something evermore inaccessible. But the mediating, nostalgic function once performed by the dumb show, its acknowledgement that the play is haunted by a text, is still necessary; it has only changed form. The design concepts of modern Shakespearean production—from Charles Kean's lavishly detailed historical stagings to William Poel's (or Mark Rylance's) 'originalist' productions to *Tempest*s or *Merchant*s set in outer space or Las Vegas—stand in relation to the Shakespearean text as (for example) the dumb shows in Heywood's *Age* plays did to Caxton's *Recuyell of the Histories of Troy*. And, indeed, these design concepts are even more nostalgic than the early modern dumb show, for they rise up out of a reverent silence in the presence of the Shakespearean text: it is all well and good to set *The Tempest* on Mars, but Caliban must under no circumstances say 'The planet is full of noises'. To take a less facetious example: Isabella may slap the Duke at the end of *Measure for Measure*, or stalk off the stage in a fury, or leap into the Duke's arms; but she cannot *say* No, or Yes for that matter. Very often modern theatre cannot *speak* the meaning it suspects (or shows) the Shakespearean text to contain. Its spectacular insistence that the play is continually meaningful, born out of a belief in the primacy of the text, comes at the price of unmooring the text from its referent. Derivative drama (all drama is derivative in some sense) longs to remember its origins; when it does, silence and noise, text and performance, become indistinguishable.

FURTHER READING

Berger Jr, Harry. *Imaginary Audition: Shakespeare on Stage and Page* (Berkeley: University of California Press, 1990).

Goldman, Michael. *Shakespeare and the Energies of Drama* (Princeton: Princeton University Press, 1972).

Weimann, Robert. *Shakespeare and the Popular Tradition in the Theater: Studies in the Social Dimension of Dramatic Form and Function* (Baltimore: Johns Hopkins University Press, 1987).

Worthen, W. B. *Shakespeare and the Authority of Performance* (Cambridge: Cambridge University Press, 1997).

CHAPTER 16

INDECORUM

ELLEN MACKAY

> nothing is harder than to determine what is appropriate.
> — Cicero, *The Orator*

Among the many reasons to like *The Defense of Poesy* is Philip Sidney's assertion that watching a show is an innocent and easy pleasure. Those who claim otherwise, mostly by denouncing the theatre as a soul-killing lie, earn Sidney's condescending rebuke: 'the poet never maketh any circles above your imagination, to conjure you to believe for true what he writeth'.[1] Having just told us that 'even a child' can understand the stage's epistemological decorum, by means of which a man, a place, or a prop is to be read as a stand-in for a fictional or fictionalized counterpart, his insinuation is not hard to catch: only an idiot can fail to navigate the 'as if' of theatrical performance.[2]

As it happens, idiots of this sort are a mainstay of the early modern English stage. A surprisingly wide array of plays, from the early Tudor to the late Stuart, depict theatre-going as an activity in which errors of spectatorship leave people at best humiliated, at worst dead. Tragedies tend to illustrate the dark end of this spectrum. Beginning with the assassinations committed by means of *The Spanish Tragedy*'s inset play,[3] early modern English dramatists have made hay with the grimmest hazards raised by the confusion of life and show. The blows struck in comedies are less

---

[1] Philip Sidney, *The Defense of Poesy*, ed. Albert S. Cook (Boston: Ginn and Company, 1890), 36.

[2] Sidney, *The Defense of Poesy*, 36. I borrow 'epistemological decorum' from Steven Shapin's book about early modern scientific practice, *A Social History of Truth: Civility and Science in Seventeenth-Century England* (Chicago: University of Chicago Press, 1994), *passim*.

[3] It is worth remembering that Kyd's example is not a beginning but a continuation of a long tradition. Jody Enders has demonstrated the centrality of fatal performance on the medieval stage; see her *Death by Drama and Other Medieval Urban Legends* (Chicago: University of Chicago Press, 2002) and *Murder by Accident* (Chicago: University of Chicago Press, 2010). In the first part of *Persecution, Plague and Fire: Fugitive Histories of the Stage in Early Modern England* (Chicago: University of Chicago Press, 2011), I discuss the classical pattern of fatal performance as it influences early modern theatre and drama.

fatal but no less keen; the takedown of Zeal-of-the-Land Busy by a puppet is a particularly satisfying example of the ridicule heaped on overcredulous and overcritical spectators, exactly of the type that Sidney mocks.[4] From this dramatic motif, it seems fair to conclude that playwrights of Sidney's age like to remind their audiences of the reciprocal principle on which theatrical performance always rests: as Bert States puts it, 'the play pretends that we don't exist...and we pretend that the play does.'[5] But just because playwrights make this principle conspicuous does not mean that they think it is easy. Given the number of plays that feature an audience's miscalibration of belief, the theatre of early modern England seems determined to show that, *pace* Sidney, the epistemological decorum of performance is hardly child's play.

The problem is an old one. Since Plato, the strain spectatorship puts on playgoers has given philosophers some disquiet. Since the mid-twentieth century, the chief expositor of this line of philosophy has been Stanley Cavell. At the start of his 1967 essay, 'The Avoidance of Love', Cavell writes that 'the first task of the dramatist' is to secure from his or her audience the 'very extraordinary behavior' of 'sitting in a crowd in the dark',[6] behaviour that he finds all the more extraordinary in light of the fact that we 'do not really understand' what we are 'being asked to accede to' when we keep ourselves quiet at the theatre. We may mock the 'yokel' who interrupts *Othello* to save Desdemona, but the 'non-factuality' of the play's violence can never be an 'empirical assertion'.[7] From our position as polite spectators, we can never know for certain whether, when, or to what extent what happens on-stage strays into the realm of actuality.

Admittedly, Cavell's theatre is not Shakespeare's. The apocryphal yokel at the centre of 'The Avoidance of Love' is imagined to leap from a hushed and darkened house onto an eighteenth-century proscenium stage. But the early modern English theatre is nevertheless strongly evoked by Cavell's philosophy, for the reason that its audiences are made subject to similar trains of thought. Consider the Prologue to Lordling Barry's 1611 satire, *Ram-Alley*, that promises 'to show'

> Things never done with that true life
> That thoughts and wits should stand at strife,
> Whether the things now shown be true,
> Or whether we ourselves now do
> The things we but present.[8]   (*Ram-Alley*, 8–13)

---

[4] The scene is found in the fifth scene of the fifth act of Ben Jonson's *Bartholomew Fair*, ed. Suzanne Gossett (Manchester: Manchester University Press, 2000).

[5] Bert States, *Great Reckonings in Little Rooms: On the Phenomenology of the Theater* (Berkeley: University of California Press, 1985), 206. I am grateful to Amy Cook for reminding me of States's formulation.

[6] Stanley Cavell, 'The Avoidance of Love', in *Must We Mean What We Say?*, 2nd edn. (Cambridge: Cambridge University Press, 2002), 326.

[7] Cavell, *Must We Mean What We Say?*, 327, 329, 328.

[8] Lording Barry, *Ram-Alley: Or Merrie-Trickes. A comedy Diuers times here-to-fore acted By the Children of the Kings Reuels* (London, 1611).

According to Barry's account, the purpose of playing is to catch the spectator on the knife's edge of an unresolvable either/or: is a play merely a presentation of 'things never done', or does it 'do' something in earnest? Though I have argued elsewhere that this quandary lies at the heart of early modern England's conceptualization of the stage, in this essay, I want to set aside the queasiness of the theatrical contract to focus instead on the etiquette of that contract's upholding. Inevitably, the problem of epistemological decorum is inextricable from this subject, for as Pierre Bourdieu has shown, good manners are at base a 'bluff' designed to 'cover lacunae' in our understanding of the way complex social interactions like the theatre work.[9] But I turn to the matter of playhouse decorum, with all the connotations of mere politesse that the term suggests, to subordinate the ontological questions that early modern English drama is famous for asking—'Is this a dagger which I see before me?' or 'What's Hecuba to him, or he to Hecuba, that he should weep for her?'—in order to consider what it is, exactly, that a play asks of us. If, as States suggests, dramatic performance is conditioned on the disposition of its witnesses, then any understanding of the theatricality of a given dramatic corpus or period depends in no small measure upon how its plays ask to be watched.

The social logic of decorum

Cavell's essay is striking for its assertion that theatrical spectatorship is behaviour that doesn't come naturally. The show-stopping yokel demonstrates that seeing a play correctly means not only suspending the reactivity of everyday life but possessing the cultural knowledge to recognize the cue for this inaction as well as the aplomb to carry it off. When done right, playgoing is thus a manner of keeping calm and carrying on that masks the fact of the theatre's epistemological complexity behind the cultivated pretence that a play is, as Sidney says, an innocent and easy pleasure. Yet the spectator's pose of insouciance—*all that happens on the stage is not happening in any way that is actually concerning*—is not simply an empty gesture of social conformity, but a bargain publicly made. Playgoers base their good conduct on the supposition that playwrights, too, must keep decorum by withholding from the field of theatrical action anything unfit for their consumption. In return for this restraint, they secure the performance to its condign outcome, for as playwrights never tire of pointing out, a play fully becomes itself only if and when an audience accords it a suitable reception.

The principle of decorum thus brings out the fundamental double-sidedness of the theatre's venture. Plays are, as Stephen Orgel has written, 'collaborative fantasies',

---

[9] Pierre Bourdieu, *Distinction: A Social Critique of the Judgment of Taste*, trans. Richard Nice (Cambridge, MA: Harvard University Press, 1984), 91.

but they are also co-requisite leaps of faith: audiences must entrust themselves to the theatre's imaginary world and workings, and playwrights must entrust a play's world and workings to the imagining of its audience.[10] The drama of England's early modern period attests to the tall task of both constituencies: to pretend the play's real existence, audiences must drop from their active notice the world-bound side of the theatrical event, leaving themselves vulnerable to the contingencies sure to arise when real people, real properties, and real actions conspire to bring dramatic fiction to life (this is Kyd's oft-emulated conceit). And to pretend the audience's non-existence, plays, in turn, leave themselves open to the contingencies bound to arise in the boisterous space of the playhouse (Cinna the poet, torn to pieces by the mob for his 'bad verses', is a good cautionary example here [*Julius Caesar*, 3.3.31][11]).

The value of decorum is its ability to mask the precariousness of this transaction by making it conventional. Though the epistemological complexity and material risks of live performance cannot be solved by the imposition of etiquette, clear-cut rules of playhouse conduct make it possible to ignore them. Indeed, for Cavell, the main purpose of theatrical decorum is to keep the audience from asking questions like, 'How do I know I am to *do* nothing?' or 'Why do I choose to subject myself to this suffering?'—questions raised by the unsteady divide between the fiction of performance and an audience's live experience.[12]

What is unusual, therefore, about the theatre culture of early modern England is how often plays keep these sorts of questions in the air, leaving 'thoughts and wits' at 'strife'. Francis Beaumont's *The Knight of the Burning Pestle* (1607) is a famous case in point. The play begins by rehearsing the negotiated peace between spectacle and spectator in terms so prescript that they are lifted verbatim from Lyly's *Saphao and Phao* (1584): 'we have endeavored to be as far from unseemly speeches to make your ears glow, as we hope you will be free from unkind reports…to make our cheeks blush' (Prologue, 14–18).[13] Yet the show itself is a metatheatrical farce on the volatility of the spectacle–spectator relation. This disparity between what Beaumont's Prologue says and what his play does—between a theatre premised on harmlessness and a theatre subject to contingency—raises the prospect that at least in some quarters, dramatists of the period want their spectators to watch with something approximating Cavell's decorum and want to strip them of it too.

The social logic of the period offers the clearest solution to this conundrum by making Beaumont's divided address—at once confrontational and placating—the effect of a divided audience. Rigid structures of social differentiation remain

[10] Stephen Orgel, 'Prospero's Wife', *Representations* 8 (1984), 1–13 (2).

[11] William Shakespeare, *Julius Caesar*, ed. David Daniel, The Arden Shakespeare (London: Thomson Learning, 1998).

[12] Cavell, *Must We Mean What We Say?*, 319.

[13] Francis Beaumont, *The Knight of the Burning Pestle*, ed. Michael Hattaway (New York: W. W. Norton, 1969).

foundational to our understanding of the early modern English theatre for two obvious reasons: first, they are so neatly manifest in the upstairs–downstairs arrangement of the open-air playhouses, and second, playwrights complain a good deal about their struggle to span the irreconcilable constituencies of the high and the low. Numerous prologues, prefaces, and inductions describe theatre houses as unevenly split between 'gentles' whose quality evinces from the quality they discern, and 'stinkard[s]' whose low standing predetermines their base, and basely aired, judgements.[14] The classic evidence of the stage thus fragmented is the contract Jonson brokers at the outset of *Barthlomew Fair*, in which judgement is to be accepted strictly in proportion to the price of each spectator's entry fee:

> It is further agreed that every person here have his or their free will of censure, to like or dislike at their own charge, the author having now departed with his right. It shall be lawful for any man to judge his six pen'worth, his twelve pen'worth, so to his eighteen pence, two shillings, half a crown, to the value of his place, provided always his place get not above his wit.   (Ind. 87–93)[15]

Other playwrights write variations on the same theme. Hamlet, for instance, is an even stronger critic of 'barren spectators' run amok; at some length, he complains that no 'excellent play', however 'well-digested in the scenes' or 'cunning[ly]' 'set down' can survive the crucible of a 'general' audience (3.2.39, 2.2.377–8, 375).[16] Hence the sad fate of the play of Pyrrhus, 'never acted, or if it was, not above once' (2.2.373), or less fictionally, the total flop of *The Knight of the Burning Pestle*, 'exposed to the wide world' and 'utterly rejected' by that breadth of (largely) unschooled humanity.[17] And hence John Webster's preface to the printed text of *The White Devil* (1612), in which the playwright bemoans the impossibility of writing well for a broad audience:

> If it be objected this is no true dramatic poem, I shall easily confess it, [...] willingly, and not ignorantly, in this kind have I faulted: For should a man present to such an auditory, the most sententious tragedy that ever was written, observing all the critical laws as height of style, and gravity of person, enrich it with the sententious Chorus, and, as it were Life and Death, in the passionate and weighty Nuntius: yet after all this divine rapture, *O dura messorum ilia*, the breath that comes from the incapable multitude is able to poison it.   (13–22)[18]

---

[14] Thomas Dekker, *The Guls Horne-booke* (London, 1609), sig. E2v.

[15] Ben Jonson, *Bartholomew Fair*, ed. Suzanne Gossett (Manchester: Manchester University Press, 2000).

[16] William Shakespeare, *Hamlet*, ed. Ann Thomson and Neil Taylor, The Arden Shakespeare (London: Thomson Learning, 2006).

[17] Francis Beaumont, 'To His Many Ways Endeared Friend, Master Robert Keysar', in *The Knight of the Burning Pestle*, 4, 7.

[18] John Webster, *The White Devil*, ed. John Russell Brown (Manchester: Manchester University Press, 1960). Brown translates the Latin phrase as 'O strong stomachs of harvesters', an allusion to 'the love of garlic among the lower sort' (20–1).

Like Jonson's monetization of the play–playgoer contract, Webster's disclaimer is a helpful index of the small faith playwrights have in the notion that unkind reports can be forestalled by the promise of seemly speeches. In a playhouse so differentiated by rank and knowledge, there is no point subscribing audiences to so general a bargain. Unlike Jonson, who seeks the well-ranked spectator's well-derived opinion, Webster throws his lot in with the 'incapable multitude', evidently in concession to its superior numbers.[19] But both playwrights share in the belief that no play will please all comers. In the socially heterogeneous milieu of the early modern playhouse, offence is inevitable; the only choice left to the poet is whom to confront and whom to placate.

It is something of an irony that the notion of decorum helps to produce, rather than resolve, this state of affairs. The high esteem in which the classical principle is held—Milton calls it 'the grand master-piece to observe'[20]—makes it a featured term in the tug of war over English dramatic standards. As Thomas McAlindon writes, 'the new drama created in the sixteenth century was felt by all the educated to be defective in one outstanding respect: its violation of decorum'.[21] McAlindon affirms what Webster predicts: that when 'critical laws as height of style, and gravity of person' are transgressed, the result must be displeasing to a refined audience. But by way of satirizing the tyranny of 'common' opinion, Jonson argues the reverse; in *The Case is Altered* (c.1597), he makes decorum the selling point of 'stale' work written for a vulgar audience by a hack 'pageant-poet':[22]

> Why look you sir, I write so plaine, and keepe that old *Decorum*, that you must of necessitie like it; Marry you shall have some now (as for example, in plaies) that will have every day new trickes, and write you of nothing but humours: indeede this pleases the Gentlemen: but the common sort they care not for't, they know not what to make on't, they looke for good matter, they, and are not edified with such toyes.[23]

Jonson, who styles himself as Horace reborn in *Poetaster* (1601), is certainly no advocate of decorum's abandonment; his argument is with unedified poets and low-minded spectators who misuse the term to defend bad theatre. Yet edification is no remedy for the problem that he mocks, for decorum is no clearer in the scholarship of the period than it is in the pageant-poet's vague and self-serving characterization. Famously, the full chapter treating decorum, or '*what it is that generally makes our speach well-pleasing & commendable,*' in George Puttenham's *The Arte of English Poesie* (1589) never progresses much beyond its dodgy etymology:

---

[19] Of course, that Webster addresses his readership to apologize for doing so indicates that he seeks the indulgence of a finer crowd, too.

[20] John Milton, 'Of Education', in *Complete English Poems, Of Education, Areopagitica*, ed. Gordon Campbell (London: John Dent & Sons, 1909), 566.

[21] Thomas McAlindon, *Shakespeare and Decorum* (London: Macmillan Press, 1973), 15.

[22] Jonson, *A pleasant Comedy, called The case is Alterd* (London, 1609), sig. A3r. The pageant-poet, named Don Antonio Balladino, is believed to be a thinly veiled jab at Antony Munday, the playwright and sometime antitheatricalist.

[23] Jonson, *The Case is Alterd*, sig. A3r.

…we in our vulgar call it by a scholasticall terme [*decencie*] our owne Saxon English terme is [*seemelynesse*] that is to say, for his good shape and utter appearance well pleasing the eye, we call it also [*comelynesse*] for the delight it bringeth comming towardes us, and to that purpose it may be called [*pleasant approche*].

As Puttenham eventually concedes, what 'the Latines call Decorum' remains a matter 'easier to conceave then to expresse':

we wil therfore examine it to the bottome & say: that every thing which pleaseth the mind or sences, & the mind by the sences as by means instrumentall, doth it for some amiable point or qualitie that is in it, which draweth them to a good liking and contentment with their proper objects.[24]

At once the 'point or qualitie' that causes a work's success as well as the feeling of 'liking and contentment' that results from this same 'point', decorum is an aesthetic judgement that retrospectively affixes its formal justification onto a supposedly intrinsic but in fact unspecified and unspecifiable trait—again, to quote from *The Arte of Poesie*: 'the matter resteth much in the definition and acceptance of this word *decorum* for whatsoeuer is so, cannot justly be misliked'.[25] Unable to pinpoint 'wherein it consisteth', Puttenham arrives at the same tautology that Jonson's pageant-poet foists on the public ('you must of necessitie like it') when he suggests that like pornography, decorum has no definition; we recognize it whenever we like what we see.

To be sure, this was not everywhere the case. On the Continent, Aristotle's *Poetics* were extrapolated to provide an ironclad dramatic covenant governing the dignity of the protagonist, the probability of the plot, the circumspection of any bloodshed, and the unities of action, time, and place. But in England, where the *Poetics* lacked this formidable (if misconstrued) influence, a hazier model of dramatic decorum was derived from Horace's *Ars Poetica*. Some poets seized on that work's early verses to deliver tendentious critiques of theatrical innovations, as in George Whetstone's complaint that 'the Englishman…is most vaine, indiscreete and out of order' when he breaks with the classical tradition of segregating high characters from low: 'they make a Clowne companion with a Kinge…: a grose *Indecorum*'.[26] Others evoked Horace's notion of *covenientia*, or the artful fitting of things together, to do quite the opposite.[27] Famously, Hamlet's address to the players—'let your own discretion / be your tutor: suit the action to the word, / the word to the action' (3.2.16–18)—draws from the Horatian discourse of decorum to thwart the stage's creakiest habits:

[24] George Puttenham, *The Arte of English Poesie* (London, 1589), sigs. Ffivr, Ffiiiv. Brackets are in the original.

[25] Puttenham, *The Arte of English Poesie*, sig. Siiir.

[26] George Whetstone, the Epistle Dedicatory to *The Right Excellent Famous Historye of Promos and Cassandra* (London, 1578), sig. Aiiᵛ.

[27] On the *Ars* and *covenientia*, see O. B. Hardison and Leon Golden, *Horace for Students of Literature: The 'Ars Poetica' and its Tradition* (Gainesville, FL: University of Florida Press, 1995), 34–6.

> O, it offends me
> to the soul to hear a robustious periwig-pated fellow
> tear a passion to tatters, to very rags, to split the ears
> of the groundlings, who for the most part are capable
> of nothing but inexplicable dumbshows and noise.
> I would have such a fellow whipped for o'erdoing
> Termagant; it out-Herods Herod. Pray you, avoid it.   (3.2.8–14)[28]

But without a more disinterested account of 'wherein it consisteth', decorum passes into popular use as the term that binds playwrights to an impossible contract. By making the worth of a play contingent upon the extent to which it purveys whatever 'pleaseth the mind or sences' of whomever happens to be watching it, decorum authorizes audiences to take their subjective feelings of displeasure—no matter how arbitrary—as the justification to watch indecorously.

Little wonder, then, that when playwrights dramatize the subject of decorum, they tend to do so derisively. In his most famous induction, at the start of *Bartholomew Fair* (1614), Jonson links the term with the stench of the Hope theatre, a sometime venue for bull- and bear-baiting: 'the author hath observed a special decorum, the place being as dirty as Smithfield, and as stinking every whit' (Ind. 151–4).[29] The joke here is at the expense of those who have reduced the ideal of the 'artfully fitting' into a witless sort of literalism. Turning back the term upon its abusers, Jonson flaunts the olfactory appositeness of playhouse-as-fairground by making decorum, in its popular misunderstanding anyway, savour of bull shit. Shakespeare, generally the milder poet, seems merely to hang an ass's head on it when he places decorum in the care of 'hard-handed men' who 'never laboured in their minds till now' (5.1.72, 73).[30] The result is the comic culmination of *A Midsummer Night's Dream* (1595), in which the tragedy of Pyramus and Thisbe is transformed into a farce of theatrical ineptitude. Shakespeare even produces a Master of the Revels to diagnose the problem, should we fail to mark it: 'There is not one word apt, one player fitted' (5.1.65).

Like Jonson, Shakespeare makes propriety's fastidious and misconceived upholding the cause of its transgression. The changes Bottom makes to the Lion's part (out of consideration for 'the Duchess and the ladies' [1.2.71]) are exemplary of this trouble:

Nay, you must name his name, and half his face must be seen through the lion's neck: and he himself must speak through, saying thus, or to the same

defect,—'Ladies,'—or 'Fair-ladies'—'I would wish you,'—or 'I would request you,'—or 'I would entreat you,'—'not to fear, not to tremble: my life for yours. If you think I come hither as a lion, it were pity of my life: no I am no such thing; I am a man as other men

---

[28] William Shakespeare, *Hamlet*, ed. Harold Jenkins, The Arden Shakespeare (London: Thomson Learning, 1982).

[29] Ben Jonson, *Bartholomew Fair*, ed. G. R. Hibbard (London: A & C Black, 1977).

[30] William Shakespeare, *A Midsummer Night's Dream*, ed. Harold Brooks, The Arden Shakespeare (London: Methuen, 1979).

are;' and there indeed let him name his name, and tell them plainly he is Snug the
joiner.   (3.1.34–43)

The joke is on Bottom, whose attempt to keep decorum brings out his weak
understanding of the theatre's aesthetic and epistemological contract. But it
also gestures at the larger costs of this sort of error. Since the effect of Snug's
amended performance is to revoke it ('I am no such thing'), we are left to see
that if theatrical production is made to cede to common standards of seemliness and decency, it will be reduced to the 'nothing, nothing in the world' of
Philostrate's discommendation (5.1.78). The same point is repeated a short
moment later, when the same self-appointed arbiter of what 'please[s]' (3.1.9)
suggests that the part of Moonshine should be assumed by the actual shining
moon ('leave a casement of the great chamber window where we play open,
and the moon may shine in at the casement' [3.1.52–4]). If for Jonson, this sort
of literalism merely stinks, for Shakespeare it revokes the very premise of theatrical performance, leaving us with the prospect of no show at all. Yet the
blame for this business is not limited to the lower sort, for even as *A Midsummer Night's Dream* holds its 'rude mechanicals' up to mockery for overestimating
the offensiveness of theatrical representation (3.2.9), it ends with a reaffirmation of
Bottom's concern:

> If we shadows have offended
> Think but this and all is mended,
> That you have but slumbered here
> While these visions did appear.
> And this weak and idle theme,
> No more yielding than a dream.
> Gentles, do not reprehend:
> If you pardon we will mend.   (5.1.409–16)

At its metatheatrical summation, the play thus asserts that keeping 'we Gentles'
unoffended requires the wholesale repudiation of its performed event. The
effect of redistributing this sentiment from the play's ass to its wiliest spirit is to
suggest that the usual complaint of a theatre held back by the ignorant multitude (viz.: these 'groundlings ... for the most part are capable / of nothing but
inexplicable dumb shows and noise') leaves out the fact that sophisticated playgoers present a like torment to the playwright. The same point is brought home
immediately prior to Puck's speech when Shakespeare leaves his audience
hostage to a court audience that is as thoroughly incapable of 'piec[ing] out
[a play's] imperfections with [its] thoughts' as Bottom predicts (*Henry V*,
Prol. 23).[31]

---

[31] William Shakespeare, *King Henry V*, ed. T. W. Craik, The Arden Shakespeare (London: Methuen,
1995).

If we take stillness and silence as the standard of good playhouse behaviour, the egregiousness of this failure is easily measured: of the 217 lines belonging to the inset performance of 'Pyramus and Thisbe', sixty-seven of them, or a full thirty per-cent, are interruptions by gentle spectators who harry the performers with such unamusing puns as, 'No die, but an ace for him, for he is but one' (5.1.296). Even if we reject this standard as anachronistic (rooted, as Cavell says, in the eighteenth-century stage), there is no denying Theseus's promise to watch 'Pyramus and Thisbe' in an accommodating spirit—'Our sport shall be to take what they mistake; / And what poor duty cannot do, noble respect / Takes it in might, not merit' (5.1.90–2)—to say nothing of his famous affirmation of the theatre's collaborative enterprise: 'The best of this kind are but shadows; and the worst no worse, if imagination amend them' (5.1.208–9). When the Duke and his cohort go on to watch the play without venturing their imaginations, choosing instead to take the performance as fodder for their empty persiflage, the disparity between what a well-mannered audi-ence ought to do and what a well-born audience actually does is made painfully explicit.

The implied critique is not unique to Shakespeare. As Beaumont writes in a poem consoling Fletcher over the wrack of *The Faithful Shepherdess* (1608), high-minded spectatorship—or rather, the hollow semblance of it—is too often to blame when good plays suffer bad receptions: 'a thousand men in judgment sit, / To call in ques-tion [the playwright's] undoubted wit / Scarce two of which can understand the laws / Which they should judge by' (13–16).[32] Against the view of the playhouse as hopelessly divided, Beaumont depicts it disastrously unified in its emulation of elite discernment:

> Among the rout, there is not one that hath
> In his own censure an explicit faith;
> One company, knowing they judgment lack,
> Ground their belief on the next men in black;
> Others on him that makes signs, and is mute;
> Some like, as he does in the fairest suit;
> He, as his mistress doth, and she, by chance.   (17–23)

In Beaumont's account, ignorance trickles down from the top: each spectator searches out the opinion of his social superior, while he in the 'fairest suit' looks to his 'mistress', apparently so devoid of judgement and so unconcerned by 'the laws' that should inform it that he leaves his taste to mere 'chance'.

Dekker lodges a similar complaint against the privileged playgoer in *The Gull's Horne-booke* (1609). While seeming to instruct men of leisure in the fashion of the time, Dekker calls out London's gadabouts for 'spread[ing]' their 'bod[ies] on the

---

[32] 'To My Friend, Mr. John Fletcher, Upon His Faithful Shepherdess', in *The Works of Beaumont and Fletcher*, 2 vols. (London: Edward Moxon, 1840), 2: 712.

stage' and 'laugh[ing] aloud in the middest of the most serious and saddest scene of the terriblest Tragedy'.[33] He then goes on to chide 'your Gallant, your Courtier and your Capten' in earnest for using the theatre to score social points:

> you publish your temperance to the world, in that you seeme not to resort thither to taste vaine pleasures with a hungry appetite, but onely as a Gentleman, to spend a foolish houre or two, because you can do nothing else.[34]

What Theseus's mannerless consumption of 'Pyramus and Thisbe' insinuates, Dekker thus states outright: status accrues to spectators who *fail* to uphold the collaborative fantasy that the theatre requires. Even Jonson, who calls himself a gentleman's playwright, corroborates this state of affairs; in *The Devil is an Ass* (1616), the highborn but dull-witted character of Fitzdottrel repairs to the theatre not to judge his half-a-crown-worth, but to air his 'rich suit':

> Today I go to the Blackfriars Playhouse,
> Sit i'the view, salute all my acquaintance,
> Rise up between the acts, let fall my cloak,
> Publish a handsome man, and a rich suit,
> As that's a special end why we go thither.   (1.4.31–5)[35]

But of course no one treats the cultivated indifference of the elite spectator more caustically than Kyd. The awful joke of *The Spanish Tragedy*'s metatheatrical finale is the obliviousness of a noble audience before the on-stage deaths of its progeny. When even Hieronimo's eighty-line, absurdly over-explicit confession—'So, Viceroy, was this Bathazar, thy son, / ... which Bel-Imperia, / In person of Perseda murdered' (135–7)—fails to alarm its addressee, Kyd shows that not even the prospect of murder and treason can overcome a nobleman's disregard for an epilogue (recall Theseus's decree: 'No epilogue, I pray you' [5.1.341]). In *The Spanish Tragedy*, bad spectatorship is a more intransigent feature of persons of quality than the instinct for self-preservation.

Kyd and his ilk offer a strong correction to the view that the early modern English playwright's greatest challenge is the task of bringing the rest of the audience in line with the perspicacity of its highest members. Still, it seems important to note that the error of elite audiences is of a different type: whereas common spectators like Bottom or Zeal-of-the-Land Busy stubbornly misunderstand the theatre's system of representation, fine ones like Kyd's Viceroy stray too far in Sidney's direction by refusing the theatre's imaginative venture. Since good spectatorship must then be a way of watching that avoids the Scylla of literal-mindedness

---

[33] Thomas Dekker, *The Gull's Horne-booke* (London, 1609), sigs. E3r–E3v.

[34] Dekker, *The Gull's Horne-booke*, sig. E3v.

[35] Ben Jonson, *The Devil is An Ass*, Revels Edition, ed. Peter Happé (Manchester: Manchester University Press, 1996).

on the one hand and the Charybdis of indifference on the other, it follows that the drama of the period tends to sit athwart the question of its own epistemological decorum, reassuring audiences that 'this weak and idle theme, / [is] No more yielding than a dream' while also asking them to wonder 'Whether the things now shown be true, / Or whether we ourselves now do / The things we but present' (*Ram-Alley*, 8–13). Provided the right constituency gets the right message, decorum in the playhouse would therefore consist of an adjustment of both ends of the social spectrum toward a happy medium: that elusive ratio of dispassion to credulity that would invite the audience to piece out a play's imperfections while at the same time preventing it from falling prey to the *fourberies* of live performance.[36]

But though a theatre that strikes out for this unobjectionable middle ground sounds a lot like the bourgeois theatre of our modernity—in which, as Brecht writes, the 'audience hangs its brains up in the cloakroom along with its coat'[37]—a theatre so thoroughly engrossed by the difficulty of its uptake as Shakespeare's, Beaumont's, or Jonson's seems unlikely to abide by Brecht's contract. Let me suggest instead that the early modern English stage holds in equal contempt two such seemingly irreconcilable models of bad spectatorship as Busy and the Viceroy not to split their difference but to mock them as two manifestations of the same bad outlook. For if we can see past the social disparity imposed between Busy's literalism (*all this is exactly what it seems*) and the Viceroy's detachment (*all this is merely an illusion*), the errors of these two characters start to look a lot alike: each holds a preconception as to what the theatre does that prevents him from seeing what the theatre is actually doing, leaving him 'confuted' and confounded, the blank of his misunderstanding held up to ridicule (*Bartholomew Fair* 5.5.102). Bad spectatorship is therefore not a function of which side one takes on the epistemological divide between the theatre as a mere show and the theatre as a true thing. Bad spectatorship is a function of taking any side at all, as if the theatre's volatile occupation of both these categories could be fixed or predicted, and as if performance was not powered by this alternating current. Since by the logic of opposition, good spectatorship must mean watching *without* this false conviction and constraint, it follows that in early modern England, plays ask to be watched in a state of engagement and uncertainty wholly incompatible with the decorum of the modern playhouse. Which is to say that like Cavell's yokel who 'doesn't know how to behave in a theater', a good spectator in early modern England is bound to look to us like a bad one.

---

[36] A case in point is the extra devil reputed to have appeared during a performance of Marlowe's *Doctor Faustus*. For a full account of this popular anecdote, see E. K. Chambers, *The Elizabethan Stage*, 4 vols. (Oxford: Clarendon, 1923), III: 423.

[37] John Willet, 'A Dialogue about Acting', in *Brecht on Theatre* (New York: Hill & Wang, 1964), 27.

The theatrical logic of indecorum

Before examining some evidence for this assertion, let me first state what I hope I have made less arguable: that the conventional representation of audiences as good (read: fine) or bad (read: common) belies the ubiquity of a problem that is neither caused by ignorance nor relieved by sophistication. How early modern England's plays ask us to watch them turns out to be a question that cannot be answered by the playhouse's social regulation. It is instead a question that the playhouse's social regulation effectively moots, since there is no means of escaping the strictures of the social to try on an alternative kind of watching. Dekker's *Horne-booke* is perhaps the best evidence of how thoroughly social imperatives trump theatrical cues in early modern England, though dramatists widely echo Beaumont's claim that audiences look to others to ascertain how a play should be watched. Particularly because their theatrical habits are a key means by which both rank and file make themselves recognizable in the period, plays are not conducive to the sort of engaged, unfiltered, and unprejudiced responses that playwrights sometimes wish for.

Moreover, the theatre could hardly have sustained itself without the 'hollow and artificial social exterior' that its practitioners complain about,[38] for the conventions of spectatorship make theatrical performance consumable. As Cavell demonstrates, it is by means of decorum that a show becomes an agreed-upon transaction and not a set of acts that demand an immediate response. Inattentive and misjudging audiences are the unavoidable cost of this commercial arrangement. But if the realities that govern the early modern English stage condition its less-than-ideal reception, the world on-stage is a blanker slate, freer, if the playwright so desires it, of such real-world entailments. In the second part of this essay, I want to take up some dramatizations of spectatorship that counter the blinkered outlook of audiences as playwrights claimed they really were to discuss the outlook of audiences playwrights set free from the constraints of real-life spectatorship. An intriguing feature of this unhindered view is that it tends to be a female one.

Jonson's *The Staple of News* (1626) is at a first glance an unlikely choice for such a discussion. Though the play features four 'gentlewomen, lady-like attired' as its inset audience, Jonson shows them venting their opinions in order to deride and contain their invidious misregard. As their names suggest, Gossips Tattle, Expectation, and Censure play the vices in a metatheatrical interlude (staggered over the prologue and four intermeans), with Gossip Mirth as their lone dissenter, tasked with blunting their bad judgements. When Tattle complains that the play lacks a good stage devil, Mirth checks her with, 'That was the old way, gossip' (Int. 2.14). When Censure spies 'abuse',

---

[38] Michael C. Leff, 'Decorum and Rhetorical Interpretation: The Latin Humanistic Tradition and Contemporary Critical Theory', *Vichiana: Rassegna de Studi Classici*, 3rd ser., 1 (1990), 107–26 (108).

Mirth tells her to 'Take heed it lie not in the vice of your interpretation' (23, 26). And when Expectation fears that the play will be 'sour' or 'rank', Mirth advises them all to 'sit down…quiet and calm', 'look…smooth and soft', 'be merry', and 'laugh' as the scene warrants (64–6). In short, in return for their predictable expressions of inattention and poor judgement (including the old standby, '[we] come to see and be seen' [9–10]), these spectators are administered a predictable correction: like Cavell's yokel, their function is to show that the role of the spectator is to sit still and keep quiet.

Staple's misbehaving female audience is thus no different from a misbehaving male one. So much does this seem to be Jonson's point that when the Gossips take their places and the Prologue nervously asks, 'But what will the noble- / men think, or the grave wits here, to see you seated on the / bench thus?' (Ind. 15–17), Mirth argues for a woman's equal right to 'arraign' the show she watches:

> Why, what should they think, but that they had mothers, as we had, and those mothers had gossips (if their children were christened) as we are, and such as had a longing to see plays and sit upon them, as we do, and arraign both them and their poets? (Ind. 18–22)[39]

But as the play continues, its representation of spectatorship changes. Or rather, its spectators seem to abandon their representational roles. By the fourth intermean, Mirth and her cohort have ceased to function as the virtue and vices they name and instead band together to draft a new ending, one in which the poet and his protagonist are made to petition for the forgiveness of both the characters and the audience. All the while, Jonson plays the hostage in this metadrama, sweating backstage over his play's reception while Mirth regales us with the sight:

> Yonder he is within (I was i'the tiring-house awhile to see the actors dressed) rolling himself up and down like a tun i'the midst of 'em, and spurges. Never did vessel of wort or wine work so! His sweating put me in mind of a good Shroving-dish…a stewed poet! (Ind. 62–7)

In a further Pirandellian twist, he is consigned by his on-stage audience to the pillory and stripped of his own creation for the sake, the Gossips say, of properly 'sustaining' it (Int. 4, 73).

The same sort of slip into metatheatrical chaos occurs in Beaumont's *Knight of the Burning Pestle*, in which a grocer and his wife take centre stage in the show that both are supposed to be merely watching. Famously, Beaumont's conceit is no mere framing device. Whereas in *Staple*, the Gossips talk apart from the play's action, bracketed by the interludic function of the intermean, here Citizen and Wife (as they are designated by their dramatic prefixes) or George and Nell (as they designate each other) mount a hostile takeover of 'The London Merchant', steering the production away 'from all that's great' (Ind. 1) with wild abandon and unabashed

---

[39] Ben Jonson, *The Staple of News*, ed. Anthony Parr (Manchester: Manchester University Press, 1988).

inexpertise—as Nell admits, 'I'm a stranger here; I was ne'er at one of these plays, as they say, before' (Ind. 50–1). Since she lacks the knowledge of what is fitting for a theatre to show, her first request is a doozy: 'Let him kill a lion with a pestle, husband; let him kill a lion with a pestle' (Ind. 42–3). In a play chock-full of intertheatrical references (to borrow from William N. West's contribution to this collection), Beaumont evokes the same creature about which Bottom was so particular ('A lion among ladies is a most dreadful thing' [3.1.24]) to indicate a spectator who is not only wholly unconstrained by theatrical decorum but also unconstrained by its ludicrous misuse.

Henceforward, the demands only accelerate. At every moment that the billed production threatens to achieve some coherence, George and Nell derail it, with the result that in the place of 'The London Merchant', the audience is presented with a veritable primer of indecorous spectatorship. Most of these lessons come at the Wife's expense, as a quick tour of her transgressions makes clear: she arrives late, assumes a place she does not seem to have a right to, and disturbs her fellow spectators in her graceless attempt to achieve it ('I pray you sir, lend me your hand', her husband asks of some unlucky audience member, pressing him to the task of hoisting her up [Ind. 47–8]).[40] Once the play is underway, she peppers her husband with inane commentary ('didst thou ever see a prettier child?' [1.92]), condoles with the characters and ministers to their fictional ailments ('How dost thou Rafe…there's some sugar-candy for thee' [2.334–6]), chastises the smokers beside her ('Now I pray, gentlemen, what good does this stinking tobacco do you?' [1.209–10]), importunes the actors for ornate detours from the plot ('let Rafe travel over great hills…and come to the King of Crakovia's house, covered in velvet' [4.33–5]) or unspecified improvements ('I would have something done, and I cannot tell what it is' [2.397–8]), eggs on the action with vulgar zeal ('kill, kill, kill, kill, kill' [3.351]), and drinks ('Come, George, where's the beer?' [Interlude 3.1]). She even undercuts the play's ending by offering her house for an after-party: 'it should go hard, but I would have a pottle of wine and a / pipe of tobacco for you' (Epilogue 6–7). Like Jonson's Gossips only far more so, Nell's indecorum is the force behind *The Knight of the Burning Pestle*'s theatrical sustaining.

Having mounted this comparison to look for signs of unfettered spectatorship, let me first admit to the obvious. The women spectators of *Staple of News* and *The Knight of the Burning Pestle* are clearly bad audiences: undiscerning, uncouth, and careless of their duty to 'draw from [the company's] labours sweet / content' (*Knight* Prol. 5–6). Cultural constructs of femininity in the period make their indecorum a plausible vice; Gail Paster's account of women's perceived inability to master 'emerging norms of bodily restraint and control' clearly informs the trouble

---

[40] As Laurie Osborne points out, the Wife commandeers the production far more often than her husband, George: 'three-quarters of the suggestions originate with Nell', 'Female Audiences and Female Authority in *The Knight of the Burning Pestle*', *Exemplaria* 3.2 (1991), 491–517 (497).

Jonson's Gossips and Beaumont's Wife have sitting tight in the playhouse.[41] In light of the standard antitheatrical complaint that 'the Poetes that write playes, and they that present them upon the Stage, studie to make our affections overflow, whereby they draw the bridle from that parte of the mind, that should ever be curbed',[42] it hardly seems surprising that women, whose leakiness Paster has shown to be proverbial, would be chosen to exemplify the inability of the theatrical spectator to contain herself.

But let me now speak to what is less evident: that the 'leaky vessel' turns out to be an unexpectedly robust participant in the theatre that Shakespeare dreams about, in which 'imagination amends' what performance can merely shadow forth. As Jean Howard has written, by way of highlighting Dympna Callaghan's important work on the subject, the absence of women from the 'presentational' side of the early modern English stage means that female characters are always 'conspicuously reliant upon the discursive citation of femininity'.[43] In the case of Beaumont's 'Wife' or Jonson's 'Gossips'—specifically, 'Tattle', 'Expectation', 'Censure', and 'Mirth'—this point is written into their nomenclature. Yet by featuring as their inset audience figures so manifestly citational, both playwrights hand over the work of spectatorship to a subjectivity that is not one, effectively loosening theatrical performance from the social logic and commercial pragmatics of its everyday reception.[44] In fine, that *it is because these 'women' spectators are evidently no such thing* that they make it possible for Beaumont and Jonson to think about spectatorship without

---

[41] Gail Paster, *The Body Embarrassed: Drama and the Disciplines of Shame in Early Modern England* (Ithaca: Cornell University Press, 1993), 23 and *passim*; Keith Thomas, 'The Place of Laughter in Tudor and Stuart England', *TLS*, 21 January 1977, 80; quoted in Paster, *The Body Embarrassed*, 23. Gail Paster discerns this construct in female characters that are depicted 'needing or failing to relieve themselves', an embarrassment of some salience to the theatre, where the demand for respectable women to keep their physical needs concealed conflicts with the unprovisioned playhouse (*The Body Embarrassed*, 23). As Tracy Davis and Peter Holland point out in their hair-raising survey of theatre toilets across the centuries, the lack of this amenity produces a 'significant and unwelcome tension in spectators' experience of a performance', no doubt because the body's urges are 'signally disruptive' of 'patterns of audience decorum' that operate on States's principle that for a show to happen, the spectator must efface herself from it. Tracy C. Davis and Peter Holland, 'Toilets', in Dennis Kennedy, ed., *The Oxford Encyclopedia of Theatre and Performance* (Oxford: Oxford University Press, 2003), 2005 / *The Oxford Encyclopedia of Theatre and Performance* (e-reference edition), http://www.oxfordreference.com/view/10.1093/acref/9780198601746.001.0001/acref-9780198601746-e-3949 [subscription necessary].

[42] Stephen Gosson, *Plays Confuted in Five Actions* (London, 1582), sig. F1v.

[43] Jean Howard, 'Staging the Absent Woman: The Theatrical Evocation of Elizabeth I in Thomas Heywood's *If You Know Not Me, You Know Nobody*', in Pamela Allen Brown and Peter Parolin, eds., *Women Players in England, 1500–1660: Beyond the All-Male Stage* (Aldershot: Ashgate, 2008), 263, 264.

[44] In pursuing this claim, I do not mean to ignore the real women who did, in fact, create and shape the theatre in early modern England, nor to whitewash the scrutiny that women's actual presence in the theatre activated, but to suggest instead that women's predominantly *conceptual* relation to the stage made them particularly well-suited to represent an unrealized, hypothetical spectatorship. See Brown and Parolin, *Women Players in England*, for a discussion of women theatre practitioners.

having to think about the real-world conditions that would make their imaginings infeasible.

By this logic, their sheer, exuberant artifice is a reason to question whether Jonson's Gossips and Beaumont's Wife practise a spectatorship that, while certainly leaky, is also necessarily bad. In *The Staple of News*, the first cue for such a reassessment occurs right at the start, in the unexpected addition of a good spectator (Mirth) among the reprobates (Expectation, Censure, and Tattle), as if to illustrate that unruliness is not a uniformly negative tendency. But the more powerful provocation comes when the Gossips are so displeased by a twist in the plot that they are moved to write the play over. Here is their revision of the fate of Pennyboy Senior, whose revival, after his apparent death, they particularly dislike:

Censure:	I would rather the courtier had found out some trick to beg him from his estate.
Expectation:	Or the captain had courage enough to beat him.
Censure:	Or the fine madrigal-man in rhyme to have run him out o'the country like an Irish rat.
Tattle:	No, I would have Master Piedmantle, her grace's herald, to pluck down his hatchment, reverse his coat armor, and nullify him for no gentleman.
Expectation:	Nay, then let Master Doctor dissect him, have him opened, and his tripes translated to Lickfinger to make a probation dish of.
Censure and Tattle:	Agreed! Agreed! (Int. 4, 50–61)

It seems a given that Jonson's view of this collective imagining unleashed by *The Staple of News* must be ironic; the frenzy of rewrites touched off by Pennyboy's resurrection suggests another indictment of the Gossips' low tastes and wagging tongues. Yet their round robin, which swiftly progresses into some breathless stichomythia, represents a very different order of engagement from the shallow preconceptions that they voice earlier. Even if we take their early foray into crowd-sourced fan-fiction as a winking display of Jonson's own virtuosity, it still demonstrates the fun of imagining a performance that is neither ignored, nor misconstrued, nor silently acceded to—as Mirth initially suggests—but instead is sustained by the active and conscious work of its audience's imaginative attempts to sustain it.

In *The Knight of the Burning Pestle*, the Wife's violations of playhouse decorum point even more explicitly at a kind of wishful theatrical thinking. We can see Nell serving the playwright's agenda from the moment she calls out the gentlemen smokers in her midst, much as Dekker does in the *Horne-booke*. But of Nell's many improprieties, the most provocative in this vein is her apparent overreaction to the scene in 'The London Merchant' in which Jasper attempts to test the faith of his stolen bride. His sword drawn, Jasper awakens Luce to proclaim, 'Come, by this hand you die; / I must have life and blood to satisfy / Your father's wrongs' (3.3.89–91), to which the Grocer's Wife responds,

> Away, George, away, raise the watch at Ludgate, and bring a mittimus from the justice
> for this desperate villain.—Now, I charge you, gentleman, see the King's peace kept!—
> O, my heart, what a varlet's this to offer manslaughter upon the harmless gentle-
> woman!   (3.92–6)

So, yokel-like, Nell fundamentally misreads the nature of the theatre's illusion. As
Cavell has written, this is a classic violation of decorum, akin to 'the visitor who drinks
from the finger bowl'. But as Cavell has also written, it is a violation that has the effect
of raising the question, 'what is *our* way' of watching a play, and why do we conform
to it?[45] Hence, Nell's classic impropriety—her failure to know what is real and what is
show—reveals an involvement in the on-stage world that ought not be dismissed as
mere ignorance. Here is Cavell working out the case of the yokel at *Othello*:

> You tell me that that woman will rise again, but I know that she will not, that she is
> dead and has died and will again die, die dead, die with a lie on her lips, damned with
> love. You can say there are two women, Mrs. Siddons and Desdemona, both of whom
> are mortal, but only one of whom is dying in front of our eyes. But what you have
> produced for me is two names. Not all the pointing in the world to that woman will
> distinguish the one woman from the other.[46]

Read in this light, the Wife's cry—'O, my heart, what a varlet's this to offer man-
slaughter upon the harmless gentlewoman!'—suggests that however fictional, the
death of a character should not be mildly acceded to. This cannot be wrong, inasmuch as to respond otherwise in like circumstances is to be Kyd's Viceroy, whose
indifference is disastrous. But neither can it be right merely in the pat sense of Nell's
qualms about 'the good of such entertainment'.[47] Instead, I want to suggest that
Beaumont orchestrates what Cavell philosophizes, namely, a theatre that is 'neither
credible nor incredible' but the expression of a fundamental 'claim' upon us to
'acknowledge' the suffering of 'others' by putting ourselves fully in its presence.[48]

Admittedly, there is not much dignity in this business. Since any attempt to rescue a play or its heroine from the script that constitutes it is bound to be read as an
expression of the sort of credulity that Sidney mocks ('the poet never maketh any
circles above your imagination, to conjure you to believe for true what he writeth'[49]),
Jonson's Gossips and Beaumont's Wife are proof of Bourdieu's assertion: 'it is not so
easy to describe the "pure" gaze without also describing the naïve gaze which it
defines itself against'.[50] My goal, however, is to propose that in a theatre that mud-
dies the distinction between things merely presented and things truly done, the

---

[45] Cavell, *Must We Mean What We Say?*, 328.

[46] Cavell, *Must We Mean What We Say?*, 328.

[47] Cavell, *Must We Mean What We Say?*, 327.

[48] Cavell, *Must We Mean What We Say?*, 327, 334.

[49] Laura Levin describes the overcredulity for which Busy is infamous as a 'naïve epistemology' in
Men in Women's Clothing: Anti-theatricality and Effeminization, 1579–1642 (Cambridge: Cambridge
University Press, 1994), 6.

[50] Bourdieu, *Distinction*, 32.

'pure' spectator is not the one who keeps 'clean' of its ethical complexity by staying 'hidden, silent and fixed'.[51] Neither is she the spectator who comes to the theatre in search of purgation. In the murky terrain of Beaumont's play, the pure spectator is the one who avoids love's avoidance, and shows in the process that the only purge that tragedy demands is the purge of our 'difference from others'. The pure spectator is thus the leaky one.

For Cavell, the tragedy of the theatre is that Nell's transgression of theatrical and bodily norms can never go far enough.

> Even the spectator who stops the play shows us how little is in our power. For that farthest extremity has not touched Othello, he has vanished; it has merely interrupted an evening's work. Quiet the house, pick up the thread again, and Othello will reappear, as near and as deaf to us as ever.[52]

In his philosophy, 'a character is not, and cannot become, aware of us'.[53] But Jonson and Beaumont espouse a different view. The plays that their female spectators interrupt are so fundamentally changed by the process that they career off in an altogether new direction: in *The Staple of News*, the prodigal parable at the play's centre cracks and falters in the wake of the Gossips' rewrites; and in *The Knight of the Burning Pestle* the role of hero transfers onto a conscripted member of the audience. More generally, though, what Nell's rescue of Luce and the Gossips' revival of the Staple both show us is theatre that proves 'we have it in us...to care about something'.[54] Jonson and Beaumont not only create spectators who risk this care, they create plays that depend on receiving it. In so doing, they revise theatrical performance from a missed encounter between two solitudes to a moment of mutual recognition.

What their representation of female spectatorship lacks, of course, is any carryover to the actual playhouse. Though Jonson's Gossips and Beaumont's Wife show regard for the suffering of others, they do so as characters in scripted fictions. By way of a conclusion, I want to return to the final act of *A Midsummer Night's Dream* to search out indecorum that while fictional, is also practiable. I hope to show that thinking with women in and about the early modern English playhouse is not only theoretically productive. It can also help us to discover unforeseen consequences in the act of sitting still and keeping quiet.[55]

While Pyramus and Thisbe succumb to their tragic fates, it is impossible to lose track of Theseus, Hippolyta, Demetrius, and Lysander, who like the Gulls in Dekker's

---

[51] Cavell, *Must We Mean What We Say?*, 330, 332.
[52] Cavell, *Must We Mean What We Say?*, 330.
[53] Cavell, *Must We Mean What We Say?*, 330.
[54] Cavell, *Must We Mean What We Say?*, 350.
[55] 'Thinking with women' is Rebecca Wilkin's phrase, which she posits as a friendly complement to Stuart Clark's 1999 title, *Thinking with Demons*. See Rebecca Wilkin, *Women and the Search for Truth in Early Modern France* (Aldershot: Ashgate, 2008).

Horne-booke, 'laugh aloud' when the play is at 'its most serious and saddest'. But invisible in the printed text are Hermia and Helena, who speak their last lines in the previous act. Given Stephen Gosson's notorious reproach of London's Gentlewomen Citizens (1579)—'you can forbidd no man, that vieweth you, to noate you, and that noateth you, to judge you'—their silence suggests a capitulation to the cultural dictum that a chaste woman who ventures into a theatre audience had best keep herself unnoticed.[56] But though it may well be fitting for the two brides to abstain from the badinage of the three grooms (and one Amazon), it is just as possible that they are abstaining from the discourtesy of the court. This uncertainty is a familiar paradox; in early modern England, silence is as readily taken as a screen for vice as it is taken as a virtue. So decorum, as it pertains to women's conduct, can also be perceived as its own breach. In dramatic practice this is a dispiriting paradox—Cavell extrapolates much of his essay's philosophy from the grief it inflicts via Desdemona's death.[57] In the theatre audience, though, this oscillation between both categories of possibility presents an example of how to watch with something approximating our modern decorum and how to violate it too.

I have argued that the reciprocal pretence that Bert States describes, in which the courtesy of not seeing is traded across both sides of the apron (i.e. *I don't see you watching; you don't see me acting*), is far from an early modern English playwright's ideal. By way of an alternative, Jonson and Beaumont give us rowdy female spectators who offer recognition, care, and even love across the play–playgoer divide. Hermia and Helena will hardly seem comparable to these creations; if they are conspicuous, it is for eschewing the raucous commentary of the men in their midst. And yet because this, too, is legible as a transgression of decorum—for it represents a failure to follow the social norms of the court audience the women partly constitute—*A Midsummer Night's Dream* models a mode of engagement whose break from convention is indistinguishable from its conventionality. What passes for 'hiddenness, silence, [and] isolation' is therefore also its reverse.

The play bolsters this claim by setting up two models of audience conduct that Hermia and Helena do not follow. On the one hand, their spectatorship represents a clear break from Theseus's aristocratic derision; on the other, it shows no affinity with the literal-minded overreaction that Bottom fears ('if you should fright the ladies out of their wits, they would have no more discretion but to hang us' [1.2.74–6]). One result is utter freedom from decorum's constraint: by leaving the women's outlook unscripted by the protocols the play establishes, *A Midsummer Night's Dream* leaves undecided, even to itself, what constitutes a manner of watching that is neither indifferent nor overcredulous. Yet because that conduct goes literally unscripted, its manner of watching can only be recognizable as hiddenness and silence: the same

---

[56] 'To the Gentlewomen Citizens of London', in *The Schoole of Abuse*, sigs. F2r, F4v.

[57] The best account of this paradox's pervasiveness and theatrical complexity is Katharine E. Maus, 'Horns of Dilemma: Jealousy, Gender and Spectatorship in English Renaissance Drama', *ELH* 54.3 (1987), 561–83.

condition that Cavell says is the theatre's duty to 'literalize': 'the conditions of theater literalize the conditions we exact for existence outside—hiddenness, silence, isolation—hence make that existence plain'.[58] A second result of Hermia and Helena's inset spectatorship is thus to show what Cavell argues: that 'acknowledgement' of the suffering of others is a confirmation of 'the final fact of our separateness. And that is the unity of our condition.'[59]

There is great beauty in this philosophy. But the reason for my return to *A Midsummer Night's Dream* is the tweak that the play's women spectators administer to it, for these unscripted characters unsettle the isolation upon which Cavell's theatricality is premised. By calling on characters to disappear into the audience of an inset play's performance, *A Midsummer Night's Dream* undercuts the recognition of 'them as separate from me'—the same recognition that makes acknowledgement possible.[60] Instead it proposes an early modern English theatricality that is uncertain of its difference from the world that watches it. True, Shakespeare's women spectators do not reach across this divide as strongly as Beaumont's and Jonson's do; we cannot know if Hermia and Helena refrain from the hauteur of their male companions to avoid love's avoidance. But it is by keeping this question undecided that hiddenness and silence can shift from a tragic expression of social isolation to a practice of shared and undivided co-presence. For if, in Shakespeare's most exquisitely self-referential work, the distinction between watching a show and being a show cannot be discerned, then watching a show, no matter how inertly, should not be misread as a capitulation to a separation that cannot be breached. The silent and still spectators of 'Pryamus and Thisbe' thus suggest that if decorum is the means later stages use to keep performance and audience safely distinct, early modern English theatricality not only spurs its invention, it also uses women characters to question the truth of this divide.

FURTHER READING

Egginton, William, *How the World Became a Stage: Presence, Theatricality and the Question of Modernity* (Albany: State University of New York Press, 2003).

Lopez, Jeremy. *Theatrical Convention and Audience Response in Early Modern Drama* (New York: Cambridge University Press, 2003).

Low, Jennifer A. and Nova Myhill, eds. *Imagining the Audience in Early Modern Drama, 1558–1642* (New York: Palgrave Macmillan, 2011).

States, Bert. *Great Reckonings in Little Rooms: On the Phenomenology of the Theater* (Berkeley: University of California Press, 1985).

Tribble, Evelyn. *Cognition in the Globe: Attention and Memory in Shakespeare's Theatre* (New York: Palgrave Macmillan, 2011).

---

[58] Cavell, *Must We Mean What We Say?*, 333.   [59] Cavell, *Must We Mean What We Say?*, 339.
[60] Cavell, *Must We Mean What We Say?*, 339.

CHAPTER 17

DESIRE

MADHAVI MENON*

How do we see desire on stage? There are, of course, the obvious signs: swooning lovers swearing undying love to one another; blazons of a lover's attributes; jealous plots to frame ex-lovers or retrieve old flames; statues that move; characters who freeze; lines that exalt; rhetoric that sweeps lovers off their feet. In the theatre, all these markers of desire depend on a body on stage to deliver lines or be the recipient of them; to be bruised or praised; to swoon or soar. But how do we see desire on stage in the absence of a body? Can desire be present without a physicality to guarantee its presence? If there is no body, then can there be desire? The problem is a peculiarly theatrical one, since the theatre is the only literary arena that calls for physical bodies to enact its tales. Taking its cue from Shakespeare's *A Midsummer Night's Dream*, this essay thinks about the story of desire in the absence of a body—whether it exists and whether it can be recognized on stage as desire. Is desire always based in a material substrate, or does theatre allow us to theorize a *non-material desire*—desire without a body?

At first glance, *A Midsummer Night's Dream* might appear to be a peculiar choice of play with which to explore this question. After all, there is no dearth of bodies on stage in the play; if anything, there is an excess. The play requires so many actors that theatrical productions since Peter Brook's RSC performance in 1970 have taken to doubling the roles of Hippolyta/Theseus and Titania/Oberon. In addition to the several bodies on stage, the play also frequently discourses on bodies and their relation to desire. Take, for instance, Theseus's famous speech on the imagination in Act 5 of the play, in which he dismisses the lovers' story about their night spent together in the forest:[1]

---

* With thanks to Gina Altavilla, Jeremy Lopez, and Henry Turner.
[1] Indeed, Theseus's speech is so famous that it has been yoked in the service of several arguments—pro- and anti-art, pro- and anti-patriarchy—all of which insist on its centrality to the play. But there has also been a strand of criticism, beginning with René Girard, 'Myth and Ritual in Shakespeare: *A Midsummer Night's Dream*', in Josué V. Harari, ed., *Textual Strategies: Perspectives in Post-Structuralist Criticism* (Ithaca: Cornell University Press, 1979), 189–212, which insists that Theseus's speech is less

> *Theseus:*...The lover, all as frantic,
> Sees Helen's beauty in a brow of Egypt.
>
> ...
>
> And as imagination bodies forth
> The forms of things unknown, the poet's pen
> Turns them to shapes, and gives to airy nothing
> A local habitation and a name.
> Such tricks hath strong imagination
> That if it would but apprehend some joy
> It comprehends some bringer of that joy;
> Or in the night, imagining some fear,
> How easy is a bush supposed a bear!   (5.1.10–11, 14–22)[2]

In an argument the play explores more fully, Theseus suggests that in order to make fantasies real, people inevitably locate desire in a body. The body is concretized *by* the desiring imagination and is thus only a phantasmatic entity. Hippolyta adds, a moment later:

> But all the story of the night told over,
> And all their minds transfigured so together,
> More witnesseth than fancy's images,
> And grows to something of great constancy;
> But howsoever, strange and admirable...   (5.1.23–7)

Though they are both talking about imaginative desire and its relation to truth, Theseus and Hippolyta fundamentally disagree with one another as the very first word of Hippolyta's response—'But'—makes clear. For her, the ability to make concrete is the reason one should heed the imagination, while for Theseus it is the reason to mistrust it. Hippolyta is convinced that the imagination bestows more credibility on its narratives, not less, but for Theseus, conjuring a coherent entity in which desire can anchor itself is mere fantasy. The imagination, for Hippolyta, is far greater than the sum of its parts—the lovers' stories together testify to the 'constancy' of love—but for Theseus, this alignment among their stories only betrays the extent of their fevered imagination. According to him, the 'bodies' that imagination brings forth are shapes intended to create a causal link between a bringer of

important than Hippolyta's. For Girard, Hippolyta returns us to the idea of myth and violence that he sees as central to the play's many doublings, suggesting that what we find in Hippolyta's lines is an instance of 'Shakespeare [being] more interested in [a] systematically self-defeating type of passion than in the initial theme of "true love"' (189). For a reading that challenges the wisdom of Hippolyta as dramatic theorist, see Kathryn Schwarz, *Tough Love: Amazon Encounters in the English Renaissance* (Durham: Duke University Press, 2000), 203–35. In *Framing 'India': The Colonial Imaginary in Early Modern Culture* (Stanford: Stanford University Press, 2002), Shankar Raman makes an argument for a similarity between Oberon and Titania's attitude towards the changeling Indian boy as an exotic commodity from the East.

   [2] Unless otherwise specified, references to Shakespeare's plays are from Stephen Greenblatt, et al., eds., *The Norton Shakespeare*, 2nd edn. (New York: Norton, 2008).

joy and the joy itself where no such link exists. Imagination thus sets up a direct correspondence between happiness–bliss–joy, on the one hand, and a body responsible for producing those feelings, on the other. This correspondence is, more forcefully for Theseus than for Hippolyta, *imaginary*. In a play in which the production and identification and transformation of bodies is crucial to both plot and rhetoric, Theseus's argument about the phantasmatic bodily materialization of an imaginative desire invites us to consider its inverse correlate: the possibility of a non-material desire that is not necessarily located in a physical body.

Theseus uses the word 'joy', which of course is not desire; in fact joy is often regarded as the opposite of desire. But the psychoanalytic term *jouissance*, which describes both pain and joy, forges a link between joy and desire in which the latter tempers the merely happy associations of the former. Untranslatable as either the one or the other, much like Theseus's speech, *jouissance* is often rendered as joy, but it is also the sundering of that joy, the moment at which one gets a glimpse of non-being and non-meaning. Describing it in Lacanian terms as the 'unnameable' remainder of the Real in the Symbolic, Lee Edelman argues that 'jouissance, sometimes translated as "enjoyment"', is 'a movement beyond the pleasure principle, beyond the distinction of pleasure and pain, a violent passage beyond the bounds of identity, meaning, and law. This passage… may have the effect, insofar as it gets attached to a particular object or end, of congealing identity around the fantasy of satisfaction or fulfillment by means of that object.'[3] In Lacanian terms, the embodied 'joy' of which Theseus speaks is the congealed object of desire, a phantasmatic solidity conjured up to tie down the 'unknown[ness]' of desire.

Might we name this congealed solidity the body? As a single name given to a collection of limbs and feelings, the body stands in a privileged relation to the self. Despite being dismissed by Descartes as the unreliable barometer of the mind's truth, bodies have made a spectacular comeback in our theoretical discourse as the basis on which identity is measured. No matter how many its peculiarities and inconsistencies, 'the body' is understood as superimposing a regime of singular legibility over it all.[4] In the case of desire, the status of the body is considered the paramount marker of identity—what a body *is* explains its desire, and then our desire for it. So what do we do with a body in *A Midsummer Night's Dream* in relation to which much desire is generated, but which is imaginary to the extent that it does not exist in the text *as* a body? A body that does not 'grow to something of

---

[3] Lee Edelman, *No Future: Queer Theory and the Death Drive* (Durham: Duke University Press, 2004), 25.

[4] Jacques Lacan's theory of the mirror stage suggests that an 'armour' is placed around the 'body in bits and pieces' as the self begins to form itself. This is done in order that the body—and by extension, the self—may be considered a uniform whole despite evidence to the contrary. See his essay on 'The Mirror Stage as Formative of the Function of the I', in *Ecrits: A Selection*, trans. Alan Sheridan (New York: W. W. Norton, 1982), 1–6.

great constancy' 'howsoever strange and admirable' its trace in the play? I am speaking about the Indian boy, the subject of Oberon and Titania's quarrel, who never appears in a speaking or non-speaking part in the text as written but who occupies significant time in the play as the subject of much conversation, since he is frequently invoked as the cause of Titania and Oberon's estrangement from one another.[5]

The boy's present yet non-materialized body performs a crucial theatrical function. From the point of view of the text, *none* of the characters has a body: they are all imaginary and implied, except insofar as the language designates physical features or an actual presence. The boy's physical absence from the playtext thus makes even more visible the fictive and 'imaginary' (in Theseus's sense) condition of the body itself. Contrary to what we often believe, characters do not actually exist on stage in bodily form—the actor's body simply takes on the character, and the boy's absent body makes this imaginary condition of all bodies in the playtext especially evident. But despite not having a body—or having only an imaginary one—the boy performatively occupies significant time on both page and stage. So why does the playtext not produce him as a fully-materialized physical body?

Generations of directors of the play have solved this puzzle simply by *materializing* the absent body and creating the Indian boy as a character on stage and on screen. The boy is never given any words, of course, but he is inevitably presented as beautiful, desirable, and mysteriously exotic. Scholars of race and colonialism have critiqued this representation as being imperialistic by reducing the Indian boy to an exotic spectacle.[6] While this may be true of certain productions, what is even more interesting is that the absence of the Indian boy from the text, the inability to conjure him from airy nothingness, creates an anxiety among textual interpreters that assuages itself by insisting on producing an object—the more spectacular the better. To ensure that the moving force behind Oberon and Titania's desire does indeed have a body, productions either exoticize the boy—not only does he have a body, but what a body it is!—or infantilize it: as if to say—'pardon the intrusion, but might we suggest the existence at least of a small body, easy to ignore, but nonetheless materially present in its embodiment?' No matter whether he is big or small, fully-dressed or naked, the embodied Indian boy is necessarily spectacular because he has nothing to do other than *be*, nothing to offer other than be *seen*. By frequently exaggerating his physical contours and making him alluring—larger than life and exotic, because that is what they assume desire looks like—productions insist on the boy's bodily presence in order to explain the desire generated by him. The 'fault' of such embodiments is not that they might be more or less racist, but

---

[5] The changeling boy is, in Shankar Raman's words, 'conspicuous only as an absent center'. Raman, *Framing 'India': The Colonial Imaginary in Early Modern Culture* (Stanford: Stanford University Press, 2002), 242.

[6] See Margo Hendricks, '"Obscured by dreams": Race, Empire, and Shakespeare's A Midsummer Night's Dream', *Shakespeare Quarterly* 47.1 (Spring 1996), 37–60.

that they are all *anxious*. And far from being a fault, this anxiety rather points to a fault-line in notions of desire that the play mines in several different ways.

There are thus two different modes of theatricality operating around the physically absent body of the changeling boy. We might hypothetically attribute the first to 'Shakespeare' and the second to 'later productions'. The first use of theatricality might hold the boy 'off-stage' as always invisible, in this way accentuating and making even more visible the imaginary, non-self-present nature of *all* bodies in the play, especially when in a condition of desire. This first use of theatricality marks the body as absent—and in doing so marks desire, and theatricality in general as a condition of desire, as *non-material*. This non-material, absent condition is also non-logical, non-causal, non-referential, and non-locatable. It implies a certain rupturing of the subject, a rupturing that is effected in several ways: by splitting the 'self' from the 'body', and by refusing a clear object for desire. The second use of theatricality would try to foreclose this theoretical insight by bringing *some* kind of physical body on-stage. It tries to assert desire (and theatre) as being physical and material, as referential, as 'caused' and contained and located. The decision about whether or not to physically produce the changeling boy on stage is thus crucial to thinking about the body and its relation to desire.

Absent body, present desire

Who is this changeling Indian boy whom no one sees—and perhaps more crucially, no character seems bothered by not seeing—in the play? While some scholars have been interested in thinking of the absence of the Indian boy as an erasure of the explicit histories of colonialism and trade from the play, I am interested, first, in the relation between his absence and the desire he nonetheless generates, and second, in the anxiety that causes productions to make his body present. The boy is introduced to us by Puck when the sprite describes the changeling's role in the fight between his master and mistress. We then see both Oberon and Titania discourse variously about the boy, the one asking for his handover, and the other one refusing it. We even get a lyrical description of his existence *in utero*, when his mother is pregnant with the foetus; but we never get a body. I do not want to speculate on the reasons why Shakespeare withholds the body of the Indian boy from us when he could have been such an interesting character.[7] But I do want to note that from the very beginning of his appearance in the play, the boy is

---

[7] According to Barry Weller's reading, in 'Identity Dis-figured: A Midsummer Night's Dream', *The Kenyon Review* 7.3 (Summer 1985), this withholding might provide fodder for the argument about Shakespeare as a sceptic of visuality: 'Shakespeare nevertheless finds a range of other ways in which to express his suspicion of the corporeal—or more broadly, the visual—and the literal mindedness into which it betrays those who trust it' (69).

positioned between presence-as-absence (his mother, now dead, then pregnant) and absence-as-presence (himself). Rather than recuperating bodily presence as the essential basis of desire, that without which desire cannot exist, I would like to argue that *A Midsummer Night's Dream* problematizes the causal link we normally attribute to that relation by giving us a non-material desire that cannot be grounded in a body.

Despite or because of not having a body, the Indian boy is always positioned in the space and time of desire. This desire attaches to him synecdochally in the mode of nostalgia—the description of his pregnant mother swimming in the perfumed and spicy Indian air—as well as practically—Oberon wants him as his page-boy, Titania wants him in her entourage. The Indian boy is desired, certainly, but in the play, this desire also *ensures* his absence, or rather, his absence is the very theme of his desirability. Titania has 'stol'n' him from an Indian king, and Oberon in turn steals the boy from Titania. Whether in India or the woods, with men or women, the boy is repeatedly configured as a thing that is lost, stolen, and even hijacked. Standing at that intersection of an absent presence and a present absence, the Indian boy is always lost from view. He cannot exist except as the backdrop to the drama, even as he is also its ostensible cause. After all, without him, Titania and Oberon would have nothing to quarrel over, the Athenian lovers would go unremarked by Oberon in the forest, Puck would not be sent to get the love potion, Bottom would not be translated into an ass, and the play within the play would not have its audience of multiple newly-weds (surely Hermia would either have been languishing in a convent, or else living outside Athens with Lysander?). Without the Indian boy, the shape of the play (its body?) would have been very different.

Even in the earliest detailed record of a production of the play—Henry Purcell's 1692 opera, *The Fairy Queen*—the Indian boy is produced as an elaborate part of the play's *machinery*. I use this word advisedly: as something that makes the play work, and that explains the workings of the play, the Indian boy is a crucial component of the production. Without him, desire cannot be explained in this play. With him, not only can it be explained, but it can also be staged. The Indian boy allows us to *see* desire and to see it as the condition of sight itself, as the material body without which, supposedly, the play cannot be seen.

Given his importance on both page and stage, then, it is only fitting that we also have a narrative about *why* he matters so much to Titania and Oberon. His life has been exchanged for his mother's—we are told that his mother died while giving birth to him—and she was a beloved votaress of Titania's. It is this exchange that gives the boy value for Titania because she wants him as a remembrance of his mother. And it is his value for Titania, we presume, that makes Oberon covet him as his own. Or maybe it is the boy's good looks, his cuteness, that attracts both Titania and Oberon, but this is precisely what we cannot know, since we never *see* the boy in the text and never get a description of him that extends beyond the adjectives 'lovely' and 'sweet'. This sweet and lovely boy, the cause of both discord and concord in the play, of 'joy' in both Theseus's and Lacan's sense of the word, does not have a body, yet it is his body that Oberon, Titania, and audiences over the years, have insistently *wanted*.

Why do we want this body? Why do we desire this body? And if, in Barry Weller's words, '[n]o theatrical fact is more unavoidable than the actor's body' (67), then why does Shakespeare avoid giving us this particular body in *A Midsummer Night's Dream*? The absent changeling child, who is both absent from the play and standing in lieu of someone or something else, does not make for a positive presence. And this lack of a positive presence begs two primary questions that Alain Badiou asks in his *Metapolitics*. First: Is it 'possible to think *subjectivity without a subject*'?[8] Is it possible to think desire without a body? Or rather, what does a body take away from our thinking about desire? By presenting us with an absent body that is very present in its effects, Shakespeare's play provides the perfect setting for thinking about this conundrum: how do we feel, recognize, and identify desire without causal reference to a material body? And second: how, exactly, are we to think about this conundrum? For Badiou, 'the whole problem is to think thought as *thought* and not as object; or again, to think that which is thought in thought, and not "that which" (the object) thought thinks'.[9] How to theatrically represent a thought—especially a thought of desire—without immediately converting it into an object? How to theatrically represent desire without immediately producing a character on stage? How to retain the drama of desire without a body?

In his introduction to the *Norton* edition of the play, Stephen Greenblatt encapsulates the commonplace understanding of desire: 'No human being in the play experiences a purely abstract, objectless desire; when you desire, you desire *someone*'.[10] It seems but a short step from the idea of desiring *someone* to desiring someone's *body*, even though as the frequent conversation about 'types' makes very clear—as in 'who or what is your type?'—this body is never reducible to or contained by only one person. Even in our day-to-day understandings, then, desire cannot be localized in a body. Rather, we seem to desire things as small as individual attributes, traits, and features, or as large as race, gender, and class, more than a body. 'The body' is both more and less than what we desire: more because we never desire it in its entirety, and less because we want it to embody all the traits we find attractive. Either way, desire for a body is a notoriously slippery phenomenon, since it rarely translates backward or forward into desire for a person, and even less for a person who can only be identified with that body. But this slipperiness of the body compels with even more urgency the need to produce a body that can claim and *own* desire. After all, a disembodied desire is rather like a changeling child—one never knows who the rightful owner is.

---

[8]   Alain Badiou, *Metapolitics*, trans. Jason Barker (London: Verso, 2005), 64.
[9]   Badiou, *Metapolitics*, 27.
[10]   Greenblatt, et al., eds., *The Norton Shakespeare*, 810.

Let us, for a moment, examine this question of bodily desire from the opposite end: how *does* a body help us to feel, recognize, and identify desire? Quite clearly, it permits us to make decisions based on visible markers: gender, race, ethnicity, and ability. If we identify as homosexual, then it becomes easy to recognize a member of the 'same' sex in order to assess one's level of attraction, and the same goes for all other categories of visibility. Incredibly, the overwhelming majority of the world's population tends to have *homo* relationships in this etymological sense of the word—like attracting like—whether in terms of race, ethnicity, class, or sexuality. This means that for the vast majority of us, desire traces itself along trajectories of identifiable similarities.[11] What a body 'does' is tell us who to choose: making a choice in the absence of a body seems like a nonsensical, even illogical, thing to do. Indeed, the absence of a body does not allow us to know who or what to desire. It takes away from us what we like to cherish as our 'choice', and in the process, allows us to see that what we used to think of as choice is not choice at all, but rather a forced consensus. We 'choose' based on what we perceive certain bodies to be; by converting bodies into identifiable categories, we perform the very translation that in the play turns Bottom into an ass—we translate the constraints on our choice into choice itself, and consider ourselves lucky to be able to do so. This is perhaps why even verbal markers of identity—names, indicators of religion, political opinions—are increasingly being translated into the register of the *visible*—skin colour, head scarves, tattoos. Verbal markers exist, and provide an identity, but that identity is not satisfying enough; it is too disembodied, too abstract, and has to be converted into a picture, an image, in order to be accessible. Almost all online romance websites insist on a photograph—not only to testify to an individual's particular looks, but also to ensure that the person matches up to the verbal description of him or herself. The valorization of the visual over the verbal in the service of *verifiable* object-choice is one of the most immediate reasons that productions of *A Midsummer Night's Dream* feel compelled to produce the Indian boy on stage and screen.

But if the body constrains rather than opens up the realm of our choice in desire, then what do we gain from having it? The obvious answer, as I have already suggested, is that we do not really want choice, what we want are constraints on choice that simplify for us which bodies do and do not lie within the realm of 'our' desire. This is why clinical tests of self-identified homophobic men yield such interesting results (the subjects were repeatedly aroused by gay male porn).[12] The horror—could

---

[11] Sara Ahmed, *Queer Phenomenology: Orientations, Objects, Others* (Durham: Duke University Press, 2006), 156: 'We don't know, as yet, what shape such a world might take, or what mixtures might be possible, when we no longer reproduce the lines we follow'.

[12] See 'Calling Out the "Blatant Bigotry" of NeoCon Editor & Fox Man Bill "I'm afraid of gays" Krystal: The Economist', http://fuhgetabotit.newsvine.com/_news/2010/02/03/3849926-calling-out-the-blatant-bigotry-of-neocon-editor-fox-man-bill-im-afraid-of-gays-krystal-the-economist (accessed June 2011). Also see the *New York Times* article, 'Homophobic? Maybe You're Gay', by Richard M. Ryan and William S. Ryan, that appeared on 29 April 2012: http://www.nytimes.com/2012/04/29/opinion/sunday/homophobic-maybe-youre-gay.html?_r=1 (accessed Nov. 2012).

we call it the *jouissance*?—resulting from these tests testifies to the horror of inter-
rupting the relation between bodies and desires. If 'our' desires do not match 'our'
bodies, then the resulting immateriality of our identities—as gay or straight or black
or white or whatever—is horrifying for two reasons. First, because of how much we
invest in the causal coupling of bodies and desires; and second, because of how convinced we are that our bodies are our 'selves'. Bodies tell us whom and what to desire,
and they tell us whom and what we desire; without a body we would neither know
nor be able to explain desire.

If we turn back now to the original version of the question of the relation between
body and desire—not what do bodies tell us about desire, but what does the *absence*
of the theatrical body tell us about desire—then we return also to the changeling
Indian boy and his present-absent body in the play. The absence of the Indian boy is
clear enough for us to understand—he does not appear physically in the text—but
his presence is even more crucial to comprehend. He is present, not only because his
name is invoked repeatedly between Oberon and Titania, but also because this invocation highlights the desire to read his role as *cause* in the play. After all, this play, like
all others, draws a connection between cause and effect such that the text has a logical
structure even when it is dealing with fairies rather than human beings. Such logic
does not have to be mathematically precise, but it does need to tell us, for instance,
why someone has been exiled if indeed he or she has been. Or why actors would
abandon their co-star when they do. Or what causes lovers to run away from family
and city when they do. No matter how flimsy the cause, there has to be one. And so
the Indian boy is conjured up to explain the cause of the fight between Titania and
Oberon which is also therefore the cause of major discord and concord in the play.

Except that the changeling boy does not present himself as an embodied cause of
desire.[13] Instead of underlining the importance of causality, his absence underlines
the importance of divorcing desire from a body that can be named as its cause.
While plot details might need to follow the logic of cause and effect, theatrical desire
does not. And so even as the boy 'explains' the stand-off between Titania and
Oberon, he cannot explain their desire for him. The boy without a body becomes
present only as a missing cause. If his presence in the play is synonymous with causality of plot, then his absence insists on a lack of causality in desire. The missing
body of the changeling Indian boy is paradoxically the cause of non-causal desire in
the play. Or rather, the missing object of desire suggests that desire cannot be pinned
down to a cause. In this play, absence itself has a causative power in relation to
desire, but this 'causality' gets mystified through the phantasmatic imposition in
theatrical productions of a body to make the absence present.

Indeed, if absence can be ascribed causality, then it is only in a way that unsettles
the very notion of cause as originary presence. Even a cursory look at the rest of the

---

[13] According to Raman, he exists 'both as cause and resolution of the play's dramatic action' (*Framing India*, 242).

play reveals that this is a pattern: desire in *A Midsummer Night's Dream* never follows the laws of cause and effect because there is always something missing in causal explanations of desire. For instance, when Helena begs Hermia to tell the secret of her attractiveness to Demetrius, Hermia responds by saying: 'I frown upon him, yet he loves me still' (1.1.194). And when Helena obsessively follows Demetrius into the woods, the man of her dreams says:

> *Demetrius*: ...do I not in plainest truth
> Tell you I do not nor I cannot love you?
> *Helena*: And even for that do I love you the more.   (2.1.200–2)

These passages do not explain desire; on the contrary, they insist on its lack of identifiable causality. In *Midsummer Night's Dream*, though much is made of the physical differences between Hermia and Helena—one is short and the other tall, for instance—that difference gets far less space than the insistence on their sameness. In the lyrical description of their love—'Two lovely berries moulded on one stem' (3.2.211)—and even before, they are described as being absolutely identical: 'Through Athens I am thought as fair as she' (1.1.227), notes Helena. Their bodies are not differentiable enough to provide the answer to the question of why one man might prefer one of them over the other; their bodies do not provide the much-sought after *cause* of love.

Even more, the physicality of appearance is repeatedly rendered suspect as a means of identification in the play. When upbraided by Oberon for having anointed the wrong man with the love juice, Puck says in his defence:

> *Robin*: Believe me, king of shadows, I mistook.
> Did not you tell me I should know the man
> By the Athenian garments he had on?   (3.2.348–50)

In this text, the body suggests not only a lack of differentiation—Lysander and Demetrius look startlingly alike, down to the clothes they wear—but also a lack of causality as the basis on which to understand desire. Hermia's preference for Lysander over Demetrius seems inexplicable to everyone. Demetrius's preference for Hermia over Helena seems inexplicable. Titania's 'choice' of Bottom with his ass's head is absurd. And Hippolyta's 'choice' of Theseus seems unmotivated. Bodies in the play do not explain or cause desire—if anything, the *absence* of bodies foments the most intense and consequential desire in *A Midsummer Night's Dream*. The absent body plots the play for us, and agrees with Theseus's dismissal of the imaginary body that desire conjures up to explain itself. This dismissal marks a break from, and interrupts, our normal association of causality among bodies, selves, and desires. For Alain Badiou, 'All resistance is a rupture with what is. And every rupture begins, for those engaged in it, through a rupture with oneself'.[14] As subject for a queer theory that would chart a somewhat different course from an

---

[14] Badiou, *Metapolitics*, 7.

identitarian gay and lesbian studies, this play's insistence on the non-material body provides plenty of food for thought.

Spectres of theatre

Despite not appearing as a character in either the Folio (1623) or Quarto (1600) editions of the play, the changeling boy has been a fixture on the *Midsummer Night's Dream* stage from the beginning of its production history. Indeed, one might argue that his backstory is so well fleshed-out in the text that it remains only to give him a local bodily habitation for him to come to life. I want to look now at the theatrical history of the changeling boy in *A Midsummer Night's Dream*, as well as at some other Renaissance renditions of absent object causes of desire. Startlingly, as we shall see, Shakespeare might have been alone in his day to opt for a non-material mode of representing desire on stage.

Currently one of Shakespeare's most frequently performed plays, *A Midsummer Night's Dream* was never seen in its entirety between 1642 and 1840.[15] Instead, directors broke off chunks of the play as it pleased them—in 1716 and 1745 the play became *Pyramus and Thisbe*, in 1755 *The Fairies*, and in 1661 *The Merry Conceited Humours of Bottom the Weaver*. But the most spectacular production was that of Purcell's *The Fairy Queen*. There are no records to indicate whether or not this was the boy's first appearance, but it is the first recorded one—according to Gary Jay Williams, '[w]e can firmly establish the presence of the Indian boy on stage in Purcell's 1692 opera'[16]—and also the most colourful. Suggesting that their love of spectacle would not have allowed theatre companies to miss out on the 'opportunity to use an attractive child, at least in an early scene', Williams goes on to give us details derived from a variant issue of the libretto: 'Titania enters first, "leading the Indian boy, fairies attending." When a sentinel enters to warn that Oberon is coming, she commands the earth to open and receive the Indian boy. Judging from the next stage direction, "He sinks," it did. Oberon then enters in perplexed pursuit of the boy.'[17] In 1816, Frederic Reynolds's operatic adaptation of the play elaborately staged the journey of the Indian boy from India to England, and his handover to Oberon.[18]

---

[15] Gary Jay Williams, *Our Moonlight Revels: A Midsummer Night's Dream in the Theatre* (Iowa City: University of Iowa Press, 1997), 38. According to Trevor D. Griffiths in *Shakespeare in Production: A Midsummer Night's Dream* (Cambridge: Cambridge University Press, 1996), 'there are only two known productions of the play under its own name between 1660 and the 1816 production by Frederic Reynolds (1).

[16] Williams, *Our Moonlight Revels*, 24.   [17] Williams, *Our Moonlight Revels*, 47.

[18] As Raman puts it, '[The Indian boy's] absence is nothing less than the immense distance that separates Europe from India, a distance double figured as death. His presence is nothing less than a bridging of that distance in the form of Europe's consumption of Eastern wares: Titania will not "part" with the boy because she has made him part of her' (*Framing India*, 244).

These intricately staged renditions of the changeling boy seem eager to make physically material what the play has already given us in rich narrative detail. However, if this is indeed the case, then we are hard pressed to explain why performances that cut out the boy's narrative backstory continue to produce him as a material character on stage.

In several nineteenth-century productions, for instance, the play's account of Titania's attachment to the boy and to his mother is excised. Without these lines the centrality of the changeling boy to the play is in jeopardy, and the mystery surrounding Titania's relationship with her votaress is removed. The passage is crucial to thinking about theatricality in Shakespeare's text, since it gives us two absent bodies and the heated desire nonetheless generated by them. This exchange between Oberon and Titania begins with Titania's complaint that their dissension has thrown the entire world—seasons, people, everything—into turmoil. Oberon in turn retorts sharply:

> Do you amend it then; it lies in you:
> Why should Titania cross her Oberon?
> I do but beg a little changeling boy,
> To be my henchman.   (2.1.17–20)

To which Titania responds:

> Set your heart at rest:
> The fairy land buys not the child of me.
> His mother was a votaress of my order:
> And, in the spiced Indian air, by night,
> Full often hath she gossip'd by my side,
> And sat with me on Neptune's yellow sands,
> Marking the embarked traders on the flood,
> When we have laugh'd to see the sails conceive
> And grow big-bellied with the wanton wind;
> Which she, with pretty and with swimming gait
> Following—her womb then rich with my young squire—
> Would imitate, and sail upon the land,
> To fetch me trifles, and return again,
> As from a voyage, rich with merchandise.
> But she, being mortal, of that boy did die;
> And for her sake do I rear up her boy;
> And for her sake I will not part with him.   (2.1.121–37)

Titania's response to Oberon gives us the entire story of the changeling boy and his mother; its excision removes the narrative details that present the boy in the play. Trevor D. Griffiths suggests that one reason for this censorship could be propriety (the votaress seems to be pregnant out of wedlock), and another could be colonialism (productions may not have wanted to humanize Indians while busy with the national project of also subjugating them). Gary Jay Williams agrees with this latter explanation: 'In nineteenth-century productions…the presence of the Indian boy become[s] more problematic, not only because this passage is cut…but also because of the context of the unmistakable scenic images of empire the pictorial stage will provide'.[19]

And so the votaress disappears but the boy appears. It is crucial to note that of the cast of two absent characters in the play, one is routinely forgotten and the other is regularly made present. Even if part of the explanation for this might lie in the fact that early productions felt it violated theatrical decorum to show an unmarried pregnant woman on stage, the more important factor, I think, is that the votaress is not the subject of desire between Oberon and Titania, and therefore, does not need to be made material. Titania's desire for the votaress does not translate into desire in and for the play; instead, the changeling child becomes the unseen scene of debate, the unmarked remark between Oberon and Titania. That almost no production of the play is complete without the production of the Indian boy—whether or not the lines about his lineage make it to the stage—attests to the anxiogenic nature of objectless desire: if Titania and Oberon want the boy, then we need to know what he looks like. It also suggests the lack of necessity in providing desire with a backstory: as long as desire has a visible object, it can be understood. Narrative plays a secondary role in thinking about desire, especially, it would seem, when that desire is being presented on stage.

These ideas raised by the absent body undergird the text of the play. As Barry Weller points out, '[t]he fact of embodiment is an obvious resource to a playwright: the audience will grant at least the existence of his character before a word has been spoken'.[20] But, he goes on to add, 'Shakespeare nevertheless finds a range of other ways in which to express his suspicion of the corporeal—or more broadly, the visual—and the literal mindedness into which it betrays those who trust it'.[21]

Is this non-corporeal, non-material, approach to theatrical desire unique to Shakespeare? The short answer is that I do not know, even though the case for Shakespeare's uniqueness seems strong. In addition to A Midsummer Night's Dream, he has two other plays in which the object-cause of desire is not presented as an object or a cause. In Romeo and Juliet, Romeo's first love Rosaline is presented as central in the first two Acts of the play, yet she is not part of the cast of characters in either of the first two quartos (1597, 1599) or the Folio (1623), and also disappears from the narrative of the last three Acts of the play. She is sometimes made present in stage productions of the play: Henry Irving's 1882 production of Romeo and Juliet in New York City featured a 'black-haired Rosaline and her companions',[22] and many twentieth- and twenty-first-century productions continue to produce

---

[19] Williams, Our Moonlight Revels, 24–5. Griffiths notes that despite the excision of this passage, '[t]he changeling child (the Indian boy) was a fixture in nineteenth-century productions' of the play (Shakespeare in Production, 126).

[20] Weller, 'Identity Dis-figured', 67.   [21] Weller, 'Identity Dis-figured', 69.

[22] From a review of the production in The New York Times on 26 March 1882.

Rosaline on stage. Interestingly, in the 1748 David Garrick edition of the play, Rosaline appears in the playbook but not in the prompt-book. In this text, the Act 2 Scene 3 conversation between Romeo and the Friar reads as follows:

> *Romeo*: She whom now I love,
> Doth give me grace for grace,
> And love for love.
> The other did not so—.

In his 1750 edition of the play, Garrick omits the last line's reference to Rosaline. Similarly, in the 1748 text, the Friar reacts with horror to Romeo's desire to marry Juliet:

> Holy Saint *Francis*, what a change is here?
> Is *Rosaline*, whom thou didst love so dearly,
> So soon forsaken?
> *Jesu Maria!* What a flood of tears.

But the 1750 speech reads:

> Holy Saint *Francis*, what a change is here!
> But tell me, son, and call your reason home,
> Is not this love the offspring of thy folly,
> Bred from thy wantonness and thoughtless brain?
> Be heedful, youth, and see you stop betimes,
> Lest that thy rash ungovernable passions,
> O'er-leaping duty, and each due regard...

The two changes between 1748 and 1750 both involve Rosaline. In the first, Romeo suggests Rosaline's lack of reciprocity is responsible for making him turn to Juliet, but the revised version omits any mention of Rosaline. In the second, the Friar moves from mentioning Rosaline as the former recipient of Romeo's love to eliding her name altogether. Taken together, these changes explicitly remove Rosaline as cause of Romeo's present and past desires. Her narrative presence in *Romeo and Juliet* consists mostly of providing the background plot for Romeo's love—she is the cause of Romeo's broken heart, and therefore in turn of the love he subsequently feels for Juliet. But it also provides a point of origin in relation to which the intensity of Romeo's love for Juliet can be measured, and this is often how Rosaline is read in the play: as the false start in the hero's career of love. No matter what his motives, Garrick's excision of Rosaline in this scene thus halts both the causal explanation of Romeo's love (if she is not physically present as a character in the text, then she can have no causal control over desire in the play), and the teleological charge of desire (in which Romeo moves from non-reciprocity with Rosaline to fulfilment with Juliet).[23] Rosaline's physical absence from the text suggests that desire is a moving

---

[23] In his 1748 Preface, Garrick says: 'Many people have imagin'd that the sudden change of Romeo's love from Rosaline to Juliet was a blemish in his character, but an alteration of that kind was thought

finger that writes, and having writ, moves on. Bringing in a body to substantialize that writing ignores the relation between desire and absence by insisting on an anchor to make the writing *manifest*.

The other notable example of such a strong desire that moulds the play through absence is in *The Two Noble Kinsmen*, commonly attributed jointly to Shakespeare and John Fletcher. Often cited for its portrayal of the intense homoerotic bond between Palamon and Arcite, the play (sourced from the same Theseus–Hippolyta story as *A Midsummer Night's Dream*) has also been noted for its depiction of a bond between women that rivals the description of Hermia and Helena's relationship. When Hippolita speaks of the intense love between the men in the play, her sister Emilia reminisces about her own love story:

> *Emilia*: …And she I sigh and spoke of were things innocent,
> Loved for we did, and, like the elements,
> That know not what, nor why, yet do effect
> Rare issues by their operance, our souls
> Did so to one another. What she liked
> Was then of me approved; what not, condemned—
> No more arraignment…
> …This rehearsal—
> Which, seely innocent wots well, comes in
> Like old emportment's bastard—has this end:
> That the true love 'tween maid, and maid may be
> More than in sex dividual.
> *Hippolita*: You're out of breath
> And this high speeded pace is but to say
> That you shall never, like the maid Flavina,
> Love any that's called man.
> *Emilia*: I am sure I shall not.
> *Hippolita*: Now, alack, weak sister,
> I must no more believe thee in this point…
> …But sure, my sister,
> If I were ripe for your persuasion, you
> Have said enough to shake me from the arm
> Of the all noble Theseus…
> *Emilia*: I am not
> Against your faith, yet I continue mine.   (1.3.60–6, 78–88, 91–4, 98–9)

It seems clear that Hippolita stands on the brink of 'conversion' to a 'faith' that prevents Emilia from being attracted to men. This is not the way in which the play

---

too bold to be attempted…'. In his 1750 preface, Garrick changes his tune completely to say: 'it was generally thought that the sudden change of Romeo's love from Rosaline to Juliet was a blemish in his character, and therefore it is to be hoped that an alteration in that particular matter be excused…'. Rosaline's behaviour towards Romeo is no longer in 2.3 cited as the cause of Romeo's change of affections.

ends, of course (Hippolita is married to Theseus, and Emilia, after many twists and turns, to Palamon), but it uses an absent character to signal its relation to dissident desire. Despite its heterosexual endings, *The Two Noble Kinsmen* is arguably one of the queerest plays in the Shakespearean canon; this queerness is due not only to the intense affective bond between Palamon and Arcite, but also and more interestingly, to the absent Flavina whose love prompts Emilia's lack of interest in men.

Neither Rosaline nor Flavina exists physically on stage, but they both excite desire. Indeed, their absence can be read as Shakespeare's insistence on a lack of causality in desire, an argument that emerges also in plays that do not have an explicitly absent character. In *Othello*, for instance, a deluded protagonist prepares to murder his wife on the grounds of alleged sexual infidelity. But even as Othello approaches Desdemona's chamber to strangle her, he cannot explain either his desire or hers, and this lack of explanation emerges as a confusion around the very idea of a cause: 'It is the cause, it is the cause, my soul; / Let me not name it to you, you chaste stars! / It is the cause' (5.1.1–3). What, one wants to ask, is the cause, and of what? But this is precisely the question that cannot be answered in any of Shakespeare's texts that deal with desire, which is to say in all his texts. *Othello* is unable to give us a cause for desire and unable also to give us a cause for the murderous end of desire. Etymologically sharing a root with the French *chose*, i.e. thing or object, cause in all these plays is the absent 'thing' that is not a *chose*, not a presence. The bodily basis of Desdemona and Othello's desire is dismissed by everyone in the play as unseemly, and there is no bodily proof that Desdemona has been unfaithful to Othello. In not depending on bodily presence as cause in the play, theatrical desire also refuses to adhere to material norms by which it can be seen and recognized as desire.

This relation between material absence and desire, writ large in several Shakespeare plays, is hard to find in the non-Shakespearean drama of the Renaissance. Indeed, the only absent characters I have found are both babies—relatives of the *Dream*'s changeling child?—who exist primarily for purposes of plot rather than to suggest the non-material basis of desire. In Webster and Rowley's *A Cure for a Cuckold* (1624–5), for instance, the sailor Compass returns from four years at sea to learn that his wife has had a child by another man. Despite this startling fact, Compass finds his bearings quickly and decides he will raise the child as his own. The biological father objects because he has purchased some land he wants to pass on to the child (his own wife cannot have children). There are two scenes where the child's custody is debated, but the baby itself never appears. There is, however, a stage direction in the final scene indicating that the baby is finally brought on, though we have no evidence to show whether such a character was produced or not. Even while largely absent, then, *A Cure for a Cuckold* indicates the presence of the baby at the end of its play, in stark contrast to *A Midsummer Night's Dream*'s resolute resistance to making visible the object-cause of desire.

In Thomas May's *The Heir* (1621), Francisco wants to marry Luce even though her father objects to the difference in their social status (his is low, hers is high). The first time we see these three characters in the play, the lovers are being upbraided by Luce's father because Francisco has got Luce pregnant. Far from letting this persuade him to let them get married, the father decides that he is going to convince Luce's rich and foolish suitor that the child is actually his, even though that suitor (whose name is Shallow) has never touched Luce. This works, because the suitor is quite foolish, and so for a while it seems like Shallow will marry Luce. Various complications and tricks ensue, and in the end Francisco and Luce get married. Luce's father accepts what has happened but says that they will never get a penny from him, adding dismissively that the baby is the only thing his daughter will get out of her marriage. At this point Luce and Francisco reveal that the 'baby' has been a pillow all along—they had faked the pregnancy in order to try and force the father's consent.

This baby does not appear on stage at all—there is not even a stage direction towards the end that indicates its presence—and certainly it acts in the interests of the lovers' desire. But even though the desires in this play are dissident in terms of class structure, the absent character does not highlight that dissidence. Instead the baby seems to exist simply as a plot device: the making explicit of its fakeness testifies also to its lack of importance at any level other than that of plot in the play.

Non-material desire

The absent cause of desire and the inability to correlate desire to a fixed body thus seems to be a hallmark specifically of Shakespearean theatricality. Posing insistently the question of what causes desire and how we can recognize it, *A Midsummer Night's Dream* suggests daringly that desire might not produce an identity we can use as the basis of subjectivity. Desire might also not produce objects that we can term material in any way because the absent body never materializes on the page. In making this suggestion, Shakespeare seems to anticipate in his own theatrical vocabulary Badiou's query to philosophy: '[h]ow can a philosophy be established within a theory of the *objectless* subject, while holding firmly to the demands of rationalism, i.e. of materialism'?[24] Materialization would seem to be the bottom-line for any understanding of subjects and objects of desire. But in *A Midsummer Night's Dream* (and *Romeo and Juliet* and *Two Noble Kinsmen*), as we have seen, it is precisely this materialization of desire that is absent. One could argue that it is only the bodily materialization that is missing: in all three texts, the subject is present as a name or title—the Indian boy/changeling child, Rosaline, Flavina. But can a name confer subjectivity? Can 'the (simple) name [rather be] that which "opens up" thought, and which must be maintained throughout the investigation, without ever

---

[24] Badiou, *Metapolitics*, 28.

being "objectified" by a definition or a referent'?[25] What exactly would it mean to maintain a name without defining it, to name a character without materializing it? In a very real sense, each character on stage always has two bodies: that of the actor and that of the character. The character's body remains shadowy—it cannot exist as an independent ontological entity. By not bringing the boy's body on stage, the play theorizes 'character' itself as the thing that *does not ever have a body*. To understand 'character' as an ontological thing is to understand it as dis-embodied: 'character' is another word for that being whose body is always absent and for whom this absence is a condition of existence. In this sense, no 'character' can ever be materialized on stage as a body. Theatricality, then, names that condition of desire in which the body is non-material. Theatrical desire neither confers subjectivity nor materializes objects.

Indeed, it also makes murky the very distinction between subjects and objects. If we are used to thinking of subjects as human beings with agency and objects as inanimate goods (or unlucky human beings) devoid of agency, then Shakespeare's use of the changeling boy calls that distinction into question. Who or what is the changeling boy? A subject with agency who causes strife in the world of fairy, or an object on which unwanted attention is concentrated? What or who are Oberon and Titania: subjects who have sway in the fairy world, or objects helplessly in the grip of desire for the Indian boy?[26] A Midsummer Night's Dream disturbs the distinction between subjects and objects in the realm of desire, just as it unsettles also distinctions of form (high and low) and genre (comedy and tragedy) and person (human and non-human). As these muddled distinctions suggest, desire in A Midsummer Night's Dream seems to possess the ability of converting subjects into objects and vice versa. The unseen boy has a powerful effect in the play while Oberon and Titania seem to spin out of control. If we assume that desire confers subjectivity, then the play argues that far from granting agency, it turns subjects into objects. The 'simple name' or title does not confer subjectivity; in this play, desire implies both subjection to its whims and an absent object. Far from presenting subjects as people who desire objects, Shakespearean theatricality insists that desire can never be seen, recognized, or controlled, and that its contours can never fully be fleshed-out. In the play it is this non-materializable desire that has the most agency of all.

Indeed, just to tantalize us even further, the play repeatedly specifies the coordinates within which the changeling boy can be found while simultaneously insisting on the boy's absence from the cast of characters. He is a 'changeling' boy from 'India': by providing him with a local habitation and a name, the play seems to make concrete what it nonetheless does not embody. However, both these locations are notoriously unlocatable. To 'be' a changeling might seem to confer a mantle of ontological

---

[25] Badiou, *Metapolitics*, 29.

[26] As Henry S. Turner has so cogently pointed out in *Shakespeare's Double Helix* (London: Continuum, 2008), this play seems to muddle the distinctions between subjects and objects in ways that resemble what science studies writers like Bruno Latour theorize as the agency of objects.

legitimacy, but that ontology is presented as always already lost—a changeling, after all, is not who he is taken to be because he has been exchanged for another body. And the 'India' to which the play repeatedly refers was imagined in Shakespeare's day to be, variously, in South Asia, Indonesia, the Americas, and Ethiopia—the so-called 'Indian' boy could be what we would understand today as Indian, Indonesian, American, or African.[27] The text gives us a changeling Indian boy who cannot be located with any precision and refuses to be embodied. To then *produce* the boy as cause, changeling, Indian, and object of desire literalizes what the play insists we read non-literally and non-materially. For Shakespeare's *Midsummer Night's Dream* desire *must* be disembodied. Only then does it qualify as desire.

FURTHER READING

Badiou, Alain. *Metapolitics*, trans. Jason Barker (London: Verso, 2005).

Edelman, Lee. *No Future: Queer Theory and the Death Drive* (Durham: Duke University Press, 2004).

Griffiths, Trevor D. *A Midsummer Night's Dream*. Shakespeare in Production Series (Cambridge: Cambridge University Press, 1996).

Harris, Jonathan Gil, ed. *Indography: Writing the 'Indian' in Early Modern England* (New York: Palgrave Macmillan, 2012).

Lacan, Jacques. *Ecrits: A Selection*, trans. Alan Sheridan (New York: W. W. Norton, 1982).

Raman, Shankar. *Framing 'India': The Colonial Imaginary in Early Modern Culture* (Stanford: Stanford University Press, 2002).

Williams, Gary Jay. *Our Moonlight Revels: A Midsummer Night's Dream in the Theatre* (Iowa City: University of Iowa Press, 1997).

---

[27] See the introduction to Jonathan Gil Harris, ed., *Indography: Writing the 'Indian' in Early Modern England* (New York: Palgrave Macmillan, 2012), for a thorough mapping of the ways in which 'India' signified in the sixteenth and seventeenth centuries.

CHAPTER 18

FORMACTION

SIMON PALFREY

> Imagine there were a machine which by its structure produced thought, feeling, and perception; we can imagine it as being enlarged while maintaining the same relative proportions, to the point where we could go inside it, as we would go into a mill. But if that were so, when we went in we would find nothing but pieces which push one against another, and never anything to account for a perception. Therefore, we must look for it in the simple substance, and not in the composite, or in a machine. And that is all we can find within a simple substance, namely perceptions and their changes; and that is all that the *internal actions* of simple substances can consist in.
>
> —Leibniz, *Monadology* (1714)

Why formaction?

1

However physical its materials, playlife is always virtual. And the forms in which this life moves are everywhere marked by gaps—between and within speeches, lines, and indeed words—all of which can produce action or elicit physically absent scenes. At every point in a playworld, life may come rushing in. Much of it is visible on-stage, in the movements or responses of interlocutors, addressees, overhearers, interrupters. But much of it is not. Some of it can be possessed coterminous with performance, as we listen to the words, watch the action, and clock things in process. But much cannot. We need to escape the approximating tyranny of eyes, as we do more broadly the limitations of our senses. There is far more life than we will see listed in a cast-list, more worlds than any putative 'location', more scenes than are marked by the entrance or exit of players. The distribution of theatre's physics—often hidden, silent, intervallic, folded, differential, time-travelling—corresponds to the nature of our own recognitions. If we notice them, we do so by stepping out of shared visible continuities, such as evident plot or articulated purpose; or stepping more deeply inside, collapsing distances, producing intimacies that disrupt the assumption of two equipoised but untouchable domains (spectators–stage). This may entail super-subtle attention to details; it might entail naïve affective permissions. Either way, scenes, lives, places, are as permeable and procreative as the forms that render them. There is nascence everywhere, yet we haven't always the time or speed to give it growth. It leaves us, or we leave it. But it hasn't gone. It waits, a living possible.[1]

2

Imagine a world that *is* the physics, the actions and passions, of theatre. What would it be to fall into the gap between two scenes, and to exist in that void? Imagine waiting inside a cue-space. Imagine the world projected by a metaphor, its unprecedented collisions, or its surprising recovery of otherwise buried actions. Or imagine that your possible world is just a single connotation of a polysemous word, or a fugitive rhyme, or a hiatus between phrases in the middle of a line. Live there, exactly there, and discover what possibilities you can. Or imagine a life not just in, but *as* disguise; imagine that identity can be ended or created by a single switch of garment. Or conceive of possibility, all memory and hope, subsisting at the end of a line, in that hanging space after the last word of one line and before the first word of the next. Or determine always and only to act before an audience, in front of faces you do not know, people that cannot intervene, and yet whose presence is the very predicate of your existing. Imagine that you are playing a role, and every word you say was there before you, and cannot be deviated from. Think of an image that no one has ever seen or heard or even entertained, a construction that neither speaker nor listeners can understand— and there you are, settling in the uncomprehending ears of strangers. Imagine that the action of these words, that and nothing else, constitutes possibility.

3

Formaction: why the portmanteau? First, it plays on *formation*, the formative or making principle that is the essential purpose of poetry and plays. Second, because form and action are always symbiotic. Play-actions are never merely random movements. They are coded, programmed, practised; they are skilful and allusive, forethought and addressed, and alive with time- and craft- and species-travelling memory. This is so even when the action is extemporary, even when the improvisation, for instance in response to a surprise in performance, is a hurried or even panicked making-do. Action alone may lack form. It is simply a deed, a something done or in the doing, whether gesture or influence or event. It need not be predicted. No one need make it but the actor of the action. It may have neither past nor future, live and die in its moment, with no more memory, no more forward recollection, than a raindrop. Let's leave mere *actions* to the off-stage world and its

---

[1] In all that follows I am thinking of theatre's possibilities. I am unsure, however, whether it truly speaks to any playmaker but Shakespeare. Perhaps it doesn't exist.

haphazard amnesia. For truly there are no such actions in a play at all: only *formactions*. Third, and somewhat more accidentally, I can hear crushed in its harsh second syllable that unloved word, *matter*, which, far from Aristotle's inert preparatory to form, or Plotinus's unsouled and unreal privation, is always and already coordinate in playlife. Consequently, I mean by formations the working parts and craft materials of playworlds—often simultaneous, clustered, overlapping, invisible—which do not simply mediate or re-present things in the world, but are themselves vitally immanent with possible life: cues, scenes, metaphors, rhymes, parts, entrances, lines, lexical repetitions, scene breaks, puns latent and overt, soliloquies, midline breaks, exits, on-stage silence, a player's type, mime shows, a present audience, and so on and on. The worlds that ensue are neither static, nor linear, nor punctual. They are *essentially* polychronic, indeed anachronic, at each moment in more than one location, endued with shapes, preformed with a purposive spirit that claims a power for itself of repeatable iteration. Each formation at once embeds pasts and *wants* futures. The action moves into, is invisibly collected by, is a satisfaction of, a premonitory ghost of the self-same action. In Herbert Blau's apt phrase, theatrical formations play to 'a skein of vanishings'.[2]

4

In the words of Bergson:

> [As] those movements are easy which prepare the way for others, we are led to find a superior ease in the movements which can be foreseen, in the present attitudes in which future attitudes are pointed out and, as it were, prefigured... Thus the perception of ease in motion passes over into the pleasure of mastering the flow of time and of holding the future in the present.... As we guess almost the exact attitude which the dancer is going to take, he seems to obey us when he really takes it: the regularity of the rhythms establishes a kind of communication between him and us, and the periodic returns of the measure are like so many invisible threads by means of which we set in motion this imaginary puppet... Thus a kind of physical sympathy enters into the feeling of grace... its affinity with moral sympathy, the idea of which it subtly suggests.... in anything which we call very graceful we imagine ourselves able to detect, besides the lightness which is a sign of mobility, some suggestion of a possible movement towards ourselves, of a virtual and even nascent sympathy.[3]

Bergson's insight (clearly indebted to Kleist's famous essay 'On the Marionette Theater') suggests the *anticipatory* power of art, a transaction that is somehow before itself, trembling on the brink, in which we take a hint and imagine its fruition, waiting deliciously or nervously for the satisfaction. In this the very form of art, precisely

---

[2] Herbert Blau, 'Elsinore: An Analytic Scenario', in *The Dubious Spectacle: Extremities of Theater, 1976-2000* (Minneapolis, MN: University of Minnesota Press, 2002), 70–1.

[3] Henri Bergson, *Time and Free Will*, trans. F. L. Pogson (London and New York: George Allen, 1913), 13–14.

as its experience, is unfinished and proleptic. This intrinsic formactive *duration* means that theatre defies what Peggy Phelan calls the 'catastrophe' of its apparent disappearance: the performance passes, of course; but unlike all other things in life, its passing is simultaneous with its recurrence, or the promise of such.[4] The crucial thing is an expectation of repetition. For plays are *not* in duration quite like the rest of life. All its active phenomena are also forms, however apparently fleeting: they compose a possible tendency or attitude; they propose a possible shape of life, capable of duration and of iteration, if only through the fact of being scripted or performed, and therefore claiming a right to repeat. Formactive time is always staggered and layered: far from a one-off happening, the event is sketched, rehearsed, performed, revised, rehearsed, performed again, an unpredictably to-and-fro process in which no single instantiation ever quite possesses the act, but in which the imperative remains to compose and animate emotion in its own perfect if momentary form. Once enacted, it is in the world, in its own way a pattern of perfection. Otherwise contingent action is granted a mime-like certainty. It could only be exactly what it is: and yet this perfection, granted by iteration, by the fact that it has all happened already, also entails the thought of future, *different* repetitions. A theatrical formaction does not merely *tell* of existent things; it does not ask us to behold a declared and completed action; it claims, through the forethought and professionalism of its coming-to-be, a kind of future. So both the processual experience of the work, and the claim of the work, pushes beyond what is simply given, and heralds the transvaluation of finished objects. Thus the artwork is not so much mimetic, as it is a moving force that models possibility. In Leibniz's apposite phrase, it is a *dynamic specimen*. Plays can be an instance *and* an abstract of things not-yet: in this the very morphology of theatre anticipates, rivals, even becomes nature.

5

Theatre's living flame is never reducible to any on-stage actant. Mind or soul can move like lightning between bodies, as between characters or signs: now dispersed immanently among many phenomena, now concentrated into one fleeting single entity. This means that the moment-by-moment attributes of a particular performer or performance are *not* themselves the formaction—a smile, a hissing sibilance, a casting eye, the easy movement of a dance or a duel, the intensified gestures of hand and face at an instant of passionate transition. These are *per-formactions*: strictly contingent, whereas formactions possess necessity. The formaction, by contrast, is the instrument that generates, and is always coincident with, these embodied iterations of it. In itself it is alive with movement, change, and counter-change, both actual *and* potential. But this changing motion will also always be embodied, in the voices, actions, exits, interruptions, and so on that are solicited, elicited, or imagined.

---

[4] Cf. Peggy Phelan, *Mourning Sex: Performing Public Memories* (London: Routledge, 1997).

Equally, the fact of the formaction releases the potential for changing bodily hosts or carriers: words can be said in different ways, the identity of actors can change, and so on. Indeed it is literally impossible that the formaction can be in the world without altering from moment to moment, as from one appearance or sounding to another. Whatever it expresses, the expression takes the form of *change*.

6

The play is a formaction, but so is every one of the working parts that make it. This follows particularly from the fact of actors' parts. The player has his part, listing cues and speeches, with no indication as to when or to whom he speaks. Rehearsal is overwhelmingly private. Much of the world is unwritten, marked by lacunae. The whole, if there is one, succeeds the part. Every point must be scanned. The slightest pause can have actorly purpose and expressive effect. Each sign in the part-text, however unglamorous and instrumental, can produce possible worlds. The putatively neutral mechanics of playmaking, the tiny levers in the machine, are no longer the affectless cogs in a contrivance. They are nested worlds, nested lives. We get a radical liberating of the fragmentary or fractional, animate with experiential possibility, endued with its own *conatus*. This teeming theatrical life posits astonishing proliferation, multiple reconfigurations of possibility.

7

The *work* that formactions perform is crucial. Each formaction has to be understood both as a functional genera or species (a rhyme, a costume) and as a particular instantiation of it (*this* rhyme, *that* costume). The genera possess certain characteristics, some of which are inevitably at work in each instant of its use: a cue cues something, a line helps to measure speaking rhythms, a metaphor suggests resemblances. An enormous reservoir of potential experience is thus latent in every formative occurrence—a kind of micro- or subvisible version of *theatergrams*.[5] Each specific application produces derivatives of this species-purpose, folds or fractions or modes of it. In turn, different moments will accentuate or extend different aspects; one metaphor will be more estranging and disordering than another; some cue-spaces function with blithe ease, others are wracked by contention or pain. No two uses will ever be exactly the same. The uniqueness of each context demands this. But there is more to this than neutral instrumentality. A kind of pathos hedges the function of each formaction: it too may be more or less at work at each singular instantiation. We need to recognize the residual *characteristics* of each formaction: how the primitive action and passion of its purpose can vitally inform the expressiveness and plaintiveness of

---

[5] See Louis Clubb, *Italian Drama in Shakespeare's Time* (New Haven: Yale University Press, 1989).

playworlds—or can do whenever a playmaker intuits the living reality of these instruments. Of course—true to the multiplicity of playmakers, human and non-human, individual and collaborative—the decisive agency might arise from anywhere, at any time, before, during, or centuries after a play's first composition or performance or reading. But with Shakespeare, a craft- and material-saturating design is very clear. Whether through immersive practice over years, or an uncanny sympathy with *any* object or condition, or species-traversing clairvoyance, he prehends what it might mean for life truly to be at stake at each particular formaction. They become existential allegories, personifications of past and future possibility.

8

This is the acme of theatricality: discovering a living *intension* in the coordinates of formactions, such that the predicates of the instrument are discovered, rediscovered, brought alive, in each instance of it. An isomorphic relation develops between playthings and playworld—a correspondence between formal-material structures and expressive-mimetic life. Every last bit is alive.

9

It might be objected that thinking like this runs the risk of hypostasizing all the instruments and techniques of theatre. In a sense that is precisely the point: to hypostasize is to endue with substance. Hypostasizing becomes a conceptual sin when it presupposes 'essential' conformity to a hegemonic ideal, one invariably rooted in the violence of ownership and the forgetting of difference. But my approach is the opposite. I want to hypostasize the quotidian stuff of theatre, in the sense of recover its multiple nodes of substance: not to wash everything in the bland light of the divine, or still less do service to a centralizing or centripetal ideologeme. Rather, I want to give what often seem to be merely 'accidents'—figurative ornaments, necessary tools of the trade, serviceable instruments of the craft—their own substance, their own reality. This is absolutely a hypostatic move on my part: but how else to respect the strange life in playworlds?

The monadic theatre

1

The metaphysics of Gottfried Leibniz offers a compelling (and astonishingly neglected) model for thinking about theatrical life, culminating in his dizzying monadology. Here is a selection of Leibnizian formulations: for the monad, think formaction:

1. Imagine there were a machine which by its structure produced thought, feeling, and perception; we can imagine it as being enlarged while maintaining the same relative proportions, to the point where we could go inside it, as we would go into a mill. But if that were so, when we went in we would find nothing but pieces which push one against another, and never anything to account for a perception. Therefore, we must look for it in the simple substance, and not in the composite, or in a machine. And that is all we can find within a simple substance, namely perceptions and their changes; and that is all that the *internal actions* of simple substances can consist in.

2. And since every present state of a simple substance is a natural consequence of its previous one...the present is big with the future.

3. In nature, everything is full. There are simple substances everywhere, genuinely separated one from another by their own actions, which continually change their relationships.

4. Each monad, together with its own body, makes up a living substance. Thus not only is there life everywhere, together with limbs or organs, but there are infinite levels of life among monads, some of which are dominant over others to a greater or lesser extent.

5. Every organized substance has in itself an infinity of others, and even has fellow creatures in its centre; no substance will perish, and those that are in the darkness of their centres will in their turn appear in the larger theatre.

6. There is in possible things a certain demand for existence—a straining to exist or (if I may so put it) a claim to exist—all possible things strive with equal right for existence in proportion to their quantity of essence or reality, or to the degree of perfection which they contain.

7. There is a world of creatures—of living things and animals, entelechies and souls—in the smallest part of matter.

8. Every portion of matter can be thought of as a garden full of plants, or as a pond full of fish. But every branch of the plant, every part of the animal, and every drop of its vital fluids, is another such garden, or another such pond.

9. And although the earth and the air in between the plants in the garden, and the water in between the fish in the pond, are not themselves plants or fish, they do nevertheless contain others, though usually they are so tiny as to be imperceptible to us.

10. Thus there is no uncultivated ground in the universe; nothing barren, nothing dead. There is no chaos, and all confusion is merely apparent.

11. Because all bodies are in a perpetual state of flux, like rivers, and parts are constantly coming into them and going out.[6]

    [6] Gottfried Leibniz, [1] *Monadology*, no. 17, in G. W. Leibniz, *Philosophical Texts*, trans. and ed. R. S. Woodhouse and Richard Francks (Oxford: Oxford University Press, 1998), 270; [2] *Monadology*, no. 22, *Philosophical Texts*, 271; [3] *Principles of Nature and Grace*, para. 3, in Woodhouse and Francks, eds., *Philosophical Texts*, 259; [4] *Principles of Nature and Grace*, para. 4, *Philosophical Texts*, 260; [5] Letter to Andre Morel (1698), *The Shorter Leibniz Texts* (trans. Lloyd Strickland [London: Continuum, 2006]), 39; [6] 'On the Ultimate Origination of Things' (1697), *Shorter Leibniz Texts*, 32; [7–11] *Monadology*, nos. 66–71, *Philosophical Texts*, 277–8.

2

One of the beautiful things about Leibniz's monads is that they are not in themselves physical. They exist in bodies—a king, a cat, a sponge, the striations of a
leaf, or the planed wood of a chair-leg—just as they exist in-between perceptible
bodies—in the wind, or in the narrowing space between hands as they draw together
to shake or clap; they exist as passions or memories, the mind-stuff of a physical
brain. But they are not these bodies. The monad precedes and survives all carriers.

3

The monad is creation's most basic substance: a soul-like entity, endued with perception and appetite, and with its own resistant, striving endeavour; sometimes, in
higher monads, blessed with apperception and memory; always expressing and
perceiving, sometimes confusedly, sometimes distinctly, everything in its world;
and defined by *change*, its substance discovered in action and alteration. These
monads—souls, minds, appetites, perceptors, expressers—are infinitely various.
Their creation is fractal—ascending or descending repetitions, endless iterations,
but every one distinct. Necessarily, there is an original cause, apperceiving all possibility (God). But the causes of each thing are immanent in it, discoverable and
renewed, moment-by-moment, as its *action*. Each is an agitated, mobile mirror of
creation: but no two mirrors will ever reflect quite the same thing. As much as Leibniz prefers unity, his monadology always discovers multiplicity and difference.

4

One of Leibniz's favourite analogues for his monads is a point in geometry, at which
an infinity of lines meet. We might think that Leibniz is comparing the monad simply to the point: a point resembles Democritus's atom, tiny and beyond empirical
observation. But Leibniz's analogy is more dynamic and dimensional than this,
closer to a kind of crystallography. The *point* is implicated in a multitude of lines or
vectors, straight and curved, which extend at once into and away from the point.
The monad is thus more profoundly a concatenation of *angles*, coming from all
directions and all times: 'Just as in a *centre* or point, in itself perfectly simple, are
found an infinity of angles formed by the lines which meet there.'[7] The criss-crossing,
looping vectors produce potentially infinite planes, glimmering in glimpsed parcels
of space and time. This point is at once supra-temporal and instantiated: the angles
collect many more than three dimensions, more than the four made up by the
dimension of time. For this *point* is virtual as well as actual, as abstract as any

---

[7] *Principles of Nature and Grace*, para. 2, Woodhouse and Francks, eds., *Philosophical Texts*, 259.

geometrical model, but also physical, because dependent on bodies if it is to live or even to be imagined (we can hardly conceive of an invisible point). The *point*, then, is more like a polymorphic crystal than an indivisible atom.

5

Each formaction is such a *point*, with all that meets in it and spools from it. Geometry can describe perfect mental pictures, and can help us in our attempts at understanding. But the world is not in truth geometrical. You will not find in nature a circle, or a line, or a triangle. The very idea of a *shape*, obedient to a prior description, is a fancy of the disciplining mind. It isn't real. The closer you look, the more things fold and unfold, endlessly fractal, endlessly unique. Every last object is a subject, and each one is a suffering in motion. In this way, the monadology is pure theatre. A substance isn't substantial unless it acts; if it does, it is also potentially a *subject*. In identifying substance with action, Leibniz is not thereby saying that *motion* is reality; nor is he saying that a perceptibly moving body is substantial, whereas an apparently unmoving body is not. Action, for Leibniz, is a much finer, less grossly sensory thing:

> There is nothing real in motion but a *momentary something* which must consist in a force striving [*nitente*] toward change.[8]

> For every finite substance is actually acted upon (for, although it is actually acting, it is also finite, i.e. imperfect, and its action is always checked, that is, to some extent impeded); moreover every passion of a body involves division.

> *Body* is a substance that can act and be acted upon.
> *Matter* is the principle of passion.
> *Form* is the principle of action.

This is Leibniz early in his career, still obedient to scholastic terminology. Nonetheless it is suggestive. Leibniz's 'passion' connotes the condition of passivity, or of being subject to alteration or suffering. Conversely, 'form' is the active agent, the force that shapes the matter. Passion and action are opposites. But Leibniz cannot rest easy in the ancient hierarchy, wherein matter is an undistinguished corporeal slurry, awaiting the shaping wand of form. For passion/matter is characterized by change, by being moved or taken by some other force; in a sense, passivity instantly becomes a misnomer, because it cannot but be active.

6

This is much more than a scientific animism. Passions themselves have substance; they go towards the constitution of the world. They are not merely 'emotions' that a

---

[8] G. W. Leibniz, 'A Specimen of Dynamics', in *Philosophical Essays*, ed. and trans. Roger Ariew and Daniel Garber (Indianapolis: Hackett Publishing, 1989), 118.

man or a woman might experience, speaking a susceptible temperament but neither here nor there when it comes to what truly matters. Passions *are*:

> [I]f anything is real, it is solely the force of acting and suffering [*vim agenda et patiendi*],
> and hence that the substance of a body consists in this (as if in matter and form).[9]

Consequently, Leibniz's strictly physical passion (a condition of being-moved or
acted-upon) garners ontological independence, and a paradoxical kind of agency.
Equally, it is inextricable from the action (as form) that it suffers: so the nominal
dualism of form and matter in fact becomes a kind of dynamic consubstantiality: a
formaction. Here we rejoin one of Leibniz's crucial moves—there is no matter without form. The two are always and already interdependent; there can no more be
formless matter than there can be a vacuum in nature. So, passion is always acted
upon, and in being so turns into an action, which produces further passions, which
issue in actions, and so on. The barest matter is inherent with *force*. This activity is
not motion (contra Descartes)—something visible and measurable—but a spontaneous internal predisposition, a dynamic futurism that is the passion's basic physics
and morphology. It becomes a simple thing to intuit a world in which the tiniest
thing might be personified, just as suffering or passion is less an excessive grief or
rare subjection and instead the basic condition of *all* being, whether a young girl in
love or a pebble.

7

The monad allows no ontological priority to humans (let alone a race or culture), or
even to 'living' organisms—for all things alter. Leibniz proposes an endlessly inter-
connected creation, exceeding even modern green ecology in the respect it grants
to all existents. In such a vision, a playworld will not be reducible to a derivative
account of a prior dispensation. For the playworld is a monad, composed of many
more monads, every one of them a mobile mirror of *actual* possibility.

> It can even be said that by virtue of these minute perceptions the present is big with the
> future and burdened with the past, that all things harmonize... and that eyes as pierc-
> ing as God's could read in the lowliest substance the universe's whole sequence of
> events.[10]

This is the crucial point: a single, lowly substance is dense with the entire 'sequence
of events'. Narrative consecution is not played out only in temporal or spatial
extension. It is *at* the instant. This is very different from the idea of a plot, divided
into scenes, which each moment incrementally serves, like a brick of a building.

---

[9] Gottfried Leibniz, *Philosophical Papers and Letters*, ed. and trans. Leroy E. Loemker, 2nd edn.
(Dordrecht: Reidel, 1976), 365; quoted in Daniel Garber, *Leibniz: Body, Substance, Monad* (Oxford:
Oxford University Press, 2009), 123–4.
[10] Leibniz, *Philosophical Papers and Letters*, 365.

The point and the moment implicates, is constituted by, all possible progression. This is what it means to say, as Leibniz does, that substance *is* change. There really is no external telos or plotmaker. Consequently, in the monadic theatre we find no void, no vacuum, no gap or interval that is not in fact dynamic with conation. The acme of this creation will be barely perceptible, quicksilver formations, waiting upon our entrance and animation—a cue-space, a line-hinge, a metalepsis. The upshot is simple but profound. In contrast to Newton's physics, there are no such abstractions as 'time' or 'space'. Nor are these things containers which precede and envelop the things or events 'in' them. Rather, time is contingent on events, and space is constituted by things: 'Space is the place of things'.[11] But Leibniz goes still further. If there were no things, there would be no space: therefore the world is full. The same applies to time: there is no time without events. If there is such a thing as future time, then it is *already* event-full. Since time is in fact only ever experienced in the present, then the present is full with all events, past and future. This present, in turn, is found in events which necessarily are manifest in bodies (of infinitely various and divisible sizes). So history—past, future, present— is immanent in bodies, in events, in places-in-motion. Precisely the same applies to each formation.

8

The challenge to common sense suppositions—which still by and large describe the methods of literary critics and historians—goes still deeper. For Leibniz's monadic perceptions are not to be understood as things that we have or observe, more or less detached products of our survey of the object-world around us. These perceptions, or expressions—the words are interchangeable—*are what we are*. Life is modelled like a language. But language is no longer the translation of something already thought; no longer even a vehicle or carriage for cognition and emotion; it is the active percipient:

> [O]ne monad in itself, and at a moment, cannot be distinguished from another except by its internal qualities and actions; which can only be its *perceptions* (that is, the representations of the composite, or of what is external, in the simple), or its *appetitions* (its tending to move from one perception to another, that is), which are the principles of change. For the simplicity of substance does not in any way rule out a multiplicity in the modifications which must exist together in one simple substance; and those modifications must consist in the variety of its relationships to things outside it—like the way in which in a *centre*, or a *point*, although it is completely simple, there are an infinity of angles formed by the lines which meet in it.[12]

---

[11] Leibniz, 4th paper to Clarke, no. 29, *The Leibniz–Clarke Correspondence*, ed. H. G. Alexander (Manchester and New York: Manchester University Press, 1956), 40.

[12] *Principles of Nature and Grace*, para. 2, Woodhouse and Francks, eds., *Philosophical Texts*, 259.

The monad utterly does away with conventional hierarchies of reference, in which the primary job of language is to denote objects, or record actions. Instead the monad, considered *as* language, is also the expressive subject, which *is* its perceptions. Leibniz thus posits 'individuals' that are symbiotically *indicated* and *constituted* by these 'insensible perceptions'. By 'individuals', we should think less of discrete people than *events*. An individual subject might constitute one such mobile event, but so too will innumerable other events (actions, passions, etc.) nested within the subject; so too may any other active thing, animate or indeed inanimate (although in truth there can be nothing inanimate in a world *full* with action). Ontology *is* perception; perception *is* expression; expression *is* being. Every discrete word, or cue-space, or costume, agitant with ongoing history, might be an event or subject, or a fold of one. Crucially, however, perception is not to be confused with what Leibniz calls 'apperception', which he associates with self-consciousness, reflection, memory. The vast preponderance of perception is not apperceptive. Understanding does not work through the precise tabulation of perceived quanta—this, then this, then the other—which need to be recognized in process if they are to be factored in—any more than the experience of a play amounts to a series of semantic equations or spatially arrested moments. We are taken by perceptions that we have no notion of owning. There is greater potential here than some rough notion of intended and unintended, conscious and unconscious meanings. For if the apperceiving, self-conscious speaker is a dominant monad, then the language he or she uses is itself animate with monads. So each metaphor, and then each shoot of possibility in the metaphor, can garner monadic potentiality: be percipient, substantial, appetitive. And each such word, as a nest of individuals, is always a concatenation of events.

9

In all kinds of ways Leibniz's monadology speaks to theatre: because a radically subjunctive take on necessity, wherein all 'possibles' *are* (being necessarily apprehended by God); because there is no separating Leibniz's understanding of what is from his understanding of what could be; because the quality of a created thing—its morphology and its morality—reflects or expresses the qualities of the creating force; because the creation is a series of differential fractals, repeated instants or nodes of everything, the same matrix of possibilities found again and again, but repeating differently rather than identically; because there are no indiscernibles, and no one thing is the same as any other; because there is no possibility of separating 'world' from its instruments, form from content, or subject from object; because the smallest, most inconspicuous trigger expresses possibility; and because the combination of lurking presence, unconscious meanings, dimly perceived relations, faint echoes, nested resemblances, all speaks for a creation which is constituted *feelingly*. Leibniz absolutely anticipates our modern world of quantum vertigo and quivering superstrings, in which what holds for big things, the measurements that seem to guarantee common sense and rectilinear order, are simply untrue when it comes to the finer particles of existing, like subatomic quarks or memory. And because every unending part of every single thing is unique, the particular *expression* of possibility at work in any one thing has its own dignity. It demands a scrupulous attention all its own, and quite possibly its own bespoke epistemology. Spectatorial eyes won't do it: like Macbeth, we need a third ear.

Perdita's waves

1

Let us then listen in to a playworld, taking our cue from two famous accounts of waves.

First, Leibniz:

> [A]t every moment there is in us an infinity of perceptions, unaccompanied by awareness or reflection; that is, of alterations in the soul itself, of which we are unaware because these impressions are either too minute and too numerous, or else too unvarying, so that they are not sufficiently distinctive on their own…I like to use the example of the roaring noise of the sea which impresses itself on us when we are standing on the shore. To hear this noise as we do, we must hear the parts which make up this whole, that is the noise of each wave, although each of these little noises makes itself known only when combined confusedly with all the others, and would not be noticed if the wave which made it were by itself.[13]

Second, Shakespeare:

> When you do dance, I wish you
> A wave o'th Sea, that you might ever do
> Nothing but that: move still, still so:
> And owne no other Function. Each your doing,
> (So singular, in each particular)
> Crownes what you are doing, in the present deeds,
> That all your Actes, are Queenes.　　　(*The Winter's Tale*, TLN 1956–62)[14]

2

There is no play more intent than *The Winter's Tale* on probing the weird magic of the theatrical medium, or more serious in its theorizing of theatrical art; no Renaissance criticism gets close to it for sophistication, or closer to being adequate to the

---

[13] Gottfried Leibniz, *New Essays on Human Understanding*, ed. and trans. Peter Remnant and Jonathan Bennett (Cambridge: Cambridge University Press, 2006), 54.

[14] William Shakespeare, *The Winter's Tale*, *The First Folio of Shakespeare: The Norton Facsimile*, 2nd edn. ed. Charlton Hinman (New York: W. W. Norton, 1996), TLN 1956–62.

worlds that theatre creates. The reports and set-pieces of the play usually have a double-aspect, at once speaking the 'tale' and apostrophizing its methods, a kind of meta-ekphrasis, in which each description echoes the others, recalling and preparing, such that we get a cumulative, mobile reflection of our own spellbound submission to play. So, much like the other reports of miraculous, reality-stealing arts in *The Winter's Tale*, Florizel's praise of Perdita is a perfect instance of and gloss upon formactions. He is talking about fluid bodily movement, but the 'dance' is not yet here, not seen on the stage; it is imagined or remembered or predicted. As ever, full presence depends upon a mixture of sensory gift and sensory deficit—we see Perdita as Florizel addresses her, and endue her visible body with the *potential* which his praises animate.

3

Thinking of Leibniz's sea-sound brings us still closer. The secret of this speech is how it understands indivisible stasis, a kind of divine perfection, as a product of Zeno-like, endlessly divisible change: there is no part so small that it cannot be divided further, into still more exquisite delicacy; no part too small for appreciation, or too fine that it does not own the singularity of action. Florizel's wordplay takes the praise beyond reiteration. 'Each your doing.../ Crownes what you are doing': the doing is spontaneously self-coronating, blessed in its motion with legitimating rightness; but *each* doing crowns the doing; it exceeds the previous, trumps it in a never-ceasing perfecting of perfection. Florizel's praise allows change, even progress, yet *without teleology*: it does not depend on a destination to confer recursive purpose or fineness; and it does so without the slightest intimation of lack. Each singular moment is complete; her continuance in the doing is simply a miraculous addition. The wistful precision of the praise, in other words, resides in the way it enacts possibility: partly because the purr of her perfection is a kind of actualized, spontaneous potentiality; partly because Florizel's modality, as befits the romantic tension of the scene, is optative: *I wish you*. The praise is for verbs and movement, not titles and statues. As such, it is perfectly metatheatrical: these acts and deeds are what we are right now hearing and seeing; what is more, as *deeds* they are a gift, or an inheritance, possessed by Perdita and yet granted simultaneously to any with ears to hear, and to anyone in the future who may attempt or attend them. The *present deeds*, at their most basic, are not so much her imagined dance as the tale enacted before us, which in the same moment claims the right to repeat. Shakespeare is everywhere invoking his own craft, the theatre's best possible worlds.

4

Much of this is encapsulated in one of Shakespeare's most marvellously monadic single lines:

(So singular, in each particular)

This line epitomizes the mix of nestedness and uniqueness that characterizes Shakespeare's formactions: each instance claiming its own gravitational field, hunkered or bracketed, peculiar to itself; yet each a metonym of all, connecting or distilling, causing or caused. This mixture of all *and* one/all *in* one is likewise instantiated in the subtle distinctions between the two words. 'Singular' means individual or separate, and so proposes a whole (or a *one*, the monad). 'Particular' means a part of a whole. But then the apparent hierarchy of parts and wholes—in which a part is subordinate to or derived from the whole—is inverted by the line's grammar: so singular *in each* particular. In other words, the whole thing is in the part; indeed every single part seems to contain the whole. It is a monadology before the (Leibnizian) monad. What is more, both words are at once nouns and adverbs, both *the* thing, and an attribute or manner of any example of the thing. The functional shift gives each word its own action or tendency: it renders it a kind of verb. The words have dynamic force; they inwardly move; potentials are *stored* as well as manifest in visible movement.

5

But as with all the nested relationships and jointed agents in this play, coordinate terms does not mean interchangeable. Imagine reversing the words: 'So particular, in each singular'. This would say that each single thing has its own bespoke fineness, a jealously guarded purpose and texture; it would suggest that each single thing has many parts, each of which demands notice and respect. Certainly both these implications are present in what Shakespeare actually gives us, with its accent upon the endlessly divisible particularity of things, and its implicit recommendation of microscopic attention: the closer we attend, the more we will notice, and the more unexpected fineness will come to life. 'So *singular*' gives to every last particular its own unique conation; it evokes a world, or a sea, or a girl, or a dance, of ceaselessly abundant procreativity, the abundance being precisely that of *more* active particulars. It is a vision of dizzying fractal replication. But 'so singular' also implies something more: it insists that each such fold, every last instant and moment, is essentially *unrepeatable*. This is the lodestone of singularity, something that 'particularity' cannot quite claim. Repetition is differential: perhaps it would be more accurate to call it replacement. Once again Shakespeare prehends Leibniz: here his Identity of Indiscernibles, the necessity that no two things can be the same, and indeed that no single thing can ever be the same from one moment to the next.

6

Florizel's beautiful repetitions—move still, *still so*—speak his sensuous wonder at his beloved, the mere fact of her, an imprecation never to cease her 'doing'. But the hint of ellipsis at the line's end delicately suggests how (even) words might fail when erotic rapture is at its zenith: still so...*something*, as the line closes and we are left hanging, searching for an adjective to do justice to such promise. We can see here how it is rhythm, or rather the symbiosis of rhythmic and sonic repetition, which at once mimics the sea-dance and admits the superior possibilities of *movement* over lexis. It isn't that semantics is unworthy of the event. The various referents of 'still' are all precisely in action, and the semantic connotations do much of the work of evoking a phenomenon that is equally in time (stay forever) and in space (stay *here*), past (as recalled), present (as self-enacting speech), and future (as prediction), a time and space which inextricably compose one another, extending via contraction, continuing via stasis. But still there is something else to which even this super-subtle exactness is subordinate: a sculpting, hypostasizing, mimical arrest of function (own no other...), epitomized in the chiasmic folding-into-one of the phrases. It evokes unsurpassable rapture and reverence, such that progression beyond *this* is barely conceivable. The genius in Florizel's conceit is thus partly Pygmalion, the patron saint of all petrifying art: *move still* clearly prepares for Hermione's breathing statue. For there is violence in this urge to miniaturize, and by miniaturizing, *selecting*: some kind of ontological absolutism in the very fact of theatre—its rage for perfection, its belief in epitomes—that can threaten to make the ragged proof of daily life seem an uncohering accident. Hence the pun, move *still*, whereby movement defers to the image of it in the mind of the beholder, as though arresting kinetic life for the greater god of reverent recollection, a snapshot for future pleasure. Like all the ekphrases in the play, the vision teeters between transformation and annihilation: after all, how can the girl, frozen as danced, not even as dancer, survive in such praise? But this in turn points to the pitiless faithfulness of Shakespeare to his art. For what ultimately survives the figure is not, at heart, an individual agent, still less a particular actor, and still less one dressed up, as Perdita is here, as they all always are, in a fleeting-false costume. What survives is the fact of repetition and iteration, in the minds of rememberers, or in future performances, or in the potential for either: this is the continuance envisaged in 'still so'. Formactions are the prior and surviving truth.

7

Theatre's modal realism, its radical materialism, is always creating worlds that go well beyond the human; in comparing humans to other things, to hares or blankets or bottles, it gives to these things their quiddity. And so it is with Perdita's waves: Shakespeare has waves of the sea genuinely in view: he sees one, and then another, and then another, each one unique, its brief claim of existing verified by the crisp glitter of its cap, of sun or salt, that he names its *crown*, like some tiny glimpsed unfolding of its secret. The wave is, just as metaphors *are*. But he isn't imagining here a nature beyond human presence, even as it is in some irreducible way beyond the human. For the life in Shakespeare's formations always derives from and depends upon the most basic crafts and coordinates of theatre. We might recall here the radical modal realism of the American philosopher David Lewis, especially what he calls 'Humean supervenience'. Essentially this is a kind of physicalism, whereby all ideas, purposes, coherences, and principles *supervene* upon the actual local properties of things:

> [A]ll there is to the world is a vast mosaic of local matters of particular fact, just one little thing and then another. (But it is no part of the thesis that these local matters are mental.)...For short: we have an arrangement of qualities. And that is all. There is no difference without difference in the arrangement of qualities. All else supervenes on that.[15]

For worlds, read *playworlds*; for the vast mosaic, read the numerous particular for-mactions, textual and material, that give to each playworld motion and matter. Metaphysics depends on the details; the master-narratives supervene on the par-ticular local points: not the other way around. This goes to the heart of theatrical ontology. It isn't just that the playtext or stage is made up of discrete physical act-ants, each of which contributes to the effect. It isn't even that each such physical instant bears a potential for feeling. It is that our very ideas of possibility are conse-quent upon each local thing, which has to be understood both in terms of its situ-ational occasion—who and what is active at it—and its potential for metaphysical or existential extension. The actual stuff of the play is *not* derivative of some pri-mary truth or place; it is not what Austin calls 'constative', or even really mimetic. Instead, each event—a line, entrance, cue-space, metaphor, disguise—produces its own laws, chances, causes, and character. So it is with Florizel's speech. For all its ideality, the vision presupposes a witness, watching or hearing or both. It presup-poses a scripter, which renders the action, however beautiful and indigenous to the mover, both an observance *and* a repetition. Without spectator and scripter, there is no dance: and so the dancer, too, is also always an actor. A dance may invite improvisation, but it is always partly imitation; the dancer moves into places that have already been moved into; we can intuit, whether we watch or perform the dance, an invisible webbing, as though of earlier dancers, moving moments ahead of the dancer, drawing her on, conferring form upon the action.

8

No wave can happen without precursors. In turn, each occurrence promises a fur-ther one. But the series does not work by the successive consecution of isolated

---

[15] David Lewis, *Philosophical Papers Volume II* (Oxford: Oxford University Press, 1986), ix–x: supervenience is a relation of ontological or morphological dependency, such that change in one state entails change in another.

elements: one wave follows another, as though drawn on by it, but this later wave is itself pushed forward by a still later one, and it by another, as each swell partakes in things subsequent to it and supplements what rolls on ahead of it. The preceding waves are hurried on, or limited in their span, by their subsequents. What appears as affectless repetition is in fact an epitome of conative force—a force that, crucially, does *not* work in only one causative direction. Things behind (in both space *and* time) act upon things ahead, which act on things behind. The 'sea', like Perdita's dance, is the very image of a monadic theatre, a theatre of successiveness and recursion, of anachrony as much as chronology, of outflowing tides and swirling currents. We cannot hear, cannot give true credit to, every single wave. Indeed each wave moves with who knows how many constituents. As Leibniz knows, the infinitesimal retains dimensions; each moment is its own conation. In turn, each 'particular' is a 'wave', constituted by an infinite series of singularities, each of them also a wave. Accordingly, every wave is also a point: an endless succession of which produces the always-moving aggregate: an aggregate we are always liable to take as the only prevailing singularity or subject.

9

Perdita is each singular wave: this one, then the next, then the next. She is each wave in the singular, *and* the flow of one into the next; she is also the aggregate, but an aggregate that derives its grace from the centred sufficiency of each wave. So Florizel's optative vision imagines, not automated repetition, but differential recurrence. Each wave is *her*; she doesn't own the wave, as one might a quality: she becomes it, as she becomes them, an irresistible flow and return and remainder. And yet as much as the speech is a rare tribute to irreducible beauty and irreducible love, the very exactitude of its terms speaks the profound melancholy of these same things, love and beauty. To be irreducible is to be composed of infinite parts, none of them yours to own. The captured, perdurable thing is no more—no less too, but certainly no more—than a ravishing sentimental abstraction. We can never quite grab the wave. In Leibniz's enigmatic formulation: the monad has no windows.

10

Any wish for fixity is at odds with the theme: *move still*. The playworld's physics are electric and magical, identities subject to instantaneous metamorphosis: 'Sure this Robe of mine / Do's change my disposition' (TLN 1949–50). No single figure is in control of this compact. So, Perdita watches herself alter, half-in and half-out of her own motions, hostage to theatre's quicksilver ontological larceny. Likewise, for all that Florizel's speech is a beautiful gloss upon formations, it cannot entirely capture those of the playworld. Adoration itself is opened out to a kind of competition, as though it might be another thing to 'tod' up and exchange in Bohemia's emergent mercantilism ('I should leave grazing, were I of your flocke, / And onely live by gazing', 1922–3; 'This is the prettiest Low-borne Lasse, that ever / Ran on the greene-ford', 1975–6; 'She dances featly', 2000). Florizel's speech is thus quickly succeeded by the visible evidence of Perdita dancing with him. Florizel's praise gives a kind of text to the dance, which at some level must aspire to the conditions of the speech. But the speech must also give way to the sensually present dance. For there may be something *more* in the visible dance, an abundance or carefreeness, qualities which will not be answerable to Florizel's speech. So it is with plays: the formations are many, and pregnant metaphor may at any moment be swept into remission by more immediate claims upon one's attention: the sound of tabor and pipe; the excited movement of immediately present dancers; the dazzling entrance of Autolicus ('O Master: if you did but heare the Pedler at the doore, you would never dance againe after a Tabor and Pipe', 2006–8); the still more astonishing twelve satyrs—they have danced before the king! they each jump twelve foot and a half! But at the same time the scene is preparing for the redundancy of pyrotechnic facility and its supersession by matters with more power of memory. The more imbricated the formaction, the more embedded in the scripting and scenography, the more it breeds: this may mean Autolicus' tales and tropes, which uncannily repeat and predict the playworld; it may mean Perdita's waves. The fact that each moment pushes into futures also requires that each moment be recursive: this is theatrical *tempo-reality*. Nothing is swept away. So, as much as one set-piece seems to render the previous one 'nothing', the play beds these possibilities down, like the dibbles and slips of flowers that Perdita sets in her garden, each one planted for memory. The visible scene, like the speech of praise, is only one measure of action. More profound is an interlacing network of verbal tableaux, each invested with a time-and-event straddling ontology: their 'eventness' is at once in their enacted moment, in their adumbration of future tableaux, and distributed among competing or complementary epitomes of the wider 'Tale'. Possibility supervenes upon specific theatrical formations, presented with varying degrees of explicitness: disguise, rehearsal, scripted impostures, pantomime, deep-lying homonyms, scenes that flash up and disappear, echoing phrases, fantastical simulations, jigs and motions and songs. The future's potential is formactive.

Is life formactive?

1

What if the instruments that render theatrical possibility are the actual model of living? I refer not to the summary-pictures that characters themselves offer, or that we give when paraphrasing this or that character; not to descriptions of types or soliloquial self-accounting or retro-rationalizing. All such things are continuous with the way we all like to make sense of our lives, as it were from a distance, if we are summing ourselves up to a stranger, or a job committee, or if we are asked to imagine our own biographies or obituaries. But these are all deceptions, or at best mollifications, smoothing out the creases, for the purposes of sociality and familiarity. No: I am referring to the fact that we are all theatre's denaturalizing vectors. We are watched, as by an audience; scripted, as by a playwright; we go disguised, carried by audacious metaphor; we need to be cued, we are rehearsed, we hope to repeat, and in repeating forget that we have done precisely this before; we live a shuttered life, as in scenes; we are made by borrowed forms, like verse and rhyme; we are *not*. We are desired, as Perdita is, because we are more or less irresistible allegory. Admittedly, any such presumption of theatre is very strange and arresting—or it *should* be felt as strange, and as arresting. And yet perhaps this is its claim upon us, and its intimacy.

2

Formactions can make us think the puzzle of a dependent ontology, or a split ontology, where what we are—not merely what we do, or the roles we must perforce play, but what we *are*—is contingent upon another's unreachable presence: our life as a kind of holograph or shadow, not ontologically self-authorizing. The playworld is the reality; it is the only reality; it only has existence as it is perceived and enacted (in reading or performance): and yet still it is *preformed*. The body that makes the move, the voice that speaks the words, even the face that smiles or grimaces, is not *quite* the thing, though it is absolutely coincident with it, and the true-thing is inadmissible, unexistent, without this body. Reality is holographic. These creatures, for all their unique self-sufficiency, are never ultimately their own. In this sense, the actor-as-carrier is merely the most obvious example of a principle that governs the whole playworld. This is the basic reality of Leibniz's monad, the true thing that can never be touched, that is never born (because nature never makes leaps) and can never die (ditto), whatever the passing appearance. And this, precisely this, is the weird ontological contract that the theatre at every point enacts. Formactions in performance come and go in a second. But then they haven't gone, they have just gone off-stage, they no more *die* than a character does when its actor passes into the wings, or a speech does once it is delivered. Formactions—as monads, as characters or events—are past and passing and to come.

3

We resist the idea that life is merely a death sentence. But perhaps the insult is less in the pre-empting arrogance of *death,* than in the presumptuous finality of *sentence.* The parts, the bits, the pieces; the lapsed intervals and buried points; the fractions and the fractals: the formactions know more. They presume a world of severed, potentially asymmetric instants, bites of time, correspondent to specific technologies, each with their own expressive conatus. The physics of this theatricality are in some senses fractional, in that each part bears some relation to an assumed whole. But the whole is not necessarily everything, or an organically complete playworld or character. There can be all kinds of series, all kinds of aggregates, none of which can claim to *be* the essential thing. But at the same time there is always the chance that the fraction really *is* the thing—that there is no whole number at all, only aggregates like Perdita, whose unity is as chimerical as a squared circle, accreting and diminishing according as occasion takes her. Her character has presence, charisma, flintiness, intelligence, perdurable unity. But at the same time 'Perdita' is a formaction, rendered by formactions, subdued to other formactions: it belongs to the playworld's fractal, nested seriality. Perhaps this is why, as Perdita's response to the speech has it, the 'praises are too large': not only because the pretence of calling her Queen depends on her pranked-up Whitsun robes; but because, rather terribly, the words move way beyond what she is sure she is, refashioning her as creation's epitome, and sublating her into spellbinding, repeating, supra-subjective art. You are what makes you; every action is a passion. Perdita, the wave, is taken.

4

Can it be that there is no difference, existentially, between an acknowledged thing-in-the-world—say, Perdita, speaking—and a metaphorized virtuality? What does it mean if the basic question of *life* is contingent on glimpses, private fancy, refined and barely shareable intellectual inferences? What if existence—the claim of an action or a passion to be in the world—depends upon fugitive recognitions, or upon the passing affective experience of a play? Or perhaps worse, upon the formal organization of what is or is not presented to us: a scene; an admitted articulation? What can it mean to live on stage, in scenic bytes? What happens when the scene is over and the actor departs? What can it mean if the character cannot exist without the actor, and yet the actor cannot travel with the character? If they do not share time and space, and yet there is no character without the actor, then where *is* the character—is it at all?—when the actor is not with it? What happens when neither actor nor character has possession of the meanings of the words they speak? Whose words are they? And what happens if the audience too is left behind? What sort of life is it if it isn't truly heard (as with latent wordplay) or truly seen (as with off-stage or reported events)? What subjects might emerge in the cleft between a mind and a meaning? Do we have to countenance layers of reality, alternative worlds, not-yet or contingent or bracketed worlds? What can it mean to depend for your life upon a silent witness, which if it once disappears, so does your hold upon life? Or upon a garrulous witness, like *The Winter's Tale*'s shepherd-clown, who apostrophizes your dying, and moves on, whistling.

5

If we don't *feel* it, does it mean it didn't happen? And if suddenly we do feel its pos-sibility, does it make it come true? Shakespeare's formactive dispensation is surely a dizzy provocation: everywhere ambiguating what is present to be reckoned with, what might be recognized, and so what asks *not* to be forgotten or, through the caprices of pleasure, simply blanked. But as Leibniz insists, the world is a *plenum*. It is full. And so too is the formactive playworld, where there is no such thing as a true blank, just as there is no such thing as true silence. The waves move upon the cries of the still-dying, of men who are not yet cold under water. If we think there is silence, that nothing is echoing—listen closer.

FURTHER READING

Blau, Herbert. *Occasions of Theatre* (New York City, Performing Arts Journal Publications, 1982).

Clubb, Louise. *Italian Drama in Shakespeare's Time* (New Haven: Yale University Press, 1989).

Kierkegaard, Søren. 'Repetition', in *Fear and Trembling/Repetition*, ed. and trans. Howard V. Hong and Edna H. Hong (Princeton: Princeton University Press, 1983).

Von Kleist, Heinrich. 'On The Theater of Marionettes', *Selected Prose of Heinrich Von Kleist*, trans. Peter Wortsman (Brooklyn: Achipelago Books, 2010).

Leibniz, G. W. *Philosophical Texts*, ed. and trans. R. S. Woodhouse and Richard Francks (Oxford: Oxford University Press, 1998).

Leibniz, G. W. *New Essays on Human Understanding*, ed. and trans. Peter Remnant and Jonathan Bennett (Cambridge: Cambridge University Press, 2006).

CHAPTER 19

NOW

SCOTT MAISANO

People like us, who believe in physics, know that the distinction between past, present and future is only *a stubbornly persistent illusion*.

—Albert Einstein[1]

In our present degeneration it is through the skin that metaphysics must be made to re-enter our minds.

—Antonin Artaud[2]

Now that you are here—and I am here—the theatrical performance can begin. Timing is everything. Timing is what distinguishes theatre from poetry, prose, painting, and the plastic arts. Theatre, unlike these other media, produces ephemeral events rather than enduring art objects. The reader of Shakespeare's sonnets can pore over the same poem for hours, can read ahead and then flip back to that particular poem again later, can set the poem aside for days, weeks, or even years and still come back to find its lines unchanged; the reader can recommend the poem to her children and grandchildren; and thus generation after generation can read the same poem across the span of a century or more. So long as Michelangelo's David stands in Florence's Galleria dell'Accademia and Leonardo da Vinci's Mona Lisa hangs in the Musée du Louvre in Paris, admirers of these early modern art objects can return to see them again and again. Even the viewer of a film on DVD can pause over a single shot for minutes or hours, can rewind to a previous scene, or jump ahead to the film's conclusion if he or she doesn't want to watch the entire movie again; and the film's conclusion, like the Shakespearean sonnet and Michelangelo's David, will be the

[1] This quotation comes from Einstein's letter, in March 1955, to the widow of his friend, Michael Besso. See Freeman Dyson, *Disturbing the Universe* (London: Basic Books, 1981), 193. For helpful criticisms of and valuable contributions to this essay, I would like to thank my undergraduate and graduate students at the University of Massachusetts, Boston, and Melissa J. Jones, Alexander McAdams, Tracey Metivier, Matthew O'Brien, Samantha Regan, Henry S. Turner, and Katie Weygand.

[2] Antonin Artaud, *The Theater and Its Double*, trans. Mary Caroline Richards (New York: Grove Press, 1958), 99.

same from one viewing to the next. For those of us born after Peter Brook's 1970 stage production of Shakespeare's *A Midsummer Night's Dream*, however, there are only photographs and a few short film clips to aid us in admiring, appreciating, and understanding why this performance proved so innovative and influential. Even those photographs and films, of course, cannot give us the experience of 'being there'—in the audience, face to face with the actors, shoulder to shoulder with other spectators—as the event unfolded in time. When Brook's *Dream* finished, it was gone, leaving not a wrack behind. The essence of theatre—ancient, Elizabethan, and modern alike—is 'now you see it, now you don't'.

Theatre can thus claim to be the most lifelike medium because, just as in real life, what's past is past and, try as we might, there's no way to recreate or to relive that past in the future. Theatre exists, therefore, only in the present, only so long as actor and audience remain present to one another. Theatre, according to twentieth-century theorists such as Antonin Artaud (1896–1948) and Jerzy Grotowski (1933–99), can do without *pages* (dramatic literature or theatrical script), and it can do without *stages* (the professional theatre); but what it cannot do without is the fleeting moment when the living, breathing bodies of actor(s) and audience(s) meet face-to-face. This moment might last for only a few seconds, as when Henry VIII dandles his infant son, Edward VI, before a window for onlookers to see; or, in the words of the Prologue to *Romeo and Juliet*, it might endure for 'the two hours' traffic of our stage'; or, longer still, for the 'nine daies wonder' of Will Kemp's morris dance from London to Norwich. But so long as it lasts, wherever it may occur, theatre is happening. Whereas in the *Poetics* Aristotle disparaged the evanescent moment of live performance, with its emphasis on spectacle and music, as accidental rather than essential to the history and philosophy of Greek theatre, twentieth- and twenty-first-century scholars and practitioners of Theatre and Performance Studies view ephemerality as the *sine qua non* of what Timothy Wiles called 'the theater event': a singular and unrepeatable occurrence. Assessing the legacy of Artaud and Grotowski in twentieth-century counter-cultural theatre, especially Allan Kaprow's script-less, theatre-less 'happenings', Wiles observes: 'The participial construction of the term "happening" points to this theater's concern with the present moment of performance, what is happening "now".'[3] And indeed the 'present moment of performance', the 'now', has increasingly taken centre stage in the half-century since the 'happenings' and avant-garde performances of the 1960s.

Peggy Phelan describes the ever-vanishing present moment—the 'now'—as absolutely indispensable to late twentieth-century 'performance art'. In 'The Ontology of Performance', Phelan insists first that 'performance's only life is in the present'; second, that 'Performance occurs over a time that will not be repeated';

---

[3] Timothy J. Wiles, *The Theater Event: Modern Theories of Performance* (Chicago: University of Chicago Press, 1980), 115.

and finally that 'only rarely in this culture is the "now" to which performance addresses its deepest questions valued'.[4] Unlike literature or painting or statuary, all celebrated for their staying power and monumentality, it is the disappearance of performance that keeps its art from being objectified, commodified, and commercialized. Philip Auslander, Phelan's most outspoken critic, assails her 'devotion to the now' and her privileging of live performance at the expense of television shows, recording artists, and new media.[5] But Auslander proves equally devoted to—and bound by—the idea of the 'now'. Explaining how cathode ray tubes create televisual images by repetitive scanning—'the first scan of the frame [is] all but gone, even from the retina, before the second interlacing scan is complete'— Auslander argues that 'disappearance may be even more fundamental to television than it is to live performance'.[6] In a subsequent essay on internet chatterbots, virtual entities that engage human users in online conversations, Auslander concludes that 'liveness is first and foremost a temporal relationship, a relationship of simultaneity'. According to Auslander, chatterbots are 'live', if not 'a-live', because these virtual, incorporeal agents 'perform in the moment'; their speech is 'heard or watched at the time of its occurrence'.[7] Even as Auslander's cathode ray tubes and chatterbots push the boundaries of who or what can perform live in the twenty-first century, performance itself never rises above nor reaches beyond 'the time of its occurrence', the 'now'.

Theatrical performance—a live art and a temporal medium—exists *for a limited time only* and this very brevity is seen as the source of its peculiar vitality. Indeed, Michael Tolaydo, the influential Shakespeare pedagogue, avers: 'A whole play does not come into being when it's in print. It breathes only when it is performed, and for that moment only'.[8] In the twenty-first-century periodic table of theatrical elements, the transitory moment of performance—the 'now'—is, like hydrogen, first and foundational. Here's the problem: according to twenty-first-century physics there's no such thing as *the* present moment or the 'now'. What, then, shall become of theatricality—the *presence* of the actor, the *immediacy* of the stage, and the *liveness* of performance—now that there is no now?

[4] Peggy Phelan, *Unmarked: The Politics of Performance* (New York: Routledge, 1993), 146.

[5] Philip Auslander, *Liveness: Performance in a Mediatized Culture*, 2nd edn. (New York: Routledge, 2008), 44.

[6] The first quotation Auslander cites is from Sean Cubitt, *Time Shift: On Video Culture* (New York: Routledge, 1991), 31; the second quotation is from Auslander, *Liveness*, 48.

[7] Philip Auslander, 'Live from Cyberspace, or, I was sitting at my computer this guy appeared he thought I was a bot', *PAJ: Performing Arts Journal* 70 (2002), 20–1.

[8] Michael Tolaydo, 'Three-Dimensional Shakespeare', in Peggy O'Brien and the Teaching Shakespeare Institute of The Folger Shakespeare Library, ed., *Shakespeare Set Free: Teaching A Midsummer Night's Dream, Romeo and Juliet, and Macbeth* (New York: Simon & Schuster, 2006), 27. The failure to think of time as a dimension in Theatre and Performance Studies is perhaps nowhere more evident than in Tolaydo's title.

The performance will continue after
this brief scientific intermission

Imagine you're at a movie theatre watching a three-hour film that requires the projectionist to switch reels halfway through the screening. During this brief intermission, however, the projectionist does not replace the reel as quickly and seamlessly
as possible; nor does he allow spectators to get up from their seats, stretch their legs,
and head into the lobby for refreshments; instead, the projectionist comes down
from his booth, positioned out-of-sight at the back of the theatre, walks through the
centre aisle dividing the seated audience and steps onto the stage in front of the
screen. He then holds up the entire film, both reels of celluloid, and explains how
the illusion of film works, how 'movie magic' *really* happens. 'Alas, folks, this is a
one-man show. And I'm your man. There's really no movement at all on the screen',
he says. 'Nor is anything moving on these reels. It's all just a very long series of static
images, a bunch of still photos shown in rapid succession. More importantly, those
characters that you've been wondering and worrying about during this cliffhanger
of an intermission, well, worry no more. Their futures and their fates were never in
question. They will live or die, prosper or come to ruin, based not on any decisions
they make or actions they take but only on these reels of film. Everything you've
seen thus far as well as everything you're waiting to see during the second half is all
right here, in my hands. Here you see the whole movie—all of it at once—and so
you may rest assured that whatever appears to be happening for the first time in a
few minutes, when we resume the screening, already exists just as much as you
and I do. And everything you've already seen, which even now seems to be fading
and receding into memory, exists too. I have it here in my hands and could come
around to each of you individually, unreel the film, and hold it up to the light so you
could see that in fact each frame, each static image, every moment of time, persists
and endures. Just because you no longer see it glowing on the screen before you doesn't
mean that it disappeared or went away. Thank you for indulging a projectionist's
ontological digression. Please enjoy the rest of the show.' With that the projectionist
steps down from the stage, returns to his booth, and resumes showing the film.

Now imagine you're not at a movie theatre but at a live theatre, watching real
flesh-and-blood actors on-stage, in a situation where presumably anything could go
wrong at any moment. And then the same thing happens. Only the 'projectionist',
who introduces himself as Albert, has a much more daunting task: he must persuade you that the future of the on-stage actor, perhaps a friend of yours, already
exists. Likewise, every single moment of your own past and future—and all the
moments throughout the entire lifetimes of every other audience member—is just
as much in existence and just as real as this present moment. Thus, there's nothing
special about what's happening right now. It might seem that way to you because

that's the only instant of time which you're able to see. But the past has not disappeared or gone away, nor is the future as yet undetermined or non-existent. Those moments are just like this moment.

My hypothetical anecdote illustrates a very contemporary problem, although it's one we rarely think about. According to Albert Einstein nothing ever begins or ends. Everything simply is—forever. In the words of theoretical physicist Paul Davies:

> Nothing in known physics corresponds to the passage of time. Indeed, physicists insist that time doesn't flow at all; it merely is... The most straightforward conclusion is that both past and future are fixed. For this reason, physicists prefer to think of time as laid out in its entirety—a timescape, analogous to landscape—with all past and future events located together. It is a notion sometimes referred to as block time. Completely absent from this description of nature is anything that singles out a privileged special moment as the present or any process that would systematically turn future events into present, then past, events... In this description, nothing happens or changes... Similar arguments go back to ancient Greek philosophers such as Parmenides and Zeno... the flow of time is unreal, but time itself is as real as space.[9]

Or, more succinctly, in the words of David Deutsch, another theoretical physicist:

> there is no single 'present moment', except subjectively... [O]bjectively, no moment is privileged as being more 'now' than the others, just as no position is privileged as being more 'here' than other positions... To exist at all at a particular moment means to exist there forever.[10]

A full explanation why 'now' is an illusion would require an entire book, and fortunately Davies, Deutsch, and other physicists have written such books for non-scientists (see also my Further Reading at the end of this chapter). But, for now, the salient questions are these: If the reality of time, notwithstanding our phenomenological experience of it, is more akin to a book or a film (where what happened in the past and what will happen in the future exist forever to either side of the present moment), is theatre screwed? That is, does theatre cease to be the most realistic art form and become, instead, the one that most closely conforms to our subjective and deceptive concept of the 'now'? How can theatre, which always takes place in time, take us outside time and thus enable audiences to experience time as a static dimension? What becomes of 1960s-style improvised 'happenings' in a world where, as Paul Davies puts it, 'nothing happens'? What might a performance based on Einstein's counterintuitive ideas—'there's no single present moment' and 'the flow of time is unreal, but time's as real as space'—look like? For answers to these questions, we need to return, somewhat unexpectedly, to Shakespeare's time. More precisely, we need to return to Shakespeare's Time.

---

[9] Paul Davies, 'That Mysterious Flow', *Scientific American* (September 2002), 40–7.
[10] David Deutsch, *The Fabric of Reality: The Science of Parallel Universes—and Its Implications* (New York: Penguin Books, 1997), 262.

Now is *The Winter's Tale*'s discontent

The most famous literary account of time as a fourth dimension is H .G. Wells's novel, *The Time Machine*, published in 1895, a decade before Einstein proposed his theory of special relativity. In the final paragraph, Wells's narrator, who has faithfully transcribed an incredible story told by the Time Traveller, wonders not where but *when* the storyteller himself might be: 'He may even now—if I may use the phrase—be wandering some plesiosaurus-haunted oolitic coral reef, or beside the lonely saline seas of the Triassic Age'.[11] The phrase 'even now' has been rendered ineffectual and obsolete in light of the discovery that both the distant past—200 million years ago when humanity did not exist but Loch Ness monsters did—and the distant future—when the Time Traveller sees life on earth extinguished by an enormous sun—are just as real as the present moment.

The same thing happens midway into Shakespeare's *The Winter's Tale*. This late tragicomic romance contains both Shakespeare's most famous stage direction, 'Exit pursued by a bear', and his most sensational *coup de théâtre*, Hermione's revivification in 'the statue scene'. But the most mind-boggling and boundary-pushing bit of stagecraft usually gets the least attention from editors and directors: 'Enter Time, the Chorus'. Training bears to chase actors across stage is no mean feat; nor indeed is getting actors to hold their composure, let alone their breath, in statue-like stillness. But 'presenting' Time—all time, past and future as well as the present—before a live audience defies the very laws of physics. Or rather this impossible-to-perform stage direction (like Wells's Time Traveller and Einstein) points the way to an alternative physics hidden behind the illusion of life as we know it.

Admittedly, Shakespeare was neither the first nor the last early modern dramatist to give body, or even voice, to Time: according to Inga-Stina Ewbank 'Time as the Father of Truth had appeared in at least three royal entries, and Middleton was soon going to use [Time] in the 1613 Lord Mayor's Show, *The Triumph of Truth*... [Thus] Shakespeare's choric Time is in a firm Elizabethan tradition'.[12] And yet nothing in the Tudor–Stuart theatrical tradition or in the illustrations of time in contemporary emblem books or even in Robert Greene's *Pandosto: The Triumph of Time*, Shakespeare's source, can account for the surprising detail that interests me here. In just 32 lines, Shakespeare's Time uses the word 'now' eight (or, including synonyms, nine) times.

---

[11] H. G. Wells, *The Time Machine*, ed. Stephen Arata (New York: W. W. Norton, 2009), 71.

[12] Inga Stina Ewbank, 'The Triumph of Time', in D. J. Palmer, ed., *Shakespeare's Later Comedies* (London: Penguin Books, 1971), 322.

Enter Time, *the Chorus.*

Time:

1. I, that please some, try all; both joy and terror
2. Of good and bad, that makes and unfolds error,
3. *Now* take upon me, in the name of Time,
4. To use my wings. Impute it not a crime
5. To me or my swift passage that I slide
6. O'er sixteen years, and leave the growth untried
7. Of that wide gap, since it is in my power
8. To o'erthrow law, and in one self-born hour
9. To plant and o'erwhelm custom. Let me pass
10. The same I am ere ancient'st order was,
11. Or what is *now* received. I witness to
12. The times that brought them in; so shall I do
13. To th'freshest things *now* reigning, and make stale
14. *The glistering of this present* as my tale
15. *Now* seems to it. Your patience this allowing,
16. Turn my glass, and give my scene such growing
17. As you had slept between. Leontes leaving—
18. Th'effects of his fond jealousies so grieving
19. That he shuts up himself—imagine me,
20. Gentle spectators, that I *now* may be
21. In fair Bohemia, and remember well
22. I mentioned a son o'th'king's, which Florizel
23. I *now* name to you; and with speed so pace
24. To speak of Perdita, *now* grown in grace
25. Equal with wondering. What of her ensues
26. I list not prophecy, but let Time's news
27. Be known when 'tis brought forth. A shepherd's daughter,
28. And, what to her adheres, which follows after,
29. Is th'argument of Time. Of this allow,
30. If ever you have spent time worse ere *now*;
31. If never, yet that Time himself doth say
32. He wishes earnestly you never may.[13]

No other speech in Shakespeare's canon repeats the word 'now' more often. Only Launce's comical re-enactment of bidding his family adieu in *Two Gentleman of Verona* ('Now come I to my father...Now come I to my mother...Now come I to

---

[13] William Shakespeare, *The Winter's Tale*, ed. John Pitcher (London: Arden Shakespeare, 2010), 4.1.1–32.

my sister') matches Time's chorus in its number of 'nows'.[14] But Time also alludes to 'the glistering of this present', another 'now' disguised and cosseted in a dramatic flourish.

Nor is it an accident that 'now' is the peculiar verbal tic (toc) of Shakespeare's Time. Scholarly editions of *The Winter's Tale* invariably explain how Shakespeare, by not keeping the action to a single revolution of the sun, flouted the neoclassical 'unity of time' derived from Aristotle's *Poetics*. But *The Winter's Tale* also holds up for examination and estrangement another Aristotelian 'unit of time', the 'now' of Aristotle's *Physics*. Here time and the now are inseparable concepts: 'if there were no time', Aristotle reasons, 'there would be no "now," and vice versa' (219b–220a).[15] 'Time, for Aristotle, is centered on Now', writes Sarah Waterlow, adding that 'in his discussion of time, the idea of Now, more than any other, confronts us at every turn'.[16] In Book 4 of *Physics*, Aristotle writes:

> [Time] either does not exist at all or barely, and in an obscure way. One part of it [the past] has been and is not, while the other [the future] is going to be and is not yet... One would naturally suppose that what is made up of things which do not exist could have no share in reality... Further, if a divisible thing is to exist, it is necessary that, when it exists, all or some of its parts must exist. But of time some parts have been, while others have to be, and no part of it is... For what is 'now' is not a part [of Time].
>
> (217b–218a)

For Aristotle, the anti-Einstein, time is *not* real but the 'now' is. The present moment, the 'now', serves as a continuously moving boundary between past and future; but, even as it bounds past and future, the 'now' itself has no boundaries because it has no extension or duration in time. If it did, then the 'now' too would be part past and part future; instead, like a geometrical point in relation to a line, the 'now' occupies no space and is, therefore, no part of time. In an effort to clarify the obscure way in which the *illusion* of time exists, Aristotle offers a spatial, even theatrical, analogy: if we think of a body in motion, the 'now' would correspond to the moving body while time would correspond to the movement traced or path taken by that body (219b). This infinitesimal moving body ('now') is real, it exists; by contrast, the larger movement or path (time itself) is something we humans observe and measure—a kind of number—but it doesn't exist independently of our observation, measurement, or enumeration.

---

[14] See *Two Gentlemen of Verona* 2.3.1–32. Apart from *The Winter's Tale*, all citations of Shakespeare refer to *The Riverside Shakespeare*, ed. G. Blakemore Evans (Boston: Houghton Mifflin, 1974).

[15] All quotations of Aristotle are from *Physics*, trans. R. P. Hardie and R. K. Gaye in Richard McKeon, ed., *The Basic Works of Aristotle* (New York: Modern Library, 2001). Aristotle's most sustained discussion of time is in *Physics* IV 10–14.

[16] Sarah Waterlow, 'Aristotle's Now', *The Philosophical Quarterly* 34.135 (April 1984), 104.

For millennia, time has been intimately and inextricably tied to the passage of the 'now'. Augustine wrestles with Aristotle's definition in *Confessions*.[17] In the twentieth century Martin Heidegger concluded his philosophical magnum opus, *Being and Time* by observing:

> Ever since Aristotle all discussions of the concept of time have clung in principle to the Aristotelian definition...Time is what is 'counted'...When one makes present that which is moved in its movement, one says '*now* here, *now* here, *now* here, and so on'. The '*nows*' are what get counted. And these show themselves in every '*now*' as '*nows*' which will 'forthwith be no-longer-*now*' and '*nows*' which have 'just been not-yet-*now*'...Thus for the ordinary understanding of time, time shows itself as a sequence of '*nows*' which are constantly 'present-at-hand', simultaneously passing away and coming along. Time is understood as a succession, as a 'flowing stream' of '*nows*'.[18]

While the New Cambridge Shakespeare edition of *The Winter's Tale* supplements its discussion of the Chorus with sixteenth- and seventeenth-century engravings and woodcuts, I submit that we'd be better off supplementing our editions with passages from Heidegger and illustrations of Einstein–Minkowski (hourglass-shaped) light cones. For Shakespeare's Time is not a hoary allegorical personification lifted from an illustrated page but a profound philosophical meditation, made specifically for the stage, about how the reality of time differs from the phenomenological appearance of its passing.[19]

If, as Stanton Garner Jr suggests, '*Theatricality*...refers to a play's existence in the moment of performance, in all its physicality and immediacy, and the many ways by which a plays calls attention to this moment...that dimension of all plays that is irreducibly here and now', then Time's chorus surpasses both the bear and the statue in terms of 'theatricality'.[20] And yet, *pace* Garner, Shakespeare's Time insists that he is *not* 'irreducibly here and now' in the present moment. Time knows and sees things, even now, which audiences will not know or see until sometime in the future. For example, the fate of Perdita: 'What of her ensues / I list not prophecy, but let Time's news / Be known when 'tis brought forth' (4.1.25–7). Indeed, like the accuracy of the Apollonian oracle in Act 3, the only way time travel into the future can occur—and this is exactly what happens at the start of Act 4—is if the future *already exists* as a travel destination. The prehistoric origins of 'order' and 'custom', events located in the audience's distant past, also remain present to Time: 'I witness

---

[17] 'In fact the only time that can be called present is an instant, if we can conceive of such, that cannot be divided even into the most minute fractions, and a point of time as small as this passes so rapidly from the future to the past that its duration is without length. For if its duration were prolonged, it could be divided into past and future. When it is present it has no duration.' Saint Augustine, *Confessions*, trans. R. S. Pine-Coffin (New York: Penguin Books, 1961), 266.

[18] Martin Heidegger, *Being and Time*, trans. John Macquarrie and Edward Robinson (New York: Harper, 1962), 473–4 (emphasis mine).

[19] William Shakespeare, *The Winter's Tale*, ed. Susan Snyder and Deborah T. Curren-Aquino (Cambridge: Cambridge University Press, 2007), 16–17, 35.

[20] Stanton B. Garner Jr, 'Theatricality in *Mankind* and *Everyman*', *Studies in Philology* 84.3 (1987), 274.

to / The times that brought them in; so shall I do / To the freshest things now reigning'. Time tangles, conflates, and confounds verb tenses here and again in his closing syllogism. But this style, which Stephen Orgel describes as 'so contorted and elliptical', is perfectly in keeping with a chorus tasked with demonstrating the relativity of simultaneity.[21]

Time's Chorus does more than call attention to the moment of performance; it calls the present, past, and future all into doubt. What can 'now' mean if the audience is situated outside Time? How can we distinguish among past, present, and future when, Time says, Time hasn't changed? By proclaiming 'The same I am ere ancient'st order was / Or what is now received' (4.1.10–11), Time not only professes his static nature but provocatively uses the present tense to speak of himself in terms of a past that his listeners perceive as 'ancient'. His boast 'in one self-born hour / To plant and o'erwhelm custom' (4.1.8–9) implies that Time is in both the past (when what we recognize as 'custom' was planted) and the future (when our deeply ingrained customs will be uprooted) even as he stands before us now. Indeed, just as the Prince of Morocco learns in *The Merchant of Venice* that 'all that glisters is not gold' (2.7.65), and just as Caliban's confederates in *The Tempest* allow themselves to be distracted by Ariel's display of 'glistering apparel' (4.1.193), Time's reference to 'the glistering of this present' hints at the showy, stagey, and phony nature of what appears to us, his audience, to be 'irreducibly here and now'.

But Time, some eagle-eyed readers will say, mentions his own 'swift passage' in a way that seems to conform to Aristotle's definition of the moving 'now'. In fact, Time appears to be asking our pardon as he requests 'Impute it not a crime / To me or my swift passage that I slide / O'er sixteen years' (4.1.4–6). Notice how the iambic pentameter stresses 'not', 'me', and 'my', as if to absolve Time, the speaker, of any wrongdoing or responsibility for the alleged 'crime'. Translation: 'when you assign blame for the lamentable fact that time flies, do *not* blame *me*'. But if Time bears no responsibility for the 'slide / O'er sixteen years', then who does? The answer becomes clearer a few lines later, as Time asks a favour of the audience: 'Let me pass…' (4.1.9). Is Time trying to tell us that, as Paul Davies puts it, 'Time doesn't flow at all; it merely is'? Might Time be suggesting that he doesn't move unless and until human spectators observe him? In his book *Shakespeare, Theatre, and Time*, Matthew Wagner remarks that

> Time's power comes across as somewhat ambiguous or contradictory…[for example] he draws our attention to both what he can do, and what he needs us (humans, the audience) for…he is asking us not to censure him for skipping all those years, and also to allow him to appear before us in his traditional image.[22]

But that's not in fact what Time asks his assembled audience to 'allow'. What does Time mean, precisely, when he says 'Your patience this allowing / Turn my glass and

---

[21]   William Shakespeare, *The Winter's Tale*, ed. Stephen Orgel (Oxford: Oxford Shakespeare, 1996), 160.
[22]   Matthew D. Wagner, *Shakespeare, Theatre, and Time* (London: Routledge, 2011), 105–6.

give my scene such growing'? One contemporary meaning of 'patience', according to the *Oxford English Dictionary*, is 'a condition which contributes to an effect by being acted upon'.[23] For example, while the combination of fire and water results in steam, fire would have been seen as the *agent*, the active cause, of steam, while water would have been classified as the *patient*, the passive cause, which produces steam as the effect of being acted upon by fire. Time itself does not move or change—it neither turns the hourglass nor grows the swelling scene—but we produce these special effects of motion and change without actively doing a thing: we passively observe and that alone 'allows', or makes possible, the impression or sense of time's passage and flow.

The fourth dimension breaks the fourth wall

My intention, despite quoting and closely reading Time's chorus in its entirety, is not to assume a 'definitive and sacred' quality about the dramatic text, an assumption, which as Antonin Artaud lamented in the 'Theatre of Cruelty', subordinates the dynamic and spatial expression of the stage as well as the physical and embodied language of performance to speeches written and characters created in advance by an off-stage author.[24] That is, I don't think it would be a big deal if an actor performing the role of Time, in Shakespeare's time or in our own, said the word only five or six or, for that matter, a hundred times. But I do think something essential is eliminated—an expression, 'half-way between gesture and thought', as Artaud puts it—whenever productions of *The Winter's Tale* either cut this chorus completely or adapt and abridge it in such a way that Time's litany of 'nows', howsoever many they may be, goes missing from the performance.[25] Time getting on-stage without his series of 'nows' would be like our hypothetical projectionist coming before us without his reels of film.

Stage directors and textual editors often draw spectators' and readers' attentions to the material props ('my wings' and 'my [hour]glass') mentioned in Time's speech, but no one to my knowledge has identified, much less exploited, this verbal prompt embedded in the verse. This is not only and not primarily Shakespeare's prompt to the actor performing the role. It is also and more importantly an actor's prompt to the audience. Time's telltale verbal tic not only registers visually on the page but chimes audibly from the stage. As John Pitcher notes, with the exception of two songs performed later in Act 4, Time's chorus contains the only end-lined rhymes in the play.[26] This first use of end-lined rhyme, withheld until the play is half over, would have rung like an alarm clock, alerting audiences to Time's unexpected entrance.

---

[23] 'patient, *adj.* and *n*.' *The Oxford English Dictionary*, 3rd edn. June 2005. *OED Online*. Oxford University Press, http://www.oed.com, accessed 8 Oct 2012 [subscription needed].

[24] Artaud, *The Theatre and Its Double*, 89.   [25] Artaud, *The Theatre and Its Double*, 89.

[26] Pitcher, ed., *The Winter's Tale*, 244, note 4.1.

This ostensible 'break in the action' is less a proto-Brechtian distancing device, meant to estrange audiences from the action on-stage and remind them that they are in a theatre, and more a proto-Artaudian attempt to 'abolish the stage' altogether and thus to eliminate any distance 'between the spectator and the spectacle'.[27]

In short, Time appears to improvise and go off-script, setting aside the prefabricated story-world in order to address the audience directly. As in a 1960s 'happening'—or a 1610s masque—the actor playing Time might mingle with members of the audience, involving them directly in the performance. If it seems outrageous or anachronistic to imagine Time as a sort of master of ceremonies in the midst of a total sensory experience—dancing The Frug while strobe lights leave spectators wondering whether Time moves forward, backward, or not at all—then we need only compare Time's surprise appearance in this play with Ariel's tactic of 'shock and awe' in The Tempest, written around the same time.[28] Ariel reports to Prospero: 'I boarded the King's ship: now on the beak, / Now in the waist, the deck, in every cabin / I flamed amazement'.[29] Faster than lightning and louder than thunder, Ariel divides himself and thus appears to show up in several places at once. Ariel gets precisely the reaction Artaud had imagined for his own 'Theater of Cruelty': spectators aboard King Alonso's ship 'felt a fever of the mad' and Prince Ferdinand, his hair standing straight on end, throws himself overboard in a desperate panic. Prospero's 'improv theatre' engages the nervous system of its targeted audience, wakes them up, and even puts their lives at risk. Time, though his intentions are different, aims to do no less. Audiences should tremble, not yawn, during his Chorus. If an actor were to call attention to each 'now' by delivering it through a megaphone or a bullhorn, following it with a pause, or complementing it with a physical pose or any theatrical gesture equivalent to the manifesto-like call-to-action that the word itself inspires (think Hamlet's 'Now might I do it pat, now he is praying; / And now I'll do't' or Oberon's 'Now, my Titania; wake you, my sweet queen'), then Time's remarkable chorus could even culminate in a crescendo of audience participation.[30] At the very moment Time requests the audience's assistance—'Of this allow'—he also cues us to complete the penultimate couplet by saying, in harmony with him, a decisive and final 'now!' But why?

Less a tragic chorus than an epic rhapsode, the figure of Time embodies a form of public storytelling that is older than—and, in some ways, the origin of—theatre itself. Historian and philosopher of the theatre Martin Puchner reminds us that in ancient Athens, before the legendary Thespis (as they say) ever stepped out of the chorus line, 'recitation of epic poetry was a staged event drawing large crowds'.

---

[27] Artaud, *The Theatre and Its Double*, 96.

[28] This 'happening' vision of Shakespeare's Time is inspired by Charles Gattnig Jr, 'Artaud and the Participatory Drama of the Now Generation', *Educational Theater Journal* 20.4 (1968), 485–91.

[29] *The Tempest*, 1.2.196–8.

[30] *Hamlet*, 3.3.73–4; *A Midsummer Night's Dream*, 4.1.75.

The public reciter, or rhapsode, is actually the first figure to instigate Plato's condemnation of stage actors:

> Plato arrives at his critique of the actor [in *Republic* and in *Ion*] only by way of a circuitous route, via the Homeric rhapsode, who narrates the action occurring in the past, the present, or the future in a mode Plato calls 'diegesis.' However, once the poet, or rhapsode, switches from the third person to the first, he no longer reports a character's speech but 'likens' his voice and gesture to those of the character; the rhapsode no longer is a narrator but is on his way to becoming an actor. At this moment rhapsodic diegesis turns into the mimesis performed by an actor ... In the eyes of Plato this switch from rhapsode to actor is fateful because it means that the poet 'hides' himself under the mask of the character, a mask made out of a false voice and false gestures.[31]

When Time appears on-stage in *The Winter's Tale*, what spectators witness is the reverse of 'this switch from rhapsode to actor' as the storyteller fatefully emerges for the first time from behind the masks he has donned and voices he has feigned up to this point. Although no one realized it till 'now', this performance has been a consummate one-man show.

Indeed, if one asks 'where has Time been until now?', the answer is that he has been 'in character', taking the part of each and every character—not to mention every prop, costume, and piece of *mise-en-scène*—on-stage. The editors of the New Cambridge Shakespeare edition of the play compare Time to 'the playwright, protean, sharing a bit of himself with almost every character and informing every scene'.[32] But this doesn't go far enough: the playwright, as Artaud insists, is both spatially and temporally distant from the on-stage action. Time, by contrast, *is* the on-stage action. And he shares more than just 'a *bit*' of himself with *almost* every character'; he puts his *whole* self into *all* the characters and every item of stage design. Stephen Orgel notes how 'the move from action [mimesis] to narration [diegesis] is ... [a] pivot, turning the drama we have experienced with such immediacy into a tale with a teller who both claims control over the apparently free play of the characters and offers a disturbingly amoral overview'.[33] Orgel's distinction between the immediacy of the dramatic action and the narration of the 'teller' again implies that Time is outside and detached from his 'characters' in the way, say, Robert Greene would be. But unlike Shakespeare's storytelling choric figure in *Pericles*, the moral Gower, whom the title page of George Wilkins's *The Painful Adventures of Pericles Prince of Tyre* depicts as reading from an open book, Time does not read his story aloud from an on-stage script. Indeed, if one asks 'where does Time go when he exits or leaves the stage?' the answer is that he gets back 'into character'—into all characters. As Soji Iwasaki argues, 'Time is ... responsible for the whole action of

---

[31] Martin Puchner, *Stage Fright: Modernism, Anti-Theatricality, and Drama* (Baltimore: Johns Hopkins University Press, 2002), 22.

[32] Snyder and Curren-Aquino, eds., *The Winter's Tale*, 34.

[33] Orgel, ed., *The Winter's Tale*, 41.

The Winter's Tale.[34] But even this claim does not go far enough. Time makes no ontological distinction between the fictional characters and action on-stage and the actual audience, objects, and events in the theatre. He takes responsibility for them all. When Time threatens to 'make stale / The glistering of this present as my tale / Now seems to it' the message is clear: not only has 'the drama we have experienced with such immediacy' been transformed, as Orgel notes, 'into a tale with a teller', but we have been reduced to agentless characters in that story too. When Time leaves the stage and goes back into character, in other words, he also goes back into *us*. Thus in the aforementioned collective and concluding 'now' Time speaks through *all* his characters, on-stage and off, at once.

Time's alternation between dramatic mimesis and narrative diegesis can also be used to iron out an apparent inconsistency in the Chorus. Alluding to an earlier appearance in the play, Time invites the audience to 'remember well / I mentioned a son o' th' King's, which Florizel / I now name unto you' (4.1.21–3). But Time has not made an appearance on-stage at any other point in the play, and so he has not mentioned the young prince until now. John Pitcher attempts to resolve the dilemma by suggesting that that 'Time refers to...[Act 1] when Polixenes talked about his son, i.e. in time passed'.[35] But Time taking credit himself for Polixenes' lines makes perfect sense, once we realize that he is an epic rhapsode who performs both third person narration, as in the Chorus, and first person impersonation, as in the rest of the play. Of course, the line might work just as well, perhaps even better, if spectators (or readers) fail to register that Time has spoken of Florizel, under the guise of Polixenes, earlier in the play. In this case, Time's impossible injunction to 'remember' causes members of the audience (and even readers of the text) to feel as though, over the course of the time of performance and as a result of our own ageing, we have forgotten something crucial. Thus the two minutes of stage (or page) time really *feels* like sixteen years. Although the passage of time is illusory, it proves incredibly *affective*—like theatre, which is also to say: like life.

But is Shakespeare's Time really that conscious of his own timing? To gloss Time's boast that 'it is in my power / To o'erthrow law', Stephen Orgel reminds us how '[Edward] Capell ingeniously suggested [in the eighteenth century] that the "law" thus overthrown is the dramatic rule of the unity of time'.[36] Capell's suggestion may well be ingenious, but it is not, I suspect, as ingenious as Shakespeare's Time. The oft-cited 'unity of time' derives from Aristotle's assertion that 'Tragedy endeavors to keep as far as possible within a single circuit of the sun' (*Poetics* 1449b), but it was not codified as an explicit rule for playwrights until Lodovico Castelvetro's 1570 Italian commentary on *Poetics*.[37] Castelvetro's neoclassicism was slow to catch on in

[34] Soji Iwasaki, '*Veritas Filia Temporis* and Shakespeare', *English Literary Renaissance* 3.2 (1973), 261.
[35] Pitcher, ed., *Winter's Tale*, 246.
[36] Orgel, ed., *Winter's Tale*, 159.
[37] *Poetics*, trans. Ingram Bywater, in McKeon, ed., *The Basic Works of Aristotle*, 1460.

England, as evidenced by Sir Philip Sidney's complaint in *Defense of Poesy* about the pre-Shakespearean early modern stage:

> For where the stage should always represent but one place, and the uttermost time in it should be, both by Aristotle's precept and common reason, but one day, there is both many days and many places, inartificially imagined.[38]

The innovation of *The Winter's Tale*, therefore, lies not in its violation of neoclassical rules, which were already more honoured in the breach than in the observance, but rather in the way it acknowledges and perhaps even adheres to the letter of the new dramaturgical law while acting contrary to its spirit.

The numbers don't quite add up when Time claims to 'slide / O'er sixteen years' between Acts 3 and 4. You do the maths: in the first half of the play Mamillius declares 'a sad tale's best for winter', but in the second half of the play Perdita distributes flowers 'Of middle summer' at a sheep-shearing festival (2.1.25; 4.4.107). Perhaps Time is rounding up from fifteen and a half years to sixteen; after all, just four lines after Time has exited the stage, Camillo remarks: 'It is fifteen years since I saw my country' (4.2.4). So which is it: fifteen or sixteen? It turns out to be both. At the beginning of the play, Polixenes identifies the moon as the standard measure of time: 'Nine changes of the watery star hath been / The shepherd's note since we have left our throne' (1.2.1–2). A remarkable feature of the lunar calendar, as anyone familiar with the Islamic observance of Ramadan can attest, is that a year is '354 days long—11 days short (roughly) of the true solar year'. As science writer Dan Falk puts it, 'Adopt such a calendar, and each New Year's celebration will be 11 days earlier that it was the year before. *A midsummer celebration would become a midwinter celebration [and vice versa] after just 16 years*.'[39] In other words, if we are on solar time, as Camillo appears to be, it's been fifteen and a half years since Act 3; but if we are on lunar time, like Polixenes, it's been sixteen years *to the day*. Thus Time upholds the neoclassical 'unity of time', taking off from Palermo and touching down in Prague on the selfsame day, despite a change in seasons and the passage of a generation. In fact, both the shift from Christmas-tide to midsummer and the generation gap are prefigured by Polixenes'—that is, Time's—boast of his son: 'He makes a July's day as short as December'.[40] Upping his own ante, Time's chorus literally digests July and December into the space of a single day.

---

[38] Sir Philip Sidney, 'From *The Defense of Poesy*', excerpted in William Shakespeare, *The Winter's Tale*, ed. Mario DiGangi (Boston: Bedford / St Martin's Press, 2008), 143.

[39] This quote and the one immediately preceding it are from Dan Falk, *In Search of Time: The History, Physics, and Philosophy of Time* (New York: St Martin's Press, 2008), 32 (my italics).

[40] 1.2.168; for more on the play's 'two fundamentally solstitial movements', though without a mention of how 16 years is precisely the amount of time required to move a lunar holiday from winter solstice to summer solstice, see Michael Bristol, *Big-Time Shakespeare* (New York: Routledge, 1996), 157.

What now?

Performance Studies has yet to interrogate or subject to critique its most privileged—and performative—keyword: now. This is why Shakespeare's character
Time remains so exciting, challenging, relevant, and indeed boundary-pushing
even today. Whereas live performance is something that happens *in* the now,
theatricality—performing the impossible—is something that happens *to* the
now.

When a clock or a wristwatch appears to move slowly, the time between each
tick—each new now—seeming to grow longer and longer, we're experiencing
what physicists call *time dilation*. Certainly, time dilation is a feature of any theatrical performance that involves asynchronous durations of mimetic stage time
and diegetic story time. If a character in Shakespeare's *Romeo and Juliet*, for example, were to observe the wristwatch of an audience member, a clock on the wall of
the theatre, or simply the sun as it passes over the Globe Theatre, it would seem
to him that the time had slowed almost to a stop, as several days would pass in his
fictional world while only a little more than 'two hours' would tick off the designated timepiece. But in all the works of Shakespeare and of his contemporaries in
the early modern theatre, there is nothing like the extreme time dilation that
occurs at 'Enter Time the Chorus'. What takes sixteen years for the characters
on-stage takes only two minutes for spectators off-stage, which in turn takes only
eight 'nows', or ticks of a clock, for a Time who is at once on-stage and off-off-
stage. Paradoxically, if Shakespeare's Time is infinite and eternal, as he claims,
then his seemingly brief chorus is infinitely larger than the play which contains it.
Exemplifying the Renaissance aesthetic of *multum in parvo* (or, in Christopher
Marlowe's incomparable phrase, 'infinite riches in a little room') the entire play,
despite spanning sixteen years, gets reduced to an infinitesimal, nigh imperceptible, part of its own chorus. In relation to eternity, *any* finite span of time—the
sixteen years that characters in the play experience, the four hundred years separating us from Shakespeare, or the whole course of human history—would appear
as if it were an Aristotelian 'now', a duration-less instant, appearing and disap-
pearing in the blink of an eye.

So how did Shakespeare—and how can we—make sense of something that is at
once an instant and an eternity? To begin, we should note that Einsteinian time
dilation was not unthinkable in medieval and early modern England, even outside
the theatre. According to Alessandro Scafi, time dilation at that time was experienced not in the vicinity of black holes (as is theorized today) but in the vicinity of
Eden: 'Many medieval legends declare that, while a fortunate pilgrim [who had
inadvertently happened upon the actual Garden of Eden] experienced Paradise for
only a brief instant or a few hours, in the outside human world many decades or

several generations had elapsed'.[41] Scafi and others have recounted the tale of three monks who accidently stumble into the Garden of Eden, where they meet Enoch and Elijah. After what seems only a few hours' bliss, the monks ask permission to stay an entire fortnight in Paradise, whereupon their hosts inform them that they've *already* been there for several hundred years.

The Winter's Tale is chock full of romantic fantasies about preserving a unique moment forever or making it possible to experience a singular instant for all eternity: the wistful longing of Polixenes' wish 'to be boy eternal' (1.2.64); the tender nostalgia of Leontes' experience when 'Looking on the lines / Of my boy's face, methoughts I did recoil / Twenty-three years, and saw myself unbreeched' (1.2.153–5); the unquenchable desire of Florizel as he tells Perdita 'When you speak...I'd have you do it ever' and 'When you do dance, I wish you / A wave o' th' sea, that you might ever do / Nothing but that, move still, still so' (4.4.140–2)—a passage for which Simon Palfrey offers a bravura Leibnizian reading in his essay on 'Formaction' in this collection—and, of course, the yearning a husband and daughter feel to look upon the likeness of a dearly departed wife and mother interminably:

> Paulina:...Shall I draw the curtain?
> Leontes: No, not these twenty years.
> Perdita: So long could I / Stand by, a looker-on.   (5.3.83–5)

And yet, while these things might seem like sentimental impossibilities, the message of Time is that, despite all appearances and all our own lived experiences to the contrary, there's no need to yearn for perseverance in a state of grace or ecstasy or happiness. Because as a mere fact of theatrical reality, it turns out, 'to exist at all at a particular moment means to exist there forever'.[42]

Is this not, after all, precisely what happens when visitors to Paulina's 'gallery' come face-to-face with the 'statue' of Hermione, existing in a sort of suspended animation? Matthew Wagner beautifully calls attention to the fact that

> Paulina's instruction to the court (and, by extension, to the audience) to 'all stand still'...produces a highly charged moment of frozen time...whereby all of the viewers [on-stage and off-stage] take on Hermione's stillness, and she can then—and only then—take on their motion...if the scene works well, one should be able to hear the proverbial pin drop in the moment just before Hermione moves.[43]

This 'highly charged moment of frozen time', as the entire theatre comes to a sudden standstill, is, I think, Time's final gift to the audience: a chance to live, to feel, to experience something approaching eternity in an instant.[44] Alas, Wagner reads it quite differently, arguing that 'this juxtaposition of stillness and motion is a

---

[41] Alessandro Scafi, 'Mapping Eden', in Denis Cosgrove, ed., *Mappings* (London: Reaktion Books, 1999), 54.

[42] Deutsch, *The Fabric of Reality*, 262.   [43] Wagner, *Shakespeare, Theatre and Time*, 110.

[44] Wagner, *Shakespeare, Theatre and Time*, 108.

temporal phenomenon, inasmuch as stillness embodies time stopped, or death, and motion embodies time active, or life'. But, as readers of Cicero's 'Dream of Scipio', or Augustine's *Confessions*, or Chaucer's *Parliament of Fowls* would have known, to be outside time is not to be dead—or at least not *only* to be dead—but to be eternal. Contemplating the implications of Einsteinian spacetime, Dan Falk writes: 'treating every "now" as equally real [leads to] a certain kind of immortality. It's not the sort of life after death that most of us would probably prefer; instead, it's something like life alongside death. Since time does not pass, we do not age... You don't have any sense in which yesterday is any less real than today'.[45] It's this kind of immortality, I think, that pervades Shakespeare's late tragicomic romance.

The time has come for Theatre and Performance Studies to sacrifice their 'sacred nows'. Artaud's 'Theatre of Cruelty' set out to disabuse its audiences of their comforting illusions and to expose them to metaphysical truths uniquely on offer in the theatre. But what devotees of Artaud have been arguing makes the theatre unique— the 'now'—is itself a comforting illusion. Whereas theatre theorists and performance artists for more than half a century have championed the 'now' as a way to bypass repetition, representation, mediation, and interpretation, the fact is that 'now' is nothing but a repetition, representation, mediation, and an interpretation of time. One further irony: even as Theatre and Performance Studies jettisoned Aristotle's *Poetics*, they have clung ever more tightly, albeit unwittingly, to his *Physics*. We can debate whether Shakespeare was 'ahead of his time', but one fact is beyond dispute: Shakespeare's Time was ahead of him. Indeed, Shakespeare's Time is ahead of us, even now.

FURTHER READING

Carroll, Sean. *From Eternity to Here: The Quest for the Ultimate Theory of Time* (New York: Penguin, 2010).

Coope, Ursula. *Time for Aristotle* (Oxford: Oxford University Press, 2005).

Maisano, Scott. 'Time', in Patricia Parker, ed., *The Shakespeare Encyclopedia: Life, Works, World, and Legacy* (Westport, CT: Greenwood, forthcoming 2016).

Schneider, Rebecca. *Performing Remains: Art and War in Times of Theatrical Reenactment* (New York: Routledge, 2011).

Shepherd, Simon and Mick Wallis. *Drama/Theater/Performance* (The New Critical Idiom) (London: Routledge, 2004).

Williams, D. C. 'The Myth of Passage', *Journal of Philosophy* (July 1957), 457–72.

[45] Falk, *In Search of Time*, 150.

CHAPTER 20

EVENTUALITY

MICHAEL WITMORE

Eventuality and theatre's 'inner touch'

What do we mean by 'eventuality' in connection with theatre? The word is difficult, even wilfully abstract. An eventuality is both something that happens and, less obviously, a quality of things that happen. The first meaning, when the word is used as a noun to describe a type of event, is common. 'We failed to consider this eventuality.' One hears such phrases in discussions of war or of legal liability—situations where the future is not clear, but one must reason about it anyway. In this sense, 'eventuality' is part of the language of prudence, foresight, and excuses: it describes an event that cannot be foreseen with certainty but which *can* be known as a fact once it has happened.[1] When eventuality is used to describe a moment in a theatrical plot, it likewise identifies a change in the state of the action that has no single, punctual cause. If we say that a particular plot twist is eventual, we mean that it is not the consequence of any single determining source of action—a character's intention to bring it about, for example, or a natural process acting in a predictable manner. As a datum of plot, the eventuality owes its theatrical existence to an obliging arrangement of actors and objects that brings it about (it 'eventuates' or comes out of the circumstances at hand). These arrangements are the object of plot and plotting, but they are also themselves contingent upon performance and so can fail to be productive: a missed cue among actors will, like a staged mishap in plot, create an outcome that no one—including the performers themselves—could have foreseen. The spatial contingency of individual eventualities in plot and performance are thus precisely what makes them difficult to explain. An arrangement as such cannot be verbally narrated but must instead be enacted, which is what makes the theatre an important place for thinking about eventualities in this first sense. I will talk further about this point in connection with several examples.

---

[1] For a detailed treatment of the language used to treat such mishaps—the language of excuses—see J. L. Austin, 'A Plea for Excuses: Presidential Address', *Proceedings of the Aristotelian Society* n.s. 57 (1956–7), 1–30.

Eventuality has a second meaning, more remote but also more precise, when we are talking about the capacity of theatre to affect its audience. If we say theatre is eventual, we mean that an entire performance has the quality of an event rather than an action: it 'comes about' in 'the way things come about'—which is to say, in an ensemble. (No one person 'does a play' in the sense that one does a favour, home-work, or a good deed.) This second meaning is more inclusive, marking first the fact that theatre as a spatial and temporal medium supports exactly the kind of eventu-alities of plot and of performance described already. But eventuality also describes the specific means by which theatrical performance involves spectators in the sen-sory play of its action and, in so doing, gives an existential and ethical urgency to their participation. Used in this more phenomenological sense, 'eventuality' is to theatrical practice as 'sexuality' is to human being: a capacity for engagement that can be recognized, experienced, and discussed. Indeed, individual eventualities of plot occurring on-stage are the means by which theatre extends its phenomenologi-cal reach, since it is precisely at such moments (when individual plots *lose* their purchase on the world) that the theatrical situation itself—the *mise-en-scène* of its bodies and props—becomes eloquent. These moments can be manufactured with great precision, and their theatrical power stems from the way in which they make characters the 'voice' of situations that have their own internal, immanent logic. Consider the moment when Lear arrives on stage with the body of his lifeless daughter, demonstrating to all that the attempt to prevent her murder has miscar-ried. Lear holds a mirror to her lips, connecting an invisible line—of breath? of sight?—between himself, the body, and the audience. 'Look there, look there' (5.3.375) he says, sensing a hint of life in the body on stage.[2] But it is really the theatre itself that is speaking.

The spectacle of such a momentary stall in action is one of the greatest things the theatre, and certainly Shakespearean theatre, has to offer. Lear's pause over Cordelia stills the interpretive impulse, engaging the senses in ways that are at once ethically, socially, and existentially demanding. What generates this spectacle is an unfore-seen meeting of causal lines of action—the delivery of a daughter's dead body to the father who had hoped to save her, or in a happier example, the discovery of an aban-doned child on the shore, as in *The Winter's Tale*. To the extent that such occur-rences appear to be, or actually are, contingent—graspable as 'what just happened' and 'what could have been otherwise'—they make special demands on a spectator. Eventualities are witnessed instead of understood; they are more seen than fore-seen. Because eventualities are rooted in the immanent fact of performance itself, they link the evanescence of stage play to specific terms of the spectators' existence,

---

[2] William Shakespeare, *King Lear*, ed. Barbara Mowat and Paul Werstine, http://www.folgerdigital-texts.org/?chapter=5&play=Lr&loc=line-5.3.375, accessed 1 January 2013. Unless otherwise noted, all citations to the plays of Shakespeare will be to the Mowat–Werstine edition of the plays available electronically at http://www.folgerdigitaltexts.org.

terms which likewise can be grasped as a momentary touch of sensation rather than an object of knowledge. Even an actor who has played a scene hundreds of times knows that a particular prop, for example, the poisoned rapier in *Hamlet*, can travel in unexpected ways during performance. If a company decides that Hamlet is to physically wrench Laertes' rapier from him in *chaude melée*, but the actor playing Laertes accidentally lets the weapon slip from his hand, all eyes will follow the rapier to the floor. Not only the plot—an internal organizing principle of events in the theatre—but the 'externalities' of performance can limit the degree to which any one person (actor, director, spectator) foresees precisely how things will develop in a particular moment.

There are thus as many sources of eventuality in theatre as there are people who do not expect things to happen as they do. But it would be a mistake to assume that, in advancing this difficult concept, we aim simply to survey the great variety of surprising turns of plots or mishaps of performance. As a fundamental capacity of theatre to engage participants precisely on the basis of what they cannot already know or expect, eventuality delivers one of the theatre's most basic pleasures—the pleasure of sensing that one exists, and of doing so in the company of others. I prefer the word 'sensing' to 'knowing' because sensation leads us away from the hermeneutic frame usually placed around drama and points us instead towards the related but distinct fields of aesthetics and phenomenology. The ancient Greek verb, *aisthanesthai*, which is at the root of our modern word 'aesthetic', means to sense, feel, or perceive. We can make use of this etymology when thinking about the nature of eventuality in the theatre, since there is something fundamentally important about the ways in which the latter mobilizes our senses and, more importantly, makes *sensation itself* something significant. While a theatrical plot certainly develops through and around shared expectations of what is likely and probable (and thus is fundamentally hermeneutic, in a Jaussian sense), it nevertheless elicits a reaction in the spectator that cannot itself be located within that horizon of expectation.[3] Such a reaction is made possible by a particular arrangement of persons and objects within the scene of performance, an arrangement that is as important now as it was in Shakespeare's time. As Henry S. Turner has shown in his work on geometry and early modern theatre, the theatre in which playwrights worked was a spatial art.[4] To the extent that the theatre still deploys space in deliberate ways, relying on

[3] The ambiguous location of sensation in general and touch in particular frustrates the spatial analogy of 'horizons' developed in hermeneutic theory; an alternative can be found in Merleau-Ponty's attempt to understand the chiasmatic intertwining of the body in the world and the world in the body. See Maurice Merleau-Ponty, *Phenomenology of Perception*, trans. Colin Smith (London: Routledge, 1962), 92. On the 'horizon of expectations', see Hans Robert Jauss, 'Literary History as a Challenge to Literary Theory', *The Norton Anthology of Theory and Criticism*, ed. Vincent B. Leitch (New York: Norton, 2001), 1556.

[4] Henry S. Turner, *The English Renaissance Stage: Geometry, Poetics, and the Practical Spatial Arts, 1580–1630* (Oxford: Oxford University Press, 2006).

productive arrangements of bodies to generate the experience we partake of as actors or audience members, theatre remains an art of contingency—an art of placing individuals in a position where the *most* they can do is see, sense, hear, and feel, rather than foresee, grasp, and know.

In what follows, I will be using a number of examples from Shakespeare's plays in order to argue that the eventuality of a stage play thrusts spectators into another drama—the drama of 'being there', of seeing and hearing 'what happens, as it happens'. It is this involving turn of events that gives theatre some of its greatest ethical and existential force, a force generated by the total arrangement of persons, props, words, and gestures that orient the senses in particular ways. To argue this point, I will be building on Daniel Heller-Roazen's work on the 'inner touch', a phrase which he employs to translate a suite of terms used by classical, medieval, and early modern thinkers to identify the reflexive capacity of humans (and, indeed, of all animals) to sense that we are sensing. In *The Inner Touch: Archaeology of a Sensation*, Heller-Roazen argues that it is this qualitatively bare capacity for 'sensing *that* we sense' which acquaints us with the fact of our own existence.[5] What is intriguing about this reading in connection with the theatre is the further claim, derived from the philosopher Georgio Agamben's reading of Aristotle's *Nicomachean Ethics*, that this reflexive power of self-sensing can itself be shared, and that it grounds a sociality that does not take 'thinking together' as its basis. Reading Aristotle's '*synaesthesia*' to mean 'joint sensing'—a shared feeling for life that is itself a form of sensation, touch, and pleasure—Heller-Roazen's analysis ends in an ethics of tact, one that provides an alternative to modern contractualism or 'intersubjectivity' and moves, instead, towards the embodied phenomenology of Maurice Merleau-Ponty. Extending that analysis here, I argue that our capacity for 'inner touch' can also explain how a certain property of theatrical performance, its eventuality, offers us the basic pleasure of sensing that we exist, and that we feel such pleasure in the company others.[6] More than simply being an aesthetic possibility of theatre, eventuality is its vital pulse, the means by which it locates us as social beings in and of the theatre's sensory world.

Eventuality and the philosophy of the event

Let us acknowledge an initial difficulty: the experience that engages this more fundamental possibility of theatre—the experience of contingency embodied in

---

[5] Daniel Heller-Roazen, *The Inner Touch: Archaeology of a Sensation* (New York: Zone Books, 2009); Giorgio Agamben, 'Friendship', trans. Joseph Falsone, *Contratemps* 5 (December 2004), 2–7.

[6] The beginnings of this analysis can be found in Michael Witmore, 'Shakespeare, Sensation and Renaissance Existentialism', *Criticism* 54.3 (Summer 2012), Special Issue: Shakespeare and Phenomenology, 419–28. See also, in the same issue, Jennifer Waldron, '"The Eye of Man Hath Not Heard": Shakespeare, Synasthesia, and Post-Reformation Phenomenology', 403–18.

spatio-temporal action—is hard to name, even in a cultural form that has been the object of analysis for thousands of years.[7] The source of this difficulty lies in the thing to be described. Eventuality is not a property of persons or even of individual actions. It is, rather, a quality of an *ensemble* of persons and actions, just as an ensemble of three points might be described, in their interconnection, as possessing the quality of an equilateral triangle. Philosophy is well positioned to provide this more diagrammatic description of the phenomenon, one in which the spatial disposition of an ensemble of bodies is itself the distributed cause of a particular event. This subfield of philosophy, now frequently referred to as the 'philosophy of the event', deals with contingent as opposed to necessary outcomes—with that which seems to eventuate or come out of (from the Latin, *ex-venire*) a novel situation rather than issuing punctually from a deliberating consciousness or regularly acting natural cause. Recalling the example of Laertes' poisoned rapier, we note first that contingency is something theatre tries to manufacture: there is a certain *sprezzatura* in the plot of *Hamlet* that makes the poisoned rapier 'happen to come within the grasp' of the wounded prince in a given performance, and do so in a way that spectators sense could have been otherwise.[8] The actors, props, and occasion of the rapier and dagger contest have all conspired to place this plot-altering possibility within reach of the hero, and to the extent that this new arrangement of things is experienced *as contingent*—'see now, there, the rapier is finally in his grasp!'—audiences become involved in the drama in a much more fundamental way.

We can understand better what is involving about such theatrical moments by examining the event's role in contemporary philosophy. Among philosophers active during the last century, the event acquired newfound status and interest: as a category of analysis, it seemed less firmly tied to the necessitarian metaphysics of substances and their essential properties, a metaphysics that began to look extravagant (and terrifying) in the twentieth century. Alfred North Whitehead, for example, develops a process metaphysics that takes 'occasions' as the most basic unit of analysis, an approach developed further by Gilles Deleuze who, like Whitehead, argues that events must replace substances as the ultimate metaphysical unit.[9] Each would

---

[7] The problem is one of 'excessive proximity', a phrase Agamben uses in describing the difficulties philosophers have thinking about friendship ('Friendship', 4).

[8] Most philosophical approaches to contingency involve counterfactual reasoning: I know that this outcome is contingent because these other outcomes are possible, and can imagine them having occurred (although they did not) in such and such a way. See, for example, Amos Funkenstein, *Theology and the Scientific Imagination from the Middle Ages to the Seventeenth Century* (Princeton: Princeton University Press, 1986), 117–52. But the contingency of specific occurrences might be apprehended in a much more immediate way, as an object of reflexive-sensation: I sense the absence of the other ways in which this thing could have come about, in their not-coming-about. See, in this connection, Heller-Roazen's remarks about the dog who reflexively senses that it *does not smell a rabbit* running down one of several pathways (*Inner Touch*, 129).

[9] See Alfred North Whitehead, *Process and Reality* (New York: Simon & Schuster, 1979) and Gilles Deleuze, *Difference and Repetition*, trans. Paul Patton (New York: Continuum Books, 2005).

argue that 'what happens' is not a necessary effect of the properties of substances (persons, objects, molecules), but rather an actualization of possibilities or virtualities already immanent to a given situation.[10] Things could always have been otherwise, and events are just those sorts of things. Indeed, in one strand of continental thought analysed by John Mullarkey, it may be the diagram rather than language which helps us understand what is truly productive about situations and events: diagrams show relations, which can be real even if the points they relate are not, and they do so outside of the causal frame of time, which makes the immanent and productive possibilities of arrangement as such difficult to grasp.[11] We can think of dramaturgy and theatrical blocking as the attempt to create a live version of this sort of diagram on stage, placing the right people in the right positions at the right time and so, by an art of theatrical *dispositio*, creating novel eventualities that seem not in and of themselves to have been premeditated by any one actor. It is this art that puts the poisoned rapier within reach of Hamlet, one whose actual mechanics we can only infer from the cryptic stage direction, 'In scuffling, they change rapiers'.[12]

Another line of thinking, focusing more explicitly on actions and performances, argues that the deliberating subject is itself a product of certain felicitous or productive conditions that might easily go another way. This group of thinkers, which includes Friedrich Nietzsche, Jacques Derrida, and Judith Butler, advances the notion that an agent or 'doer' is something we add to 'the deed' after the fact, and only under conditions that satisfy conventions which are themselves historically contingent.[13] Particular performances—signing a document, granting forgiveness, being oneself (as Polonius urges)—are thus not simply a matter of sincerity and conviction. Rather than being purely deliberate actions, such performances are themselves eventualities, fundamentally dependent on a happy and semi-stable conjuncture of conventions and circumstances that allow us to confer upon them the status of deeds after the fact. While this line of argument emphasizes the limits of deliberate action, it also holds out the possibility that unforeseen convergences (the rapier lying within the reach of the hand) may be revelatory or conducive to new—because eventual—forms of action. Whether it is a political revolution, a

---

[10] See John Mullarkey, *Post-Continental Philosophy: An Outline* (London: Continuum Books, 2007). See especially ch. 5.

[11] The most extreme version of this philosophy of contingency, one which takes 'things could have been otherwise' as a radical, foundational condition, is developed by Quentin Meillassoux in his *After Finitude: An Essay on the Necessity of Contingency*, trans. Ray Brassier (New York: Continuum, 2010).

[12] On the rapier exchange, see James L. Jackson, ' "They Catch One Another's Rapiers": The Exchange of Weapons in Hamlet', *Shakespeare Quarterly* 41.3 (1990), 281–98. As the article suggests, the uncertainties of theatrical action can be tracked on the textual and editorial level as well.

[13] Some seminal texts in this tradition: Friedrich Nietzsche, 'On Truth and Lie in the Non-Moral Sense', *Philosophy and Truth: Selections from Nietzsche's Notebooks in the Early 1870s*, trans. Daniel Braezeale (Atlantic City, NJ: Humanities Press, 1979); Jacques Derrida, *Limited Inc.*, trans. Samuel Weber (Chicago: Northwestern University Press, 1988); Judith Butler, *Gender Trouble* (New York: Routledge, 2006).

divine revelation, or a piece of street theatre, contingency is the fickle friend of all those who act in circumstances that are not of their own choosing.[14] This limitation can be productive, since it makes of eventualities a curious sort of way out, an escape from the self-same repetitions of history, ideology, habit, or psychic repression. Like the pirates in *Hamlet*, eventualities can turn things around unexpectedly. But there is a catch: the very qualities that make something eventual—its singular unpredictability, its arrival from a future that could not be reliably foreseen—are what makes it rare, the experiential equivalent of an eclipse.

Let us leave aside for a moment the fact that theatre itself regularly tries to simulate this kind of eclipse, that there is an almanac in the script that says when the sun must darken. The significance of eventuality, both as a type of occurrence in the theatre and as a category of experience, is that it acquaints us with certain structural limits of agency, limits that become clear when an individual's desire to act is interrupted by something unforeseen. This limit applies to performance itself, as a temporal phenomenon, since the total event that is a stage play may always go astray, and so is itself subject to 'consenting' circumstances.[15] Actors can always miss their cues; audience members can faint, requiring immediate medical attention. This basic plight of performance is itself sometimes reproduced on the level of plot: Hamlet wants to kill his uncle, but the man is now at prayer, asking forgiveness for the very murder Hamlet wants to revenge. In this unhappy arrangement of persons and intentions, resolution gives way to inaction, suggesting that action itself—in the sense of something deliberately undertaken and then accomplished—is only possible when the facts on the ground oblige. As Derrida, Butler, and others have argued, there is something basic about our inability to prosecute our designs in the absence of a certain enabling disposition of circumstances, circumstances that are beyond any one actor's control. In this same sense, there is always something about the intention to act that is subject to circumstances being 'just so', of 'place, time and fortune...coher[ing]', to use a wonderful phrase from Shakespeare's *Twelfth Night* (5.1.261).

There is a tragic version of this convergence, which I have already gestured towards. The convergence of circumstances that precipitate Hamlet's revenge is certainly unforeseen: once armed in the exchange of rapiers, he manages to wound mortally his opponent and so to precipitate the confession that will damn Claudius. Recall too the other enabling occurrences: pirates had to rescue Hamlet and bring him back to Denmark, and Claudius' plan to kill the prince with a poisoned drink

---

[14] This more utopian view of the event is evident in the work of Alain Badiou, *Being and Event* (New York: Continuum, 2006) and Peter Hallward's, *Alain Badiou: A Subject to Truth* (Minneapolis: University of Minnesota Press, 2003).

[15] On the intimate connection between contingencies of this kind and early modern theatre, see Ellen MacKay, *Persecution, Plague, and Fire: Fugitive Histories of the Stage in Early Modern England* (Chicago: University of Chicago Press, 2011).

has to miscarry: all of these contingencies simply amplify the theatrical power of the concluding action, suggesting that it might easily have *not taken place*. I have argued elsewhere that such moments were startling to early modern spectators, engaging buried suspicions about a providential hand that might be guiding dramatic action and, perhaps, their own lives.[16] This was and is its own ideological reflex arc, one enabled by historical conditions Shakespeare himself witnessed: the rise of theatre as a professional art form, the attenuation of a particular providential view of the world with Calvinism, perhaps even the multiplication of deliberate 'accidents' in an urban, mercantile world that matched buyers and sellers.

But there is an important sense in which theatrical eventualities like the ones that occur in *Hamlet* exceed the ideological frames—authorial, providential, generic—that can be placed around them. There is something gratuitous, excessive, and spectacularly unentailed about this kind of dramatic sequence that closes out the tragedy. True, we can infer some divine 'doer' orchestrating the events that conspire to bring about this or any other eventual conclusion—we can, in other words, read providence, policy, authorial intention, and perhaps even genre in the complexities plot. But the way in which we are asked simply to witness these events leads away from such inferences. What is most powerful about the eventualities of the theatre—whether they are simulated deliberately in a series of chance events in the plot or are 'real' in the sense of a mishap during performance—is that they are more objects of sensation than of cognition. In claiming priority for what is *sensed* in the theatre, I do not in any way want to detract from the fine work of scholars such as Subha Mukherji and Holger Syme, both of whom have shown how judicial canons of witnessing and evidence may have patterned what early modern audiences made of the evidence presented to their senses on stage.[17] I do, however, want to suggest that a certain kind of occurrence—one whose presence in a sequence is unentailed by any of the intentions thought to have brought it about—mobilizes the evidence of the senses in a way that upends the sort of hermeneutic 'case-building' we engage in as we try to match actions to intentions in the theatre. We are interested not so much in the way that certain kinds of events speak *as evidence* to those witnessing them as we are in the fact that such contingent events— say, Desdemona's handkerchief falling to the ground in sight of Emilia—carry theatrical force because of the (equally contingent) fact *that they are experienced by an audience*. Once seen or heard, that which has become the object of sensation can be turned into evidence, say in the hands of a skilful Iago. But it must first be seen, heard, or sensed, and it is the fact of that apprehension that drives us towards a more epistemologically narrow, but also more vivid, sense of our participation in theatrical events.

---

[16] See Michael Witmore, *Culture of Accidents: Unexpected Knowledges in Early Modern England* (Stanford: Stanford University Press, 2001).

[17] Subha Mukherji, *Law and Representation in Early Modern England* (Cambridge: Cambridge University Press, 2006); Holger Schott Syme, *Theatre and Testimony in Shakespeare's England: A Culture of Mediation* (Cambridge: Cambridge University Press, 2012).

If certain types of theatre help found our sense that we exist with and among others, how do they do it? What quality of eventual occurrences nudges audiences towards what they see and hear rather than what they know, or will later know? For a play to contract within itself the force of eventuality, it must first convince an audience to adopt, at least provisionally, the limited view of theatrical action that belongs to those characters who cannot foresee them. An example, the first of many: Viola does not know that Sebastian has just crossed whatever imaginary line plots the boundary of Illyria, and Sebastian does not know that his sister awaits. It is with these characters' ignorance, rather than their own apparent omniscience, that audience members greet the final scene. While an audience may know the underlying facts, and enjoy knowing them, it must *nevertheless wait* to see if, eventually, the twins encounter one another face to face. The position of the adverb in the previous sentence suggests that there is some cause for the happy encounter that concludes the play. But that cause is illusory, even if we are using 'eventually' as a shorthand way of referring to 'whatever plot mechanisms the playwright has devised in order to bring about the ending'. The point of using the word is to show that there is no single line of narrative action that comprehends, in advance, the decisive conjuncture that is the reunion itself. The physical and spatial convergence on which the plot turns is itself *under*determined: it is the starting point for all subsequent explanation, the 'thinnest slice' of time we can consider in a sequence of plot. (A 'thicker' one would be the presence of poison on the tip of Laertes' rapier: it is comprehended, as it were, in Laertes' prior intention to put it there.)

All this is to say that the meeting of brother and sister in *Twelfth Night* is an eventuality, something to be experienced as singular, rare, and therefore causally out of the hands of those who experience it. Here the link between what we might call the 'epistemological thinness' of contingent events and the necessity of waiting to see 'what eventually happens' becomes clear: the most one can know of an eventuality is *that it happens*, and this only once it *has happened* or *is happening*. The convergence of apparently independent agents that takes place at the end of *Twelfth Night* cannot itself become an object analysis; rather, it is the only starting point. (All the action that has preceded the reunion makes sense once the meeting itself becomes a 'given'.) Epistemological thinness here does not mean that eventualities are simply a blank in experience. Rather the opposite: because they are known as facts rather than as effects, eventualities place sensation at the centre of the show. We are dealing with an overall geometry here in which each point contributes to the pattern: no single point can project the shadow that we call theatrical action as it plays out on stage.

And if the eventuality of a complex plot is tangled, there is an even deeper thicket that awaits us in the actual performance of a play. Because it is a physical, embodied art form, the theatre is always open—constitutively open—to accidental events, which range from a missed cue to fire in the theatre, from broken props and fainting patrons to rowdy audience members who interrupt the show. Both actor and audience members are, in a sense, passengers in the romance that is performance:

they agree to go where the wind takes them, setting out on a sea of 'whatever happens'. But this structural dependence upon circumstance is only part of the way in which theatre highlights its own eventuality and, so, its claim on the equally thin slice of existence embodied in the spectator him or herself. Indeed, the presence of any given spectator at any given moment of performance is *itself* one of the conditions that could have been otherwise: for something to be merely seen, merely sensed on stage, there must also be someone who is merely there (and could easily not be). Eventuality here becomes a lure for our own experience of historical and social complexity—plighted, incomplete, never fully informed. Indeed, eventuality is that specific mode whereby the theatre invites audience members to experience, in an immediate because reflexive way, their own specific being as plighted—located in a scene that exceeds any one individual yet nevertheless resolves our being on a limited number of axes: here, now, with others.

I admit that this is a big bill to foist on the theatre, one the theatre is not often able to pay. But if we cannot rehearse all of the moments in which theatre actually does produce this effect, we can nevertheless say what it aspires to and, in the end, put a name to this aspiration. 'Eventuality' is that name: it helps us narrow down the ways in which we might talk about an experience that I believe is the remotest part of our specific, conscious existence: the slender fact that we exist and do so in the company of others. We can debate whether or not this fact is prior to other more properly social categories, whether or not this bare sensing 'that I exist' may be grasped alongside predicates such as class, position of desire, gender, and the like. But in getting a sense of oneself—sensing oneself sensing—in the theatre, we arrive at a specific person or being who is conceptually distinct from the social categories that define us and that seem to coincide with the very fact of our existence. By grasping that bare fact of existence conceptually and saying how we apprehend it, we build a bridge between what makes the theatre experientially involving and what grounds us, eventually, in the categories of communal life.

As an initial sounding of this set of phenomenological relays, I now propose a series of theses about eventuality. I offer them as a means of whittling down the quality of eventuality to its contingent core: the bare fact 'that something happens'. Such a whittling down involves separating the consequences of an unforeseen occurrence (and the intentions or causes that led to it) from the phenomenal surplus that such an occurrence represents for an audience, the sensed fact that something is happening before us. What needs to be understood now is how an experience of certain apparently felicitous events in the theatre—the fact that it is this, and not another, thing that is happening—can itself become the basis for an even more proximate act of self-sensation in the audience, one through which audience and actor meet in a kind of mutual ethical stare. We need to understand, in other words, how the network of dependencies surrounding an eventuality—its pell-mell emergence from an arrangement of circumstances that 'bring it about'—actually concentrate attention on 'the fact that things are so', a fact that brings the *existence* of the spectator into the theatre's weird, illuminating glow. The theses here are offered as partial glimpses of a fugitive phenomenon, an analysis 'on the hoof' of what we see and hear in the theatre. I then conclude, in a brief closing section, with some reflection about the word 'eventuality' and what it names.

Six theses on eventuality

Thesis 1. An eventuality is something that doesn't have to happen but *does* happen. Like the following:

> Hamlet does meet pirates and returns to Denmark.
> Sebastian does show up in time for a duel with Sir Andrew.
> Perdita does get discovered on the shores of Bohemia.
> Cymbeline, Posthumus, Imogen, Belarius, Guiderius, and Arviragus do meet at the end of the battle with Rome.

Each of these examples represents a point of convergence, one that is unambiguously narrative but also spatial. In the example of Hamlet's rescue by pirates, the convergence happens off-stage and is recounted in speech: the speaker would not even be able to tell the story of his rescue had the chance meeting with pirates not taken place. *I was sailing one way, to my death; meanwhile, pirates were sailing another, looking for booty. We met at sea, and in the confusion, I escaped and returned to Denmark.* The pirate rescue of Hamlet is eventual because, in narrative and developmental terms, it blooms from no particular seed. Hamlet didn't set out on his journey with a plan to meet pirates, much less to befriend them. His captors, for their part, did not head out to sea to meet a Danish prince: as pirates, they seek 'any ship whatever' that serves their ends. The event grows organically—perhaps we should say, automatically—out of a chance meeting in the open seas of narrative.

Thesis 2. An eventuality follows from circumstances being just so—from a situation in which, as Viola says in *Twelfth Night*, 'place, time, fortune do cohere' (5.1.264).

Eventualities *require* productive arrangements of persons, things, and even statements. An example I have already mentioned: the two twins need to walk on stage at the same time for *Twelfth Night* to come to an end. But they must also fail to meet on stage throughout the action, and they must do this for a long time (most of the play). Everything, eventually, works out: just so.

Thesis 3. An eventuality might in some sense be explained, but only by rehearsing circumstances in a narrative. As if I write:

> First I washed up on shore, then I met a Sea Captain. He introduced me to a melancholic Duke, who asked me in turn to plead his suit to a Lady. She, for her part...

As I continue to summarize the sequence, recitation fatigue might set in, leading me to compress the sequence by using a word such as 'eventually'. As in:

> 'Eventually, I met my brother...'
> 'Eventually, I was captured by Roman soldiers...'
> 'Eventually, I met my father on a ship...'

Shakespeare has his own strategies for compressing stretches of reported action, using words like 'anon' and 'by and by' to fill in a sequence in which one thing does not lead directly to another (i.e. in the intervening time, a person must arrive, a choice must be made, etc.). Consider, for example, this short but extreme case of narrative recounting, in which the Page in *Romeo and Juliet* reports to the Prince the complicated comings and goings around the Capulet tomb which resulted in his departure to seek help:

> Page: He [Romeo] came with flowers to strew his lady's grave
> And bid me stand aloof, and so I did.
> Anon comes one with light to ope the tomb,
> And by and by my master drew on him,
> And then I ran away to call the watch.   (5.3.291–5)

The need for such vocalized ellipsis in reported action is directly related to the underdetermined, causally thin sequentiality of eventual narrative. One state of affairs has given way to another in recitation, but that does not mean that the first was the determining cause of the second. Indeed, it is not simply the sequence of arrivals the Page is struggling to recount but also the indifferent containing power of place, the Capulet tomb, and the brute durative presence of Romeo in that place over the intervening time, which supports the eventual convergence of independent lines of deliberate action in the final, tragic scene of the play. When, in our own modern parlance, we insert 'eventually' into the sequence of an explanation, we acknowledge that words fail us and that what we really need is a diagram—a plot in space, like a stage full of actors moving about the Capulet tomb, which *plays out* the thing to be explained. Verbal plot summary, in fact, is a failed diagram in words, and elliptical particles like 'anon', 'by and by', or 'eventually' mark the fact that no sequence of statements will capture the simultaneity of converging causal paths in space which is precisely what the theatre places before us.

Thesis 4. An eventuality can be sensed and discussed, reflexively, as it happens. Consider these two examples taken from *Twelfth Night* and *Cymbeline*, in which the speaker's words possess theatrical power precisely because they touch on facts that are being witnessed, as they are witnessed:

> Viola [to Sebastian]: If nothing lets to make us happy both
> But this my masculine usurped attire,
> Do not embrace me till each circumstance

> Of place, time, fortune do cohere and jump
> That I am Viola…(5.1.261–5)
>
> Cymbeline [to Imogen]: When shall I hear all through?…
> Where, how lived you?
> And when came you to serve our Roman captive?…
> See…
> Posthumus anchors upon Imogen;
> And she, like harmless lightning, throws her eye
> On him, her brothers, me, her master, hitting
> Each object with a joy; the counterchange
> Is severally in all.   (5.5.465–83)[18]

If an eventuality is the product of an arrangement of persons in time, speech is the line that connects different points on the stage's living diagram. In this passage, 'The counterchange / Is severally in all', is a present tense recognition: Cymbeline sees that a polygon of glances links every person on the scene ('severally in all'). This recognition is itself transformative, as the speaker is now several persons, an agent who speaks and sees, but also a 'patient' who is seen and spoken about. In this final scene, the king and his company become a troupe of mythical creatures, each a plurality of eyes, ears, and mouths. Like Newton's vast *sensorium* of universe, the theatre has become an integrated space of distributed sensation.

Thesis 5. When the eventuality of an outcome is touched on in speech, as in the examples here, that speech becomes evidence of some form of sensation—of a momentary seeing or hearing. To return to the example from *Cymbeline*:

> Cymbeline [to Imogen]: See…
> Posthumus anchors upon Imogen
> And she…throws her eye
> On him.

The speaker, in this situation, states 'that' something is so because someone has sensed that it is so. The epistemologically slender fact of sensation, whether seeing or hearing, is indicated by the word 'that' in sentences describing eventualities ('that I am Viola'). The same sensation is buried in the auxiliary verb 'do', as in Viola's 'each circumstance of place, time, fortune do cohere and jump'. What do these words, 'do' and 'that', accomplish in such sentences? They are fossils of perception, the mineral traces of eventuality itself.

Thesis 6. Eventualities make spectators and characters equally dependent on sensation: at such moments, both actor and audience are sensing that something is the

---

[18] William Shakespeare, *Cymbeline*, ed. Barbara A. Mowat and Paul Werstine (New York: Washington Square Press, 2003).

case, and doing so in real time. Neither character nor audience can get behind the 'that-it's-happening' of an eventuality, which is what makes it a levelling force in theatre. A sort of theatrical chime sounds when this sensing-together, a collective *synaesthesia*, occurs. 'Are you seeing what I am seeing? As I am seeing it? Did we just hear that, you and I?' Ping.

Such moments of consonance have an important role to play within the ethics of tact that Heller-Roazen develops around reflexive sensation. For in grounding the relationship between self and what Aristotle calls 'another self' (*heteros autos*) in a moment of joint sensing, Heller-Roazen helps us identify the phenomenological plane on which theatrical eventuality must itself operate: certain moments gather together a group of 'other selves' (actors and audience members) without assuming anything like a political or contractual basis for their interrelation. Tact has become contact. When Hamlet looks at the poisoned rapier, the actor, character, and spectator are all—at least potentially—touched by the sight of the weapon the same way, touched because it is *sense alone* that can say why the blade ended up here rather than there. The actor is included in this quorum because, setting aside the script that he or she tries to know by heart, there is never any way to know with certainty how the actor playing Laertes is going to lose touch of the weapon in a given performance. (An eventuality is precisely that which characters and actors lose touch of.) All of the hermeneutic questions we ask about the meaning of words, objects, and events begin, in such eventualities, to acquire parallel questions in the realm of sensation. *Are you seeing what I am seeing, as I am seeing it?* If we are able to ask such questions during or after the fact, it is because interpretive cognition has itself, during theatrical performance, become a species of sensation. Heller-Roazen asks what he calls an untimely question about the history of consciousness, one that should be asked of theatre as well: 'What if the activities of awareness and self-awareness attributed to the modern faculty [of consciousness] were forms not of cognition but rather, as Aristotle maintained, of sensation? What if consciousness, in short, were a variety of tact?'[19]

Putting a name to what happens

In the third volume of Proust's *In Search of Lost Time*, the narrator recurs to one of his favourite themes: the difficulty of matching the rich associations of a particular name (Mme de Guermantes) with the physical presence of that person and the environs in which she lives.[20] Eventuality, as a contemporary concept for thinking

---

[19] Heller-Roazen, *Inner Touch*, 40.

[20] Marcel Proust, *In Search of Lost Time*, ed. Christopher Prendergast, vol. 3, *The Guermantes Way*, trans. Mark Traherne (New York: Penguin, 2002), 22.

about theatricality, is like one of Proust's names: it designates something specific and definite, but its ultimate meaning takes shape over time, and with respect to specific examples. I have offered a few such examples with explanatory glosses, but I am aware of the fact that my own attempt to provide a phenomenology of theatre's eventual power is both un-Proustian and crude. Nevertheless, I hope to have made some real gain in saying that eventuality designates theatre's most basic form of existential appeal, a real corner we turn in an imagined world of play. If we hear the 'ping' of joint sensation described already; if theatre is designed to produce such a chime in the collective *sensorium* of performance, then at least one meaning of eventuality is the capacity of stage play to engage the spectator in a social awareness of his or her specific existence.[21] Certain types of drama, certainly Shakespearean drama, are designed to manufacture this experience and, like all plots and designs, the ideal effect will sometimes fail to materialize in performance. Actual results may vary, and—to take the converse view for a moment—clearly some of the most profound experiences of the theatre can occur around the failure of audiences to feel engaged by its simulation of contingent occurrences. One imagines a sceptical early modern spectator of *Cymbeline* looking at the giddy crowd and despairing at the delight others take in what is arguably a silly ending. It is possible to be an orphan of the theatrical experience, and this possibility of being left behind by the spectacle—of seeing through the pretence, not meeting the actor face to face at a moment of live, ethical decision or reaction—is part of what lures spectators to drama in the first place.

But for those charmed by the theatre's pretence to self-eventuating action, of action springing from its own mechanism, automatic and so indifferent to whatever proximate causes could have premeditated it, there is a certain creaturely reward: a pleasure in the sensed fact of one's existence, which blooms in the absence of designs and causes. This is a pleasure as evanescent and difficult to describe as anything Proust tried to pin on the sensations of his narrator. The difficulty lies in its simplicity, since the pleasure and fact of sensation itself—unique as an experience without quality—cannot but open onto yet other sensations; it cannot, as Heller-Roazen suggests, coincide with itself, just as the faculty of touch cannot itself be touched.[22] Theatre may offer a touch of the real, but it does so by deflecting it onto an 'inner touch', the reflexive capacity of spectators to 'jointly sense' what might have been otherwise. What we attempt to exhaust, in probing the eventuality of theatre, is the ongoing human capacity for being affected in ways that—like the event itself—seem unaccountable, lacking a foregoing cause.

---

[21] One meaning of the word 'specific' here might be found in Peter Hallward's 'The Limits of Individuation, or How to Distinguish Deleuze and Foucault', *Angeliki: The Journal of Theoretical Humanities* 5.2 (2000), 93–111.

[22] See Heller-Roazen, *Inner Touch*, 294–6 and Witmore, 'Shakespeare, Sensation and Renaissance Existentialism', 422–4.

One might add other contingent facts that shape events in performance, for example: the fact that it is this actor (Burbage) playing the part, this costume that is being worn (the vestments of a former priest), this audience is taking in the performance (a group of apprentices on holiday). These too are circumstances that must be folded into a properly historical phenomenology of the theatre, one that attends to the centripetal and centrifugal forces that converge on theatrical experience, the inward pull of the individual and the outward reach to the crowd.[23] Yet in this welter of pushes and pulls, there is a fugitive experience—an experience of something, but what?—that may be the theatre's alone to provide. Whatever it is, it is occasioned by a certain kind of event, one that becomes sensible as the thinnest slice of experience, unentailed, under-determined, aimed at sense itself, witnessed aloud as something seen, felt, or heard. When we call that something eventual, we say what that experience is.

FURTHER READING

Heller-Roazen, Daniel. *The Inner Touch: Archaeology of a Sensation* (New York: Zone Books, 2009).

Mullarkey, John. *Post-Continental Philosophy: An Outline* (London: Continuum Books, 2007).

Nietzsche, Friedrich. 'On Truth and Lie in the Non-Moral Sense', *Philosophy and Truth: Selections from Nietzsche's Notebooks in the Early 1870s*, trans. Daniel Braezeale (Atlantic City, NJ: Humanities Press, 1979).

Witmore, Michael. *Culture of Accidents: Unexpected Knowledges in Early Modern England* (Stanford: Stanford University Press, 2001).

---

[23] See Kevin Curran and James Kearney, 'Introduction', 353–64 and Bruce Smith, 'Phenomophobia, or Who's Afraid of Merleau-Ponty', 479–83, in *Criticism* 54.3 (Summer 2012), Special Issue: Shakespeare and Phenomenology.

CHAPTER 21

DUEL

PAUL A. KOTTMAN

In this essay, I want to discuss an abiding challenge to theatricality exemplified by philosophical reflections on drama. I have in mind here not what Jonas Barish called an 'anti-theatrical prejudice' characteristic of certain philosophical discourses; nor what I have elsewhere described as political philosophy's constitutive expropriation of theatrical categories (such as 'representation' or *mimesis*).[1] Rather, I will be talking about a challenge to theatricality that comes from a powerful philosophical appropriation of drama—which I will call 'philosophical dramaturgy'. This challenge is less an attack on theatricality's legitimacy as a public practice than it is a claim that drama—as a mode of human self-understanding—can and does free itself from needing re-enactment or sensuous expression in order to present an understanding of human agency, historical existence, and inter-personal dynamics. The aim of my discussion— towards the end of this essay—will be a consideration of whether Shakespeare might be understood to offer an answer to this challenge or 'philosophical dramaturgy'.

To preface what I have to say—and to get this challenge into better focus—I will, in the first section of this essay, recall a few aspects of what are probably our two most far-reaching philosophical accounts of drama: that of Aristotle and that of G. W. F. Hegel. I will then turn in the second and third sections to what I see as an exemplary instance of 'philosophical dramaturgy' in modern philosophy: the presentation of the life-and-death struggle (or 'duel') in Thomas Hobbes's *Leviathan* and Hegel's *Phenomenology of Spirit*, which is presented as the primal act (albeit a kind of idealized act, or mythologeme) through which human life in its normative dimension is achieved. The final sections of the essay will be devoted to sketching a Shakespearean response to this philosophical dramaturgy.

---

[1] See Jonas Barish, *The Anti-Theatrical Prejudice* (Berkeley: University of California Press, 1985); Paul A. Kottman, *A Politics of the Scene* (Stanford: Stanford University Press, 2008).

Aristotle and Hegel

Since Aristotle's *Poetics*, dramatic works have been understood to be graspable apart from—at a minimum—the sensuousness or 'theatricality' of their material performance.[2] Recall, for instance, Aristotle's well-known assertion that plot (*mythos*), rather than diction or spectacle (*opsis*), is the soul of tragedy—and that, furthermore, 'the plot [of a tragedy] ought to be so composed that, even without seeing a performance, anyone...will experience terror and pity as a result of the outcome'.[3] For Aristotle, tragedies are gripping quite apart from their reliance on theatrical, sensuous representation—indeed, for the author of the *Poetics*, it is enough to recall to mind a tragic *mythos* in order to be moved by it.

Of course, Aristotle's reflections presuppose—that is, they historically follow—the ritual, public enactment of tragic drama in a manifestly theatrical setting. However, once dramas had actually been performed in fifth century BC Athens, *once tragedy had become a self-consciously ritual activity* distinct from epic, it became possible to see (as Aristotle did) that what was being sensuously represented were not only idealized theatrical (visual, choreographed, sensuously perceptible) representations of human beings—characters like Oedipus, to stick with Aristotle's favourite example—but the *actions themselves* of these figures, their words, their gestures, their individual deeds.

And furthermore, once it became clear that tragedies represented human *actions*—that tragedies were sensuous representations *of* an action and its consequences for the agent and his world (*mimeseos praxis*, to use Aristotle's famous definition of tragedy)[4]—then the specific power of drama with respect to the other arts (image, narrative, dance) was seen to lie, significantly, *not* in its status as sensuous performance (*mousike*) but rather in its capacity to yield a special understanding about what it is for human beings to act among others in a given social world, a philosophical understanding in light of which the poetic mimesis of action (the *mythos*) becomes philosophically defensible, as in Aristotle's own account.[5]

---

[2] By 'theatricality' I mean what Henry S. Turner has described in Chapter 1 as 'a cluster of mimetic and symbolic techniques: the objects, bodies, conventions, and signs, the collective habits of apprehension and affective response' that are 'shared across individual theatrical occasions and that even motivate performances that take place outside of a conventional theatre building'.

[3] See Aristotle, *Poetics* 1453b1–4, trans. Stephen Halliwell (Chapel Hill, NC: University of North Carolina Press, 1987), 45.

[4] *Mimeseos* is the genitive form of *mimesis*, indicating that the representation 'belongs' to the action, not the reverse.

[5] That tragic drama—the most refined representation of human actions, more refined than epic or lyric—yields a special understanding not available elsewhere was, of course, central to Aristotle's defence of tragedy in the face of Plato's criticism of tragic drama. Note: Aristotle did not defend tragedy as sensuous performance [*mousike*] against Plato's attack; his defence of tragedy lay in his view of tragedy as yielding an understanding of an action in light of its unintended consequences.

And once it was recognized that the chief accomplishment of the theatrical performance of tragedy was, at bottom, a new understanding of human *praxis* through its mimetic representation, then tragic drama ended up *by means of its ritualized sensuous performance* obviating—in Aristotle's own view—the need for that very theatrical performance.[6] That this obviation was not only Aristotle's idiosyncratic opinion is, in a sense, borne out by the historical fact that performances of tragic dramas were well on the wane in Athens by the time Aristotle composed the *Poetics*.

In light of all this, it could be said that the self-dissolution of the *sensuous* material performance of drama belongs, already, to its classical milieu as a formal artistic practice.[7] Classical theatricality (when it comes to tragedy, at least) *lends itself to this self-dissolution* inasmuch as it succeeds in bringing what it represents—human actions—to the understanding. The understanding, as it were, takes over for our eyes and ears—hence, again, Aristotle's claims about the ability of a tragic *mythos* to move us independent of its sensuous performance. Dramatic performance alone among the classical fine arts emerges as a practice that tends towards its own self-dissolution because the medium of its artifice—the here-and-now performance of human words and deeds—invariably evacuates the here-and-now, leaving behind only an *ex post facto* practical understanding of the deeds that have been represented.[8] In another context, it would be important to consider tragedy's special significance for Greek philosophy's own self-authorization in light of its distinctiveness in this regard.

So, by sensuously representing human beings in action, classical tragedy obviates the need for the sensuousness of that very representation. *This obviation is nothing*

---

[6] The obviation of the sensuous performance is expressed by Aristotle when he argues that the soul of tragedy is its plot-structure, 'the intrinsic structure of events', and distinguishes the *mimesis* particular to the composition of tragedy from the 'material resources' required to produce spectacular performances. See Aristotle, *Poetics*, 45–6.

[7] I offer a longer elaboration of these arguments—those gathered in Section 1 here—in my essay, 'Shakespeare and the Self-Dissolution of Theatrical Drama', *Memoria di Shakespeare*, 1.1. My discussion here is an effort on my part to rethink some aspects of that essay; both are 'works-in-progress' in that sense.

[8] The same self-dissolution does not, I would argue, apply to the other arts in their classical forms. Epic narrative still requires the spoken word if it is to represent *the past* (that is, the temporal distance between the speaker and that of which he speaks)—so the fate of epic narration is, as Walter Benjamin aptly suggested, tied to a tradition in which the physical act of speaking is capable of transmitting historical experience. Cf. Walter Benjamin, 'The Storyteller', in *Selected Writings*, vol. 3 (Cambridge, MA: Harvard University Press, 2002). Similarly, the performance of music obviously requires the hearing of sound; images require light and surfaces. Unless, of course, one sees in the Pythagorean (or Platonic) conception of music as an invisible *harmonia* (a 'harmony of the spheres') a similar 'philosophical' self-dissolution of the sensuousness of music. See the discussion in Adriana Cavarero, 'The Harmony of the Spheres', in *For More Than One Voice: Toward a Philosophy of Vocal Expression* (Stanford: Stanford University Press, 2005). But here philosophy would silence music from the outside, in mute opposition to its sonority—whereas I am arguing, pace Aristotle, that drama is self-dissolving and that this historical self-dissolution is noted by, but not enacted by, philosophy.

less than the temporality of the performance of drama itself—its resistance to sensu-ous reification, its dependence on a shared here-and-now context, its inevitable vanishing at the 'end' of the play, its iterability, its retrospective fulfilment in the understanding or collective judgement (*phronesis*) that the performance occasions.[9] From the perspective of tragedy, theatrical performances are intrinsically self-dissolving as a sensuous practice—both as a historical-artistic practice and at the level of each individual performance.

In his *Lectures on Fine Art*, G. W. F. Hegel offered a more historically self-aware version of Aristotle's reflections. In Hegel's account, the development of artistic practices—that is, of historically shifting, context-specific needs for different 'arts' (e.g. the need for pyramids in Egypt, for classical sculpture in Greece, or for paint-ing in Christian Europe), as well as internal developments within those arts (from 'symbolic to classical to romantic', for example, or from epic to lyric)—presents an ongoing and increasing denaturalization or 'spiritualization' of our self-understand-ing. According to Hegel, the more that we see ourselves as—or teach ourselves that we are—free and self-determining subjects, the less we are limited to artistic expres-sions that work with 'natural' or sensuous media in order to understand ourselves, and our world. The twist in Hegel's story is that sensuous, representational artistic practices *are* a primary way we teach ourselves this lesson—because by transform-ing natural-sensuous material in modes that we can regard as 'free' from material or instrumental needs, we express our own liberation and, in this way, *become* free. (Art, claims Hegel in a famous passage, allows a free human being to 'strip the external world of its inflexible foreignness and to enjoy in the shape of things only an external realization of himself'.[10]) And once this lesson is absorbed—that is, once we see ourselves as liberated from nature, inasmuch as the terms of our self-under-standing no longer depend upon, and are no longer fully limited by, something 'out there' called 'Nature' or 'God' or the 'One' or whatever—we find ourselves less need-ful of the sensuous representational works by which we 'taught ourselves' this les-son. Coming to understand ourselves as free and self-determining entails (and perhaps even requires) a diminishing need to make sensuous, representational art-works, even as it entails a heightened need for 'philosophical' reflection on our (past) need for sensuous representation. This is what Hegel means when, famously, he claims—'art, considered in its highest vocation, is and remains for us a thing of the past'.[11]

---

[9] It is this last element, especially, that distinguishes the performance of spoken drama from the acoustics of music in classical accounts like Aristotle's.

[10] G. W. F. Hegel, *Lectures on Fine Art*, trans. T. M. Knox (Oxford: Clarendon Press, 1975), 1: 31.

[11] As many others have pointed out, Hegel's argument is not that art has come to an end, but rather that we can outlive, culturally, our need for sensuous, representational art as a deeply essential mode of self-understanding. So, this is not to say that there are not other ongoing critical 'needs' for sensuous, represen-tational art—only that these needs are now less essential to our deepest efforts at self-understanding, what

Furthermore, for Hegel, this ongoing denaturalization unfolds (or has unfolded) through an increased awareness *within* artistic practices *of* artistic practices as medium-specific. So, for instance, classical architecture manifests a higher awareness of its own status as architecture—of itself as a freestanding, artificial, material construction—than does symbolic architecture.[12] Similarly, as Robert Pippin has convincingly argued, the deepening self-reflexivity of modernist and abstract painting—paintings about painting as such—might be understood to fall within the purview of the overall narrative that Hegel offers.[13] Perhaps the easiest way to see the point here is to consider how artworks—once they no longer *need* (for a given historical community) to be about this or that content 'out there' (a material purpose, an animal quarry, a 'god', the afterlife, a bit of shared history)—are freed up to determine *for themselves* their own content. And this 'freeing up' is perhaps most clearly manifested when artworks start to be about themselves. Self-reflexive artworks and practices undeniably assert the autonomy of human artistry.

Now—to move closer to our topic here—thinking along these lines also led Hegel himself, at the end of his *Lectures on Fine Art*, to consider dramatic poetry as 'the highest stage of poetry and of art generally' because 'in contrast to the other perceptible materials, stone, wood, color and notes, speech is alone the element worthy of the expression of spirit'.[14] Such statements seem to place Hegel close to a view prevalent in Jena Romanticism—found especially in the thought of Lessing and Friedrich Schlegel—according to which poetry holds a privileged place among the arts because its medium (speech, language) places fewer material constraints on the freedom of the imagination.[15]

Hegel calls 'the deepest interests of mankind, and the most comprehensive truths of spirit [*Geist*]'. Hegel, *Lectures on Fine Art*, vol. 1: 7. For more on this point, see, as a start, the discussions of Hegel—and the debates over this pronouncement—in Dieter Heinrich, 'Art and Philosophy of Art Today: Reflections with Reference to Hegel', in *New Perspectives in German Literary Criticism*, ed. R. Amacher and V. Lange, trans. D. Wilson et al. (Princeton: Princeton University Press, 1979), 107–33; Arthur Danto, *The Philosophical Disenfranchisement of Art* (New York: Columbia University Press, 1986), especially 81–115; Stephen Houlgate, 'Hegel and the "End" of Art', *Owl of Minerva* 29.1 (1997), 1–19; Gregg Horowitz, *Sustaining Loss: Art and Mournful Life* (Stanford: Stanford University Press, 2001); Eva Geulen, *The End of Art: Readings in a Rumor After Hegel*, trans. James McFarland (Stanford: Stanford University Press, 2006), especially Chapter 2.

[12] 'The peculiarity of Greek architecture', writes Hegel in a typical formulation, is that by fluting and other means 'it gives shape to...supporting *as such* and therefore employs the column as the fundamental element in the purposiveness of architecture'. Hegel, *Lectures on Fine Art*, vol. 2: 666, my emphasis.

[13] I realize, of course, that I am skipping over a number of important questions—for example, those having to do with the differences between the fates of classical and romantic art in Hegel's account. But I think my overall point about denaturalization as self-reflexivity can stand, for the moment, without tackling those questions. See Robert Pippin, 'What was Abstract Art? (From the Point of View of Hegel)', *Critical Inquiry* 29 (August 2002), 1–24.

[14] G. W. F. Hegel, 'Dramatic Poetry', in Paul A. Kottman, ed., *Philosophers on Shakespeare* (Stanford: Stanford University Press, 2009), 57.

[15] See Gottfried Ephraim Lessing, 'Laocoön: An Essay on the Limits of Painting and Poetry', trans. A. W. Steel; and Friedrich Schlegel, excerpts from 'Critical Fragments', 'Athenaeum Fragments', 'Ideas', 'On Goethe's *Meister*', 'Letter about the Novel', and 'On Incomprehensibility', in J. M. Bernstein, ed., *Classic and Romantic German Aesthetics* (Cambridge: Cambridge University Press, 2003).

However, although Hegel apparently analyses drama in the *Lectures on Fine Art* under the heading of poetry, he does not reduce drama to linguistic or poetic expression. Drama, he writes, 'also displays a complete action', and it is this centrality of *action* (not of the poetic free imagination) that, for Hegel, permits and requires drama to suture subjective experience and objective reality more fully than the other arts.[16] Hence, dramatic poetry is, for Hegel, inherently more self-reflexive than sculpture, painting, or architecture not only because both its 'medium' and its content—namely, speech, and action—are from the start 'spiritual', human, denaturalized; drama's self-reflexive potential is also tied to its resulting capacity to hold together both a first-person (subjective) and a third-person (objective) viewpoint.[17] For all of these reasons, drama is for Hegel already freer than the other arts when it comes to choosing its content, when it comes to the expressive capacities of its medium.

Another quick way of grasping the stakes of Hegel's high regard for dramatic poetry is to recall his idiosyncratic (for a German writer of his period) disinterest in natural beauty, his assertion that 'the beauty of art is *higher* than the beauty of nature'.[18] Recall, for instance, Hegel's blunt declaration that in landscape painting 'the work of spirit acquires a higher rank than the mere natural landscape'; or, similarly, his provocative assertion that Titian, Dürer, and others have painted portraits that are 'more like the individual than the actual individual himself'; or, still more plainly, 'even a single fancy as may pass through a man's head … is higher than any product of nature'.[19] Only in being transformed artistically do natural materials (stone, sound, colour, and so on) acquire a specific meaning for us.[20] In Hegel's view, nature and natural materials are in and of themselves boring, lacking a plot (as Hayden White once quipped to me, as we gazed upon a choice piece of California

---

[16] Hegel, 'Dramatic Poetry', 57. To repeat, and to distinguish Hegel from Lessing and Schlegel in this regard, I am suggesting that drama's privileged status arises, for Hegel, not just from its status as 'poetry' (as de-materialized sign or linguistic object) but from its status as action; hence, drama's self-reflexive capacities need to be grasped in light of drama's capacity to connect subjective experience and objective reality—not in light of the aesthetic-poetic reason defended by Lessing or the Jena romanticism of Schlegel. It is true that Lessing also thought that 'actions' are the real content of poetry—but he did not regard, as did Hegel, action to be also poetry's *medium*. See the discussion in Lessing, 'Laocoön', Chapter xvi.

[17] For more on this last point, see my 'No Greater Powers Than We Can Contradict', *Criticism*, special issue on Phenomenology and Shakespeare, ed. James Kearney and Kevin Curran, 54.3 (Summer 2012), 445–54.

[18] Hegel, *Lectures on Fine Art*, vol. 1: 2. On this point see also Pippin, 'What was Abstract Art? (From the Point of View of Hegel)', 9.

[19] Hegel, *Lectures on Fine Art*, 1: 29; 2: 866–7.

[20] At a minimum, a bit of 'nature-wrought-into-art' expresses the capacity of stone, sound, or colour to transmit meaning for a particular community and its practices. Art, as Hegel puts it, creates a reality that is 'besouled' ['für sich beseelt']—by which, as Robert Pippin aptly states, Hegel does not mean that human freedom re-enchants the world through artistic means but rather that art 'elevates us above the need for [the] enchantment [of the natural world]'. See Hegel, *Lectures on Fine Art*, 2: 834; and Pippin, 'What was Abstract Art? (From the Point of View of Hegel)', 8.

real estate).[21] Northrop Frye expressed the same thought about drama when he wrote that dramatic poetry fully 'belongs to the world man constructs, not to the [natural] world he sees; to his home, not his environment'.[22]

If artistic practices are medium-specific modes of self-understanding, goes the thinking here, then what medium could be more adequate to our reflexive self-understanding than that which, so to speak, we know to be 'ours' from the get-go? Not elements ripped from an indifferent domain of nature (sound, colour, hard materials like stone or marble), in other words—nor only linguistic elements which, to borrow Lessing's definition, articulate sounds in time—but rather what Giambattista Vico described in terms of 'poetic wisdom': elements of culture and history, words and deeds, social principles and passionate aims, conflicts between individual characters.[23] Because all of these are the 'stuff' of poetry—and in particular of dramatic poetry—to work in the dramatic arts entails, relative to other artistic media, a heightened degree of historical self-awareness.

Moreover—apropos our topic here—we will do well to remember not only that Hegel ranks dramatic poetry as the highest (the most prevalently 'spiritual') of artistic practices, but also the fact that he thought among modern dramatists 'you will scarcely find any . . . who can be compared with Shakespeare'.[24] And so, although Hegel does not say so explicitly, we can nevertheless infer—from the perspective of my highly condensed account here—that Shakespeare's pre-eminence in Hegel's account of the history of human artistic development should have something to do with Shakespeare's heightened degree of self-reflexivity, his dramatic presentation of drama *as such* and of the sort of self-understanding it affords.[25]

---

[21] Hegel's way of putting it is to say that nature is 'spiritless'.

[22] Northrop Frye, *The Educated Imagination* (Toronto: Canadian Broadcasting Corporation, 1963), 8.

[23] Lessing, 'Lacoön', 81.

[24] Hegel, *Lectures*, vol. 2: 1228. Shakespeare's pre-eminence in Hegel's account—the fact, for instance, that Hegel's discussion of Shakespeare comes at the culmination of his *Lectures on Fine Art*—would, of course, require some qualification. Hegel also seems to claim that Greek art is more fulfilled *as art* than modern art, and his high regard for Sophocles seems of a piece with that view. 'There is,' as Robert Pippin notes, however, 'another sense in which he claims that the ethical life behind Shakespeare's presentation and the kind of self-awareness visible in Hamlet, say, does represent an advance or moment of progress'. Robert Pippin, *The Persistence of Subjectivity: On the Kantian Aftermath* (Cambridge: Cambridge University Press, 2005), 84 n. 12. See further the discussion of Hegel and Shakespeare in Henry and Anne Paolucci, *Hegelian Literary Perspectives* (Smyrna, DE: Griffon House rpt, 2002), and, especially, in Jennifer Ann Bates, *Hegel and Shakespeare on Moral Imagination* (Albany: State University of New York Press, 2010), 5–20.

[25] Of course self-reflexivity (or self-referential theatricality) abounds in other pre- or non-Shakespearean dramatic works and practices—for example, in the formal composition of the Chorus in Greek Tragedy, or the self-referential character of gestures and costumes in Japanese Noh or Kabuki (not to mention in the architectonics and choreographic practices of various types of world drama, whether or not such dramas are 'scripted'). So, too—to move closer to Shakespeare's original context—it is by now a scholarly truism to note that sixteenth- and seventeenth-century English drama comprised a set of highly self-conscious artistic practices, in which a dramatic work's standing as 'theatre' was reflexively presented in both the composition and performance itself.

I would now like to take seriously Hegel's depiction of Shakespeare as a highly self-reflexive dramatist in order to further explore Shakespeare's dramatic presentation of drama as such. My broader ambition—which cannot be realized in the space of this essay—would be to bring into better focus Shakespeare's historically self-conscious understanding of human agency and human freedom. Here I will only try to begin sharpening some features of Shakespeare's own dramaturgy—by contrasting it to a particularly influential dramaturgical understanding of human action offered by modern philosophers, including above all Hegel himself: the duel, or life-and-death struggle.

I will have two claims to defend by way of this contrast. First, whereas Hegel's and Hobbes's 'philosophical dramaturgy' is meant to show how human life in its historical-institutional-normative dimension distinguishes itself from nature or mere living, Shakespeare nowhere presents anything like a natural state or biological viewpoint on the basis of which the achievement of human life might be grasped.[26] For Shakespeare any difference between human-historical life and 'mere living' already belongs to human history. Second, and correlated, if the achievement of human life is to be regarded as historical through and through, then it must be enactable, stageable before an audience—it must be something whose implications *we*, some particular historical community, can recognize as a concretely 'playable' human situation. For Shakespeare and his contemporaries, this took the form not of drama but of *theatre*, or of something we could call a *theatricalized drama*. We can leave open the form that such enactments might take for us: theatrical, a close-up shot of an actor in a film, or something else entirely.

Life and death struggles as philosophical dramaturgy

Before going any further, let me now make an observation, on the basis of which I hope to (at least partly) defend these theses. The observation is this: while modern philosophers, from Thomas Hobbes and G. W. F. Hegel to Alexandre Kojève, Heidegger, and Derrida, have regarded the life-and-death struggle as central to the emergence of the modern self-conscious individual, Shakespeare did not seem to regard duelling as such to be an elemental scene for human beings. If anything, in play after play and throughout his career—from *Romeo and Juliet* to *Richard II*, from *Hamlet* to *Macbeth*, from *Coriolanus* to *Cymbeline*—Shakespeare depicts idiosyncratic, aborted, perverted, botched, or failed struggles to the death: as if there is simply no such thing as an idealized 'struggle to the death' whose motivation and upshot can be staged as such.

[26] Some might argue that this is what Shakespeare does with the Forest of Arden in *As You Like It*, or the heath in *King Lear*, or Prospero's Island. I would argue that each of these is a historical predicament; see my comments on these plays in *Tragic Conditions in Shakespeare* (Baltimore, MD: Johns Hopkins University Press, 2009).

What to make of this?

First, we should recall that when Thomas Hobbes speaks of 'the state of nature' as a 'war of all against all', he is suggesting that a battle to the death is not a socio-historical practice but rather that this *bellum omnium contra omnes* aptly characterizes a pre-historical or 'natural' circumstance *out of which* human life in its institutional, political, normative dimension emerges.[27] So, while Hobbes's *Leviathan* is clearly a reflection on the stakes of the English Civil War, he does not have in mind a *particular* enacted (or enactable) battle or duel. The 'war of all against all' functions, rather, as a dramatic mythologem or idealized primal scene in his philosophy.[28] Similarly, when Hegel speaks of a 'struggle to the death' as the predicament in which human self-consciousness is forged, he thinks he is putting his finger on a drama—on a particular action—that not only does not depend upon a given set of historical circumstances in order to be meaningful, but that might actually explain the emergence of historical-institutional life as such.[29] He does not, therefore, mean to set a *theatrical scene*—he does not give the combatants proper names, nor arrange a particular *concrete* conflict for an audience. And though Hegel is elaborating a primal, dramatic scene that might perhaps take any number of 'lived' phenomenal shapes, it is far from clear that the struggle to the death as related in the *Phenomenology* lends itself to any *particular* re-enactment. At any rate, important differences between these philosophers notwithstanding, both regard the life-and-death struggle as a dramatic predicament through which human, historical life *tout court* emerges—rather than as a function of the duel's relation to some socio-historical form of life, or concrete 'theatrical' moment.

These assertions, I think, raise fundamental questions about drama that scholars of literature and theatre, too, must address: what if certain human actions are compelling not only because of their meaning within an pre-existing form of cultural, human, socio-historical life but because of their function at, or as, the threshold of what makes a life 'human'? What if certain actions are paradigmatic not because they reflect this or that social world but because sociality as such comes to light through these actions?

My point here is not primarily to determine whether Hobbes and Hegel are 'correct' to privilege life-and-death struggles in what I am calling their 'philosophical dramaturgy' (although I will try to say something about what I think it means that Shakespeare does not privilege duelling in the same way).[30] My point, rather, is that

---

[27] Thomas Hobbes, *Leviathan* (New York: Penguin, 1968).

[28] See Kottman, *A Politics of the Scene*, Chapter 3.

[29] G. W. F. Hegel, 'Self-consciousness', in *The Phenomenology of Spirit*, trans. A. V. Miller (Oxford: Oxford University Press, 1977).

[30] It should be underscored that what interests Hegel and Hobbes, primarily, are not fights in which one side (or both) is killed. There are, of course, many such scenes in Shakespeare—but these are not our primary focus. Instead, Hegel and Hobbes focus on how the relationship between the surviving combatants—and their very way of life—is irrevocably altered by the fight.

instead of seeing drama solely as the depiction of the values, rituals, and practices of a *particular* culture or social-historical world, 'philosophical dramaturgy' also tries to depict the threshold of social-historical life, our *becoming* human, by offering an idealized picture of *how* human (socio-historical, cultural, institutional) values and practices take shape or crumble through the performance of certain paradigmatic actions. Struggles to the death are, for these philosophers, part of our self-distancing from mere life or nature (for Hobbes, the 'state of nature'; for Hegel, 'the sphere of life') and are essential to the achievement of our humanity as a form of historical, and not merely natural-biological, existence.

To avoid confusion, by 'philosophical dramaturgy' I do not mean that Hobbes or Hegel (or, for that matter, Shakespeare) are 'dramatizing' a philosophical position—as if drama were a handmaiden of philosophical claims or positions that could stand on their own, non-dramaturgically. I am not talking about something like what Colin McGinn has revealingly called 'the ideas embedded in Shakespeare's text'.[31] Rather, I am assuming that philosophy makes itself dramaturgical whenever it depicts the emergence of the human through a paradigmatic action—like a battle to the death—and that, therefore, philosophers like Hobbes or Hegel are *already* dramatists of a kind, even if they are not theatrical practitioners. And I mean, further, that such dramaturgy—understood as the search for those paradigmatic actions that make us who we are—is necessarily 'philosophical' inasmuch as it understands such actions to reflect something other than theatrical display, historical contingency, or residual habits and traditions. Philosophical dramaturgy, in short, shows certain human actions to be compelling—worth reflecting on—not only because they reveal something about the conditions of theatrical action, or this or that historical moment or sociality, but also because they also depict human life being achieved by discovering its historicity and its possibilities.

I would now like to contrast Shakespeare to the 'philosophical dramaturgy' of Hobbes and Hegel. Again, I want to claim that whereas both Hegel and Hobbes are concerned to show—'dramatically', through the duel—how human life distinguishes itself from 'nature' or from mere living, Shakespeare shows through a manifold of scenes that there is no single paradigmatic action which can fully capture the stakes of human life's self-distinction in this way. Moreover, he shows that the 'achievement' of our humanity is best grasped not by a proper suturing of 'nature' and 'culture', but rather by provisional historical self-understandings which, because never properly idealized, must be 're-enactable' in manifold concrete scenes *to ourselves*—that is, before historically situated audiences.

In order to begin sketching a contrast between Shakespeare's and Hegel's 'philosophical dramaturgy', let me offer a few words about the centrality Hegel accords to the life-and-death struggle in the chapter on 'Lordship and Bondage', towards the beginning

---

[31] Colin McGinn, *Shakespeare's Philosophy: Discovering the Meaning Behind the Plays* (New York: Harper, 2006), vii.

of the section on Self-Consciousness in the *Phenomenology of Spirit*.[32] Given the many pages Hegel devotes explicitly to dramatic poetry, and to Shakespeare in particular—in the *Lectures on Fine Art* and elsewhere—my focus on these pages from the *Phenomenology* might seem out of place. However, I simply wish to take— as many others have—Hegel's *Phenomenology* as a kind of dramaturgical presenta- tion, in which various shapes of human consciousness unfold (albeit obliquely) in Hegel's writing as concrete predicaments or scenes. Some well-known instances of such Hegelian dramaturgy include the *Phenomenology*'s presentation of Antigone, the Unhappy Consciousness, and Pleasure and Necessity. In such passages, Hegel's tack is not only—as was Aristotle's—to philosophically describe an object of study. Rather than talk *about* human self-consciousness, Hegel instead offers a perspective in which the drama of human self-consciousness unfolds *through* dramatic predica- ments, scenes, and actions. These are not necessarily 'theatrical' scenes, though Hegel often seems to be inspired by (or to be condensing and refining) literary or dramatic representations, which he seems to want to offer as structural predica- ments endemic to the struggle for human self-realization.[33]

My reason for focusing especially on the life-and-death struggle is that it is the predicament through which Hegel turns from a descriptive account of consciousness to a phenomenological-dramatic staging of self-consciousness. Here, in other words, Hegel stops *explaining* what a human being is and starts *showing* how, from the inside, the doing of certain actions and the suffering of their outcomes makes us who we are. In this sense, as I have been intimating, Hegel is changing what it is to be a philoso- pher. For his task is now indistinguishable from a dramatist: to stage a uniquely grip- ping and consequential scene. Indeed, Hegel himself refers to the life-and-death struggle as the 'turning point' of the *Phenomenology*, and the chapter in which it occurs now seems a defining moment for modern philosophy.[34] Although Hegel was

---

[32] One crucial question raised by this passage from Hegel is the appropriateness of the 'pair' or the duo as the most elemental form of human relationality. Many have asked whether all mediating 'thirds' can be so easily bracketed. Although I do not have the space to take up this question here, I will do so in other contexts.

[33] So, there are, in a sense, 'characters' in Hegel's philosophical dramaturgy—"The unhappy con- sciousness', and so on. And these are not just blank names; they are also 'characters' with a 'history' or 'baggage' (namely, the historical development of *Geist*). So, I would not want to deny the many ways in which Hegel's presentation is akin to that of a dramatist. My point here, rather, is that Hegel's text *need* not be enactable in order to be *philosophically* compelling. For a good discussion of Hegel's use of literary-dramatic figures, see Robert Pippin, 'The Status of Literature in Hegel's *Phenomenology of Spirit*', in Richard T. Gray, Nicholas Halmi, Gary Handwerk, Michael A. Rosenthal, and Klaus Vieweg, eds., *Inventions of the Imagination: Interdisciplinary Perspectives on the Imaginary since Romanticism* (Seattle: University of Washington Press, 2011); also, Allen Speight, *Hegel, Literature and the Problem of Agency* (Cambridge: Cambridge University Press, 2001); more recently, to give another example, Terry Pinkard has explored the significance of Mozart's *Don Giovanni* for Hegel's depiction of pleasure and necessity in a paper presented at the New School for Social Research in February, 2012.

[34] For a recent and excellent discussion of this, see Robert Pippin's *Hegel on Self-Consciousness: Desire and Death in the Phenomenology of Spirit* (Princeton: Princeton University Press, 2011), 3–4 and *passim*.

not the first to consider a fight to the death as the elemental scene of human self-realization—again, Hobbes's *bellum omnium contra omnes* is one precursor—his account is notable for its inspiration of a wide swath of modern thought.

This influence is due in no small measure to the interpretation of Hegel given by Alexandre Kojève in a set of lectures attended by Jacques Lacan, Georges Bataille, André Breton, Maurice Merleau-Ponty, and many others. In fact, Kojève's interpretation of the 'duel' as a struggle for recognition—though influential and well known—is somewhat off the mark. Kojève takes Hegel to be staging a 'fight to the death between two beings that claim to be men' as 'a fight for prestige carried on for the sake of "recognition" by the adversary'.[35] In this sense, Kojève perceives the distinctiveness of human desiring in its orientation towards a non-natural object, towards something that cannot be the object of 'animal desire'—namely, another's desire. This desire to be desired (to be recognized by another) is the core of Kojève's explanation of Hegel's battle:

> ... anthropogenetic Desire is different from animal Desire (which produces a natural being, merely living and having only a sentiment of its life) in that it is directed, not toward a real 'positive,' given object but toward another Desire... Thus, an object perfectly useless from the biological point of view (such as a medal, or the enemy's flag) can be desired because it is the object of other desires. Such a desire can only be a human Desire, and human reality, as distinguished from animal reality, is created only by actions that satisfy such Desires: human history is the history of desired Desires.[36]

However, as Paul Redding has rightly pointed out, Kojève's account is beset by a circularity that Hegel himself sought to avoid.[37] On the one hand, Kojève wants to follow Hegel in seeing the life-and-death struggle as an elemental drama through which human self-consciousness, historical being, as such is forged—as a struggle whose need cannot be fully explained by pre-existing social norms. On the other hand, Kojève understands the quarrel to be *already* motivated by a distinctly 'human' (or historical) desire—namely: the desire for prestige or social recognition. Since the 'humanity' (or socio-historicity) of our desire cannot *both* 'come to light' in the battle and be the (already 'socio-historical') 'motivation' for the battle—something in Kojève's interpretation is amiss.

To cut to the chase, I tend to agree with Redding that, for Hegel, the duel is meant to depict the primal scene in which human-historical life is achieved—and, therefore, meant also to show human life to *be* an achievement rather than some essence attributable to a substantive, biological, or metaphysical 'human nature'. Human-historical life is achieved, first of all, by *actively proving* its independence from species-specific

---

[35] Alexandre Kojève, *Introduction to the Reading of Hegel: Lectures on the Phenomenology of Spirit* (Ithaca: Cornell University, 1980), 11–12.

[36] Kojève, *Introduction to the Reading of Hegel*, 6.

[37] See Paul Redding, *Hegel's Hermeneutics* (Ithaca: Cornell University Press, 1996), especially chapters 5 and 6.

requirements for life and self-preservation—human Desire [wins] out over the desire for preservation. One fights to *prove* one's humanity—and, by the same token, only in such an active demonstration does one come to have the standing (for oneself and for others) as human, as part of history.

Shakespeare understood this, too, I would argue. Indeed, on this point at least, Hegel and Shakespeare seem to meet. Consider, for example, the opening of *Romeo and Juliet*, which forces us to ask: Why do the men fight? If our answer is that the men fight because they happen to be Capulets and Montagues, then we are left with something like *West Side Story*—a pre-existing ethnic, tribal context or 'gang war', in which the characters are caught up and by which they are defeated. As if they all merely had the misfortune of being in the wrong place at the wrong time among the wrong people. We might also answer that the brawl gives each participant the chance to prove his manhood.[38] But by 'manhood' we would have to mean not just some desired social standing, masculine virtue or 'manliness'—such as the 'man at arms' described in Castiglione's *Book of the Courtier*. Such a standing may indeed be desirable in certain contexts, and may be obtainable in some circumstances by prevailing in violent conflict. However, because violent conflict is not absolutely *necessary* for the acquisition of such a standing—if anything, in Shakespeare's Verona, one's civic status appears to depend upon keeping the peace—the desire to be recognized *by others* as 'manly' (or as a 'Montague', or a 'Capulet') cannot explain the necessity of the fight to the death here. And it is the fight to the death that we need to explain.

At stake, therefore, is something more elemental.

I risk my life in a battle to the death—say the men—*not for prestige, nor as an act of tribal duty or animal aggression; but rather to show that the desire to stay alive (mere instinct) does not drive me absolutely.* ('Draw if you be men' [1.1.59].)

'I' am more than my desire to live. My bodily vitality is not the highest value for me; biological life is not a higher 'good' by which my existence is measured. I take measure of my own life by risking it.

If I cannot stake this claim, then no social standing or recognition of my manhood can be meaningful for me.[39] (This is exactly how Hegel describes the motivation for the life-and-death struggle in the 'Lordship and Bondage' section of the chapter on 'Self-Consciousness'.)

So, at this point at least, Shakespeare seems to see the duel much as Hegel does—as a scene in which a longing for social recognition, while it may well follow the struggle, does not *motivate* the battle.[40] Recall, as further evidence, the exchange

---

[38] There is no use denying that a display of sexual prowess is also motivational for the men. ('I will push Montague's men from the wall, and thrust his / maids to the wall' [1.1.15–17].) But 'sexual prowess' is not only a form of social prestige; it is also a struggle for self-realization.

[39] See Hegel, *The Phenomenology of Spirit*, 114, paragraph 187.

[40] For a longer discussion of this, see my 'Defying the Stars: Romantic Love as the Struggle for Freedom in *Romeo and Juliet*', *Shakespeare Quarterly* 63.1 (2012).

between Benvolio and Mercutio at the opening of Act III, which explains that the socio-historical occasion for a fight—a hot day, a 'Capel abroad', a drunken tavern—is not to be confused with the motive for fighting. A hot day, and two young desiring beings who stand ready to risk their lives to prove themselves, will suffice. Fighting is its own motive—the quarrel urges itself:

> Thou wilt quarrel with a man that hath a hair more or a hair less in his beard than thou hast. Thou wilt quarrel with a man for cracking nuts, having no other reason but because thou hast hazel eyes. What eye but such an eye would spy out such a quarrel? Thy head is as full of quarrels as an egg is full of meat, and yet thy head hath been beaten as addle as an egg for quarreling. Thou hast quarreled with a man for coughing on the street, because he hath wakened thy dog that hath lain asleep in the sun.... (3.1.16–26)

Now, if Hegel and Shakespeare at least agree on the motivation of 'quarrelling' as the threshold of socio-historical life, then it is striking that Shakespeare nowhere organizes one of his dramas around the consequences of the 'duel' as depicted by either Hegel or Hobbes. After all, while *Romeo and Juliet* contains life-and-death struggles (Romeo slays Tybalt and then Paris) the play does not seem to be primarily *about* the consequences of those struggles.

Put simply, if Shakespeare agrees with Hegel and Hobbes about the *motive* for the duel—that it belongs to those actions in which the achievement of our humanity is on display—then it would seem that Shakespeare does *not* share the philosophers' vision of the upshot of the duel. Nor, significantly, does Shakespeare think that duels, in all of their perverse specificity, *need not be shown theatrically*. Hamlet's fight with Laertes, Macbeth and Macduff, Tybalt and Romeo—all these must lend themselves to re-representation. Let me now turn, then, to my discussion of the implications of Shakespeare's departure from Hegel and Hobbes on these two points.

First, on the upshot of the battle. Neither Hegel nor Hobbes is really interested in a struggle that leaves one (or both) of the combatants dead.[41] As Hegel puts it, 'death is the *natural* negation of consciousness . . . which thus remains without the required significance of recognition'. Or, put less floridly, dead is dead is dead: end of story. Duelling generates historical life not through the destruction of one or both combatants but through a transformation effected when both survive and begin to interact in norm-governed ways, as in Hobbes's 'commonwealth' and 'pact', or Hegel's 'Lord and Bondsman'.

Moreover, both Hobbes and Hegel focus on the fear of death in which the battle results, when it does not end up destroying one or both combatants. 'This consciousness,' writes Hegel of the combatant who becomes the bondsman, 'has been

---

[41] So, Hegel's interest is quite different from that of, say, Elias Canetti—for whom the survival of the victor is the crucial point of political–ethical interest. See Elias Canetti, *Crowds and Power* (New York: Macmillan, 1984), 72 and *passim*.

fearful, not of this or that particular thing or just at odd moments, but its whole being has been seized with dread; for it has experienced the fear of death, the absolute Lord'.[42] If this fear only expressed a species-imperative or a survival instinct, then the 'natural' response of the fearful combatant would be to take flight—to run away from the enemy and avoid his company. But remember that what Hegel and Hobbes envision are not battle scenes in which one side simply turns tail and runs—evading all further interaction with the enemy. Instead, they want to explain *why* the fear of death that arises in the duel leads, somewhat counter-intuitively, to a *relationship* between the combatants—indeed, to an enduring, institutionalized, norm-governed, 'human' relationship.[43] For Hobbes, this fear produces the 'pact' whereby the combatants agree to submit to the terrifying authority of a sovereign power; for Hegel, the Bondsman does the Lord's bidding inasmuch as he labours in submission to the fear of death.

For both philosophers, in other words, the fear of death is the impetus to norm-governed, historical interactions—and registers far more than just an instinctive response to this or that frightful thing in the world (*this* enemy or *that* mortal danger). Leaving aside the many differences between them, each sees the fear of death as distinguishing human life from mere natural instinct inasmuch as this fear transforms one's relation to life and living *tout court*. Unlike the flight of a deer from a predator, or the flinch of a hand from a hot stove, the institutionalized submission of one human being to another is urged not simply by the unthinking preservation of life and limb but—more deeply—by a reflective estimation of one's life and limb as *worth preserving*. Rather than an innate instinctual reflex to stay alive—what Robert Pippin calls a 'species imperative'—there emerges an individual who reflects upon *her attachment to her own life* and comes to see her life as valuable.[44] This is not a natural (species) imperative, in other words, because her life is now individually *hers*—valuable *to her*. For both Hobbes and Hegel, this reflexive movement through which *life becomes worthwhile* to the one(s) living—and not just a species imperative—is a threshold or passage from something like sheer natural consciousness to self-conscious, historical existence. Why? Because now the former combatants must and do *interact* with one another in norm-based, rather than merely biologically driven, ways: they *take up* a life together. In Hobbes, for instance, this

---

[42] Hegel, *Phenomenology of Spirit*, 117, paragraph 197. Hegel's fear of the 'absolute Lord' [Death] has a parallel in Hobbes's suggestion that the 'Gods were at first created by human feare'—a 'perpetuall feare, always accompanying mankind'. See Hobbes, *Leviathan*, 169–70. This is captured, as well, by Carl Schmitt in his description of the relevant moment in Hobbes's *Leviathan*: 'The state of nature drives anguished individuals to come together; their fear rises to an extreme; a spark of reason (*ratio*) flashes, and suddenly there stands in front of them a new God'. Carl Schmitt, *The Leviathan in the State Theory of Thomas Hobbes* (Chicago: University of Chicago Press, 2008), 31.

[43] This also explains why they focus on a fear of death occasioned by violent conflict with another—rather than some generic fear of dying, or of what Hamlet called 'the undiscovered country'.

[44] Robert Pippin, *Hegel on Self-Consciousness*, 79 and *passim*.

means that the former combatants 'obey' the sovereign; in Hegel, it means at a minimum the ritual acts by which the Bondman demonstrates his submission to the Lord.

'Social-historical interaction' thus turns out be co-extensive with the self-conscious estimation of life as *worthwhile*—and furthermore with an estimation of *ourselves* (rather than Nature, or God or biology) as the final arbiter of that worth. Hence, this self-arbitration is more than an intellectual exercise or pious belief. Self-conscious reflection upon one's life as worth living must amount to the *doing* of certain routine, norm-based actions—such as wearing the required uniform, bowing deeply, or saying 'yes, sir'. Historical forms of life—with all of their ritual practices, customary modes of interaction, and divisions of labour—turn out to be, at bottom, practical reflections of the value of our lives, estimations of our lives as worth living.

There would, of course, be much more to say about all of this. At this point, however, I would like to characterize the perspective of Hegelian or Hobbesian 'philosophical dramaturgy' as the search for paradigmatic acts that allow human life to distinguish itself from mere living or from nature. And in this way, 'philosophical dramaturgy' also suggests that socio-historical forms of life are invariably practical estimations of the worth of our 'natural' lives. Certain actions—such as duelling, at least for Hobbes and Hegel—might even constitute zero-degree dramas through which a mere life might begin to appear worth living, worth preserving, worth something as 'human'.

Shakespeare's difference

In a sense, of course, dramatic poets have always asked us to reflect upon whether our lives are worthwhile or desirable. They invite us to regard our lives not only in terms of species-level requirements for living but also in light of social practices that—when laid bare—show themselves to be occasions for weighing the value of particular lives, opportunities for their *self-evaluation*. This is as true of Shakespearean drama as it was, for instance, of Sophoclean or Aeschylean drama.[45]

Consider, as one striking instance of both points, Shylock's agreement to convert to Christianity at the end of the *Merchant of Venice*. Here the 'dramatic' predicament is inseparable from a self-consciously *theatrical staging* of it—namely, both Shylock's appearance before all of Venice, and the appearance of this scene before an audience (us). This self-conscious presentation—a 'courtroom drama' with both an internal audience (the Duke and those gathered) and an external audience

---

[45] For more on this comparison, see the close of my 'Introduction' in *Tragic Conditions in Shakespeare*.

(us)—seems designed in part to *test*, as in Greek tragedy, whether the action is as meaningful to us as it is to the protagonists. And, if it is, then it must be in large measure because we have achieved, by watching the enactment, some sense of what this conversion must mean to Shylock as a Jew or as a Venetian, or because we somehow 'identify' with his predicament. We squirm, that is, because we have seen (through the enactment of the drama) that circumstances have forced Shylock to reflect upon the value of his own life—in light of the occasion furnished by his attachment to his Judaism, to his money, to his community. The stakes of that reflection are not separable, I think, from our sense of how the other onlookers—in 'Venice' and in the audience—gauge their importance. All of this parallels Aristotle's view of how our affective response to a classical tragic drama is an expression of its social stakes.[46]

This also allows us to hear Shylock's 'first-person' experience of the threat of being reduced to abject poverty—to hear, that is, Shylock offer an evaluation not only of what owning property means in Venice generally but also, above all, a declaration of what owning property in Venice means to *him*:

> Nay, take *my* life and all; pardon not that:
> You take *my* house when you do take the prop
> That doth sustain *my* house; you take *my* life
> When you do take the means whereby *I* live.   (4.1.372–5) (emphasis mine)

The moment is riveting, I want to suggest, because we sense that what hangs in the balance is not only the fate of Venice, of *that* historical world or way of life, nor simply the fate of Shylock's or Antonio's standing, nor even the future of Shylock's biological life. We are mesmerized, rather, because we see that Shylock is in the process of discovering *for himself* whether his life is worth preserving. We watch him ask himself if his own life matters to him at all—whether there are conditions under which it might no longer appear worth living. Shylock's consent to the conversion—like his seemingly relentless pursuit of the pound of flesh at the scene's opening—grip us, then, because they are moments at which we see someone *discover* that which, for him, is worth living or dying for. After all, we do not simply watch Shylock act on what he has already *decided* is most important to him—his biological life, his money, or his social standing as a Jew. Instead, we see him forced by circumstance into actively evaluating his own life's worth *to him*. In doing so, we ask ourselves the very questions that also signal our investment in the drama: how far will Shylock go? Is he willing to die in order to see Antonio die? Will he be pushed over the edge, to the point of devaluing his life utterly? Or, does he love his life enough to go on living bereft of property? Does he love life enough to renounce Judaism and to live as a Christian?

---

[46] See my 'Avoiding Tragedy in *The Merchant of Venice*', *The Journal of Cultural and Religious Theory* 8.3 (Fall 2007), 53–65.

Now, we may or may not feel that how Shylock answers these questions bears on the worth of *our own* life—collectively or individually—as well. We may or may not see Shylock as one of us. But we do not *need* Shylock's self-evaluation to bear immediately upon our own lives in order to perceive the stakes of his predicament for *him*. We look on as Shylock weighs his attachment to his own life as such. And we perceive, further, that only in light of this reflective evaluation will his place in Venice—will the social meaning of his actions—be decided. Thus, his acceptance of his new social standing as a Christian is the outcome, not the origin, of this self-evaluation. Indeed, there is nothing about being a Jew or a Christian—nothing about belonging to an historical community—that can fully decide whether it is worth clinging to one's life by means of that belonging.[47] Shylock's practical commitment to a community, finally, must be the upshot—and not the full means—of his evaluation of his own life as worth living or not. As Shakespeare knows, the particularities of the Venetian world—the conflict between Jews and Christians, the realities of a mercantile economy and so on—merely occasion a self-evaluation that Shylock alone must undergo.

Everything I just said sounds, I think, consistent with the questions motivating Hegel's philosophical dramaturgy, or, for that matter, with many aspects of Aristotle's reflections on ancient tragedy. So what is Shakespeare's difference?

First, if for Hegel (and Aristotle) the particularities of the structural predicament do not need to be tested through the concrete enactment or re-enactment of *this* particular protagonist—then, in Shakespeare, the theatrical enactment seems crucial. Indeed, in light of our earlier discussion of the philosophers, the conspicuous specificity of Shylock's predicament cannot but strike us here. Whereas Hobbes and Hegel perceived a general, indeterminate 'battle to the death' as the elemental scene in the self-evaluation of human life, Shakespeare offers the singular predicament of deeds of *this* man, Shylock the Jewish moneylender of Venice—a person whose historical 'baggage' is as particular and personal as it is historically determined.

Shylock is a well-known instance, but in every play he wrote, Shakespeare offered predicaments of such vivid and particular detail that they defy all paradigmatic or generic descriptions (including paradigmatic descriptions such as 'Duel'). At the same time, Shakespeare supersedes classical tragedy by offering no final guidelines—theatrical, ritual, psychological, physical, or other—for *how* Shylock is, finally, to be played or *mise-en-scène*. In this sense, the nearly infinite *enactability* or stageability of Shakespearean drama is expressive of, and essential to, its presentation of our historicity. Because the very conditions for human activity are historically transformable—and must therefore be seen as transformable still—our

---

[47] This is not at all to say that the particularities of the Venetian world—or the differences between Judaism and Christianity—do not matter to Shakespeare. They matter absolutely to the full presentation of the predicament in the drama; I mean to say, here, that these cannot *decide* the matter for Shylock himself. And that this, too, is essential to the drama's presentation.

presentation of these activities must be manifold, transforming and transformable: replayable, re-enactable, rethinkable. This radical mutability, I think, explains both our need for Shakespeare's drama in its multiplicity—for *all* the plays—as well as for the sheer variety of critical responses (theatrical, cinematic, and other) that Shakespeare's work has occasioned in universities and playhouses since the eighteenth century. J. G. Herder praised Shakespeare for just this quality: 'Is there anyone in the world who is indifferent to the time and place of even trivial events in his life?' writes Herder:

> Is it not place and time and the fullness of external circumstances which endow the whole story with its direction, duration, and existence?...From out of all the scenes and conjunctures in the world, Shakespeare chose, as though by some law of fatality, just those which are the most powerful, the most appropriate to the feeling of the action; in which the strangest, boldest circumstances best support the illusion of truth; in which the changes of time and place over which the poet rules, proclaim most loudly: 'This is not a poet, but a creator! Here is the history of the world!'[48]

In *The Merchant of Venice* alone, we see a 'strange' suit for a pound of flesh, a Venetian merchant whose fortune has been ruined by three shipwrecks, the inimitable legalisms of Portia, the utterly contingent motivations of love and friendship that lie just beneath her words—to say nothing of the convergence of Jewish and Christian interests in Venice, or of the weight of flesh and gold in that world, or of Shylock's own motivations. The particularities of these scenes stem not only from Shakespeare's peerless skill as a dramatic poet, from his imaginative energy. They also reveal, I am suggesting, a crucial difference between Shakespeare's dramaturgy—which *must* pass through the theatre—and the philosophical dramaturgy of Hegel and Hobbes.

Unlike Hobbes and Hegel, Shakespeare does not think that the actions by which our humanity is achieved—by which we *evaluate* our attachment to our individual lives, and to our lives together—unfold at the emergence of socio-historical life, out of what Hobbes calls the 'state of nature' or what Hegel calls 'the sphere of life'. Shakespeare, that is, does not derive his dramatic energy from the cusp of culture's denaturalization of life, or at the moment at which animal desire is transformed into human longing. Shakespeare nowhere looks for those actions that supposedly raise us out of nature, thereby making us human. Shakespeare never depicts, imagines, or stages wholly pre-institutional desires or strivings. In Shakespeare's theatrical dramaturgy, there is no 'state of nature' or 'sphere of life'—there is, instead, always an enactable *scene*.

Rather than proceed, as do Hobbes and Hegel, from 'nature to culture'—Shakespeare remains firmly within the particular contingencies of the social, which seem

---

[48] Herder, 'Shakespeare', in Kottman, ed., *Philosophers on Shakespeare*, 31.

to require something like their enactability. Shakespeare, that is, *begins* with the facts of historical existence, the nitty-gritty of social interactions and communal practices. Even where Shakespeare seems to depict a kind of pre-institutional setting—such as the cave in *Cymbeline*, or Prospero's island, or the forest of Arden, or the heath and cliffs of Dover in *King Lear*, or the world of Oberon and Titania—he never lets us forget that these settings are historical predicaments through and through. Savageness, deprivation, raging desires, fear, deep despair, the 'churlish chiding of the winter's wind'—for Shakespeare, these are not the origins but rather the direct fallouts and expressions of specific human interactions, histories, relationships.

And the 'proof' of this theatrical dramaturgy is the enactability of these scenes before an audience. To say it all at once: for Shakespeare, that which cannot be reenacted as a scene before an audience cannot be understood as historical, as human, as implicating *us*. Our dramatic practices are, in this sense, a test of our historical self-understanding—its limits and possibilities. This is how Shakespeare differs from the 'philosophical dramaturgy' exemplified by the Hegelian and Hobbesian 'duel'. Rather than imagine that there is an elemental dramatic 'structure'—a fight to the death that transforms animal desire into a human relationship, that takes us from biological life to institutional-human-historical life—Shakespeare shows how we invariably begin to act, in some here-and-now setting, from within a specific human-historical setting, with all its attendant baggage and precise conundrums. The lustre of our humanity shines brightest when this baggage weighs most concretely, here and now (as in a tense theatrical or cinematic moment), when the specificity of our socio-historical existence crushes us most. And because it is *as a specifically weighty circumstance*—which, I think, is Shakespeare's sense of what any performance self-consciously displays—that historical life becomes drama, there can be no single 'human' scene through which others are encompassed and explained. If dramas—loss, joy, fulfilment, desperation—are to be found in all our words and deeds, at different moments and in disparate ways, then dramatic performances afford a historically self-aware human *practice* through which to better grasp the implications of this knowledge.

Shakespeare thinks, too, that we can never really see the 'origins' of our historical baggage or social quandaries; to *really* inhabit a human predicament means accepting this blindness as an insight. Agnes Heller has it right when she says that, in Shakespeare, 'truth is revealed about history' because Shakespeare shows us 'what' happens and 'how' it happened without bothering to show us 'why'.[49] In Shakespeare we grasp *what* happens when we stop asking *why* it happens. For Shakespeare, we see our sociality most clearly when we cease looking for its pre-historical

---

[49] Agnes Heller, from 'The Time is Out of Joint: Shakespeare as Philosopher of History' in Kottman, ed., *Philosophers on Shakespeare*, 188.

motivation and attend, rather, to its possible expressions as theatrical performance. *That* Capulet and Montague quarrel matters more than why; *that* Duke Senior has been banished to Arden matters more than why; *that* Jews live in the ghetto in Venice matters more than why; *that* Fortinbras marches matters more than why. *That* we fight and have fought matters more than *why*. Let us admit this, says Shakespeare, and strive to show how the inevitable historicity of our practices—the unavoidable *baggage* that comes with being born into a historical world—shoves our face in the mud of self-evaluation, whether we like it or not. There needs no murderous enemy on the desert plain come to force us to reflect on the worth of our lives. Anyway, there is no such desert plain. We encounter one another in the world, not on the moon. What murderous enemies there are live in our midst; they speak our language; we can know their names.[50]

If Shakespearean dramaturgy dovetails with, but differs from, that of Hobbes and Hegel, then it is because Shakespeare sees the manifold, concrete specificity of our communal rituals, re-enactments, social practices, and values as the only occasions—and *only* the occasions—for ongoing, reflective evaluations of our lives' worth.

FURTHER READING

Hegel, G. W. F. *Lectures on Fine Art*, trans. T. M. Knox (Oxford: Clarendon Press, 1975), volumes I and II.

Hegel, G. W. F. 'Lordship and Bondage', in *The Phenomenology of Spirit*, trans. A. V. Miller (Oxford: Oxford University Press, 1977).

Kojève, Alexandre. *Introduction to the Reading of Hegel: Lectures on the Phenomenology of Spirit* (Ithaca: Cornell University, 1980).

Kottman, Paul A. 'Defying the Stars: Romantic Love as the Struggle for Freedom in *Romeo and Juliet*', *Shakespeare Quarterly* 63.1 (2012), 1–38.

Pippin, Robert. *Hegel on Self-Consciousness: Desire and Death in the Phenomenology of Spirit* (Princeton: Princeton University Press, 2011).

Redding, Paul. *Hegel's Hermeneutics* (Ithaca: Cornell University Press, 1996).

---

[50] At any rate, quarrelling Capulet boys are probably the least of our worries. We should be so lucky that all our relationships are forged from out-and-out duels! But, alas, murderousness does not always present itself immediately as such—as Othello, Banquo, Edgar, Claudio, and company find out. Enmity can also arise as a betrayal of trust, in the wrecking of a world that we have no choice but to share. The experiences of such betrayals, too, make us who we are—introduce us to our humanity, such as it may be.

CHAPTER 22

HOSPITALITY

JULIA REINHARD LUPTON

'Theatricality' usually designates a phenomenon distinct from drama and its humanist spaces and institutions, while also capturing an essential feature of dramatic art, namely its appearing, its phenomenal passage into a special kind of space that is brought into being by the fact and act of that transit. For this reason, Bert States identified theatre as 'a place of disclosure, not a place of reference',[1] and Samuel Weber insists that theatricality 'does not merely "reproduce" and yet also does not simply "create"'.[2] Theatricality is affiliated with non-linguistic elements of performance such as lighting, sound, and props; yet the suffix -ality also implies a reflexive fold and self-distilling movement that sublimates stage craft into consciousness and towards language. Finally, theatricality names a gestural mode that can travel far from formal performance spaces, enlivening (or contaminating) everything from political speech and social exchanges to dress codes, gender norms, and teaching styles.

What might hospitality have to do with theatricality? What do they share, and what does each render visible in the other? The rituals of hospitality incubate the theatricality incipient in all human exchange, and do so in a manner that remains close to bodily wants and the comportments and technologies that accompany them: in hospitality events, life manifests itself as theatre. Because of this primary conjunction of vitality, welcoming, and performance, scenes of accommodation and conviviality and their refusal or violation abound in the mythic situations of dramatic literature. From masked balls, slaughtered guests, and cannibal banquets to resident aliens, exotic sojourners, and heavenly hosts, hospitality gathers together a diverse yet coherent repertoire of narrative scenarios, physical routines, and

---

[1] Bert O. States, *Great Reckonings in Little Rooms: On the Phenomenology of Theater* (Berkeley: University of California Press, 1985), 4.

[2] Samuel Weber, *Theatricality as Medium* (New York: Fordham University Press, 2004), 14.

cosmic musings.[3] Hospitality feeds the thematics of Renaissance drama in part because acts of reception are built into the conditions of theatrical performance, whether via the memory of innyards embedded in the architecture of the public theatre, as the occasion for court entertainments, or as a customary script in the theatre of daily life. Hospitality is always simultaneously a narrative event and a sumptuary instance, the unfurling of a panoply of socio-symbolic relationships and the ceremonial setting forth of material things for enjoyment and display. Hospitality crafts scenes for appearing: both the tremulous and risky appearing of persons to each other in moments of quasi-public encounter and acknowledgement, and the appearing of things as vessels of affect and allure that overflow their use.

The dramatic character of hospitality—its generation of occasions for consumption, enjoyment, and wonder as well as resistance, scepticism, and betrayal—weds it fundamentally to theatricality as a simultaneously formal and material effect. As Henry S. Turner argues in his essay 'Generalization' in this volume, 'theatricality... was never exclusively a material phenomenon. Certainly theatre is "material" in the sense that specific objects, bodies, and structural elements become integral aspects of a performance and make it possible...But theatre is also always intellectual, mental, fictional, abstract'. Hospitality is embodied thought and thoughtful practice: this doubleness of hospitality in and for Renaissance theatricality constitutes the object of this inquiry. *Hospitality is embodied thought*: the theoretical aspirations of hospitality always bear the lived dimension of entertainment within them as the ground and occasion for their speculative processes. *Hospitality is thoughtful practice*: culinary, decorative, and sheltering efforts bear their own ideational tendencies to analyse and archive, to curate and conserve.

Although hospitality has yielded many rich literary readings when pursued from the ethical perspectives of Levinas and Derrida,[4] I have chosen to track the confluence of hospitality's *biopolitical, political–theological,* and *political–ecological*

[3] On hospitality and Renaissance theatre, see excellent studies by Daryl Palmer, *Hospitable Performances: Dramatic Genre and Cultural Practices in Early Modern England* (West Lafayette, IN: Purdue Research Foundation, 1992), Chris Meads, *Banqueting Set Forth: Banqueting in English Renaissance Drama* (Manchester: Manchester University Press, 2001), and David Goldstein, *Eating and Ethics in Shakespeare's England* (Cambridge: Cambridge University Press, 2013). See also Felicity Heal, *Hospitality in Early Modern England* (Oxford: Clarendon Press, 1990), for an historical account of hospitality and social policy and practice, 1400–1700. My work is indebted to that of my student, Tracy McNulty, *The Hostess: Hospitality, Femininity, and the Expropriation of Identity* (Minneapolis: University of Minnesota Press, 2007). On 'repertoire' as those aspects of theatre not associated with the dramatic text, see W. B. Worthen, *Drama: Between Poetry and Performance* (Chichester: Wiley-Blackwell, 2010).

[4] In Renaissance studies, see David Goldstein, 'Emmanuel Levinas and the Ontology of Eating', *Gastronomica* 30.1 (2011), 1529–62; and Kevin Curran, 'Hospitable Justice: Law and Selfhood in Shakespeare's Sonnets', *Law, Culture and the Humanities* (2011), 1–16. Other developments of the Derridean line outside our field include Mireille Rosello, *Postcolonial Hospitality: The Immigrant as Guest* (Stanford: Stanford University Press, 2001) and Richard Kearney and Kascha Semonovitch, eds., *Phenomenologies of the Stranger: Between Hostility and Hospitality* (New York: Fordham University Press, 2011).

investments, that is, its ritual regulation of life processes for purposes that range from the immunization of vitality against its own creative–destructive tendencies to the staking out of affective labour as the ground for new forms of politics. Hospitality is *biopolitical* insofar as it cultivates the threshold between the *oikos* or household and the *polis* or city, bidding a provisional politics to pitch its tent on the scene of bodily care. Hospitality is *political–theological* insofar as gifting, greeting, feasting, and sanctuary institute visions of community and social order within corporate, creaturely, and cosmological frames of reference. Finally, as the symbolic organization of bodily and affective needs within environments that host us, hospitality's enacted poetics of vitality is nested within complex ecologies of creaturely exposure and biotechnical extension. Hospitality's seasonal scripts gather up and mobilize not only human actors but also non-human actants, including foods and fabrics as well as animals and furniture, while hospitality's library houses husbandry and housekeeping guides alongside biblical commentaries, classical myths, and the texts of plays and entertainments. The arts of hospitality, as provisional public spheres, environmental assemblages, and phantasmatic memory palaces, have much to tell us about the fundamentally mixed conditions and several destinations of Renaissance theatricality.

Hospitality between biopolitics and political theology

There are many ways to approach the ideational topography formed by political theology, biopower, and their peculiar tracing of early modernity as moment, canon, and question.[5] Primary texts by Carl Schmitt, Hannah Arendt, Michel Foucault, and Giorgio Agamben all figure into current elaborations of the relationship between *zoë*, *bios*, and sovereignty: that is, between biological vitality and the kinds of care it solicits (*zoë*); civic virtue and its exercise of a freedom from bodily need secured by the labour of others (*bios*); and sovereignty understood as the mythic metaphors animating and unifying the body politic by means of originary identifications of the monarch with God, metaphors that are constitutionally fraught by the pressure of more distributive, self-organizing, and immanent collectivities. The ritual practices of hospitality draw together these regions of concern by creating a provisional politics out of acts focused on meeting those needs for nourishment, shelter, and security that affiliate human beings with other forms of life.

---

[5] For a set of contemporary responses, see Graham Hammill and Julia Reinhard Lupton, eds., *Political Theology and Early Modernity* (Chicago: University of Chicago Press, 2012).

Hannah Arendt anticipated Foucault in diagnosing the modern state as a form of housekeeping organized around the physical health rather than the civic virtues of the people. Thus she writes in *The Human Condition* that the classical division between 'activities related to a common world and those related to the maintenance of life' have become 'entirely blurred, because we see the body of peoples and political communities in the image of a family whose everyday affairs have to be taken care of by a gigantic, nationwide administration of housekeeping'.[6] Whereas classical politics identified virtue with the exercise of freedom through public speech and deliberative action, modern politics—no politics at all in Arendt's judgement—takes as its *raison d'être* the management of the needs of life through offices of public health, whose home remedies include eugenics, ethnic cleansing, and homeland security alongside universal education and childhood vaccines. For Arendt, the minor monarchies of the Middle Ages as well as the absolutist enterprises of early modernity muffled the possibilities of the *polis* by glorifying the king as the master of a giant household. The Tudor offices of wardrobe and bedchamber, though not synonymous with the operations of governmentality in the modern sense, contributed both conceptually and pragmatically to the expansion of the royal *oikos* into the modern state by linking household matters to public functions.[7] Whereas the *vita activa* of the classical *polis* defines itself by its freedom from the cares of the *oikos*, courtly space, as the architectural support and reflection of the royal household and its bodily ministrations, retains domestic concerns at the centre of its ceremonials.

Hospitality belongs to housekeeping as one of its finest arts, elevating bodily care into a social offering, a seasonal symbol, and an aesthetic opportunity. Indeed, in the practical literature of householding, hospitality and housekeeping are sometimes synonymous, especially when they bear on social welfare: in *Five Hundreth pointes of good husbandrie*, Thomas Tusser writes, 'Of all other doings, housekeeping is cheere, / for dailie it helpeth, the poore with reliefe'.[8] Periodic proclamations by Elizabeth and James 'requiring the Residencie of Noblemen, Gentlemen, Lieutenants, and Justices of Peace, upon their chiefe Mansions in the Countrey, for the

---

[6] Hannah Arendt, *The Human Condition* (Chicago: University of Chicago Press, 1958), 28.

[7] See G. R. Elton, *The Tudor Constitution: Documents and Commentary* (Cambridge: Cambridge University Press, 1982). Elton claims, 'The revival of monarchy by the Yorkists and Henry VII relied in great part on the renewed exploitation of the Household as a means of administration. In particular this meant the development of the Chamber as a financial department' (130). Elton argues that these expanded household offices were displaced by more properly statist forms of administration under Cromwell's reforms. Household positions such as membership in the Office of the Bedchamber remained important posts in the court of James. See Neil Cuddy, 'The Revival of the Entourage: The Bedchamber of James I, 1603–25', in David Starkey et al., eds., *The English Court from the War of the Roses to the Civil War* (Harlow: Longman, 1987), 173–225. Cited by Kevin Curran, *Marriage, Performance, and Politics at the Jacobean Court* (Farnham: Ashgate, 2009), 57.

[8] Thomas Tusser, *Five Hundreth pointes of good husbandrie* (London: Richard Yardley and Peter Short, 1593), 44.

better maintenance of Hospitalitie, and discharge of their duties' were designed to ensure the proper distribution of charity; such actions also dispersed the nobility, weakening their influence at court and, in Daryl Palmer's formulation, 'confin[ing] the nobility in their imagination of themselves'.[9] Meanwhile, court entertainments used the commemoration and symbolization of life functions to seal deals, broker compromises, and communicate organic visions of the polity.[10]

In our own time, the language of hospitality helps shape the biopolitical administration of refugees, guest workers, and other stateless persons; in this sense, hospitality's techniques and procedures contribute to the neutralization of classical politics by the social state as diagnosed by Arendt. In *The Winter's Tale*, Hermione anticipates the biopolitical punch of state-sponsored hospitality when she asks Polixenes if he would rather remain in Sicily as her prisoner or as her guest (I.ii.52), a rhetorical question that manifests the dark affinity between these two forms of sequestering.[11] Shylock is a guest turned prisoner, his provisional rights as a resident alien suspended when his suit threatens the life of a citizen. In *The Taming of the Shrew*, as Nichole Miller has argued, Petruchio's farmhouse hospitality employs techniques of starvation, sleep deprivation, and sexual shaming that anticipate biopolitical manipulations of bodily functions as a means of rebooting or annihilating the personhood of impounded subjects.[12]

If hospitality harbours a dark area in which sanctuary can turn into encampment, hospitality also builds a temporary platform for actors normally excluded from public speech. Collective labour followed by collective celebration—as dramatized, for example, in the sheep-shearing festival in *The Winter's Tale*—suggests the protopolitical capacities of hospitality in agrarian settings not formally included in the operations of the state.[13] In his artisanal novels, Thomas Deloney praises shoemakers and clothiers for 'their worthy deeds and great hospitality'.[14] *The Shoemaker's Holiday*, which draws on Deloney's worlds of craft and community, is one of a

---

[9] Proclamation by James I, 9 December 1615 (London: Robert Barker, 1615), one of several such proclamations. On the political as well as social uses of these calls to fight 'the decay of hospitalitie', see Palmer, *Hospitable Performances*, 7–9.

[10] On theatricality and marriage at court, see Curran, *Marriage, Performance, and Politics*.

[11] All citations from Shakespeare are from David Bevington, ed., *The Complete Works of Shakespeare* (New York: Longman, 1997).

[12] Nichole E. Miller, 'The Sexual Politics of Pain: Hannah Arendt Meets Shakespeare's Shrew', *Journal of Cultural and Religious Theory* 7.2 (Spring 2006), 18–32.

[13] Thomas Tusser enjoins his husbandmen to end the harvest with a party: 'In harvest time harvest folke, servants and all, / Should make altogether, good cheere in the hall' (*Five Hundreth pointes*, 102). This is commoning by the commoners themselves.

[14] Thomas Deloney, *The Gentle Craft: A Discourse . . . Shewing what famous men have been Shoemakers* (London: Robert Bird, 1637) and *The Honour of the Cloathworking Trade; Or, the Pleasant and Famous History of Thomas of Reading* (London: J. Deacon, 1612), frontispiece. See Palmer, *Hospitable Performances*, 99 on hospitality in *The Shoemaker's Holiday*: 'Like George a Greene, Eyre envisions a government deriving from the topography of the community, from Fleet Street to Tower Street, enlivened by his mad hosting'.

number of Renaissance plays that dramatize the self-organizing capacities of lower-class hosting, as Daryl Palmer has demonstrated.[15] In *Othello*, Desdemona exits the privacy of 'house affairs' and enters into the circle of narrative performance when her father entertains Othello, her active audition ('with a greedy ear / She did devour up my discourse') ultimately achieving the status of an act when she elects him as her beloved (I.iii.130–72). In *The Travels of the Three English Brothers*, a play by John Day, George Wilkins, and William Rowley, the entertainment of English visitors at a Persian court becomes an occasion for exploring and indeed performing religious pluralism, as Sheiba Kaufman is arguing in new work.[16] In *Edward II* Gaveston enters the play planning a series of entertainments for the new king ('Italian masques by night, / Sweet speeches, comedies, and pleasing shows').[17] As an exile from England, a Frenchman by origin, and an Italian in taste, Gaveston is a barely tolerated guest in England, subject (not unlike Shylock) to disenfranchisement, conspiracy, and ambush, yet he will play host to the king by providing him with cosmopolitan entertainments and thus secure a favourite's foothold in the court. In each of these instances, hospitality events clear a stage for actors unaccustomed to or excluded from political speech, including women, artisans, foreigners, and sexual outlaws.[18] In prepolitical societies, such as the great households depicted in the *Odyssey* and the Book of Genesis, the laws of hospitality supplement the lack of a sovereign instance with customary procedures for encounter, exchange, and affiliation. Manifesting the originary inmixing of *oikos* and *polis* that remains imminent within later hospitality formations, the arts of entertainment set the table for more formal deliberations and decisions. Considered under the aspect of biopower, then, hospitality can be enjoined to signal both the *end of politics* (the disappearance of civic virtue into public house-keeping) and the *beginning of politics* (the calling into speech and action of beings without recourse to a formal public sphere).

Whereas biopower concerns the isolation and cultivation of life as the object of governmental activity and social action, political theology is associated with the phantasmatic ensouling of collective bodies, most prominently the natural body of the monarch as an image of the national community, but always also community itself as a potentially constitutional displacement of the monarch's single body by

---

[15] Palmer, 'Powerful Pinners and the Dispersion of Genre', in *Hospitable Performances*, 89–117.

[16] John Day, William Rowley, and George Wilkins, *The Travels of the Three English Brothers*, in Anthony Parr, ed., *Three Renaissance Travel Plays* (Manchester: Manchester University Press, 1995), 55–134. My student Sheiba Kaufman is working on the hospitable conditions of the performance of pluralism in this drama. 'Improbable Hospitality: Staging the Sherleys and Shakespeare's Sophy', MA thesis, University of California, Irvine, 2011.

[17] Christopher Marlowe, *Edward II*, ed. Matthew Martin (Ontario: Broadview, 2010), 1.1.52–4.

[18] On the figure of the gay outlaw read from a biopolitical perspective, see James Kuzner, *Open Subjects: English Renaissance Republicans, Modern Selfhoods and the Virtue of Vulnerability* (Edinburgh: Edinburgh University Press, 2011), 91–2.

the many bodies of a looming collective.[19] Such social bodies gather under the names of *corpus mysticum, politeia*, and the rule of law as well as the commons, the people, and the multitude, to which we might also add the more creaturely spectres of the crowd, the swarm, and the hive. As Lorna Hutson and Victoria Kahn have reminded us, Ernst Kantorowicz's ultimate goal in *The King's Two Bodies* was not to glorify the mortal body of the king but rather to account for the generation of abstract concepts and institutions of the public good out of, and in tension with, the singularity of his person.[20] So too, the picture of court entertainments emerging in current scholarship is surprisingly pluralist; as Kevin Curran has argued, Jacobean court performances were not monolithically oriented around the single voice and vision of the king, but rather forwarded a number of interests and agendas that divided the king's body according to opposing visions of political union, including Parliamentarian ones.[21] Suited to the welcoming and provisional integration of strangers, the semi-theatrical rites of hospitality organize this pluralized space of the court in order to immunize it against the foreign bodies it hosts.

Hospitality is indeed political–theological insofar as it feeds and feeds on the sacred body of the king. Yet hospitality also stages fictions of equality that render it a blueprint for political theology's more lateral, commensal, and even messianic fantasies of collective belonging. In the famous banquet scene of *Macbeth*, the newly invested king, put into power by no claim to primogeniture or natural succession, bids his guests to sit down according to their own degrees:

> Ourself will mingle with society
> And play the humble host.
> Our hostess keeps her state; but, in best time
> We will require her welcome. (III.iv.3–6)

Although the scene is organized by the ritual proprieties of enacted status, Macbeth chooses to engage in the practice of 'commoning', in which the host joins the guests at the lower table.[22] It is a supremely theatrical moment—'Ourself will...*play* the humble host'—in which everyone knows who's king, yet it is precisely the theatricality of hospitality, its repertoire of assumable and exchangeable roles, that makes

---

[19] The key text here remains Ernst Kantorowicz, *The King's Two Bodies: A Study in Medieval Political Theology* (Princeton: Princeton University Press, 1957) and its many responses in Renaissance studies. For a helpful survey, see Jennifer Rust, 'Political Theology and Shakespeare Studies', *Literature Compass* 6.1 (Nov. 2008), 175–90.

[20] Lorna Hutson, 'Imagining Justice: Kantorowicz and Shakespeare', *Representations* 106 (Spring 2009), 118–42; Victoria Kahn, 'Political Theology and Fiction in *The King's Two Bodies*', *Representations* 106 (Spring 2009), 77–101. On corporate metaphors in the Renaissance, see Henry S. Turner, 'Toward an Analysis of the Corporate Ego: The Case of Richard Hakluyt', *differences* 20.2–3 (2009), 103–47.

[21] On Anne's court, the decentred character of entertainments under James, and competing visions of the king's bodies, see Curran, *Marriage, Performance, and Politics*, 6–7, 62–5.

[22] Lady Macbeth exclaims, 'When all's done, / You look but on a stool' (III.iv.66–7). See commentary by J. P. Dyson, 'The Structural Function of the Banquet Scene in *Macbeth*', *Shakespeare Quarterly* 14.4 (Autumn 1963), 374.

such commoning a potential vehicle for social experiment.[23] This mingling is not without its own political–theological motifs; consider the equalizing power of table fellowship and communion in Christianity and Jesus's own act of commoning when he chooses to wash the feet of his guests at the Last Supper (John 13:1–17).

Public hospitality at inns always entailed a form of commoning, even if visitors could be segregated by rank.[24] In his artisanal novel *Thomas of Reading*, Thomas Deloney remarks of his travelling band of clothiers that they 'were the chiefest Guests that travailed along the Way; and this was as sure as an Act of Parliament, that *Tom Dove* could not digest his Meat without musicke, nor drinke Wine without women'.[25] The reference to Parliament imbues this scene from the Renaissance hospitality industry—oikonomic through and through—with a sense of political process rooted in artisanal habits of work, travel, and commerce. Deloney's sketches of communal enjoyment mix equality in rank with diversity in pleasures and provincial origins, serving up an urban and artisanal pluralism that is hard not to love.[26] It is some dose of these commensal pleasures that Macbeth finds forever out of reach, not because he is now a king but because in some sense he is no longer a man; by violating the hospitable contract to succour the guest, Macbeth has destroyed for himself the concordance of sociability and satisfaction promised by convivial routines. In Paul Kottman's analysis, 'Rather than being sentenced to death, Macbeth is thus thrown back into life, but now as a stranger to it. Nothing makes this clearer than the fact that Banquo's ghost appears in Macbeth's *own* seat, effectively alienating Macbeth from…his place in life with others.'[27] The scene in *Macbeth* ends with the disordered departure of the guests, an anti-masque that dissolves the studied informality of the scene's opening into another, more chaotic mingling of society, the dream of a festive commons becoming the nightmare of insomnia and indigestion.

In *King Lear*, Goneril complains that her father's knights are 'so disordered, so debauched and bold / That this our court, infected with their manners / Shows like a riotous inn…More like a tavern or a brothel / Than a graced palace' (I.iv.239–43). When inn, tavern, and brothel, common outposts of the hospitality industry, overrun the decorum of court and palace, centres of aristocratic largesse, Deloney's

---

[23] On 'commoning', see John Astington, *English Court Theatre 1558–1642* (Cambridge: Cambridge University Press, 1999), 37, and Michelle O'Callaghan, *The English Wits: Literature and Sociability in Early Modern England* (Cambridge: Cambridge University Press, 2007), 30–60.

[24] Beat A. Kümin and B. Ann Tlusty, *The World of the Tavern: Public Houses in Early Modern Europe* (Aldesrshot: Ashgate, 2002).

[25] Thomas Deloney, *The Pleasant Historie of Thomas of Reading*, ed. Charles Roberts Aldrich and Lucian Swift Kirtland (New York: J. F. Taylor, 1903), 15. The whole novel unfolds as a series of hospitality events, ending with the murder of Thomas of Reading by inn hosts who drop him (Barabas-like) into a scalding cauldron.

[26] Deloney's presentation of music as a digestive for meat is a commonplace he shares with Lady Macbeth, who tells her distracted husband, 'The sauce to meat is ceremony' (III.iv.36).

[27] Paul Kottman, *Philosophers on Shakespeare* (Stanford: Stanford University Press, 2009), 7.

world meets Macbeth's. More than a simple inversion, Goneril's complaint manifests the fundamental homology among Renaissance environments of entertainment. In the limited building typologies of the period, great halls and open courtyards were designed to house multiple functions—from task work and sleeping to dining and theatrical entertainment—depending on the pressures of the occasion. 'Played before the Kings Maiestie at Whitehall upon S. Stephans night in Christmas Hollidayes',[28] *King Lear* would have itself been performed in a great hall rezoned for theatrical use during a period of seasonal festivity, with Goneril delivering those lines from a temporary stage erected on trestles for easy assembly and disassembly. Such a stage could 'show like' a riotous inn or a graced palace depending on the shifting action of the play, the setting reset through the most minimal indicators. Hospitality and theatricality converge here as practices intimately bound up in shared forms of commoning, which are also forms of 'showing'.

The host, writes Benveniste in his etymological essay on hospitality, is a despot, since it is only 'the master who is eminently "himself" (*ipsissimus*)'.[29] Insofar as the ancient privileges of the host are linked mythically and ritually to the authority of God, hospitality enforces a conservative blueprint of political theology. Yet the possibility that the guest might himself be a god or angel in disguise partially disables the sovereignty of the host by asserting the rights of the stranger. Commensality itself harbours both hierarchical and egalitarian impulses that stretch hospitality in opposing directions of respect and service, the reassertion of rank and the fantasy of a truly round table. The ritual frameworks, real offerings and spatial routines of hospitality, itself divided among courtly, public, and domestic service economies, help us to avoid the temptation of identifying political theology exclusively with monarchical formations or relegating the motifs of biopower to later modernity. Whether stifling action or inviting it, hospitality's orchestrations of vitality are always incipiently theatrical in their management of the spaces and conditions of appearing.

Hospitality and creaturely life:
from political theology to political ecology

Performances of hospitality shelter and make apparent the captivation and reorganization of life functions within mythic, liturgical, and legal orders that are simultaneously biopolitical (in their management of need) and political–theological (in their cosmic references and spectral operations). What political theology and

---

[28] Title page of the 1608 Quarto, reprinted in *King Lear: Norton Critical Edition*, ed. Grace Ioppollo (New York: W. W. Norton, 2008), 2.

[29] Emile Benveniste, 'Hospitality', in *Indo-European Language and Society*, trans. Elizabeth Palmer (Miami: University of Miami Press, 1973), 71.

biopower share is a fascination with 'life' in both its real, pulsating insistence as thirst, hunger, and exposure to the elements and its symbolic abstraction as a mesmerizing value cultivated apart from, and sometimes at the expense of, living beings and the systems in which they dwell. Most accounts of hospitality focus on exchanges among human actors, and this has been true of my examples so far. Yet by meeting bodily wants through provisions culled from the natural world within settings often marked by seasonal decor, hospitality also always involves an environmental dimension.

In political–theological terms, we might call these concerns *creaturely*, a term that quarries and clothes the bare life of biopolitics within a scene defined by the signifying force of Scriptural laws and liturgical calendars. 'Creature' indicates a made or fashioned thing, identifying an element of technicity in the natural world while also naming a relationship of continued subjection to signifying forces that lie outside the person. Eric Santner, building on Franz Rosenzweig and Walter Benjamin, writes,

> By 'creaturely' I do not simply mean nature or living things or sentient beings, or even what the religiously minded would think of as the whole of God's creation, but rather a dimension specific to human existence, albeit one that seems to push thinking in the direction of theology. It signifies a mode of *exposure* that distinguishes human beings from other kinds of life: not exposure simply to the elements or to the fragility and precariousness of our mortal, finite lives, but rather to an ultimate lack of foundation for the historical forms of life that distinguish human community…We could say that the precariousness, the fragility—the 'nudity'—of biological life becomes potentiated, amplified, by way of exposure to the radical contingency of the forms of life that constitute the space of meaning within which human life unfolds.[30]

In Santner's account, creatureliness both embeds human beings in the natural world and distinguishes them from other creatures insofar as our most scarring vulnerability is not to the needs of life per se but to the terrifying groundlessness of the civilizing processes, including the arts of hospitality, designed both to meet those needs and to keep them at bay. Benjamin wrote of the Baroque sovereign, 'However highly he is enthroned over subject and state, his status is confined to the world of creation; he is the lord of creatures, but he remains a creature'.[31] The sovereign's situation replicates that of man himself, who may have been put in charge of other creatures in Genesis 1:25–7, but also finds himself adrift in creation, caught up in affiliations that shadow human dominion with the prospect of alternative constitutions, as

---

[30] Eric Santner, *The Royal Remains: The People's Two Bodies and the Endgames of Sovereignty* (Chicago: University of Chicago Press, 2011), 5–6. See also Santner, *On Creaturely Life* (Chicago: University of Chicago Press, 2006). On creaturely life in Shakespeare, see Julia Reinhard Lupton, 'Creature Caliban', *Shakespeare Quarterly* 51.1 (Spring 2000), 1–23.

[31] Walter Benjamin, *Origins of the German Tragic Drama*, trans. John Osborne (London: New Left Books, 1977), 85.

Laurie Shannon has argued.[32] If the routines of hospitality gravitate around human hosts and guests, considerations of creatureliness bid us to consider the extent to which creation as environment and habitat hosts us, today as guest and tomorrow as prisoner. Such considerations discover in the creaturely topographies of biopower and political theology the dimension Jane Bennett calls 'political ecology', which addresses the 'active powers issuing from nonsubjects', including trash, food, cells, and gases.[33]

Both *As You Like It* and *A Midsummer Night's Dream* bring these other, environmental forms of hosting into view. The Duke and Jaques's famous disquisitions on the deer as 'native burghers of this desert city' highlight the status of the outlaws from the court as guests in the forest.[34] As Rob Watson has argued, *A Midsummer Night's Dream* is more microbial in its sense of scale and perspective; when Puck claims responsibility for keeping the barm from developing in beer (II.i.39), he hails from a region of 'culture' shared with the moulds that congregate in cheeses and yogurts.[35] Puck manifests these biotechnologies as collaborative initiatives among forms of life rather than the dominium of art-wielding men and women over a fundamentally passive nature. In his *Delightes for Ladies*, a popular housekeeping guide, Hugh Plat attributes a similar capricious and living character to beer; if bottled too early, 'ale is both...windie and muddy, thundring and smoaking', since 'his yeast being an exceeding windy substance...doth incorporate with the drink'.[36] Between the beer and the brewer, writes Bruno Latour, 'there was something that sometimes acted and sometimes did not'.[37] Before Pasteur identified that third party as yeast, Puck gave a face and a name to the unruly behaviour and uncanny agency of ale. Jane Bennett would call the beers of Puck and Plat instances of 'vibrant matter': 'the capacity of things—edibles, commodities, storms, metals—not only to impede or block the wills and designs of humans but also to act as quasi-agents or forces with trajectories, propensities, or tendencies of their own'.[38]

---

[32] Laurie Shannon, 'The Eight Animals in Shakespeare; or, Before the Human', *PMLA* 124.2 (March 2009), 472–9, and 'Poor, Bare, Forked: Animal Sovereignty, Human Negative Exceptionalism, and the Natural History of King Lear', *Shakespeare Quarterly* 60.2 (Summer 2009), 168–96.

[33] Jane Bennett, *Vibrant Matter: A Political Ecology of Things* (Durham: Duke University Press, 2010), ix.

[34] *As You Like It*, ed. Heather DuBrow for the Evans Shakespeare (Boston: Wadsworth, 2012), 2.1.23. On *As You Like It* and the origins and destinies of ecocriticism, see Robert Watson, *Back to Nature: The Green and the Real in the Late Renaissance* (Philadelphia: University of Pennsylvania Press, 2006), 77–107.

[35] Rob Watson, 'The Ecology of Self in *A Midsummer Night's Dream*', in Lynne Bruckner and Daniel Brayton, eds., *Ecocritical Shakespeare* (Farnham: Ashgate, 2011), 33–56.

[36] Hugh Plat, *Delights for Ladies, to adorn their Persons, Tables, closets, and distillatories* (London: Printed by H. L., 1608.) 'Cookerie and Huswiferie', Recipe 47 (for 27), 'The true bottling of beere' (F12v). On early modern beer, see Richard W. Unger, *Beer in the Middle Ages and the Renaissance* (Philadelphia: University of Pennsylvania Press, 2004).

[37] Bruno Latour, *The Pasteurization of France*, trans. Alan Sheridan and John Law (Cambridge, MA: Harvard University Press, 1988), 33.

[38] Bennett, *Vibrant Matter*, viii.

Channelling the sinister side of Renaissance housekeeping literature, Jan Kott was one of the first visitors to the Shakespearean forest to punk up its pastoral naturalism with queer urbanisms and crawling life forms, a biotechnical and crea-turely reboot given new theoretical heft in recent work by Henry Turner.[39] The forest of *A Midsummer Night's Dream*, writes Turner, 'teems with forms of life at every scale of ontology and across every boundary, from God to mortal, human to animal, and beyond'.[40] Turner borrows the phrase 'forms of life' from cybernetics, where the term life, far from naming a vital substance or mystic ensoulment, sim-ply marks the threshold at which matter achieves enough complexity to cohere and persist. Turner cites Norbert Wiener: 'We are not stuff that abides, but patterns that perpetuate themselves'.[41] Both Santner and Turner use the phrase 'forms of life' in order to gather up the constitutive identification of vitality with writing. Santner, however, favours the linguistic, cultural, and theological side of this pri-mal tattooing, while Turner inclines towards the scientific, technological, and posthuman dimensions of life as information. As a consequence, Santner ulti-mately conscripts the creature into a renewed definition of the human, while Turner presses forms of life into the ambassadors of what he calls a 'posthuman Enlightenment'.[42]

The theatre of hospitality, I'd like to argue, draws a fluid figure eight composed by these two creaturely turns, codifying a set of routines designed to distinguish and elevate the human in response to cosmic exposure (Santner) precisely by reminding its participants of the power and complexity of things (Turner). As intersubjective moments of greeting, hospitable rituals are humanizing events, calling on us to appear to each other as social and ethical agents capable of reciprocal acknowledge-ment in a shared world.[43] If, as the old proverb goes, it's the people who make the party, the party also makes us people; under situations of extreme dearth, nothing can be made into something worth offering another, through the operation, say, of

---

[39] Kott writes, 'The bestiary of the *Dream* is not a haphazard one. Dried skin of a viper, pulverized spiders, bat's gristles appear in every medieval or Renaissance prescription book as drugs to cure impo-tence and women's afflictions of one kind or another.' *Shakespeare Our Contemporary* (Garden City: Doubleday, 1964), 219. Kott also envisions an urban palace rather than a country house as the setting of the play's entertainments.

[40] Henry S. Turner, 'Life Science: Rude Mechanicals, Human Mortals, Posthuman Shakespeare', *South Central Review* 26.1–2 (Winter and Spring 2009), 199. See also Turner's monograph, *Shake-speare's Double Helix* (London: Continuum, 2008). Other significant contributions to Shakespeare object studies conducted from a perspective other than that of cultural or material history include Jonathan Gil Harris, *Untimely Matter in the Time of Shakespeare* (Philadelphia: University of Pennsyl-vania Press, 2008), and Julian Yates, *Error, Misuse, Failure: Object Lessons from the English Renaissance* (Minneapolis: University of Minnesota Press, 2002).

[41] Turner, 'Life Science', 210.

[42] Turner, 'Life Science', 214. Shannon's use of the creature is closer to Turner's than to Santner's.

[43] See Paul Kottman, *A Politics of the Scene* (Stanford: Stanford University Press, 2007) for a defini-tive account of drama as a scene of human appearing.

a blessing.[44] Acts of thanksgiving constitute us as human precisely by insisting that we lay claim to our insufficiencies, our fundamental dispossession, by what surrounds and sustains us. Hospitality, especially perhaps in its breach, provides a menu of theatrical occasions for considering the worth and definition of human being as it emerges within and separates from its species dimension. Hospitality is always a response to the threat of exposure: both exposure to the elements and exposure to each other in our capacity to insult, shame, avoid, or betray. The spatial and temporal rituals of hospitality as a form of domestic theatre zone the spaces in which we struggle to manage these double exposures. The hostess's kitchen consciousness, her keen attention to setting and atmosphere, her curation of a multimedia sensorium, and her seasonal sensibilities foster some of the comportments of affiliation, care, and obligation in response to other forms of life advanced by political ecology. She does so, moreover, through arts of arrangement, display, roleplaying, and temporal sequencing whose indigenous theatricality plays out against the background composed by the counter-arts of withdrawal and reserve (frugality, thrift, modesty, keeping).

The division within creaturely life between humanist and posthuman orders of interest and experience reappears as the hinge between assembly and assemblage. Whereas *assembly* concerns the gathering of persons for conversation, celebration, courtship, and the confirmation of prestige, *assemblage* names the amalgams of objects, symbols, and environments cultivated in the labours of hospitality. Assemblage is a key term for Turner, Bennett, Latour, De Landa, and other commentators seeking to draft new models of agency and vitality that include an expanded set of potential players on the scene of action. In *The Melancholy Assemblage: Affect and Epistemology in the English Renaissance*, Andrew Daniel uses Deleuze's concept of the assemblage alongside avant-garde art practices to conceive of melancholy as an always emergent combine of affective, material, epistemological, and iconographic elements that disperse and regroup without losing their identifying signature.[45] As a pattern of practices recognizable over time and space yet subject to mutations and metastases, hospitality is also an assemblage, while each hospitality event is itself a gathering of diverse agents of cheer. A banqueting tray might feature 'Cream Cheeses', 'small Fruit', 'a Dish of Jellies of several colours', 'some of your fine Drinks',[46]

---

[44] I am thinking here of the prayer for *chametz* (leavened foods) recited in the concentration camps in lieu of matzah and now incorporated into many Passover seders. In a common Jewish folktale, the poor couple who tries to accommodate the stranger despite an empty cupboard is magically surprised with provisions for the Sabbath.

[45] Drew Daniel, *The Melancholy Assemblage: Affect and Epistemology in the English Renaissance* (New York: Fordham University Press, 2013).

[46] Menu adapted from Hannah Woolley, 'A Bill of Service for extraordinary Feasts in the Summer' and banqueting instructions', in *The Queen-like Closet or Rich Cabinet* (London: R. Chiswel and T. Sawbridge, 1669), 315–16 and 348.

and a brace of rabbits and pigeons moulded out of marzipan,[47] set off by candles hanging in the air,[48] women's faces whitened with powdered bone,[49] and madrigals recently Englished.[50] The mixed company of foods, fabrics, lighting techniques, and acoustic accents gathered up in a festive affair are actively solicited by the energy of the occasion to make their own showing as ongoing contributors to the enjoyments at hand.

Not all such solicitations are benign. Gloucester has already become a prisoner in his own house when Cornwall orders his men to bind their erstwhile host to his chair. The chair's stately arms and solid back normally support the dignity of the master of the house or his most honoured guest; now those very same features afford very different actions as Gloucester's 'corky arms' (III.vii.30) are tied to the wooden arms of the chair, which is then tilted backwards to receive Cornwall's blinding foot. The brutal repurposing of Gloucester's chair rezones the castle into a 'hard house' (III.ii.63) and a 'dark tower' (III.v.181), a theatre of cruelty that convenes human, inhuman, and non-human actors within its executive circle, in order to probe the lendings and borrowings that connect these forms of life.

Out on the heath, Kent urges Lear to take refuge in a shack suited for animals: 'hard by here is a hovel: / Some friendship will it lend you 'gainst the tempest' (III. ii.61–2). Finding unexpected affordances under the pressure of necessity, Kent's personification of the hovel as 'friendly' manifests the 'naïve orientation to the thing' that Bennett urges us to bring to our environments.[51] Kent's homely hovel manifests the rudimentary character of hospitality's migratory building forms (tent, canopy, pavilion, picnic blanket), rezonable spaces (banqueting house, great hall, courtyard, mezzanine), and ambidextrous furniture types (joint-stools, trestles, folding chairs, table skirts, air mattresses, convertible couches, roller bags). Even in hospitality's more elaborate orchestrations of space—Cleopatra's barge, Titania's bower, or the Field of the Cloth of Gold, to which we might add hotel ballroom, synagogue basement, and hash-tagged food truck—hospitality favours assemblages-for-assembly, mixed congeries of available affordances toggled together in order to support a temporary commons that reminds its denizens to attend to their own creatureliness.

In plays as various as *Romeo and Juliet*, *A Midsummer Night's Dream*, *Macbeth*, *King Lear*, *Othello*, and *The Winter's Tale*, hospitality draws dramatic scenarios of

---

[47] Plat, *Delights*, 'The Arte of Preserving', Recipe 10, 'A most delicate and stiff sugar paste…' (B4r).

[48] Plat, 'Cookerie and Huswifery', Recipe 40, 'How to hang your candles in the aire without candle-sticke', a 'strange shew to the beholders that know not the conceite'. (G7r).

[49] Plat, 'Sweet Powders and Ointments', Recipe 7, 'A white focus or beauty for the face' (G9v).

[50] Nicholas Yonge, *Musica Transalpina* (London: William Byrd, 1588). Palmer notes that this song book is 'addressed to "Gentleman and Merchants"' who, feeling the obligation to host, will pay for instruction in the making of hospitable madrigals' (17).

[51] Jane Bennett, 'The Force of Things: Steps toward an Ecology of Matter', *Political Theory* 32.3 (June 2004), 356.

enacted personhood out of the theatrical offerings of home entertainment and courtly spectacle, nudging the *oikos* to give birth to actions ranging from the comic to the catastrophic. At the same time, the hospitable arts in their conjunction with the affective labours of husbandry, housekeeping, and stagecraft beckon non-human forms of life to appear, whether in the diegesis of the plays themselves, in the technical apparatuses of theatrical and domestic making, or in the memorial tracery of metaphor and ekphrasis. I'd like to end this essay by visiting some poetic soundings of hospitable assemblage in the plays of Shakespeare.

Assemblages for assembly: a selection

A nest of martlets frames Duncan and Banquo's fateful approach to the castle of the Macbeths:

> Banquo: This guest of summer,
> The temple-haunting martlet, does approve,
> By his loved mansionry, that the heaven's breath
> Smells wooingly here: no jutty, frieze,
> Buttress, nor coign of vantage, but this bird
> Hath made his pendent bed and procreant cradle:
> Where they most breed and haunt, I have observed,
> The air is delicate. (I.vi)[52]

Banquo weaves a kind of virtual welcome mat that Banquo sees, or wants to see, decking the halls of Macbeth's castle with the promise of succour. As a figure of place-making, the martlets' nests figure the spatial efforts of both theatrical and home entertainment. *Macbeth*'s martlet image is an imaginative blueprint of the residual spaces activated by the anticipation of summer guests, evoking the readying of dormant spaces—guest rooms, porches, floors, trundles, tents, stables—for the temporary housing of visitors and their things. As a map of leftover spaces carved out of permanent structures through skilled acts of care, the martlet image begins to visualize hospitality as an orchestration of spatial and temporal remainders. The Globe itself was essentially a system of open galleries set up around a canopied stage, a disposition of porch-like spaces recalling the possible origins of the public theatre out of innyards.[53] The birds' 'loved mansionry'—their animal

---

[52] See Dyson's reading of this passage as a synthesis of the values disrupted by Macbeth's act, 'Banquet Scene', 369–70. See also Carolyn Spurgeon's search for the real nests, *Shakespeare's Imagery and What It Tells Us* (Cambridge: Cambridge University Press, 1965), 374, 189. I provide a longer reading of this passage in '*Macbeth*'s Martlets: Shakespearean Phenomenologies of Hospitality', *Criticism* 54.3 (Summer 2012), 365–76.

[53] Once a commonplace, the role of innyards in the architectural and performance history of English drama is now a matter of considerable debate. See Robert B. Graves, *Lighting the Shakespearean Stage, 1567–1642* (Carbondale, IL: Southern Illinois University Press, 1999), 26–8.

architecture—creates 'pendent bed(s) and procreant cradle(s)' that knit together physical construction work with emotional and biological expenditures. As we gaze with Duncan and Banquo at these imagined nests, we gain a passing phenomenological access to our own coigns of vantage in the accommodations of theatre, inn, and household.

The entwining of martlet nests around protrusions of sculpted stone models the relationship of 'softscape' to 'hardscape', as I will call them, in the spatial techniques of hospitality. In landscape architecture, 'hardscape' encompasses the permanent elements that make up a garden (landforms, paved paths, fountains, grottos, retaining walls), while 'softscape' gathers all those plantings whose colours, textures, mass, and fragrance change with the seasons and over time. Renaissance environments of entertainment were often shaped out of fabric, in the form of hangings, tents, canopies, and backdrops whose mobile membranes could partition chambers, cushion walls, lower ceilings, or simply drape and mask rougher surfaces like table tops or timber frames.[54] Titania's bower, 'quite overcanopied with luscious woodbine' (II.i.251) is an instance of soft architecture, as is Cleopatra's barge, a sheltering, framing pavilion built of 'cloth of gold of tissue' and propelled by 'purple sails' (II.ii.209).

A key feature of the Renaissance softscape is its mobility—both the capacity of its components to be assembled and disassembled on short notice and the susceptibility of fabric and foliage to sway, drift, and billow. Aby Warburg, in an aesthetics of motion deeply responsive to the confluence of the poetic and material features of Renaissance pageantry, called attention to what he called 'accessories in motion' (*bewegte Beiwerke*)—fabric, ribbon, and hair on women as well as boughs and leaves on trees—that wound their way into the metamorphic vision of the landscape celebrated in Renaissance entertainments.[55] Although Warburg focuses on the flowing accoutrements of dancing nymphs and frantic maenads (in Warburg's neurasthenic imagination, grace and agitation are kissing cousins), bowers and barges can also be accessorized. In *The Merchant of Venice*, Salarino imagines his melancholy host Antonio reading the fate of his ships in every moment of daily life:

> Should I go to church
> And see the holy edifice of stone
> And not bethink me straight of dangerous rocks
> Which, touching but my gentle vessel's side,

[54] On temporary stages and seating built on trestles and covered in fabric, see John Astington, *English Court Theatre 1558–1642* (Cambridge: Cambridge University Press, 1999), 93–4. On Renaissance England as a cloth culture, see Ann Rosalind Jones and Peter Stallybrass, *Renaissance Clothing and the Materials of Memory* (Cambridge: Cambridge University Press, 2000).

[55] Aby Warburg, 'Sandro Botticelli', in *Renewal of Pagan Antiquity* (Los Angeles, CA: Getty Research Institute for the History of Art and the Humanities, 1999), 88–156, and commentary by Phillipe-Alain Michaud, *Aby Warburg and the Image in Motion*, trans. Sophie Hawkes (New York: Zone Books, 2004).

> Would scatter all her spices on the stream,
> Enrobe the roaring waters with my silks,
> And, in a word, but even now worth this,
> And now worth nothing?   (I.i.29–36)

Salerio's image of Antonio's rich vessels 'enrob[ing] the roaring waters with [their] silks' offers a magnificent portrayal of textile's fluid affordances. Earlier in the exchange, he had pictured Antonio's argosies as parading their 'portly sails / Like signors and rich burghers on the flood, / Or as it were the pageants of the sea' (I.i.9–11); the two figures together, imaginatively linking the sails on the ships to the soft goods in their holds, acknowledge the role of fabrics in shaping the spaces of entertainments of all kinds. In civic celebrations, for which Venice was famous, the city plays host to itself, enjoining its 'signiors and rich burghers' to put the city's corporate constitution on display.[56] These well-wrought images are themselves little hostess gifts, tiny tokens of comfort and wit offered by Salerio to his host like so many pieces of gilded marzipan. Antonio's spilt silks offer a moving metonym of hospitality's flow among commercial, municipal, and maritime channels while also expressing the breathless luxury of a certain abandonment to things displayed in the radical self-expenditure of the host, who is most *ipssimus* when he gives himself away. Secret pleasures and dangers gather in the folds of the hospitable softscape: both Madhavi Menon and Drew Daniel point to the onanistic rhythms of Cleopatra's and Antonio's fabric effusions, while the fate of Desdemona reminds us that bedclothes can smother as well as shelter.[57]

In *The Winter's Tale*, Autolycus, who declares that his 'traffic is sheets' (IV.iii.23), sells a whole passel of Warburg's *bewegte Beiwerke* to Perdita's guests:

> Lawn as white as driven snow,
> Cyprus black as e'er was crow,
> Gloves as sweet as damask roses,
> Masks for faces and for noses,
> Bugle bracelet, necklace amber,
> Perfume for a lady's chamber,
> Golden quoifs and stomachers,
> For my lads to give their dears,
> Pins and poking-sticks of steel,
> What maids lack from head to heel,
> Come buy of me, come. Come buy, come buy.
> Buy lads, or else your lasses cry.
> Come buy.   (IV.iv.218–30)

---

[56] Edward Muir, *Civic Ritual in Renaissance Venice* (Princeton: Princeton University Press, 1986).

[57] Madhavi Menon, *Unhistorical Shakespeare: Queer Theory in Shakespearean Literature and Film* (New York: Palgrave Macmillan, 2008), 141. Drew Daniel, "'Let me have judgment, and the Jew his will": Melancholy Epistemology and Masochistic Fantasy in *The Merchant of Venice*', *Shakespeare Quarterly* 61.2 (Summer 2010), 206–34.

Autolycus not only uses music to sell his accessories and sewing notions but includes ballads in his basket, contributing his many wares to the media architecture of the sheep shearing party. Autolycus is a purveyor of the Renaissance version of what modern marketers call the experience economy, the theatricalized display of sensory stimuli and orchestrated interaction that characterizes contemporary branded retail and service environments, including the so-called 'hospitality industry'.[58] The rogue's ribbons and pins[59] are tricks of the theatrical trade, tools of assemblage that manifest an environment cross-hatched by courtly, rural, urban, artisanal, and news networks. Each of these assemblages is itself composed of the things, meanings, knowledges, and routines that contributed their techniques to both stage management and household management in Renaissance theatres of hospitality.

The martlet's nests, Titania's bower, Antonio's ships, Cleopatra's barge, and Autolycus' wares, are, each in its way, assemblages-for-assembly: composite structures culled out of diverse environments and bundled together in compact images of worlds in motion. Such images distil the hospitable affects, efforts, and ambience of Renaissance theatricality, providing proprioceptive traces of those less articulated and codified arts of reception that create cushioned encampments of holiday and refuge within the firmer spaces of the work week and the hard house. These moving thing-pictures have the capacity to superimpose the physical conditions of viewing (our coigns of vantage as guests in the theatre) with the forms of attentive workmanship shared by craft work, housekeeping, and theatrical making. Madhavi Menon argues that the image of Cleopatra is all accessory, no human figure at all: the words of Enobarbus 'metonymically describe her boat, the water, and the furnishings in her barge, but as for Cleopatra herself—she beggars all description'.[60] Yet such assemblages, which bid their own homely ingredients to shimmer and billow in the special visibility of performance, come into play in order to solicit human and almost-human actors into some form of subjective manifestation and encounter. The martlet's nest overhangs the entry where Lady Macbeth will raven-like greet her guests. Titania's bower frames the encounter between fairy queen and translated weaver, a nest for epiphany and disclosure around and beneath which the play's other transactions feverishly unfold. Cleopatra's barge provides the floating stage upon which this 'most triumphant lady' can first be glimpsed by Antony, unmooring history's course (II.ii.194). As Kevin Curran notes in a thoughtful review of Renaissance object studies, most claims to non-humanism are actually

---

[58] On the experience economy as the shape assumed by the contemporary *theatrum mundi*, see B. Joseph Pine II and James H. Gilmore, *The Experience Economy: Work Is Theatre and Every Business a Stage* (Boston: Harvard Business School Press, 1999) and Anna Klingman, *Brandscapes: Architecture in the Experience Economy* (Cambridge, MA: MIT Press, 2007).

[59] On the recovery of a remarkable number of pins in the archaeological dig of the Rose Theatre, see Jenny Tiramani, 'Pins and Aglets', in Tara Hamling and Catherine Richardson, eds., *Everyday Objects: Medieval and Early Modern Material Culture and Its Meanings* (Farnham: Ashgate, 2010), 86–94.

[60] Menon, *Unhistorical Shakespeare*, 141.

part of 'a "new" humanism, one that finally acknowledges Man's inescapable enmeshment within a larger ecology of organic and non-organic agents'.[61] The theatre of hospitality, with its multiple scales and economies of action, is the *mise-en-scène* of this enmeshment.

FURTHER READING

Ahmed, Sara. *Queer Phenomenology: Orientations, Objects, Others* (Durham: Duke University Press, 2006).

Balmori, Diana and Joel Sanders. *Groundwork: Between Landscape and Architecture* (New York: Monacelli Press and Random House, 2011).

Worthen, W. B. *Drama Between Poetry and Performance* (Malden, MA: Wiley-Blackwell, 2010).

[61] Kevin Curran, 'Renaissance Non-humanism: Plants, Animals, Machines, Matters', *Renaissance Studies* 24.2 (Spring 2009), 315.

CHAPTER 23

BECOMING-INDIAN

JONATHAN GIL HARRIS

Theatricality and antitheatricality

'All the world's a stage' (2.7.9): Jaques's aphorism from *As You Like It* has become such a cliché that we can easily lose sight of its peculiar ethnographic resonances at a time when 'all the world' was opening up in unprecedented ways to European knowledge.[1] Early modern English travellers to Asia and the Americas may not have seen Shakespeare's play, but Jaques's words would doubtless have rung true for them. Take, for example, John Smith's description of what he calls a 'Virginia Maske' in his *Generall History of Virginia* (1624). The performance was not an actual masque; it was a spontaneous Algonquian greeting ritual that Smith and his fellow Jamestown colonists witnessed in 1608, performed by Pocahontas and several other dancing women. But Smith describes it in terms strongly reminiscent of an anti-masque at court:

> Thirtie young women came naked out of the woods, onely covered behind and before with a few greene leaves, their bodies all painted, some of one colour, some of another, but all differing, their leader had a fayre payre of Bucks hornes on her head, and an Otters skinne at her girdle, and another at her arme, a quiver of arrows at her backe, a bow and arrows in her hand; the next had in her hand a sword, another a club, another a pot-sticke; all horned alike: the rest every one with their severall devises. These fiends with most hellish shouts and crycs, rushing from among the trees cast themselves in a ring about the fire, singing and dauncing with most excellent ill varieitie, oft falling into their infernall passions, and solemnly again to sing and daunce; having spend neare an houre in this Mascarado, as they entred in like manner they departed.[2]

For Smith, all Virginia is a stage. To describe the behaviour of the native inhabitants of the land, he deploys the language of theatrical form, both explicitly ('this Mascarado') and implicitly, describing a demarcated theatrical space ('a ring about the fire'), costumes ('a fayre payre of Bucks hornes on her head'), stage properties and

---

[1] All quotations from Shakespeare are from Stephen Greenblatt et al., eds., *The Norton Shakespeare*, 2nd edn. (New York: W. W. Norton, 2008).

[2] John Smith, *The Generall Historie of Virginia, New England, and the Summer Isles* (Bedford, MA: Applewood, 2006), 139–40.

iconography ('every one with their severall devises'), histrionic utterances ('shouts and cryes'), and movements on- and off-stage ('as they entred in like manner they departed'). But what stands out above all in Smith's description is the way it puts the language of theatricality in the service of ethnography. He describes foreign cultural forms through the lens of performance, a heuristic move familiar to students of the work of modern cultural anthropologists from Victor Turner to Johannes Fabian.[3] Indeed, the anthropologist Clifford Geertz, who compellingly teases out the theatrical dimension of cultural forms in a study of what he calls the nineteenth-century Balinese 'theatre state' and whose work was so influential on the first wave of New Historicism, himself took inspiration from Shakespeare, evoking Jaques's aphorism when he says that 'the drama analogy for social life has been around in a casual sort of way—all the world's a stage and we but poor players who strut and so on—for a very long time'.[4]

But Smith's use of theatre as a mode of ethnography is also rather different from Geertz's. In modern cultural anthropology, and in New Historicist work indebted to Geertz, the Shakespearean metaphor has informed an interpretive model in which all aspects of everyday life can be read in broadly performative terms. For this model, the crucial words in Jaques's speech are not 'all the world's a stage' so much as 'one man in his time plays many parts' (2.7.12). This has led to rich theoretical understandings, bolstered by J. L. Austin's linguistics, of identity as fundamentally performative, inasmuch as it is culturally scripted and materialized only through discursive iteration.[5] From Stephen Greenblatt's *Renaissance Self-Fashioning* (1980) to Judith Butler's *Excitable Speech* (1997), this anthropological-linguistic understanding of performativity has proved enormously influential in literary studies.[6] But in the process, it has become somewhat detached from the formal and conceptual features that distinguish the theatre in general and early modern theatre in particular. Smith's 'Virginia Maske' reminds us how the specific textures of early modern theatricality rather than a generalized, abstract notion of performance

[3] There is a long anthropological tradition of understanding culture as performance. Victor Turner developed his conception of 'social drama' to explain the forms of ritual and religious practice; see his influential book *Dramas, Fields, and Metaphors: Symbolic Action in Human Society* (Ithaca: Cornell University Press, 1974). Johannes Fabian elaborated a slightly different notion of cultural performance, one that saw local theatrical forms as modes of political knowledge, in *Power and Performance: Ethnographic Explorations though Proverbial Wisdom and Theater in Shaba, Zaire* (Madison: University of Wisconsin Press, 1990); and 'Theater and Anthropology, Theatricality and Culture', *Research in African Literatures* 30.4 (1999), 24–31.

[4] Clifford Geertz, 'Blurred Genres: The Refiguration of Social Thought', in Henry Bial, ed., *The Performance Studies Reader* (New York: Routledge), 64–7. See also Clifford Geertz, *Negara: The Theatre State in Nineteenth Century Bali* (Princeton: Princeton University Press, 1980).

[5] See J. L. Austin, *How to Do Things with Words* (Oxford: Clarendon Press, 1962); and 'Performative Utterances', in *Philosophical Papers* (London: Oxford University Press, 1970), 233–52.

[6] See Stephen Greenblatt, *Renaissance Self-Fashioning: From More to Shakespeare* (Chicago: Universtiry of Chicago Press, 1980); and Judith Butler, *Excitable Speech: A Politics of the Performative* (New York: Routledge, 1997).

shaped travellers' understandings of 'all the world's a stage', and in ways that have a rich potential for our own critical thinking.

By characterizing the Algonquian women's greeting ritual as a masque, Smith also underscores the asymmetrical power relation between ethnographer and foreign spectacle that often informs the practice of cultural anthropology. The English masque was conventionally performed at the royal court; it presumed the primacy of the monarch's gaze, which—as Stephen Orgel and others have noted—possessed a shaping power in relation to the performance, lending both perspectival and interpretive order to it.[7] This power was crucial also to the famous 1550 entertainment at Rouen, in which an entire Brazilian village was recreated for the gaze of the French king Henri II. The spectacle showcased fifty Tupinamba Indians joined by two hundred and fifty French sailors dressed up as Indians who hunted, danced, and cut Brazil-wood amongst trees full of parrots and monkeys.[8] The entertainment at Rouen, like Smith's 'Virginia Maske', amounted to theatrical ethnography for an imperial spectator. Foreign culture in both instances is a spectacle decoded by a European eye that organizes it, glosses it, and converts its disorder into intelligibility. All the world may be a stage, but the knowledge of the world that this stage provides is not for all the world to possess.

But was ethnographic spectacle the only form of theatricality available to early modern English travellers? Another, more dangerous version is hinted at in Smith's 'Virginia Maske'. When he describes Pocahontas and her fellow dancers as 'fiends' who utter 'most hellish shouts and cryes', Smith also uses language remarkably similar to that of the Puritan antitheatricalists, notably William Rankins, whose *A Mirrour of Monsters* (1587) characterizes the early modern playhouse as the abode of the 'damned fiend, attired to be the second in this masque, appointed to seduce men's souls'.[9] To Rankins, the playhouse is an engine of diabolical seduction, a 'bellows of desire... That Satan may send', and his conviction finds a counterpart in Smith's alarmed observation that Pocahontas and her fellow 'fiends' concluded their 'masque' by 'crowding, pressing, and hanging about him, most tediously crying, Love you not me? Love you not me?'[10] Theatre as spectacle, yielding meekly to the imperial ethnographic gaze, here blurs into something else: a sensuous, demonic 'crowding' that spills off the stage, touching and potentially transforming the bodies of its spectators.

---

[7] Stephen Orgel, *The Illusion of Power: Political Theater in the English Renaissance* (Berkeley, CA: University of California Press, 1979). For a recent study of masque that offers a substantial revision of Orgel's enormously influential argument, see Lauren Shohet, *Reading Masques: The English Masque and Public Culture in the Seventeenth Century* (Oxford: Oxford University Press, 2010).

[8] The relationship between the Rouen entertainment and English theatrical forms is discussed by Steven Mullaney, 'Strange Things, Gross Terms, Curious Customs: The Rehearsal of Cultures in the Late Renaissance', *Representations* 3 (1985), 40–67.

[9] William Rankins, *A Mirrour of Monsters* (London, 1587), fol. 22v.

[10] Smith, *Generall Historie of Virginia*, 140.

This transformative power lay at the core of the antitheatricalists' fear of the early modern playhouse. Although their critique of playing was fuelled in large part by a Protestant aversion to fraudulent images—an aversion grounded in the equation of Catholic ritual with histrionic imposture—the antitheatricalists' iconoclasm shaded into a fear of bodily contamination by other senses.[11] In particular, they feared the tactile properties of theatre; like Smith, they saw theatre as coupling toxic contact with perverse desire. In his *Treatise against Dancing, Dicing, Plays, and Interludes* (1577), John Northbrooke denounces theatre as 'contagiousness' and prays that 'vice shall not enter our hearts and breasts, lest the custom of pleasure touch us'.[12] And as Henry Crosse argues in his antitheatrical jeremiad, *Vertues Commonwealth* (1603), theatrical spectacles are 'baits to entice people to lightness…it cannot be but that the internal powers must be moved at such visible and lively objects'.[13] This 'movement' is no metaphor: it presumes a fully embodied understanding of spectacle. Sight *touches* the spectator, provoking within his or her body a transformative motion of desire. Much like Smith's Virginia, the antitheatricalists' playhouse was a 'contact zone', although in a more pathological sense than that famously theorized by Mary-Louise Pratt.[14] Theatricality may underwrite the language of ethnography, but it also models a protean bodily transformation grounded in contagious touch and desire. The tension between the two modes is, I would argue, particularly apparent in early modern scenes of theatricality involving English encounters with Indian cultures.

In what follows, I consider the theatricality of the court of the Mughal Emperor, Jahangir, as described in 1616 by a pair of Englishmen: King James's and the East India Company's ambassador, Sir Thomas Roe, and the eccentric global perambulator Thomas Coryate. I begin with the theatrical dimensions of Roe's ethnographic descriptions of Mughal culture as a prelude to a particularly spectacular scene: Coryate's Persian oration, in Indian dress, to Jahangir. Roe and Coryate disagreed about the propriety of his oration. Their disagreement shows us that, if all the world's a stage, then the nature of the world differs according to how one participates in its scene. In Roe's and Coryate's divergent attitudes to theatricality, we can recognize the prehistory of two radically divergent conceptions of embodied selfhood: an essential, ethnicized identity, on the one hand, and on the other what we might term a 'becoming-Indian' that refuses bodily and identitarian fixity.[15] In the process,

---

[11] For a discussion of the antitheatricalist fear of the senses, see Tanya Pollard, *Drugs and Theatre in Early Modern England* (Oxford: Oxford University Press, 2005), esp. 123–43.

[12] John Northbrooke, *Treatise Against Dicing, Dancing, Plays, and Interludes, with Other Idle Pastimes* (London: Shakespeare Society, 1843; reprinted, New York: AMS Press, 1970), 62.

[13] Henry Crosse, *Vertues Commonwealth, Or Highway to Honour* (London, 1603), sig. P2v.

[14] See Mary-Louise Pratt, 'Arts of the Contact Zone', *Profession* 9 (1991), 33–40.

[15] As some readers might recognize, I am adapting here Gilles Deleuze and Félix Guattari's exfoliations of 'becoming' in *A Thousand Plateaus: Capitalism and Schizophrenia*, trans. Brian Massumi (Minneapolis: University of Minnesota Press, 1987), especially chapter 10, '1730: Becoming-Intense, Becoming-Animal, Becoming-Imperceptible…', 233–309.

Roe's and Coryate's stand-off tells a subjunctive story of the early modern English traveller's body. This story is ultimately a theatrical one: it illustrates the tension between the view that 'all the world is an ethnographic spectacle', in which exotic bodies and cultural forms are to be decoded by European eyes, and the counter-view that 'all the world is a protean contact zone', unleashing universally transformable and transformative bodies.

Mughal ethnography: Sir Thomas Roe's scenes of imperial power

The traveller's embodied experiences are often suppressed in early modern English ethnographic narratives that purport to describe the foreignness of India, its inhabitants, its religious customs, and its arrangements of power. This suppression is apparent in the writings of Sir Thomas Roe, King James I's ambassador to the court of Jahangir from 1615 to 1619. Roe's journal enumerates, often with haughty disdain, the customs of the Mughal court.[16] He is a character in his own story, but he is simultaneously absent from it, inasmuch as his narrative often focuses on the strange, theatrical bodies of Indians—especially that of Jahangir—while leaving his own body just out of view. Take, for example, Roe's account of his first visit to Jahangir's court in Ajmer in January 1616:

> *January 10.*—I went to Court at 4 in the euening to the *Durbar*, which is the Place wher the Mogull sits out daylie, to entertayne strangers, to receiue petitions and presents, to giue Commandes, to see, and to be seene. To digresse a little from my reception, and declare the Customes of the Court, will enlighten the future discourse. The king hath no man but Eunuchs that comes within the lodgings or retyring rooms of his house: his women watch within, and guard him with manly weapons. They do Justice one vpon another for offences. He comes every Morning to a window called the *Jarruco* [*Jharukha*, or interview window] looking into a playne before his gate, and shows him selfe to the Common People. At one hee returns thither and sits some howers to see the fight of Eliphants and willd beasts; vnder him within a rayle attend the men of ranckel from whence hee retiers to sleep among his woemen.   (I.106)

Jahangir's aim, Roe tells us, is 'to see, and to be seene'. The spectacular theatricality of the Great Mughal's daily regimen is underscored by Roe's terminology: as if remembering a performance of Shakespeare's *Antony and Cleopatra*, the English ambassador presents Jahangir's androgynous attendants ('Eunuchs' and 'women' who 'guard him with manly weapons') as entering and exiting from 'retyring rooms of his house'—a phrase that recalls the tiring rooms of the early modern English

---

[16] All references to Roe's journal are to *The Embassy of Sir Thomas Roe to the Court of the Great Mogul, 1615–19*, ed. William Foster, 2 vols. (London: Hakluyt Society, 1894), and are cited in the main body of the text.

playhouse. Arguably the key phrase in this passage, however, is 'To digresse a little from my reception'. Roe was immensely invested in his 'reception' and its outcome, which resulted in the East India Company gaining unprecedented trading privileges. But this immense expansion of English mercantile power here becomes secondary to Roe's expansion of English ethnographic authority, a dilation effected by placing himself out of frame in order to describe the details of the scene. And 'scene' *is* the operative word, since (like Victor Turner, Johannes Fabian, or Clifford Geertz after him) Roe sees the customs of the foreign culture in theatrical terms. He continues:

> The king sits in a little Gallery ouer head; Ambassidors, the great men and strangers of quality within the inmost rayle vnder him, raysed from the ground, Couered with Canopyes of veuet and silke, vnder foote layd with good Carpetts; the Meaner men representing gentry within the first rayle, the people without in a base Court, but soe that all may see the king. This sitting out hath soe much affinitye with a Theatre—the manner of the king in his gallery; The great men lifted on stage as actors; the vulgar below gazing on—that an easy description will informe of the place and fashion.
>
> (I.108)

Roe's eye, panning down from Emperor through ambassadors to gentry to common people, records numerous details of Mughal social hierarchy. Even as he describes the body of the sovereign—a body whose power is understood in terms of how it is spatially and spectacularly positioned in relation to other human and even non-human bodies[17]—Roe grants himself a sovereign power as ethnographer by removing his body from the scene he describes. The gesture is an extraordinary recuperation of what Roe concedes to be an effective Mughal strategy of power over *him*. The Emperor's spectacular theatrical self-display, calculated, like that of James or Charles, to subordinate those who visibly gaze upon him, now facilitates an English heuristic privilege akin to that of the king himself in the early modern masque, as Roe becomes the invisible, knowing spectator. Even as he describes one imperial power, then, Roe performs another: his own empirical power to *understand*.[18]

---

[17] For a discussion of the spatial dynamics of Roe's ethnography, see Pramod K. Nayar, 'Colonial Proxemics: The Embassy of Sir Thomas Roe to India', *Studies in Travel Writing* 6 (2002), 29–53. Jyotsna G. Singh interprets Roe's descriptions of Mughal spectacle as a mode of proto-colonialist knowledge in *Colonial Narratives/Cultural Dialogues: 'Discoveries' of India in the Language of Colonialism* (London: Routledge, 1996), especially 26–32. For a reading of Roe that sees him as less a proto-colonist than a mercantile ally of the Mughals, see Rahul Sapra, *The Limits of Orientalism: Seventeenth-Century Representations of India* (Newark, DE: University of Delaware Press, 2011), especially 62–72.

[18] The analogy between the Mughal court and the London stage is one that evidently stuck with Roe. He described his audience with Jahangir in more or less identical terms in a letter to Lord Carew, written from Ajmer on January 17: 'I found him in a Court, set aboue like a King in a Play and all his Nobles and my selfe below on a stage couered with carpets—a iust Theater; with no great state, but the Canopies ouer his head, and two standing on the heads of two wooden Elephants, to beat away flies' (cited in Foster, ed., *The Embassy of Sir Thomas Roe*, I.112n). Here, Roe writes himself into the scene from which he absented himself in the more ethnographic account that distinguishes his journal.

If Roe uses metaphors of theatre to describe the Mughal court, however, his discourse has a decidedly antitheatrical dimension. Mughal power, in his view, shades into theatrical imposture. Granted an audience with Jahangir's son Pervez in Brampur in late 1615, en route to Ajmer, Roe—upset because he believed he had not been treated by Pervez as an 'equal' of the other ambassadors—complained that 'The place was Covered overhead with a Rich Cannapie, and vnderneath all Carpetts. To discribe it rightly it was like a great stage, and the Prince satt aboue as the Mock kings doth thear' (I.91). The analogy between royal court and theatrical stage here pivots on the capitalized adjective 'Mock'. Roe draws on the common antitheatrical sentiment, voiced virulently by William Prynne in *Histrio-Mastix: The Player's Scourge, or Actor's Tragedy* (1632), that theatrical performance entails an illicit transformation: a 'counterfeiting of persons, affections, manners, vices, sexes, and the like, which is inseparably incident to the acting of Playes . . . [and] transformes the Actors into what they are not'. For Prynne, such 'counterfeiting' is more than simply deceptive; it also prompts actual bodily transformations that pervert God-given identities. As he says, 'I may likewise condeme these Play-house Vizards, vestments, images and disguises, which during their usage in outward appearance offer a kinde of violence to Gods own Image and mens human shapes, metamorphosing them into those idolatrous, those brutish formes, in which God never made them'.[19] Prynne doesn't mean that Christian actors play idolatrous characters but rather that acting itself is a form of idolatry. As David Hawkes has argued, the antitheatricalists understood idolatry as a form of semiotic abuse. In idolatry, God's creations, whose proper 'use' is to signify their creator, mock their true purpose by becoming the ends rather than the means of human devotion.[20] Signifier is thus valued over divine signified, matter over spirit. Theatrical idolatry transforms audiences as much as actors by making them enter into perverse alliances with mere things. In antitheatrical discourse, therefore, 'Mock kings' are both theatrical counterfeits of kings *and* real kings who make a mockery of sovereignty by over-valuation of their theatrical trappings—and, in Roe's case, undervaluation of their English ambassadors.

Both senses of the 'Mock' king are everywhere evident in Roe's descriptions of the Mughal court's ostentatious theatricality. Perhaps the most glaring instance is his extended discussion of Jahangir's *durbar* (or public audience) in October 1616 with the Persian ambassador. As the subtitle of this section of the journal makes clear, Roe was both fascinated and troubled by Jahangir's 'Super-exceeding Pompe' (II.299). The entire scene plays out for Roe as an antitheatricalist's nightmare: the Persian ambassador greeted Jahangir with so many garish gifts that 'he appeared, rather a Iester or Iugler, then a person of gravity, running vp and downe and acting all his words like a Mimicke Player' (II.300). And Jahangir was costumed in such

---

[19] William Prynne, *Histrio-Mastix: The Players Scourge* (London, 1633), 946.

[20] David Hawkes, *Idols of the Marketplace: Idolatry and Commodity Fetishism in English Literature, 1580–1680* (New York: Palgrave Macmillan, 2001), esp. 78–86.

finery that he resembled Enobarbus' description of Cleopatra in her barge on the river Cydnus: with music playing, he made his entrance in 'his coat of cloath of Gold', attended by eunuchs and a servant 'who was cloathed as such as any Player, and more gaudy' (II.307). Even though Roe seems to have furnished some of the stage properties for this scene—he had gifted Jahangir an English-style coach, a version of which makes an appearance in the durbar—he again remains at a remove from the spectacle, choosing to offer a detailed description of what he revealingly calls the 'strange ensignes of Maiesty' (II.307). Here ethnography and antitheatrical discourse blur into each other: Roe decodes the gaudy signs of a 'strange', or foreign, culture, but he also protests the *estrangement* of such signs from their proper purpose.

So long as such estrangement happens within the circumscribed space of Mughal spectacle, Roe's antitheatrical discourse works for him. But the 'strange ensignes of Maiesty' occasionally refuse to be contained within their ethnographic frame, with consequences that serve to theatricalize Roe and his otherwise invisible body. One such instance is his receipt in November of 1616 of a gift from Jahangir's favourite son, Prince Khurram:

> By and by came out a Cloth of gould Cloake of his owne, once or twice worne, which he Caused to be putt on my back, and I made a reverence very unwillingly. When his Ancestor Tamerlane was represented at the Theatre the Garment would well have become the Actor; but it is here reputed the highest of favour to give a garment warne by the Prince, or, being New, once layd on his shoulder.   (II.334)

As Ellorashree Maitra has noted, Roe here describes—and misrecognizes—the Islamic tradition of *khil'at*, the gift of clothes as tokens of imperial favour.[21] The ritual performed an important political function by producing bonds of cross-cultural reciprocity. But Roe understands it only as the theatrical performance of a 'Mock king'. His reference to Tamburlaine—simultaneously Khurram's historical ancestor and Christopher Marlowe's histrionic character—works to theatricalize the Mughal line, and all the more so because Edward Alleyn's famous performance as the title character of Marlowe's play had made Tamburlaine a byword for an over-the-top histrionicism associated with loud declamation, frantic gesture, and eye-catching apparel.[22] Khurram's gold cloak is, for Roe, a gaudy garment more suited to the playhouse than an imperial court; as such, it is a particularly unwelcome addition

---

[21] In an as-yet unpublished paper, 'Replaying *Tamburlaine* at the Mughal Court: Auto-ethnography as Theatre in the Contact Zone' (presented at the 2011 meeting of the Modern Language Association in Los Angeles), Ellorashree Maitra offers a brilliant reading of how Roe's theatrical ethnography is shaped by the oriental drama of the early modern English stage, especially Christopher Marlowe's *Tamburlaine*.

[22] See Richard Levin, 'The Contemporary Perception of Marlowe's Tamburlaine', *Medieval and Renaissance Drama in English* 1 (1984), 51–70. I discuss the denigration of Tamburlaine as a figure of histrionic excess in *Untimely Matter in the Time of Shakespeare* (Philadelphia: University of Pennsylvania Press, 2009), 78–81.

to the briefly visible 'back' of an English ambassador who saw his clothes not as theatrical costumes but, rather, as natural and irrevocable signs of his God-given national identity. Edward Terry, Roe's chaplain, noted that 'For my Lord Ambassador and his Company, we all kept to our English habits, made as light and coole as possibly we could haue them; his wayters in Red Taffata cloakes, guarded with green Taffat, which they always wore when they went abroad with him; myself in a long black Cassock.'[23] Not the best attire for the hot Ajmer sun, perhaps, but certainly powerful 'ensignes' of authentic Englishness for Roe's theatre of antitheatricality.

Roe thus spurns not just the theatrical vestments of Mughal self-display but any demand that he himself wear them. Early modern antitheatricalists, horrified that costumes might contagiously transform the identity of the player, reserved particular outrage for the cross-dressed boy actor. The antitheatricalist fear of cross-dressing has been studied largely in relation to early modern ideas of gender and sexuality. But it potentially extended also to cross-national migration and transformation: in an extended jeremiad against the vogue for the lovelock, a curly hair extension, William Prynne castigated this 'effeminate' accessory as a barbarous prosthesis, derived from non-Christian cultures in the New World and the Orient. In his vituperative assessment, it had succeeded in transforming Englishmen not only into Englishwomen but also into idolatrous Indians.[24] Roe's response to Khurram's gift betrays some of Prynne's phobia: he is horrified that, placed on his back, it might turn him into an ethnically cross-dressed player-Tamburlaine. Imagine Roe's horror, then, when another ethnically cross-dressed English body—a body possessed, moreover, of a very different disposition to the theatrical Tamburlaine—walks on stage. Enter Thomas Coryate.

Becoming-Indian: Thomas Coryate's Persian oration

'Odd Tom' Coryate was a self-conscious eccentric.[25] Born in approximately 1579 and raised in the small Somerset village of Odcombe—Coryate repeatedly claimed that he embodied the 'odd' of his village's name—he studied at Oxford in the late 1590s before moving to London by 1603. He arrived there having already cultivated an interest in theatre. His father, a church rector, had been reputed for his public

---

[23] Edward Terry, *A Voyage to East-India: Wherein Some Things Are Taken Notice Of, In Our Passage Thither, But Many More in Our Abode There, Within That Rich and Most Spacious Empire of the Great Mogul* (London, 1655), 205.

[24] William Prynne, *The Unloveliness of Lovelocks* (London, 1628). I am immensely grateful to Jessica Roberts Frazier for bringing Prynne's text to my attention.

[25] For details of Coryate's biography, I am indebted to Dom Moraes and Sarayu Srivatsa, *The Long Strider: How Thomas Coryate Walked from England to India in the Year 1613* (Delhi: Penguin India, 2003) and R. E. Pritchard, *Odd Tom Coryate: The English Marco Polo* (Stroud: Sutton Publishing, 2004).

orations; the son followed in his father's footsteps with histrionic flair. Coryate's skill may have been honed by his exposure, whether in London or earlier, to the drama of Christopher Marlowe. As we will see, he was certainly familiar with *Tamburlaine the Great*, and Marlowe's well-known promise in the play's opening lines to dazzle the audience's ears with 'high astounding terms' may well have grabbed Coryate's imagination.[26] In any case, Coryate seems to have cultivated a distinctive, highly theatrical, wilfully eccentric style of public speaking. This style was probably responsible for his appointment to Prince Henry's court as a *de facto* jester. There he also met a number of theatrical practitioners—amongst them Ben Jonson and Inigo Jones, both of whom he counted as friends.[27]

In 1607, Coryate left the court to tour Europe on foot. His journey, which lasted a little more than eight months, took him through France, Switzerland, Italy, Germany, and Holland. It is clear that, from the outset, he intended to convert his experiences into a published travelogue: he took copious notes about all the places he visited. But this was to be no straightforward ethnographic report. Coryate's inspiration was not the current vogue for chorographical writing about cities, typified by the antiquarian John Stow's *Survey of London* (1603), but a theatrical precedent: the actor-clown Will Kemp's famed morris dance from London to Norwich, performed over nine days in 1600 in front of cheering crowds. As John Straingeway's prefatory poem to the *Crudities* says of Coryate, 'Kemp yet doth live' (I.34).[28] In other words, if Coryate sought to experience foreign cultures, it was in a very different fashion from Roe: he intended to be a leading participant in the spectacles he described. The frontispiece to the resulting narrative, *Coryates Crudities* (1611), makes this participation spectacularly clear (Figure 13).

Unlike Roe's invisible body, Coryate's is prominently displayed—transported by ship and palanquin across the English channel and the Swiss alps (left); chased by a Venetian Jew brandishing a knife (bottom left); riding a gondola, pelted by rain and fruit thrown by an angry courtesan (bottom right); even vomited on by a figure representing Germany (or so a caption tells us at bottom centre). Coryate's body is thus not just the object of spectacle: it is repeatedly exposed to foreign elements. This much is suggested even by the extended gastronomic metaphor of the *Crudities*' title. Coryate didn't simply *see* foreign cultures; he *tasted* them (or 'gobbled' them up), hoping that his readers would find the flavours of his foreign experience

---

[26] Christopher Marlowe, *Tamburlaine*, ed. Thomas Crawford (Toronto: Dover Publications, 2002), Prologue, line 5.

[27] Whether Jonson and Jones reciprocated Coryate's claim of friendship is less clear. Jonson wrote commendatory lines for Coryate's *Crudities*, but they are somewhat ambivalent, describing Coryate as 'an Engine, wholly consisting of extremes, a Head, fingers, and toes'; Thomas Coryate, *Coryats Crudities*, 2 vols. (Glasgow: University of Glasgow Press, 1905), I.16. All further references to Coryate are to this edition.

[28] Kemp's feat was written up and published as *Kemps Nine Daies Wonder* (London, 1600). For a discussion of Kemp's career, see David Wiles, *Shakespeare's Clown: Actor and Text in the Elizabethan Playhouse* (Cambridge: Cambridge University Press, 1987), 24–42.

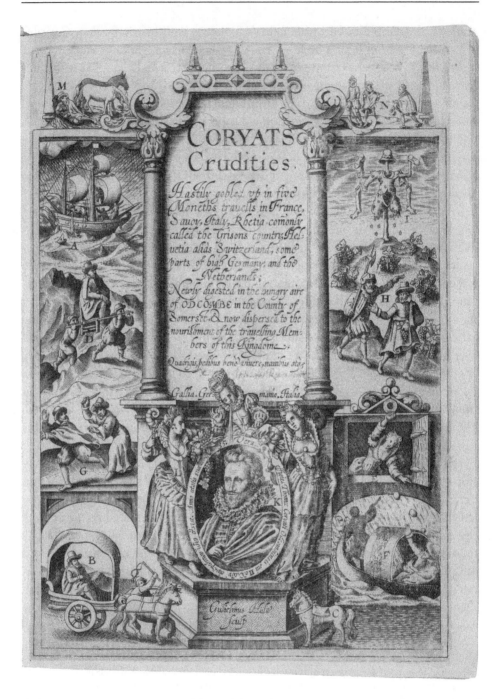

Figure 13 Title page, *Coryats Crudities* (London, 1611). STC 5808 copy 2. By permission of the Folger Shakespeare Library.

similarly appetizing. It is no accident that Coryate is responsible for introducing to England the fork, which he had encountered in Venice while dining there. This typifies how his response to Italy was not that of an invisible, disembodied ethnographer who sought to codify foreignness: it was that of a highly embodied actor, training his body how to work with unfamiliar stage properties. As Richmond Barbour notes, Coryate repeatedly sought 'to graft himself to foreign objects in his report'.[29] To travel, he had to become-Italian—not *be* Italian but rather enter into assemblages with human and non-human Italian actors. In other words, his goal was not the ethnographic delimiting and description of identity (or being). Instead it was the altogether more improvisational task of self-transformation (or becoming) by extending and altering his body in concert with foreign people and objects.

To be sure, the ethnographic optic is fundamental to Coryate's narrative. He describes much of what he sees as exotic spectacle, in terms that draw explicitly on antitheatrical discourse. As we might expect from the son of a Protestant rector, his account of a Catholic Mass in Calais recoils from the theatricality of the 'superstitious geniculation' (I.152)—Coryate's term for the Catholic ritual of praying on one's knees. But he often responds to foreign spectacle not by adopting a knowing ethnographic distance but rather by embracing its power to touch and transform him. Describing his first view of the Piazza de San Marco in Venice, for example, Coryate pronounces it to be 'the most glorious and heavenly shew upon the water that any mortal eye ever beheld, such a shew that did ravish me both with delight and admiration' (I.299).[30] This ravishment is of a piece with Coryate's persistent desire to be touched and transformed by his experiences. It is important to recognize how much he seeks to get outside himself, or seeks to make his body do things that it didn't or couldn't do previously. Hearing the Italianate Latin spoken by the residents of Bergamo, for example, he resolves 'to abandon my old English pronunciation' (II.60), which implies studying hard to change the motor habits of his tongue, lips, and facial muscles. His tour of Europe is for him not a luxurious holiday, therefore, but *travail*, the original meaning of travel: it is *work*, both labour that he performs and work performed on his body.

The transformative effort of travel is clear from Coryate's subsequent and final journey. In 1612, basking in the success of his *Crudities*, he decided to walk east to Asia. We don't know if India was part of his original travel itinerary; but after

---

[29] On the one hand, we might see this ravishment—and, indeed, the sustained eating metaphor of the *Crudities*—as illustrating the tourist's unique brand of possessive individualism, according to which foreign culture is reduced to so many pleasing 'crudities' whose consumption sustains rather than contagiously transforms the touristic subject. Yet it is crucial to note here also how much Coryate willingly submits to the possibility of bodily alteration. For a discussion of Coryate as tourist, see Richmond Barbour, *Before Orientalism: London's Theatre of the East, 1576–1626* (Cambridge: Cambridge University Press, 2003), 121.

[30] Compare Barbour's discussion of Coryate's writings, which is entitled 'Thomas Coryate and the Invention of Tourism', in *Before Orientalism*, 115–45.

dallying in Constantinople and Jerusalem, he joined a caravan that crossed Persia on foot, via the Silk Route, to Lahore, which he reached in 1615. From there he made his way to Delhi and Agra, before heading to Ajmer, where Jahangir and his court were temporarily based in order to subdue a revolt by a Rajput king. Coryate met Thomas Roe en route to Ajmer, greeting him, of course, with a theatrical oration—Coryate's 'exercise here or recreation is making or repeating orations', Roe observed tartly (I.104). After many months in Ajmer, Coryate returned to Agra and then proceeded to Surat. His untimely death there from dysentery in 1617 has robbed us of what would have been a stupendous travel narrative about the thousands of miles he ended up walking. All that survives from his Asian journey are reminiscences by some of the travelling Englishmen he met while abroad and five letters he sent back to England, most of which were published posthumously. These letters insist on the 'travail' by means of which Coryate transformed himself and his body.

The title page to one of his published letters, *Thomas Coryate, Travailer for the English Wits and the Good of This Kingdom* (1616), mines the Coryate 'brand' made famous by the *Crudities*, resorting to the same theatrical display of his body that had characterized his European travelogue (Figure 14). Here the publisher responds to Coryate's express desire '(by Gods leave) to have my picture expressed in my next booke sitting upon an elephant' (247).[31] Coryate sits imperially atop the animal, clutching his book—a repository of ethnographic mastery—and attired in English clothes. But this is more the publisher's fantasy than Coryate's. The image of the traveller in the title page duplicates Coryate's likeness from another woodcut in *Coryate's Crudities*, which depicts him—again in English garb—atop the Great Tun of Heidelberg, an enormous beer vat (Figure 15).[32] The publisher's doubling of Coryate's image generates the illusion of an unchanging English body, one that masters foreign cultures by topping their accoutrements. But this illusion is belied by Coryate's letters. For there was little that was recognizably English about Coryate or his body by the time he reached India. When he met Thomas Roe en route to Ajmer, he was wearing Turkish and Persian clothes; he was also speaking fluent Farsi. He had also been eating little, living on the equivalent of two English pennies a day. In other words, Coryate's body had been radically transformed by his journey through central Asia. Underscoring the 'Travailer' of the title to the pamphlet in which the illustration of Coryate riding an elephant appeared, he himself insisted on the embodied 'travail' that his journey had entailed, distinguishing its fruits from other forms of knowledge purchased 'without labour or travel'. His was an embodied knowledge, he argued, derived from 'continuall... practice'[33]—that is, from the repetitions of bodily training, a transformative knowledge not unlike the muscle-memory on which both

---

[31] All references to Coryate's Indian writings are to *Early Travels in India 1583–1619*, ed. William Foster (London: Humphrey Milord and Oxford University Press, 1921).

[32] For a discussion of this image, see Barbour, *Before Orientalism*, 130.

[33] Foster, ed., *Early Travels in India*, 274.

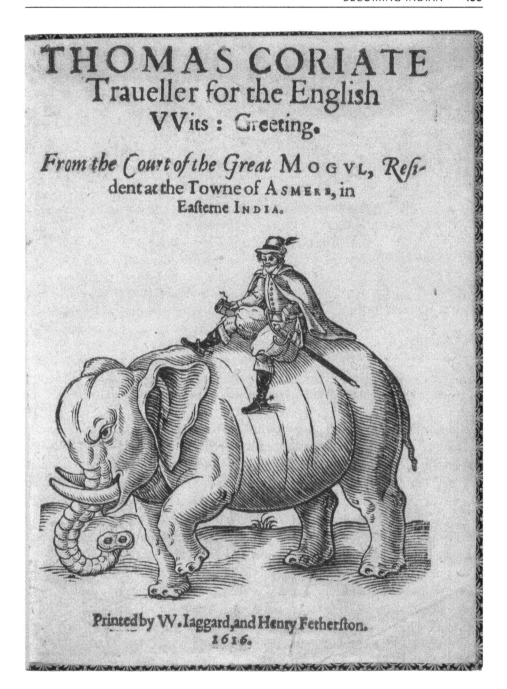

Figure 14 Title page, *Thomas Coriate Traueller for the English Wits: Greeting. From the Court of the Great Mogvl, Resident at the Towne of Asmere, in Easterne India* (London, 1616). STC 5811. By permission of the Folger Shakespeare Library.

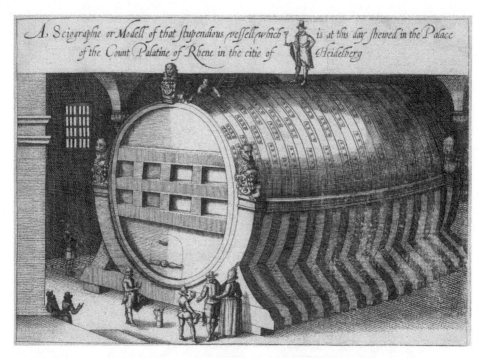

A Sciographie or Modell of that stupendious vessell which is at this day shewed in the Palace of the Count Palatine of Rhene in the citie of Heidelberg

Figure 15 Coryate standing on the tun of Heidelburg. *Coryats Crudities* (London, 1611). STC 5808 copy 2. (Fold-out after p. 486.) By permission of the Folger Shakespeare Library.

the athlete and the actor depend. It was this 'continuall practice' that allowed Coryate to speak to those he met without the mediation of a translator. As in Europe, Coryate travailed particularly hard in the acquisition of language, making a point of formally studying Turkish and Arabic while in Ajmer. He also picked up the local vernacular. Edward Terry tells a story of how Coryate so out-talked a feisty washing-woman in her own language that 'she had not one word more to speak'. [34]

Coryate's linguistic aptitude also gave him access to Jahangir of a kind that was denied to the exclusively Anglophone Roe. This access bespeaks the 'continuall practice' by means of which he trained his body to become a histrionic, expressive medium legible to its Mughal audience. Dressed in the clothes of an Indian beggar, Coryate delivered a lengthy oration to Jahangir at Ajmer's Akbari Fort in formal Farsi, the language of the Mughal court. Coryate transcribed the oration in one of his letters, supplementing it with a translation. It is a remarkable document. His Farsi is somewhat garbled, but it is hard to tell whether this is because of his own inadequacies in the

[34] Foster, ed., *Early Travels in India*, 284. Coryate's xenophilia did not extend to religion, however; he used his command of Hindustani also to denounce a *mu'ezzin* by a proclamation that Christ was the true prophet and Muhammad an impostor—a potentially dangerous oration that was dismissed because its audience believed 'the English *fakir*' to be mad (Foster, 274). This replicated his attempt to persuade a Venetian rabbi, in Latin, to give up his Jewish beliefs and embrace Christ or face eternal damnation (Coryate, *Crudities*, I.374).

language or the incomprehension of the English typesetter. From Coryate's opening words, however, he speaks in a stylized mode of address suited to his royal audience: '*Hazaret Aallum pennah salamet, fooker Daruces ve tehaungeshta hastam kemia emadam az wellagets door, ganne az mulk Inglizan*'.[35] He translates these lines as follows: 'Lord protector of the world, all hail! I am a poor traveller and world-seer, who am come here from a far country called England'.[36] Yet this translation finesses how, in Farsi, Coryate had begun to characterize himself as Indian. His term for himself is a '*fooker Daruces*', or *fakir dervish*, a wandering Sufi ascetic who begs for alms.

Coryate's make-over as a Sufi *fakir* is all the more remarkable given his readiness elsewhere to inveigh against what he regarded as the heresies of Islam. In a letter to his mother, he transcribes yet another oration he had delivered, this time in Italian, tediously enumerating the supposed errors and impostures of Muhammad to a Muslim who had lived in Florence.[37] Yet Coryate's self-identification as a *fakir* in his oration to Jahangir is more than an instance of self-serving legerdemain. It also gives some indication of how he had transformed his body during his time in Ajmer, following the model of the many poor *fakirs* who begged outside the *dargah* (or shrine) of Ajmer's medieval Sufi saint Moin-Ud-Din Chishti. Coryate, in other words, had learned not only the Farsi spoken by the Mughals but also the theatrical bodily practices—of scant clothing, respectful prostration, and pleading for alms—that he needed to master in order to be legible to Jahangir as a worthy supplicant. Sitting at his *jharoka* or public window at the Akbari Fort, Jahangir was sufficiently impressed by the English *fakir*'s oration that he immediately made him a gift of 100 rupees[38]—a not insubstantial sum at the time, especially for a man who had lived on tuppence a day throughout his long Asian walk.

But Roe was not so pleased by the oration. Coryate complains that Roe 'nibbl[ed] at me', fearing that his performance 'might redound to the discredit of our nation, for one of our country to present himself in that poor and beggarly manner before the king, to crave money from him by flattery'.[39] Roe doubtless felt that Coryate had damaged the reputation of the English, and hence his own precarious standing as King James's unremunerated (and therefore financially struggling) ambassador. But one might also sense an antitheatrical component in Roe's response to the sight of an Englishman becoming-Indian. Like the lovelock wearer demonized by Prynne, Coryate had consented to be transformed by foreign objects. And Roe's animus may have been occasioned also by what he perceived to be a theatricality that paid homage to, rather than scorned, Marlowe's stage-Tamburlaine.

In his journal, Roe observes that Coryate's desire was to visit 'Samarcand in Tartarya, to kisse Tamberlans tombe'. One can hear a note of Protestant derision in

---

[35] Foster, ed., *Early Travels in India*, 263.   [36] Foster, ed., *Early Travels in India*, 264.

[37] For the wording of this oration, see Foster, ed., *Early Travels in India*, 271–5.

[38] This is the figure alleged by Edward Terry; see Foster, ed., *Early Travels in India*, 284.

[39] Foster, ed., *Early Travels in India*, 266.

Roe's language, which hints at how Coryate's wish is an embodied act simultane-ously of religious and theatrical idolatry. Not surprisingly, Coryate describes the desire somewhat differently in his oration to Jahangir, referring to Tamburlaine by his Persian honorific 'Lord of the Corners':

> I have a strong desire to see the sepulchre of the Lord of the Corners for this cause: that, when in Constantinople, I saw a notable old building in a pleasant garden near the said city, where the Christian emperor, Emanuel, made a sumptuous banquet to the Lord of the Corners, after he had taken Sultan Bajazet in a great battle near the city of Brusa, when the Lord of the Corners bound Sultan Bajazet in golden fetters, and put him into an iron cage.[40]

Coryate here is referring to the historical Tamburlaine. But his imagination is clearly inspired by the theatrical one. The historical Timur took Sultan Beyezid captive; yet Coryate's story of Bajazeth's enslavement inside an iron cage is a later embellish-ment that would have been unknown to Jahangir.[41] It is, of course, one of the most memorable pieces of stage business in Marlowe's play. So why should Coryate have been so curious to see the tomb of the stage Tamburlaine's historical counterpart? Coryate evidently saw Tamburlaine not as a 'Mock king', as Roe did, but rather as a legitimate object of fascination. Is it too much to speculate that Coryate identified with Marlowe's version of Tamburlaine—less Tamburlaine the imperial invader, perhaps, than Tamburlaine the highly histrionic shape-shifter of humble provincial origins who got to perambulate around Asia delivering mighty lines?

This suggests how much Coryate's 'becoming-Indian' was not a teleological pro-gression towards an endpoint of pure otherness; it was, rather, a dynamic theatrical assemblage of both English and non-English elements. Yet this assemblage served to radically de-territorialize the authentic English ethnicity in which Roe was so invested. If, as Jyotsna G. Singh argues, Roe's journal is an early exercise in colonial-ist epistemology that asserts a clearcut and even racialized difference between the-atrically embodied Indian and largely disembodied English ethnographer, Coryate is the fly in Roe's ointment.[42] Not only does Coryate publicly flaunt his body in the Mughal court; he also makes it part of a transnational body, as his hyperbolic

---

[40] Foster, ed., *Early Travels in India*, 265.

[41] The story of Bajazeth and the cage seems to be of Arabian provenance; but the details as Coryate understands them were fleshed out by George Whetstone in Marlowe's source for *Tamburlaine*, *The English Myrror* (London, 1586). For an extended discussion of Marlowe's possible debt to Ibn Arab-shah's 1436 account of Tamburlaine's life, *Ajaib al-maqdur fi nawa'ib Timur: The Wonders of Destiny Concerning the Calamities Wrought by Tamerlane*, see Ahlam Maijan Alruwaili, 'Ibn Arabshah: The Unacknowledged Debt of Christopher Marlowe's Tamburlaine', MA Thesis, University of Nebraska at Lincoln, 2011. I am grateful to Julia Schleck for bringing this work to my attention.

[42] Singh, *Colonial Narratives/Cultural Dialogues*, 17–44. Roe's ethnographic strategy of self-disem-bodiment is contradicted by his private letters from India, in which he draws sustained attention to how he spent most of his time in India suffering from protracted illnesses. I discuss these letters in my essay 'Sick Ethnography: Recording the Indian and the Ill English Body', in Jonathan Gil Harris, ed., *Indog-raphy: Writing the Indian in Early Modern England* (New York: Palgrave Macmillan, 2011), 133–47.

hyphenated self-description makes clear: 'the Hierosolymitan-Syrian-Mesopotamian-Armenian-Median-Parthian-Persian-Indian Leggestretcher of Odcomb in Somerset'.[43]

If all the world's a stage, then, for Coryate it is not simply an ethnographic spectacle to be decoded. His extraordinary histrionics in the Mughal's court at Ajmer embody much that the English antitheatricalists would have deplored; yet their understanding of the playhouse as a contact zone in which subjects touch and are transformed by foreign objects arguably offers us a powerful hermeneutic, one far richer than that modelled by the modern anthropological concept of 'performativity', with which to theorize early modern theatricality in general and the theatricality of cross-cultural encounter in particular. Coryate indeed believes that all the world's a stage. But to function in it and to profit from it, he enthusiastically leaps onto that stage and submits to what the antitheatricalists regarded as its contagious touch. Contra Roe, he embraces the theatricality of becoming-Indian.

FURTHER READING

Barish, Jonas. *The Antitheatrical Prejudice* (Berkeley: University of California Press, 1985).

de Certeau, Michel. 'Ethno-Graphy: Speech, or the Space of the Other: Jean de Léry', in *The Writing of History*, trans. Tom Conley (New York: Columbia University Press, 1988), 209–43.

Deleuze, Gilles. 'Literature and Life', in *Essays Critical and Clinical*, trans. Daniel W. Smith (Minneapolis: University of Minnesota Press, 1997), 1–7.

Subrahmanyam, Sanjay. *Three Ways to Be Alien: Travails and Encounters in the Early Modern World* (Boston: Brandeis University Press, 2011).

---

[43] Foster, ed., *Early Travels in India*, 258.

CHAPTER 24

POOR

ROBERT HENKE

The theatre and the street

In early modern theatre, poverty in the form of hunger, physical degradation, begging, charity, and economically induced crime is omnipresent as theatrical energy: a fertile source for actor's gags and author's conceits. But in relation to the rest of the scripted or performance text, poverty is at the same time usually de-centred in some manner: it is marginalized, fictionalized, carnivalized, criminalized, repressed, or present in vestigial forms. From these processes emerge the micro-forms of poverty that characterize European early modern theatre: the gestures, poses, and stances of the actor simulating (and sometimes actually experiencing) degradation; the dyadic forms of exchange between a supplicator and his or her 'audience'; the responses to degradation by fictional characters that are distorted and exaggerated in striking formal ways, like hypertropic masks or distended elements of costume. Suffering poverty from want or degradation—whether imagined or actually experienced by the actor—really could be the mother of invention.

These energies and forms moved between the institutionalized theatre and the quotidian performances of those living on the edge of subsistence, but not in ways that would render the dramatic script or the theatrical performance text a simple mirror of social reality. As a paradigm for the relationship between the historical–social arena and the aesthetic artefact, we may take the *commedia dell'arte*. In the *Arte*, the hierarchical organization from master-parents to children to servants is fundamental, and the romantic themes of blocking parents and amorous children shape the plot's spine. But the social contradictions of a bourgeois society requiring servants (and occasionally slaves) do point us to something like Jameson's 'political unconscious': the starvation, degradation, and oppression of the labouring class bubble to the surface through distorted aesthetic forms such as the 'hunger gag' played for laughs by the emaciated servant character, or *zanni*. To be sure, the fact that the actor was sometimes not just impersonating hunger but actually experiencing it provides a theatrical complication to the layered techniques of reading such as Jameson's: in Pierce's semiotic terms, the actually starving actor would represent hunger iconographically, not merely symbolically. In general, however, early modern theatrical forms of poverty, which 'compensate for and rectify a structural lack at some lower or earlier level of production', in Jameson's terms,[1] are produced by the active work of processes such as distortion, exaggeration, displacement, and condensation. The raw and disturbing stuff of acute need and depravation is transformed into complex theatrical forms: the tortured and grotesque lines, impressions, and cavities of a *zanni* mask deployed by the actor as a distilled map of his very body; the impossibly complex (and usually doomed) plot strategems of the *zanni* to obtain food. On the street, there is nothing funny about hunger; in the theatre, the grotesque, desperate *zanni* actor serves his empty belly up for laughter. But this laughter is often of a precarious and disturbing nature that leads the audience, consciously or unconsciously, back to some recognition of socio-economic life.

Beggar as actor

Since the demonstrable spike in early modern European poverty in the early stages of capitalism did not respect national boundaries, and since this socio-economic phenomenon was absorbed everywhere by theatre and performance, one can identify micro-forms, or 'theatregrams', of destitution passing across geo-linguistic borders.[2] The new institutional theatres of England, Italy, Spain, and France, whether centred on national capitals and fixed stages (England, Spain, and, to a certain degree, France) or based on a system of diffused patronage and itinerancy (Italy), were largely made possible by new capitalist forms of accumulation, entrepreneurship, and marketing, and they represent both the self-fashioning of individuals 'freed' by new market possibilities and those judged to be corrupted by the traditional sins of greed and avarice, now enhanced by the latest economic technologies (as in plays such as Ben Jonson's *Volpone* [1606] or *The Devil is an Ass* [1616]).[3] As the Marxist critics Robert Weimann and Walter Cohen have demonstrated, each of the emerging national theatres in this early stage of capitalism exhibited salient contradictions, partly because of the contradictions of capitalism itself, and partly because the theatres were not yet fully capitalist but still retained vestiges of feudal, pre-capitalist structures.[4]

---

[1] Fredric Jameson, *The Political Unconscious: Narrative as a Socially Symbolic Act* (Ithaca: Cornell University Press, 1981), 44.

[2] The useful term 'theatregram' was coined by Louise George Clubb in *Italian Drama in Shakespeare's Time* (New Haven: Yale University Press, 1989).

[3] Dates for plays refer to the first known performance.

[4] See Robert Weimann, *Shakespeare and the Popular Tradition in the Theater: Studies in the Social Dimension of Dramatic Form and Function* (Baltimore: Johns Hopkins University Press, 1978) and

In forming companies that would not just perform at ecclesiastical and political occasions but *all year long*, and at diverse kinds of venues, the emerging Italian professional theatre provided a model of company organization and market rationalization that would directly influence the emerging professional theatre in Spain, beginning with the famous 1545 actors' contract signed in Padua.[5] Still, successful companies such as the Gelosi, Confidenti, and Fedeli were bound to a network of northern Italian court patronage and were rewarded by playing market-based public venues such as the Teatro di Baldracca in Florence only after having established themselves securely at court.[6] Upon the ebbing of the northern courts' prestige and power after the 1620s, the *commedia dell'arte* had to emigrate, moving to Paris in order to survive. The professional Spanish stage, like its English counterpart, enjoyed a public market with a national centre. Still, the companies did also perform for the court and leased the *corrales* in which they played from the confraternities who owned them. In addition, the Spanish companies were obliged to distribute a regular portion of their profits to the poor.[7] The London professional troupes, meanwhile, organized as profit-sharing joint-stock companies and blessed with a fixed theatre and dependable markets except in plague seasons, were the most advanced capitalist engines. But as the 'King's Men', especially during the Christmas season, Shakespeare's company were required to function as King James's servants in more than name; the very requirement that troupes had to wear aristocratic or royal livery may be seen as a feudal vestige.

These were neo-medieval vestiges characteristic of the liminal historical position of early modern theatre. But the inherent contradictions of early capitalism also left their mark. As the great historian of poverty Bronislaw Geremek has argued, capitalism structurally required the generation of new modes of impoverishment, much of it coming from the countryside, as well as new wealth.[8] For landowners to amass profits and take advantage of new agricultural technologies, the accumulation and consolidation of land and capital was essential; if smaller landowners were not constrained to sell their land for economic reasons, they were often forcibly evicted by enclosure or other means.[9] By the end of the seventeenth century, across Europe, higher yields were being extracted from the land—and more former small landowners had been thrust into poverty.

Walter Cohen, *Drama of a Nation: Public Theater in Renaissance England and Spain* (Ithaca: Cornell University Press, 1985).

[5] For the text and a discussion of the 1545 contract, see Esther Cocco, 'Una compagnia comica nella prima metà del secolo xvi', *Giornale storico della letteratura italiana* 65 (1915), 55–70.

[6] Annamaria Evangelista, 'Le compagnie dei Comici dell'Arte nel teatrino di Baldracca a Firenze: notizie dagli epistolary 1576–1653', *Quaderni di Teatro* 24 (1984), 50–72.

[7] N. D. Shergold, *A History of the Spanish Stage From Medieval Times Until the End of the Seventeenth Century* (Oxford: Clarendon Press, 1967), 177–208.

[8] Bronislaw Geremek, *Poverty: A History*, trans. Agnieszka Kolakowska (Oxford: Blackwell, 1994), 102.

[9] Geremek, *Poverty: A History*, 107.

In keeping with the contradictory nature of early modern capitalism, the new institution of theatre revealed persistent, if often hidden, forms of poverty as the marginalized but insistent underside of the early modern world that they staged to the world. The first public Spanish theatres, or *corrales*, can be said to emerge from the very opposition between new scarcity and new plenty. Speaking of the growth of charitable institutions in the midst of the increasing poverty in sixteenth-century Spain, J. E. Varey writes, 'If the obvious misery and poverty of a large number or people provoked this reaction [the foundation of new charitable institutions], it was the relative prosperity of a minority that made it possible.'[10] By renting the *corrales* from religious confraternities dedicated to charitable work and by being obliged to give a portion of their profits to the poor, the professional Spanish theatre that emerged in the 1560s and 1570s was directly dependent on the new forms of charity.

The English professional theatre buildings and revenue system was not structurally tied to poverty and charity, like the Spanish, but the institutional formation of the English professional actor certainly was. Amending and consolidating previous royal edicts, the 1572 'Acte for the Punishment of Vagabondes, and for the Relief of the Poore and Impotent' mandated whipping, stocking, and branding for 'Comon Players in Enterludes and Minstrels' without a licence of two Justices of the Peace.[11] The result was the consolidation of acting companies into those, like the Earl of Leicester's Men or the Queen's Men, patronized by lords or royalty and protected by the new law. But for their aristocratic protection, the actors in these early companies would have been placed in the same class as beggars and vagabonds. It could hardly be said that a member of the King's Men was one step away from a beggar, but just as prosperous Arlecchini like Tristano Martinelli and Domenico Biancolelli could draw back on the historical legend of the famished *zanni*/servant, it would be possible for an English player to summon a vestigial past—and in some cases a threatening future—of destitution.

If, as Mario Apollonio has argued and as documents from the 1540s and 1550s bear out, the core of the early *commedia dell'arte* was based on the opposition between the traditionally hungry servant *zanni* and the prosperous urban merchant Pantalone,[12] then poverty is foundational to the early modern professional Italian theatre. The fiction of the *zanni*, based on the social reality of many new

---

[10] 'Si la evidente miseria y pobreza de gran número de personas provoca esta reacción, es la relativa prosperidad de una minoría lo que la hace posible.' Luciano Garcia Lorenzo and J. E. Varey, *Teatros y vida theatral en el siglo de oro a traves de las fuentes documentales* (London: Tamesis Books, 1991), 10. All translations are my own.

[11] C. J. Ribton-Turner, *A History of Vagrants and Vagrancy* (London: Chapman and Hall, 1887), 106–10.

[12] Mario Apollonio, 'Il duetto di Magnifico e Zanni alle origini dell'arte', in Maria Teresa Muraro, ed., *Studi sul teatro Veneto fra rinascimento ed età barocca* (Florence: Olschki, 1971), 193–220, and Robert Henke, *Performance and Literature in the Commedia dell'Arte* (Cambridge: Cambridge University Press, 2002), 69–84.

Bergamasque immigrants to Venice, is that he is a former Bergamasque peasant displaced from his land by war or the new agri-business who seeks his fortunes in the city, where life may not be any easier but where there is at least the possibility of eking out a living all year round. If, for Marx, the ironically 'freed' Italian serf came to the city and 'found his master waiting for him',[13] the indigent Bergamasque peasant inventing the role of *zanni* on the streets of Venice may be said to find not only his stingy master but also his scene partner waiting for him, at the 'origins' of *commedia dell'arte* theatricality itself. Despite the prosperity and success of the famous troupes, the *commedia dell'arte* was fundamentally based on itinerancy, and subject to the vagaries and persecutions of the road. The actors travelled the same roads used by vagrant beggars, and would have been an injured mule or horse away from being taken as vagabonds, which the actor-writer Domenico Bruni claims to have happened in his *Le fatiche comiche* (1623).[14] Tristano Martinelli, the actor who alchemized the folk figure of Arlecchino into a specifically theatrical mask during the 1580s in Paris, worked many years for the Mantuan court as the 'supervisor' of the charlatans and street performers working the piazzas and streets of Mantua because of 'information' that he had about them, presumably gained from having practised the profession himself.[15] As Robert Tessari has argued, the professions of penurious street performer and that of the new professional actor were culturally and economically adjacent.[16]

The structural capitalist opposition between poverty and wealth, whereby extreme wealth seems to be inevitably counterbalanced by its opposite (examples abound in the early twenty-first century, if taking different forms) is reflected in many dramatic texts of the period. Counterpointing, as if by a kind of hidden law, the ostentatious new gentleman cavorting himself in the 'Poet's Royal Exchange' of the theatre, as Thomas Dekker dubbed it,[17] are the incarcerated paupers of Dekker's own *The Honest Whore*, Part 1 (1604) and the criminal poor in his prose tracts, such as *The Belman of London* (1608). In Calderón's *auto sacramental El Gran Teatro del Mundo* (c.1633–6), the 'Autor' dispenses the archetypal part of 'Pobre' as the binary (but not dialectical, given Calderón's rather conservative position) counterpart of the 'Rico', with an entire constellation of theatrical, stageable gestures and attitudes built into the role that include 'la desdicha' (misfortune), 'la pasión' (passion), 'el suspirar' (sighing), 'el gemir' (groaning), 'importunar y rogar' (importuning and begging), 'la vergüenza' (shame), 'el hambre' (hunger), 'la desnudez' (nakedness),

[13] Karl Marx, *Capital: A Critique of Political Economy*, trans. Samuel Moore and Edward Aveling, 3 vols. (New York: International Publishers, 1967), 1: 715.

[14] See Ferruccio Marotti and Giovanna Romei, eds., *La commedia dell'arte e la società barocca: La professione del teatro* (Rome: Bulzoni, 1991), 346.

[15] See Siro Ferrone, *Arlecchino: Vita e avventure di Tristano Martinelli attore* (Rome: Laterza, 2006), and Robert Henke, 'Representations of Poverty in the Commedia dell'Arte', *Theatre Survey* 48.2 (2007), 237–9.

[16] Robert Tessari, *La commedia dell'arte: la maschera e l'ombra* (Milan: Mursia, 1989).

[17] Thomas Dekker, *The Gull's Horn-Book*, in *Selected Writings*, ed. E. D. Pendry (London: Stratford-upon-Avon Library, 1967), 4: 98.

'el llanto' (crying), 'la immundicia' (filthiness), and 'la bajeza' (abjectness).[18] For readers of Shakespeare, the prospect of on-stage 'desnudez' and 'bajeza' recalls the stage picture of '*poor* Tom' in *King Lear*: that 'unaccommodated man' who generates his own set of characteristic postures and stances and also elicits reflections on economic inequality and redistribution from royal (Lear) and ducal (Gloucester) authorities—reflections that are both traditional and radical in their stance towards capitalist norms.[19] As surely as the starving *zanni* and the wealthy Pantalone are linked to one another, the destitute Edgar is linked to the King, whose tragic course has brought him to question the relationship between need and superfluity, most tellingly in the 'Poor naked wretches' uttered just before Poor Tom's entrance. A theatre of kings seems to have required not only the fool, but also the beggar. As William C. Carroll has put it in his aptly titled book *Fat King and Lean Beggar: Representations of Poverty in the Age of Shakespeare*,[20] the figure of the beggar counterpoints the wealthy king as an obverse principle, well expressed in Hamlet's grim, carnivalesque logic: 'Your fat king and your lean beggar is but variable service—two dishes, but to one table' (*Hamlet* 4.3.23–4).[21]

If Edgar has often been noted as a consummate performer, proceeding through a dizzying array of impersonations once he has been cast out of his fixed role of 'legitimate' brother, his first and most fundamental part is that of a destitute, mad, and *naked* beggar. The extended, implicit stage direction, as he gradually assumes the role, enumerates the postures and forms of the actor's body as he assumes the part of 'Poor Tom', which may be seen as the grounding fiction of the emerging actor, in the athletic and ascetic manner of Grotowski's 'poor theatre'. For Grotowski, the figure of the naked, suffering, vulnerable actor, stripped of the distractions of stage lighting, props, and even costume, is fundamentally compelling in a way that returns us to the elemental power of theatricality itself. If an actor can play naked poverty—one of the base, archetypal roles in Calderón's 'gran teatro del mundo'—then he can play anything. So Edgar, in his role-assuming speech, names the ground zero of acting:

> While I may scape
> I will preserve myself, and am bethought
> To take the basest and most poorest shape

---

[18] Calderón de la Barca, *El Gran Teatro del Mundo*, ed. Eugenio Frutos Cortés (Madrid: Ediciones Anaya, 1969), 50.

[19] For the argument that Lear's and Gloucester's articulations of economic injustice and calls for redistribution are radical in relationship to contemporary economic norms, but traditional in their theological basis in the Church fathers and canonized authors such as Thomas Aquinas, see Debora K. Shuger, 'Subversive Fathers and Suffering Subjects: Shakespeare and Christianity', in Donna Hamilton and Richard Strier, eds., *Religion, Literature, and Politics in Post-Reformation England, 1540–1688* (Cambridge: Cambridge University Press, 1996), 46–69.

[20] William C. Carroll, *Fat King and Lean Beggar: Representations of Poverty in the Age of Shakespeare* (Ithaca: Cornell University Press, 1996).

[21] William Shakespeare, *Hamlet*, ed. Ann Thompson and Neil Taylor, Arden Shakespeare (London: Thomson Learning, 2006).

> That ever penury in contempt of man
> Brought near to beast. My face I'll grime with filth,
> Blanket my loins, elf all my hair in knots
> And with presented nakedness outface
> The winds and persecutions of the sky.
> The country gives me proof and precedent
> Of Bedlam beggars, who, with roaring voices,
> Strike in their numbed and mortified bare arms
> Pins, wooden pricks, nails, sprigs of rosmary;
> And with this horrible object, from low farms,
> Poor pelting villages, sheepcotes and mills
> Sometime with lunatic bans, sometime with prayers,
> Enforce their charity.   (*King Lear* 2.2.176–91)[22]

Begging is such a powerful form of theatricality because of its inborn paradox: on the one hand, it must be distilled, exaggerated, and performed; on the other hand, if it is to be successfully received, the 'performance' must be read as indicating true need.

That the role of 'Poor Tom' is partially constructed from the 'Abraham Man' category in contemporary 'beggar books' such as Thomas Harman's 1567 *A Caveat for Common Cursetors* does not make it any less theatrical, or diminish its theatrical power. In fact, the pan-European genre of the beggar book—a form cataloguing types of dissembling, fraudulent beggars that the innocent passer-by might be likely to encounter—gives powerful voice to the theatricality of poverty, despite the form's ostensible function of debunking and disenchantment. The 'Abraham Man' role that Edgar very deliberately performs in front of an audience is described by Harman to be such as those who 'feign themselves to have been mad, and have been kept either in Bedlam or in some other prison a good time'.[23] Harman's litany of false beggars, which derives from a pan-European genre with a German lineage going back to 1342 municipal registers in the town of Augsburg, minutely catalogues the various kinds of disguises that illegitimate beggars will cannily use to fleece the naïve passer-by: lazy but clever scoundrels simulating blindness, lameness, deafness, epilepsy; discharged soldiers, priests, hermits, relic-sellers, and sometimes even itinerant professors.[24] Texts like Harman's are unexpectedly rich documents of performance, since they attentively describe, as Edgar himself does, the theatrical techniques employed by these consummate actors: make-up on the face and body, costume (or, rather, anti-costume for the

---

[22] William Shakespeare, *King Lear*, ed. R. A. Foakes, Arden Shakespeare (London: Thomson Learning, 1997).

[23] Thomas Harman, *Caveat for Common Cursitors Vulgarly Called Vagabonds*, in *Rogues, Vagabonds, and Sturdy Beggars*, ed. Arthur F. Kinney (Amherst: University of Massachusetts Press, 1990), 127.

[24] The most detailed account of the European beggars book is provided by Bronislaw Geremek in *Les fils de Cain: L'image des pauvres et des vagabonds dans la littérature européenne du XVème au XVIIème siècle*, trans. Joanna Arnold-Moricet et al. (Paris: Flammarion, 1991), 75–128.

naked Poor Tom), gesture, voice, narrative, and verbal formulae that would include set prayers as well as lunatic ravings. In perhaps the single most influential book, the German *Liber vagatorum. Der Betler Orden* (first published around 1509), only the first two categories of beggars provide legitimate objects of charity, for they are the only figures who play just themselves and not a theatrical role.[25]

All of these texts attempt to void the paradigmatic, medieval holy beggar of his aura and sacred power, but in their hyperbolic paranoia, and in their imputation to these quotidian street performers of near-miraculous powers of histrionic transformation, they implicitly return us to that elemental capacity for self-transformation and enchantment that is so powerful in *King Lear* (witness Edgar's transformative effect on Lear and Gloucester). To be sure, there is an important difference between Harman's accounts of fraudulent beggars disguising themselves—usually via secondary testimonials of spies sent by Harman to expose the beggars' dissimulations[26]—and Edgar's speech given directly before our eyes, in which it is clear that the fictional role that he adopts overlaps significantly with his real, existential condition of disgrace, displacement, exile, and hunger. But the difference here may lie more in Harman's dogged scepticism than in the quotidian reality of the indigent, whose 'overlap' between need and performativity was perhaps closer to the compelling figure of Edgar than to Harman's brazen impostors.

One of the best representations of this paradoxically dual nature of begging comes from Spain, a Catholic country where traditional medieval charity tended to survive vestigially in the midst of the same aggravation of poverty under early capitalism that was dogging the rest of Europe. In early modern Spanish literature, the most powerful engagement with poverty and charity comes not in the regular *commedia*, where we might expect it, but in the picaresque novel, which despite its non-theatrical form can eloquently express the self-consciously performative quality of begging. In the third chapter in the anonymous *Lazarillo de Tormos*, the famished, eponymous protagonist is forced to take to the streets, and the author represents him as 'lying like truth':

> When I saw that it was two o' clock and he still hadn't come back, and I was going through the tortures of hunger, I shut the door and put the key where he'd told me to and went back to plying my old trade. In a low, sickly voice, with my hands drooping over my breast with God in front of my eyes and His Name on my tongue, I set about begging bread at the doorways of whichever big houses looked most promising. It was a calling which I'd sucked in with my mother's milk.[27]

[25] For an English translation, see *The Book of Vagabonds and Beggars with a Vocabulary of Their Language*, trans. J. C. Hotten, ed. D. B. Thomas (London: Penguin, 1932).

[26] See, for example, the exposure of the 'Counterfeit Crank' Nicholas Jennings, whom Harman's agents espy 'renew[ing] his face again with fresh blood, which he carried about him in a bladder, and [he] daubed on fresh dirt upon his jerkin, hat, and hosen' (Kinney, ed., *Rogues, Vagabonds, and Sturdy Beggars*, 130).

[27] *La vida de Lazarillo de Tormes y de sus fortunas y adversidades*, ed. Alberto Blecua (Madrid: Castalia, 1972), 139, translated by W. S. Merwin, in *The Life of Lazarillo de Tormes: His Fortunes and Adversities* (New York: New York Review of Books Press, 2005), 68.

We see clearly the constitutive paradox of theatrical poverty, in which enhanced performance is not a diversion from but a means towards truthful revelation; the fact that Lazarillo's begging is the accomplished product of many years of training does not necessarily compromise its truth, since the 'trade' has been forged under conditions of real indigence. Even here, in narrative, one can glimpse the micro-forms of 'poor theatre' as performed across Europe, both on and off the stage, since Lazarillo's exaggerations are no less formal than the hyperbolic lines of a *commedia dell'arte* mask.

The Lazarillo passage is interesting, too, for suggesting the possible passage of performed poverty between the street and the theatre, as it is refracted through aesthetic form. The great historian of Venetian poverty Brian Pullan has observed the congruence of some of the routines described in the beggar books with archival records.[28] If the early modern period was characterized both by the dissolution of older forms of medieval charity and by increasing suspicion and scrutiny of the poor, then begging only became more and more like a performance: up for grabs, seeking its own new forms, not subject to the institutional securities of the medieval period. The early modern beggar was performing for his supper, and sometimes his life. And the changes in social welfare policy were less neat and linear than many historians have believed. Despite the series of official poor laws, remarkable both for their similarity and contemporaneity across national boundaries—from Venice to London, most poor edicts emerge between 1520 and 1540—the story of poverty and charity did not chart a simple transition from medieval contractual exchange (alms for prayers) to early modern surveillance, control, and rationality inexorably leading to Foucault's 'great confinement'. As Paul Slack has shown for England and a group of recent town-based historians have for continental Europe, social welfare reforms proceeded by fits and starts, often clinging onto the old practices of individual, voluntary charity.[29] The new edicts and transnational anti-poor literature of the beggar books scrutinized the new beggar to reveal the charlatan, but it was still possible to discover the holy man, or at least someone who could still do your soul some good in an alms-for-prayer exchange.

If the beggar–almsgiver dyad, with its dynamic of performance and reception, was patently theatrical, theatre was also the place where the inconsistencies, the contradictions, and the 'aleatory' elements of early modern poverty and charity could quite literally be played out. But this process was rarely as transparent as the Lazarillo begging episode cited already. Although there were significant structural connections between the *commedia dell'arte* actors and the new facts of poverty,

---

[28] See Brian Pullan, 'Poveri, mendicanti e vagabondi (secoli XIV–XVII)', in *Storia d'Italia* (Turin: Einaudi, 1978), 1: 1013.

[29] Paul Slack, *Poverty and Policy in Tudor and Stuart England* (London: Longman, 1988). For a fine collection of essays taking a town-based approach to the issue of poverty and charity, see Thomas Max Safley, ed., *The Reformation of Charity: The Secular and the Religious in Early Modern Poor Relief* (Boston: Brill, 2003).

most of the Italian actors did everything they could to occlude this connection. The internationally renowned diva Isabella Andreini once campaigned to extirpate mountebank performers from Milan because of the ways in which they disgraced the acting profession.[30] Andreini and other actor-writers used print to transform theatre into less embodied modes of literary discourse: she wanted to be known as a poet just as much as an actor. Andreini never mentions the mercenary aspects of the acting profession, and certainly not its connections with poverty.

The forms of poverty

We may now consider the different ways in which the themes and energies of poverty are indeed staged in plays and performance, but in *de-centred* and aesthetically transformed ways. The conceptual headings that follow are meant to indicate different kinds of strategies; they are not mutually exclusive, and the examples are meant to be suggestive rather than comprehensive.

Marginalization

A good example of marginalization may be found in the scenario collection of Flaminio Scala, published in 1611 with a view to memorializing past performances and to providing a blueprint for future ones.[31] It is probably the case that in the 1540s and 1550s, before the advent of the actress and while the fledgling professional theatre was dominated by the *zanni*–Pantalone dyad, a key form of theatrical poverty was the dialectic of hunger and stinginess that these two characters had come to represent. The few documents that survive from the period mostly feature exchanges between the *zanni* and his master, with Pantalone frequently suffering Carnivalesque reversals at the hand of the trickster *zanni* but also giving as good as he gets, hoarding his excessive but precious Venetian mass of capital at the expense of the indigent *zanni*. The *zanni*, supplicating for food, may stand as the object of charity wrested from the secure, institutionalized medieval world and plunged into the harsher arena that followed the radical social welfare reforms of the 1520s. In principle (but not always in practice), this is now a brave new world of scrutiny, control, and discipline where Pantalone is the gate-keeper, sceptically rewriting the ostensibly deprived and famished *zanni* as a lazy, gluttonous drone.

But poverty, penury, and plaint are not, by and large, what we discover in the pages of Scala. What Scala memorializes is the mature, post-actress era of the *Arte*,

---

[30] See the 12 October 1601 letter written by Isabella Andreini to the Governor of Milan, beseeching him to suppress the piazza performers: Antonio Paglicci Brozzi, *Contributo alla storia del teatro: Il teatro a Milano nel secolo xvii* (Milan: G. Ricordi, 1891), 12.

[31] Flaminio Scala, *Il teatro delle favole rappresentative*, ed. Ferruccio Marotti, 2 vols. (Milan: Il Polifiolo, 1976).

which privileges romantic plots centring around the dazzling actresses and actors playing the *innamorati* roles, and based on plots largely appropriated from the scripted comedy, or the *commedia erudita*. Even though the *Arte* was frequently attacked for perceived sexual immorality both on- and off-stage, it was securely post-Tridentine in outlook and ideology, so that one would not expect a frontal attack on the institutional engines of social economy. In Scala, we find that that poverty is almost literally marginalized, identifiable in the props lists located at the margins of the page, which include bread (dispensed in the scenarios to real or pretended beggars); travellers' clothing fit for a vagabond; begging instruments such as stools; and eye patches for actors impersonating blind beggars within either the first- or second-order fictions of the plays.

Scala marginalizes but still deploys the theme of poverty in a second, distinct way: by outsourcing it to an underground social level even below (but connected to) the servants, who themselves rank beneath the *vecchi* (old men) and *innamorati* (lovers). Culled, in fact, from the overcrowded piazzas and streets of northern Italian cities, the following kinds of figures emerge from Scala's scenarios, usually not listed by individual name but generically: beggars, pickpockets, gypsies, card sharks, rogues, fugitives, courtesans, prostitutes, and madmen. The *zanni*'s constant employment to his *vecchio* usually staves off hunger, but he frequents masterless men who have been cast from the social net. The social unconscious seeps up from the servant level.

In *Le burle d'Isabella* [The Tricks of Isabella], poverty does not supply the central theme, but rather a resonant undercurrent, first introduced by the main characters and then staged with performative bravura by subsidiary characters in a detachable action lying somewhere between a subplot and a gag. Pantalone has had his way with his servant Franceschina, and covered it up by funding a marriage between her and the impoverished Burratino, promising them an extra one thousand ducats if they produce a male child. (If lust and stinginess constitute Pantalone's two chief personality traits, and motors of action, here he sacrifices the second for the first.) Scala explicitly names the socio-economic issue, indicating that Franceschina views the offer as a potential 'escape from poverty'. Recognizing Burratino's destitution, the Capitano provides him what amounts to alms. When Burratino sits down to eat, outside of his inn, the food that he has bought, he is accosted by two rogues. Declaring that they come from the country of 'Cuccagna', they beguile Burratino with tales of the fantastic paradise where hunger has been eliminated, food fairly drops from the sky, and one is punished for working. This narrative opium, of course, merely serves to distract Burratino from the food that he has set before him, which the two rogues devour. Emotionally, the Tantalian hunger gag works unstably, for Burratino's tears after the event may well taint the audience's laughter. Then, in a scene that only contributes to the servant subplot, after Pedrolino has become at odds with Burratino later in the scenario, Pedrolino solicits him for charity in the guise of a beggar, with an eye patch and a walking stick. (In this unstable economic world, the beggar can become the almsgiver, and vice versa.) As if observing the new social welfare laws, Burratino rebukes him for laziness and tells him to work, whereby Pedrolino protests that where he comes from (the same Cuccagna) one is actually punished for working. A character explicitly named in the cast list as 'Beggar' (Guidone) then enters, disguised as a merchant, who hails Pedrolino for having helped him get his wife pregnant with a male child—the very thing needed by Burratino. Poverty, in *Le burle d'Isabella* is the underside of Pantalone's wealth; it is that which he wishes to buy off and a painful topic that 'motivates the device' (as the Russian Formalists would have put it[32]) of Cuccagna narratives.

Fictionalization

In *Le burle d'Isabella*, the figure of the beggar materializes as a fiction performed by Pedrolino: more often than not in Scala's *favole*, beggars are impersonated. In *La travagliata Isabella* [The Travails of Isabella] Pantalone, '*uomo di ricca fortuna*' [a man of rich fortune], hastily leaves the state of Venice after hiring two thugs to murder two importunate suitors of his daughter. Arriving in Rome with his servant Pedrolino, he assumes the role of a beggar, asking alms from door to door. Although there is some overlap between role and reality here (like Shakespeare's Edgar, Pantalone is a self-imposed exile, itinerant and probably hungry), his servant Pedrolino plays the role in earnest, 'asking alms in a loud voice' and betraying his acute need. Perhaps suggesting the kinship between the actor and the beggar, the disguise of destitution is in fact ubiquitous in the scenario, including Capitano Spavento and his servant Arlecchino. In *Il finto cieco* [The Disguised Blind Man], Flavio is compelled to wander for three years in the disguise of a blind beggar; again, we find significant overlap between role and reality, since Flavio has actually been thrust into a state of itinerancy whereby he is actually supported by mendicancy: the role of beggar operates something like a love penance, with 'beggar' carrying symbolic valance. The *commedia dell'arte* actors did not brandish their very real connections (especially salient for the less successful troupes) with vagabonds and beggars. But as for Edgar, the role was available as a second-order fiction.

In Richard Brome's *The Jovial Crew* (1641), the fiction of poverty, in the form of an assumed disguise, finishes by revealing the central socio-economic contradiction of the play: that Oldrent's happy wealth is in fact founded on his grandfather's exploitation of his neighbour Wrought-On to the point of forcing him into beggary. At the beginning of the play, both Oldrent's steward Springlove and his daughters Rachel and Meriel are drawn to the life of a nearby group of vagabond beggars, which fiction they assume. The beggars themselves, though their poverty is real enough, are also creatures of theatricality, since they perform as strolling players. The play that they eventually perform before Oldrent and other gentlemen,

---

[32] And mentioned by Jameson, *The Political Unconscious*, 44.

moreover, reveals the Oldrent's grandfather's ur-crime. What emerges is that the leader of the beggars, the Patrico, happens to be Wrought-On's grandson, and Springlove turns out to be the son of the illegitimate union of Oldrent's grandfather and Wrought-On's beggar-sister. Both the fiction of the servant and daughters' adoption of the beggar role and the fiction of the play-within-the play reveal the deep structural connections between capitalist land accumulation and new poverty, and help work towards the restitution of those wrongs. In Edgar's stage persona of Poor Tom, in the destitute roles taken on by *commedia dell'arte* characters within the scenarios, and in the *The Jovial Crew* poverty is de-centred but crucially staged in the forms of assumed fictions.

Carnivalization and exaggeration

The destitute rogues who, in Scala's *Le burle d'Isabella*, mesmerize Burratino with tales from Cuccagna, suggest a general principle of the *commedia dell'arte* and the related piazza and banquet literature from which it draws: where there is gluttony (actual or, quite often, fantasized), hunger is not far behind. The proverbial hunger of the *zanni*, behind which the social reality of rural displacement, emigration, and urban poverty can be glimpsed, stages the trope of gluttony as its photographic negative. As Dario Fo's *commedia*-inspired *Sogno dello Zanni* has recently demonstrated, a ravenous *zanni* drifts into an extended dream of a fantastic, Rabelaisian-style meal that he prepares with delirious joy—only to wake up again, of course, to his cruel reality.

The famous Arlecchino actor Tristano Martinelli nicely played starvation and gluttony against each other. In a private publication issued to Henri IV and Maria de' Medici in earnest of their 1601 *tournée* in Paris, Martinelli plays the beggar to the king, in another twist on the role that Edgar plays for Lear. In one image, he entreats an advanced payment in a strange mixture of bravado and destitution, abjectly falling to his knees in a traditional posture of supplication. In another image, we meet him on the perilous highway, armed against bandits, a bowl for food attached to his waist with protruding spoon, and perched in a basket on his back, accompanied by his destitute 'Allichineria', a family of little Arlecchinos. Two mid-sized progeny are on the ground, one voraciously devouring food and the other imploringly holding out an open bowl.[33] But in a series of letters written to Maria de' Medici, Ferdinando Gonzaga, and other sovereigns, he plays the glutton, invoking the delicious food that he has eaten at their tables during previous visits.[34]

[33] Search 'Compositions de rhétorique' online or see Henke, *Performance and Literature*, 165 (image of the supplicating Arlecchino) and 168 (image of Arlecchino and his family).

[34] See, in particular, the 26 October 1612 letter written to Ferdinando Gonzaga in Claudia Buratelli, Domenica Landolfi, and Anna Zinani, eds., *Comici dell'Arte: Corrispondenze* (Florence: Le Lettere, 1993), 386.

As the Fo routine suggests, carnivalesque exaggeration and the representation of gluttonous servants do not come *ex nihilo* but rather from modes of mental distraction or hallucination that, in turn, are generated out of real need. Piero Camporesi even argues that in times of famine peasants were forced to eat bread adulterated with poppy seeds and other mild hallucinogens.[35] Many late sixteenth-century *zanni* poems performed in banquet halls and piazzas nicely match Fo's gag by framing gluttony as a fantastic, desperate dream, extravagant but securely nestled within the parameters of socio-economic reality.[36] Ruzante's desperate peasants in *Dialogo facetissimo* (1529), who have taken to eating animal food, liken themselves to mad and rabid dogs. The hallucinatory 'gag of a hundred men', a version of which Shakespeare plays in Falstaff's multiplying buckram men, occurs first in Ruzante's *Dialogo facetissimo*; after the peasant Menego is mugged by his love rival Nale, he imagines that he has been attacked by no fewer than a hundred men. And at the end of *Il parlamento de Ruzante che iera vegnú de campo*, the character Ruzante rises from a similar beating at the hands of his estranged wife's new thug-protector, similarly complaining to his sceptical compadre Menego that he has been attacked by a hundred men. At the beginning of this play, Ruzante had straggled into St Mark's square in Venice as a war deserter: a destitute, emaciated figure who wonders if he has become a ghost.[37] The prank or 'dream' played by the Lord on Christopher Sly—described in the 1623 Folio text of *Taming of the Shrew* (c.1589–95) as a 'beggar' and as near a Warwickshire indigent as any other character in Shakespeare's plays—is cognate with the dynamic of scarcity-based fantasy that we have identified in the Italian tradition: he will be carried to the Lord's 'fairest chamber', surrounded with 'wanton pictures', bathed, scented, entertained with dulcet music, attended like a grand Lord, and treated to an Italian play.

Vestigial presence

Even for economically successful troupes such as the Gelosi and the Comédie Italienne in Paris, the trope of the hungry *zanni* was encoded in the *Arte*'s DNA, easily retrievable in the gags of Domenico Biancolelli, the great Arlecchino/Harlequin of Molière's time who performed in Paris, and, occasionally, the *zanni* of Goldoni. For Shakespeare and other English early modern dramatists, the hungry *zanni*, along with a few other tropes of the Italian players, such as lascivious old men and lustful servants, never played centre stage (with the exception of Falstaff in *Merry Wives*). What we can observe in Shakespeare, however, is the presence of the starving

---

[35] Piero Camporesi, *Il pane selvaggio* (Milan: Garzanti, 1980).

[36] Henke, *Performance and Literature*, 126–9.

[37] Falstaff's own alternation between self-professed gluttony and his ludicrous, but perhaps real fears that he is 'shrinking' provide another example of this dynamic. My thanks to Henry Turner for pointing this out.

zanni–stingy master encounter in vestigial form. In Shakespeare, it is in the back-story to Launcelot Gobbo and Shylock that we most closely approximate the ratio of scarcity and plenty that plots the *gestus* of the starving *commedia zanni* and his ostensively wealthy master Pantalone. Shylock, who in his age, avariciousness, obsession with money, and other respects, bears striking similarities to the Vene-tian figure Pantalone, animates the Italian *lazzo* of wildly divergent perceptions between master and servant: the former sees gluttony where the latter sees starva-tion. Shylock holds Gobbo to be a gluttonous, shiftless, 'drone', whom he is glad to release to Bassanio, where, Shylock maintains, he will not be able to continue the 'high life' that he experienced under the Jew: 'Thou shalt not gurmandize, / As thou has done with me.../ And sleep and snore, and rend apparel out' (2.5.3–5).[38] Lance-lot, however, is running away from Shylock because his stingy master has left him emaciated. Via dyslexic malapropism, Launcelot declares: 'I am famished in his service; You may tell every finger I have with my ribs' (2.2.106–7).

And as both blind and destitute (he calls himself 'an honest exceeding poor man' [II.ii.52–3]), Old Gobbo on stage would have evoked beggars, whether genuinely blind (like Gobbo himself), or counterfeiting blindness, as in the beggar books and in *commedia dell'arte* scenarios such as *Il finto cieco*. Although Launcelot poses above his station, both in the delayed recognition scene with his father and before Bassanio, he is always a masterless man performing for his livelihood, playing lin-guistic and physical gags with his sidekick, the blind man. The father–son duo tri-umph; liking his wit, Bassanio takes Launcelot into his service, granting him a special livery that some scholars have argued to be the fool's motley. Bassanio's granting of livery to the otherwise destitute Launcelot, therefore, could have easily evoked the noble patronage of acting troupes following the 1572 Act for the Pun-ishment of Vagabonds. Hunger, at least according to Launcelot's own narrative, drives him into a brief 'servant of two masters' gag in search of more food.

Repression

Poverty, especially in neoclassical early modern theatre, may operate as a repressed origin story, barely lying beneath the surface. The vicious quarrel between Lovewit's servant Face and Subtle, the alchemist, that begins Jonson's play quickly betrays the fact that the ingenious devices constructed by both rogues have been launched from the engines of extreme poverty and hunger. Subtle accuses the now 'Suburb-Captain' Face to have been nothing more than a lowly menial servant with a pitiful annual wage of three pounds per year. Quickly, and viciously retorting, Face lays bare Sub-tle's destitute origins, in what is one of the most compelling evocations of poverty and hunger in early modern English drama:

[38] William Shakespeare, *The Merchant of Venice*, in *The Riverside Shakespeare*, 2nd edn., Vol. 1 (Boston: Houghton Mifflin, 1997).

> But I shall put you in mind, sir, at Pie Corner,
> Taking your meal of steam in, from cooks stalls,
> Where, like the father of hunger, you did walk
> Piteously costive, with your pinched-horn-nose,
> . . .
> When you went pinned up, in the several rages
> You'd rakd, and picked from dunghills, before day,
> Your feet in mouldy slippers, for your kibes,
> A felt of rug, and a thin threaden cloak,
> That scarce would cover your no-buttocks—   (*The Alchemist* 1.1.25–8, 33–7)[39]

According to Face, what translates Subtle from a starving, desperate, thread-bare beggar, one who desperately takes but 'meals of steam' from street kitchens, is not the machinations of Subtle's 'dozen of trades' but the capital ('credit for your coals', etc.) that Face claims he has provided him. For Subtle's part, and more mystically, he claims nothing less to have 'sublimed' and 'exalted' Face from his the degradation of his former condition: 'So poor, so wretched, when no living thing / Would keep thee company, but a spider, or worse?' (*The Alchemist* 1.1.65–6). Jonson probably considered Face's narrative of Subtle and Subtle's of Face to be coterminous, capitalism itself a form of mystifying alchemy, in the wake of which is generated the poverty from which the two rogues originally arise. A few of Molière's rogues chart a similar history. Tartuffe, whom Orgon first meets in a condition of beggary and degradation, is clearly motivated by hunger but comes to rule the household and nearly triumphs; the disturbingly charismatic Trissotin from *Les femmes savantes* (1672) similarly rises from the dust and also nearly wins the day.

Criminalization

It is not difficult to see how the disgust and degradation evoked by the two Carriers in the innyard scene in Act II, Scene 1 of *Henry IV, Part One* (1597) translates itself into organized crime. In one of the few direct complaints of poverty in Shakespeare's canon, the two food carriers in the Rochester inn, readying themselves in the early morning to carry their foodstuffs to London, lament the impoverishment and suffering of their horse, and the 'starving' and pitiful turkeys that they are hoping to sell, displacing implicit human suffering onto animals. (*Displacement*, in fact, might be considered as another formal mechanism operating at the passage of social reality into an aesthetic object.) The 'poor jade', suffering from a worn-out saddle that cuts through his hide, has contracted intestinal worms from mouldy food. The carriers simultaneously voice nostalgia, lament, and social critique when they allude to happier times under the previous ostler, who was apparently so keenly attuned to the welfare of his animals that the rise in the price of oats hastened his early death:

---

[39] Ben Jonson, *The Alchemist*, ed. Elizabeth Cook (London: Norton, 1991).

'Poor fellow never joyed since the price of oats rose. It was the death of him' (*Henry IV, Part One* 2.1.11–12).[40] (The play was entered in the Stationers' Register two years after the famine of 1596.) Just as the character Ruzante, in *Il parlamento*, has brought back lice as his only trophy from the wars, the carriers are infested with fleas, and for reasons that Shakespeare chooses to make particularly explicit and disgusting. Because their superiors do not provide them with chamber pots, they are obliged to urinate in the chimney, breeding fleas which then turn back to feast on them as if they were rotting fish. This repulsive food cycle, reminiscent of Hamlet's meditations to Claudius after Polonius' death, returns humankind to the lowest level of animal existence.

The response to such devastating poverty is criminal activity, which via the inn's chamberlain reaches Prince Hal across three degrees of separation. The chamberlain living in the destitute inn overhears the wealthy Franklin plotting a charitable 'pilgrimage' to Canterbury (he means to bequeath 300 gold marks to the cathedral), the chamberlain conveys this information to Gadshill, who relays it to Poins, who informs Falstaff and the Prince. The Franklin's wealth (ironically juxtaposed to the poverty of the inn); the fact that he is accompanied by an accountant; Poins's observation that the London–Canterbury route is also frequented by wealthy merchants: all of these details tend to taint the *geste* of the Franklin's 'charity'. Poins and company just possibly become types of Robin Hood engaged in redistributing wealth, but less as a socialist band of 'merry men' (half of them of course turn on the other) than as part of a Robert Greene-style criminal network. What I wish to emphasize about this particular scene is Shakespeare's frontal engagement with raw poverty, which remains visible through its displacement and the clear connection that the scene establishes between poverty and criminality.[41]

The German, Italian, and English beggar books, in fact, aim to show us that nearly all beggars and vagabonds, save an honest few, have become criminals. As Linda Woodbridge has demonstrated,[42] these texts temper the *utile* of censoriousness and social rebuke with the *dulce* of the humanist jest book, figuring the wily strategems of the fraudulent beggars as so many merry pranks that the culturally and socially superior laughter of the reader can 'correct' in the Bergsonian 'rire'. But despite the acuity of Woodbridge's analysis, we should not follow the way of the beggar books by placing undue emphasis on the colourful figures of the vagabond rogue. Or when we do, we can follow Richard Brome's lead in analysing the 'merry

[40] William Shakespeare, *Henry IV, Part One*, ed. David Bevington (Oxford: Clarendon Press, 1987).

[41] For an excellent theoretical discussion of early modern English criminal culture, see Bryan Reynolds, *Becoming Criminal: Transversal Performance and Cultural Dissidence in Early Modern England* (Baltimore: Johns Hopkins University Press, 2002).

[42] Linda Woodbridge, *Vagrancy, Homelessness, and English Renaissance Literature* (Urbana: University of Illinois Press, 2001).

beggar' in the context of capitalist accumulation and dispossession: the original tragedy of exploitation revealed by the vagabond players. Partly because of an Anglophone bias, studies of poverty on the early modern stage have tended to concentrate on the colourful figure of the criminal rogue, who does frequent the pages of dramatic and non-dramatic English literature. What this essay has attempted to show, however, is that a pan-European, transnational approach can provide a fuller account of the many different forms that the performance of poverty could take, as it was refracted through indirect lenses that, nonetheless, reveal it lying at the heart of early modern theatricality.

FURTHER READING

Carroll, William C. *Fat King and Lean Beggar: Representations of Poverty in the Age of Shakespeare* (Ithaca and London: Cornell University Press, 1996).

Cruz, Anne J. *Discourses of Poverty: Social Reform and the Picaresque Novel in Early Modern Spain* (Toronto: University of Toronto Press, 1999).

Fumerton, Patricia. *Unsettled: The Culture of Mobility and the Working Poor in Early Modern England* (Chicago and London: University of Chicago Press, 2006).

Jameson, Fredric. *The Political Unconscious: Narrative as a Socially Symbolic Act* (Ithaca: Cornell University Press, 1981).

Pugliatti, Paola. *Beggary and Theatre in Early Modern England* (Aldershot and Burlington: Ashgate Publishing, 2003).

CHAPTER 25

FOREIGN

SUSANNE L. WOFFORD

The foreign is intrinsic to theatricality and perhaps is even its essence. Theatre lays bare the fact that the self is as foreign as the foreign characters it plays, and so theatre must seize the foreign, use it, and become it: we cannot have theatre without the foreign. Theatre is and feels like the foreign, but in doing so it becomes most deeply expressive of our local and native identities.

Theatre often appears to be a fantastical form of tourism, in which audiences are presented with the awesome and bizarre nature of foreign places and characters. Examples are easily found on the early modern stage, whether in a *Tamburlaine*, or in subtle parodies of national characteristics and costumes, as in the Dauphin in *Henry V* (he of the sonnet to his horse fame, and the comment 'my horse is my mistress'),[1] the Italians and Frenchman in the wager scene in *Cymbeline* (a chance to stage national parodies), or the Illyrians. This sense of the enjoyment of unusual foreign traits or customs—the fun of the foreign character—can also take subtler form in plays like *Twelfth Night*, where Orsino's foreignness, and the foreignness of Illyria itself, seem to serve as crucial boundary markers in the play: the action takes place in a strange border space between Ottoman and Christian lands, a border place that surprisingly in some scenes comes to seem almost English, for Illyria in moments is 'Englished', as Puttenham says of the translation of figures of speech. Theatre often puts the foreign before our eyes as spectacle and entertainment— taking us to see somewhere else is one of the great capacities of theatre—and, as in the Egypt of Antony and Cleopatra, the foreign can also be the past, that 'foreign country' that we incorporate into our seemingly unitary national identities.

On the other hand, paradoxically, one could say that there is nothing that can truly be called the foreign on stage, although I do not mean this in the way that some materialist readings have suggested, that is, that the foreign is somehow 'contained' or domesticated in any of a variety of ways. If audiences of *Tamburlaine* must have included spectators who identified passionately with the transgressive

---

[1] William Shakespeare, *Henry V*, ed. Gary Taylor (Oxford: Oxford University Press, 1982; 1998), 3.7.42.

foreigner and thrilled to see kings and rulers of any nationality put in cages, we cannot always assume either a xenophobic, nationalistic, or a narrowly moralistic (or even Christian) response to the foreign.[2] In fact, this is precisely one point of the foreign on stage: it can present emotional and political opportunities not acceptable or imaginable in the home culture. Theatre is entirely about bringing the foreign home—putting on the image of something not native and using it to define new local and native possibilities.

Models of theatrical practice imported from abroad profoundly reshaped English theatre from the late 1580s to the early 1600s, of course, as both Robert Henke and Anston Bosman show in their chapters for this collection. The importation of narrative and dramatic traditions into England from the Continent in the 1560s and 1570s, a generation before the so-called golden age of English drama, created a significant intercultural literacy that only intensified with the subsequent flourishing of an international English theatre culture in the 1580s–1610s. Focusing at once on what makes a device, or stage topos, or 'theatregram' (to use Louise Clubb's term)[3] 'foreign', and on what that strangeness meant for the creation of English theatre, one may identify four kinds of foreignness as essential to theatre:

(1) theatrical practice learned from actors, usually travelling actors from the Continent bringing both *commedia dell'arte* scenarios and performative *lazzi*, as well as female performers and performance techniques both courtly, professional, and informal (the work of street performers);
(2) the reshaping of narratives into drama, especially from the rich Italian narrative traditions but also from the French, and the particular theatricality associated with the compression thereby created;
(3) the importing of Italian scripted dramatic conventions, including those of pastoral and tragicomedy, and the emotions associated with baroque intensity on the Continent;
(4) the importing and translating of writing from the ancient world, especially from Latin, into English, in this way importing into plays, at the level of both form and in some cases of plot, Roman formulations of political, ethical, and emotional concerns.

Moreover, attending more closely to these the 'foreign' aspects of English drama has brought with it the need for a new critical vocabulary: 'intertextuality', for instance, has had an old and distinguished career but recently has been re-purposed as a way of understanding the problem of dramatic sources, as Stephen Guy-Bray demonstrates in his essay. With the notion of 'intertextuality' has come the related notion of the 'intertheatrical', as William N. West has argued elsewhere in this collection, in

---

[2] See Thomas Cartelli, *Marlowe, Shakespeare, and the Economy of Theatrical Experience* (Philadelphia: University of Pennsylvania Press, 1991), 67 ff.

[3] See Louise Clubb, *Italian Drama in Shakespeare's Time* (New Haven: Yale University Press, 1989).

which theatrical conventions and performance techniques traverse the English play from afar. But the question of when the 'intertextual' or the 'intertheatrical' become the 'intercultural' is a central one that criticism is only beginning to answer, and as it does so, the notion of 'translation', in all its senses, becomes central. Perhaps it is not a paradox but rather a fundamental definition of theatricality to say that the foreign is always en route to the local, if not already arrived there—to say, therefore, that most of early modern English drama is itself already foreign.

We may begin our approach, therefore, by identifying three troping actions that describe the transformations brought about by the foreign on stage. First, the foreign as intertext, or the trope intertextual. Central to interpreting this trope is the question of how much cultural knowledge is imported when a novella text, say, or a story from Plutarch, is adapted for the stage by an English playwright. Such transportation of cultural knowledge can occur in an intertextual view of theatricality without any authorial agency or 'intentionality', because this knowledge is embedded in the foreign culture and foreign text being transported by the trope. Here the metaphorical action of carrying over cultural meanings and possibilities not assumed or even articulated in an English context becomes quite literal, and it poses a challenge for the historicist thinking of the past few decades, which sought to query the notion of authorial agency but did so without recognizing the 'formal' agency, as it were, of intertextual tropes that carried foreign cultural meanings into English dramatic texts.

Second, the closely related question of the foreign as intertheatrical, or of the intertheatrical trope. Here we move beyond 'text' to the question of performance, the conventions of acting and staging, of emotion and personation. How much cultural knowledge is imported by the very theatrical techniques used to enact a text that has been borrowed and adapted? When a *commedia dell'arte* scenario is imitated, for example, how much of the comic performance tradition that is embodied in the roles is transported into the new work? How many layers of physical and emotional experience are overlaid in one action? If we cannot dismiss these multiple meanings—and I do not think that they can be dismissed—then we must acknowledge the folded, or doubled, or textured meaning of the action that is both expressing the foreign emotion—indeed the entire imaginary interiority of the self—while at the same time being recognized as clearly foreign. What do we make of an emotional register, such as the wonder associated with tragicomedy, imported by performance conventions into English drama and felt to be foreign to the English self, while at the same time beginning to define it?[4]

To highlight what it means to import foreign theatrical techniques and forms of acting as modes of intertheatrical troping, we might take the opening of Middleton and Dekker's *The Honest Whore, Part 1* as an example. It begins with a mourning

---

[4] See Jonathan Gil Harris, *Untimely Matter in the Time of Shakespeare* (Philadelphia: University of Pennsylvania Press, 2008), 69, for another account of intertheatricality, this time in Shakespeare's Henry plays, that links present to past through acting traditions as well as history, and so argues that intertheatricality creates a doubled and different moment of presence.

procession in which a coffin is carried across the stage followed by a mourning father, while a distraught lover (Hippolito) responds by exclaiming his distress and demanding to see the coffin opened. The trick of this scene (the father is only pretending that his daughter is dead to get rid of the suitor) appears in several of Scala's *commedia dell'arte* scenarios, and its transmission into England in this period may have come in part from travelling *commedia* troupes which had been in London in the 1580s, or from other travellers.[5] The play is set in Milan, so it has already marked its Italian roots, and, while we feel the scene to be potentially comic, it nonetheless allows Hippolito a significant tragicomic emotion. How much does the comparison with Pantalone and his style of acting change the perspective, form, and action of the Duke of Milan who is pretending his daughter is dead to thwart the lover? The performance tradition behind the scripted scene subtly undermines the Duke, reminding us of his comic theatrical roots, but such a suggestion is muted, hidden in the folds of the dramatic tradition: the Duke remains a serious and threatening figure, whose authority has nonetheless been subtly questioned. The traditional identification of the play and audience with the lovers against the angry father *senex iratus* has been implied through a theatrical memory, even while the scene remains tragicomic in tone.

Third, translation and the trope intercultural. Here we touch upon what is perhaps the broadest mode of foreign exchange that constitutes early modern theatricality. For the transposition of the foreign onto the English stage does not depend upon a specific intertext, source, verbal allusion, or performative technique but rather draws on a more generalized cultural interchange that enables wholescale assumptions, values, or ideologies to be transported and incorporated into new works. The complexity of such intercultural translation and importation is precisely that broad aspects of cultural practice, foreign and even in a sense unrecognized, can be imported with a plot, a cultural meme, a staged geography, a text, or any kind of foreign theatre practice. While the English actor or playwright may or may not know what Italian burial practices were, the novellas on which *Romeo and Juliet* or *Much Ado About Nothing* were based encode that knowledge and make it available to an audience in a different culture. Given Protestant shifts in burial and mourning practices, these imports may also have created a window onto a cultural past: a dramatic reminder that English culture itself was an historical braid that twisted into itself practices considered foreign in Shakespeare's London.

The intercultural trope contains two opposed features, then: it relies on a certain intercultural literacy that emerges in the period, and it also can enable an importing of foreign cultural knowledge that may not be recognized or understood but becomes

---

[5] See the introduction to Richard Andrews, ed. and trans., *The Commedia dell'Arte of Faminio Scala: A Translation and Analysis of 30 Scenarios* (Lanham, MD: Scarecrow Press, 2008) for a discussion of the comic plots including pretend death scenes. The scenarios were created and performed by the sixteenth-century *commedia dell'arte* troupe *i Gelosi* and written down by Scala. One example of these scenarios is *The Lady Who Was Believed Dead*, also seen as source for *Romeo and Juliet*.

present and available for interpretation as that intercultural literacy increases. Thus, the widespread reading of romances of chivalry in the 1570s and 1580s and the popularity of Painter's *Pallace of Pleasure* in the 1570s as a source of knowledge about French and Italian novellas (not to mention Livy and Plutarch, along with other foreign texts) produced a public with some knowledge of the expectations of many genres imported from non-English literary traditions.[6] It is reasonable to assume, then, that when a novella was staged, for instance, in the 1590s, an English audience would have had a significant cultural competency in understanding the inner form of the genre and in recognizing dramatic shifts in generic possibilities.[7] At the same time, this same audience might not recognize the cultural meanings in certain forms or events staged from these texts. Thus the intercultural trope was at once legible in some aspects of its functioning and was in others invisible as a formal function of the intercultural play.

A good example of the *intercultural* effect of intertheatrical practice around 1600 is the role of Hymen at the conclusion of *As You Like It*, a case where the influence of Italian pastoral drama clearly shapes the ending of the play. In modern productions, Hymen is often played as a villager, a rural person, or anyone else the director can invent, and in the 2010 production at the Brooklyn Academy of Music directed by Sam Mendes with his Bridge Company, Hymen was played as and by Corin, who also sang Hymen's songs as local folk songs. But rarely in modern productions or criticism is Hymen interpreted as a god, nor is the ending seen as incorporating the tragicomic emotion evoked by the presence of a god. In Italian pastoral drama, which was exploding as a genre in the 1560s through the 1590s, the presence of the god Hymen on stage formed a serious part of the fiction. And the possibility that the god might have appeared on-stage at the end of the play to endorse Rosalind's seizing of performative power—here and earlier—changes the degree to which Rosalind's assertion of control for her own romantic goals is itself endorsed. The notion that this final scene concerns the nature of divine presence, or that it shows how love, in finding a solution to the political wounds created by the system of primogeniture, can actually invoke the god and bring him into presence as an endorsement of the lovers' fictional deeds, would seem completely outside the arena of acceptable ironic action in many modern productions, powerful as they may be in other ways. But in fact the play blends its witty ironic heroine with an Italian nymph who can indeed perform magic—a magic highlighted by bringing the god on stage.

---

[6] See, for instance, John J. O'Connor, *Amadis de Gaule and its Influence on Elizabethan Literature* (New Brunswick: Rutgers University Press, 1970) for the enormous popularity of the *Amadis de Gaule* books, as evidenced by their publication histories.

[7] On staged novellas and their importing of or resistance to the foreign, see Melissa Walter, 'Dramatic Bodies and Novellesque Spaces in Jacobean Tragedy and Tragicomedy', in Robert Henke and Eric Nicholson, eds., *Transnational Exchange in Early Modern Theater* (Farnham: Ashgate, 2008), 63–79.

England is a foreign country

The foreign, then, does not remain an outsider to the worlds we imagine we inhabit. The world represented on stage creates a stage metaphor that uses the foreign to present possibilities for the local. This stage metaphor is a not a simile or analogy, as if the local were seen as 'like' or 'similar to' the foreign; rather, it is powerful metaphoric equation. Illyria *is* England, especially in the scenes involving Sir Toby and his contingent and in the resolutely beef-eating Sir Andrew,[8] but the converse is also true: England, including the English stage but also including by extension the English audience, *is* Illyria, and what could happen in Illyria could happen in England too. This paradox states that we cannot have theatricality without the foreign, and yet nothing on stage can ever be separated cleanly from the local, in this case from English identity.

We may say, then, that the 'Foreign' on stage sometimes shapes theatrical experience by naming a place as foreign and then treating it as English: for instance, when Mistress Overdone in the second scene of *Measure for Measure* asks if 'all our houses of resort in the suburbs be pulled down?' (1.2.84–5), the reference to a 'plucking down' (1.2.80) of houses of prostitution in the suburbs turns Vienna into London, so that we wonder how such English figures as Mistress Overdone, with her London geography in mind, or Dogberry and Elbow for that matter, found their places in Vienna?[9] In the meantime, foreign stage techniques, devices, and forms of acting are used to denote subjects that are both English and 'foreign' simultaneously. In both these cases, the foreign can open possibilities for the self and the culture that then can be claimed for the audience and playwright. Here, too, the representation of foreign emotions has its place as a way in which theatre opens emotional possibilities that begin as unusual or even as culturally excluded categories of emotional, religious, or political experience.

Speeches from *As You Like It*, for example, also show us that 'foreign' could mean someone from the other side of the county as well as from the other side of the world or from another metaphysical world entirely (as in the case of Hymen). Foreign can be opposed to 'an inland man', as Rosalind in *As You Like It* claims her imaginary uncle was, and Orlando uses the same phrase about himself: 'Yet am I inland bred'.[10] Even the most common modern meaning, 'from another country or

---

[8] See Robert Applebaum, *Aguecheek's Beef, Belch's Hiccup, and other Gastronomic Interjections: Culture and Food among the Early Moderns* (Chicago: University of Chicago Press, 2006), 4, for beef-eating as a practice marking Englishness.

[9] William Shakespeare, *Measure for Measure*, ed. Brian Gibbons, New Cambridge Shakespeare (Cambridge: Cambridge University Press, 1991). All references to *Measure for Measure* are from this edition.

[10] William Shakespeare, *As You Like It*, ed. Alan Brissenden, Oxford World Classics (Oxford: Oxford University Press, 1993). All references to *As You Like It* are from this edition. Rosalind's comment is at 3.2.331; Orlando's is at 2.7.96.

nation; not domestic or native' has the sub-meaning of 'Unfamiliar or Strange' (meanings 8a and 8b in the *OED*). But much narrower senses of the foreign seem to have been more common in the early modern period:

> 6a. Situated outside an estate, manor, district, parish, province, etc.
>
> 6b. Belonging to or coming from another district, county, society, etc.

Or as a noun:

> B 1b. One not a citizen, or more particularly not a member of the guild, a stranger, an outsider.
>
> B 3a. That part of a town which lies outside the borough or the parish proper.

Most of these are not meanings that attach to the term 'foreign' today, and they highlight the difficulty of generalizing about the foreign on stage. They suggest how it is that almost all characters in a play are by definition 'foreign': most plots begin with someone from elsewhere arriving at a destination that is treated as 'home' or 'native', but that 'elsewhere' can be somewhere quite geographically close.

A similar set of meanings attach to 'outland', which could refer to what we mean by foreigners today: 'Of or belonging to another country; foreign, alien'. But it also could mean someone from the next valley or parish:

> Outlying land (opposed to <u>inland n.</u> 1); *spec. (a) Anglo-Saxon Law* and *Feudal Law*, the portion of a manor or estate not retained by the lord but granted to tenants (now *hist.*); *(b) Sc.* the (usually rougher or less easily cultivated) outskirts of an estate or arable area; also *fig.*

Rosalind's use of the term 'inland' links it with courtliness, furthering the sense that foreignness can also be a measure of distance in social status:

> Rosalind: I have been told so of many; but indeed an old religious uncle of mine taught me to speak, who was in his youth an inland man; one that knew courtship too well, for there he fell in love. I have heard him read many lectures against it, and I thank God I am not a woman, to be touched with so many giddy offences as he hath generally taxed their whole sex withal.   (3.2.329–35)

Orlando too includes courtly manners in his use of the term:

> Duke Senior: Art thou thus boldened, man, by thy distress?
> Or else a rude despiser of good manners,
> That in civility thou seem'st so empty?
> Orlando: You touched my vein at first. The thorny point
> Of bare distress hath ta'en from me the show
> Of smooth civility. Yet am I *inland* bred,
> And know some nurture.   (2.7.91–7, my emphasis)

We know that Orlando does not believe he has been nurtured sufficiently by his brother, but by acknowledging that he has had some proper upbringing, he also acknowledges a certain social status which seems to blend in his mind with *not* being taken for a rude foreigner.

Here some of the central conventions of the pastoral come into play, as the rough-handed Corin is revealed to be more polite, more generous within his limits, more well-mannered, and less 'foreign' than Rosalind, Celia, and Touchstone on the one hand or Orlando on the other. While the play is not certain whether it is set in England or France, or whether the conventions of pastoral so parodied and so enjoyed in the Phoebe–Silvius plot involve an invasion from Roman and Italian Pastoral of an international foreignness, the play is clear that those from very high aristocratic worlds (dukes, for instance, and their heirs) can learn much about how to be a native and how to value local generosity as a centre of humanity from at least one of the pastoral residents of the forest, Corin, who seems in this sense more 'English' than the aristocratic purchasers of his master's hut may be.

It might be worth noting that 'Corin' seems to have been a name associated with pastoral in the English tradition, though he does not appear in Lodge's *Rosalynde*, the source for *As You Like It*, where the character he is modelled on is named Corydon. But that character in turn may be modelled on an older English romance, *Sir Clyomon and Sir Clamydes* (1570), in which the name Corin does appear. The name may first appear in English in relation to pastoral in Tottel's *Miscellany*, where one of the anonymous poems is 'Harpelus complaint of Phillidaes love bestowed on Corin who loved her not and denied him that loved her'.[11] The line may be echoed indirectly by Titania in *A Midsummer Night's Dream* when she accuses Oberon:

> but I know
> When thou hast stol'n away from fairyland
> And in the shape of Corin sat all day,
> Playing on pipes of corn, and versing love
> To amorous Phillida.[12]

As David Bevington has commented, 'Corin's recognizably Arcadian Pastoral name is meant to seem comically inappropriate in that he is not the stereotypical shepherd of Virgil's Eclogues'.[13] Corin's name seems to simultaneously echo the English pastoral tradition and remind listeners of its foreign origins. He is resolutely non-courtly and more grounded in the real limits of hospitality than the literary shepherds Phoebe and Silvius, and more determined to suggest that a local and native wisdom is appropriate to the place of the play. In his own unusual way, he reminds us that the foreign

---

[11] *Tottel's Miscellany: Songes and Sonettes* (1557), ed. Edward Arber (New York: Kessinger Publishing, 2008), 138.

[12] William Shakespeare, *A Midsummer Night's Dream*, ed. Peter Holland (Oxford: Oxford University Press, 2008), 2.1.64–8.

[13] See David Bevington, 'Shakespeare and the Theatrical Performance of Rusticity', in Paul Edward Yachnin and Patricia Badir, eds., *Shakespeare and the Cultures of Performance* (Farnham: Ashgate, 2008), 19.

(the pastoral tradition; the 'French' story of Rosalynde) can relocate and find an English setting if it remains grounded in rustic simplicity and not aristocratic play.

Identifying your 'country' as the county or parish or village within which you live and seeing others as foreigners is common usage in early modern vernaculars. We see it when Rabelais's Panurge refers to the Touraine as his 'pays' ('country'), and a residue of that usage remains in the contemporary French 'vin de pays'. It is what Rosalind and Orlando mean when they refer to themselves or to the fictional uncle as 'an inland man'. Indeed, some recent studies on the extent to which English culture can be seen as having its own ethnicity follow this older usage of foreign or outland, by defining what might be called 'English culture' not as what is national but as what is local in an imaginary sense—in the case of Shakespeare, as the culture typical of midlands gentry in a past far from rural life today. Such a view of rural England as the source of value that has its own strange 'foreign' customs was both idealized and also satirized by Jez Butterworth in his recent play *Jerusalem* ('England's green & pleasant Land').

This quality of the 'foreignness' that is an essential trait and result of theatricality can be recognized in a different form in current critical work on the question of 'Englishness'. Willy Maley, Andrew Hadfield, and others who have led the way in studies of the Celtic component of the 'United' Kingdom have commented on how the new British History (more knowledgeable as it is of an Irish, Scottish, and Welsh presence in Shakespeare and in early modern British political and artistic life) has had little to say about the English component of this union, as though what made something 'English' were transparent and self-evident.[14] In an essay entitled 'Shakespeare-land', Graham Holderness argues that the concept of rural English life developed by the Shakespeare industry and used to characterize 'England' all over the British empire is itself a fantastical construction: 'there is no return to the Stratford of Shakespeare-land: it was never there in the first place'.[15] His point is not just that we have created an imaginary and idealized image of early modern rural life and named it as 'England' but that this very concept of 'England' is itself more foreign and more different than we might imagine, foreign and different from us (scholars

[14] See among others Andrew Hadfield, *Literature, Politics and National Identity: Reformation to Renaissance* (Cambridge: Cambridge University Press, 2009); Antony Easthorpe, *Englishness and National Culture* (New York: Routledge, 1999); Willy Maley and Margaret Tudeau-Clayton, eds., *This England, That Shakespeare: New Angles on Englishness and the Bard* (Farnham: Ashgate, 2010); Brendan Bradshaw and Peter Roberts, eds., *British Consciousness and Identity: The Making of Britain, 1533–1707* (Cambridge: Cambridge University Press, 2003); Philip Schwyzer, *Literature, Nationalism, and Memory in Early Modern England and Wales* (Cambridge: Cambridge University Press, 2009); Willy Maley and Philip Schwyzer, eds., *Shakespeare and Wales: From the Marches to the Assembly* (Farnham: Ashgate, 2010).

[15] Graham Holderness, 'Shakespeare-Land', in Maley and Tudeau-Clayton, eds., *This England, That Shakespeare*, 201–19 (219). Francis Barker, too, has stressed the 'synthesis of possession and loss' essential to Englishness; see Francis Barker, 'Nationalism, Nomadism and Belonging in Europe', in John Joughin, ed., *Shakespeare and National Culture* (Manchester: Manchester University Press, 1997), 233–65 (256).

of Shakespeare), from students introduced to 'England' from across the former British colonies, or even from early modern English life itself. This 'English' way of life—and the values extolled by late nineteenth- and twentieth-century writers such as Sir Walter Raleigh (1861–1922) to idealize English identity—was itself often defined by not being something else: the English were *not* French (cf. the Norman conquest), nor were they Scots (even if they accepted a political union in 1603), nor were they Welsh (even if the Tudor line claimed its legitimacy from its distant Welsh blood and connection to Arthur). This sense of Englishness as a national identity defined by absence, Holderness comments, took on a remarkable complexity during the centuries of colonial and then post-colonial cultural development, when England and Englishness become explicitly the distant place and the foreign identity to be claimed and possessed or criticized and even rejected.

Similarly, in an essay tracing references (most of which are from the later sixteenth century) to the 'motley' character and dress of the Englishman, Margaret Tudeau-Clayton comments that 'more recently the motley character of the English has again been mobilized against xenophobia as well as to promote unity of heterogeneous multiplicity. This is no longer the United Kingdom, which is rather perceived today as falling apart, but a multicultural global unity'.[16] It should not perhaps surprise us to find that Shakespeare's 'England' becomes a place not located exactly in the UK but somewhere else. After all, Jonson already lauded Shakespeare as being beyond the national, even though he does see that transcendence of the national as a source of British pride: 'Triumph, my Britaine, thou hast one to showe / To whom all scenes of Europe homage owe. / He was not of an age, but for all time!' Holderness concludes by arguing that ' "Englishness" as the alien and nomadic, structured by loss and absence, is precisely the kind of nationality we seek today. And if it is to be found anywhere, it will be found in Shakespeare'.[17] Shakespeare is again to be central to 'Englishness', even if that English identity is now found to be foreign.[18]

This might be what the Puritan critics of the theatre also felt: that early modern theatre was fundamentally alien, the nation and the selves it portrayed dangerously foreign. One reason Shakespeare critics have found this foreign, alien, or even nomadic identity of the English in Shakespeare, I believe, is because of the way his plays, like those of many of his contemporaries (who are incorporated into the imaginary state of 'Shakespeare-land'), embrace this central feature of theatricality.

---

[16] Margaret Tudeau-Clayton, 'The "trueborn Englishman": *Richard II, The Merchant of Venice,* and the Future History of (the) English', in Maley and Tudeau-Cayton, eds., *This England, That Shakespeare,* 63–85 (83).

[17] Holderness, 'Shakespeare-Land', 213. See also David Starkey, 'Hooray, England doesn't exist', *The Sunday Times,* 26 April 1998, 5; cited by Tudeau-Clayton, 'The "trueborn Englishman" ', 83.

[18] See Michael Dobson, *Shakespeare and Amateur Performance: A Cultural History* (Cambridge: Cambridge University Press, 2011) for a study that recovers less ironically the values of what Holderness calls 'Shakespeare-land' in the traditions of amateur theatricality characteristic of rural and small town local life.

Indeed, this capacity to dramatize the foreignness of our identities both personal and national—their embrace of and staging of this theatricality—may well be why sixteenth-century dramatic practice is felt to be so modern.

The foreign and class

One effect of this carrying over of the foreign in the English stage is to highlight the many kinds of difference that separate many audience members and actors from the elite of their own nation. Thus, for the actor performing Orsino, does his character feel more foreign because he is an Illyrian or because he is a Duke?[19] Playing the king may have been more shocking in an early modern context than playing the girl or woman, although to us that difference is usually inverted. Differences of rank and status may also have been felt more keenly than differences of language or geography. Thus, towards the end of Dekker's *The Shoemaker's Holiday*, when Margery warns Simon Eyre to speak with care before the king, Eyre responds:

> Away, you Islington whitepot! hence, you hopperarse, you barley pudding full of maggots, you broiled carbonado! Avaunt, avaunt, avoid, Mephistophilus! Shall Sim Eyre learn to speak of you, Lady Madgy? Vanish, Mother Miniver-Cap; vanish! Go, trip and go, meddle with your partlets and your pishery-pashery, your flews and your whirligigs! Go, rub, out of mine alley! Sim Eyre knows how to speak to a pope, to Sultan Soliman, to Tamburlaine an' he were here. And shall I melt, shall I droop before my sovereign? No, come, my Lady Madgy; follow me, Hans; about your business, my frolic freebooters. Firk, frisk about, and about, and about, for the honour of mad Simon Eyre, Lord Mayor of London.   (scene 20, 45–56)[20]

At first it seems that Sultan Soliman and Tamburlaine come to Eyre's mind as images of powerful foreign forces—exaggerated military killers who might terrify someone not as brave as the shoemaker. But then the English King is himself included in this same list, and all of a sudden we are thinking that Soliman, Tamburlaine, and Henry all have something more in common than they are different: that they should frighten lowly shoemakers but won't frighten Simon Eyre. Moreover, not only does Simon Eyre express a comfortable familiarity with the King, but the names of Soliman and Tamburlaine correspond to his own excessive rhetoric, which invokes a mock furor against his wife's caution in a rhetorical mimesis of carnival violence. In other words, not only will Eyre stand up to these foreigners, he is himself like them in rhetoric and power (at least in *his* mind), even if he pricks with an awl and not a

---

[19] See Susanne L. Wofford, 'Foreign Emotions on the Stage of *Twelfth Night*', in Henke and Nicholson, eds., *Transnational Exchange in Early Modern Theater*, 141–58, for a more extended exploration of these issues.

[20] Thomas Dekker, *The Shoemaker's Holiday*, ed. Jonathan Gil Harris (London: Methuen Drama, 2008). All quotations from *The Shoemaker's Holiday* are from this edition.

sword. Like Tambulaine, Eyre comes from a modest origin; he takes on his greater status through the casting on of elaborate costume, and he then lives up to his claims rhetorically. One is in a comic and one a heroic vein, but the hyperbole and over-reaching similar to Eyre and Tamburlaine is part of what makes Eyre's claims about his lack of fear dramatically believable. Given Eyre's remarkable comic excessive rhetoric, how could he be cowed by meeting with the king?

Similarly, the Dutch disguise of Sir Rowland Lacy *seems* to be a typical example of a stereotyped foreigner being made fun of—and he is funny—but he turns out to be a truer Englishman then the other aristocrats in the play, perhaps because he has learned a trade while abroad (as many critics have noted, the play endorses a merchant class anti-aristocratic ideology as the mark of Englishness) but perhaps also because he has incorporated or even become the foreign persona he plays. In a typical form of comic 'both/and' logic, this foreign disguise allows Rose to marry both a shoemaker and an aristocrat, but the 'foreign' element of Lacy's character, the craftsman in Eyre's workshop, earns a rightful place for the aristocrat as someone who will be an appropriate embodiment of English values. *The Shoemaker's Holiday*, a play interested in presenting the myth of origins for a local institution (Leadenhall) and the history of the guild of the Worshipful Company of Cordwainers (which it borrows from popular folk tale and romance), is concerned with what is appropriate to the English; the play clearly presents the aristocracy as practically un-English and suggests that spending time with Dutch shoemakers is the best school for a true Englishman's identity. Here, one effect of the theatrical troping of the foreign is precisely to heighten rank and status associations while de-emphasizing some national differences.[21]

The foreign, then, is a marker of adaptation and intercultural translation and transportation, creating a doubled meaning. Read in one way, the foreign provides a new way to embody and represent the English self. Thus the 'foreign' on stage provides another marker of apparent difference, but often the plays invoke it to underline the ways in which theatricality—and the experience of being in the theatre—is about the crossing of these lines of difference.

The foreign and tragedy

Shakespeare, as we have recently been reminded by Lynn Enterline's magisterial study, *Shakespeare's Schoolroom*, lived in a bilingual culture, and the role of Latin drama in particular, as well as Latin oratory, in shaping notions of what the self should be (especially the gentlemanly self) were deeply inculcated in boys in the

---

[21] On the treatment of the Dutch in London and on the Dutch disguise of Lacy, see Christian Billing, 'The Dutch Diaspora in English Comedy 1598–1618', in Henke and Nicholson, eds., *Transnational Exchange in Early Modern Theater*, 119–40.

schoolroom and from thenceforth throughout their education. Enterline's study has shown us how central drama—playing the role, learning the speech, and perfecting the hand gestures—was to English grammar school education. The base of humanist Latin education in the theatrical imaginary helps to suggest how much the educated self was a foreign, and indeed a Latin self—and, as Enterline notes, sometimes even a self of another gender.[22] If foreign geography becomes a place to locate English experience, then, foreign language (Latin, Shakespeare's French, Irish, Welsh, and Scottish; Dekker's and Marston's Dutch, and so forth), foreign theatrical practice, foreign settings, and foreign emotions, all become sources from which to build an English identity.

Many of the preceding examples have come from comedy, where the stakes of importing the foreign might seem to be generically limited by the fact that comedy aims to reconcile opposites and incorporate differences (as symbolized by the role of marriage in comic closure). Considering this problem in *Hamlet*, then, might provide a useful final example. When Horatio says, 'I am more an antique Roman than a Dane' (5.2.323) and wishes to be able to kill himself with what he hopes is the remaining poison, Hamlet stops him with the words 'Absent thee from felicity a while, / And in this harsh world draw thy breath in pain / To tell my story' (5.2.329–31).[23] For Hamlet, suicide is felicity, and being able to commit suicide with dignity, as the Romans did, was a situation to be valued (one reason Shakespeare as a dramatist may have appreciated Roman history was the opportunity to stage honourable suicide). Horatio may truly be more like an antique Roman. 'Dane' here stands for the harsh world of the present tense *in* the play (set, of course, in the distant past), with its monosyllabic words and words rooted in Old English, like 'a while' (from the Northern Anglo-Saxon *a whīl*); it connects the temporality of the modern with Old English archaic roots and separates both from the Roman world, a world of 'felicity' and, we might note, of 'story'. 'Denmark' is characterized as a 'harsh world', where one draws one's breath in pain: it is the world of the living, while the world of 'felicity' and 'story' or 'history' is the world of the dead. Hamlet asks his philosopher friend to stay alive and forfeit being a Roman in order for his version of events to be told, while Hamlet will leave Denmark for the world of story. The intertwining of words with Anglo-Saxon and Latinate roots in this famous example re-dramatizes the story on the level of language, showing us what the English language can do while reminding us that as English speakers we all must be partly Roman.

In this example, where the foreign enters the closed poisoned inner chambers of the castle by conquest, by imported books, or by 'story', the foreign—here the Roman—is felt as a closer measure of what the self would like to choose as its

---

[22] See Lynn Enterline, *Shakespeare's Schoolroom: Rhetoric, Discipline, Emotion* (Philadelphia: University of Pennsylvania Press, 2011), esp. 25–32 (on the 'habits of alterity' inculcated by the Latin grammar school) and 33–48 (on the centrality of acting and dramatic impersonation).

[23] All references to Hamlet are to *Hamlet: Case Studies in Contemporary Criticism*, ed. Susanne L. Wofford (Boston: St Martin's Press, 1994).

identity, while the Dane seems more alien. Hamlet may be more Dane than antique Roman, but he wishes it were otherwise, for he recognizes the Roman as a state of felicity. The audience only twice escapes the poisoned confines of the castle, once to see Fortinbras on the plain, and once to the graveyard. Here tragedy defines the physical space and the generic boundaries of the dramatic experience. But it is arguable that Hamlet's capacity to finish the action and conclude the play comes in significant degree from his luck in being rescued by another genre, foreign to tragedy: battle and rescue by pirates, a classic Renaissance romance plot.

Hamlet feels himself to be a stranger in his own court, and not only because the King who is 'more than kin', is 'less than kind' (1.2.65). He explains Danish customs to Horatio, and laments them ('More honor'd in the breach than the observance', 1.4.16). His education has taken him to Protestant Wittenberg, and the book he is reading in Act 2 may be *The Praise of Folly* by Erasmus. He seems briefly more Danish when he laments the fact that the King had 'Popp'd in between th' election and my hopes' (5.2.65), a rare allusion to tanistry and to his political ambitions (the next after his comment about being 'too much in the sun' in 1.2.67) and to his rivalry with Claudius for the throne. But in most ways Hamlet feels himself to be a foreigner forced to accept 'kin' who are both too close and very alien. We might consider whether discovering oneself to be the foreigner at home can be read as a mark of tragedy, while discovering oneself to be at home in foreign places, as occurs for all the court characters in *As You Like It* or for Viola in *Twelfth Night* (where she finds herself at home in Illyria and in a foreign gender) could be a mark of comedy. In each case, however, the central recognition is that the self is both foreign and native, whether that recognition is painful or fulfilling.

How foreign then is the Roman or the Dane, the Italian or the Illyrian? No more foreign than the self, its interiority unknown, its emotions hidden, its secrets offstage and undisplayed. Playing the foreign makes it possible to stage and even perhaps to recognize the foreign within the self—and for that reason acting and the theatricality of the early modern English stage drew on foreign models, foreign dramatic techniques, and foreign selves. In so doing, the theatre opened the world within and outside the plays to culturally excluded emotions, political possibilities, and arenas for action. These, while not being native, provided an articulation of a complex English identity, one that was never simply nationalist or native, but hybrid and 'foreign'. The bilingual education of the English and their 'foreign' theatre, in which the characters, actions, and plots all come from afar, suggest that English national identity in this period can best be understood through its deep immersion in and growth from foreign performances, foreign plots, and foreign politics.

FURTHER READING

Enterline, Lynn. *Shakespeare's Schoolroom: Rhetoric, Discipline, Emotion* (Philadelphia: University of Pennsylvania Press, 2011).

Henke, Robert and Eric Nicholson, eds. *Transnational Exchange in Early Modern Theater* (Farnham: Ashgate, 2008).

Hoenselaars, A. J. *The Italian World of English Renaissance Drama: Cultural Exchange and Intertextuality* (Newark: University of Delaware Press, 1998).

Levin, Carole and John Watkins. *Shakespeare's Foreign Worlds: National and Transnational Identities in the Elizabethan Age* (Ithaca: Cornell University Press, 2009).

Marrapodi, Michele. *Shakespeare, Italy, and Intertextuality* (Manchester: Manchester University Press, 2005).

Redmond, Michael J. *Shakespeare, Politics, and Italy* (Farnham: Ashgate, 2009).

CHAPTER 26

MOBILITY

ANSTON BOSMAN

I

At the border checkpoint, a familiar scene plays itself out. The travellers approach the booth, shuffling luggage along the ground and smoothing out their paperwork. The agent scans the faces. He notes the clothes, the sacks bulging with equipment, how the bodies move and how they stand still. They lean in towards one another, whispering; he listens for the rhythm of the words. Now here they are before him, eye to eye, passing the documents over. In a cool tone, his practised questions begin: What are their names? Where are they from? What is their final destination? Their religious affiliation? Will they be staying locally? Where and for how long? As they speak, the agent takes note of their accent and checks their responses against the documents he has unfolded:

> Messieurs, Comme les presentz porteurs, Robert Browne, Jehan Bradstriet, Thomas Saxfield, Richard Jones, auec leurs consortz estanz mes Joueurs et seruiteurs ont deliberé de faire vng voyage en Allemagne, auec Intention de passer par les païs de Zelande, Holande et Frise. Et allantz en leur dict voyage d'exercer leurs qualitez en faict de musicque, agilitez et joeuz de comedies, Tragedies et histories, pour s'entretenir et fournir à leurs dispenses en leurs dict voyage. Cestes sont partant pour vous requerir leur monstrer et prester toute faueur en voz païs et Jurisdictions, et leur octroyer en ma faueur vostre ample passeport soubz le seel des Estatz, à fin que les Bourgmestres des villes estanz soubz voz Jursdictions, ne les empeschent en passant d'exercer leur dictes qualitez part tout. Enquoy faisant, je vous en demeuray à tous obligé, et me trouuerez très appareillé à me reuencher de vostre courtoisie en plus grand cas. De ma chambre, à la court d'Angleterre ce xme jour de Febvrier 1591.
>
> Vostre tres affecsionné à vous fayre plaisir et sarvis
> C. Howard

Fair enough. These people match their papers. The agent clears his throat: everything, he says, appears to be in order. The group will need a health certificate—he slides the form across the desk—for which the town charges a small fee. Each member of the company will also receive a ticket to give to the innkeeper, who will then provide a confirmation to be taken to the town hall for entry into the register. Certificate, fee, tickets: the agent waves the travellers on. These are foreigners, Englishmen no less, but hardly trouble. On the other hand, he thinks, hardly profit either. Trouble is what gets you the big tips.

The passport as comic script

The vignette here is a fragment of what one might call, adapting a phrase from Caroline Walker Bynum, theatre history in the comic mode. A historian of the fragmentary body, Bynum characterizes her scholarship as similarly partial and perspectival, a discourse playfully resistant to the tragic hero, the total narrative, and the inexorable conclusion. 'In comedy,' she writes, 'there is resolution for only a moment,' and so 'a comic stance towards doing history is aware of contrivance, of risk. It always admits it may be wrong. A comic stance knows there is, in actuality, no ending (happy or otherwise)—that doing history is, for the historian, telling a story that could be told another way'.[1] My subject in this essay—what difference mobility once made to early modern theatre and now makes to our accounts of it—seems to me paradigmatically comic in Bynum's sense, and I therefore began this exploration by setting a single piece of evidence in a fictive frame.

Facing a document over four centuries old, a passport written in London and now archived in The Hague, I realized it captured not merely what I'd been looking for, namely theatre in motion, but also something unexpected: evidence that the very movement of culture across borders appears structured as a theatrical scene. This passport, in other words, is a script. Originating in the office of Charles Howard, the Lord High Admiral, it anticipates and aims to control interactions between its bearers, some named and unnamed English actors who were members of the Admiral's Men, and unspecified officials on the European continent. To bridge the gap between English, Dutch, and German, it is written in French. Let us re-examine it in translation:

> Sirs, Since the present bearers, Robert Browne, Jehan Bradstriet, Thomas Saxfield, Richard Jones, with their company, being my players and servants, have decided to make a journey into Germany, with the intention of passing through the countries of Zeeland, Holland, and Friesland, and in taking their aforementioned voyage to exercise their skills in music, agility, and playing comedies, tragedies, and histories, in order to support themselves and to defray their expenses during their aforementioned voyage. I write this to request that you show and extend them every favour in your countries and jurisdictions, and that you grant them on my behalf your full passport under the state seal, to the end that the mayors of towns under your jurisdiction should

---

[1] Caroline Walker Bynum, 'In Praise of Fragments: History in the Comic Mode', in *Fragmentation and Redemption: Essays on Gender and the Human Body in Medieval Religion* (New York: Zone Books, 1991), 23–5.

not hinder them from practising their art everywhere. In so doing, I remain indebted to all, and find myself very bound to repay your courtesy in greater measure. From my chamber at the English court this tenth day of February 1591.

Most affectionately yours, at your pleasure and service,
C. Howard

We may read this passport as a script for theatrical mobility on at least three levels. Working inwards in concentric order, we could term these levels geographical displacement, physiological dynamism, and ontological instability. On the other hand, following Bynum's ludic prompt, we might call them the Comedy of the Touring Company, the Comedy of the Agile Player, and the Comedy of the Shifting Identity.

Practising their art everywhere

The outermost movement described by the passport—the travels of acting troupes across regions, countries, and continents—has long been mentioned in histories of the English stage. Yet it was typically relegated to the margins as a curiosity and has only lately begun to gain acceptance as a pattern for early modern theatricality. In a brief section on 'International Companies' in his four-volume theatre history published in 1923, E. K. Chambers included Howard's letter as proof of English players active on the Continent, but he neither translated nor analysed its contents.[2] In 1980, Willem Schrickx provided a fresh transcription of the document and locked horns with Chambers over whether the actors were servants of the Lord Admiral, but again no claim was made for the wider significance of the company's travels.[3] The passport was briefly noted in later studies, including Jerzy Limon's *Gentlemen of a Company* (1985), but only in the past decade have the passport and its context of transregional and transnational theatre come into anything like sustained focus. In 2004, I published the first of several essays on the subject under the rubric of 'Renaissance intertheater', while Ralf Haekel came out with a German monograph that approached the problem, as it were, from the opposite side.

Subtitled 'An Inquiry into the Origins of the German Professional Theatre', Haekel's probing book *Die Englischen Komödianten in Deutschland* interpreted the English comedians, including those mentioned in the 1591–2 passport, as a formative influence on the German stage. Haekel argued that the hallmark of those comedians was their mobility, and that the itinerant stage, characterized by ensemble work, the repertory principle, and deployment in multiple social and religious spheres, was their necessary theatrical form.[4] Tracking the companies' movements between courts and cities as well as between Catholic and Protestant regions, Haekel

---

[2] E. K. Chambers, *The Elizabethan Stage* (Oxford, Clarendon Press, 1923), II: 274.

[3] Willem Schrickx, 'English Actors at the Courts of Wolfenbüttel, Brussels and Graz', *Shakespeare Survey* 33 (1980), 153–68.

[4] Ralf Haekel, *Die Englischen Komödianten in Deutschland. Eine Einführung in die Ursprünge des deutschen Berufsschauspiels* (Heidelberg: Winter Verlag, 2004), 321.

took earlier scholars to task for stressing the actors' residencies on the model of musicians; in fact, he insisted, the players' default mode was one of frequent migration. In showing how Elizabethan acting founded the tradition of professional itinerant performance in Germany, Haekel reminded us how late into the eighteenth century a fixed national theatre came to be founded in that country.

Meanwhile, in Britain and the United States, new scholarship was uncovering mobility as a driving force in early English theatre. Supported by data from the Records of Early English Drama (REED) project and the Malone Society, Anglo-American historians began to document the vibrancy of performance outside London and its playhouses, revealing a well-established network of travelling players who brought a range of entertainments to diverse audiences in a variety of spaces. Siobhan Keenan's *Traveling Players in Shakespeare's England* (2002), for instance, reconstructed 'provincial dramatic culture' in churches, taverns, schools, markets, and country houses; and the last of these places was a focus of an important article by Barbara Palmer in a *Shakespeare Quarterly* symposium titled 'Theatrical Movements' (2005).[5] 'The Elizabethan players,' Palmer wrote, 'perpetuated a legacy of mobility, a rich inheritance of tested routes, circuits and communication networks, which they no doubt altered to their own needs but which they most surely did not invent'.[6] Palmer's bemusement at 'how it is possible so persistently to misunderstand, underestimate, or distort the mobility of traveling players' was echoed by the symposium editor S. P. Cerasano, who diagnosed inertia in standard accounts of 'actors, companies, playbooks, literary sources, audiences, theatrical financiers' and urged scholars to remap the history of early modern theatre.[7]

To be sure, work on the intercultural dimension of the period's drama was increasingly making clear that the infrastructure of roads, waterways, commerce, and communications that made theatrical mobility possible also extended beyond England, which was then less insular by geography than may now appear, and was certainly never so by attitude or practice. Comparatists have mapped early modern theatre 'both in the ways that it represented transnational exchanges and in the ways that it enacted them', as Robert Henke has put it, 'by means of border-crossing acting troupes; the transmission of theatrical tropes and gags between actors and playwrights; the exchanges of actors, playwrights and theatrical culture at the aristocratic and thus "supranational" level; the representation of "foreign" identity; the transmission and translation of printed plays across national borders' and other vehicles'.[8] Such studies implied a relay between theatrical materials and dramatic

---

[5] Siobhan Keenan, *Traveling Players in Shakespeare's England* (London: Palgrave Macmillan, 2002), 86.

[6] Barbara Palmer, 'Early Modern Mobility: Players, Payments, and Patrons', *Shakespeare Quarterly* 56.3 (2005), 263.

[7] Palmer, 'Early Modern Mobility', 263–4; S. P. Cerasano, 'Theatrical Movements', *Shakespeare Quarterly* 56.3 (2005), ix.

[8] Robert Henke, 'Introduction', in Henke and Eric Nicholson, eds., *Transnational Exchange in Early Modern Theater* (Aldershot: Ashgate, 2008), 1.

imagination by which migration in one domain spurred innovation in the other and vice versa. On a grander scale, Stephen Greenblatt has signalled just this circularity in a recent 'mobility studies manifesto' that directed attention to 'the physical, infrastructural, and institutional conditions of movement' in order to understand larger cultural tensions, mixtures, and flows: 'Almost every one of these metaphorical movements,' he argued, 'will be understood, on analysis, to involve some kinds of physical movement as well.'[9] The 1592 passport, to return to our example, should be investigated as a key not merely to the actors' route, with its conduits, controls, and costs, but also to the difference movement makes to their productions as creative translations of a mobile culture.

Their skills in music, agility, and playing

The passport-as-script does more than forecast the geographical displacement of its bearers. It promises the detonation of each actor's body into energetic performance. The study of early modern theatricality, however, has rarely considered 'agility' a worthy subject; in fact, undervaluing the physical dexterity of travelling companies in favour of their linguistic and literary skill dates back to the sixteenth century.[10] Thus Fynes Moryson, travelling in the Netherlands, noted disdainfully that 'when some cast Players of England came into those partes, the people not vnderstanding what they sayd, only for theire Action followed them with wonderfull Concourse.'[11] Popular admiration for musical and acrobatic virtuosity is a commonplace in foreigners' accounts of the English players abroad (similar fandom attached to *commedia dell'arte* troupes working in France). But it equally typifies foreigners' accounts of what they liked most on London stages: the Swiss medical student Thomas Platter, for instance, noted in his travel diary seeing a performance of *Julius Caesar* at the Globe in 1599 'most skilfully acted' ('gar artlich agieren').[12] In sixteenth-century German, the verb *agieren*, which shares the Latin root *agere* with the English nouns 'action' and 'agility', is the dynamic antonym to static terms like *vorlesen* (to recite) or *deklamieren* (to declaim).[13] Often specified by phrases like *mit den Händen* or *Armen* or *Beinen*—with the hands, arms, or legs—it is exemplified in the account Platter gives of the graceful dance concluding the play.

Neither Moryson nor Platter attends here to the content of the drama. In both examples, 'action' or 'acting' is a formal category, a process of embodiment rather than representation, and its goal is to shape compelling gestures and seductive

---

[9] Stephen Greenblatt et al., *Cultural Mobility: A Manifesto* (Cambridge: Cambridge University Press, 2010), 250.

[10] See, however, Evelyn Tribble's essay on 'Skill' in this volume.

[11] *Shakespeare's Europe: Being unpublished chapters of Fynes Moryson's Itinerary*, ed. Charles Hughes (New York: Benjamin Blom, 1967), 373.

[12] Chambers, *Elizabethan Stage*, II: 364.

[13] *Deutsches Fremdwörterbuch*, ed. Hans Schulz, Otto Basler, and Gerhard Strauss (Berlin: Walter de Gruyter, 2004), 1: 211.

movement. Early modern playwrights displayed some ambivalence towards this histrionic agility. John Webster, for instance, wrote of an 'excellent actor' (probably Richard Burbage) that 'by a full and significant action of body he charmes our attention: sit in a full Theater, and you will thinke you see so many lines drawne from the circumference of so many ears, whiles the *Actor* is the *Center*'.[14] Note how what begins as praise of the performer's full-bodied 'action' narrows as the actor is connected to the 'ears' of theatre-goers: it turns out to be the play's *language* that holds the audience spellbound. Webster's own metaphor immobilizes the scene by fixing the audience's hearing-lines in an idealized geometry—one to which early modern stage design gives the lie. In practice, acoustic distractions beset the theatres of the age no less than visual obstructions, and players had to move around a lot merely to keep the largest number of people engaged. On travels in the provinces or overseas, where obstacles to audience comprehension ranged from makeshift stages to a language barrier, the deployment of 'action' was an imperative.

No member of an itinerant troupe showcased his agility to the same degree as the clown. By the time Thomas Platter visited the Globe, the London amphitheatres had mostly confined the clown's rhyming and dancing, which had earlier been interspersed throughout the story and given free rein at its conclusion, to the separate and structured jig that Platter enjoyed.[15] But touring versions such as Moryson witnessed in Holland broke that confinement, exploiting a more flexible blend of scripted plot and bravura improvisation. Not coincidentally, extant stage directions for these versions echo the peripatetic rubrics of medieval drama, epitomized by the instruction in the Coventry Shearmen and Tailors' nativity play that '*Herod rages in the pageant [wagon] and in the street also*'.[16] Such comic exuberance, transgressive in both tone and space, is what Shakespeare's Hamlet targets in his rebuke to the travelling company of actors arrived at Elsinore to 'let those that play your clowns speak no more than is set down for them' and to 'avoid' a histrionic style that 'out-Herods Herod'.[17]

Yet when *Hamlet* itself travelled beyond London, in English and foreign-language versions alike, the power relation between princely text and clownish performance was rebalanced. In the First Quarto, abridged for provincial touring, Hamlet mugs and quips in exactly the style he appears to be censuring, and the German version *Der Bestrafte Brudermord* is stuffed with the kinds of supercharged effects that rely on a player's virtuoso 'action'. Like the Coventry play, these scripts convey only a hint of what must have been a chief source of the production's appeal. Imagine, for instance, the musical or acrobatic skill required of the clown in a German rendition

[14] Sir Thomas Overbury, *New and Choice Characters of Several Authors* (1615), sig. M5v, cited and attributed to Webster in Chambers, *Elizabethan Stage*, IV: 257–8.

[15] David Wiles, *Shakespeare's Clown: Actor and Text in the Elizabethan Playhouse* (Cambridge: Cambridge University Press), 43.

[16] Hardin Craig, ed., *Two Corpus Christi Plays* (London: Oxford University Press, 1931), line 783 stage direction.

[17] William Shakespeare, *Hamlet*, ed. Ann Thompson and Neil Taylor (London: Thomson Learning, 2006), 3.2.13–14.

of Thomas Dekker's *Old Fortunatus*, the surviving text of which includes a stage direction, occurring five times in the first three acts, that declares 'Allhier agiret Pickelhering'. We might translate this elliptical instruction as 'here Pickleherring acts' or better, to preserve the sense of *agieren*, 'performs actions'.[18]

Highlighting the virtuosity of early modern players should not, to be sure, lead one crudely to equate them with today's gymnasts, concert musicians, or even stand-up comedians. For whereas those modern performers are trained to deliver a set routine with minimal improvisation, the 'action' practised by itinerant companies in the sixteenth and seventeenth centuries needed to be profoundly contextual, extemporized, and interactive. Rather than a fixed and discrete unit of imitation— what the Italianist Louise George Clubb has called a 'theatregram' and, in a broader context, the biologist Richard Dawkins termed a 'mimeme' or 'meme'—'action' on the early modern stage is better described as a mutable form of engagement, an exertion of force contoured in terms of place and moment in order to provoke a reaction from specific addressees.[19] For this reason the *audience* is crucial to understanding early modern theatrical mobility. In the antithetical responses of Moryson and Platter, for instance, we see how the players repulsed or attracted beholders in a metaphorical sense; but Moryson's remark on the company's literal followers suggests measurable knock-on effects of histrionic agility. The 'wonderfull Concourse' with which he says admirers 'followed' the supposedly incomprehensible troupes 'only for theire Action' concedes how agility extended beyond actors to include an audience whose bodies they moved no less than their minds.[20]

Moryson's account of foreign reception exaggerates. Accounts of early modern performance make clear that actors engaged audiences on both an embodied and a fictional plane; indeed, they suggest that the capacity to move between these planes of engagement may itself constitute a higher-level form of agility. Besides his interest in dance, for instance, Platter was intrigued by dramatic plot; his diary reconstructs the story of an unnamed play he attended at another London theatre. Another traveller, the German court physician Johannes Rhenanus, was so fascinated by what he saw on stage in London that he contrived to observe a play in rehearsal and subsequently attempted to write drama in the English style. In the preface to his translation of Thomas Tomkis's university comedy *Lingua*, which he entitled *Speculum Aestheticum* (1613), Rhenanus praises the 'composition' as well as the 'action' demanded by English plays, attributing their pre-eminence in Europe to

---

[18] *Comoedia von Fortunato und seinem Seckel und Wuenschhuetlein*, in *Spieltexte der Wanderbühne*, vol. I, pp. 137 (end of act I), 146 (end of act II), 150, 154, 159 (in course of act III). This citation is drawn from Tom Pettitt, 'Opening the Gutenberg Parenthesis: Media in Transition in Shakespeare's England', MiT5 [Media in Transition 5], Massachusetts Institute of Technology, 27–29 April 2007, http://www.web.mit.edu/comm-forum/mit5/papers/Pettitt.Gutenberg%20Parenthesis.Paper.pdf (accessed Jan. 2013).

[19] Louise George Clubb, *Italian Drama in Shakespeare's Time* (New Haven: Yale University Press, 1989), 6 and Richard Dawkins, *The Selfish Gene* (Oxford: Oxford University Press, 2006 [1976, second edn. 1989]), 192.

[20] That audience was, to be sure, more diverse and discerning than Moryson claims.

a double expertise in poetry and performance.[21] What these witnesses record has been theorized by Robert Weimann as a permeable division between 'the world of the play' and 'the play in the world' that affords an 'interplay of presentation and representation, game and fiction, theatrical craftsmanship and classical story' in which 'a performer...is, and is not, lost in a character'.[22] In this theory, an actor's dramaturgical to-and-fro across stage space corresponds to an epistemological flexibility between sport and role; although the literal positions of player and theatre-goer are residually present in his analysis, Weimann in fact scrutinizes the figurative moves by which the actor/character approaches or distances the audience. A term he sometimes uses for this skill is 'agility': to be agile in this sense is to play the changes between stillness and motion, actor and audience, and physical and meta-phorical mobility.[23]

Yet the paradoxical tendency of this argument is to pattern contingencies into configurations, and thereby to subsume restless movement into reassuring stasis. This balancing propensity of theory will be revisited in the second half of this chapter, which examines the textual legacy of the itinerant companies. For now, the pressing question is how the precarious identity of the early modern actor changes when he starts to travel. What was the effect of transcultural migration on the actor's capacity to manage a subjectivity that was already relational and mobile? The formal agility required by conventions of performance on the established stages of the homeland needed to be recalibrated when players journeyed into unfamiliar terrain. At its worst, such destabilization threatened ruin; at its best, it promised reinvention. 'We can be bankrupts on this side,' one writer asserted in 1625 on behalf of the actors, 'and gentlemen of a company beyond sea: be burst at London, and pieced up in Rotterdam.'[24] But what did casting off the anchorage of one's identity look like in these cases? What can they teach us about the intersection and the interference between theatre and travel?

The present bearers...being my players

Let us return one last time to the 1592 passport. I have called this document a script for theatrical mobility, inasmuch as it charts the itinerancy and vaunts the athleti-cism of certain members of the Lord Admiral's Men. Yet this essay's opening vignette points to a more fundamental sense in which Howard's letter is at once the promise and vestige of border-crossing performances. Beneath the legal formulas, assertions

---

[21] See the reprinting of the preface in Wilhelm Creizenach, *Die Schauspiele der englischen Komödi-anten* (Darmstadt: Wissenschaftliche Buchgesellschaft, 1967), 328.

[22] Robert Weimann, *Author's Pen and Actor's Voice* (Cambridge: Cambridge University Press, 2000), 67–8.

[23] Weimann, *Author's Pen*, 75.

[24] B. V., *The Run-awayes Answer to a Booke called, A Rodde for Runne-awayes* (London, 1625), sig. B3r.

of patronage, and certifications of state power lies the basic claim the document shares with any modern passport: that the persons carrying the paper really are the individuals named within it. Denoting its 'present bearers' as persons appearing in the here and now, the spatio-temporal rhetoric of the 1592 letter anticipates the best-known interrogation in early modern drama. The passport promises a reliable answer to the question with which Shakespeare's Barnardo opens *Hamlet*: 'Who's there?'

But should it not make a difference that these particular bearers are in the same gesture being certified as 'players', that is, specialists in the falsification of place, time, and personhood? After all, the skill that modern critics such as Weimann have praised as '[traversing] the intricate field between present actors and their absent dramatic identities' is precisely what early modern moralists denounced as hypocrisy.[25] Like the actor's part, the passport is a paper out of which the bearer generates a persona. This insight depends on recognizing that a passport is not, as we conventionally think, an inert 'identity document'. It is rather an active 'identification document', one that *produces* a new identity distinct from that of the bearer, who is then bound to perform that identity within the specific contexts— linguistic, institutional, and geographical, to name only a few—that secure 'identification' itself.[26] In other words, 'Who's there?' cannot be answered before the question 'Where are you?' Recalling our circles of mobility, we may imagine responses to the latter question in concentric topologies: in England or Germany, at the border post or in a theatre, far upstage or close downstage, etc. Each performance of identity will be 'framed' within the constraints of social structure and organization.[27] So let us ask: What are the restrictions and affordances of the passport-as-script here, and how much control does the bearer have in the shaping of his role?

Consider how the 1592 passport identifies the persons presenting it. Between 'bearers' and 'players' appears the following list: 'Robert Browne, Jehan Bradstriet, Thomas Saxfield, Richard Jones, with their company.' Not all the actors are named; nor is the number of travellers specified. Yet even some of the named individuals, whose authority in this context is second only to that of the Lord Admiral, appear in unfamiliar guise. We easily recognize Robert Browne and Richard Jones, but presume that 'Thomas Saxfield' was Thomas Sackville, and 'Jehan Bradstriet' was John Bradstreet. So far, so good: erratic spelling, especially of proper names, is ubiquitous in the early modern age. That Shakespeare's

---

[25] Weimann, *Author's Pen*, 75. On hypocrisy, see Jonas Barish, *The Antitheatrical Prejudice* (Berkeley: University of California Press, 1981), 91–3.

[26] See Craig Robertson, *The Passport in America: The History of a Document* (Oxford: Oxford University Press, 2010), 263–4, fn. 22.

[27] See Erving Goffman, *Frame Analysis: An Essay on the Organization of Experience* (Harmondsworth: Penguin, 1975), 13.

name was commonly spelled in half a dozen ways, and more rarely in the same number of variations again, is the standard measure of what scholars call 'a semantic field that, not yet ruled by lexical statute, accommodates verbal vagrancy'.[28]

Except that not all vagrants or variations are equal. It is harder simply to dismiss the multiple forms that Sackville's name took in Europe in the context of what we might call, to borrow a phrase from Bacon, other 'migrating instances' of translated identities: John Coprario, the composer, who changed his name from plain John Cooper or Cowper after studying music in Italy, later securing the patronage of Sir Robert Cecil; or the eminent Anglo-German violist Dietrich Stoeffken, Steffkin, or Steffkins, often called Theodore; or the Jesuit playwright Emmanuel Lobb, who entered the English College at Rome under the pseudonym of Joseph Simons, by which he became generally known; or the Flemish-born Nicholas Tooley, listed among the 'principal actors' in Shakespeare's first folio, whose original name appears to have been Wilkinson, and who appended both surnames to his will.[29] Nor can it be a coincidence that the name of the period's most elusive dramatist, covert traveller, and secret agent should occur in no fewer than nineteen forms: Marlowe, Marley, Mario, Morley, Marlyn, Marlin, Marlen, Malyn, Marly, Marlye, Marlinge, Marlyne, Marline, Merlin, Marlow, Marloe, Morle, Marlynge, and Marklin.[30]

These examples open up the shadow world of the early modern traveller, in which identities were fissured and fashioned to secure celebrity and privacy alike. When later biographies of actors stitch together identities that their bearers may have had an interest in keeping separate, they erase mobility as a hallmark of artistic practice. The diaries of Thomas Platter illustrate the point. Platter's now-famous attendance at the Globe in 1599 was preceded by studies in France and travels there and throughout the Continent. His meticulous records include transcriptions of travel documents and accounts of border passage and control, and they reveal that in the years before he praised the English players he had proved to be something of an actor himself. Time and again the young man finessed problems in his journeys that could not be solved through connections or bribes by stating a false name, birthplace, or religion. In papal Avignon he posed as a Catholic and his Polish companion claimed to be French: 'We gave

---

[28] See David Kathman, 'The Spelling and Pronunciation of Shakespeare's Name', http://shakespeareauthorship.com/name1.html (accessed Jan. 2013); and Margreta de Grazia and Peter Stallybrass, 'The Materiality of the Shakespearean Text', *Shakespeare Quarterly* 44 (1993), 264.

[29] On *instantiae migrantes* or 'travelling instances', see Francis Bacon, *Novum Organum*, ed. Thomas Fowler (Oxford: Clarendon Press, 1878), II: 23, 413. The biographical facts derive from Chambers, *The Elizabethan Stage*, vol. 2; Edwin Nungezer, *A Dictionary of Actors* (London: Oxford University Press, 1929); and a series of articles on 'Elizabethan Actors' by Mark Eccles in *Notes & Queries* 236 (1991), 38–49 and 454–61; 237 (1992), 293–303; and 238 (1993), 165–76.

[30] R. M. Cornelius, *Christopher Marlowe's Use of the Bible* (New York: Peter Lang, 1984), 297 fn. 16.

our names, too,' Platter writes, 'but not our proper ones'.[31] At the border with Spain, his group claimed to be French merchants; in Perpignan, he acquired a Catalan safe-conduct under the name 'Tomas Plateros'; and in Barcelona he passed himself off as a German Catholic come for the marriage of the Spanish queen and to worship relics. As Valentin Groebner writes in his study of early modern surveillance: 'To what extent was the traveling citizen of Basel himself while on his journey throughout Europe?'[32] Groebner situates Platter's tour within the larger rise of impostors or impersonators and proxy persons or doppelgangers, the former assuming the identity of real persons presumed dead, often using fake insignia, and the latter inventing whole life histories backed up with credit notes or letters of recommendation. To insist against this background that Thomas Platter was 'identical' to Tomas Plateros would be to ignore the self-fashioning strategy by which variable orthography shades into the creation of an alias and, in bureaucratic terms, a new person.

The world of early modern theatre offers intriguing variations on these types of counterfeit performances. On the side of the impersonators we find the case of Ralph Reeve (alias Rodolphus Reeffe, Rudolphus Riweus, Rudoplphus Riuius, or Robertus Riuius), who for the better part of a decade led a troupe of English players performing regularly at the Frankfurt fair and the court of Maurice of Hesse. On his return to England in 1611, Reeve brought a company to Norwich and presented a licence issued to the actor Philip Rosseter, claiming to be Rosseter himself. But the civic authorities uncovered the deception and Reeve was forced to confess to it. Did Reeve take this risk because his long absence made him harder to recognize? And to what extent, if any, was Rosseter, who was very much alive and later became a co-patentee of a new playhouse with Reeve, a conspirator in the scheme? On the side of doppelgangers, *mutatis mutandis*, we might consider the identity shift by which an actor steadily becomes merged with the character that has made him famous. Nowhere is this more obvious than in the case of popular clowns. Thus it is that Robert Reynolds appears in records as 'Robertt: Pickelheringk', Thomas Sackville as 'Johannes Bouset', and John Spencer as 'Hans Stockfisch'. The most piquant example is probably the identification of John Green with his character of Nobody—an ironic fusion, since the role is precisely what made Green *somebody* in the theatre. In fact, like several English comedians, we know of Green only through activity on the Continent, so one could say that in England he was literally a dramatic nobody. That his theatrical movements enabled his social mobility derives from the ontological instability of the actor, but also owes much to the transculturation of dramatic character, a process of textual mediation, adaptation, and translation to which we now must turn.

---

[31] Valentin Groebner, *Who Are You?: Identification, Deception, and Surveillance in Early Modern Europe* (New York: Zone Books, 2009), 204.

[32] Groebner, *Who Are You?*, 206.

II

This chapter opened by reconstructing a scene of early modern theatrical mobility. In centring that scene on a passport and its agents—a network of writers, bearers, and inspectors—I aimed not only to depict performers in transit but also to evoke the social performances of identification and control to which the passport functioned as a protocol or script. My argument so far has been that inasmuch as theatre in the period was far less fixed than is traditionally supposed, it is equally true that early modern dislocations of stage people and properties were undertaken and regulated in highly theatrical ways. This interplay between migration and performance— the mobility of theatre and the theatricality of its movements—should make a difference in how we read early modern dramatic texts. It explains, to start, why so many plays transported and transformed by itinerant companies thematize the opportunities and risks of setting words, artefacts, and identities in motion. But it will not suffice to mine early dramatic texts for representations of travel, commerce, diplomacy, conversion, or other changes in physical or symbolic capital. What is needed besides is an account of how the medium of theatre (including books and productions and, where identifiable, writers and actors) was swept up in such flows beyond mere relocation to the point of being disfigured and subsequently reshaped.

As a complement to the passport-as-script, then, we must consider the script as a passport. What can the dramatic archive reveal about early theatre's displacements and metamorphoses? To answer this question we will need to extend our idea of 'the script' to cover the full range of stage documents that Tiffany Stern has characterized as 'all the papers created by authors and theatres by the time of the opening performance'.[33] Not, to be sure, that opening performances spell an end to the matter; on the contrary, the paper patches out of which a play was constructed and into which it might again be disassembled only proliferated as the play was disseminated, translated, and adapted. Like a passport with its stamped dates and times, these scripts allow us to survey theatrical border-crossings and to organize those entries and exits into patterns and zones: more than representational documents, they also function as 'logistical media' or 'media of orientation', tracking the movements of their intercultural agents over time and space.[34] Moreover, like almost all passports from medieval Europe onwards, the archive of such scripts is multilingual, simultaneously demonstrating the elasticity of a dramatic work across regions or nations and the ideological stress that may deform the material as it moves. Having noted these general features of

[33] Tiffany Stern, *Documents of Performance in Early Modern England* (Cambridge: Cambridge University Press, 2009), i.

[34] John Durham Peters, 'Calendar, Clock, Tower', lecture, Media in Transition 6 conference, Massachusetts Institute of Technology, Cambridge, MA, 25 April, 2009. See also Judd Ammon Case, 'Geometry of Empire: Radar as Logistical Medium', dissertation, University of Iowa, 2010, http://ir.uiowa.edu/cgi/viewcontent.cgi?article=1659&context=etd (accessed April 2013).

the documentary evidence, we can now proceed to consider individual playtexts and productions, remaining alert to the presence of mobility and its limits as internal literary themes and external social forces alike.

In February 1591–2, the same month in which Charles Howard composed his letter of introduction for itinerant members of the Admiral's Men, their rivals the Strange's Company were performing at the Rose a play that Howard's travelling actors might well have taken abroad—a play that begins with an application for a passport. The Induction to Thomas Kyd's *Spanish Tragedy* (1587) explains how and why the ghost of Andrea, a courtier slain in war, returns from the underworld to seek revenge, but in doing so it reveals that his initial access to the world of the dead was a bureaucratic nightmare.[35] Andrea's spirit had to wait three days and nights until his burial rites had been performed among the living, when 'churlish Charon' (1.1.19) would agree to ferry him over the river Acheron; then Cerberus had to be placated at the 'foremost porch' (31) before Andrea passed to what twenty-first-century border control now terms secondary inspection:

> Not far from hence, amidst ten thousand souls,
> Sat Minos, Aeacus, and Rhadamanth,
> To whom no sooner 'gan I make approach,
> To crave a passport for my wandering ghost,
> But Minos, in graven leaves of lottery,
> Drew forth the manner of my life and death.   (1.1.32–7)

Yet the august judges do not find Andrea's application materials determinative. Should he spend the afterlife among lovers or warriors? The decision is referred to the court of Pluto: 'To this effect my passport straight was drawn' (54). When Andrea, with all due humility, presents this document to the rulers of the underworld, Queen Proserpine is moved to summon Revenge to lead Andrea back up among the living on his mission.

'I showed my passport' (77): Andrea's display of this logistical medium licenses the bewildered traveller's reorientation in terms of space (upward), time (forward), and identity (he is made into an avenger). Comparing this scene to its source, the episode of the golden bough in *Aeneid IV*, critics have emphasized Andrea's ignorance and passivity, pointing out that, unlike Virgil's hero but like many other characters in Kyd's drama, he finds himself working through a script that others have written.[36] The play returns obsessively to the structural constraints on individual, social, and cultural mobility. Over and over, the possibility of a liberating movement is raised only to be disappointed. Andrea's famous opening lines complain that his soul used to be 'imprisoned' (2) in his body and portray the court of Spain,

---

[35] Thomas Kyd, *The Spanish Tragedy*, ed. J. R. Mulryne (London: A & C Black, 1989).

[36] See Eugene D. Hill, 'Senecan and Vergilian Perpective in *The Spanish Tragedy*', *ELR* 15 (1985), 150–1; Katharine Eisaman Maus, 'Introduction', *Four Revenge Tragedies* (Oxford: Oxford University Press, 1995), xxii.

with its rigid hierarchy, as no less confining; but death subjects his soul to another courtly patron, Proserpine, whose 'doom' (79) forces him back among the living. Like its plot, the Induction's dramaturgy also chafes vainly against stasis: when Andrea's opening speech, a vestige of one-handed prologues of earlier plays, is interrupted by the figure of Revenge, the audience expects a debate that will develop both characters—certainly not the non sequiturs and narcolepsy Revenge presents.[37] The dismal rhyme with which Revenge declares they have 'arrived' to see Balthazar 'deprived' of life is confirmed by the fact that they will 'sit [themselves] down to see the mystery' (86–90). They will not need to budge for the tragedy to unfold.

Less a passport than a sort of place card, Andrea's papers afford him observer status only, fixing him in front of an action Revenge presents as a foregone conclusion. Yet to call the entire play 'deeply pessimistic, even nihilistic', as Katherine Eisaman Maus does, surely overstates the case.[38] A more balanced view is offered by Lukas Erne, who identifies 'a tension between the determinist universe suggested by the allegorical figure Revenge in the play's frame, on the one hand, and the play's protagonist, who shapes his own destiny, on the other'.[39] One should add that both Hieronimo and his fellow avenger Bel-Imperia shape their destiny in part by writing texts. Whereas Andrea had to petition for documents, the living avengers manage to create their own, the first of which passes from Bel-Imperia to Hieronimo at the mysterious stage direction 'A letter falleth' (3.2.23 stage direction). In a striking reversal of the deceased Andrea's passport to nowhere, which traps where it might have liberated, Bel-Imperia's letter comes out of nowhere, escaping her sequestration and enlivening her revenge with the imprint of her own blood.

Yet no papers in *The Spanish Tragedy* rewrite identities and reorient the action as forcefully as the documents surrounding the playlet of Soliman and Perseda. Balthazar's request for a 'pleasing motion' (4.1.66) to entertain his father, the Portuguese viceroy, prompts Hieronimo to offer the '*book*' (79 stage direction) of a tragedy he wrote as a student in Toledo and to cast the courtiers by distributing 'abstracts' (141) or outlines. His model for the playlet, he declares, will be the improvisation of the *commedia dell'arte*:

> The Italian tragedians were so sharp of wit,
> That in one hour's meditation
> They would perform anything in action.   (4.1.164–6)

To this commendation Lorenzo adds testimony of seeing 'the like / In Paris, 'mongst the French tragedians' (167–8), words that match the historical trajectory of

---

[37] S. F. Johnson links the sleeping figure of Revenge to God's slow punishment of wickedness via Calvin's commentary on Genesis; see '*The Spanish Tragedy*, or Babylon Revisited', in Richard Hosley, ed., *Essays on Shakespeare* (Columbia: University of Missouri Press, 1962), 28–9.

[38] Maus, 'Introduction', xxii.

[39] Lukas Erne, *Beyond the Spanish Tragedy: A Study of the Works of Thomas Kyd* (Manchester: Manchester University Press, 2001), 192.

scenario-based theatre from sixteenth-century Venice to Spain, France, England, and beyond. Nor does that performance style jar with the serious content of the playlet; on the contrary, what Hieronimo proposes is a kind of *tragedia dell'arte*, known in its time as *opera regia*, which the Venetian actors seem to have developed to suit work drawing on Spanish influences.[40] This incorporation of local elements within a cross-cultural style is a hallmark of the *commedia*, which Robert Henke has aptly called 'the perfect transnational machine'.[41] Viewed in this light, Hieronimo's instruction that each of his cast members should 'act his part / In unknown languages' (172–3) pays tribute to the mixture of dialects and languages that lent itinerant theatre across early modern Europe its opacity and allure. Though Hieronimo presents *Solimon and Perseda* as a writer's conceit fashioning 'poetry' (72) into 'argument' (107) glossed with an 'oration' (184), Lorenzo recognizes the playlet's deep source in the 'action' of intercultural performance.

Once transnational theatre is acknowledged as an enabling context for the playlet, it becomes possible to grasp its paradoxical simultaneous effects of turbulence and fixity. On the one hand, the 'motion' set before Balthazar and the on-stage and off-stage audiences includes, to import a taxonomy proposed elsewhere by Bruce R. Smith, emotion, locomotion, and commotion; the performance is a vortex of action and languages.[42] Literary critics have focused on the spinning of that vortex, interpreting Hieronimo's promise to 'see the fall of Babylon, / Wrought by the heavens in this confusion' (195–6) as re-enacting God's punishment of the Tower of Babel in order to 'confound language and dull the perceptions of the villains to his and Bel-imperia's real purposes'.[43] On the other hand, scholars interested in the theatrical effects of the playlet have attended also to the still centre of the vortex, finding the hermeneutic breakdown wrought by the 'confusion of languages... freezing the event as image in order to compel the spectator into a deep engagement with its horror'.[44] The latter argument suggests why the playlet needed performing 'in sundry languages' (4.4.10), even as the note from the playwright or publisher justifies printing the text, for the benefit of readers, 'in English more largely'.[45] We have here

---

[40] Cesare Molinari, *La Commedia dell'Arte* (Milan: A. Mondadori, 1985), 49, cited by Ellen Rosand, *Opera in Seventeenth-Century Venice* (Berkeley: University of California Press, 1991), 35.

[41] Henke, 'Border-Crossing in the *Commedia dell'Arte*', in Henke and Nicholson, eds., *Transnational Exchange*, 19. See also Henke's essay on 'Poor' in this volume.

[42] Bruce R. Smith, 'E/loco/com/motion', in Peter Holland and Stephen Orgel, eds., *From Script to Stage in Early Modern England* (Basingstoke: Palgrave Macmillan, 2004), 131–50.

[43] Johnson, '*The Spanish Tragedy*, or Babylon Revisited', 27. Scholars have noted that Babylon was also associated with Rome and therefore with Catholic Spain.

[44] Janette Dillon, *Language and Stage in Medieval and Renaissance England* (Cambridge: Cambridge University Press, 1998), 185.

[45] Dillon calls this announcement a 'printer's note' (185). Erne grants that the English text of the playlet in the 1615 edition is likely Kyd's, but adds that we cannot know if it was originally written alongside a multilingual text or produced at a later point.

a case of the tension between mobile 'meaning effects' and still 'presence effects' whose simultaneity, according to Hans Ulrich Gumbrecht, accounts for early modern theatre's 'provocative instability and unrest'.[46] In this respect, Kyd's play is a worthy follower of the itinerant performance tradition it pointedly cites.

In its own right *The Spanish Tragedy* was soon in vigorous motion, migrating across the country and onto the Continent, generating parodies, adaptations, and translations en route. In England, the play's success in print and performance—Henslowe records staging it twenty-nine times between 1592 and 1597, and we know of eleven editions by 1633—assured it a place in the touring repertoire, probably up to the closings of 1642.[47] Unfortunately, records of performances in the provinces do not survive, unless one counts the moment in Dekker's *Satiromastix* (1602) when Horace (a pseudonym for Ben Jonson) is taunted for having played Hieronimo in a company of strolling players: 'Thou hast forgot how thou amblest (in leather pilch) by a play-wagon, in the high way,' says Dekker's character, 'and took'st mad Ieronimoes part, to get seruice among the Mimickes' (4.1.130–2).[48] To be sure, jibes demoting ambitious playwrights to common players were regularly aimed at Shakespeare and others.[49] Still, when Dekker mocks Jonson as a 'Iorney-man Player', his pun on 'journey' as 'a day's travel' and 'a day's wages' reminds us that great parts like Hieronimo's also guaranteed revenue on tour.

The journey of *The Spanish Tragedy* stretched well beyond England. Travelling actors took the play abroad to widespread acclaim, performing it from 1601 in towns and courts across Northern and Central Europe. Adaptations were recorded in manuscript and print between 1615 and 1729, of which three German and three Dutch versions have survived. This evidence shows not only that the play flourished overseas even while receding into obscurity at home, but also that both its 'composition' and 'action' were reinvigorated by European literary and stage contexts. At the crossroads of these cultural systems, *The Spanish Tragedy* shed qualities that had overdetermined its reception in early modern England; it became newly mobile. This chapter cannot adequately survey the play's many intercultural transpositions, but their general characteristics may be noted. First, the adaptations typically minimize or omit the mythological frame; second, they add plentiful vernacular clowning; third, they refocus on the character of Bel-Imperia; and fourth, they extend the play-within-the-play. The overall tendency is to foreground the norms of the target culture. Given time, one could detail the variants on these general rules; for now,

[46] Hans Ulrich Gumbrecht, *Production of Presence: What Meaning Cannot Convey* (Stanford: Stanford University Press, 2004), 106–8.

[47] The figures in this paragraph and the next are drawn, with modifications, from Erne, *Beyond the Spanish Tragedy*, 127.

[48] Thomas Dekker, *Satiromastix*, in Fredson Bowers, ed., *The Dramatic Works of Thomas Dekker* (Cambridge: Cambridge University Press, 1953), 1: 4.1.129–32.

[49] Bart van Es, '"Johannes fac Totum"?: Shakespeare's First Contact with the Acting Companies', *Shakespeare Quarterly* 61.4 (2010), 551–77, esp. 562–4.

however, let us examine a pair of cases—the earliest in Dutch and German respectively—that represent a stark opposition. Whereas the German work boosts *The Spanish Tragedy*'s theatricality, the Dutch version instead mutes it, forcing open a gap between cultural translation and the mobilization of performance.

The Dutch text in question, which constitutes the earliest printed adaptation of Kyd's play, is neither complete nor free-standing nor, for that matter, in dramatic form. It appeared at Antwerp in 1615 embedded in a work of translation by Everaert Siceram (*c*.1560–*c*.1620), a jeweller who belonged to a major chamber of rhetoric, or literary guild, in Brussels. The volume, *Il divino Ariosto oft Orlando furioso*, translates the first twenty-three cantos of the 1532 Italian epic into a Dutch poem that contains, in partial and dispersed form, the first half of *The Spanish Tragedy* in around 93 stanzas of *ottava rima*.[50] Siceram begins his third canto by announcing a curious substitution: instead of rendering Ariosto's genealogy of the House of Este, which he thinks of little interest to the Low Countries, he will provide a tale that reflects on Pinabello's treachery towards Bradamant, one that shows 'what the wages are of a wicked heart laden with sins'.[51] This is the point at which Kyd's drama is unexpectedly incorporated into Ariosto's narrative.

Convinced that he has dispatched Bradamant, Pinabello is riding through a wood when he comes upon a wounded knight who mistakes him for the figure of Revenge. This knight turns out to be the ghost of Andrea, and he proceeds to relate the circumstances of his return from the underworld. The ensuing stanzas are a close translation of the Induction to *The Spanish Tragedy*—bizarrely close at times, since Siceram even transfers printing errors from early English editions. (When he writes of Andrea's spirit passing through the 'gaten van Hor' (40: 7), for example, he seems to offer a strange image of a pharaoh's tomb—the pits of Horus?—but the phrase proves instead to be a false construal of 'gates of hor', which is how 'gates of horn' is misprinted in the 1592 and 1594 editions of Kyd's drama.) As Siceram's poem continues, the characters of *The Spanish Tragedy* serve as intermittent foils to those of the *Orlando Furioso*, appealing to its Netherlandish readers by showing their Hapsburg overlords in a gruesome light. Since the work is unfinished, one cannot finally judge how successfully Siceram would have interleaved Kyd's story within Ariosto's, but his cultural and generic transposition is plain enough. The new poem labours to integrate the Elizabethan dramatic material with the Baroque culture of seventeenth-century Flemish rhetoricians. Siceram embellishes the plot with biblical and classical allusion and furnishes it with an ornate style, contorted syntax, and diction turgid with foreign loanwords and Brussels colloquialisms.[52] As dramatic

---

[50] The relevant text appears in Rudolf Schoenwerth, *Die niederländischen und deutschen Bearbeitungen von Thomas Kyd's Spanish Tragedy* (Berlin: E. Felber, 1903).

[51] 'Hoort my eens Heeren wat den loon is vol on-lust / Van een quaet ghemoet beswaert met sonden' (26: 1–2); Schoenwerth, *Niederländischen un deutschen Bearbeitungen*, 3.

[52] Henri Plard, 'Adaptations de la *Tragédie espagnole* dans les Pays-Bas et en Allemagne (1595–1640)', in Jean Jacquot, ed., *Dramaturgie et Société* (Paris: C.N.R.S., 1968), 2: 643.

verse and prose are alchemized to epic poetry, the work demonstrates a trade-off between mobility and theatricality: to travel into this form, Kyd must be disembodied.

Yet if we view Siceram's text as a passport recording the curious journey of *The Spanish Tragedy*, then we must admit that the passport is missing crucial information. Far from acknowledging Kyd's material as a source, Siceram presents Andrea's tale as his own invention. So how did Siceram come to choose the play in the first place? Did he discover it as a text or in performance? That *Il divino Ariosto* relies upon one or two specific printed editions—a unique provenance among foreign adaptations of *The Spanish Tragedy*—does not prove that Siceram encountered the play first, much less only, as a reader. On the contrary, there is every chance that he witnessed a production of Kyd's drama by the itinerant English companies whose various passages through or sojourns in early seventeenth-century Brussels have been amply documented.[53] These professional actors did not enter a cultural vacuum, but rather intruded upon a theatrical sphere dominated by amateur rhetoricians with established socio-political functions and dramaturgical conventions. The rivalry between *commedianten* such as Robert Browne and *rederijkers* such as Everaert Siceram was heated enough to be mentioned on the Dutch stage, including a well-known passage debating the merits of the two styles of performance.[54] Yet the most cunning riposte to the migrant players was to convert their showmanship and ironic perspectives into humanist verse expressing a moral allegory. Whether or not Siceram saw *The Spanish Tragedy* in performance, his poem retains Kyd's anxiety over Spanish power while transposing his drama into Italianate poetry. As befits a rhetorician who was by trade a jeweller, Siceram cuts, shapes, and mounts Kyd's text in a larger setting, bringing some facets to light while leaving others in shadow.

By contrast, the play's earliest German adaptor made a living as an ironmonger, and his version is a rougher but sturdier construction that forges old and new elements together. Jakob Ayrer (1544–1605) belongs to a group of writers on whose work the tours of the English comedians in the German-speaking lands had a well-documented influence.[55] Among these Ayrer holds a unique place: the city of Nuremberg, where he was born and died and where his plays were posthumously

[53] Thomas Heywood's *Apology for Actors* (1612), written about 1607 and touched up in 1608, reports that 'the Cardinall of *Bruxels*, hath at this time in pay a company of our *English* musicians'; cited in Chambers, *Elizabethan Stage*, IV: 250–3. Willem Schrickx adduces a 1607 passport in the Brussels Archives begging safe passage for seventeen 'Comédiens Angloys' through Holland to Brunswick, and cites a document alluding to a 'compagnie royale anglaise [qui] obtint l'autorisation de donner à Bruxelles des representations' in 1605; see his 'English Actors at the Courts of Wolfenbüttel, Brussels and Graz during the Lifetime of Shakespeare', *Shakespeare Survey* 33 (1980), 163–5.

[54] Gerbrand Bredero, *Moortje*, ed. P. Minderaa and C. A. Zaalberg (Leiden: Nijhoff, 1984), lines 1450–63. The original and my translation appear in Anston Bosman, 'Renaissance Intertheater and the Staging of Nobody', *ELH* 71.3 (2004), 567–8.

[55] Others include Heinrich Julius of Wolfenbüttel, Hector Conradus, Johannes Nendorf, Johann Georg Schoch, and Johann Rist; see Haekel, *Englischen Komödianten*, 141–58.

brought out, maintained a thriving native theatre that attracted numerous international acting companies. The dominant playwright of the previous generation had been Hans Sachs, the Meistersinger, whose dramatic subjects, structural principles, and didactic purpose Ayrer inherited.[56] Yet since Nuremberg was an artistic and commercial hub, local tradition was supplemented by performers from further afield, including the visiting troupes of the *commedia dell'arte* and, from the early 1590s on, a succession of English groups led by actor-managers such as Robert Browne or Thomas Sackville.[57] So Ayrer's collection of plays and entertainments, published in 1618 as *Opus Thæatricum*, advertises a mix of indigenous and imported influences: besides comedies and tragedies, the volume contains Shrovetide plays (Fastnachtsspiele) and singing plays (Singspiele) indebted to Sachs, but its foreword specifies that even these traditional forms are to be acted 'in the new English style' ('auff die neue Englische manier vnnd art').[58] We can observe such amalgamation in Ayrer's reworking of *The Spanish Tragedy* as the *Tragedia von dem griegischen Keyser zu Constantinopel und seiner Tochter Pelimperia mit dem gehengten Horatio*.

That both the matter and the manner of *Pelimperia* testify to the mobility of early modern theatre does not, to be sure, imply that specific features of the new drama are easily ascribed to particular agents of writing or performance. An obvious example is the plot's relocation to Constantinople, a move which fuses Kyd's Spanish King and Duke of Castile into the Greek emperor (Keyser) of Ayrer's title—though the *dramatis personae*, speech prefixes, and dialogue refer throughout to him as Amurates, the King (König). Who is responsible for this change of setting, and what was his or their motivation? Early critics saw a strategy of displacement on the author's part, suggesting that Ayrer wished to separate the play's violence from Christendom or, more especially, Hapsburg Spain.[59] This reading underestimates the appeal of Turkish topics for early modern writers from Camões and Tasso to Dryden and Racine, a tradition to which Ayrer added three plays apart from *Pelimperia*: the comedies *Vom Soldan von Babilonia* and *Von dem getreuen Ramo*, and the sensationally titled tragedy *Vom Regiment vnnd schändlichen Sterben des türkischen Keisers Machumetis des andern dis namens, wie er Constantinopel eingenommen vnd gantz grausam tyrannisirt* (*The Reign and Shameful Death of the Turkish Emperor Mahomed, How He Captured and Cruelly Tyrannized Constantinople*). German carnival plays had

[56] See Andrea Grafetstätter, 'Foreign Culture in a Foreign Town. The Nuremberg Poet Jakob Ayrer and the Reception of Sixteenth-Century Comedy Plays in Germany', in Grafetstätter et al., *Islands and Cities in Medieval Myth, Literature, and History* (Frankfurt: Peter Lang, 2011), 153; and Christine Baro, *Der Narr als Joker: Figurationen und Funktionen des Narren bei Hans Sachs und Jakob Ayrer* (Trier: Wissenschaftlicher Verlag, 2011), 222–3.

[57] On the *commedia*'s influence on German theatre, see Karl Trautmann, 'Italienische schauspieles am bayerischen Hofe', *Jahrbuch für Münchener Geschichte*, I (1881), 225. On English players in Nuremberg, see Trautmann, 'Englische Komödianten in Nürnberg bis zum Schlusse des Dreissigjahrigen Krieges (1593–1648)', *Archiv für Litteraturgeschichte* 14 (1886), 113–36.

[58] Jakop Ayrer, *Dramen*, ed. Adelbert von Keller (Stuttgart: Litterarischer Verein, 1865), 1: 6.

[59] Schoenwerth, *Niederländischen und deutschen Bearbeitungen*, 125–6.

depicted Turks since the fifteenth century, and Hans Sachs incorporated lurid fantasies of Ottoman violence throughout his writings, so that Ayrer had an abundant stock of Turkish material with which to develop Kyd's drama afresh, less to spare Spain than to critique German ideas under the veil of the Ottoman threat.[60]

Yet the complex media shift that, following Randall McLeod, we might call *The Spanish Tragedy*'s 'transformission' into *Pelimperia* would be oversimplified by an interpretation that emphasized authorial strategy at the expense of theatrical context.[61] In stark opposition to the case of Siceram's poem, there is no textual evidence that Ayrer was working from a copy of Kyd's play; on the contrary, the elision of the framework, addition of a clown, extension of the playlet, and profusion of stage directions all point to the 'new English style' that the travelling players displayed to the citizens of Nuremberg. Any of these adaptations may stem from the actors just as easily as from the playwright, and the relocation to Constantinople is no exception.[62] Ayrer's *Keiser Machumet* play, for instance, has been linked by source-hunters with John Spencer's troupe's contemporary show play *Türkische Triumphkomödie*, probably a version of George Peele's lost tragedy *The Turkish Mahomet and Hyrin the fair Greek*.[63] If this provenance holds, then the travellers would have known how popular Ottoman subjects were in the German-speaking lands, and they could have adapted repertory standards like *The Spanish Tragedy* accordingly. A milder version of the hypothesis is that the English comedians' Turk plays emboldened Ayrer to revive his Oriental interests; but perhaps that concedes too much. For scholars have advanced a far narrower theatrical reason for the change of location, namely that the actors' extension of the Soliman and Perseda playlet might have rendered a wardrobe change undesirable, leading the Turkish theme to spill from the inset into the main action of the drama. In this case presentation torques representation, and the costume ('a Turkish cap, / A black mustachio and a fauchion' [4.1.144–5]) drives the plot in topsy-turvy fashion. Movable objects extended the mobility of the theatre.

The trajectories of the early Flemish and German reworkings of *The Spanish Tragedy* diverge strikingly in formal, chronological, and geographical terms. Siceram turns the play southwards, pulling it backward into the Renaissance verse of Italian epic. Influenced by travelling players, Ayrer reorients the play northwards,

---

[60] On the Ottomans in early modern German drama, see Nina Berman, *German Literature on the Middle East: Discourses and Practices, 1000–1989* (Ann Arbor: University of Michigan Press, 2011), 91–7. A more specialized study is Claudia Kleinlogel, *Exotik-Erotik: Zur Geschichte des Türkenbildes in der deutschen Literatur der frühen Neuzeit* (Frankfurt am Main: Lang, 1989).

[61] Randall McLeod, 'Information on Information', *TEXT* 5 (1991), 240–81.

[62] That the venue change is not maintained consistently over the drama—references to the Portuguese subplot unexpectedly surface—further indicates that theatrical impact rather than literary unity was the aim of the performers or the playwright, or quite possibly both.

[63] Carl Kaulfuss-Diesch, *Die Inszenierung des deutschen Dramas an der Wende des Sechzehnten und Siebzehnten Jahrhunderts* (Leipzig: R. Voigtländer, 1905), 40; Lawrence Marsden Price, *The Reception of English Literature in Germany* (Berkeley: University of California Press, 1932), 23–4.

embodying allusion in early modern action through a blend of clowning, topical plots, and Protestant morals. Criticism today neglects these adaptations because each tends to an opposite extreme: thus a typical commentary deplores the 'pedantry' of Siceram's 'prolix' and 'often obscure' poetry, but then also rejects Ayrer's drama as 'flat' and 'of only historical interest', approvingly citing a comparison of the play to a mere puppet-show.[64] This double dismissal restates familiar and only recently contested efforts to sideline entire modes of early modern theatricality as either too poetic (such as so-called closet drama) or too performative (pageants or masques). Scholars who relegate these modes to subgenres complain that each polarizes elements that ought to be artfully combined in a dynamic equilibrium. Here we discern the aesthetic criterion most inimical to understanding mobile theatricality—the subtle but resilient critical ideal of *balance*.

Among early modernists, no critic has limned this ideal more deftly than Robert Weimann, whose influential cultural poetics rests on the assumption that '[t]he precariously relative balance of word and action on the Elizabethan stage is probably unique'.[65] Weimann understands late Tudor theatre as an equipoise, variously described as complementarity or tension, in which humanist mimesis squares off against the skill of common players. These polar qualities are pegged to social forces—embodiment is allied with popular ritual and imitation with the rhetoric of the elite—which are viewed as evenly matched. Explaining late sixteenth-century English culture as manifest in the shifting emphases of a drama's framing texts, Weimann cites Victor Turner on moments of social transition when 'everything, as it were, trembles in the balance'.[66] Yet this dialectical method worryingly reproduces the commonplaces to be found in, of all places, the New Criticism, whose supreme good, whether realized in the artwork's design or its effect on the reader, was a state I. A. Richards termed 'balanced poise'.[67] When Weimann praises Shakespeare's oeuvre as a 'unity of contrasts', for instance, we glimpse the stability of a Marxian synthesis in which balance subsumes tension so that Shakespeare, as others have noted, 'appears as the genius at the end of the evolutionary trail'.[68]

But what if authors or actors were to wander from that trail? What if theatre lost its balance? The versions of *The Spanish Tragedy* we have examined showcase the errancy, disproportion, and mutability that upset the equipoise championed by critics like Weimann. For such harmonizers, moving beyond 'the Elizabethan stage', its

---

[64] Plard, 'Adaptations de la *Tragédie espagnole*', 637–9 and 641–3.

[65] Weimann, *Author's Pen and Actor's Voice*, 4.

[66] Victor Turner, *From Ritual to Theatre: The Human Seriousness of Play* (New York: Performing Arts Journal Publications, 1982), 44; cited in Robert Weimann and Douglas Bruster, *Prologues to Shakespeare's Theatre: Performance and Liminality in Early Modern Drama* (London: Routledge, 2004), 41 fn. 35.

[67] I. A. Richards, *Principles of Literary Criticism* (London and New York: Routledge Classics, 2001 [1924]), 232.

[68] Annabel Patterson, 'Bottom's Up: Festive Theory in *A Midsummer Night's Dream*', *Renaissance Papers* (1988), 31.

spatial and temporal coordinates as fixed as its pantheon of playwrights and performers, means losing critical balance, so that mobility amounts to freefall. What
conceptual frameworks, then, can best capture the mobility of early modern plays?
The default option is *translatio*, but the term binds the dissemination of culture too
closely to a nationalist vision of rebuilding the ruins of *imperium* into a foundation
for future empire. Such teleology stabilizes texts and authors and stratifies places
and times of composition. In this process theatricality—porous, provisional, and
performative—easily disappears. To render it visible anew we might learn from
debates in transcultural literary studies, a field currently recasting its object as
'world literature' in the sense not of a canon of global masterpieces but rather a
mode of circulation in which the travels of texts (and, we might add, performances)
generate a dynamic network of ingenious hybrids, visualized by one scholar as 'a
montage of overlapping maps in motion'.[69] Each adjustment in this geography of
cultural power may shift the balance point of an artwork and even transform its
core. David Porter envisages charting these new patterns in a history 'not of points
but of vectors, not of fixed and bounded aesthetic objects but of functional trans-
missions, connections, and recombinations'.[70] Drawing on the work of David Damrosch, Franco Moretti, and Pascale Casanova, Porter has proposed a fresh taxonomy
for the study of world literature: in place of the category of nation, Porter substitutes
that of *trajectory*; instead of period, *life cycle*; and instead of genre, *function*. Though
Porter nowhere mentions plays, his new taxonomy could hardly suit them better,
for an effective way to quicken the history of theatricality beyond calcifications of
identity and origin is to ask instead what a play has done, when it has flourished,
and where it has travelled. The interrogation reconstructed at the start of this chapter could, in 1592, have yielded only crude data about the itinerant performers and
their craft; but if we now aim to restore some of early modern theatre's resonance
and mobility, we need to inquire further and accommodate a wider variety of
evidence.

Such accommodation has already been modelled in the most famous scene to
feature travelling players, which is the arrival of the 'tragedians of the city' at Elsinore (*Hamlet* 2.2.392). The company's ambiguous provenance—their city ought to
be Copenhagen but looks, as the scene continues, ever more like London—is
matched by the flexibility of their adaptive work and the uncertainty of their final
destination. Like *The Murder of Gonzago* reinvented as *The Mousetrap*, the troupe at
the centre of *Hamlet* fits Porter's description of a text as 'always a hybrid product of

    [69] Vinay Dharwadker, 'Introduction: Cosmopolitanism in Its Time and Place', in Dharwadker,
ed., *Cosmopolitan Geographies: New Locations in Literature and Culture* (New York: Routledge,
2001), 3. See also David Damrosch, *What is World Literature?* (Princeton: Princeton University
Press, 2003), 24.

    [70] David Porter, 'The Crisis of Comparison and the World Literature Debates', *Profession* (2011),
255.

multiple origins and…always on its way to someplace else.'[71] The deep mobility of players and their plays frustrates neat definitions and evaluations, thwarting the bureaucratic aim of Polonius to 'use them according to their desert' (465–6). As scholars and critics, we would do better to follow Hamlet's lenient rejoinder, welcoming them without foreknowing their nature or worth, not putting them in their place so much as granting them space to set their art in motion. 'Will you see the players well bestowed?' Hamlet replies (460). 'Use every man after his desert, and who shall scape whipping?'

FURTHER READING

Adey, Peter. *Mobility* (London: Routledge, 2010).

Canzler, Weert, Vincent Kaufmann, and Sven Kesselring, eds. *Tracing Mobilities: Towards a Cosmopolitan Perspective* (Aldershot: Ashgate, 2008).

Cresswell, Tim. *On the Move: Mobility in the Modern Western World* (New York: Routledge, 2006).

Cronin, Michael. *Across the Lines: Travel, Language, Translation* (Cork: Cork University Press, 2000).

Henke, Robert and Eric Nicholson, eds. *Transnational Exchange in Early Modern Theatre* (Aldershot: Ashgate, 2008).

Papastergiadis, Nikos. *The Turbulence of Migration: Globalization, Deterritorialization, and Hybridity* (Malden, MA: Polity Press, 2000).

Sanders, Julie. *The Cultural Geography of Early Modern Drama, 1620–1650* (Cambridge: Cambridge University Press, 2011).

Urry, John. *Mobilities* (Cambridge: Polity Press, 2007).

[71] Porter, 'Crisis of Comparison', 253.

CHAPTER 27

HONESTAS

PHIL WITHINGTON

In his *Humble Motion to the Parliament of England Concerning the Advancement of Learning* (1649), the precocious John Hall developed a powerful, if rambling, argument for the *Reformation of the Universities*.[1] Hall marshalled a range of points in the name of an agenda common to the 'Hartlib Circle' to which he belonged, and one of his more striking suggestions was to create archives of *all* surviving historical documents, so that students could learn the full round of 'those particularities and circumstances, without which a History is but dead'.[2] Frustrated by the way in which contemporary works were 'so larded and pestered with the private discourses and conceptions of the Writers, that they seem to have been composed for no other end', he called for History to teach lessons 'naturally enforced from the things themselves'. To this end he called for a:

> catalogue of characters, and that of the lives of some of the more eminent; which I should not care, how much they had been stuffed with particular actions, because Man in business is but a Theatrical person, and in a manner but personates himself, but in his retired and hid actions, he pulls off his disguise, and acts openly.[3]

Hall concluded that 'I judged by that means that characters were the best and faithful to be gained, and we should come to a higher knowledge and judgment of Vertue, and the Passions. For I had seen abundance of things related as high acts of generosity, which possibly were but the effects of weakness, cruelty and despair'.[4]

With his materiality, his empiricism, his scepticism, and his desire to know the real nature of things (including both 'Men' and 'Nature'), Hall may seem a very 'modern' writer. It is no surprise that one of his heroes was Francis Bacon and that

---

[1] John Hall, *An Humble Motion to the Parliament of England Concerning the Advancement of Learning, and Reformation of the Universities* (1649).

[2] Hall, *An Humble Motion to the Parliament*, 6, 8, 16–17; 36; G. H. Turnbull, 'John Hall's Letters to Samuel Hartlib', *Review of English Studies*, n.s. 4 (1953), 221–33.

[3] Hall, *An Humble Motion to the Parliament*, 37.

[4] Hall, *An Humble Motion to the Parliament*, 37.

he was admired by Bacon's friend, Thomas Hobbes, the perpetrator of what James Harrington called 'modern prudence'.[5] Certainly Hall's contention that public life involved 'Theatrical persons' hiding their real passions and motives was reminiscent of Hobbes's view of human psychology.[6] As Hall explained, one function of the new learning would be to find ways 'of discovering and judging the many inclinations and natures of men: And so by that means a greater facilitation of business, and possibly greater success in it, than have yet commonly happened'.[7]

I have two reasons for starting my chapter with Hall. First, he clearly espouses a concept of what might be called 'quotidian theatricality'. Hall associates the term not with the theatre per se or indeed other kinds of carefully choreographed, ritualized, or representational performance—the usual inference of the word at this time. Rather he uses 'theatrical' to delineate the ways in which people interacted and 'personated' in the course of their everyday lives. As such, he at once points to the performative aspects of ordinary sociability and invokes the sense of self required to cope with, and function effectively in, a society conceived in theatrical terms. This notion of selfhood involves a clear distinction between an interiority of inner passions and, as Hobbes would have it, the will to power; it presumes an exterior face which communicates with the outside world through words, gestures, and actions. Second, in sketching as a commonplace this dialectic between public theatricality and interior reality, Hall was using new words to invoke an idea which was, in fact, very familiar to educated contemporaries. This was the Latin concept of *honestas*: the notion that, in order to live civilly and honestly together, people needed to be able to assess their place or role within any social context, to recognize the conventions and behaviour required for that context, and in this way to act and speak appropriately and profitably. Since the early sixteenth century, a range of words had been used in English to denote the skills and attributes of *honestas*, including 'decorum', 'discretion', 'courtesy', 'seemliness', 'handsomeness', 'civility', and 'honesty'. In the decades after Hall's death, the very same skills would become equally important to those notions of civil and polite society which are now so central to eighteenth-century historiography.[8] What Hall's astute intervention nicely

---

[5] James Harrington, *The Commonwealth of Oceana*, ed. J. G. A. Pocock (Cambridge: Cambridge University Press, 1992), 9, 10, 13. John Davies recorded in 1657, a year after Hall's early death, that Hobbes had intimated that 'Had not [Hall's] debauches and intemperance diverted him from the more serious studies, he had made an extraordinary person; for no man had ever done so great things at his age'; see John Davies, 'An Account of the Author of the Translation, and his Work', in John Hall, *Hierocles upon the golden verses of Pythagoras; teaching a vertuous and worthy life* (1657), sig. A.

[6] Thomas Hobbes, *Leviathan*, ed. Noel Malcolm, 3 vols. (Oxford: Oxford University Press, 2012), 2: 132–4, 150–4.

[7] Hall, *An Humble Motion to the Parliament*, 38.

[8] Peter Borsay, *The English Urban Renaissance: Culture and Society in the Provincial Town, 1660–1770* (Oxford: Oxford University Press, 1989); Lawrence E. Klein, *Shaftesbury and the Culture of Politeness: Moral Discourse and Cultural Politics in Eighteenth-Century England* (Cambridge: Cambridge University Press, 1994); Anna Bryson, *From Courtesy to Civility: Changing Codes of Conduct in Early Modern England* (Oxford: Oxford University Press, 1996).

captures, however, is how the capacity for theatricality had always informed these terms: that theatricality, indeed, was essential to emerging notions of seventeenth-century public life.

This chapter outlines the long genealogy of quotidian theatricality embedded in the idea of *honestas*, which characterized Renaissance and early Enlightenment notions of normative sociability. In so doing, however, it traces something of a conceptual Trojan horse. This is because for many commentators 'theatrical' was deeply pejorative in the manner of its root term, 'theatre': it implied hypocrisy, insincerity, Popery, Paganism, and a host of associated vices. Yet even as explicit examples of theatricality were roundly and regularly condemned, so the practice of theatricality in everyday life was implicitly sanctioned by *honestas*. This remarkable tension at the heart of Renaissance culture is explored in three sections. The chapter considers the predominant meanings and inferences of 'theatrical' over the course of the sixteenth and seventeenth centuries, before turning to some of the ways and genres by which *honestas* was recommended to the wider reading public. It concludes with William Shakespeare's *Othello*, a play which, in dissecting the many and conflicting meanings of honesty (including *honestas*) dramatizes the profound social dangers of an accomplished 'Theatrical personality' that could manipulate conversations and interactions at will.[9]

Papists, stage-players, and hypocrites

It is difficult to find an affirmative use of the word 'theatrical' and its cognates in English printed texts during the later sixteenth and early seventeenth centuries, and this is largely because of the kind of writers who deployed it. While the term seems to have entered printed discourse in the 1570s—the decade when commercial theatres began to become a fixture in the metropolitan landscape—its initial deployment was invariably by puritan polemicists critiquing the traditional church. The tone was set by the influential reformer and Church of Scotland minister David Ferguson in his sermon to the Scottish nobility at Leith in 1572, in which he derided 'all the vain theatrical toys prescribed in papistrie to penitentis [sic]'.[10] South of the border in London, the popular preacher and Cambridge-educated Calvinist, William Fulke, likened the spoils of Babylon to the 'merchandise of the church of Rome, that is in masses, in images, in the theatrical or player like shewes of there temples, and in other papisticall ceremonies'.[11] Now Master of Pembroke College in

---

[9] William Shakespeare, *Othello*, ed. and intro. E. A. J. Honigmann (London: Arnold Shakespeare, 1987).

[10] David Ferguson, *Ane sermon preichit befoir the Regent and nobilitie upon a part of the thrid chapter of the prophet Malachi* (1572), 125v.

[11] William Fulke, *Praelections upon the sacred and holy Revelation of S. John* (1573), 121r.

Cambridge, Fulke continued with the trope in 1583, noting that 'in the Popish Church, they have none but offices about idle ceremonies, and vain pageants of their Masses, consecrations, ordinations, and such like theatrical pomps, and shows'.[12] While these early uses of the term drew attention to the material culture of Catholicism, the behaviour and demeanour it encouraged was also invoked. As the Danish Lutheran Niels Hemmingsen argued in 1581, the 'canon of the Mass' was 'brought into the Church by the devil himself, the author of all idolatry, and super-stition. For the mumbling with their theatrical gestures agreeth to the incantation, and cursed superstition of the Gentiles, rather than to the institution of Christ'.[13]

The turn of the century saw more concerted and direct discussion of the concept in print. Whilst theatricality continued to be a metaphorical stick with which to beat Catholics, its classical provenance and the nature of the literary forms associ-ated with it were also debated. As a result, arguments about theatricality began to echo the claims and counter-claims made for the theatre more generally. Important in this respect was the intervention in 1599 by John Rainolds, a leading Oxford puritan, over the rights and wrongs of university interludes; and the translation of Plutarch's moral essays by Philemon Holland in 1600.[14] Rainolds was at pains to distinguish sports and 'lawful recreation' from your 'Theatrical sports, and plays' on the grounds that theatrical performance imprinted itself on the bodies and minds of those doing the acting. University students were not simply playing 'womanly raiment; of *Melanthos* kissing; of *Phaedras* furious rage; her *Nurses* and the *Nymphs* bawdry; of wantonness and scurrility shewed in sundry speeches, actions and ges-tures; of the loose and beastly behaviour of the mariners, with the rest of like qual-ity'.[15] Rather these roles and scenarios became embodied in the person and a template for living. Rainolds was equally incensed by the suggestion that the ire directed by the early Christian fathers at classical theatre was irrelevant today. Not only were 'your theatrical sights…of the same kind that the *Fathers* have *decreed in their Councils, and written in their books against*'. Such criticisms were even more relevant in the light of

> *Popish Priests*, who, being *corrupted from the simplicity* that is in *Christ*, as they have transformed the celebrating of the Sacrament of the *Lords supper* into a *Masse-game*, and all other parts of *Ecclesiastical service* into *theatrical sights*; so, instead of *preaching the word*, they caused it to be played; a thing put in practise by their flowers, the *Jesuits*, among the poor *Indians*.[16]

---

[12] William Fulke, *A briefe confutation, of a popish discourse* (1583), 38r.

[13] Niels Hemmingsen, *The faith of the church militant moste effectualie described in this exposition of the 84. Psalme* (1581), 206.

[14] John Rainolds, *Th'overthrow of stage-playes, by the way of controversie betwixt D. Gager and D. Rainoldes wherein all the reasons that can be made for them are notably refuted* (1599); Philemon Holland, *The philosophie, commonlie called, the morals vvritten by the learned philosopher Plutarch of Chaeronea* (1603).

[15] Rainolds, *Th'overthrow of stage-playes*, 24.

[16] Rainolds, *Th'overthrow of stage-playes*, 161.

Holland's Plutarch likewise acknowledged the peculiar transformative power of theatre but reasoned that just as the joys of wine can be safely appreciated in moderation, so 'strange fables and Theatrical fictions therein, by reason of the exceeding pleasure and singular delight that they yield... is not without some fruit nor void of utility'. Indeed so long as 'theatrical fictions' were consumed carefully, 'there let us bring in withal the reason of Philosophy, and make a good medley of pleasure and profit together'.[17]

Depending on its context, then, theatricality raised two related problems for these educated contemporaries. As a basis for Christian worship, it signalled a profound deviation and distraction from the authentic and original word of God. As a mode of pagan literary performance, it was a powerful—too powerful—style of representation, whereby actors and audiences alike were transfigured by experiencing it, usually in ways that encouraged vice and excess. As William Prynne insisted in his infamous *Histro-mastix, The Player's Scourge* (1633), God could not countenance 'men's degenerating into beasts, or Devils, either in their minds or manners, be it but for a season':

> therefore it cannot approve of these theatrical, bestial, and diabolical *transfigurations of their bodies*; which are inconsistent with the *rules of piety, gravity, honesty, modesty, civility, right reason, and expedience, by which all Christians actions should be* regulated.[18]

Underpinning these fears was the problem of pretence and reality. For Prynne and others, theatricality always risked becoming reality. For the great Elizabethan and Jacobean churchman Lancelot Andrewes, in contrast, theatricality hid reality. Andrewes implored his congregation not to '*play religion*' and warned 'of this *Scenical, theatrical, histrionical godliness*, there is good store abroad in the world'. But 'GOD grant it be not found in *Israel*. Be not then *like stage-players*, when about any *religious act*; Not, when about any'.[19] Andrewes explained that the alternative was to become hypocrites, a 'Greek word' for those 'whom the *Latin* term *Histriones*, and we in English, *Stage-players*: Such as in disguised attire and hair present themselves on a stage, and there oft represent those, whom (GOD knows) they are far from; but yet, outwardly take upon them their *persons*, as if they were'. The key was to '*judge* them (not by their *Player's coat* above, but) by that, they are *underneath* in their own, when their *gorgeous* and *gay attire* is of[f]'. He also noted that 'the word (in the tongue CHRIST spake) is as much to say, as one in a *vizour, Assumens vultum*, a *face-taker*; one that hath got him a *taken-on-face*, which is none of his owne, nor nothing like it'. On this basis Andrewes extrapolated two kinds of hypocrite. On the

---

[17] Holland, *Plutarch*, 19.

[18] William Prynne, *Histrio-mastix The players scourge, or, actors tragaedie, divided into two parts* (1633), 879.

[19] Lancelot Andrewes, *XCVI. Sermons* (1629), 232.

one hand, there was the '*Stage-players*' formally defined. 'And at the second hand, all others, which do off of the stage, that which they doe upon it; and in *Court*, *City*, or *Country*, carry themselves with other *faces* then their own, as these do on the *Stage*, at *Play-houses*'.[20]

This notion of generic hypocrisy coincided with the identification of theatricality, beyond the church and playhouse, as a feature of everyday relations. The Separatist John Robinson noted how 'Men say, *Familiarity breeds contempt*; whereupon many fearing to be *contemned* by others, dispose themselves to *contemn* others by a supercilious, and overly behaviour'. He argued that it was primarily those 'in jealousy, and consciousness of their own wants, take up a theatrical, and affected strangeness, and stateliness, specially towards their inferiors, and equals'. Such people were 'like the ass in the Lions skin: but by braying when they should roar, are discovered, and become more ridiculous, then if they had always shewed their asses' ears'.[21] Or as Ben Jonson put it, if 'our whole life is like a Play: where in everyman, forgetful of himself, is in travail with expression of another. Nay we so insist on imitating others, as we cannot (when it is necessary) return to our selves'. The result of these shifting selves was that eventually 'everyman' becomes like those 'Children, that imitate the vices of Stammerers so long, till at last they become such; and make the habit to another nature, as it is never forgotten'.[22] In his 1635 potted history of human knowledge, Edward Kellett discerned a decisive moment for the ancients when '*the sciences began to be theatrical, and all their profit was thought to be able to deceive in disputing, and throw dust before the eyes by a most ignorant dexterity and with words coined at pleasure, the Logic and Physic books of Aristotle seemed to be more fit*'.[23] And by 1665 John Hall's friend, Robert Boyle, took it as given that 'Theatrical persons' were 'Courtiers and Gallants' emasculated by 'the glittering and deluding outside of Greatness' and the 'Vanity of the World'.[24]

Civil philosophy

This brief narrative of theatricality suggests the term was a powerful if select weapon in the armoury of the early modern moralist. Whether critiquing Catholic mass, university interludes, court masques, or generic hypocrisy and superficiality, it

---

[20] Lancelot Andrewes, *XCVI. Sermons* (1629), 231–2.

[21] John Robinson, *Observations divine and morall* (1625), 217.

[22] Ben Jonson, *Timber, or Discoveries*, in Ian Donaldson, ed., *Ben Jonson* (Oxford: Oxford University Press, 1985), 551.

[23] Edward Kellett, *Miscellanies of divinitie divided into three books, wherein is explained at large the estate of the soul in her origination, separation, particular judgement, and conduct to eternall blisse or torment* (1635), 15.

[24] Robert Boyle, *Occasional reflections upon several subjects, whereto is premis'd a discourse about such kind of thoughts* (1665), 22.

raised the fraught problem of where reality and authenticity ended and representation and pretence began. Prima facie its changing point of reference—from depicting acts of formalized representation in the 1570s to everyday social interaction by the 1620s—can in itself explain, perhaps, Hall's plea for an archive of 'retired and hid actions'. Crucially, however, this was neither the only nor possibly the primary story of quotidian theatricality in early modern England and Scotland. Even as the term theatrical emerged as an explicit and pejorative descriptor of sociability, so the concept of *honestas* valorized precisely the same qualities as a normative and requisite feature of social relations.

The most recent and subtle account of this process is Jennifer Richards' genealogy of the idea of 'civil conversation'. Richards shows that this idealized conversational mode, promulgated by Tudor humanists, enshrined a Ciceronian concept of honesty (*honestas*) that was less about truth-telling, integrity, and simplicity—as moderns tend to define the term—and much more about maintaining constructive and mutually profitable interaction between separate interests. Richards notes the various attributes with which Cicero endowed the concept—wisdom, justice, fortitude, decorum—and shows that, when enacted or represented in civil conversations, these encouraged 'the self-restraint of potentially domineering speakers'. This led to the paradox—at least for modern readers—that 'apparently dissembling conduct is also honest when it facilitates negotiation between different and conflicting interests'.[25] Yet we receive the idea as paradoxical only because the conflation of *honestas* with our 'honesty' did not survive the seventeenth century, the concept of *honestas* coming to reside in the language of civility, discretion, and the public performance of the self instead. As William Temple observed at the end of the seventeenth century, 'what we call an honest man the Romans called a good man, and honesty in their language, as well as in French, rather signifies a *composition of those qualities* which generally enquire honour and esteem'.[26]

One of the most cogent accounts of the practical application of *honestas* occurs in the most canonical and influential humanist texts of the sixteenth century. This was Thomas More's *Utopia* (1516), translated into English by Ralph Robinson in 1551.[27] The timing and context of Robinson's translation, which allowed *Utopia* to appear in English for the first time, is significant. Not only did it coincide with the complex upheavals of the Edwardian reformation and Marian counter-reformation, but it was sponsored by a group of London citizens and merchants deeply engaged in civic and parliamentary politics (Robinson himself was a clerk of the Company

---

[25] Jennifer Richards, *Rhetoric and Courtliness in Early Modern England* (Cambridge: Cambridge University Press, 2003), 2.

[26] Cited in Samuel Johnson, *A Dictionary of the English Language: in which the Words are Deduced from their Originals, and Illustrated in their Different Significations by Examples from the Best Writers*, vol. I, 4th edn. (London, 1776), 'honest'.

[27] The text was republished in 1556. Quotations are taken from Thomas More, *Utopia*, ed. and intro. David Harris Sacks (Boston: Bedford St Martin's, 1999), which uses the 1556 text.

of Goldsmiths).[28] Moreover, it was patronized by William Cecil, a member of the network of Cambridge humanists which was instrumental in disseminating the Ciceronian ideal of civil conversation.[29] For both sponsors and patrons, that is, the dialogue between Hythloday (the traveller who has been to Utopia) and More (the character who records his conversation with Hythloday) about the nature of political discourse and counsel was not simply an abstract or fictional concern but one of very real and immediate relevance.

This discussion occurs towards the end of the first book of *Utopia* and addresses the classical conundrum of whether philosophy and morality can ever be squared with political self-interest and pragmatism. For Hythloday, who espoused the conventional Platonic separation between the higher world of contemplation and the dirty pit of politics, it was patently obvious that, given the self-interest, wilfulness, and irrationality of rulers, 'philosophy had no place among kings'.[30] The assertion provokes, however, an unusually sharp and (in the context of the dialogue) extenuated response from More the narrator:

> 'Indeed', quoth I, 'this school philosophy [i.e. scholastic learning] hath not, which thinketh all things meet for every place. But there is another philosophy more civil which knoweth, as you would say, her own stage, and thereafter ordering and behaving herself in the play that she hath in hand, playeth her part accordingly with comeliness uttering nothing out of due or order and fashion'.[31]

Not only does the narrator put forward a concept of counsel at once attuned to social context and dependent on communicative acuity and skill. He explicitly emphasizes the theatrical qualities required of the counsellor:

> And this is the philosophy that you must use. Or else, whiles a comedy of Plautus is playing and the vile bondmen scoffing and trifling among themselves, if you should suddenly come upon the stage in a philosopher's apparel and rehearse out of Octavia the place wherein Seneca disputeth with Nero, had it not been better for you to have played the dumb person than by rehearsing that which served neither for the time nor place to have made such a tragical comedy or gallimaufry [hodgepodge].[32]

Continuing with the theatrical analogy, he explains:

> For by bringing in other stuff that nothing appertaineth to the present matter, you must needs mar and pervert the play that is in hand, though the stuff that you bring be much better. What part soever you have taken upon you, play that as well as you can and make the best of it, and do not, therefore, disturb and bring out of order the

---

[28] Jennifer Bishop, '*Utopia* and Civic Politics in Mid-Sixteenth Century London', *Historical Journal* 54.4 (2011), 933–53.

[29] Richards, *Rhetoric and Courtliness*; Stephen Alford, 'The Political Creed of William Cecil', in John F. McDiarmid, ed., *The Monarchical Republic of Early Modern England. Essays in response to Patrick Collinson* (Aldershot: Ashgate, 2007), 74–90; C. L. S. Davies, 'Slavery and Protector Somerset: The Vagrancy Act of 1547', *Economic History Review* 19.3 (1966), 533–49.

[30] More, *Utopia*, 121.   [31] More, *Utopia*, 121.   [32] More, *Utopia*, 121.

whole matter, because that another which is merrier and better cometh to your remembrance.[33]

The nub of More's point is that the impossibility of truthful and disinterested ratiocination 'in the consultations of kings' should not preclude counsel, and the possibility of morally orientated decision-making.[34] Instead:

> you must with a craft wile and subtle train study and endeavour yourself, as much as in you lies, to handle the matter wittily and handsomely for the purpose, and that which you cannot turn to good so to order it that it be not very bad, for it is not possible for all things to be well unless all men were good, which I think will not be yet these good many years.[35]

It was this self-reflective theatricality—all directed to a moral end—which for More denoted a 'philosophy more civil': a politics of counsel conducted according to the principles of Ciceronian *honestas* and designed to work in a world in which self-interest, custom, and blinkeredness inevitably militated against honest debate.

Whereas More described this quotidian theatricality as civil, his successor translated *honestas* more literally as 'honest'. Honest and honesty were, of course, venerable and complex English words with meanings which ranged from honour and liberality to female chastity and trustworthiness.[36] But Thomas Elyot's extraordinarily influential Latin–English dictionary confused the lexicon even further. This styled '*Honestas, tatis*' as 'honesties', '*Honestus, ta, tum*' as 'honest', and '*Honour, oris, honos, noris*' as 'honour, dignity, sometime beauty, also reverence, honesty'. Elyot also defined '*Decorum*' as 'a seemliness, or that which becomes the person, having respect to his nature, degree, study, office, or profession, be it in doing or speaking, a grace, sometime it signifies honesty' and '*Decorus, ra, rum*' as 'honest, seemly, fair'.[37] Most revealing about Elyot's own understanding of the term was the way Elyot himself used 'honest' in his dedication of the dictionary to Henry VIII. He opined that the purpose of government was that people 'should be kept and preserved in quiet life, not exercised in bestial appetite, but passed forth in all parts of honesty' (A2r). He praised Thomas Cromwell, who had patronized the dictionary, as a 'favourer of honesty, and next to your highness chief patron of virtue and cunning' (A2v). And he thanked his prince 'for the good estimation that your grace retains of my poor learning and honesty, promising... that during my life natural, I shall faithfully employ all the powers of my wit and body, to serve your majesty in everything' (A3v).

A third canonical writer—no less than Hall's admirer Thomas Hobbes—was equally enthralled by the prospect of *honestas*. However, Hobbes does not frame

---

[33] More, *Utopia*, 121.   [34] More, *Utopia*, 122.   [35] More, *Utopia*, 122.

[36] William Empson, *The Structure of Complex Words* (Cambridge, MA: Harvard University Press, 1985), chapters 9 to 11.

[37] Thomas Elyot, *The dictionary of syr Thomas Eliot knight* (1538), definitions of *Honestas, Honestus, Honour, Decorum, Decorus*.

this discussion in terms of honesty and civility—or, indeed, theatricality—but rather wit, fancy, and discretion. He suggests that the 'natural wit' manifest in all people 'consisteth principally in two things; *Celerity of Imagining*, (that is swift succession of one thought to another) and *steady direction* to some approved end'.[38] Those quick to draw links between thoughts and 'observe their similitudes' had 'a *Good Fancy*'; those able to 'observe their differences, and dissimilitudes, which is called *Distinguishing*, and *Discerning*, and *Judging* between thing and thing…are said to have *good Judgment*'. Hobbes noted that 'particularly in matter of conversation and business; wherein, times, places, and persons are to be discerned, this Vertue is called DISCRETION'.[39] Of fancy and discretion it was the latter which was the primary mental and conversational virtue. In any given social situation, 'Besides the Discretion of times, places, and persons, necessary to a good Fancy, there is required also an often application of his thoughts to their End; that is, to some use to be made of them'. With discretion, fancies could be effectively and appropriately applied; without it, 'a great Fancy is one kind of Madness; such as they have, that entering into any discourse, are snatched from their Purpose, by everything that comes in their thought, into so many, and so long digressions, and Parentheses, that they utterly lose themselves'.[40]

The capacity to judge time, place, and person and speak and act accordingly applied to any conversational moment, whether written or spoken. It was especially pertinent to Plutarch's 'Theatrical fictions': in 'a good Poem', in 'a good History', in 'Orations of Prayse, and in Invectives', in 'Hortatives, and Pleadings', in 'Demonstration, in Councell, and all rigorous search of Truth'. Indeed 'in any Discourse whatsoever, if the defect of Discretion be apparent, how extravagant soever the Fancy be, the whole discourse will be taken for a sign of want of wit; and so will it never when the Discretion is manifest, though the Fancy be never so ordinary'.[41] Discretion enabled the speaker to interact appropriately, and so profitably, according to context. It also prevented the 'secret thoughts of a man [to] run over all things'.[42] In these ways, for Hobbes discretion—or civility and honesty—described the repertoire and skills of Hall's 'Theatrical person'. An archive of 'retired and hid actions' offered, in contrast, some clue into the real passions and 'secret thoughts' of past events.

Quotidian theatricality

We have seen how the concept of *honestas* and the theatrical skills it demanded of the person was very much apparent in three of the canonical political treatises of the

---

[38] Hobbes, *Leviathan*, 104.   [39] Hobbes, *Leviathan*, 105.   [40] Hobbes, *Leviathan*, 106.
[41] Hobbes, *Leviathan*, 106–8.   [42] Hobbes, *Leviathan*, 108.

English Renaissance. But it is even more integral to another genre of early modern text: conduct books. These texts were crucial in propagating the ideals of *honestas*—not simply for English gentlemen, as Anna Bryson's otherwise consummate history of the genre tends to assume, but rather for any social group willing to purchase the texts and read the advice.[43] Whereas Bryson regards the normative culture of civility so engendered to be essentially genteel and masculine, writers and publishers also appealed, for example, to urban tradesmen and women. Indeed two of the most cogent and accessible statements of *honestas* in English were made precisely for these groups: in William Scott's 1630s advice to drapers, and Hannah Woolley's 1670s companion for gentlewomen. And as befits accounts of this early modern theory of social practice, the theatrical person was very much in evidence.

Scott's explicit aim was to outline the skills and principles by which drapers could become 'complete citizens' by trading at once 'justly', 'pleasingly', and 'profitably'.[44] He accordingly noted that the 'foundation' of drapery 'is Honesty': 'He cannot be a good Draper which is not first a good man … opening his conscience, living as if he were always in Publique, rather fearing himself than others'. Without honesty, the draper's 'wisdom'—defined by Scott as 'the beautiful and noble composition of him in all his words, his actions and all his motions'—would be 'erroneous' and 'his policy will be knavery'. On the other hand, 'honesty without wisdom is unprofitable'.[45] Scott accordingly described a draper who was quite as accomplished at 'philosophy more civil' as More's counsellor. He explained:

> That which he perform, he must be assisted by behaviour: without this, his other qualities will not help him. It cannot but be distasteful to any man, coming into a Shop, when he sees a man stand as if he were drown'd in phlegm and puddle; having no other testimony of his being awake, than that his eyes are open. It is expected that the outward carriage should promise what's within a man.[46]

It transpires, however, that for Scott exterior and interior are very different spheres. The former is an elaborate performance constructed by the latter, which must pay careful attention to 'ceremonies', to 'behaviour and countenance', and, most of all, to 'conversation'.[47]

To this end, the mind of Scott's shopkeeper must 'be stuffed with sufficiency to produce pleasing discourse, wherein he must not be so lavish as to hinder his observation, and become tedious to him he deals with'.[48] Like some Ciceronian fantasy figure, 'Eloquence will make him more excellent than other men'.[49] This involved consummate theatrical and rhetorical skills, 'wherein a man may see the visage, hands, and members of the man to speak with his mouth; and thus persuading his

---

[43]   Bryson, *From Courtesy to Civility*, chapter 2.
[44]   William Scott, *An Essay on Drapery: or The Complete Citizen* (1635), frontispiece.
[45]   Scott, *An Essay on Drapery*, 3.
[46]   Scott, *An Essay on Drapery*, 85–6.   [47]   Scott, *An Essay on Drapery*, 86–8.
[48]   Scott, *An Essay on Drapery*, 89.   [49]   Scott, *An Essay on Drapery*, 94.

Customer to the liking of his commodity, he must put on the same liking himself; for putting on the same passion he would stir up in others, he is most like to prevail'. However, performance had to be adjusted from one customer to the next: 'Yet in as much as he is to deal with men of divers conditions, let him know that to speak according to the nature of him with whom he commerce, is the best Rhetoric.'[50] Thus:

> To his superior, his words must carry much humility in them; to his equals, familiarity, which because he shall be sure of from them, must be mingled with a little state. To his inferiors familiarity too, but not too much of it, lest he breed contempt; yet his words may carry a great deal, for with inferiors he shall be sure of reverence.[51]

Scott concluded 'that my Citizen may deal pleasingly with all men; I would have him be a good Linguist, getting so many Languages, and those so well that if it were possible, every man he deals with, should think him a Countryman.'[52] The result is a 'composition' of 'honesty and profit' which Bancroft would have understood only as hypocrisy and which Scott described as an 'extraordinary skill, which may be better practiced then expressed'.[53]

Hannah Woolley and her publisher, Dorman Newman, made an altogether better job at defining the 'extraordinary skill' lionized by Scott in their *Gentlewoman's Companion* (1673).[54] Whereas Scott had used the 'composite' of honesty, profit, and wisdom to denote the concept, and Hobbes talked in terms of discretion, fancy, and wit, Woolley more conventionally harked back to More and talked in terms of civility. She explained to her readers that 'Civility, or gentle plausibility, of which I intend to give you information, is in my slender judgment nothing else but the modesty and handsome decorum, to be observed by everyone according to his or her condition; attended with a bonne grace and neat becoming air'.[55] Woolley noted that insofar as natural attributes are concerned, 'It lies not in my power to lay you down rules and precepts for the procuring this charming air, and winning agreeableness'. This was because 'Nature hath reserved this to herself, and will not bestow this inexpressible boon, but to her choice favourites, and therefore I do not see how Art with her utmost skill can imitate it to any purpose'.[56] However, natural charms were more or less irrelevant. It was learned skills and their strategic application which mattered. This was because:

---

[50] Scott, *An Essay on Drapery*, 94.   [51] Scott, *An Essay on Drapery*, 94.
[52] Scott, *An Essay on Drapery*, 94.   [53] Scott, *An Essay on Drapery*, 136–7.
[54] Hannah Woolley, *The Gentlewoman's Companion: or, A Guide to the Female Sex* (1673). For Woolley see Elaine Hobby, *Virtue of Necessity: English Women's Writing, 1646–1688* (London: Virago, 1988), 172–6; Hobby, 'A Woman's Best Setting Out is Silence; the Writings of Hannah Woolley', in Gerald Maclean, ed., *Culture and Society in the Stuart Restoration: Literature, Drama, History* (Cambridge: Cambridge University Press, 1995), 181; Phil Withington, *Society in Early Modern England: The Vernacular Origins of Some Powerful Ideas* (Cambridge: Polity Press, 2010), 195–7.
[55] Woolley, *Gentlewoman's Companion*, 44.   [56] Woolley, *Gentlewoman's Companion*, 44.

whether you are afflicted with any natural or accidental deformity, or not, you can never be truly accomplished till you apply yourself to the Rule of Civility, which is nothing but a certain Modesty or *Pudor* required in all your actions; this is the virtue I will labour to describe, which description I hope will be sufficient to direct you towards the acquisition of that agreeable deportment which hath the power to conciliate and procure the applause and affection of all sorts of people.[57]

Thus while Elyot defined *honestas* as honesty, More applied the concept to counsel, Scott embedded *honestas* in shopkeeping, and Hobbes integrated it into his general philosophical system, Woolley explained to her female readers that 'Civility may be thus understood; it is a science for the right understanding ourselves, and true instructing how to dispose of all our words and actions in their proper and due places'. There were, she noted, 'four circumstances which attend Civility, without which, according to its Rules, nothing can be done exactly'. These circumstances included self-knowledge, in terms of one's relative age and condition; an appreciation of the 'quality of the Person you converse withal'; and a sense of the time and place 'where you are'.[58]

Although Woolley was describing a means of coping with patriarchy, her reasons for adapting this theory of social practice were the same as those for counsel or retailing. By developing social acuity and theatrical competence, women could negotiate the many dangers of conversation, whether with inferiors, peers, or superiors. In this way they served their personal interests as effectively as possible while respecting the social conventions which protected each from the 'will' of others. The implications for each woman were, as for counsellors and drapers, considerable. Not only did civility demand a repertoire of habits, gestures, and responses so that people behaved appropriately for the context they found themselves in. It also encouraged pronounced degrees of self-reflectivity and performative skill. Women, like shopkeepers and counsellors, were expected constantly to interpret company and their place within it and also learn the appropriate and most efficacious ways to act. Thus Woolley continues:

> These circumstances relating to the knowledge of ourselves, and all persons in all conditions, having respect of time and place, are of such great consequence, and necessary import, that if you are deficient in any of these, all your actions (how well soever intended) are the rags of imperfection and deformity.

As befits a social anthropologist, she added:

> I shall find it somewhat difficult to prescribe the exact rules of Civility, so as to render them compliable with all times, places, and persons, by reason of variety of Customs: You may fall accidentally into the society of some exotic and foreign person of quality; and what may seem civil and decent in you, may seem indecent and ridiculous to another Nation.[59]

---

[57] Woolley, *Gentlewoman's Companion*, 45.   [58] Woolley, *Gentlewoman's Companion*, 45–6.
[59] Woolley, *Gentlewoman's Companion*, 46.

All of which served to reiterate that civility was not a list of rules and conventions which a gentlewoman learned and followed slavishly, but rather an ethos and set of skills enabling her—like counsellors or drapers—to adjust to and cope with whatever company she found herself in.

'Honest, honest Iago'

Although they used different vocabulary, Elyot's *Dictionary*, Robinson's *Utopia*, Hobbes's *Leviathan*, Scott's *Drapery*, and Woolley's *Companion* all disseminated the attributes of *honestas* to an English reading public. In so doing they also provided a largely positive gloss on the concept, presenting it as mode of practice to benefit interlocutors in various conversational settings. This was in sharp contrast to the language of theatricality, which for moralists was a byword for hypocrisy and false-consciousness. With its remorseless interrogation of the language of honesty, Shakespeare's *Othello* exposes the theatricality at the heart of *honestas* and the dangers the theatrical basis of public life entailed. In Iago Shakespeare reveals, painfully and tragically, how a character fully inured to the ways of 'craft wile and subtle train', as More put it, can dominate and destroy everyone around them; he dramatizes, indeed, how quotidian theatricality was quite as perilous as its more overtly religious or stage-playing forms. In this way Shakespeare might well be said to have enabled or encouraged the discursive reorientation in the word 'theatrical' itself, away from the heightened ceremony and ritual of church and theatre to the more mundane spaces of tavern, shop, and bedroom.

The language of honesty was important to Shakespeare. With over 350 appearances across his corpus of plays, 'honest' and its derivatives appear much more often than other terms to describe the self, such as 'ingenious' and 'discretion' (under 50 appearances each), 'civility' (57), 'courtesy' (103), and 'wit' (332).[60] Viewed in quantitative terms, *Othello* is easily Shakespeare's most honest play. The word appears no less than 37 times in *Othello*, over ten times more than its nearest rivals, *Timon of Athens* (24) and *The Merry Wives of Windsor* (22). And in *Othello* it is Iago who dominates this language. Almost all uses of honest involve Iago, with Iago either describing someone else as honest, someone else describing Iago as honest, or Iago describing himself as honest.

The assumption that Shakespeare is using a modern and simple conception of honesty to denote truth and sincerity makes for a perfectly good reading of this language, invoking a sharp and deep sense of irony and pathos. However, the reading is enormously enriched, and certainly more fully historicized, if the

---

[60] Phil Withington, '"Tumbled into the Dirt": Wit and Incivility in Early Modern England', *Journal of Historical Pragmatics* 12.1–22 (2011), 156–77.

complicated classical sense of honesty as *honestas* is borne in mind, along with the strong performative dimension it carried. Indeed, this is precisely the definition of 'honesty' which Shakespeare provides in the play. After the famous drinking scene, in which Iago engineers for his commanding officer, Cassio, to become involved in a drunken brawl, Othello asks Iago for an account of what has happened. Iago gives a perfectly judged speech which incriminates Cassio while giving the impression to Othello that he is moderating the truth in order to protect him. Deceived by this rhetorical double-bluff, Othello says: 'I know, Iago / Thy honesty and love doth mince this matter, / Making it light to Cassio' (2.3.242–5). That is, Othello recognizes Iago's *honestas* ('honesty') even as Iago uses these skills to destroy Cassio. Likewise in the crucial counselling scene, when Iago manages to sow the seeds of doubt in Othello's mind about Desdemona's trustworthiness and chastity, Othello repeatedly uses 'honesty' to refer to his *de facto* counsellor's *honestas*. Iago says 'My lord, you know I love you', to which Othello replies 'I think thou dost. / And for I know thou'rt full of love and honesty / And weighs't thy words before thou giv'st them breath, / Therefore these stops of thine fright me the more' (3.3.119–23). And as Iago's rhetoric begins to take effect, Othello ruminates 'This fellow's of exceeding honesty / And knows all qualities, with a learned spirit, / Of human dealings' (3.3.262–5).

This conception of 'honesty' as *honestas* forces attention not merely on Iago's motives for destroying Othello—the traditional concern of literary scholars—but also on his remarkable social acuity, decorum, and theatricality in achieving this end. As E. A. J. Honigmann notes, he is a character blessed with 'outstanding dramatic talents' and 'verbal dexterity and psychological insight'.[61] As critics since Auden have pointed out (and as the 2011 production for the Sheffield Crucible, with Dominic West as Iago, beautifully demonstrates) Iago is also the play's 'chief humourist'.[62] Iago can accordingly play the quintessential 'good-fellow', singing ballads and calling toasts in order to get Cassio drunk: 'Some wine, ho! And let me the cannikin clink, clink, / And let me the cannikin clink. / A soldier's a man, / O, man's life's but a span, / Why then let a soldier drink! Some wine, boys' (2.3.64–70). He can play the witty flirt, bantering with Desdemona (2.1.125–30). He can play the sage counsellor, persuading Othello to follow his advice and suspect Desdemona without any grounds whatsoever: 'I am glad of this, for now I shall have reason / To show the love and duty that I bear you / With franker spirit: therefore, as I am bound, Receive it from me. I speak not yet of proof: / Look to your wife, observe her well with Cassio' (3.3196–200). And so on.

Iago is versed, in effect, in each of the senses of *honestas* I have considered here: More's 'craft and wile', Hobbes's 'fancy and discretion', Scott's 'extraordinary skill',

---

[61] E. A. Honigmann, 'Introduction', in William Shakespeare, *Othello*, 37.

[62] Honigmann, 'Introduction', 39; W. H. Auden, *The Dyer's Hand and Other Essays* (London: Faber, 1975), 253.

and Woolley's 'science for the right understanding ourselves'. In Othello, however, Shakespeare reverts to Elyot's descriptor in order to depict these traits, with the result that the numerous exchanges about honesty throughout the play are charged with a complex and ambiguous piquancy. Not least is the moment when the truth finally begins to dawn on Iago's hapless victims:

> Othello: Ay, 'twas he [Iago] that me on her first;
>   An honest man he is, and hates the slime
>   That sticks on filthy deeds.
> Emilia: My husband!
> Othello: What needs this iterance, woman? I say thy husband.
> Emilia: O mistress, villainy hath made mocks with love!
>   My husband say she was false?
> Othello: He, woman;
>   I say thy husband: dost understand the word?
>   My friend thy husband, honest, honest Iago.   (5.2.140–50)

The difficult word here, of course, is not 'husband', as Othello sardonically suggests, but rather 'honest'. Emilia knows Iago to be as far from honest as any man can be—'he lies to th'heart' (5.2.152). But insofar as the attributes of *honestas* are concerned, Othello knows Iago to be adept as they come: viewed in these terms, the epithet 'honest, honest Iago' is far from inappropriate. This skill gives Iago an extraordinary power, which he uses not for the common good—as the 'philosophy more civil' was intended to do—but for his own somewhat inexplicable ends. It also means that he is defined entirely through his theatricality and eloquence. There can be few more finite departures than 'Demand me nothing. What you know, you know. / From this time forth I never will speak word' (5.2.300–1). When Iago stops speaking, he stops being.

Theatre as history

As a character who not only practises *honestas* but in many respects personifies it, Iago raises obvious doubts about the possibility of ever stripping back the 'Theatrical person' in order to discover their 'retired and hid actions' in the manner of John Hall. When such skills are so deeply embodied and acquired, is there anything left that 'retired' and interior to the self? *Othello* suggests there is. Iago's metaphorical 'stammering', to use Jonson's phrase, was clearly orchestrated through a keen and calculating intelligence, and it varied from one social context to the next. His was not an acquired and involuntary *habitus* so much as a prolonged and careful performance based on the highly attuned skills of stage-player: an act, that is, of quotidian theatricality. Viewed in these terms, *Othello* can be viewed as a revelatory moment in which the dramaturgical foundations of civil and honest society were exposed. Indeed, *Othello* and other plays like it performed precisely the kind of role identified by Hall for his modern kind of history, dramatizing and recording the 'craft wile and subtle train' of 'Theatrical persons' across the ages. That the 'Romans call those who act comedies and other theatrical plays, *Histories*', and that 'theatrical plays' were still outlawed in England in 1649, helps explain, perhaps, his plea for an expanded historiography.[63] The theatrical archive of quotidian theatricality—the Renaissance theatre—was no more. Rather, in 1649 the *only* theatricality permitted in England was *honestas*—the theatricality of everyday life.

In conclusion, it is worth noting three aspects of early modern linguistic change which the word 'theatrical' and the various English words used to describe *honestas* highlight. Most obviously, they show that the recent historiographical interest in the theatrical and rhetorical dimensions of social and political life—not to mention the instability and mutability of selfhood—is not simply a reflection of modern concerns.[64] Rather it resonates deeply with the preoccupations of early moderns themselves. Second, the words demonstrate the complicated and sometimes inde-terminate relationship between language and concepts.[65] This is especially the case for those classical ideas introduced into English through an intensifying engage-ment with ancient and continental culture.[66] In this sense, the large and diffuse number of referents for *honestas*—from honesty and civility, to discretion and wis-dom, to seemliness and handsomeness, to theatricality—nicely illustrates what a semantically fecund and fluid era this was. So, too, does the burgeoning accretion of pejorative inferences for theatrical, from Popish false-consciousness to drama-turgical transfiguration to moral corruption to everyday hypocrisy, affectation, and honesty. Finally, the words illuminate the varied ways by which classical ideas and practices insinuated themselves into the vernacular and the potential breadth and social depth of their cultural impact. By the seventeenth century, one did not

[63] Holland, *Philosophie*, 885.

[64] For some recent approaches see Karin Sennefelt, 'The Politics of Hanging Around and Tagging Along: Everyday Practices of Politics in Eighteenth-Century Stockholm', in Michael J. Braddick, ed., *The Politics of Gesture: Historical Perspectives* (Oxford: Past & Present, 2009); Phil Withington, 'Com-pany and Sociability in Early Modern England', *Social History* 32.3 (2007), 291–307; Markku Peltonen, *Rhetoric, Politics and Popularity in Pre-Revolutionary England* (Cambridge: Cambridge University Press, 2013); Chris R. Kyle, *Theatre of State: Parliament and Political Culture in Early Stuart England* (Stanford: Stanford University Press, 2012); Laura Gowing, ' "The Manner of Submission": Gender and Demeanour in Seventeenth-Century London', forthcoming in *Cultural and Social History*, 10.1 (2013).

[65] Quentin Skinner, 'The Idea of the Cultural Lexicon' and 'Retrospect: Studying Language and Conceptual Change', in *Visions of Politics: Volume I: Regarding Method* (Cambridge: Cambridge Uni-versity Press, 2002); The Early Modern Research Group, 'Towards a Social and Cultural History of Keywords and Concepts by the Early Modern Research Group', *History of Political Thought* 31 (2010), 427–48.

[66] Withington, *Society*, chapter 6; Early Modern Research Group, 'Commonwealth: the Social, Cultural, and Conceptual Contexts of an Early Modern Keyword', *The Historical Journal* 54.3 (2011), 659–87.

need to read Cicero to learn about *honestas* or to come across Plutarch to know about theatricality. One could read Robinson and Hobbes, Scott and Woolley. One could listen to sermons. One could learn the conventions and skills of civil society. One could go to the theatre, if it was open.

FURTHER READING

Bryson, Anna. *From Courtesy to Civility: Changing Codes of Conduct in Early Modern England* (Oxford: Oxford University Press, 1996).

Klein, Lawrence E. *Shaftesbury and the Culture of Politeness: Moral Discourse and Cultural Politics in Eighteenth-Century England* (Cambridge: Cambridge University Press, 1994).

Peltonen, Markku. *Rhetoric, Politics and Popularity in Pre-Revolutionary England* (Cambridge: Cambridge University Press, 2013).

Richards, Jennifer. *Rhetoric and Courtliness in Early Modern England* (Cambridge: Cambridge University Press, 2003).

Withington, Phil. *Society in Early Modern England: The Vernacular Origins of Some Powerful Ideas* (Cambridge: Polity Press, 2010).

CHAPTER 28

READING

ANN BAYNES COIRO

The closing of the theatres in 1642 is one of the most clearly demarcated dividing lines in literary history, the decisive end of a great theatrical age. This division can certainly be debated and nuanced. To a limited extent theatre itself lived on: in contraband stagings of plays, Cromwell's commissioning of masques, and the performance late in the interregnum of Davenant's post-masque proto-operas.[1] Theatricality, as an idea or metaphor, remained an important ideological flashpoint, as Phil Withington shows in his chapter on '*Honestas*' in this volume. Royalists, for example, routinely targeted antitheatricality as prime evidence of destructive Puritan ignorance.[2] Political argument on every side consciously explored the metaphorical space between the stage and the public sphere.[3] Pamphlets from various perspectives were written in play form.[4] Parliament deliberately staged Charles's execution in front of the Banqueting House where court masques had been performed. And the king understood that he too could appropriate the theatre of

---

[1] On performances between 1642 and 1660 see Leslie Hotson, *The Commonwealth and Restoration Stage* (Cambridge, MA: Harvard University Press, 1928), 2–59, 133–66; Gunnar Sorelius, '*The Giant Race Before the Flood': Pre-Restoration Drama on the Stage and in the Criticism of the Restoration* (Uppsala: Almqvist & Wiksell, 1966), 34–5; Dale B. J. Randall, *Winter Fruit: English Drama 1642–1660* (Lexington: University Press of Kentucky, 1995); Susan Wiseman, *Drama and Politics in the English Civil War* (Cambridge: Cambridge University Press, 1998); and Janet Clare, *Drama of the English Republic, 1649–60* (Manchester: Manchester University Press, 2002).

[2] Jonas Barish has documented the abiding concerns of antitheatricality: the degenerate role of the actor, the unsavouriness of public display, and the dangers of mimesis for the audience in *The Antitheatrical Prejudice* (Berkeley: University of California Press, 1981). Ben Jonson's satires of Puritan antitheatricality (such as Zeal-of-the-Land Busy in *Bartholomew Fair*) provided royalists a venerable template for this stereotype.

[3] See Bronwen Wilson and Paul Yachnin, eds., *Making Publics in Early Modern Europe: People, Things, Forms of Knowledge* (New York: Routledge, 2010), particularly the editors' introduction, 1–24.

[4] Nigel Smith, *Literature and Revolution, 1640–1660* (New Haven: Yale University Press, 1994), 70–92.

execution to his advantage, a political and theatrical competition that royalists would decisively win.[5]

Yet the consequences of English theatre's long intermission were undoubtedly profound. Performance became at best private and, potentially, illegal. When the theatres opened again, almost twenty years later, the market was severely constricted to two closely monitored companies. The reconstituted theatre audience of the Restoration was also distinctly different from the audiences of the pre-revolutionary theatre, including the more select audiences of Caroline private theatres.[6] Theatrical fashion now privileged sophisticated spectacle and broad-stroke rhetoric. French drama and continental romance enjoyed even greater influence than they had in the 1630s, and the neo-Aristotelian unities undergirding French theory and practice exerted an intimidating influence on English conceptions of their own theatrical tradition. Like all acts of nostalgia, the 'restored' stage intended to evoke, not to recreate, the past.

When the theatre reopened, printed plays were the essential component of the memories shaping a revived theatricality. This fact reveals what is perhaps the single most important effect of the closing of the theatres: most people grew accustomed to experiencing 'theatricality' through reading.[7] Two generations earlier, Ben Jonson had tried, without much success, to elevate masques and plays above theatre's transitory materiality by printing them as dramatic 'poems'.[8] After the collapse of press censorship in 1642 and the resulting flood of pamphlets and books, however, print had lost its stigma. And the combination of print's dominance and the concomitant stage ban finally accelerated theatre's alchemical change into dramatic poetry.

---

[5] Nancy Klein Maguire, *Regicide and Restoration: English Tragicomedy, 1660–1671* (Cambridge: Cambridge University Press, 1992) and Maguire, ed., *Renaissance Tragicomedy: Explorations in Genre and Politics* (New York: AMS Press, 1987). On the success of *Eikon Basilike*, see Philip Knachel's introduction to *Eikon Basilike* (Ithaca: Published for the Folger Shakespeare Library by Cornell University Press, 1966), Elizabeth Sauer, *'Paper-Contestations' and Textual Communities in England, 1640–1675* (Toronto: University of Toronto Press, 2005), 57–76, and Elizabeth Skerpan Wheeler, 'The First "Royal": Charles I as Celebrity', *PMLA* 126.4 (2011), 912–34.

[6] Jessica Munns observes that 'although the audience was somewhat mixed, these were coterie theatres under direct royal control and patronage, and the court and those who followed the court made up a significant part of their spectators'; see her 'Theatrical Culture I: Politics and Theatre', in Steven N. Zwicker, ed., *The Cambridge Companion to English Literature 1650–1740* (Cambridge: Cambridge University Press, 1998), 82–103 (87). In 1668, though, Samuel Pepys records in his diary a 'mighty company of citizens, prentices, and others' in attendance near him at a play; *The Diary of Samuel Pepys*, ed. Robert Latham and William Matthews, 11 vols. (Berkeley: University of California Press, 1970–83), 9: 2.

[7] See Lois Potter, *Secret Rites and Secret Writing: Royalist Literature, 1641–1660* (Cambridge: Cambridge University Press, 1989) and Sauer, *'Paper-Contestations'*, 77–99.

[8] In his 1616 *Works*, Jonson reproduces the dedicatory prefaces to his plays, where he calls them a 'legitimate Poeme' (*Catiline* [London, 1616], 681) and a 'poeme...that out-liv'd' the 'malice' (*Sejanus*, 357) of the audience of the play. In the long dedication of *Volpone*, Jonson contrasts his own 'poetrie' in the play that follows to the offending 'stage-poetrie' of other writers (443).

Printed theatrical works pose important questions, and particularly so in the fraught, politicized circumstances of a state-darkened theatre. Were plays performed in private and semi-private settings using printed texts? When they encountered plays only in books, had readers considered themselves actors? What were the protocols, the conventions, of reading something that had been a script but was repurposed as a 'dramatic poem'? When we discuss drama that is written to be read rather than performed we call it 'closet drama', a term that even those who deploy it find inadequate. It is certainly not adequate to describe plays that were explicitly written to be performed and that evoke lingering memories of past performances. No matter how hard we now strive to throw off the book, reading profoundly shapes our own notions of early modern theatricality. The impetus for our present literary framing lies significantly in the cultural contests of the mid-seventeenth century: the same literary framing indelibly changed Restoration theatre. As Milton astutely observed in *Areopagitica*, censorship can have unintended effects.

Memory itself is a judgement, a working theory of what is worth remembering. When the theatres reopened, no one wanted to go back to the ways things were in the uncouth, untutored, and politically dangerous old days. For the theatres of the Restoration were charged not only with the greatness of England's theatrical past but also with the deep cultural strife theatre had engendered. Antitheatricality had certainly contributed to the closure of the stages, but it had been stalking theatre throughout the early modern period. It had also been answered by a rich tradition of theatrical defence: from Sidney's justification of theatre as an experiential pedagogy called 'poesy', to the knowing metatheatricality of plays such as Shakespeare's *Midsummer Night's Dream* and *Hamlet*, Jonson's *Bartholomew Fair*, or Massinger's *The Roman Actor*, all of which valorize theatrical practice, even while mocking their audiences and announcing their distrust of their own actors. During the revolutionary and post-revolutionary years, the dialectic of theatricality and antitheatricality then became a memory game played for high cultural stakes and long-term influence. The criss-crossing polarity of popular culture and canon, of theatre and drama, of theatricality and antitheatricality, of stage and page can be charted across the history of theatre. But because late sixteenth- and early seventeenth-century theatre is crucial in Western culture, it is particularly important that we trace its movement off the stage, into books, and back again, irrevocably changed.

Plays in print were, for example, open to retroactive rewriting. After 1660, plays from the age 'before the Flood' were subject to a grafting of the old collaborative theatrical practices with the new work of literary criticism that characterizes the 1660s.[9] Although Restoration playwrights would eventually gain new legal rights and develop a distinctive body of work, pre-revolutionary plays were subject to

---

[9] The phrase is Dryden's from his 1694 poem 'To My Dear Friend, Mr. Congreve, On His Comedy, call'd *The Double Dealer*', in *Works*, ed. A. B. Chambers and William Frost (Berkeley: University of California Press, 1974), 4: 432.5.

startlingly thorough adaptation or imitation so blatant it can be called plagiarism, or samplings and mash-ups that created weird DNAs with multiple life potencies.[10] At the same time, previously suspect theatrical audiences were newly reconceived as discerning readers and granted greater power to shape stage practice. In this highly collaborative atmosphere, old practices and current theories negotiated a new theatricality.

This essay explores the question of early modern theatre and its relationship to the emerging concepts of drama and literary criticism through the example of two gifted and astonishingly influential bookmen, both of whom were responsible for the re-conceptualization of theatre after the Restoration: Humphrey Moseley, who curated English literature from his bookshop in St Paul's throughout the wars and interregnum, and John Dryden, who brilliantly shaped the past and theorized the future in *An Essay of Dramatick Poesie*.

'The presse shall give to ev'ry man his part'

Restoration theatre started out with the past: two pre-war playwrights as company managers and a repertoire of old plays. Charles II rewarded the Caroline playwright and *bon vivant* Thomas Killigrew with the King's Company and William Davenant, a theatrical innovator before and during the wars and interregnum, with the Duke's Company.[11] In 1660 there were no active English playwrights: Shirley was still alive but not writing, and Davenant, who had been strikingly innovative in the late 1650s, was devoting his considerable theatrical talent to adapting and translating plays and to running his theatre company. Basically, therefore, the two Restoration companies could directly perform earlier plays or they could adapt early modern plays to Restoration taste. Their scripts came either from the grey market of old plays, still unpublished, or from already published plays (sometimes repeatedly).[12] Whatever route they travelled, this reservoir of pre-war plays is obviously crucial to re-establishing Restoration theatricality. By the 1670s, Restoration theatre, as we now conceive it, was recognizably taking shape. But performances of older plays,

---

[10] In Eric Rothstein's formulation, Restoration drama developed 'by subverting the tradition on which it drew. By a sort of half-aware fifth column work, camouflaged with cheerfully ambiguous terminology, it...reviewed and revised and remolded its Renaissance critical models', *Restoration Tragedy: Form and the Process of Change* (Madison: University of Wisconsin Press, 1967), 3. On the development of playwright's rights, see Paulina Kewes, 'Plays as Property, 1660–1710', in Alan Houston and Steve Pincus, eds., *A Nation Transformed: England After the Restoration* (Cambridge: Cambridge University Press, 2001), 211–40.

[11] I am indebted to Sorelius, '*The Giant Race*'; Rothstein, *Restoration Tragedy*, 51–9; and Robert D. Hume, 'Securing a Repertory: Plays on the London Stage, 1660–5', in Antony Coleman and Antony Hammond, eds., *Poetry and Drama: Essays in Honour of Harold F. Brooks* (London: Methuen, 1981), 156–72.

[12] See Alfred Harbage, 'Elizabethan-Restoration Palimpsest', *MLR* 35 (1940), 287–319.

with or without adaptation, would continue—and, indeed, would dominate stage offerings—for many years.

Robert Hume has called the 1660s 'an isolated freak' in theatrical history.[13] But early Restoration revivals and experimentation are in crucial ways precisely the opposite of isolated: the London theatre was crowded with old theatrical memories and new demands.[14] During these years, theatricality returned to the stage. Having passed through books, having become a national canon and the subject of theoretical analysis, however, it could not come back the same. Killigrew tried to look back to the plays and performance norms of the theatrical past, and Davenant looked forward, experimenting with music and state of the art theatrical spectacle, but for each company the restored stage was a volatile crucible combining theatricality and the dramatic poetry plays had become. The early years of the decade— between the theatres' reopening in 1660 and the extended hiatus beginning in June 1665 when the great plague once again closed them—form a natural experiment, allowing us to see how theatricality was reconstituted out of memories embraced and rejected.

Killigrew's company had a significant advantage when the stage officially reopened, because it had been awarded the rights to hundreds of old plays. This boon may have been granted, at least in part, because Killigrew's troupe included '[t]he scattered Remnant' of older actors from pre-1642 theatres.[15] The core of Davenant's company, on the other hand, was a troupe of younger actors who had worked with John Rhodes in the last years of the Protectorate and at the Cockpit in Drury Lane during the military rule of General Monck in early 1660. Yet Davenant was given only temporary access to the most desirable of the twelve plays that Rhodes's troupe had in their repertoire; in fact, Davenant had to petition the Lord Chamberlain to perform even his own plays. Davenant, however, was granted the right of 'reformeinge some of the most ancient Playes that were playd at Blackfriars and of makeinge them, fitt, for the Company of Actors appointed under his direction and Comand'.[16] Of these eleven 'ancient Playes' available for Davenant's rehabilitation, nine are by Shakespeare, including *The Tempest*, *Measure for Measure*, *King Lear*, *Macbeth*, and *Twelfth Night*.[17] The remaining two are Webster's *The Duchess of Malfi*, whose violence and plot structured over an extensive time period made its appeal in 1662 decidedly retro, and *The Sophy*, Sir John Denham's only play, a blank verse

[13] Hume, 'Securing a Repertory', 169.

[14] Rothstein argues that the development of Restoration tragedy 'owes a great deal to the presence, for the first time in the history of English drama, of a backlog of plays large enough to permit conscious borrowing, conscious imitation, conscious archaism', *Restoration Tragedy*, 53.

[15] According to John Downes, *Roscius Anglicanus, or an Historical Review of the Stage* (London, 1708), 1.

[16] Hume, 'Securing a Repertory', 158–9.

[17] The other Shakespeare plays are: *Much Ado About Nothing*, *Romeo and Juliet*, *Henry VIII*, and *Hamlet*. According to Downes, 'No succeeding Tragedy for several Years got more Reputation, or Money to the Company' than *Hamlet*, first performed by Davenant's company in 1662 (*Roscius Anglicanus*, 21).

tragedy published in 1642.[18] Although we now would consider this 'ancient' repertoire (almost entirely) enviable and not in need of 'reformeing', it was not a group of highly desirable theatrical properties in the Restoration.

A measure of what was actually valuable might be found in the six plays from Rhodes's repertoire that the Duke's Company was allowed to perform for just two months so that they could get themselves established: Fletcher's *The Mad Lover*, *The Maid in the Mill*, *The Spanish Curate*, *The Loyal Subject*, and *Rule a Wife*, plus Shakespeare's *Pericles, Prince of Tyre*.[19] Even during the two-month period when these plays were allowed to the Duke's Company, the King's Company was poaching them. The King's Company also poached and continued to poach five of the six other Rhodes company plays that the Lord Chamberlain's decree implicitly seems to have left to the Duke's Company: Fletcher's *The Wild Goose Chase*, *A Wife for a Month*, and *The Woman's Prize*, Massinger's *The Bond-Man*, and Suckling's *Aglaura*. The only play there is no record of the King's Company performing is Middleton and Rowley's *The Changeling*. In other words, the play in this group most highly regarded by twenty-first-century literary criticism was apparently the least attractive theatrical vehicle to Restoration taste: a chastening warning that literary history is always in danger of being blinkered by anachronistic judgements.

Where did these twelve plays, so valuable at this transitional moment when theatre was re-emerging, come from? Most arrived on stage via a detour through Humphrey Moseley's printing press. Moseley published *Aglaura* in 1646 and in 1653 published *The Changeling* for the first time (it had first been performed in 1622).[20] Seven more of the Rhodes company's twelve plays were published for the first time in Moseley's great 1647 Beaumont and Fletcher Folio. Because he bought up as many play copyrights as he could, the pattern of Moseley's strong connection with the Rhodes company plays is repeated across the rest of the existing theatrical canon. As a result, the range of plays Restoration audiences saw and the 'optick' through which they viewed them, to use Shirley's term in his dedicatory epistle to the Beaumont and Fletcher Folio, were both significantly shaped by one interregnum bookseller.[21]

---

[18] The *Duchess of Malfi* was performed in 1662, 1668, and at court in 1686; Downes calls it 'one of the Best of Stock Tragedies' (*Roscius Anglicanus*, 25). The 1642 title page claims that *The Sophy* had been 'acted at the Private House in Black Friars by his Majesties servants', but Brendan Ó Hehir, Denham's editor and biographer, calls the evidence for such a performance 'extremely tenuous'; see *Expans'd Hieroglyphicks: A Critical Edition of Sir John Denham's Coopers Hill* (Berkeley: University of California Press, 1969), 27 and Ó Hehir, *Harmony from Discords: A Life of Sir John Denham* (Berkeley: University of California Press, 1968), 38–40.

[19] Downes names the plays, *Roscius Anglicanus*, 18.

[20] Both plays were published as part of Moseley's octavo series. Suckling had published *Aglaura* himself in a much mocked folio edition (with copious white space) in 1638. The other three Rhodes plays were Fletcher's *Rule a Wife and Have a Wife*, Shakespeare's *Pericles, Prince of Tyre*, and Massinger's *The Bond Man*, all perennially popular both before and after the revolution.

[21] James Shirley, 'To the Reader' (sig. A4v, 35–6). Shirley also has a prefatory poem, the last to appear before Moseley's own, called 'Upon the Printing of Mr. John Fletchers works' (sig. G1v).

Early modern English literature, as we know it today, was Humphrey Moseley's business.[22] Moseley saw a new market in this revolutionary world where coterie manuscript circulation was no longer an effective circuit for fine poetry, no court had the gravitational field to define cultural tastes, and there were no legal public theatres. From 1645 until his death soon after the Restoration, Moseley defended royalism by advancing the cause of poetry, dramatic and otherwise. He had already had a long publishing career when he published Edmund Waller's *Poems &c* in 1645 and fully discovered his calling.[23] After publishing Waller and receiving the 'incouragement' of 'the most ingenious men', Moseley soon brought out Milton's *Poems*, comparing this relatively unknown poet and masque writer favourably with the worth of Waller.[24] Moseley paired Waller and Milton in a physical and commercial way as well; each volume appeared in octavo with similar front matter. From 1645 until 1651, Moseley published a number of literary writers in what became a series: besides Waller's *Poems &c* and Milton's *Poems* (and *A Maske*) in 1645, Moseley published Suckling's *Fragmenta Aurea* and Shirley's *Poems &c* in 1646, and in 1651 Stanley's *Poems*, Carew's *Poems, with a Maske*, and William Cartwright's *Comedies, Tragi-comedies, with Other Poems*.[25] David Scott Kastan has gone so far as to argue that Moseley's recognizable volumes of poetry, printed so that they could be collected as a matched set and prefaced with Moseley's confident introductions, made 'a coherent literary field visible' and 'invented' English literature.[26] Without a doubt, Moseley understood seventeenth-century poetry as a print discourse, as a political vehicle and as valuable culture on sale for anyone.[27]

But Moseley's special franchise became drama. He more or less cornered the market on the stock of pre-war plays, and as a result his impact on Restoration theatre was incalculable. For one thing, Moseley created a drama series imitating his publishing endeavour with the English poets. Over a five-year period, using the

[22] I am indebted to John Curtis Reed, 'Humphrey Moseley, Publisher', *Oxford Bibliographic Society Proceedings and Papers* 2.2 (1928), 57–142; Pauline Kewes, ' "Give me the sociable pocket-bookes…": Humphrey Moseley's Serial Publication of Octavo Play Collections', *Publishing History* 38 (1995), 5–21; and Peter Lindenbaum, 'Humphrey Moseley', in James K. Bracken and Joel Silver, eds., *The British Literary Book Trade, 1675–1700* (Detroit: Gale, 1996), 177–83.

[23] Moseley began his career in 1619 as an apprentice to Matthew Lownes, who had published the works of Sidney in 1605 and 1613 and of Spenser in 1609, 1611, and 1617.

[24] Moseley, 'The Stationer to the Reader', in *Poems* (London, 1645), sig. A4r.

[25] On Moseley's poetry series, see Peter Lindenbaum, 'Milton's Contract', *Cardoza Arts and Entertainment Law Journal* 10 (1992), 451.

[26] David Scott Kastan, 'Humphrey Moseley and the Invention of English Literature', in Sabrina Alcorn Baron, Eric Lindquist, and Eleanor Shevlin, eds., *Agent of Change: Print Culture Studies after Elizabeth L. Eisenstein* (Amherst: University of Massachusetts Press, 2007), 114, 105. For a somewhat different account of Waller and Moseley see Ann Baynes Coiro, 'The Personal Rule of Poets: Cavalier Poetry and the English Revolution', in Laura Lunger Knoppers, ed., *The Oxford Handbook of the Literature of the English Revolution* (Oxford: Oxford University Press, 2012), 206–37.

[27] Ann Baynes Coiro, 'Milton and Class Identity: The Publication of *Areopagitica* and the 1645 *Poems*', *JMRS* 22 (1992), 261–88.

poetry series' octavo-with-author-portrait format, Moseley published: Brome's *Five New Plays* (1653), Shirley's *Six New Plays* (1653), Massinger's *Three New Plays* (1655), Lodowick Carlell's *Two New Plays* (1657), and Middleton's *Two New Plays* (1657).[28] The plays in the series are 'new' in the sense that they had not appeared in print before; when Moseley published other, already printed, plays by these authors, he did so in octavo so that they could be bound together with the 'new' plays. Lined up on a shelf or bound together, the plays could achieve an authorial, literary presence.

Meanwhile Moseley bought up copyrights to as many previously published and unpublished plays as he could get his hands on; his subsidiary interest in publishing continental romance would also be a major resource for the plots of Restoration drama. In 1653 he registered more than forty plays in the Stationers' Register.[29] He published many of them, but others he didn't, and Moseley reasserted his claims in 1660, when all these plays became highly valuable.[30] Moseley died early in 1661 and therefore did not directly realize the profits from his visionary investments. But in a letter he wrote to Sir Henry Herbert in August 1660 Moseley is clearly keeping his options open: 'I never so much as treated with [Mr. Rhodes, of the Cockpitt playhouse] ... neither did I ever consent directly or indirectly, that hee or any others [the Whitefryers playhouse and players] should act any playes that doe belong to mee, without my knowledge and consent had and procured'.[31] The cache of scripts Moseley had accumulated was potentially worth a great deal of money and influence.[32]

The volume that most boldly established Moseley as the primary shaper of English dramatic literature is deliberately different from his playwrights' series. Moseley's *Comedies and Tragedies Written by {Francis Beaumont and John Fletcher} Gentlemen. Never printed before, And now published by the Authours Originall Copies*, published in 1647, performs the role of memory and print consciously and brilliantly.[33] First of all, rather than the octavo format suitable for lesser playwrights, Beaumont and Fletcher deserve a Folio. By imitating Shakespeare and Jonson's Folios, Moseley ostentatiously creates a triumvirate of England's greatest dramatists (Beaumont and Fletcher meld into one person, called Fletcher), a triangulation that many of the poets contributing to the volume's front matter underscore. Denham,

---

[28] On Moseley's drama series, see Kewes, 'Give me the sociable pocket-bookes ...'.

[29] *A Transcript of the Registers of the Worshipful Company of Stationers. 1640–1708 AD* (London: 1913), 1: 428–9.

[30] *Transcript*, 2: 271.

[31] *The Dramatic Records of Sir Henry Herbert*, ed. Joseph Quincy Adams (New Haven: Yale University Press, 1917), 90.

[32] See Harbage, 'Elizabethan-Restoration Palimpsest', and James Anderson Winn, *John Dryden and His World* (New Haven: Yale University Press, 1987), 139–40.

[33] The Folio's imprint includes Humphrey Robinson as well, but Moseley says Robinson's role was purely financial and claims sole responsibility himself for recovering the texts and arranging the volume.

for example, hails Fletcher as part of the 'Triumvirate of wit', and several writers emphatically place Fletcher on that pyramid above both Shakespeare and Jonson.[34] Secondly, the Folio is clearly intended as a political statement. Moseley and most of the more than thirty contributors write strongly marked royalist paeans to Fletcher, to Beaumont, and to both; these elegiac panegyrics mourn 'this Tragicall Age' even as they praise the elegance and moral passion of the plays to follow.[35] Finally, the Beaumont and Fletcher Folio deliberately supplants the stage with the book; the end of the theatre becomes the beginning of a glorious literature. The Beaumont and Fletcher repertoire had been so invaluable on stage that acting companies had kept these plays out of print for years, but now they are celebrated in a new medium.[36] In his prefatory poem, Thomas Stanley rejoices in the darkening of the stage, a place where Fletcher had lived only a shadowy afterlife. But now he is reborn:

> His losse preserv'd him; They that silenc'd Wit,
> Are now the Authours to Eternize it;
> Thus Poets are in spight of Fate reviv'd,
> And Playes by Intermission longer liv'd.[37]

The death of the theatre brings the life of the Poet. Milton has never been more right when he argues, in 1644, that 'books are not absolutely dead things, but do contain a potency of life in them to be as active as that soul was whose progeny they are'.[38]

Although the Beaumont and Fletcher Folio remains an obligatory footnote in book history, Fletcher has fallen out of our pantheon of dramatic immortals. This strange book is nevertheless worth reconsidering more closely. To begin with, the meme 'Beaumont and Fletcher' immediately obscures the authorial claims the Folio makes.[39] Fletcher is the primary author recognized by the Folio panegyrists (Beaumont is occasionally praised directly in poems written years before, but in most cases he is praised for the rational judgement that tempered Fletcher's creativity or simply for his friendship). Yet the memory of collaboration powerfully shapes Moseley's collection. No one then or now publishes a volume of Shakespeare and Fletcher or Massinger and Fletcher. But the panegyrists of the 1647 volume are happy to accede to Beaumont and Fletcher's blurry aura in spite of the fact that

---

[34] 'On Mr. John Fletcher's Workes' (sig. b1v, 30). The most extreme statements are William Cartwright's two poems under the heading 'Upon the report of the printing of the Dramaticall Poems of Master John Fletcher, collected before, and now set forth in one Volume' (sig. d1v–d2v) and John Birkenhead, 'On the happy Collection of Master Fletcher's Works, never before Printed' (sig. E1v–E2v).

[35] Shirley, 'To the Reader' (sig. A3r, 31).

[36] Hume, 'Securing a Repertory', 157.

[37] 'On the Edition' (sig. B4v), 33–6.

[38] John Milton, *Areopagitica*, ed. Merritt Y. Hughes [Rpt.] (Indianapolis: Hackett Publishing Company, 2003), 720.

[39] See Jeffrey Masten, *Textual Intercourse: Collaboration, Authorship and Sexualities in Renaissance Drama* (Cambridge: Cambridge University Press, 1997) and Philip J. Finkelpearl, *Court and Country Politics in the Plays of Beaumont and Fletcher* (Princeton: Princeton University Press, 1990).

Beaumont remains only a ghostly presence.[40] Moseley says he could not, try as he might, find a likeness of Francis Beaumont (an author portrait, usually engraved by William Marshall, is a standard Moseley book feature), so John Fletcher alone looks out from the front of the book. Fletcher thus plays the role of the great, remembered author, and yet is ill-defined, a collaborative author who has neither a clear corpus nor identity.

Similarly, the Folio's date of publication is at once predictable and peculiar. Moseley's publication of the Folio in 1647 is an intentional rallying cry for royalists, and historians of the wars and interregnum often cite it as an example of cultural resistance. That such a flagrantly royalist group statement was not censored demonstrates, at the least, the degree to which interregnum authorities were tolerant of (or uninterested in) cultural criticism. It is, however, remarkable that the royalists chose the plays of Beaumont and Fletcher as the cultural monument on which to stake their claims. The Folio appears more than two decades after Fletcher, its primary author, had died (in 1625, the year Charles I took the throne).[41] The first Folio of Shakespeare's works had been published seven years after his death, in 1623 and the second Folio in 1632. Ben Jonson famously published a Folio edition of his *Works* in his lifetime (1616); soon after his death in 1637, another Folio edition appeared (1640/1). The very belated appearance of Fletcher (and Beaumont)'s great Folio is evidence of how enduringly popular these plays had been while the theatres were open—and of how their value has shifted into print in the absence of the stage.

The 1647 Folio is both an act of historical memory and a deliberate tool to shape the future. But that act of memory is even more complicated than the two decades elapsing between the author's death and his celebration in folio might imply. Fletcher was already an occasion of nostalgia in the 1630s—precisely because he had failed on the popular stage and had transmuted a play into poetry. Fletcher's *The Faithful Shepherdess* infamously flopped in its original performance, and its resulting publication in 1608 is a defining moment in the story of early modern theatricality's transformation into dramatic poetry. Published soon after its disastrous staging,

---

[40] Sir Aston Cockayne (who praised Fletcher in the 1647 Folio) later expressed unease about the joint attribution. He protested 'To Mr. Humphrey Moseley and Mr. Humphrey Robinson' the absence of Massinger because he had collaborated on some of the plays, but he particularly protested the slighting of Fletcher's importance:

> In the large book of Playes you late did print
> (In Beaumonts and in Fletchers name) why in't
> Did you not justice? give to each his due?
> For Beaumont (of these many) writ in few:
> And Massinger in other few; the Main
> Being sole Issues of sweet Fletchers brain.   (*Chain of Golden Poems* [London: W.G., 1658], 117)

[41] Francis Beaumont died in 1616.

The Faithful Shepherdess includes Fletcher's address 'to the Reader' explaining his conception of tragicomedy: 'a tragie-comedie is not so called in respect of mirth and killing, but in respect it wants deaths, which is inough to make it no tragedie, yet brings some neere it, which is inough to make it no comedie'.[42] Tragicomedy will remain a vexed critical problem for years to come; here it explains stage failure in the face of an illiterate audience.

The 1608 edition of *The Faithful Shepherdess* also includes what amounts to an excoriating attack on theatre audiences written by Fletcher's fellow playwrights. Fletcher's own complaints are mild by comparison:

> First the infection, then the common prate
> Of common people, have such customes got
> Either to silence plaies, or like them not.   (493.4–6)

Nathan Field praises the pastoral 'Clad in such elegant proprietie / Of words, including a morallitie' (489.11–12), far beyond the ken of a theatrical audience that, even when pleased by something less fine, is merely 'a monster [that] clapt his thousand hands, / And drownd the sceane with his confused cry' (490.33–4). Beaumont mocks the illiterate audience who judges 'Headlong according to the actors clothes' (491.28) and congratulates Fletcher on 'this second publication' (490.40) in print rather than on stage, where 'Your censurers must have the quallitie / Of reading, which I am afraid is more / Then halfe your shreudest judges had before' (491.44–6). George Chapman pays a Sidneian compliment to Fletcher's 'golden world' (493.21). And Ben Jonson writes indignantly of the play's mixed audience of knights and shop foremen, ladies and whores: 'The wise, and many-headed *Bench*, that sits / Upon the Life, and Death of *Playes*, and *Wits*' (492.1–2). Jonson makes an eerily prescient prediction, calling the stage failure of *A Faithful Shepherdess* a 'Martirdome' that 'crown[s]' 'thy murdred *Poëme*: which shall rise / A glorified worke to Time, when Fire, / Or moathes shall eate, what all these Fooles admire' (492.13–16).

Indeed, *The Faithful Shepherdess* did rise, over and over. It was printed again in 1629; performed at Charles and Henrietta Maria's court in 1633; and published in 1634 with its successful court performance prominently part of its title page: *Acted at Somerset House before the King and Queene on Twelfe night last, 1633. And divers times since with great applause at the Private House in Blacke-Friers, by his Majesties Servants.* Because it had already been published, *The Faithful Shepherdess* was not included in Moseley's 1647 Folio, but it is referenced several times in the Folio's prefatory poems and provides the model for praising fine poetry disdained by the ignorant mob. Fully laden with courtly nostalgia (down to the reference to the

---

[42] The first edition of *The Faithful Shepherdess* is not available on EEBO. Because it is based on the first edition, I am using Cyrus Hoy's edited edition, part of Fredson Bowers' *The Dramatic Works in the Beaumont and Fletcher Canon* (Cambridge: Cambridge University Press, 1976), 3: 497.

Twelfth Night 'last, 1633'), *The Faithful Shepherdess* appeared in print in 1656 and again in 1665.

The long arc of *The Faithful Shepherdess*'s failure, influence, and success, perhaps even more than the Beaumont and Fletcher Folio, accurately tracks what happens to theatricality through the Jacobean and Caroline reigns, the stage's closure, and its return at the Restoration. It also reminds us how selective our own memories of the early modern stage can be. For us, Shakespeare is the defining playwright, and his working circumstances form the basis of our thinking about early modern theatricality. But theatricality kept changing, and by the 1630s, the decade before theatres were closed, theatrical experience was quite different. Although the popular theatre we remember nostalgically was still active, especially in the summer, theatre was, to a significant degree, court centred and shaped by court fashions.[43] The vogue for Neoplatonic pastoralism, and the greater involvement of women as patrons, writers, and even actors pushed theatre ever more strongly towards the 'poetic'. Milton's 1634 *Maske presented at Ludlow Castle*, for example, echoes *A Midsummer Night's Dream* but is also saturated with the influence of *The Faithful Shepherdess*, seeding Fletcher's play far into the literary future.[44] Nor is it a surprise that Moseley put Massinger, Brome, and Shirley into his little octavo volume series but gave Fletcher the full star treatment as England's treasure.[45] Fletcher was a Caroline court favourite, at once ostensibly high-minded and kinky, influenced by continental fashion and free of Jonson's gnarly wit or Shakespeare's vivid characters from across the social spectrum. The influence of Charles I and Henrietta Maria's court profoundly determined the future of theatricality after the revolutions, including its continental, literate taste and its concomitant debasement of impatient, ignorant theatrical crowds. When the Restoration remembered theatre, it remembered Fletcher first and foremost.[46]

[43] Martin Butler provides an authoritative account of the Caroline theatre: 'Adult and Boy Playing Companies, 1625–1642', in Richard Dutton, ed., *The Oxford Handbook of Early Modern Theatre* (Oxford: Oxford University Press, 2009), 104–19.

[44] Ann Baynes Coiro, 'A Thousand Fantasies: The Lady and the Masque', in Nicholas McDowell and Nigel Smith, eds., *The Oxford Handbook of Milton* (Oxford: Oxford University Press, 2010), 89–111.

[45] Martin Butler argues convincingly for the political and artistic independence and importance of professional drama during these years, particularly the work of Massinger, Shirley, and Brome. In order to make his revisionary argument, however, Butler downplays the extent of the court's powerful influence, something that becomes especially evident over the long term; *Theatre and Crisis, 1632–1642* (Cambridge: Cambridge University Press, 1984).

[46] See Arthur C. Sprague, *Beaumont and Fletcher on the Restoration Stage* (Cambridge, MA: Harvard University Press, 1926); John Harold Wilson, *The Influence of Beaumont and Fletcher on Restoration Drama* (Columbus: Ohio State University Press, 1928); and Robert Markley, '"Shakespeare *To Thee Was Dull*": The Phenomenon of Fletcher's Influence', in Robert Markley and Laurie Finke, eds., *From Renaissance to Restoration: Metamorphoses of the Drama* (Cleveland: Case Western Reserve University Press, 1984), 89–126. Neander remarks in Dryden's *An Essay of Dramatick Poesie* that 'Their Playes are now the most pleasant and frequent entertainments of the Stage; two of theirs being acted through the year for one of *Shakespeare's* or *Johnson's*: the reason is, because there is a certain gayety in their Comedies, and Pathos in their more serious Playes, which suits generally with all men's humours'; *Works*, ed. Samuel Holt Monk (Berkeley: University of California Press, 1971), 17: 57.

Just as *The Faithful Shepherdess* was properly performed on the page for a literate audience, the Fletcher immortalized in the 1647 Folio is meant to be read. Moseley explains how carefully he has sought out the manuscripts of every one of the remaining unpublished plays, promising that this book 'is all New' and 'you have not onely All I could get, but All that you must ever expect' (he could not find one play, *The Wild Goose Chase*, but asks anyone who knows its whereabouts to get in touch at once).[47] He knows there is nothing 'Spurious or impos'd' because 'I had the Originalls from such as received them from the Authours themselves; by Those, and none other, I publish this Edition'.[48] It is unlikely that Moseley could trace his manuscripts directly back to Fletcher (and close to impossible for Beaumont) given the length of time since his death. Moseley's purpose, though, is to underscore the value of owning the author's full intention, unaltered by the vicissitudes of performance. When the plays were performed the actors 'omitted some Scenes and Passages' (albeit 'with the Authour's consent'): 'But now you have All that was Acted, and all that was not', Moseley proclaims, 'even the perfect full Originalls without the least mutilation'.[49]

Moseley is not, however, setting up an invidious polarity where the stage 'mutilates' and the printed book perfects. In fact, the Beaumont and Fletcher Folio is a collaborative effort between Moseley and the King's Company itself. In a close imitation of the dedication of the 1623 Shakespeare Folio, the Beaumont and Fletcher Folio is prefaced by a dedication to the Earl of Pembroke and Montgomery signed by all surviving members of the King's Company, led off by the joint managers, John Lowin and Joseph Taylor.[50] After 'many calme yeares' when the troupe 'derive[d] a subsistence to our selves, and Protection to the Scene (now withered, and condemn'd, as we feare, to a long Winter and sterilitie)', the actors, who have only been 'Trustees to the Ashes of the Authors', present the plays in print.[51] The plays in print are another kind of performance, a bid for patronage in their theatre's long winter. When someone *did* find *The Wild Goose Chase*, Moseley published it in 1652 (in folio, so it could be bound with its other 'new' brethren) not only for the 'publick delight of all the Ingenious' but also for the 'private benefit' of the two company managers, Lowin and Taylor: a benefit performance for the old actors at the end of their lives.[52]

---

[47] Moseley explains: 'for a Person of quality borrowed it from the Actours many yeares since, and (by the negligence of a Servant) it was never return'd; therefore now I put up this *Si quis*, that whosoever hereafter happily meetes with it, shall be thankfully satisfied if he please send it home'; 'The Stationer to the Readers' (A4 v), 7, 11, 16–19.

[48] Moseley, 'The Stationer to the Readers', 7–9.

[49] Moseley, 'The Stationer to the Readers', 28–32.

[50] John Heming and Henry Condell, Lowin and Taylor's predecessors as managers of the King's Company, dedicated the first Folio to Philip Herbert, First Earl of Montgomery and his older brother, William Herbert, Third Earl of Pembroke.

[51] Sig. A2v, 1–3; sig. A2r, 9.

[52] Proclaimed on the title page, where Moseley also praises the 'Person of Honour' who 'Retrive'd' the play (*The Wild-Goose Chase* [London, 1562]).

As the actors let go of the plays, the readers assumed their roles. In the massive front matter of the Beaumont and Fletcher Folio, reading a play becomes better than seeing it performed. James Shirley brilliantly redefines stage 'liberty' in his address 'to the Reader': 'in this *Tragicall Age* where the *Theater* hath been so much out-acted, congratulate thy owne happinesse that in this silence of the Stage, thou hast a liberty to reade these inimitable Playes'.[53] The theatre was only 'a conjuring glasse', magical and superstitious; the press is now a better 'optick', a scientific instrument for the educated.[54] John Webb tells the ghosts of Beaumont and Fletcher that 'the vast world' is now 'your Theater' because 'The presse shall give to ev'ry man his part, / And we will all be Actors; learne by heart / Those Tragick Scenes and Comicke Straines you writ'.[55] Perhaps the oddest, yet most predictive praise comes from Robert Herrick. His poem in the Folio is characteristically ritualistic:

> For now behold the golden Pompe is come,
> Thy Pompe of Playes which thousands come to see,
> With admiration both of them and thee,
> O Volume worthy leafe, by leafe and cover
> To be with juice of Cedar washt all over;
> Here's words with lines, and lines with Scenes consent,
> To raise an Act to full astonishment;
> Here melting numbers, words of power to move
> Young men to swoone, and Maides to dye for love.[56]

Herrick's speaker metaphorically washes the pages of Beaumont and Fletcher's plays with cedar to make them eternal. Preserved in print, the plays can now reach 'thousands' and move those readers physically and powerfully: to swoon, even to die.

Moseley embraced his mission as the saviour of high culture in a desperate time, and he succeeded. He was already being thanked in the front matter of the 1647 Beaumont and Fletcher volume:

> 'Tis not all Kingdomes joyn' d in one could buy
> (If priz' d aright) so true a Library
> Of man: where we the character may finde
> Of ev'ry Nobler and each baser minde.[57]

---

[53] Shirley, 'To the Reader', sig. A3r, 31–3.

[54] Shirley, 'To the Reader', 34–5. William Habington demonstrates the ways in which this embrace of printed drama (or print in general) is still painfully new and uncomfortable. Addressing Fletcher as the 'Great tutelary Spirit of the Stage', Habington expresses his righteous 'rage' ''gainst their officious crime / Who print thee now, in the worst scaene of Time' (sig. b3v, 1, 2, 3–4), but by the end of his impassioned poem, of course, Habington comes round to the importance of Moseley's publication of Fletcher's plays.

[55] 'To the Manes of the celebrated Poets and Fellow-writers, Francis Beaumont and John Fletcher, upon the Printing of their excellent Dramatick Poems', sig. c2v, 26–9.

[56] 'Upon Master Fletchers Incomparable Playes', sig. E1r, 2–10.

[57] Grandison, 'To the Stationer' (sig. A5r, 5–8). The author is probably George Villiers, Third Viscount Grandison.

'To the Stationer' nicely supports Moseley's commercial ambition while employing the common mid-century trope that a private realm is better than striving for national kingdoms. In that private realm, stage actors become 'characters' read in libraries.

When the theatres reopened, therefore, the stage faced a world where theatrical texts had become dramatic literature and where the audience was imagined not as illiterate fools but as sophisticated readers who have learned to play dramatic roles themselves. What is the effect of a long period of communal reading on theatricality once the playhouses reopen in the Restoration? And what can it tell us about the nature of theatricality itself?

3 June 1665

John Dryden was eleven in 1642 when the London theatres closed; he became the most innovative and protean playwright of the Restoration. His long and important career in the theatre begins with memory.

During the first years of the theatres' reopening, Dryden is the only writer who could be called a professional playwright, but his work is still journeyman stuff.[58] Dryden's first plays are typical, in many ways, of the quasi-original theatre that the duopoly put up before the plague closed theatres again in June 1665. His first, *The Wild Gallant* (1663), is probably a revision of a pre-revolutionary manuscript by Richard Brome that came to Dryden's hands via Humphrey Moseley and his invaluable stash of unpublished plays.[59] In the play's prologue Dryden admits the Restoration's dependence on the great writers of the past and the sense of futility it could engender:

> Nature is old, which Poets imitate,
> And for Wit, those that boast their own estate,
> Forget *Fletcher* and *Ben* before them went,
> Their Elder Brothers, and that vastly spent:
> So much 'twill hardly be repair'd again.[60]

---

[58] I am indebted throughout to Winn, *John Dryden and His World*.

[59] Sir Robert Howard's *Duke of Lerma* (1668) is another likely instance where one of Moseley's pre-war plays was adapted without acknowledgement, in this case a play by John Ford. Dryden may have been attacking Howard when he mocked literary theft (in a prologue to *Albumazar*, another play in revival), those who 'Joyn the dead living, to the living dead' (Winn, *John Dryden and His World*, 189–90 and Harbage, 'Elizabethan-Restoration Palimpsest').

[60] John Dryden, *Works*, ed. John Harrington Smith and Dougald MacMillan (Berkeley: University of California Press, 1962), 3: 5.42–6. When the play was published in 1669, Dryden acknowledged that 'The Plot was not Originally my own: but so alter'd, by me (whether for the better or worse, I know not) that, whoever the Author was, he could not have challeng'd a Scene of it' (3: 3).

The Rival Ladies (1663), Dryden's next play, is an adaptation of a Spanish tragicomedy.[61] Then he worked with Howard on a rhymed heroic tragedy, *The Indian Queen* (1664). Davenant's interregnum experiment, *The Siege of Rhodes*, which had been a spectacular success when revived by the Duke's Company, was their chief model.[62] Its 1665 sequel, *The Indian Emperor*, is a significant advance in which Dryden begins to make heroic drama his own. Nevertheless, when the theatres closed on 5 June 1665, Dryden was still in a formative stage as a playwright, adapting and imitating.

But in 1668 Dryden published what may be his greatest dramatic achievement, and certainly one of the most brilliant literary critical analyses ever written. For *An Essay of Dramatick Poesie*, despite its title, is itself an emotionally and intellectually complex drama. A dialogue among four characters, it is wittily constructed around the unities: one afternoon, 3 June 1665; one place, a boat; one action, to debate 'who writ the best Plays'.[63] Audiences had long been distrusted by public authorities and antitheatrical polemicists, and audiences were conventionally demonized by playwrights and actors as well because of their purported ignorance and superficiality. In *An Essay of Dramatick Poesie*, however, Dryden creates a discerning, knowledgeable, and articulate audience, divided but enjoying its disagreements. In the process, as Samuel Johnson first claimed, Dryden becomes 'the father of English criticism'.[64] *An Essay of Dramatick Poesie* invents English criticism by working with theatre's self-consciousness, theorizing drama as it writes it. *An Essay of Dramatick Poesie* might fairly be called, therefore, a closet drama or a metadrama that remembers the theatre's past in order to theorize modernity.[65]

An Essay of Dramatick Poesie can also be understood as theatrical, in a Brechtian sense. Its witty conflict on a boat demands a constant intellectual adjustment, calibrating the differences between the past and the present, role-playing and sincerity, theory and practice. *An Essay*, in other words, asks its readers to distance themselves

---

[61] It is a direct imitation of Sir Samuel Tuke's successful imitation, *The Adventures of the Five Hours*.

[62] On the significance and influence of Davenant's 1656 *The Siege of Rhodes*, see Richard Kroll, 'William Davenant and John Dryden', in Susan J. Owen, ed., *A Companion to Restoration Drama* (Malden, MA: Blackwell, 2001), 311–25.

[63] John Dryden, *An Essay of Dramatick Poesie*, in *Works*, ed. Monk, 17: 14. Further references to *An Essay* will refer to this volume parenthetically.

[64] Samuel Johnson, *Prefaces, Biographical and Critical, to the Works of the English Poets* (London, 1779), III.168.

[65] Martin Puchner has characterized closet drama as a 'resistance to the theater', but a resistance so thoroughgoing that theatre is constitutive of drama: *Stage Fright: Modernism, Anti-Theatricality, and Drama* (Baltimore: Johns Hopkins University Press, 2002), 2. Dryden's dedication of *An Essay* to Buckhurst in 1668 hints at its complexity. Because it is an essay, 'all I have said is problematical' (17: 3). Dryden's own opinions are unreachable since 'Sometimes, like a Schollar in a Fencing-School I put forth my self, and show my own ill play, on purpose to be better taught. Sometimes I stand desperately to my Armes, like the Foot when deserted by their Horse, not in hopes to overcome, but onely to yield on more honourable termes' (17: 5).

and analyse the stage. It also dramatizes (on a boat rather than a coffee-house) the nuanced public debates that Habermas argued inaugurated the 'public sphere'.[66] But the best theoretical framework for *An Essay of Dramatick Poesie* is the one Dryden consciously built upon: the sceptical, free-play of discussion between intelligent interlocutors developed by Plato and Cicero, what Martin Puchner has recently called the 'drama of ideas'.[67] Dryden himself explained that the 'whole Discourse was Skeptical, according to that way of reasoning which was used by *Socrates*, *Plato*, and all the Academiques of old, which *Tully* and the best of the Ancients followed, and which is imitated by the modest Inquisitions of the Royal Society'.[68] Whatever we call *An Essay of Dramatick Poesie*—closet drama, metadrama, distancing exercise, drama of ideas—it is a work that attempts to reconstitute theatre by means of dramatic analysis.

An Essay of Dramatick Poesie is almost entirely made up of dialogue among four characters (a narrator opens and closes the work and provides brief narrative links to explain the flow of conversation). Its opening paragraph sets the scene following the rules of a dramatic poem:

> It was that memorable day, in the first Summer of the late War, when our Navy ingag'd the Dutch: a day wherein the two most mighty and best appointed Fleets which any age had ever seen, disputed the command of the greater half of the Globe, the commerce of Nations, and the riches of the Universe. While these vast floating bodies, on either side, mov'd against each other in parallel lines, and our Country men, under the happy conduct of his Royal Highness, went breaking, by little and little, into the line of the Enemies; the noise of the Cannon from both Navies reach'd our ears about the City: so that all men, being alarm'd with it, and in a dreadful suspence of the event, which they knew was then deciding, every one went following the sound as his fancy led him; and leaving the Town almost empty, some took towards the Park, some cross the River, others down it; all seeking the noise in the depth of silence. (8)

The paragraph is a tour de force. Dryden opens his piece with a framing anecdote, much like the opening of England's first great critical essay where Sidney remembers learning horsemanship 'at the Emperor's court' and compares the passion of an Italian riding instructor to his own passion for his avocation, poetry.[69] But Dryden's essay never abandons his framing conceit. And, unlike Sidney's *Defense*, Dryden's *An Essay of Dramatick Poesie* elaborately deflects away from its author; it is the

[66] Jürgen Habermas, *The Structural Transformation of the Public Sphere: An Inquiry into a Category of Bourgeois Society*, trans. Thomas Burger and Frederick Lawrence (Cambridge, MA: MIT Press, 1989; orig. published in 1962).

[67] *An Essay*'s great editor Samuel Holt Monk has carefully detailed Dryden's classical models: *Works*, 17: 348–59. Puchner, *The Drama of Ideas: Platonic Provocations in Theater and Philosophy* (Oxford: Oxford University Press, 2010).

[68] Dryden, *Defence of An Essay*, ed. John Loftis, in *Works* (Berkeley: University of California Press, 1966), 9: 15.

[69] Philip Sidney, *A Defence of Poetry*, ed. J. A. Van Dorsten (Oxford: Oxford University Press, 1966), 17.

audience that matters, not the maker. The cavalier is replaced with sea power, and the battle is over 'the command of the greater half of the Globe, the commerce of Nations, and the riches of the Universe'. The expansive rhetoric contrasts with Sidney's self-deprecatory wit, but for both Sidney and Dryden England's cultural destiny is at stake. Dryden's battle fought 'in parallel lines' 'under the happy conduct of his Royal Highness' models the neoclassical debate about rhyme and heroic elevation of style to follow. Although the battle is fought in marshalled lines, however, each member of the audience follows 'the sound as his fancy led him'. Some of the key debates in the essay are foreshadowed in the stage setting: the combination of discipline and wandering fancy, for example, and the sound of cannons off-stage while the audience 'all [seek] the noise in the depth of silence'.

The four characters who share the dialogue to follow teasingly seem 'real' and yet are never fully identifiable. A scholarly guessing game has gone on for years (beginning, no doubt, when *An Essay* was first published) about the actual people disguised by pseudonyms.[70] As a key to the rivalries, friendships, and shifting terms of debate in the early Restoration, such speculation certainly enriches the work. But reading *An Essay* as a *roman-à-clef* also diminishes its rich dramatic coherence—its complex characters and the relationships the work creates among them. These four critics try to understand the best direction English theatre can take in a new age of dramatic poetry and scientific rationalism. Their arguments are based on classical learning, courtly sophistication, memory, and practice. They debate whether the Ancients or the Moderns, the French or the English have written the 'best Plays' (14), whether rhyme or blank verse is appropriate for the stage, wrestling throughout with memories of what English theatre was in the oft invoked 'last Age' (12).[71] Their most profoundly theatrical focus is on the audience—its perceptions, its feelings, its imaginative power and limits, its national character and its new role in a modern age. Nevertheless, the debate continuously skitters between theatre and printed drama, or what we would now call 'literature'.

Crites is 'a person of a sharp judgement, and somewhat too delicate a taste in wit, which the world have mistaken in him for ill nature' (9). He gets so overheated in his objections to the bad poetry that a naval victory will surely elicit that he proposes the virtues of censorship, until his friends smile at him. Crites is, in some ways, a stodgy reactionary. He champions the plays of the Ancients and sees everything since as a falling off. On the other hand, he delivers a brief but powerful argument (proven right by time, past, present, and future) that blank verse is a better theatrical tool than heroic couplets. Eugenius is a modern man, dismissive of Aristotle across the board. This present, scientific age better understands nature, which is the very soul of drama. Complex experience of human psychology should now

---

[70] The speakers are usually identified as Sir Robert Howard (Crites), Charles Sackville, Lord Buckhurst (Eugenius), Sir Charles Sedley (Lisideius), and Dryden (Neander).

[71] This is the first use of the recurring phrase 'the last Age'.

supersede old genre rules. Lisideius is profoundly disappointed by the behaviour of the last generation. According to him, the high point of 'the last Age' was when '*Beaumont, Fletcher*, and *Johnson*' reigned, and England's theatre was the best in the world (33). But since then 'we have been so long together bad *Englishmen*' (33) that everything, including theatre, has devolved. Lisideius therefore champions the careful propriety of the French dramatists.

Neander is clearly, in many ways, Dryden himself, the new man, the one outsider among the other three 'persons whom their witt and Quality have made known to all the Town' (8). He gets elliptically scolded by Lisideius for his past Cromwellian loyalties (33); he is deferential about intervening in the aristocratic conversation, but once he starts he can't stop talking ('*Neander* was pursuing this Discourse so eagerly, that *Eugenius* had call'd to him twice or thrice ere he took notice that the Barge stood still, and that they were at the foot of *Somerset*-Stairs, where they had appointed it to land' [80]). His position, as the ambitious new man, is that the English playwrights are better than the French, and that rhyme, Charles II's strongly expressed preference, is more appropriate for tragedy than blank verse or prose. But Neander is ambivalent, hedging his support for rhyme and adding provisions to his endorsement of the popular playwrights of the 'last Age'.

Neander strongly defends English drama over any other nation's. Nevertheless, the restored stage does face a serious crisis, even if it is facing it stoutly: 'though the fury of a Civil War, and Power, for twenty years together, abandon'd to a barbarous race of men, Enemies of all good Learning, had buried the Muses under the ruines of Monarchy; yet with the restoration of our happiness, we see reviv'd Poesie lifting up its head, & already shaking off the rubbish which lay so heavy on it' (63). Neander here deploys a key rhetorical switch that royalists had devised when the stage was dark; theatre becomes 'Poesie'. Puritans could thus be accused of ignorant antitheatricality, while royalists could avoid a wholesale endorsement of popular theatre. In this way, the printed drama of the interregnum had beaten its enemy at its own game by feeding off and thriving upon antitheatricality, inflaming fears that English culture was under threat and must be preserved in print if it could not live on the stage.

But now, five years into the Restoration, Neander faces a problem. Freeing theatre from the rubble of its destruction is relatively simple; the difficult part is freeing theatre from the 'Poesie' it has become. Theatre must now get back out of the closet and on to the stage. Dryden clearly fears that, for one thing, a national, English drama could again be repudiated. Even as theatre is supposed to rise up and banish the revolution, it brings with it a demeaning stigma of uncouth Englishness. But the most immediate and intense anxiety throughout *An Essay of Dramatick Poesie* is not about the worth of the Ancients vs. the Moderns or the French vs. the English: it is always about how, and even whether, the English stage is going to be able to reconstitute itself. The first five years of revived London theatre have not been promising. When Crites proposes to limit the debate about poetry to dramatic poetry, Eugenius, who had already volunteered to be the defender of modernity, acknowledges he has 'undertaken a harder Province than I imagin'd' because the plays 'we now see acted, come short of many which were written in the last Age' (13). Neander, too, admits that 'it cannot be deny'd but we have had some little blemish either in the Plot or writing of all those Playes which have been made within these seven years' (63–4).[72] The playwrights of 'the last Age' were so impossibly good 'that not onely we shall never equal them, but they could never equal themselves, were they to rise and write again… There is scarce an Humour, a Character, or any kind of Plot, which they have not us'd' (72–3). In fact, this theatrical exhaustion is Neander's pragmatic argument for rhymed heroic drama—at least it is different from what has come before.

The memory of the stage from the 'last Age' is of authors and their dramatic poems, as reconstituted by printed editions such as Moseley's. The early modern playwrights remembered in *An Essay* are those canonized by Folio publication: Shakespeare, Ben Jonson, and Beaumont and Fletcher. All four debaters refer to these playwrights of 'the last Age' as a commonly accepted canon (no other playwright is once mentioned by name), but Neander has the privilege of evaluating their strengths and weaknesses. Beaumont and Fletcher 'represented all the passions very lively, but above all, Love. I am apt to believe the *English* Language in them arriv'd to its highest perfection; what words have since been taken in, are rather superfluous then ornamental' (56–7). Jonson is the most learned, most faithful to the 'Dramatique lawes' (55), the best at plotting and at portraying humours, but lacks wit. But where he may 'admire' Jonson, Neander 'loves' Shakespeare (58). In spite of his many sins against regularity and his weakness for low jokes and 'Bombast' (55), Shakespeare 'was the man who of all Modern, and perhaps Ancient Poets, had the largest and most comprehensive soul' (55).

The drama of *An Essay* lies in the teasing tension between dramatic theory and theatrical practice, the same intractable tension that Jonson had tried so hard to reconcile throughout his career. All the Thames debaters agree on the definition of a play: '*A just and lively Image of Humane Nature, representing its Passions and Humours, and the Changes of Fortune to which it is subject; for the Delight and Instruction of Mankind*' (15). But what is a 'just Image', how best can the stage make it 'lively'? And how is 'Mankind' delighted and instructed? Lisideius is the closest adherent to Sidney's *Defense of Poesy* (a witty turn, since he is defending the French). He mocks Shakespeare's history plays, which put 'the business many times of thirty or forty years' into 'two hours and a half' (36). To a greater degree than his friends, Lisideius understands drama as an intellectual rather than a bodily experience. He privileges the diegetic over the mimetic, and his strongest evidence is stage fighting and death: 'I have observ'd that in all our Tragedies, the Audience cannot forbear

---

[72] Seven years reflects the essay's publication, rather than the day on which it is set (although it is dated 1688, *An Essay* probably appeared in late 1667).

laughing when the Actors are to die; 'tis the most Comick part of the whole Play. All *passions* may be lively represented on the Stage, if to the well-writing of them the Actor supplies a good commanded voice, and limbs that move easily, and without stiffness: but there are many *actions* which can never be imitated to a just height' (39–40). The only actor who could properly represent death on stage, Lisideius says sardonically, is 'a *Roman* Gladiator' (40). It is the poet, not the actor, who can persuade us.

Lisideius firmly loses his argument about mimetic violence, however, and Eugenius, the most enamoured of the present moment, praises the modern actor's excellence at expressing the passion of love, which 'cannot better be express'd than in a word and a sigh, breaking one another. Nature is dumb on such occasions, and to make her speak, would be to represent her unlike her self' (31–2). For him, bodies on stage are more expressive and natural than long speeches. Later, Neander directly addresses the theatrical power of representing fighting and death, which is often demanded by audiences. His only objection ('the indecency of tumults') has a political tenor; theatrically, he sees no problem: 'For why may not our imagination as well suffer it self to be deluded with the probability of it, as with any other thing in the Play?' (50). Even Jonson, who espoused the classical rule that death happens off stage, is not always correct in practice and rightly so (51). Shakespeare and Fletcher are particularly irregular in several ways; nevertheless, 'there is a more masculine fancy and greater spirit in the writing, then there is in any of the *French*' (54).

Despite these moments of theatricality, however, throughout *An Essay of Dramatick Poesie* discerning readers ultimately trump the theatrical audience. The group's final argument, about the merits of blank verse or rhyme, demonstrates the authorial and theoretical power of dramatic poetry, even as it acknowledges the role of the audience more fully. Perhaps because Dryden at some level knew that Crites, the defender of blank verse, was right, he allots him only a brief space to defend blank verse over rhyme. Yet the concision of Crites' arguments only makes them stronger. He begins pragmatically, with English tradition: it is 'in vain...to strive against the stream of the peoples inclination; the greatest part of which are prepossess'd so much with those excellent Playes of *Shakespeare*, *Fletcher*, and *Ben. Johnson* (which have been written out of Rhyme)...'(65). Next he turns to Aristotle: since 'a Play is the imitation of Nature' (65), dialogue should seem natural in order to seem true. 'We know we are to be deceiv'd, and we desire to be so' when we go to a play; 'but no man ever was deceiv'd but with a probability of truth, for who will suffer a gross lie to be fasten'd on him?' (67). Theatrical experience is the bedrock of Crites' argument, but it lies behind a scrim of classical theory and canonical printed plays.

As evening falls and the boat approaches the Somerset House stairs, Neander launches into his defence of rhyme. Neander, who had embraced the power of the imagination and excused Shakespeare's irregularities because of the greatness of his soul, now must argue differently in order to imagine the future. The political realities of Charles II's preference for rhymed drama and of post-revolutionary reactions against tumult and enthusiasm combine to push the new man away from the theatricality of 'the last Age'. Although it is true that 'the people are not generally inclin'd to like' (73) rhymed drama, 'if by the people you understand the multitude, the *hoi polloi*, 'tis no matter what they think; they are sometimes in the right, sometimes in the wrong; their judgment is a meer Lottery' (73). 'The Noblesse' (73) like rhyme, and although theatre should be 'true', it is also political, a reflection of national identity. Its reappearance under the aegis of 'Monarchy' (63) is premised on a theoretical reality where elevated persons speak elevated language and where the distribution of stage time among characters is a political calculation. Rhymed verse is like 'Statues which are plac'd on high' so as to be 'greater then the life, that they might descend to the sight in their just proportion' (75) or like painting where the 'shadowings' contribute to the work's power but become invisible to the eye (77).

The confident brilliance of *An Essay of Dramatick Poesie* is complicated and deepened by its doubts and disagreements. It ends evocatively: the evening of 3 June, almost midsummer, two days before the theatres will again close, and before the naval victory turns to humiliating defeat. The 'company' is reluctant to separate 'and stood a while looking back on the water, upon which the Moon-beams play'd, and made it appear like floating quick-silver' (80). Metaphor, allusion, magic stand behind them. Before them, 'a crowd of *French* people who were merrily dancing in the open air, and nothing concern'd for the noise of Guns which had allarm'd the Town that afternoon' (80–1). Dryden's *Dramatick Poesie* turns to the future, but the future is haunted now by the past.

FURTHER READING

Bennett, Benjamin. *All Theater is Revolutionary Theater* (Ithaca: Cornell University Press, 2005).

Kivy, Peter. *The Performance of Reading: An Essay in the Philosophy of Literature* (Oxford: Blackwell, 2006).

Peters, Julie Stone. *Theatre of the Book, 1480–1880: Print, Text, and Performance in Europe* (Oxford: Oxford University Press, 2000).

Sorelius, Gunnar. *'The Giant Race Before the Flood': Pre-Restoration Drama on the Stage and in the Criticism of the Restoration* (Uppsala: Almqvist & Wiksell, 1966).

CHAPTER 29

PASSIONS

BLAIR HOXBY

The title of *Character and Conflict: An Introduction to Drama* says a great deal about twentieth-century interpretations of theatre. Edited and introduced by the distinguished critic Alvin Kernan, who taught Shakespeare to generations of students at Yale and Princeton, the volume presents 'in a condensed and simplified form the methods of analysis now used in the majority of college classrooms' while at the same time advancing a 'theory of drama' founded on the criticism of 'T. S. Eliot, William Empson, Kenneth Burke, R. P. Blackmur, Francis Fergusson, Alan Downer, W. K. Wimsatt, and Northrop Frye, to name a few'. It strives, in other words, to be a digest of the best dramatic criticism published by 1963. Although Kernan believes that he and his contemporaries have developed a critical vocabulary that allows readers to get closer than ever to the true nature of literature, he also insists that there is a deep continuity between the analysis of drama that he offers and that which Aristotle advanced long ago in the *Poetics*. 'When we see a play,' Kernan argues, 'our attention first focuses on character', 'a dramatist's primary [image] of human nature'. Any character is like an arrow 'shot outward toward a target', 'not pointed inward to a still center of consciousness'. He must therefore reckon with other characters and with 'that force, or forces, expressed' by the 'stage world'. When the key forces of a play—its characters and its world—'seek fulfillment', they produce the dramatic conflict that we call plot. The knowledge that a play produces is its 'meaning'. Kernan believes that his four categories of character, world, plot, and meaning capture what is most valuable in the six parts of tragedy that Aristotle names in the *Poetics* and that Kernan renders (archaically but accurately enough) fable, manners, sentiments, diction, decoration, and music.[1]

For all his efforts to translate the ancient parts of drama into contemporary terms, Kernan's critical vocabulary omits a category that was fundamental to early modern discussions of the art in both its ancient and contemporary aspects: the passions.

---

[1] Alvin B. Kernan, *Character and Conflict: An Introduction to Drama* (New York: Harcourt, Brace & World, 1963), 4, 8, 26, 137, 253, 323.

Consider the 'Description' of a play that Lisideius offers in John Dryden's *An Essay of Dramatick Poesie* (1667): 'a Play ought to be, *A just and lively Image of Humane Nature, representing the Passions and Humours, and the Changes of Fortune to which it is subject; for the Delight and Instruction of Mankind*'. Although Crites observes that this definition does not distinguish the ends of drama from the ends of literature as a whole, it is 'well received by the rest' of the interlocutors.[2] And if no one in Dryden's dialogue thinks to object that 'character and conflict', to use Kernan's terms, must figure prominently in any definition of drama, it is because these categories are not timeless elements of drama but critical concepts that only emerge to prominence in the late eighteenth century. Judging by Kernan's principles, we might suspect Dryden of ineptitude or carelessness, were it not for Milton's nearly contemporary definition of tragedy, which also omits all mention of character, conflict, and action: 'Tragedy, as it was antiently compos'd, hath been ever held the gravest, moralest, and most profitable of all other Poems: therefore said by *Aristotle* to be of power by raising pity and fear, or terror, to purge the mind of those and such like passions, that is to temper and reduce them to just measure with a kind of delight, stirr'd up by reading or seeing those passions well imitated'.[3] Milton knew perfectly well that Aristotle defined tragedy as the imitation of an action, for he quotes the passage on the title page of *Samson Agonistes* (1671). Yet he himself omits all mention of action. For him, the passions are the crucial objects of tragic imitation, and their arousal and purgation in the souls of the audience is at once a profit and a pleasure. How could Dryden and Milton consider the passions central to any definition of drama in the mid-seventeenth century, while Kernan could notice nothing missing when he failed to mention them in 1963?

The answer, I would argue, lies in a critical sea change that took place in the last decades of the eighteenth and the first decades of the nineteenth centuries. Prior to that epistemic shift, dramatic critics spoke not of character and conflict—which could scarcely be said to exist as conceptual categories at all—but of the actions, manners, and passions of men. They invoked these categories when analysing the mimetic powers not just of dramatists but of historians and epic bards, but they did not assume that each object of imitation was of equal importance to these genres. Whereas historians were bound to record the truth of actions, poets could distil the more general truths contained in a natural history of manners and passions. And whereas epic bards could depict a range of customs because they were not bound to respect the unities of time and place as playwrights were, they could not deploy all the wonders of theatrical presentation to sway the passions. It was precisely the performative aspect of tragedy that seemed to account for its peculiar property of

    [2] John Dryden, *An Essay of Dramatick Poesie* in *The Works of John Dryden*, ed. Edward Niles Hooker and H. T. Swedenberg, Jr, 20 vols. (Berkeley: University of California Press, 1956–89), 17: 15.
    [3] John Milton, *Complete Shorter Poems, with Original Spelling and Punctuation*, ed. Stella P. Revard (Oxford: Wiley-Blackwell, 2009), 460–1; subsequent quotations from *Samson Agonistes* follow this edition and are cited parenthetically.

catharsis.[4] Thus when the Restoration's greatest actor Thomas Betterton insisted that 'The Stage ought to be the *Seat* of *Passion*', he was not just giving sound advice to his fellow actors; he was asserting that passion held the key to early modern theatricality: that passion was inherently theatrical and that drama could become theatre only when the passions of its dramatis personae were embodied on stage.[5] It is no accident, we shall see, that the emergence of conflict and character as critical categories in the early nineteenth century coincided with a denigration of staged performance. The passions and early modern theatricality stood and fell together.

The passions in dramatic criticism

If we wish to understand the place of the passions in early modern dramatic theory, we must begin with the reception of the *Poetics*, for the efforts of Francesco Robortello and Vincenzo Maggi to explicate Aristotle's notion of tragic catharsis in the mid-sixteenth century drew attention to a more general feature of the writings of ancient critics: that they located the essence of tragedy in the passions that it imitated and aroused.[6] Indeed, it was precisely the affective power of tragedy that disturbed its ancient critics, from Plato, who burned his own tragedies in remorse, to Tertullian, who denounced tragedy for arousing violent emotions in even the most respectable members of the audience, to St Augustine, who admitted that in his youth he had felt an 'unseemly itch' to sorrow over the 'fictitious passions of the stage', taking most pleasure in the actors who could 'draw tears' from his eyes.[7] In response to Plato, Aristotle offered a viable defence of theatrical emotionalism by defining tragedy as an imitation that, 'by means of pity and fear, accomplishes the catharsis of such emotions' (*Poetics* 1449b).[8] His early modern commentators could not agree entirely on what catharsis meant, but his description of the effect left no doubt that, in his view, the state of passionate excitement induced at tragic festivals was a harmless pleasure, not a danger to the city-state.

---

[4] See Giovambattista Strozzi, *Lettione in Lode Poema Eroica* (Rome, 1594), in *Orazioni Et Altre Prose* (Rome, 1635), 189–203.

[5] Thomas Betterton, *The history of the English stage from the restauration to the present time*, compiled by William Oldys, Edmund Curll, and William Egerton (London, 1741), 54.

[6] W. B. Stanford, *Greek Tragedy and the Emotions: An Introductory Study* (London: Routledge & Kegan Paul, 1983).

[7] Diogenes Laertius, *Vitae philosophorum* 3.5, in *Diogenis Laertii Vitae philosophorum*, ed. H. S. Long, 2 vols. (Oxford: Clarendon Press, 1964); Tertullian, *De Spectaculis* 15, in *Apology, De Spectaculis, Minucius*, trans. T. R. Glover and Gerald H. Rendall, Loeb Classical Library (Cambridge, MA: Harvard University Press, 1953); St Augustine, *Confessions*, trans. William Watts, ed. W. H. D. Rouse, 2 vols., Loeb Classical Library (New York: Macmillan, 1912), 3.2.

[8] I follow the text in Gerard F. Else, *Aristotle's Poetics: The Argument* (Cambridge, MA: Harvard University Press, 1967), but I depart from his translation when it differs from the sense typically accepted in the early modern period.

Given the importance that the ancients attached to displays of pathos, Aristotle's early modern commentators were not surprised to find him saying that all mimetic arts imitate the manners (*ethoi*), passions (*pathê*), and actions (*praxis*) of men (*Poetics* 1447a), even though it was not easy to see how this claim squared with the three objects of tragic imitation that he listed: *mythos*, *ethos*, and *dianoia*, or fable, manners, and sentiments (*Poetics* 1449b). Some commentators maintained that the movements of a soul torn by competing passions were themselves actions, others contended that the portrayal of manners encompassed the imitation of passions, but the largest number thought that the passions were the most important form of *dianoia*. For in his discussion of *dianoia*, Aristotle especially praises those moments when dramatis personae rage or express dejection in the most natural way, leading spectators to recognize the same potential in themselves and to enter into the feelings of the actors on stage (*Poetics* 1455a–56a). Identifying *dianoia* with imitations of the passions led to a neat alignment of the three objects imitated by all the mimetic arts and the first three parts of tragedy: *mythos* was a dramatic action, *ethos* a portrayal of manners, and *dianoia* an expression of sentiment or passion. The gulf separating Kernan from this early modern tradition is thus especially evident in his unconvincing claim that 'sentiment (*dianoia*) apparently refers to the "theme" of the play, the ideas in it, and this I have enlarged to the topic "Meaning"'.[9]

It may seem surprising to us that early modern commentators should place so much emphasis on passion at the expense of dramatic action, but they found their justification in another passage of the *Poetics*, in which Aristotle exalts the poet, who tells what could happen (striving, like a philosopher, to distil universal principles), above the historian, who simply tells what did happen (1451a–b). To Sir William Davenant this distinction could be translated into a contrast between action and passion. Only a historian thinks it worthy to 'record the truth of actions' or to describe 'particular persons, as they are lifted, or levell'd by the force of Fate', he explains, which amounts to no more than a 'selected Diary of Fortune'. 'Wise poets think it more worthy to seek out truth in the passions', which hold the key to a 'general history of nature'. Even 'Painters', he maintains, 'are no more than Historians, when they draw eminent persons (though they term that drawing to the life) but when, by assembling diverse figures in a larger volume, they draw passions (though they term it but Story) then they increase in dignity and become Poets'. Playgoers, says Dryden's Eugenius, 'watch the movements' of persons' 'minds' on stage 'as much as the changes of their fortunes. For the imaging of the first is properly the work of a Poet, the latter he borrows from the Historian'.[10]

The passions were so important to the early modern conception of drama that they could serve as the basis of the generic distinctions that were one of the most

[9] Kernan, *Character and Conflict*, 4.

[10] Sir William Davenant, *A Discourse upon Gondibert, an Heroick Poem Written by Sir William D'Avenant, With an Answer to It by Mr. Hobbs* (Paris, 1650), 6–7; Dryden, *An Essay of Dramatick Poesie*, in *Works*, 17: 32.

original aspects of sixteenth-century poetic theory. Comedy was expected to imitate suspicions, fears, sudden passages from good to evil and from evil to good, rescues, and contentment; tragedy to imitate hopes, desires, despair, weeping, mourning, and deaths; and tragicomedy to mix these passions, avoiding only terror. Yet generic theory also suggested that if the passions were especially important to one dramatic genre, it was tragedy. For in their New Comedy, as Dryden's Neander observed, the ancients had sought to depict the *ethos* (or 'humour') of mankind, while in their tragedy they had always sought to express its *pathos*.[11] Dramatists and actors paid so much attention to the imitation of the passions in tragedy because the ends of tragedy yielded by their syncretic reading of Horace's *Ars Poetica* and Aristotle's *Poetics*—instruction, catharsis, and pleasure—could be defined in its terms.

Catharsis was the most important term in this triad, for neither the instruction nor the pleasure afforded by tragedy seemed explicable without reference to this enigmatic process. As Robortello explained,

> There is nothing that men must need be more exercised in than in becoming accustomed to judge rightly and to enjoy gentle and sound morals and praiseworthy actions...when poets, in the recitation of their tragedies, show persons and events which are utterly worthy of commiseration and by which a wise man will be terrified, men learn what things rightly move pity and lamentation and inspire fear.[12]

The theatre, affirmed Heinsius, 'is a kind of training hall for our passions which (since they are not only useful in life but necessary) must there be readied and perfected'.[13] René Descartes' *Les Passions de l'âme* (The Passions of the soul, 1649) explained how the theatre could be such a training hall: the passions of a player, or for that matter of the audience who sympathized with him, were accompanied by vehement movements of the animal spirits that could accentuate the convolutions of the brain, thus disposing player and audience alike to react the same way on future occasions.

But perhaps the most famous example was that of St Genesius, the patron saint of actors portrayed in several Latin, French, and Spanish plays of the seventeenth century, including Lope de Vega's *Lo fingido verdadero* (The true make-believe, 1608) and Jean Rotrou's *Le Véritable Saint Genest* (The True Saint Genesius, 1645). In Rotrou's version, the Roman actor Genest loses himself in his part as he rehearses the role of Adrian, a Roman minister who converted to Christianity and died as a martyr. Upon performing the role, Genest is constantly put in the position of judging, or at least of acting as *if* he is properly judging, what characters and events should be rightly feared or pitied: a tyrant should not be feared, despite his alarming

---

[11] See Bernardino Tomitano, *Ragionamenti Della Lingua Toscana* (Venice, 1545), 228; Battista Guarini, *Il Verato Secondo Ovvero Replica Dell'Attizzato Accademico Ferrarese In difesa del Pastorfido* (Florence, 1588), esp. 19v, 27–9; quotation from Dryden, *An Essay of Dramatick Poesie*, in *Works*, 17: 60.

[12] Francesco Robortello, *In librum Aristotelis De Arte Poetica Explicationes* (Florence, 1548), 53.

[13] Daniel Heinsius, *De Tragoediae Constitutione: On Plot in Tragedy* (1611), trans. Paul R. Sellin and John J. McManmon (Northbridge, CA: San Fernando Valley Stage College, 1971), 12.

physical displays of wrath, and a backsliding Christian should not be pitied, even by those who are bound to him by ties of affection. At last, Genest interrupts the performance, declaring that the play is not a play and that he is both the image and the player of himself (ll. 1325–30). He has experienced one sort of purgation—an intellectual clarification and rectification of his passions—which is in turn consummated by another sort of purification through the blood sacrifice of his martyrdom.[14]

Other critics stressed the importance of Aristotle's medical analogy for catharsis in the *Politics*, where he asserted that participants in sacred ritual were 'restored as a result of the sacred melodies…as though they had found healing and purgation'. Lorenzo Giacomini argued that catharsis referred to the use of homoeopathic substances that drew off humours. Just as rhubarb, aloe, or black hellebore could attract the humours by dint of their natural virtues, so the natural sympathy existing between humans meant that the actor's display functioned like a cure, drawing out and purifying the passions of the audience.[15] The numerous descriptions of purgation by fire and water that Paolo Beni gleaned from classical sources could support a view of catharsis that emphasized the overwhelming or ravaging effects of the experience. The most colourful of these accounts was that of Hermes Trismegistus, who said that God purged the earth by means of floods, fires, epidemics, and cataclysms. Reasoning that what worked for the macrocosm must obtain in the microcosm of man, Beni suggested that tragic purgation might be a similar form of destructive purification. It was a suggestion rife with dramatic possibilities. When the Serapion of Dryden's *All for Love* (1677) says in the tragedy's opening speech that the Nile 'flow'd ere the wonted Season, with a Torrent / So unexpected, and so wondrous fierce, / That the wild Deluge overtook the haste / Ev'n of the Hinds that watch'd it', he is insinuating that the audience will be overtaken in a similar manner—and purged by the flood.[16]

But why should this process be pleasurable, especially if it involved painful feelings such as pity and fear? Answers ranged from the pleasure we take in imitation, to the relief we feel in being spared the misery of others, to the satisfaction we experience in reflecting on our own capacity for benevolent involvement. But one of the most durable explanations rested squarely on the passions: the physical stimulation of the animal spirits was itself pleasurable, provided it was harmonious and not so

[14] For the text, see Jean Rotrou, *Le véritable Saint Genest*, ed. François Bonfils and Emmanuelle Hénin (Paris: Flammarion, 1999). Also see Robert J. Nelson, *Immanence and Transcendence: The Theater of Jean Routrou, 1609–1650* (Columbus: Ohio State University Press, 1969); and Mary Ann Frese Witt, 'From Saint Genesius to Kean: Actors, Martyrs, and Metatheater', *Comparative Drama* 43 (2009), 19–44.

[15] Aristotle, *The Politics*, trans. Benjamin Jowett, rev. Jonathan Barnes, ed. Stephen Everson (Cambridge: Cambridge University Press, 1988), 1342a; Lorenzo Giacomini, *Sopra la Purgazione della Tragedia*, in *Orationi e Discorsi* (Florence, 1597), 29–52. Also see Baxter Hathaway, *The Age of Criticism: The Late Renaissance in Italy* (Ithaca: Cornell University Press, 1962), 251–60.

[16] Hermes Trismegistus, *De Mundo* 7.1, in *The Theological and Philosophical works of Hermes Trismegistus, Christian Neoplatonist*, trans. John David Chambers (Edinburgh: T. & T. Clark, 1882); Paolo Beni, *In Aristotelis poeticam commentarii* (Padua, 1613), 194–212 ; John Dryden, *All for Love*, 1.1.3–6, in *Works*, 13: 24.

overwhelming as to damage the nervous system. 'A man naturally takes delight to feel himself moved to all sorts of Passions, yea, even Sadness, and Hatred', said Descartes, 'when these Passions are caused only by strange adventures, which he sees personated on a stage, or by such like occasions, which not being capable of troubling us any way, seem to tickle the Soul by touching it'. René Rapin drove the point home in his *Réflexions sur la poétique d'Aristote et sur les ouvrages des poètes anciens et modernes* (Reflections on the *Poetics* of Aristotle and on the works of poets ancient and modern, 1674): 'Nothing is more sweet to the Soul than Agitation, and of all Passions Fear and Pity are those that make the strongest Impressions on the Heart of Man'. For Rapin, this agitation of the soul was not just one of many sources of pleasure afforded by tragedy, it was the sole source: 'in this *Agitation* consists all the *Pleasure* that one is *capable* to *receive* from *Tragedy*'.[17]

The passions in dramatic poetry

Theatre thus has a peculiar power to present the ebbs and flows of the passions together with all the physical symptoms wrought by them. The Stoics might observe that anger is a short madness, remarked Sir Philip Sidney, but 'let Sophocles bring you Ajax on stage, killing and whipping sheep and oxen, thinking them the army of Greeks with their chieftains Agamemnon and Menelaus, and tell me if you have not a more familiar insight into anger than finding in the schoolmen his genus and difference'.[18] Yet even if poets could surpass philosophers in the mimetic energy of their representations, they still had to work with a theory of the passions. What precisely were passions in the early modern imaginary? They were perturbations of the soul caused by movements of the spirits in the body, which might be set in motion by either the body or the mind. 'As the body works upon the mind by his bad humours, troubling the spirits, sending gross fumes into the brain, and so *per consequens* disturbing the soul, and all the faculties of it', explained Robert Burton in his rambling but influential *Anatomy of Melancholy* (1632), '...so, on the other side, the mind most effectually works upon the body producing by his passions and perturbations miraculous alterations, as melancholy, despair, cruel diseases, and sometimes death itself'.[19]

Because the ancients frowned on the dissection of humans, Hippocratic and Galenic physicians were compelled to posit a resemblance between the processes they could observe in nature and those that were concealed within the body. They

---

[17] See Earl Wasserman, 'The Pleasures of Tragedy', *ELH* 14 (1947), 283–307. Quotations from René Descartes, *The passions of the soule in three books* (London, 1650), 75; René Rapin, *Monsieur Rapin's Reflections on Aristotle's Treatise of Poesie*, trans. Thomas Rymer (London, 1694 / first pub. 1674), 112.

[18] Sir Philip Sidney, *Apology for Poetry*, ed. Forrest G. Robinson (Indianapolis: Bobbs-Merrill Company, 1970), 28–9.

[19] Robert Burton, *The Anatomy of Melancholy* (1632), ed. Thomas C. Faulkner, Nicholas Kiessling, and Rhonda Blair, 2 vols. (Oxford: Clarendon Press, 1989), 2: 250.

therefore spoke of tempests in the soul. 'A double tide tosses me, uncertain of my course, as when rushing winds wage warfare, and from both sides conflicting floods lash the seas and the fluctuating waters boil', says Seneca's Medea, 'even so is my heart tossed'.[20] Such imagery proved irresistible to early modern dramatists. Consider the lament of Shakespeare's Titus Andronicus, who finds his own passions whipped up by the tears and sighs of his raped and mutilated daughter:

> When heaven doth weep, doth not the earth o'erflow?
> If the winds rage, doth not the sea wax mad,
> Threatening the welkin with his big-swollen face?
> And wilt thou have reason for this coil?
> I am the sea. Hark how her sighs doth blow.
> She is the weeping welkin, I the earth.
> Then must my sea be moved with her sighs,
> Then must my earth with her continual tears
> Become a deluge overflowed and drowned,
> For why my bowels cannot hide her woes,
> But like a drunkard must I vomit them.   (*Titus Andronicus* 3.1.222–32)[21]

King Lear's cries on the heath initially suggest a more obscure relationship between the storm without and the coil within, but he too eventually insists on the connection:

> Thou think'st 'tis much that this contentious storm
> Invades us to the skin: so 'tis to thee;
> But where the greater malady is fix'd,
> The lesser is scarce felt. Thou'ldst shun a bear;
> But if thy flight lay toward the roaring sea,
> Thou'ldst meet the bear i'th'mouth. When the mind's free
> The body's delicate; this tempest in my mind
> Doth from my senses take all feeling else
> Save what beats there—filial ingratitude!   (*King Lear* 3.4.6–14)

Here, the storm without is the bear, a fearful threat but nothing like the tempest within, which is a roaring sea. Such imagery would become so conventional in arias in the next century that it can be hard to remember that the basis of the topos was a somatic experience of overmastering force.

The tempests that the early moderns felt roiling inside them did not necessarily find their origin or their termination within the boundaries of the self. This is an important point to stress to readers reared in the conventions of character criticism, with its assumption of autonomous personhood. Sermons, spiritual autobiographies,

---

[20] Seneca, *Medea*, ll. 938–44, in *Seneca*, vol. 8., *Tragedies*, vol. 1, trans. Frank Justus Miller, Loeb Classical Library (Cambridge, MA: Harvard University Press, 1979).

[21] All quotations from Shakespeare follow these Arden editions: *Titus Andronicus*, ed. Jonathan Bate (London: Routledge, 1995); *King Lear*, ed. Kenneth Muir (London: Routledge, 1989); *Hamlet*, ed. Harold Jenkins (London: Routledge, 1989); *Othello*, ed. E. A. J. Honigmann (Walton-on-Thames: Thomas Nelson and Sons, 1997); *The Second Part of King Henry IV*, ed. A. R. Humphreys (London: Methuen, 1966).

and medical treatises all attest that the early moderns, unlike most of us today, experienced their selves not as bounded egos but as voids open to spiritual influences—whether those influences were from the stars, from the waters, from demons, or from the Holy Spirit. In the colourful imagery of Lancelot Andrewes, 'a house will not stand empty long. One spirit or other, holy or unholy, will enter and take it up'; to be yourself, as Debora Shuger has observed, was to be inhabited by something other than yourself.[22] To men and women who experienced passions as imperious strangers who presented themselves uncalled, the sudden movement of animal and vital spirits associated with them could feel like a spiritual influx. In a Jesuit tragedy such as Bernardino Stefonio's *Crispus* (1597), an evil demon might goad the shade of Phaedra into stoking the breast of a living mortal with her former lust and vengeance, thus bringing the same sorrow on the house of Constantine that Phaedra once brought on the house of Theseus. Milton's *Samson Agonistes* (1671), on the other hand, withholds any authoritative interpretation of the 'intimate impulse' (l. 223) and 'rouzing motions' (l. 1382) that Samson feels. Is he shaken by a rush of animal and vital spirits, or has he been inspired by the Holy Spirit, or may both claims be true? To those possessed of a 'pneumatic self', the flux and reflux of their vital and animal spirits, those intermediaries between body and soul, could never be ignored: they might be tokens of grace, signs of damnation, or whispers from Providence.

But whatever the origins of the passions might be, dramatists had to rely on speeches, first and foremost, to express them. "'Tis not the admirable Intrigue, the surprising Events, and extraordinary Incidents that make the Beauty of a Tragedy', said Rapin in a passage that Dryden repeated with approval, 'it's the Discourses, when they are Natural and Passionate'.[23] Yet neither critics nor dramatists agreed on what a natural and passionate speech should sound like. The disagreement turned on whether dialogue should reproduce what men and women actually said when fraught with passion (thus leaving the audience, as it were, in the position of witnesses), or should instead create an audible similitude of their hidden thoughts and feelings.

Proponents of the first approach tended to admire the brisk dialogue of the Elizabethan stage. Dryden's Neander maintained that 'short Speeches and Replies are more apt to move the passions, and beget concernment in us then the other: for it is unnatural for any one in a gust of passion to speak long together, or for another in the same condition to suffer him, without interruption'. The same standard of verisimilitude and naturalness suggested that illustrious persons in the heat of action or the grip of passion might employ apostrophes, exclamations, ironies, imprecations, interrogations, and exaggerations but would not have the patience to concoct

---

[22] On the 'pneumatic' self, see Debora Shuger, *Habits of Thought in the Renaissance: Religion, Politics, and the Dominant Culture* (Berkeley: University of California Press, 1990), 97–105 (100), where she quotes *The Works of Lancelot Andrewes*, 11 vols. (Oxford: Oxford University Press, 1854), 3: 191.

[23] Dryden, *Heads of an Answer to Rymer* (1677–78), in *Works*, 17: 193.

comparisons, allusions, antitheses, and maxims. Thus a speech like King Lear's 'O me! my heart, my rising heart!—but down!' (2.4.118) might win high praise from Joseph Warton:

> By which single line the inexpressible anguish of his mind, and the dreadful conflict of opposite passions with which it is agitated, are more forcibly expressed than by the long and laboured speech, enumerating the causes of his anguish, that ROWE and other modern tragic writers would certainly have put in their mouth.

On the other hand, Shakespeare's passionate speeches were often faulted for being too pregnant of simile and his soliloquies censured for being too long, sedate, and disconnected from the action. Charles Gildon went so far as to insist that there was not a single soliloquy in Shakespeare, including Hamlet's 'To be, or not to be', that could be 'excus'd by nature or reason'.[24]

On the other hand, Hamlet's 'To be, or not to be' soliloquy *could* be defended by poets who considered the inner movements of the soul to be the objects worthiest of imitation. These poets tended to prefer simpler dramatic actions in order that they might, as Dryden's Lisideius puts it, 'have leisure to dwell on a subject which deserves it; and to represent the passions (which we have acknowledg'd to be the Poets work) without being hurried from one thing to another'.[25] The ideal of this sort of dramaturgy was to set a passion in motion, propel it with a series of reasons, images, and examples, and then bring it to a point of plenitude. In some cases, like the famous stanzas that end Act 1 of Pierre Corneille's *Le Cid* (1634), such a speech might be set off formally. In six stanzas of ten lines each, written in an irregular metre intended to express irresolution and anxiety, Roderick endures a wild storm in his breast as he works through his intolerable options: he can kill the father of his beloved, thus defending his honour but alienating Chimène; or he can spare her father, thus losing his honour and becoming unworthy of her. It is little surprise that Marc Antoine Charpentier, perceiving the musical quality of the stanzas, set them as a series of operatic airs linked by recitative and ritornellos.

The artistic imperatives that drove the amplification of pathetic speeches in declaimed tragedy also encouraged the development of *dramma per musica*. Disappointed that neither their dramatic representations nor their music possessed the marvellous power to move the affections that they found described in ancient texts, and impelled by that disappointment to re-examine the performance practices of the Greeks, a handful of Italian humanists came to two fateful conclusions: Greek tragedies had been sung throughout, and rather than confusing the emotional point of their melodies with polyphony, the Greeks had used modes whose pitch and rhythm could sustain imitations that were close to actual passions and that could therefore transform the souls of listeners. These conclusions encouraged

---

[24] Dryden, *An Essay of Dramatick Poesie*, in *Works*, 17: 48; on figures of speech see Abbé d'Aubignac, *La Pratique du théâtre* (1657), trans. as *The Whole Art of the Stage* (1684), bk. 4, ch. 8; Joseph Warton, *Adventurer*, 153 (4 December 1753); Charles Gildon, *The laws of poetry* (London, 1721), 207.

[25] Dryden, *An Essay of Dramatick Poesie*, in *Works*, 17: 37.

experiments with a style of sung monody performed over a continuous bass that, by synthesizing textual, musical, and expressive content, sought to speak the natural language of the affections and paved the way for the dramatic form we know as opera. In early operas such as Claudio Monteverdi's *Orfeo* (1607), *Arianna* (1608), and *Il Ritorno d'Ulisse in patria* (The return of Ulysses, 1640), the long pathetic speeches are usually characterized by a more pronounced use of metre, rhyme, and affective text repetitions that set them off from the surrounding recitative. In some cases such as the immensely influential lament of Arianna, the music takes its form from the rhetorical emphases and refrains of the verse itself, as the heroine's passions progress from despair ('Lasciatemi morire'), to disbelief ('Dove, dove è la fede'), to a furious desire for revenge ('O nembi, o turbi, o venti'), and then through shame ('Non son, non son quell'io') to resignation ('Mirate, ove m'ha corto empia fortuna'). In other cases, such as the many laments that Monteverdi and his pupil Cavalli set over a descending ostinato bass, the heroine's attempts at self-expression and self-direction are constrained by a more coercive musical form, suggesting the downward pull of despair, death, or necessity. Either way such pathetic speeches are *long*—fifty to eighty lines of verse.[26]

By the late seventeenth century, however, most librettists had begun to alternate passages of action and dialogue (written in free verse and set as recitative) with passages in which the dramatis personae could respond to the action in closed poetic forms set as arias. The text of such arias was usually brief: two stanzas of four to six lines, with the first stanza announcing a passion or determination and the second qualifying or contradicting it. But its musical development was ample.[27] The length of da capo arias could vary considerably, but Geminiano Giacomelli's 'Sposa non mi conosci', an aria performed by the great castrati Farinelli and Caffarelli, gives a sense of their magnitude in the early eighteenth century. The aria is a recognition duet *manqué*—Epitide's expression of dismay at the failure of his mother and his wife to recognize him in Act 3 of Apostollo Zeno's *Merope* (Naples, 1746)—and occupies about ten minutes in performance.

---

[26] On the developments that led to opera, see Claude V. Palisca, 'Girolamo Mei: Mentor to the Florentine Camerata', *Musical Quarterly* 40 (1954), 1–20; Girolamo Mei, *Letters on Ancient and Modern Music to Vincenzo Galilei and Giovanni Bardi: A Study with Annotated Texts*, ed. Claude V. Palisca (n.p.: American Institute of Musicology, 1977); Nino Pirrotta and Elena Povoledo, *Music and Theatre from Poliziano to Monteverdi*, trans. Karen Eales (Cambridge: Cambridge University Press, 1982); Palisca, ed., *The Florentine Camerata* (New Haven: Yale University Press, 1989). On these laments, see Ellen Rosand, 'The Descending Tetrachord: An Emblem of Lament', *Musical Quarterly* 65 (1979), 346–59; Gary Tomlinson, 'Madrigal, Monody, and Monteverdi's "Via Vaturale alla Immitatione"', *Journal of the American Musicological Society* 34 (1981), 60–108; and the special issue on laments that appeared in *Early Music* 27 (1999).

[27] On the early development of arias in Venetian opera, see Ellen Rosand, *Opera in Seventeenth-Century Venice: The Creation of a Genre* (Berkeley: University of California Press, 1991), 281–321. On its forms in the eighteenth century, see James Webster, 'Aria as Drama', in Anthony R. DelDonna and Pierpaolo Polzonetti, eds., *The Cambridge Companion to Eighteenth-Century Opera* (Cambridge: Cambridge University Press, 2009), 24–49.

Although an aria-based opera advances an action and depicts the manners of its dramatis personae, the importance it attaches to arias means that what is presented on stage is, first and foremost, a gallery of monuments to the passions. To be sure, the inexhaustible variety of melodic and motivic development, rhythm and texture, made the aria form immensely expressive in the hands of masters such as Handel, Hasse, and Mozart, but its conventional association of certain keys, tempos, and motives with particular passions and classes of person nevertheless meant that its arias could be categorized into types (such as the rage aria) and even transposed from one opera to another (hence the 'suitcase arias' of travelling virtuosi). The effect was to emphasize the primacy of passion over character or action. The appeal of ensemble pieces in which all the persons of the drama were brought to feel the same passion at the same time only underlines where the priorities lay. Examples of the form include the ensemble that ends Act 1 of Mozart's *La Finta Giardiniera* (1775), in which all the dramatis personae are brought to sing of their rage ('Che smania orribile!'), and the quartet of Act 3 of Mozart's *Idomeneo* (1781) ('Soffrir più no si può'), in which the four principal persons declare that they can bear no more, that their sorrow is worse than death, that no one has ever borne greater pain. Such ensembles must be distinguished from choral scenes in which a crowd responds spontaneously and unanimously to the same stimulus. What makes them such *coups de théâtre* is that the personages converge on the same passion at the same time, even though they have arrived at it by different routes and for different reasons.

Because theorists of the passions thought that the body had a tendency to remain fixed in the same state once its spirits had been deranged by a vehement passion, dramatists had only four plausible options open to them once they had developed a passion to the point of plenitude. They could allow the personage to regain equilibrium off-stage—hence the popularity of the exit aria. They could drive him through an ascending or descending scale of passions like the one that David Garrick could perform on call, changing from 'wild delight to temperate pleasure, from this to tranquility, from tranquility to surprise, from surprise to blank astonishment, and from that to sorrow, from sorrow to the air of one overwhelmed, from that to fright, from fright to horror, from horror to despair'.[28] They could take advantage of the fact that passions could combine into compounds and then disaggregate into simples to stage-manage affective transformations, as John Ford does in *The Queen* (1621), shifting the king from simple hate to pure love by way of jealousy, a passion that contained the two. Or they could introduce fresh stimuli to set the spirits of their characters into motion again, thus making them susceptible to different passions. These might be provided by the entrance or exit of persons, but they could also be provided by dreams, prophecies, messages, even unlooked-for thoughts,

---

[28] Denis Diderot, *Le paradoxe sur le comédien*, trans. W. H. Pollock, in *'The Paradox of Acting' and 'Masks or Faces?'* (New York: Hill & Wang, 1957), 33.

like the one that elicits Lear's, 'O! that way madness lies; let me shun that; / No more of that' (3.4.21–2).

The dramatic imperative to renew the passions explains a great deal about the way Dryden constructs his scenes. Act 4 of *Aureng-Zebe* (1674) opens, for instance, with the imprisoned hero contemplating the prospect of his own death to the sound of '*Soft Music*' and in tones reminiscent of Hamlet's: 'Death, in itself, is nothing; but we fear / To be we know not what, we know not where'. We would expect him to react with aversion to the entrance of his stepmother, whom he believes to be working against his interests, but he is too tired of life to care about the intrigues of the court. When she begins to address him with winning words, he is struck with amazement: she has presented herself in a new light that he can only wonder at. He becomes slowly mollified as she assures him of her good will, but when he realizes that she is making an incestuous proposition his attitude hardens into odium. Like a Roman mime, Aureng-Zebe strikes one affective pose after another, but Dryden always furnishes him with a fresh stimulus for what he conceives to be a pneumatic reaction. Similarly, it is impossible to feel the power of the final scene of Racine's *Bérénice* (1671) without understanding that the stage movements are somatic expressions of disarranged spirits. Towards the conclusion of the tragedy, Titus penetrates the queen's plans to kill herself, and she sinks down on a seat in despair at the discovery—an almost unthinkable loss of self-possession for a queen on the French stage. When Antiochus enters to confess that he has been the emperor's rival in love and to announce his own determination to end his life, Bérénice musters the physical strength and the moral courage to rise to the inevitable: 'Je l'aime, je le fuis; Titus m'aime, il me quitte' (I love him, I flee him; Titus loves me; he forsakes me). Bérénice's heroic feat is to contradict her instinctive desire to approach Titus; instead, she exits and forbids Titus to follow. Only if we understand that exits and entrances can be the purest theatrical expressions of the most deeply felt passions, the most basic forms of appetite and aversion, can we appreciate how Bérénice's final withdrawal could be received by seventeenth-century audiences as a grand gesture, a brutal display of the will's costly triumph over desire. Such bold stage movements convey the impression that the speeches of the persons are more than mere rhetoric. They are revelations of passions that are rooted in the body and that can overcome it.[29]

The passions on stage

And what of the actor's approach? The example of Andrea Perucci's *Dell'Arte rapp-resentativa, premedita ed all'improviso* (A Treatise of acting, from memory and improvisation, 1699), one of the earliest treatises devoted to the art of acting, is

---

[29] Dryden, *Aureng-Zebe*, 4.1.3–4, in *Works*, 12: 209; Jean Racine, *Bérénice*, ll. 1512/1500, in *Œuvres complètes*, vol. 1, ed. Georges Forestier (Paris: Gallimard, 1999), 508.

instructive, for we find that he covers two main topics: how to portray the manners of types such as old men, young lovers, and women, and how to express passions and sentiments such as requited love, despairing love, and defiance of fortune. Manners and passions had to be considered in tandem because age, gender, humoral complexion, and national custom could all inflect the expression of passion, however universal the passions might be. Indeed, it was considered one of the peculiar excellencies of Betterton that he could suit his displays of passion to his role: 'Those wild impatient Starts, that fierce and flashing Fire, which he threw into *Hotspur*, never came from the unruffled Temper of his Brutus (for I have, more than once, seen a *Brutus* as warm as *Hotspur*) when the *Betterton Brutus* was provok'd, in his Dispute with *Cassius*, his Spirit flew only to his Eye'.[30]

Nevertheless, when it came to interpreting any given speech, the actor's first duty was to translate the poet's verse into an affective script. James Burgh's *The Art of Speaking*, which appeared in at least seven British and eight American editions between 1761 and 1804, outlines the procedure in an introductory 'Essay, in which are given Rules for expressing the principal Passions and Humours, which occur in Reading, or Public Speaking' and then provides exercises for the reader by printing numerous speeches under headings that outline the sequence of passions that should be performed. For instance, the unsuccessful attempt of Claudius to pray in *Hamlet* appears as Lesson 'LIX. REMORSE. Attempt at REPENTANCE. OBDURACY. DESPAIR' (Figure 16). Burgh's marginalia provide a more detailed affective script that the orator is asked to enact by following Burgh's instructions on the expression of the passions. Not just individual speeches but whole roles could be translated into a passionate sequence with a definite shape and rhythm. What distinguished a great actor from a mediocre one, maintained Denis Diderot in *Le paradoxe sur le comédien* (The paradox of the actor, 1770–8), was that 'His passion has a definite course—it has bursts, and it has reactions; it has a beginning, a middle, and an end'.[31]

Both the dignity of its personages and the grandeur of its passions dictated that tragedy should be performed in the high style that Quintilian described as slow, weighty, and marked by wide vocal modulation and protracted harmonies. Racine reportedly wrote down the pitch in which Mademoiselle Champmeslé should deliver every syllable of his tragedies, and Elkanah Settle praised Charles Hart for a 'perfectly Musical' voice that had made the Theatre Royal 'all *Harmony*'. The abbé Dubos considered the musical line that actors took through lines of tragic verse to be too important to be entrusted to them: he suggested that poets adopt a musical system of notation for

---

[30] Colley Cibber, *An Apology for the Life of Colley Cibber* (1740), ed. B. R. S. Fone (Ann Arbor: University of Michigan Press, 1968), 62; on early modern acting styles, see Joseph R. Roach, *Player's Passion: Studies in the Science of Acting* (Newark: University of Delaware Press, 1985); Dene Barnett, *The Art of Gesture: The Practices and Principles of 18th Century Acting* (Heidelberg: Carl Winter, 1987).

[31] James Burgh, *The Art of Speaking*, 7th edn. (London, 1787), title page, 213; Diderot, *Paradox of Acting*, 15.

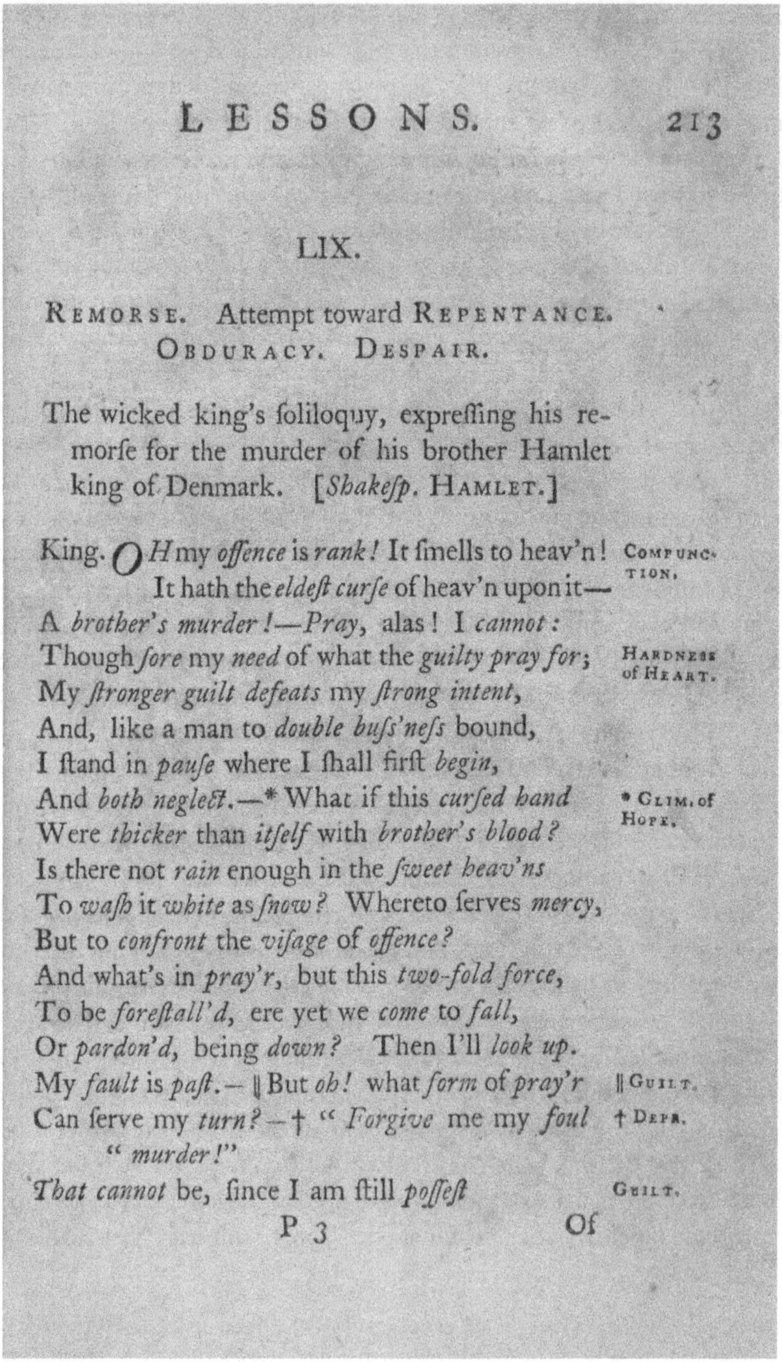

LIX.

REMORSE. Attempt toward REPENTANCE.
OBDURACY. DESPAIR.

The wicked king's foliloquy, expreffing his re-
morfe for the murder of his brother Hamlet
king of Denmark. [*Shakefp.* HAMLET.]

King. *O H* my *offence* is *rank!* It fmells to heav'n!   COMPUNC-
          It hath the *eldeft curfe* of heav'n upon it—   TION.
A *brother's murder!*—*Pray*, alas! I *cannot:*
Though *fore* my *need* of what the *guilty pray for*;   HARDNESS
My *ftronger guilt defeats* my *ftrong intent,*   of HEART.
And, like a man to *double bufs'nefs* bound,
I ftand in *paufe* where I fhall firft *begin,*
And *both neglect.*—* What if this *curfed hand*   * CLIM. of
Were *thicker* than *itfelf* with *brother's blood?*   HOPE.
Is there not *rain* enough in the *fweet heav'ns*
To *wafh* it *white* as *fnow?* Whereto ferves *mercy,*
But to *confront* the *vifage* of *offence?*
And what's in *pray'r*, but this *two-fold force,*
To be *foreftall'd,* ere yet we *come* to *fall,*
Or *pardon'd,* being *down?*   Then I'll *look up.*
My *fault* is *paft.—* ‖ But *oh!* what *form* of *pray'r*   ‖GUILT.
Can ferve my *turn?—*† " *Forgive* me my *foul*   † DESP.
      " *murder!*"
That cannot be, fince I am ftill *poffeft*   GUILT.
                    P 3   Of

Figure 16 A lesson from James Burgh, *The Art of Speaking*, teaching how to read texts for the passions implied by them. Shown here in the 7th edn. of 1787, the text was first published in 1761. Houghton Library, Harvard University (9280.761.70).

their plays. Perhaps intrigued by the idea, the conductor of the Comédie-Française recorded the pitches used by the great actress Mademoiselle Clairon when reciting the same monologue on four different occasions, and he reported that they were precisely the same each time. Tragic pronunciation and recitative were kissing cousins. Indeed, Voltaire remarked that if readers wanted to know how tragedians had declaimed on stage when he was young, they should listen to the recitative at the French opera.[32]

In the silent language of the body, composure was expressed by adopting a contrapposto stance, which embodied an ideal of repose and tranquillity animated by a potential for action. French tragedians underlined the ethical significance of this stance by using the word 'repos' to refer to the state of peace that personages enjoyed when they were free from vehement passions.[33] In Racine's *Phèdre et Hippolyte*, for example, the heroine recalls the moment before her fatal passion in just these terms: 'Mon repos, mon bonheur semblait être affermi' (my tranquillity, my happiness seemed to be secure).[34] This repose of the soul was assumed to manifest itself in the balanced opposition of forces on display in the resting body, in hand gestures that followed the line of beauty, and in the S-shaped stage movement of actors in full command of their bodies and their environment. When confronted with a new object or surprising news, the tragic actor would often express silent wonder by opening his eyes, mouth, and nostrils wide, standing stock still with his legs close together, and holding his arms up with his hands open as if he were uncertain whether to welcome or to avert the object before him (Figure 17). If his wonder hardened into astonishment, thus depriving his muscles of spirits, he might remain still like a statue. Otherwise, as he came to form an opinion of whether the object was good or evil, his wonder would yield to a passion that depended on his judgement. If he felt joy at the sight, his body would express his elevation of spirits (Figures 18 and 19); if he felt sorrow, it would respond to his depression (Figures 20 and 21). When, on the other hand, he was reacting to some desired good or a dreaded evil, his expectation would more often be expressed on the horizontal axis. When King Lear shuns the thought of his ungrateful daughters, exclaiming, 'O, that way madness lies; let me shun that; / No

[32] Quintilian, *The Institutio Oratoria of Quintilian*, trans. H. E. Butler, 4 vols., Loeb Classical Library (London: William Heinemann, 1920), 11.3.93, 84, 111–12, 60; Elkanah Settle, Dedication to *Fatal Love* (1680), 1; Jean-Baptiste Dubos, *Réflexions critiques sur la poésie et sur la peinture* (Paris, 1719), trans. Thomas Nugent as *Critical Reflections on Poetry, Painting, and Music*, 3 vols. (London, 1748), 3: 234–44. On Voltaire's remark, which comes from his entry 'Chant', in the *Dictionare philosophique*, see G. Lote, 'La déclamation du vers français à la fin du XVIIe siècle', *Revue de phonétique* 2 (1912), 329. On the ties between tragic declamation and recitative more generally, see Lois Rosow, 'French Baroque Recitative as an Expression of Tragic Declamation', *Early Music* 11.4 (1983), 468–79; James Winn, 'Heroic Song: A Proposal for a Revised History of English Theater and Opera, 1656–1711', *Eighteenth-Century Studies* 30 (1996–7), 113–37.

[33] On *repos* as a spiritual ideal, see Domna C. Stanton, 'The Ideal of "Repos" in Seventeenth-Century French Literature', *L'Esprit Créateur* 15 (1975), 79–104.

[34] Racine, *Phèdre et Hippolyte*, l. 271, in *Œuvres complètes*, 831.

Figure 17 Charles Le Brun. A figure expressing wonder and astonishment. Musée du Louvre, Cabinet des Dessins. © RMN-Grand Palais/Art Resource, NY.

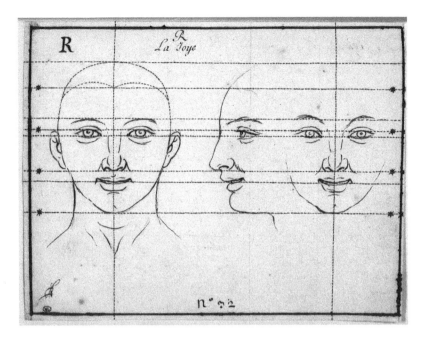

Figure 18 Charles Le Brun. The expression of 'la joie' (joy). *Conference sur l'expression des passions*. Musée du Louvre, Cabinet des Dessins. © RMN-Grand Palais/Art Resource, NY. The ebullient spirits associated with joy and ecstasy force the facial features and hands upwards.

Figure 19 Extasis (ecstasy), a detail from D. Fermin Eduardo Zeglirscosac, *Ensayo sobre el origen y naturaleza de las pasiones, del gesto y de la accion teatral* (Essay on the origin and nature of the passions, of gesture, and of theatrical action) (Madrid, 1800). Bibliothèque Nationale de France. The figures provided by D. Francisco de Pazula Marti display habits and passions, the chief units of theatrical significance in the early modern period.

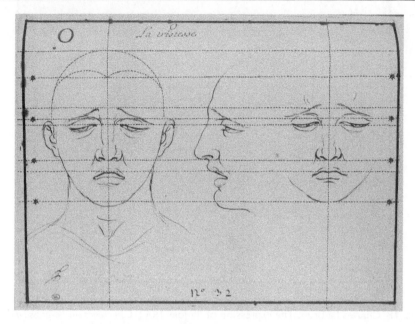

Figure 20 Charles Le Brun. The expression of 'la tristess' (sadness). *Conférence sur l'expression des passions*. Musée du Louvre, Cabinet des Dessins. © RMN-Grand Palais/Art Resource, NY. The languid spirits associated with sadness weigh down the features of the face and the gestures of the hands.

Figure 21 Tristeza (sadness), a detail from Zeglirscosac, *Ensayo sobre el origen y naturaleza de las pasiones* (Essay on the origin and nature of the passions). Bibliothèque Nationale de France.

Figure 22 Jakob Engel, *Ideen zu einer Mimik* (1785–6). Illustration of the gesture to accompany, 'O, that way madness lies; let me shun that; / No more of that!' (*King Lear* 3.4.21–2). Houghton Library, Harvard University (Typ 720.85.363, vol. 1).

more of that!' (3.4.21–2), he should, then, turn his back on it and repel it with a gesture (Figure 22). Thus the most basic unit of tragic action consisted of an actor being dislodged from his posture of repose and driven through wonder to some other vehement passion that impelled his features and limbs in one or more of the cardinal directions. Passions such as adoration and contempt combined two of these actions, for those who adore look up to the object they desire and seek to approach it, while those who feel contempt look down on the object they spurn and seek to repel it.

That the passions tended to follow each other in natural sequences—infinite in variety, yet nevertheless bound by natural laws—was suggested by the way they could be developed from proximate passions. Wonder could be transformed into terror by drawing the eyebrows together, raising the trembling hands higher, and drawing a foot backward to prepare for flight. This is the stance that Betterton assumed when, as Hamlet, he saw the ghost of his father in Gertrude's closet; an engraving from the edition of Nicholas Rowe depicts the prince's terror at the apparition of the ghost and Gertrude's amazement at the conduct of her son (Figure 23). By averting his gaze and extending his hands more forcefully, the actor could express aversion, raising his hands high in recognition of its superior force if he was terrified (Figure 24), holding them lower if he felt simple odium (Figure 25). Garrick could reportedly make the transition from one passion to another at will, as if practising scales.[35]

Did actors have to *feel* these powerful passions in order to incite them in the audience? No lesser authority than Horace seemed to answer yes: 'If you will have me weep, grief must first be yours: then, O Telephus or Peleus, will your misfortunes hurt me.' But Quintilian undertook a more subtle investigation of the problem. Distinguishing between true affections and fictive ones, he observed that the former erupt naturally but lack art and must be formed by methodical training,

---

[35] Diderot, *Paradox of Acting*, 33.

Figure 23 The closet scene depicted in Nicholas Rowe's edition of Shakespeare (1709). With his overturned chair and backward step, Hamlet displays terror, while Gertrude, who does not see the ghost, remains seated, expressing simple amazement at the conduct of her son. Courtesy Department of Special Collections, Stanford University Libraries.

while the latter imply art but lack the sincerity of nature: 'consequently in such cases the main things is to excite the appropriate feeling in oneself, to form a mental picture of things, and to exhibit an emotion that cannot be distinguished from the truth'. This mental picture was a fantasy or vision 'whereby things absent are presented to our imagination with such extreme vividness that they seem actually to be before our very eyes'. Quintilian implied that for an actor, the dramatic text could supply that vision. He had noticed that the 'mere delivery of words written by another' had the power to set the souls of actors 'on fire with fictitious affection'. This is the process that Hamlet memorably describes after listening to the Player's speech:

> Is it not monstrous that this player here,
> But in a fiction, in a dream of passion,
> Could force his soul so to his own conceit
> That from her workings all his visage wann'd,
> Tears in his eyes, distraction in his aspect,
> A broken voice, and his whole function suiting
> With forms to his conceit? And all for nothing!
> For Hecuba!   (*Hamlet* 2.2.545–52)

Figure 24 Jakob Engel, *Ideen zu einer Mimik* (1785–6). The figure of Terror contains a gesture of aversion whose raised hands imply a feeling of inferiority to the feared object. Houghton Library, Harvard University (Typ 720.85.363, vol. 1).

Figure 25 Odio (odium), a detail from Zeglirscosac, *Ensayo sobre el origen y naturaleza de las pasiones* (Essay on the origin and nature of the passions). Odium contains the same gesture of aversion displayed by Terror, but the downward slope of the arms implies contempt for the object. Bibliothèque Nationale de France.

Polonius' distaste for the actor's performance should remind us that such raw portrayals of passion were not to everyone's taste, but in the early modern period, stories of actors becoming lost in their passions were more often repeated with approval. Aesopus' performance of 'Atreus deliberating the revenge of Thyeste' was one of the most frequently retold: according to Plutarch, he became 'so transported beyond himself in the heat of action, that he struck with his scepter one of the servants, who was running across the stage, so violently that he laid him dead on the place'. Such was the power of a vision when it had taken full possession of the mind to affect the spirits, direct the movement of the blood, and overmaster the body. This physical expression of passion had the same power over the body of the audience that the actor's vision had over his own, for the action of a thespian exhibiting pathos, said Thomas Wright, cried out 'with all the universal life and body… "Thus we move because by the passion we are moved, and as it has wrought in us so it ought to work in you" '.[36]

But the actor did not have to rely on the poet for his visions: he could muster them from his own psychic history. As Michel Le Faucheur (an important influence on Betterton's conception of acting) explained, ancient actors 'kept their *Imagination* still at work upon *real Subjects* and *private Afflictions* of their own, which they lay very much to *Heart*; and not upon *Fables* or *Fictions* of the *Play they acted*, which did not touch them at all in effect'. To illustrate this procedure, he told the story of the actor Polus, recorded by Aulus Gellius and recounted in the sixteenth and early seventeenth centuries by the likes of Giacomini, Nicolò Rossi, the Jesuit Louis de Cressoles, and the playwright Georges de Scudéry. When Polus (*c.*300 BC), the finest actor his age, returned to the stage after a hiatus occasioned by the death of his son, he appeared as Electra in Sophocles' tragedy, a work 'whose plot is so constructed that Electra, thinking that she carries her brother's remains, bewails and bemoans his death'. 'Clad in Electra's mourning garb', Gellius recounts, Polus received into his arms no mere stage prop but the urn of his dead son, so that he might fill the theatre 'not with imitations and feignings, but with true and living grief and lamentations. Thus while it appeared that a fable was being enacted, what was acted out was his pain'.[37]

---

[36] Horace, *Ars Poetica*, ll. 102–4, in *Horace, Satires, Epistles and Ars Poetica*, trans. H. Rushton Fairclough, Loeb Classical Library (London: W. Heinemann, 1932); Quintilian, *Institutio Oratoria*, 11.3.61–2, 6.2.29, 35; Plutarch, *The Lives of the Noble Grecians and Romans*, trans. John Dryden, rev. Arthur Hugh Clough (New York: The Modern Library, 1932), 1043; Thomas Wright, *The Passions of the Mind in General*, ed. William Webster Newbold (New York: Garland, 1986), 213–14.

[37] Michel Le Faucheur, *An Essay upon the Action of an Orator* (London, 1680), 186; Gellius, *The Attic Nights of Aulus Gellius*, trans. John Carew Rolfe, Loeb Classical Library (Cambridge, MA: Harvard University Press, 1927), 6.5.1–5. See Leofranc Holford-Stevens, 'Polus and His Urn: A Case Study in the Theory of Acting, *c.* 300 B.C.–*c.* A.D. 2000', *International Journal of the Classical Tradition* 11.4 (Spring 2005), 499–523.

From passion to character

When Betterton asserted that 'The Stage ought to be the *Seat* of *Passion*', he had every reason to feel confident that the theatre should be a privileged locus for *any* consideration of the passions. The reasons are not far to seek. Because the early moderns conceived of the passions both as the meeting point of the body and the mind within persons and as a means of communication from body to mind between persons, no art could be more perfectly suited to their expression than one founded on the actor's physical embodiment of the word and his transmission of affects to theatrical audiences. But the theatre also illustrated a subtler point: that inner excitations of the soul could coexist with bodily passions that were their opposite. As Descartes put it:

> …when we read strange adventures in a book or see them personated on a stage, it sometimes excites Sadnesse in us, sometimes Joy, or Love, or Hatred, and generally all the Passions, according to the diversity of the objects, that offer themselves to our imagination; but withall, we take a delight, to feel them excited in us, and this delight is an intellectual Joy, which may as well spring from Sadnesse, as all the rest of the Passions.

For Descartes and his contemporaries, the passions were not just emotions; they were experiences that demanded to be seen, entered into, contemplated, rehearsed, and remembered, both in the cool still centre of the soul (which could take a pure, intellectual joy in a passion well realized) and in the society of men (which could confirm the common sense of the passions).[38]

Yet if the theatre was the seat of passion in the seventeenth century, it was no longer so by the early nineteenth century, when the passions were displaced from their pride of place in dramatic theory. In his *Lectures on Dramatic Literature* (1808), A. W. Schlegel took exception to *Ideen zu einer Mimik* (Ideas on mimicry, 1785–6), an acting manual published by the actor and dramatist J. J. Engel: 'the grand error of the author is, that he considered it a complete system of mimicry or imitation, though it only treats of the expression of the passions, and does not contain a syllable on the subject of the exhibition of character'.[39] There was, however, nothing negligent about Engel's focus on the passions for its period. Preconditions for the change were already being established in the early eighteenth century, but as the publication of Joanna Baillie's *Plays on the Passions* (1798) should suggest, the change was gradual. How did it occur?

In the first place, a new emphasis on sympathy in the writings of men such as the third earl of Shaftesbury, Francis Hutcheson, Edmund Burke, Adam Smith, and Diderot began to colour or entirely supplant the Aristotelian notion of catharsis. To be sure, a handful of critics stretching all the way back to J. C. Scaliger had declared

---

[38] Descartes, *The passions of the soule*, 119–20.
[39] A. W. Schlegel, *A Course of Lectures on Dramatic Art and Literature*, trans. John Black, rev. A. J. W. Morrison (London: Henry Bohn, 1846), 513.

that catharsis was an improbable or unnecessary effect of tragedy, but the vast majority of critics writing in the sixteenth and seventeenth centuries assumed that a great deal hung on their interpretation of the vexing concept. It was therefore a sign of the changing spirit of the times when Bernard le Bovier de Fontenelle, the polymath nephew of Pierre and Thomas Corneille, announced blithely that he was going to skip the subject in his *Réflexions sur la poétique* (Reflections on the *Poetics*, 1742): 'I have never understood the purging of the passions by means of the passions themselves; so I will say nothing of it'. Others, like the author of *Cursory Remarks on Tragedy* (1754) and the French Encylopedists, omitted to mention catharsis altogether as an end of tragedy. Catharsis simply could not outlast a philosophy that lionized sympathy, that held that nature had implanted social passions in all men and women, and that conceived of the audience's imagination as an active participant in the theatre. For whereas Aristotle's sixteenth-century commentators believed that tragedy could teach when it was appropriate to feel passions, their late eighteenth-century successors only wanted it to provide occasions for instinctive benevolence. Whereas the former parsed the passions and believed that they stemmed from cognitive judgements, the latter were more inclined to say with Edmund Burke that they resulted from 'the mechanical structure of our bodies, or from the natural frame and constitution of our minds', not from reason. Whereas the former thought of tragedy as a means of instruction and social control and spoke of poets leading the psyches, impressing the imaginations, or igniting the passions of the audience, sympathetic philosophers often assumed that tragedy's beneficial effects could only be fully enjoyed by those who were 'most exquisitely susceptible to all the influences of the pathetic', in the words of George Campbell. For those who believed that it was more important to awaken the natural social affections of citizens than to tutor or temper their unruly passions, that it was more crucial to cultivate the sensibilities of men and women than to subject them to a flood of feeling that might skim off the impurities in their souls, catharsis ceased to be a crucial end of tragedy.[40]

A new emphasis on sympathetic identification in turn prepared the way for character to emerge as a more important unit of dramatic meaning than passion. The word *character* could not even be applied to one of the persons of a drama until the late seventeenth century. Critics translated the Greek *ethos* via the Latin *mores* into terms such as *manners, habits, customs, mœurs,* and *costumi.* Following Horace's *Ars Poetica* (ll. 114–18, 153–78), they demanded that these be appropriate to the nationality, age, profession, and sex of dramatis personae, but they did not look for the development of character. When an early modern actor 'personated' a role, he adopted the manners appropriate to a man with a certain

---

[40] Bernard Le Bovier de Fontenelle, *Réflexions sur la poétique* (1742), in *Œuvres complètes*, 9 vols. (Paris: Fayard, 1990–2001), 3: 138–9. Edmund Burke, *A Philosophical Enquiry into our Ideas of the Sublime and the Beautiful* (London, 1757), 22–3; George Campbell, *The Philosophy of Rhetoric*, 2 vols. (London, 1776), 1: 278.

natural disposition occupying a particular station in life, but he did not create a character with a backstory as an actor today might; he gave somatic expression to a sequence of passions. This is why Margaret Cavendish, writing in 1662, praises Shakespeare's 'persons' rather than his 'characters' for their manners, humours, and passions: 'Shakespeare did not want Wit, to Express to the Life all Sorts of Persons, of what Quality, Profession, Degree, Breeding or Birth soever; nor did he want Wit to Express the Divers, and Different Humours, or Natures, or Several Passions of Mankind'. In the seventeenth century, a person acquired a 'character' only if someone else on stage painted a succinct verbal portrait of him. Even when critics such as Dryden began using the word 'characters' on occasion to refer to dramatis personae, they applied the criteria of distinctness and consistency and therefore judged Ben Jonson, whom we usually consider a coiner of dramatic types, to be a greater master of the art of characterization than Shakespeare.[41]

Before the late eighteenth century, critics rarely praised the radical individuation of stage persons. The whole tenor of Renaissance theory taught that poets should distinguish themselves from what Sidney described as 'the meaner sort of painters (who counterfeit only such faces as are set before them)'. Poets ought to model themselves on those more idealizing painters who 'bestow that in colors upon you which is fittest for the eye to see: as the constant though lamenting look in Lucretia's eye when she punished in herself another's fault. Wherein he painteth not Lucretia, whom he never saw, but painteth the outward beauty of such a virtue.' 'In Plays,' as James Drake explained, characters should be neither 'General' nor 'so Singular as to extend no farther than single Individuals'. We do, to be sure, hear Alexander Pope saying that 'every single character in Shakespeare is as much an Individual as those in Life itself', but Pope's point is that Shakespeare did not copy from other authors. And we can still find Samuel Johnson praising Shakespeare on the opposite grounds in 1765: 'His persons act and speak by the influence of those general passions and principles by which minds are agitated, and the whole system of life is continued in motion. In the writings of other poets a character is too often an individual; in those of Shakespeare it is commonly a species'. Elsewhere Johnson maintains that Shakespeare's 'chief Skill was in Human Actions, Passions, and Habits'—in other words in manners, not character.[42]

That character could be a unit of dramatic meaning at all—and indeed a fourth unity more important than the rest—was one of the great critical discoveries of

---

[41] Margaret Cavendish, Letter 123 from CCXI Sociable Letters (London, 1664), 245; Dryden, Grounds of Criticism in Tragedy, in Works, 13: 239. Also see Peter Womack, Ben Jonson (Oxford: Basil Blackwell, 1986), 34.

[42] Sidney, Apology, 20; James Drake, The Antient and Modern Stages survey'd (London, 1699), 288; Alexander Pope, 'Preface to The Works of Shakespeare' (1725) and Samuel Johnson, 'Preface to The Plays of William Shakespeare' (1765), both in D. Nichol Smith, ed., Eighteenth Century Essays on Shakespeare, 2nd edn. (Oxford: Clarendon Press, 1963), 45, 106; Johnson, dedication to Charlotte Lennox, Shakespear illustrated, 2 vols. (London, 1753), 1: ix.

the mid-eighteenth century, a discovery that had to await the publication of works such as John Locke's *An Essay Concerning Human Understanding* (1690), David Hume's *A Treatise of Human Nature* (1739–40), and Samuel Richardson's *Clarissa* (1748). It now made sense to write about characters as if they were the record of minds shaped in childhood, scarred by experience, and distinguished by their own peculiar chains of remembrance and anticipation. If the persons of a drama were sufficiently *whole*, it could even be warranted, maintained Maurice Morgann in his *Essay on the Dramatic Character of Sir John Falstaff* (1777), to 'account for their conduct from the *whole* of character, from general principles, from latent motives, and from policies not avowed'. The romantics' emphasis on organic development and *Bildung* led them to demand that characters, like living beings, should *develop* and find their *own* form, not just be distinct and consistent as Horace had demanded. They declared Shakespeare the master of conferring such freedom on his creations. 'Hamlet is not a person whose nativity is cast, or whose death is foretold by portents', says William Hazlitt appreciatively in 1826; 'he weaves the web of his destiny out of his own thoughts'. By conferring 'intelligence and imagination' on his characters, says Hegel, Shakespeare allows them 'to contemplate themselves objectively' as works of art, thus making them 'free artists of themselves'. That character was a recent discovery of critics and readers of novels is underlined by Lamb's contention that Shakespeare should not be acted because 'the form of *speaking*', much like the epistolary form of *Clarissa*, 'is only a medium, and often a highly artificial one, for putting the reader or spectator into possession of that knowledge of the inner structure and workings of mind in a character', while 'the glory of the scenic art is to personate the passions, and turns of passion', and 'the more coarse and palpable the passion is, the more hold upon the eyes and ears of the spectators the performer' enjoys.[43]

Yet however much nineteenth-century critics might praise Shakespeare for his allegiance to spiritual truths rather than spectacular actions, they tended to accept Hegel's contention that it was through the life of volition and action that Spirit

---

[43] On character as a unity, see Samuel Foote, *The Roman and English Comedy Consider'd and Compar'd* (London, 1747), 20–1; Elizabeth Griffith, *Essay on the Genius and Writings of Shakespeare* (London, 1775), 26. For the quotations, see Maurice Morgann, 'An Essay on the Dramatic Character of Sir John Falstaff' (1777), in *Eighteenth Century Essays*, 231; William Hazlitt, 'Sir Walter Scott, Racine, and Shakespeare' (1826), in *Hazlitt's Criticism of Shakespeare: A Selection*, ed. R. S. White (Lewiston: Edwin Mellen Press, 1996), 65; G. W. F. Hegel, *The Philosophy of Fine Art*, trans. F. P. B. Osmaston, 4 vols. (London: G. Bell and Sons, 1920), 4.337; Lamb, 'On the Tragedies of Shakespeare, considered with reference to their fitness for stage representation' (1811), in *The Works of Charles and Mary Lamb*, ed. E. V. Lucas, 6 vols. (London: Methuen, 1906), 1: 99. A high point (but by no means an endpoint) of character criticism is marked by A. C. Bradley's *Shakespearean Tragedy* (Oxford: Oxford University Press, 1904); for accounts that rightly point to the emergence of character as a literary ideal in the eighteenth century, see Womack, *Jonson*, ch. 2; and Deidre Lynch, *The Economy of Character: Novels, Market Culture, and the Business of Inner Meaning* (Chicago: University of Chicago Press, 1998).

manifested itself in the world. Discounting the notion that dramatic action might comprise the movements of a soul buffeted by passions, critics in Hegel's generation redefined dramatic action in stringent terms as a *deed* entailing will, performance, and reflection. Whereas Sidney, Davenant, and Dryden had been at pains to distinguish the poet from the historian—and had therefore privileged passion above action and sought to avoid the mere particulars of persons and deeds—Hegel looked to the stage to exhibit the same creative process of collision and resolution that he had outlined in his philosophy of history. Neither Aristotle nor his early modern heirs had stressed the importance of conflict on the stage because doing so would only have confirmed Plato's reasons for banishing the poets from the republic. Once Hegel was able to imagine conflict as an indispensable part of a historical process in which Spirit violently embodied itself in the world and revealed itself through the dissolution of antitheses in a higher synthesis, the way was clear for critics from A. W. Schlegel, through A. C. Bradley, to Kernan to treat character and conflict as if they were constants of drama.[44]

It would be hard to imagine many critics today writing precisely as Kernan does. For since the 1960s, post-structuralists have questioned the possibility of inward, agential personhood; some New Historicists have maintained that even if *we* experience inwardness, the early moderns may not have; and new bibliographers and theatre historians have amassed evidence—from the absence of lists of dramatis personae and the inconsistency of speech tags in Elizabethan texts, to the doubling of roles—that suggests that the seventeenth century did not necessarily share the nineteenth century's sense of whole and integral characters. Yet character and conflict continue to provide the starting point for influential introductions to early modern theatre—especially when the subject is Shakespeare. 'In Shakespeare, characters develop rather than unfold', writes Harold Bloom in the opening of *Shakespeare: The Invention of the Human* (1998). 'We know perfectly well that the characters have no inner lives apart from what we see on the stage, and yet we believe that they continue to exist when we do not see them, that they exist apart from their represented words and actions, and that they have hidden dimensions', concurs the New Historicist Stephen Greenblatt in his introduction to the *Norton Shakespeare*. But that is, of course, just half of what recommends Shakespeare's tragedies according to Greenblatt, for they are also 'concerned with dynastic struggles...; with violent conflicts between social classes...; with world-historical events...; with the clash of civilizations'. In short, with character and conflict.[45]

---

[44] See Michelle Gellrich, *Tragedy and Theory: The Problem of Conflict Since Aristotle* (Princeton: Princeton University Press, 1988).

[45] Harold Bloom, *Shakespeare: The Invention of the Human* (New York: Riverhead Books, 1998), xvii; Stephen Greenblatt, 'General Introduction' and 'Shakespearean Tragedy', in *The Norton Shakespeare*, ed. Stephen Greenblatt, Walter Cohen, Jean E. Howard, and Katherine Eisaman Maus, 2nd edn. (New York: W. W. Norton, 2009), 61, 923. Representative New Historicist treatments of character include Jonathan Goldberg, 'Shakespearean Inscriptions: The Voicing of Power', in Patricia Parker and Geoffrey

It is beyond the scope of this essay to explore the extent to which Shakespeare's practice may lie outside the mainstream of early modern dramaturgy, thus justifying the analysis of his plays in these terms. I would suggest in passing, however, that if these concepts are to be set on a firm historical footing, then they should be grounded on the practice of two of Shakespeare's chief sources, Raphael Holinshed and Plutarch, who consider it part of their charter to portray the manners and dispositions of men and to narrate lives that are co-terminal with historical contentions.[46] But the mainstream of early modern tragedians preferred to dispense with the severity of history in order that they might unlock a more general treasury of nature by portraying the passions. We must remember this when we interpret neoclassical tragedy, the solemn tragedy of the Jesuits, *opera seria*, and other early modern theatre that relies on persons, not characters in our modern sense, to advance the action of the drama and to exhibit passions.

For a century and a half after his death, readers who brought the standards of Aristotelian criticism to Shakespeare's plays often faulted him for the conduct of his fables and the obscurity of his diction, but they praised him for his admirable drafts of manners and his mastery of the passions. In the view of such readers, what distinguished Shakespeare from other tragedians was not that his plays presented something other than imitations of the passions—such as, for example, G. Wilson Knight's structures of metaphor—but that, in the words of an *Examen* of 1747, his 'amazing Superiority' lay 'in his great Knowledge and Use of the *Passions*'. Some readers, such as Leonard Welsted, fingered his ability to interweave the sublime and the pathetic in passages such as Othello's final speech, 'Set you down this, / And say besides, that in Aleppo once…' (5.2.349–50). Others praised his ability to *build* a passion. Sir Richard Steele pointed to the scene from *Henry IV, Part Two* when Morton is preparing to tell Northumberland of his son's death:

> the whiteness of thy cheek
> Is apter than thy tongue to tell thy errand;

Hartman, eds., *Shakespeare and the Question of Theory* (New York: Methuen, 1985); Peter Stallybrass, 'Patriarchal Territories: The Body Enclosed', in Margaret Ferguson et al., eds., *Rewriting the Renaissance: The Discourse of Sexual Difference in Early Modern Europe* (Chicago: University of Chicago Press, 1986), 123–42; Katherine Maus, *Inwardness and Theater in the English Renaissance* (Chicago: University of Chicago Press, 1995); Stephen Orgel, 'What Is a Character?', in *The Authentic Shakespeare and Other Problems of the Early Modern Stage* (New York: Routledge, 2002), 7–13; Randall McLeod, '"The Very Names of the Persons": Editing and the Invention of Dramatick Character', in David Scott Kastan and Peter Stallybrass, eds., *Staging the Renaissance: Reinterpretations of Elizabethan and Jacobean Drama* (New York: Routledge, 1991), 88–98. For a recent attempt to inaugurate a 'new character criticism', see Paul Yachnin and Jessica Slights, eds., *Shakespeare and Character: Theory, History, Performance, and Theatrical Persons* (Basingstoke: Palgrave Macmillan, 2009).

[46] I develop this argument in *What Was Tragedy? Theory and the Early Modern Canon* (forthcoming), ch. 5.

> Even such a man, so faint, so spiritless,
> So dull, so dead in look, so woe-begone,
> Drew Priam's curtain at the dead of night,
> And would have told him half his Troy was burnt:
> But Priam found the fire ere he his tongue,
> And I my Percy's death ere thou report'st it.   (1.1.68–75)

What Steele admired was Morton's gradual ascent to his affliction, from a state of composure that enabled him to employ a simile to the utter loss of all patience upon confirmation of the death:

> Now let not Nature's hand
> Keep the wild flood confin'd! Let order die!
> And let the World no longer be a stage,
> To feed contention in a ling'ring act....   (1.1.153–6)

And yet, as *An Examen* observed, Shakespeare was also prepared to omit any 'Transition from one Passion to the other' altogether, blending them together in passages like these:

> And let not women's weapons, water-drops,
> Stain my man's cheeks—! No, you unnatural hags,
> I will have such revenges on you both....   (*King Lear* 2.4.275–7)

> Ay, let her rot and perish, and be damned tonight, for she shall not live. No, my heart is turned to stone: I strike it and it hurts my hand. O, the world hath not a sweeter creature: she might lie by an emperor's side and command him tasks.   (*Othello* 4.1.177–82)

It may have been such unprepared transitions that led Alexander Pope to emphasize Shakespeare's ability to take us unprepared: 'The *Power* over our *Passions* was never possess'd in a more eminent degree... Yet all along there is seen no labour, no pains to raise them; no preparation to guide our guess to the effect or be perceiv'd to lead toward it'.[47]

Such practical criticism bears witness to the remarkable variety of Shakespeare's dramaturgy while underlining how it differs from that of French tragedians or Italian librettists, but it also reminds us that Shakespeare did *not* lie outside the mainstream of early modern theatre in one important respect: he too sought to represent and sway the passions. If we want to rest our critical interpretations on a sound theoretical foundation in the twenty-first century, we cannot afford, like Kernan, to neglect the heart and soul of early modern theatricality.

---

[47] For a representative example of G. Wilson Knight's approach, see *The Wheel of Fire: Essays in Interpretation of Shakespeare's Sombre Tragedies* (London: Oxford University Press, 1930). Quotations from *An Examen of the New Comedy, Call'd 'The Suspicious Husband'* (London, 1747), in Brian Vickers, ed., *Shakespeare: The Critical Heritage* (London: Routledge, 1975), 3: 260; Leonard Welsted, *Remarks on Longinus*, 3rd edn. (Dublin, 1727), 118; Sir Richard Steele, *Tatler* 47 (27 July 1709); *An Examen*, once again, in *Shakespeare: The Critical Heritage*, 3: 264; Pope, 'Preface', in *Eighteenth Century Essays*, 45.

FURTHER READING

Campbell, Lily B. *Shakespeare's Tragic Heroes: Slaves of Passion* (Cambridge: Cambridge University Press, 1930).

Dixon, Thomas. *From Passions to Emotions: The Creation of a Secular Psychological Category* (Cambridge: Cambridge University Press, 2003).

James, Susan. *Passion and Action: The Emotions in Seventeenth-Century Philosophy* (Oxford: Clarendon Press, 1997).

Levy, Anthony. *French Moralists: The Theory of the Passions, 1585 to 1649* (Oxford: Clarendon Press, 1964).

Mace, Dean T. 'Dryden's Dialogue on Drama', *Journal of the Warburg and Courtauld Institutes* 25 (1962), 87–112.

Roach, Joseph R. *Player's Passion: Studies in the Science of Acting* (Newark: University of Delaware Press, 1985).

Rowe, Katherine. 'Minds in Company: Shakespearean Tragic Emotion', in Richard Dutton and Jean E. Howard, eds., *A Companion to Shakespeare's Works: The Tragedies* (Oxford: Blackwell Publishing, 2003), 47–72.

INDEX OF PLAYS

Includes partial plays, entertainments, scenarios, songs, and other para-theatrical works. Dates are approximate; titles have been shortened to familiar usage, with alternate titles in brackets. ? after author's name indicates uncertain attribution. English titles and dates follow Alfred Harbage, rev. S. Schoenbaum, *Annals of English Drama 975–1700*, 3rd edn. rev. Sylvia Stoler Wagonheim (London and New York: Routledge, 1989).

GENERAL INDEX